PEASANTRIES OF EUROPE

THE
PEASANTRIES OF EUROPE
from the Fourteenth to the Eighteenth Centuries

Edited by
TOM SCOTT

LONGMAN
London and New York

Addison Wesley Longman Limited
Edinburgh Gate,
Harlow, Essex CM20 2JE, United Kingdom
and Associated Companies throughout the world.

Published in the United States of America by Addison Wesley Longman, New York.

First published 1998

ISBN 0–582–10132–8 CSD
ISBN 0–582–10131–X PPR

British Library Cataloguing in Publication Data

catalogue entry for this title is available from the British Library

Library of Congress Cataloging-in-Publication Data

The peasantries of Europe : from the fourteenth to the eighteenth
centuries / edited by Tom Scott.
p.   cm.
Includes bibliographical references and index.
ISBN 0–582–10131–X (ppr). — ISBN 0–582–10132–8 (csd)
1. Peasantry—Europe—History.   2. Peasantry—Europe—Case
studies.   3. Economic history.   I. Scott, Tom, 1947–   .
HD1531.5.P4   1998
305.5′633′094—dc21
97–41897
CIP

Set by 35 in 11/12pt Garamond
Produced by Longman Singapore Publishers (Pte) Ltd.
Printed in Singapore

Contents

List of Maps	vii
Notes on Contributors	viii
Note on Usage	xi

1. Introduction   1
   Tom Scott

2. The Peasantries of France, 1400–1789   21
   Jonathan Dewald and Liana Vardi

3. The Peasantries of Iberia, 1400–1800   49
   Teófilo F. Ruiz

4. The Peasantries of Italy, 1350–1750   75
   S. R. Epstein

5. The Peasantries of Western Germany, 1300–1750   111
   Thomas Robisheaux

6. Village Life in East-Elbian Germany and Poland, 1400–1800   145
   William W. Hagen

7. Peasantries under the Austrian Empire, 1300–1800   191
   Hermann Rebel

8. The Russian Peasantries, 1450–1860   227
   Edgar Melton

9. The Ottoman Peasantries, c.1360–c.1860   269
   Fikret Adanır

10. The Peasants of Scandinavia, 1300–1700   313
    David Gaunt

CONTENTS

11. The English Peasantry, 1250–1650   339
    Richard M. Smith

12. Conclusion: The Historical Geography of European
    Peasantries, 1400–1800   372
    John Langton

Index of Names and Places   401

Select Subject Index   413

List of Maps

Map 2.1   France   20
Map 3.1   Iberia   48
Map 4.1   Italy   74
Map 5.1   Western Germany   110
Map 5.2   Types of Village Settlement in Germany   113
Map 6.1   The Prussian Region in 1793   144
Map 6.2   The Polish-Lithuanian Commonwealth in 1772   155
Map 7.1   The Lands of the Austrian Empire   190
Map 8.1   Russia   226
Map 9.1   Ottoman Lands in Europe and Anatolia   268
Map 10.1 Scandinavia   312
Map 11.1 England   338

Notes on Contributors

Fikret Adanır is Professor of South-East European and Ottoman History at the Ruhr University in Bochum. His many essays on rural society in south-eastern Europe include 'Tradition and rural change in Southeastern Europe during Ottoman rule', in Daniel Chirot (ed.), *The Origins of Backwardness in Eastern Europe* (University of California Press, 1989).

Jonathan Dewald has written widely on French provincial society. His most recent books include *Aristocratic Experience and the Origins of Modern Culture: France, 1570–1715* (University of California Press, 1993), and *The European Nobility 1400–1800* (Cambridge University Press, 1996). He is Professor of History at the State University of New York at Buffalo.

Stephan R. Epstein is Reader in Economic History at the London School of Economics. In addition to numerous articles on comparative economic development in the Italian peninsula, he has published *An Island for Itself: Economic Development and Social Change in Late Medieval Sicily* (Cambridge University Press, 1992). He is currently completing a book on the political economy of markets in Renaissance Europe.

David Gaunt is Senior Lecturer in History at University College of South Stockholm, and has written extensively on problems of rural society and demography in Scandinavia. His publications include *Memoir on History and Anthropology* (Swedish Research Councils Publications, 1982) and the chapter on Scandinavia in André Burguière *et al.* (eds), *A History of the Family* (Harvard University Press, 1996).

William W. Hagen is Professor of History, Society and Culture at the University of California at Davis. Since his study of *Germans, Poles and Jews: The Nationality Conflict in the Prussian East 1772–1914* (University of Chicago Press, 1980), he has turned his attention to rural society in early modern Brandenburg and Prussia, on which he has published many articles.

John Langton is Fellow in Geography at St John's College, Oxford. His research on historical geography and demography has ranged from the coal-mining industry of south-west Lancashire to population growth in early modern Sweden. His most recent major study, written with Göran Hoppe, is *Peasantry to Capitalism: Western Östergötland in the Nineteenth Century* (Cambridge University Press, 1996).

Edgar Melton is Professor of History at Wright State University in Dayton, Ohio. After his doctoral research on serfdom and the peasant economy in Russia, 1780–1861, he has written numerous articles from a comparative perspective on seigneurial authority and peasant subjection in both Russia and east-Elbian Germany.

Hermann Rebel teaches at the University of Arizona in Tucson. His research on the transformation of rural society in Austria appeared as *Peasant Classes: The Bureaucratization of Property and Family Relations under Early Habsburg Absolutism, 1511–1636* (Princeton University Press, 1983). He is at present completing a book on family formations, disinheritance and the progress of a social pathology in provincial Austria, 1649–1948.

Thomas Robisheaux's main work has focused on south-west German village life, notably his *Rural Society and the Search for Order in Early Modern Germany* (Cambridge University Press, 1989), and he has recently translated Arthur E. Imhof's *Lost Worlds: How Our European Ancestors Coped with Everyday Life* (University of Virginia Press, 1996). He is Professor of History at Duke University in Durham, North Carolina.

Teófilo F. Ruiz teaches history at the University of California at Los Angeles. He has written widely in both Spanish and English on Iberian rural society, including his latest book *Crisis and Continuity: Land and Town in Late Medieval Castile* (University of Pennsylvania Press, 1994), which received the *Premio el Rey*, the American Historical Association's biennial award for the best book on Spanish history before 1564.

Tom Scott is Reader in History at the University of Liverpool. Though his interests include the German Peasants' War and the social history of the Reformation in Germany, on which he has written extensively, his principal research has concentrated on town–country relations and rural economic life. In 1997 he published *Regional Identity and Economic Change: The Upper Rhine, 1450–1600* (Oxford University Press).

Richard M. Smith FBA is Director of the Cambridge Group for the History of Population and Social Structure, and fellow of Downing College, Cambridge. His many studies of medieval society, demography and anthropology include *Land, Kinship and Life-Cycle* (Cambridge University Press, 1984). Most recently he has edited, with Zvi Razi, *Medieval Society and the Manor Court* (Oxford University Press, 1996).

Liana Vardi is Professor of History at the State University of New York in Buffalo. Her most recent monography is a study of proto-industrialization: *The Land and the Loom: Peasants and Profit in Northern France, 1680–1800* (Duke University Press, 1993). She is currently writing a history of the harvest in western Europe from 1500 to 1800.

Note on Usage

Throughout the text in order to avoid confusion, upper case is used to designate Estates as social orders or political corporations, whereas lower case is used to denote estates as landed possessions. There is no agreed English usage to translate the economic and social systems prevalent in much of eastern Europe, *Gutswirtschaft* and *Gutsherrschaft*. For a discussion of their meaning and evolution readers should refer in particular to the chapter by William W. Hagen. Other technical terms are explained in the text as they arise.

CHAPTER ONE

Introduction

Tom Scott

DEFINING EUROPEAN PEASANTRIES

Until the recent past, the majority of men and women in almost all societies have lived by working the land in family groups to secure their own survival. These men and women have commonly been called peasants. Because peasants have been such a universal feature of human history, it has also been assumed that they shared certain characteristics which recur throughout time and space. The 'peasant' has been taken as an unvarying archetype, whose identifying marks are rootedness to the soil and a commitment to economic subsistence, sufficient to ensure that the peasant family or household can reproduce itself as both a social and an economic unit, without thought of additional gain.

There are three immediate drawbacks to this definition, and they bear closely upon each other. The first is that the category 'peasant' is so broad as to become not so much an archetype as a stereotype, unable to distinguish, let alone explain, significant variations in peasant social and economic formation throughout history. The second is that to fix upon peasants as individuals may obscure differences between peasants as groups. A 'peasantry' in one particular place or time may display characteristics which other 'peasantries' elsewhere do not share, even if their constituents are all in the widest sense peasants. But thirdly, and decisively, what is to distinguish a 'peasant' from any other kind of family farmer – from, say, a small-scale farmer today relying largely upon family labour to sell his produce in a capitalist market? By drawing attention to these difficulties of definition, we are already alerted to the fact that 'peasants' and 'peasantries' are not to be seen as unmediated and unvarying categories – as some kind of Platonic ideal form – but as historically contingent formations whose emergence, therefore, has as much to do with their relation to other forces and groups in society as it has to any qualities supposedly intrinsic to and inherent in their mode of social reproduction.

To try to come closer to what a peasant might be, Frank Ellis has suggested three main desiderata which should be borne in mind. It is necessary in the first place, he argues, to be able to distinguish peasants not simply from other social groups not engaged in agriculture, but from other kinds of farm producers as well, whether they are workers on an estate or plantation, tied to a capitalist economic system, or workers on a commercial family farm. Secondly, the historian must beware of treating peasants as if they existed in a timeless vacuum. Peasants are never just 'subsistence' or 'traditional' cultivators, whose lifestyle never varies and whose mentality is one of conservatism leading to stagnation. He also emphasizes the wisdom of focusing on the family or household group, so as to register its interaction with the wider economy. Starting from these premises, he concludes that peasants are agriculturalists who are 'only *partially* integrated into *incomplete* markets' – in contrast to commercial family farms, whose members are wholly integrated into fully working markets.[1] We will return to this verdict in detail later on.

In the first instance, however, it is worth pausing to reflect on the more general implications of this definition. Its most obvious merit is that it identifies the essentially fluid, rather than static, nature of peasant economy and society. Peasants are not isolated in a world of their own, yet at the same time their links with the wider economy and society are attenuated; they constitute what is commonly termed a 'part-society'. We might almost say that the peasant is Janus-faced: concerned primarily with the survival of his own family or household, but also alive to the possibilities of a wider market economy. If that is so, then two further reflections must logically follow. Historically, peasants only exist when markets exist, even if they do not fully participate in them; or, to take the argument a stage further, those whom we call peasants are reliant upon markets for the distribution of some of their produce, but they do not control these markets – they are drawn into them. And that in turn raises the question whether peasants voluntarily or involuntarily engage with markets, an issue not merely pragmatic, but one which goes to the heart of what we understand 'peasant' predisposition or mentality to be.

The apparent indeterminateness of peasants is precisely what for Eric R. Wolf constitutes their essence: they stand, in his words, 'midway between the primitive tribe and industrial society'. Along that spectrum the mid-point may be hard to determine. In any case, he goes on, it requires more than chronology to define peasants: their 'social location' is vital, too. 'It is only when . . . the cultivator becomes subject to the demands and sanctions of power-holders outside his social stratum that we can appropriately speak of peasantry.'[2] It is to the legal and political constraints operating upon the peasantry that Wolf, and virtually all other scholars who have studied peasant societies, would trace the hallmarks which distinguish peasants from (earlier) primitive cultivators or (later) commercial farmers. That is not to deny that there are structural differences between peasants, on the one hand, and nomadic herdsmen or hunter-gatherers, on the other; or that functional distinctions exist between a peasant household and the life of a slave in Greek or Roman antiquity (or, indeed, a hired hand today).[3]

1. Frank Ellis, *Peasant Economics: Farm Households and Agrarian Development* (Wye Studies in Agricultural and Rural Development) (Cambridge, 1988), pp. 4–5.
2. Eric R. Wolf, *Peasants* (Englewood Cliffs, NJ, 1966), p. 11.
3. Werner Rösener, *The Peasantry of Europe* (Oxford/Cambridge, MA, 1994), p. 18, following Reinhard Wenskus (ed.), *Wort und Begriff 'Bauer'* (Göttingen, 1975), pp. 13f.

But crucial to the definition of a peasant are power-relations (or class-relations) between dominant and subordinate groups – rudimentary in primitive societies, perhaps, but fundamental to peasant ones.

In primitive societies, anthropologists have observed, cultivators, whether settled or nomadic, may accumulate surpluses, but they do so not for economic gain by exchange but to build up necessary replacement stocks or else for ceremonial purposes (the ritual exchange of gifts). Peasants, by contrast, are obliged to generate surpluses which they render as tribute to power-holders beyond their own ranks. 'It is this production of a fund of rent', Wolf argues, 'which critically distinguishes the peasant from the primitive cultivator.' Yet the types of tribute and, more importantly, the means by which that tribute is exacted vary so that 'there are consequently many kinds of peasantry, not just one'.[4]

EUROPEAN PEASANTRIES IN THEIR WORLD-HISTORICAL CONTEXT

That insight is the starting-point for the present collection of essays on the peasantries of Europe. All the contributors share the view that, whatever common features may be discerned, peasants on the land-mass of Europe displayed significant differences, and it is a principal task of the essays which follow to explain why that should be so – whether the reasons, for instance, are to be sought in differing ecologies, inheritance rights, patterns of production and consumption, as well as the configuration of power-relations. That view, however, rests in turn upon two further assumptions which need to be spelled out. The first is that the differences within Europe cannot be appropriately demarcated by actual or historical political or national frontiers. There is no such thing as a 'national' peasantry, peculiar to one country. And that caveat applies just as much at the boundaries of Europe (or at the boundaries of Christianity, we might say), which is why the volume includes a comparative chapter on peasantries in both the European land-mass and the Near East under Ottoman rule, by Fikret Adanır. But at the same time the contributors accept that European peasantries differ in important respects from their counterparts in Africa, Asia or Latin America. Before discussing the various peasantries within Europe, therefore, we need to set them in the context of general attempts by historians and anthropologists to describe peasantries past and peasant. The most succinct of such studies remains Eric R. Wolf's classic account, simply entitled *Peasants*, which appeared over thirty years ago.

Taking up his point (to which we have already referred) that it is the 'appearance of the state' (that is, external power-relations brought to bear on cultivators) which marks the threshold of the transition between food cultivators in general and peasants, we can detect the emergence of peasants as early as

4. Wolf, *Peasants*, p. 10.

3500 BC in the Middle East, though only around 1000 BC in central America.[5] In Europe, too, peasants in this sense existed well before the Christian era, but the formation of a distinctive peasantry – as a separate caste or social group – was the achievement of the High Middle Ages. We will pursue this point in a moment. But at the outset we need to revert to a more basic level of analysis in order to identify which peasant ecosystems were characteristic of Europe, in order to be able to determine what distinguished European peasants from those in other parts of the globe. Here Wolf offers a helpful typological distinction between what he terms 'paleotechnic' and 'neotechnic' ecosystems (which some might be tempted – unwisely – to render as 'static/backward' and 'progressive/innovative'). Of the five types of paleotechnic ecosystems which he describes, only three occur in Europe, and of these three one, namely the permanent cultivation of favoured plots by means of an infield-outfield system, is rarely encountered except in deltas on the Atlantic seaboard. The two remaining types both rely on some form of crop alternation which allows part of the land to regenerate by lying fallow. Long-term fallowing is necessary where soil is poor and the climate harsh (cold and damp), as in Europe's most northerly latitudes. In Scandinavia, indeed, a particular variant of long-term fallowing can be found, known as swidden, a form of slash-and-burn husbandry in afforested areas, described in detail in David Gaunt's essay on Scandinavian peasantries. But swidden can only support a peasant economy in exceptional circumstances, or in conjunction with some other crop. The other type is short-term fallowing, characteristic of Eurasian grain farming. Here a further distinction must be drawn between Mediterranean and transalpine (or Continental) ecotypes, the former using a lighter plough (scratch-plough), often on a two-field rotation worked by family groups, the latter requiring a heavier, wheeled plough in a three-field rotation, sometimes using labour beyond the family unit.[6]

Onto these paleotechnic systems may be grafted a variety of neotechnic ecotypes, which encompass diversified or specialized cultivation. Among these may be counted horti-, arbori- and viticulture, as well as the cultivation of industrial crops (flax, cotton, dyestuffs). Dairy farming, mixed farming (a balance between animal and cereal husbandry) and plantation crops represent other neotechnic ecotypes. All of these, except the last, which is confined to the tropics, can be found in Europe, with a natural concentration of dairying in transalpine regions and specialized horticulture in the Mediterranean.[7]

This brief taxonomy of peasant ecotypes is helpful in identifying basic differences between European and non-European peasants. In Europe, peasants hold (though they do not necessarily own) land on which they grow crops or raise beasts using family labour. They are extensive rather than intensive cultivators such as rice-growers in permanent cultivation systems reliant upon water. European peasants are not peons, indentured wage-labourers working on plantations. The incidence of neotechnic ecosystems in many parts of Europe also

5. Ibid., p. 11.
6. Ibid., pp. 20–1, 25, 32–3.
7. Ibid., p. 36.

underlines the integration of the peasant economy, however partial, into the market. This gives us, therefore, the image of a peasantry of some independence, able to reproduce itself, with a stake in the land, but beholden to an ecology and technology which do not facilitate intensive land use or permit rapid increments in agricultural output. These are features which have persuaded some observers to infer an essentially conservative cast to the mentality of the European peasant, averse to innovation, risk or profit-maximization. Whether this view is justified comes under scrutiny in the essays which follow.

THE EMERGENCE OF PEASANTRIES

When we turn to the origins of peasantries in Europe, what immediately strikes us is that the terms used in the vernacular to describe peasants rarely make any mention of their occupation as tillers of the soil. The English word 'peasant' derives from the French *paysan*, which means no more than a country-dweller; both it and its equivalents in Spanish and Italian stem from the Latin *pagus*, a district or landscape (as in the modern French *pays*). The Scandinavian term *bonde* also indicates a land-dweller. In German, the word *Bauer* can easily lead to false conclusions. While in modern German the verb *bauen* does indeed mean to till the soil (as well as to build), the roots of the noun *Bauer* go back to the Old High German *bur*, meaning house, or more broadly the family group dwelling therein. The *gebure* were the members of the house community, while the *burschap* denoted, not the peasantry as a social corporation which its modern equivalent *Bauernschaft* implies, but the inhabitants of a locality, indeed a 'neigh*bour*hood' in its English cognate form.[8] The Latin sources themselves, it is true, as well as referring to country-dwellers (*rustici*), do also mention cultivators (*agricolae*), but in the early Middle Ages the commonest definition of such men and women was by their legal status – whether they were free (*liberi*), half-free (*liti*), or unfree (*servi*). The transition from a society in which peasants were present to a society in which the peasantry formed part of the social order can indeed be traced in part by the linguistic shift from legal to occupational designations. Peasants become identified primarily as tillers of the soil at the point where the beginnings of a division of labour between themselves, on the one hand, and those who fight (the knightly class) and those who pray (the clergy), on the other, can be discerned. The evolution from the clan or tribal retinue, whose members bore arms and tilled the soil, which had prevailed among the Germanic peoples, to a settled society with a separation of functions or duties was the achievement of the High Middle Ages. The first inklings can be seen in the army reforms under Charlemagne in the years 807 and 808, whereby military service was restricted to those who held at least three, and subsequently four, hides of land. With that, the Frankish monarchy effectively excused from military duty the vast majority of country-dwellers, whose landholdings were too small

8. Werner Rösener, *Peasants in the Middle Ages* (Urbana, Il./Chicago, 1992), pp. 12, 161.

to qualify.[9] Much later, the public peace proclaimed throughout the German Empire in 1152 at Mainz banned peasants from owning weapons at all, thereby excluding them from infantry as well as cavalry duty.[10] The twelfth century marks the full emergence of the peasantry in Europe as an identifiable order or Estate within a society of Estates, no longer simply a *Bauernschaft* but a *Bauernstand*, as the German usage makes plain. This recognition underscores several points already made. The peasantry was a historically mediated phenomenon, not a timeless category; a peasantry is distinct from peasants; and the emergence of a peasantry was determined by its relations with other social groups.[11] The formation of the peasantry as a separate social class by the twelfth century was underpinned in the two centuries which followed by the consolidation of the peasant community at local level, in village, parish or district. The reasons for the rise of the rural commune, which are customarily traced to the disintegration of the manor and the loosening of the seigneurial bonds which it had imposed on those dependent upon the landlord's jurisdiction, need not detain us here. What is important to remember is that, even where *land*lordship lost its power of judicial coercion, lords still had an arsenal of weapons of dominion at their disposal. Seigneurialism did not disappear; rather, it was displaced or transformed by the growth of public or state authority in the later Middle Ages. The peasant commune, therefore, defined itself not only as a response to the crumbling of traditional landlordship (manorialism) but also against a background of consolidating authority in the hands of a continuing power elite.

Peasant communes were not peculiar to Europe from the later Middle Ages onwards, and even within Europe their diffusion and resilience varied greatly. But in its specifically European form as a 'closed corporate community', whose membership was restricted by birth and endogamy, and which collectively controlled the allocation of land and regulated external claims upon it for tribute, it developed, according to Eric Wolf, in the context of a social system which left intact the peasant base of production while appropriating the peasantry's fund of rent. These communes developed where the peasant ecotype was essentially paleotechnic, and where seigneurial authority was patrimonial (feudal) or prebendal (Max Weber's term to describe estates acquired not through inheritance but by state grant).[12] But – and here is the paradox – these types of domain were being superseded in parts of western Europe from the thirteenth century onwards by the mercantile domain (as Wolf calls it): land treated as a commodity, to be bought and sold for profit.[13] In its most advanced form, the spread of the mercantile domain, by subordinating social relations on the land to the dictates of the market and capitalist enterprise, could cause the peasantry and the peasant commune to disappear altogether, leaving capitalist landowners on one side, and wage-dependent farm-workers on the other. This is the pattern which is held to have emerged in England in the later Middle Ages.

9. Ibid., p. 21.
10. Ibid., p. 13; Rösener, *Peasantry of Europe*, p. 19.
11. Ibid., pp. 18, 20; Rösener, *Peasants*, pp. 12–13.
12. Wolf, *Peasants*, pp. 85–6; cf. p. 51.
13. Ibid., pp. 54, 56–7.

PEASANTS AND THE MARKET

At the very point, therefore, that we can discern a separate peasant class in Europe and its manifestation at local level in the rise of the commune, the European peasantry was increasingly being drawn into a web of commercial relations which had the potential to transform the basis of its social and economic existence. That underscores once again the essential indeterminateness of the European peasantry from its flowering in the thirteenth and fourteenth centuries until its virtual disappearance in the eighteenth and nineteenth, the chronological bounds of the present volume. For in these centuries peasant economy and society in Europe were always in flux, exposed in varying degrees at different times to market pressures and their social repercussions.

The attitude of peasants towards the market has been the subject of intensive historiographical debate, of which it is only possible of give a flavour here, since our main purpose is to unravel how commercial pressures served to distinguish between different peasantries. Two points should be stressed at the outset. In the first place, the commitment of peasants to markets varied, and when times were hard peasants tended to revert to subsistence agriculture. In the second place, peasants resorted to the market to raise cash for tribute payments to the power elite before they came to engage in commercial competition with other peasants or with non-peasants. This was particularly the case where no free market in land existed – indeed, the rise of a land market is often taken to herald the decline or eclipse of a traditional peasant society and economy.[14] However, when we speak of markets we need to be clear that three distinct (though obviously related) phenomena are involved. The market is a physical entity, a place where goods are exchanged; it also denotes the system of commercial exchange itself; and it describes the existence of a resource or a demand. In all three senses the markets with which peasants in pre-industrial Europe engaged were deficient or underdeveloped. Market foundations by lords often owed as much to political and territorial imperatives as to purely economic objectives; their location and operation were accordingly often skewed or stilted (to use Robert Dodgshon's term).[15] Poor communications and transport, and with that poor dissemination of information, impaired the working of a perfect market system. And, not least, the rudimentary development of capital markets meant that peasants had to borrow from their own landlords, merchants or moneylenders at rates of interest which fluctuated unpredictably and which were not driven by purely economic criteria: credit and interest might be tied to the price of land or labour and thus were in part socially determined.[16] Here the contrast between peasants and commercial family farms is most evident. Although even markets in modern capitalist economies, despite the claims of certain monetarists, do not function perfectly either, credit is freely available,

---

14. Ellis, *Peasant Economics*, pp. 10–11.

15. Robert A. Dodgshon, *The European Past: Social Evolution and Spatial Order* (Houndmills, Hants/London, 1987), pp. 238–9.

16. Ellis, *Peasant Economics*, pp. 11–12.

rates of interest are economically driven, technical knowledge is widely diffused, and there is a free market in land. These are the variables which enabled Frank Ellis to reach the definition of peasants cited earlier, and to distinguish them from commercial family farmers (who will *not* return to subsistence farming in times of adversity). His conclusion deserves to be spelled out in full:

Peasants are farm households, with access to their means of livelihood in land, utilizing mainly family labour in farm production, always located in a larger economic system, but fundamentally characterized by partial engagement in markets which tend to function with a high degree of imperfection.[17]

But if markets in capitalist societies are not 'perfect' either – a woman's work in the home is rarely paid for by her husband; wage-workers often grow some of their own food on allotments, as John Langton points out in the Conclusion – then we need to find a more fundamental feature by which to determine peasants' relations to markets. This is suggested in Karl Polanyi's classic work *The Great Transformation*, where he describes the markets in labour, land and money as they exist today under capitalism (in the form of wages, rent and interest) as essentially fictional, for what they trade in are not commodities at all, for none of them originally exists or is produced for sale. In that sense, markets under capitalism rely upon a commodity fiction which 'supplies a vital organizing principle in regard to the whole of society'.[18] Peasants in pre-industrial Europe clearly did not engage in such fictional markets as a rule, so that the issue no longer turns simply on whether we can construct an evolutionary chronology of peasant integration into markets, but at what point we can trace the rise of fictional markets, for they did indeed finally spell the end of a peasantry as it is customarily understood. If we follow Polanyi, that did not occur – perhaps could not have occurred, even in England – before the end of the eighteenth century. Nevertheless, the process of peasant integration into the 'non-fictional' market, that is to say, into a web of relations of commercial exchange, began much earlier. One notable attempt to plot such integration was undertaken by George Dalton in the very first issue of the *Journal of Peasant Studies* in 1973. He argued that traditional peasant markets existed in Europe until the late Middle Ages, in which more than half the peasants' output was not transacted at market but instead directly consumed or yielded in tribute to lords. But from the late fourteenth century onwards until the dawn of the industrial era (the span of the present volume) peasants entered a new phase in which they were exposed to the pull of burgeoning regional and even international markets, especially if they were engaged in specialized production of high-value commodities (quality viticulture, or silk-manufacturing, for instance).[19]

But that does not altogether address the question whether peasants' involvement in emerging markets was voluntary or involuntary. In the 1920s Alexander

17. Ibid., p. 12.

18. Karl Polanyi, *The Great Transformation: The Political and Economic Origins of Our Time* (Boston, MA, 1957), pp. 68–9, 72–3.

19. George Dalton, 'Peasant markets', *Journal of Peasant Studies*, 1 (1973), pp. 240–3. Quoted in Richard Hodges, *Primitive and Peasant Markets* (Oxford, 1988), pp. 5–6.

Chayanov (going somewhat out on a limb against the prevailing Marxist orthodoxy in the Soviet Union) suggested that there might indeed be some truth in
the notion that peasants wished to buy and sell at market with thought to profit.
What hindered them, he argued, was not so much the lack of intrinsic desire,
but the fact that the expenditure of peasants' time, energy and money might
amount, in their perception, to nothing more than extra drudgery.[20] Nowadays,
the argument has moved on. Simply put, peasant participation in the market
has been given a positive rather than a negative charge. That is to say, on the
assumption that everyone has infinitely expandable wants, has self-interest,
and believes themselves to be guided by rational choices, then they will exploit
market opportunities (or, if they do not, there will be good economic reasons
why), so that in this light regional specialization is not something which sucks
peasants reluctantly along in its wake but something which peasants actively
pursue if the opportunity presents itself.[21] Here a note of caution must in any
case be sounded. While it is true that a primary motive for peasants entering
markets was the need to provide tribute to those with power over them, it
should not be thought that peasants' willingness to trade over and above what
social relations dictated meant that they became free economic agents once
the requirement of tribute had been satisfied. It has been emphasized, most
recently by Stephan Epstein, that lords exercised dominion not simply over
production (the classic Marxist assumption) but by controlling distribution as
well. Markets were important not simply as places of exchange or distribution, but also as a means of appropriating surpluses and redistributing profits
from production and trade. Markets are not simply economic or commercial,
but political and social instruments as well, which are shaped by institutions
and property relations as well as by the more immediately obvious factors of
resources and location.[22] It would be wrong, therefore, to suppose that peasants 'escaped' from social constraints governing production into an apparently
autonomous sphere of exchange beyond power-relations where only the 'laws
of the market' operated. Hence it is dangerous to infer that increasing commercialization within the late medieval European economy automatically spelled the
replacement of 'feudal' by 'capitalist' relations and the gradual disappearance of
a traditional peasantry. The trajectories along which that might occur will be
examined below, but there was no teleology in the process.

THE DISAPPEARANCE OF TRADITIONAL PEASANTRIES

The difficulties in pinning down peasants' involvement in markets, and therewith
their exposure to pressures which might ultimately lead to the disappearance of

20. Ibid., p. 13. Cf. A. V. Chayanov, *The Theory of Peasant Economy*, ed. Daniel Thorner *et al.* (Homewood,
IL, 1966).
21. Cf. Hodges, *Primitive and Peasant Markets*, pp. 14–15; S. R. Epstein, 'Cities, regions, and the late
medieval crisis', *Past and Present*, 130 (1991), p. 8.
22. Cf. S. R. Epstein, *An Island for Itself: Economic Development and Social Change in Late Medieval Sicily*
(Cambridge, 1992), pp. 21–2.

a traditional peasantry, can be illustrated by examining three classic 'deviations' from the model of a traditional peasant household economy and social structure. The first is sharecropping, which has commonly been regarded as a form of subsistence agriculture, but which is sometimes seen as being to all intents and purposes capitalistic.[23] In Europe, sharecropping was practised between landowners and their tenants, rather than between the former and landless labourers, as in much of South-East Asia. That might appear to reinforce the impression of sharecropping as a form of subsistence agriculture in Europe, given that it embraced peasants with a stake in the land, not entirely dependent upon wage labour at the behest of the power elite. And yet it was prevalent in areas of intense commercialization and urbanization, such as Tuscany and Lombardy in northern Italy, where it evidently developed in response to the obvious market opportunities to maximize returns from agricultural output. A solution to this conundrum has been suggested by Frank Ellis, who stresses the dependence of sharecropping on two input markets which operated in different ways – the lord's ownership of land and the peasant's provision of labour. Where sharecropping was chiefly undertaken by tenant labour, it tended towards inefficiency since the use of labour was less than optimal, that is, the peasant had only a partial incentive to increase productivity (for that share of the crop, usually but not invariably 50 per cent, which he retained himself). But where the landowner had full control of all the inputs, that is, when he could determine the allocation of land *and* labour, then the only constraint was what wage-rate the market dictated, for the land-working tenant must – for sharecropping to make any sense – be allowed to earn as much as he would by being a full-time wage-labourer. In these circumstances, sharecropping could become efficient and truly responsive to the market, with the landowner turned effectively into a capitalist farmer.[24] In practice, though, in pre-industrial Europe the landowner rarely had complete freedom to dispose of the size and number of tenancies or to stipulate the labour input of the tenant. Nevertheless, since to work the land while retaining part of the crop was more attractive to peasants than being degraded to mere agricultural wage-labourers, sharecropping in principle, Ellis believes, tended to encourage efficiency rather than inefficiency, because peasants had a greater motivation to improve output if they kept part of the yield rather than none. What may have thwarted that tendency in our period, however, was the imperfect nature of the market (as we have argued above), in which calculations of risk – potential profit and loss – not only had a different arithmetic for peasants as opposed to landlords, but were reached in any case in a context of market rigidities and deficient information.[25]

In the context of northern Italy (to take the example cited earlier) the spread of sharecropping in fact worked to the detriment of secular economic transformation towards capitalist agriculture, not because it was not profitable, but

---

23. Cf. Epstein, 'Cities, regions, and the late medieval crisis', p. 7.
24. Ellis, *Peasant Economics*, pp. 142–7.
25. Cf. ibid., pp. 148–9. Ellis develops his analysis of sharecropping in considerably greater detail and with much more refinement than can be considered here. Cf. ibid., pp. 150–3.

rather precisely because it was – at least in the short term. The prevalence of sharecropping in the more fertile and prosperous agricultural areas, where peasants already had a stake in the land, inhibited, in Epstein's view, commercialization and specialization while emphasizing peasant self-sufficiency, because it offered lords a high rate of return for low initial investment and, by contracting the market, increased the possibility of gain by speculation. That landlords were thus able to distort the market for their own advantage (switching in and out of sharecropping when it suited them, changing the crops to be grown, and altering the terms of sharecropping contracts at will) is explained by the fact that the urban oligarchies of the north Italian cities were largely made up of sharecropping landowners! In the short term, then, the gains were considerable, but the long-term effects – in the case of Florence a general economic sclerosis and an inability to free itself from the necessity of importing grain until the mid-fifteenth century – were either ignored or not anticipated by the immediate beneficiaries within the power elite.[26]

Another path towards the dissolution of a traditional peasant society was trodden by the northern Low Countries from the sixteenth century onwards. This was predicated upon the abandonment of any attempt at cereal self-sufficiency; instead, grain imports, chiefly from the Baltic, allowed the rural economy of the Dutch Republic to flourish and diversify as never before. This came about because the rural population in parts of the Netherlands rejected a 'peasant' mode of existence in favour of what Jan de Vries has termed a 'specialization' mode of production. Since there is no separate essay on the Low Countries in the present volume, it is worth tracing de Vries's argument in some detail here. His starting-point is the difficulty experienced by all pre-industrial populations in raising agricultural output to meet demographic pressure. The precarious balance between population and resources is disrupted; famine and disease (or plague) ensue in what is known as the 'Malthusian check', until mortality has restored the population to a sustainable level once more. The question is whether that cycle could ever be broken in pre-industrial European society. In de Vries's 'peasant' model the answer is no. In response to population pressure peasants subdivided their holdings and increased their labour input to cultivate the land more intensively in order to satisfy a growing demand for food. Farm incomes declined, so that peasants were obliged to supplement their earnings through by-employments. At the same time, peasants were unable to produce enough grain to feed their own households and were consequently forced to buy additional stocks elsewhere, but because they were faced with rising cereal prices their available cash surplus to spend on other goods (such as craft manufactures) dwindled, and so peasants began to shun the urban markets. In effect, they drew in their horns and hunkered down to a subsistence economy, tumbling into debt and falling prey to institutional landowners (whose holdings remained intact) with spare capital to invest, who whittled away their tenancy rights. A burgeoning class of landless farm-labourers appeared in

26. Epstein, 'Cities, regions, and the late medieval crisis', pp. 39–40.

the countryside alongside peasant smallholders. But, above all, the weakening of commercial ties between town and country inhibited urban growth and put a brake upon wider economic development.[27]

That was the pattern which obtained throughout most of the European continent. In the northern Netherlands, by contrast, peasants embraced an entirely different strategy of 'specialization'. Faced with a demographic crisis, they kept their farms intact, resisted subdivision, abandoned non-agricultural by-employments and concentrated instead on raising agricultural output in order to sell their surplus on the open market to townsfolk, buying craft goods in exchange. In this situation peasants could actually benefit from the rise in cereal prices, and thereby gained some financial protection from the clutches of predatory urban capitalists. The surplus rural population no longer degenerated into a cottar class but either emigrated to the towns or else took up new full-time employment in the countryside in road- and canal-building, ironmongery or petty trading. The interaction of town and country stimulated local and regional trade, which was a decisive precondition of urban growth. The countryside was thus divided between specialized farmers, on the one hand, and artisans, on the other, living and working in quasi-urban settlements quite distinct from purely agricultural villages, which were known in the northern Netherlands as *vlekken*. As a result, the peasantry was no longer 'the' rural class, but merely 'a' class of farmers alongside other rural inhabitants.[28]

De Vries is careful to point out that this pattern of 'specialization' did not occur throughout the whole of the northern Netherlands (the Dutch Republic, as it became); it was essentially confined to the maritime provinces of the northwest and centre, those which had never been fully 'feudalized' in the Middle Ages, and where a free peasantry had been able to establish itself. In the provinces further to the east or south seigneurialism continued, as did a traditional peasant social and economic regime. Where 'specialization' prevailed, however, the farming population remained stable, while the output from pastoralism and dairying improved steadily. Here it was the non-farming population which grew, independently of any urban investment or early-capitalist 'putting-out' of work on piece-rates to rural wage-labourers; indeed, it engaged in businesses which directly helped the farming sector to grow (shipbuilding to facilitate transport, petty trading to supply consumer goods to farmers). In the *vlekken* new local markets sprang up to enable more frequent and convenient selling of agrarian and craft products. Although the older urban centres protested loudly, these new markets intensified rather than disrupted the existing market network, in which the chartered towns remained the prime centres of commodity exchange and credit.[29]

Although de Vries paints a picture of significant change within the traditional peasant economy and society in the northern Netherlands – which does indeed bear some of the hallmarks of capitalist agriculture worked by commercial family

27. Jan de Vries, *The Dutch Rural Economy in the Golden Age, 1500–1700* (New Haven/London, 1974), pp. 4–7.
28. Ibid., pp. 7–11.
29. Ibid., pp. 125–7, 137, 155–7.

farms – he is too shrewd a historian to be carried away by the impressive evidence of the early modern period on its own, the 'Golden Age' of the Dutch Republic. Not only, as we have seen, did the 'specialization' model not apply to certain provinces of the Netherlands, even in the areas where it did develop there was no decisive transformation towards industrialization or modern capitalism. Towards the end of the seventeenth century agricultural output began to stagnate and urban industrial output to decline. The reasons which de Vries advances – notably the lack of a cottar class which could have provided the labour to feed the growth of proto-industries, and more widely the very openness of the Dutch rural population to urban or bourgeois cultural values which may have acted as a barrier to industrialization (with its implication that the workforce would be reduced to a proletariat)[30] – rest upon assumptions about the inherent dynamic of proto-industrialization, and the location of its preconditions in rural indigence or immiseration rather than affluence, which recent historiography on the subject has called into question.[31] Not only was there no teleology of development in the 'specialization' model, it is doubtful whether any can be found in the spread of proto-industries either. Here it is salutary to be reminded of the wider human constraints upon economic development which John Langton highlights in the Conclusion to this volume.

Is it the case, therefore, that before the coming of the industrial age the peasantries of Europe, like the poor, were 'always with us'? The third path to a possible supersession of peasantries by commercial family farmers, the case of England, suggests not. The classic argument has been that the enclosure of open fields to permit intensive pastoral farming in the sixteenth century transformed the social and economic relations of production in the countryside to the point where agricultural output was geared to an emerging national market and hence became fully commercialized, while land and the labour required to work it became fully commoditized. Customary tenures worked by peasant households were replaced by leaseholds, whose rental value was determined entirely by the market, the laws of supply and demand. Those who had once been peasants were either degraded to landless, wage-working farm hands, or else became yeomen leasing tenancies at commercial rates from capitalist landowners, with the network of feudal obligations swept away, their households instead fully integrated into a market economy. In England, large aristocratic landowners gained control of around three-quarters of the land by the late seventeenth century, a proportion far higher than anywhere else in western Europe, where a traditional peasantry with hereditary tenures protected by custom and latterly by the state was able to entrench itself, owning perhaps as much as 40 per cent of cultivable farmland.

As a broad statement of fact, this account is widely though not universally accepted (as we shall see below), but why developments in England should have

---

30. Ibid., pp. 234–5, 239.
31. For the most recent surveys, with extensive bibliographical references, cf. Sheilagh C. Ogilvie, 'Institutions and economic development in early modern Central Europe', *Transactions of the Royal Historical Society*, 6th series, 5 (1995), pp. 221–50; Sheilagh C. Ogilvie and Markus Cerman (eds), *European Proto-Industrialization* (Cambridge, 1996).

differed so markedly from the continent of Europe (except the Low Countries), or indeed the rest of the British Isles (for a peasantry is certainly regarded as having survived in Scotland, Wales and Ireland), remains highly controversial. Only the outlines of recent debate can be sketched here. Some historians have believed that the decline of serfdom in England after the Black Death in the mid-fourteenth century played a decisive role, for the feudal constraints ('extra-economic coercion') which had prevented the emergence of purely market-driven agricultural production were thereby removed.[32] But the decline of serfdom is at best a necessary, not a sufficient, explanation: necessary, inasmuch as commercial family farming fully integrated into the market is clearly incompatible with the survival of feudal obligations; but insufficient, since serfdom disappeared (or was radically transformed) in many other parts of Europe without paving the way for capitalist agriculture or the disappearance of a peasantry. Indeed, in parts of eastern Europe the rise of vast grain-exporting latifundia geared to overseas markets in western Europe was facilitated from the sixteenth century onwards by the reimposition of feudal obligations accompanied by the erosion of secure peasant tenures to create a wage-working rural labour force, part cottar class, part quasi-proletariat. This picture, of course, has been subject to much retouching, and cannot perhaps be sustained at all in its original colours (as William Hagen's essay shows); and there are those who would argue that any system of agricultural production which uses servile labour cannot, by definition, be fully capitalist. However, the east European latifundia of the early modern period can plausibly be compared to the colonial economies of the eighteenth century in the Caribbean or Latin America, where indentured labour was used to work sugar, coffee or cotton plantations, whose mode of production seems eminently capitalist.

In other words, there are two separate issues at stake: the rise of capitalist agriculture, on the one hand, and the disappearance of serfdom and of a traditional peasantry, on the other, the latter a feature specific, though not exclusive, to England. A sweepingly ambitious explanation of the peculiarity of English development was offered twenty years ago by Robert Brenner. His analysis, not only Marxist in its categories, but privileging the role of relations of production (the social conditions governing land and labour) over the role of factors of production (such as technological change), was intended to refute what had become the prevalent assumption among historians, namely that demographic change holds the key to secular economic transformation. Those who had argued that the demographic and economic slump of the late medieval agrarian crisis could explain such change were, in Brenner's view, profoundly mistaken, for what was a pan-European phenomenon (with pockets of exception, to be sure) led to radically different outcomes in England and on the continent. The explanation, he insisted, must lie in the differing configuration of class relations in the two societies. Brenner's thesis provoked a vigorous debate, which unfortunately has remained inconclusive. Those who disagreed with his analysis

---

32. The best survey of the decline of serfdom (which stresses that the benefits accruing to the peasantry should not be overstated) remains R. H. Hilton, *The Decline of Serfdom in Medieval England* (Studies in Economic History) (London/Basingstoke, 1969).

(particularly those who questioned whether the differences between France and England were as stark as he claimed) failed to budge him from his original position; indeed, in his magisterial summing-up of the debate, a massive riposte of over one hundred pages, Brenner gave barely an inch to his critics.[33] There is no space here to rehearse the arguments in detail, but one feature of Brenner's analysis deserves to be highlighted. In England, he suggests, the landholding gentry and magnates were at once weak and strong: weak, because they were unable to reimpose serfdom effectively after the Black Death (the Statute of Labourers being reduced to a dead letter); but strong enough to erode (or transform) some customary peasant tenures, replacing them with commercial leaseholds. Faced with the impossibility of any further recourse to serfdom, lords switched tack and committed themselves to extracting surplus value from their labour force by means of market-driven rental income alone. There is, however, no consensus on why landlords should have been able or indeed willing to do so, apparently uniquely, in England. Is the explanation to be found in the peculiarities of English land law, which facilitated the buying and selling of land; in the particular character of the English state, as a strong centralized monarchy which had no need to succumb to the kind of trade-off which the French monarchy entered into with its nobility, whereby their liberties (particularly their fiscal immunity) were guaranteed, but which at the same time required a strong and stable peasantry as a vital financial milch-cow; or was it because of the unusual degree of commercial integration within the late medieval English economy, in short, the emergence of a national market, which gave an external impetus to the transformation of property relations in the countryside? These possible explanations are, needless to say, not mutually exclusive, though most recently it is the last of the three which has received the most attention. Richard Britnell has argued that commercialization cannot be deployed as a catch-all explanation for the collapse of serfdom and the transformation of property relations in England, but he notes that the 'possibilities for liberty were objectively greater in the later fifteenth century than they had been, at much the same level of population, in the late twelfth'.[34] In order words, similar structural circumstances within English agrarian society produced, three centuries apart, a different outcome, and the reason, he contends, is that the quantity and productive capacity of resources other than labour had increased. Britnell waves no magic wand; least of all is he susceptible to claims that technological innovations were decisive (though recently Bruce Campbell has sought to reaffirm the importance of technological change, especially the use of windmills).[35] Rather, Britnell argues that 'commercialisation . . . encouraged and permitted increases

33. T. H. Aston and C. H. E. Philpin (eds), *The Brenner Debate: Agrarian Class Structure and Economic Development in Pre-Industrial Europe* (Cambridge, 1985). For a useful discussion of the Brenner debate see S. H. Rigby, *English Society in the Later Middle Ages: Class, Status and Gender* (Houndmills/London, 1995), pp. 127–43.

34. R. H. Britnell, *The Commercialisation of English Society 1000–1500* (Cambridge, 1993), p. 223.

35. Bruce M. S. Campbell, 'Progressiveness and backwardness in thirteenth- and early fourteenth-century agriculture: the verdict of recent research', in Jean-Marie Duvosquel and Erik Thoen (eds), *Peasants and Townsmen in Medieval Europe: Studia in Honorem Adriaan Verhulst* (Centre Belge d'Histoire Rurale, 114) (Ghent, 1995), pp. 546–9.

in productivity' and so aided 'the development of traditional activities'.[36] Commercialization was a reciprocal process: it stimulated economic specialization while simultaneously promoting the growth of new regional markets and fairs. The former made agriculturalists more dependent on the latter, but, equally, the latter encouraged the former. (He also remarks that all this was quite compatible with a survival of serfdom.[37]) Because of the role of the national monarchy, the institutional barriers which impeded trade throughout much of the continent (local franchises, immunities, or tolls in the hands of often competing princes or cities) were greatly diminished in England, so that, as Christopher Dyer has suggested, a 'great chain of being' from rural specialization at local level to regional or national distribution, not to mention a burgeoning export trade, could develop, linked by an interlocking hierarchy of central places.[38] In that sense, there are some obvious parallels to Jan de Vries's 'specialization' model for the Netherlands, but we are still left with the question of why England achieved a decisive transformation into fully capitalist agriculture, both economically *and* socially, and on that foundation into the first capitalist industrial economy, whereas the Netherlands stagnated. It is not the primary task of a volume on the peasantries of Europe to attempt to solve that conundrum, though it is hoped that the essays which follow may offer some suggestions.

But this rapid consideration of the English anomaly cannot be brought to an end without mentioning an altogether heretical explanation of the peculiarity of England. In 1978, when the Brenner debate was beginning to pick up speed, Alan Macfarlane published a highly controversial account of the development of English society, *The Origins of English Individualism*, which argued, in essence, that the debate over the transition from feudal to capitalist agriculture, and therewith the disappearance of the English peasantry, was fundamentally flawed, because a traditional peasantry had never existed in England in the first place.[39] It has to be said at the outset that Macfarlane's thesis left his colleagues, especially medieval historians, entirely baffled (though it found favour with certain right-wing journalists). It is striking, at any rate, that none of the contributors to the Brenner debate, not even Brenner himself, gave Macfarlane a second glance. Indeed, Macfarlane's argument – apart from one stinging review by Rodney Hilton[40] – has been passed over in dignified silence by most historians. Before we judge whether this scholarly death by neglect is justified, the outlines of Macfarlane's case must be sketched.

In its essentials, his argument rests upon two assumptions. The behaviour of English 'peasants', not only in the sixteenth century but in the centuries before, was entirely and resolutely individualistic. They bought, sold, transferred, bequeathed land as a commodity, heedless of the interests and claims

36. Britnell, *Commercialisation*, p. 229.
37. Ibid., p. 230.
38. Christopher Dyer, 'Market towns and the countryside in late medieval England', *Canadian Journal of History*, 31 (1996), pp. 17–35.
39. Alan Macfarlane, *The Origins of English Individualism: The Family, Property and Social Transition* (Oxford, 1978).
40. R. H. Hilton in *New Left Review*, 120 (1980), pp. 109–11.

of other family or household members, and of the peasant's emotional stake in the land as a social, as well as an economic, good. This behaviour, he goes on, stands in glaring contrast to the attitudes of those within his model of a traditional peasantry, constructed exclusively from east European evidence, where peasants displayed all the attributes described earlier in this Introduction. What are we to make of this hypothesis? It cannot be denied that a certain unease pervades Macfarlane's argument, where he concedes that the peasantries of *western* Europe (the comparison at the heart of the Brenner debate) may have behaved rather more like their English counterparts than their other neighbours to the east. But even in eastern Europe, Macfarlane's belief in the essentially collectivist and conservative character of peasantries cannot stand up to the evidence of peasant land-dealing and marketing in, for instance, Russia (see Edgar Melton's contribution in this volume, and the fundamental study of peasant farming by R. E. F. Smith[41]). As far as England itself is concerned, it is not clear why Macfarlane assumes that 'individualist' behaviour in one dimension (even assuming his interpretation of the evidence is sound) should preclude collective behaviour in another. If the peasants of fourteenth-century England were already such thoroughgoing individualists, how are we to understand the rebels in the English Peasants' Revolt of 1381 at Smithfield, as recounted by Henry Knighton, the Leicester chronicler, who reported that they were demanding 'that all preserves of water, parks and woods should be made common to all: so that throughout the kingdom the poor as well as the rich should be free to take game in water, fish ponds, woods and forests as well as to hunt hares in the fields . . .'?[42] This demand, for the communal control of resources held to be common to all and whose usufruct should benefit the commonweal, echoes very closely aspirations voiced in the German Peasants' War of 1525, whose participants stand in no danger of being disqualified as peasants. It is regrettable that the debate over these issues has all but petered out, as if the contestants have fought themselves to a standstill. Those who address the issues in future, it might be concluded, would be well advised to bear in mind that explanations which focus exclusively on relations of production at the expense of the forces governing distribution are unlikely to take us much further.

What is so striking about all the attempts to explain the alleged disappearance of the English peasantry is that their terms of reference are essentially legal rather than social or economic. Whatever the differences between Macfarlane and Brenner (and they are huge), or even between Postan and his critics in an earlier generation, historians of English rural society have been obsessed with legal status, and inheritance and property rights, in a tradition stretching back through Vinogradoff to F. W. Maitland himself. How far this historiographical straitjacket has impeded an understanding of the determinants and characteristics of the peasantries of England is explored in Richard Smith's contribution to this volume.

41. R. E. F. Smith, *Peasant Farming in Muscovy* (Cambridge, 1977). Cf. also Gilbert Rozman, *Urban Networks in Russia, 1750–1800, and Pre-Modern Periodization* (Princeton, NJ, 1976).
42. R. B. Dobson (ed.), *The Peasants' Revolt of 1381*, 2nd edn (Houndmills, Hants/London, 1983), p. 186.

COMPARATIVE PEASANTRIES: AN AGENDA FOR RESEARCH

Given the volume's premise that differences between the peasantries of Europe may be as significant as the similarities, the contributors were not invited to write their chapters according to a rigid brief; indeed, the diversity of approach evident in the volume is testimony to the eagerness with which the contributors have sought to emphasize the particular characteristics of the peasantries of their own regions. However, to prevent the volume becoming of unmanageable length, and bearing in mind that it represents the beginning, not the end, of an intellectual enquiry long overdue, contributors were encouraged to pay most attention to the fundamental aspects of peasant life. As well as analysing the structure of peasant economy and society, questions of demography and standards of living, peasants' relations to lordship and the state, as well as the broader issue of peasant involvement in politics (including the politics of resistance, though a separate volume could easily have been devoted to peasant rebellions alone), were placed deliberately in the foreground. That is not to say that either the editor or the contributors regard the issues of peasant religion, culture or mentality as being of no importance (and from time to time these are accorded considerable prominence in the essays which follow, notably in Teófilo Ruiz's contribution on Iberia), but to aid a comparative understanding of peasantries in Europe it seemed appropriate to concentrate on the material conditions of peasant life, a decision vindicated by the sobering reflections contained in John Langton's Conclusion, which offers a historical-geographical perspective on the variations in peasant life. Comparative research will in the future undoubtedly add further dimensions to our understanding of peasantries over time and space, and many of the conclusions reached in the present volume are likely to be nuanced, revised, or even overthrown. None of the contributors would be alarmed at the thought. On the contrary, the comparative perspective which underpins this volume positively encourages the questioning of current assumptions, particularly those located in national historiographies. The present volume cannot lay claim to being the final word, if only because we still know too little about the peasantries in several areas of Europe. Portugal is one obvious example. Elsewhere, it would have been possible, even desirable, to devote two chapters to the British Isles, one comparing regional variations within England, and another contrasting Scotland, Ireland and Wales; to explain the survival of peasantries in the Celtic regions of the British Isles alongside their apparent disappearance in much of England is a task of comparative historical research which needs urgently to be addressed. A chapter on the peculiarities of the Low Countries, comparing late medieval Flanders and Brabant with early modern Holland and Zeeland, would also have made sense, since developments in fourteenth-century 'Belgium' seem to prefigure those in the sixteenth-century Netherlands; here the barriers of national historiography are particularly obtrusive. And the treatment of eastern Europe, notwithstanding Fikret Adanır's survey of the lands under Ottoman rule, should ideally have been more comprehensive. For that the editor offers no excuse, except to say that it is often easier to articulate a demand than to satisfy it, and that the volume is already much longer than originally planned. But a start must be made somewhere. This volume's aim is modest: to offer a new perspective on understanding the peasantries of Europe, in the hope that others will be encouraged to take the investigation further.

Map 2.1 France

CHAPTER TWO

The Peasantries of France, 1400–1789

Jonathan Dewald and Liana Vardi

'Peasants', '*paysans*': France gave Europe one of its preferred terms for describing country-dwellers, and for centuries the French peasants have held a powerful place in European imaginations. The images have been complex and often contradictory. French peasants have symbolized terrifying collective rage, as in the Jacquerie of 1358 and the château-burning of 1789. But they have also seemed to exemplify a baffling political apathy; in 1852 their indifference to political events provoked Karl Marx to dismiss peasants' political potential altogether. Many Europeans believed the French peasants to be especially impoverished, a miserable contrast to the dignity of English yeoman farmers; yet the French peasants have also seemed models of greed and canny economic calculation.

In part because they point in such different directions, these commonplace images raise basic questions that a historian of the French peasantry needs to ask. There are questions about the peasants' wealth or poverty, and about the sources of these. There are questions about the peasants' relations with other social groups, and above all with those who dominated French society: with the nobles, clerics and city-dwellers who held most of the society's wealth and enjoyed most of its privileges. There are questions about peasants' relations with one another, especially in the setting of village communities, and questions about peasants' culture, their beliefs about how life should be lived and their expectations as to what life would hold.

In each of these domains, the historian confronts the underlying problem that upset Marx and so many others, that of the French peasants' apparent backwardness. Numerous observers used this or similar terms in the early modern period, especially in the eighteenth century, when interest in agricultural development became widespread. But recent historical writing has begun to question the assumptions behind these observations. Historians no longer believe French agriculture to have fallen so far behind the English, nor do they see the French peasants as so apathetic as they once did. They have begun to portray the

French peasantry as wealthier, more energetic and less tradition-bound than was once believed.[1]

THE REGIONS OF FRANCE

At the start of any such inquiry lies a basic fact. At all points between 1400 and 1789, the French peasantry constituted an enormous mass of population: 15 million people in 1500 (nearly three times the total population of contemporary England), almost 26 million in 1800. Throughout the period, they made up about 90 per cent of the French population. France only ceased to be a primarily rural society in the late nineteenth century, well after the onset of the industrial revolution.[2]

Spread among some 40,000 rural communities, such a huge population resists generalization. No single interpretation could apply to so many people and so many villages. Although generalizations will always admit of exceptions, however, historians have traditionally divided France into four broad zones of rural life, zones shaped by a combination of natural and human geography. These geographical differences affected nearly all areas of human life. They meant that, despite many common experiences and common pressures, 'the French peasantry' in certain respects should be seen as several different peasantries, with divergent experiences and outlooks.

A first zone, the largest and most populous, occupied the broad plains of northern France, stretching from the Loire river in the south to Flanders in the north, from upper Normandy in the west to Burgundy in the east. Flat and open, these were areas of wheat production, though the region's agriculture yielded numerous other products as well: throughout our period, for instance, hillsides near the Seine continued to grow grapes for wine production. At the centre of the region was Paris, in 1600 Europe's largest city, a source of both opportunities and pressures for country-dwellers anywhere near its influence. In all, about one-third of the French population lived within this region.[3]

A second zone lay in western France, in the provinces of lower Normandy, Brittany, Anjou and Maine, and counted for about one-quarter of the French

---

1. A large historical literature on the French peasants developed between 1931, the first publication of Marc Bloch's *French Rural History: An Essay on Its Basic Characteristics*, trans. Janet Sondheimer (Berkeley, CA, 1966), and the mid-1970s. Two important efforts to synthesize this literature are Georges Duby *et al.* (eds), *Histoire de la France rurale*, 4 vols (Paris, 1975), and Emmanuel Le Roy Ladurie, *The French Peasantry 1450–1660*, trans. Alan Sheridan (Berkeley, CA, 1987), first published 1977. Studies of the French peasants have been far less numerous since 1975, but they have also brought a change in interpretive emphasis: from stress on the immobility of the countryside to exploration of its potential dynamism. See, for example, Philip T. Hoffman, *Growth in a Traditional Society. The French Countryside 1450–1815* (Princeton, NJ, 1996).

2. E. Anthony Wrigley, 'Urban growth and agricultural change: England and the Continent in the early modern period', *Journal of Interdisciplinary History*, 15: 4 (Spring 1985), pp. 683–728.

3. Population statistics calculated from Jacques Dupâquier, *La population rurale du bassin parisien à l'époque de Louis XIV* (Paris/Lille, 1979), pp. 159–66.

population. Here the terrain is hillier and soils are less rich, hence less suited to grain production. But the most important aspects of the landscape resulted from human effort. Already in the fifteenth century, hedges and small, enclosed fields dominated the landscape, and habitations tended to be more widely dispersed, with fewer residents in large villages, more in isolated hamlets. Together, these facts of human geography produced isolation for the region's rural population. In western France, the divide between urban and rural seemed far more absolute than in the Paris basin.

The third area was that of Mediterranean France – the provinces of Languedoc, Provence, Guyenne. This was a region of fundamentally different climate from the northern plains, a region of hot and dry summers. Climate allowed for agricultural possibilities that did not exist in the north (the production of olives, fruits, eventually silk worms), but it denied others – wheat grew well in many parts of the region, but the hot climate and light soils limited yields. On the northern plains, farmers produced crops two years out of every three; in the south, only in alternate years. On the other hand, in the south grain production required a lighter, cheaper ploughing apparatus and fewer draught animals; and the wide variety of agricultural products brought benefits to the small property-holder, whose small acreage could produce valuable crops. In the south, climate encouraged a degree of economic democracy. Partly for that reason, the region supported a surprisingly dense population: nearly as many villagers lived in the dry and hilly south as in the fertile plains of the Paris basin.

Finally, there were the large stretches of France that were ill-suited to permanent cultivation. These included the mountainous regions of the south-west and east, the Pyrenees and the Alps. Much of central France was barren and mountainous, and even in the fertile north large tracts remained forested. Regions like these were thinly populated, but by no means empty. They supported important trades that required forest resources, such as metallurgy and glass- and tile-making, and they provided pasturage. Some 15 per cent of French population – between 2.5 and 3 million people – lived within these regions, but many depended on the supplementary incomes provided by temporary migration.

How alien were these different regions from one another? Much more than geography and economic habits divided them. Residents of different regions spoke different forms of French, so different that they could scarcely have understood one another, and their religious beliefs might also differ. The French Revolution would make such differences dramatically evident: villagers in the Paris basin tended to support the Revolution's secularizing policies in far greater numbers than those in the west, south or centre.[4] On the other hand, every year thousands of men and women crossed these regional boundaries, either permanently or temporarily. In the late eighteenth century, at least 200,000 workers migrated annually, finding temporary jobs as harvesters and urban

---

4. For strong emphasis on the importance of such differences, Eugen Weber, *Peasants into Frenchmen: The Modernization of Rural France, 1870–1914* (Stanford, CA, 1976), pp. 67–94 and passim; Timothy Tackett, *Religion, Revolution, and Regional Culture in Eighteenth-Century France: The Ecclesiastical Oath of 1791* (Princeton, NJ, 1986), pp. 52–4.

labourers.[5] Though regional boundaries seemed impermeable, in other words, villagers in fact managed to negotiate the differences and fit themselves into new economic and social arrangements. Permanent migrations were equally important. French cities only survived because of regular immigration from the countryside, much of it from distant provinces. In the eighteenth century, two-thirds of all Parisians had been born outside the city, and about half the residents in provincial cities.[6] Such movement was common in earlier periods as well, although the documents do not permit quantitative estimates. Martin Guerre, today the best-known of sixteenth-century peasants, travelled across France and even lived for a time in Spain. Like the millions of eighteenth-century migrants, he (and the impostor who took his place in his native village) seems to have had little difficulty fitting into alien environments.[7]

GOOD YEARS AND BAD

If French peasants' experiences varied according to place, they also changed dramatically over time. Divided between good times and bad, the centuries from 1400 to the French Revolution fall into four eras, eras not quite overlapping the centuries themselves. The first half of the fifteenth century constituted a period of intense difficulty. The plague had reached Europe in the previous century, and repeatedly killed very large numbers. Still more destructive, however, was war, and the Hundred Years War ranked among the most destructive that Europe ever experienced. In mid-fifteenth-century Normandy (one of the regions especially hard-hit by warfare), the population fell to about 30 per cent of its thirteenth-century level. Even those who evaded the war's worst sufferings lost capital – livestock, crops, savings. All of Europe suffered dark times after 1348, but nowhere was the situation so bleak as in France.[8]

Conversely, France recovered vigorously from the fifteenth-century depression. The end of the Hundred Years War in 1453 ushered in a period of rebuilding and rural prosperity that lasted more than a century. The plague remained endemic in these years, but France enjoyed relative peace – only relative, it must be emphasized: there remained occasional civil wars and some destructive foreign invasions in these years. For villagers who had survived the depredations

5. Olwen Hufton, *The Poor of Eighteenth-Century France, 1750–1789* (Oxford, 1974), pp. 70–92; see also Jean-Pierre Poussou, 'Les Mouvements migratoires en France et à partir de la France de la fin du XVe au début du XIXe siècle: approches pour une synthèse', *Annales de démographie historique* (1970), pp. 11–78, and Abel Poitrineau, *Remues d'hommes: Essai sur les migrations montagnardes en France au XVIIe et au XVIII siècles* (Paris, 1983).

6. Pierre Goubert and Daniel Roche, *Les Français et l'Ancien Régime*, vol. II: *Culture et société* (Paris, 1984), p. 302.

7. Natalie Zemon Davis, *The Return of Martin Guerre* (Cambridge, MA, 1983), pp. 6–10, 21–6, 36–41; Daniel Roche, *Le Peuple de Paris* (Paris, 1981), pp. 20–33; T. J. A. Le Goff, *Vannes and its Region: A Study of Town and Country in Eighteenth-Century France* (Oxford, 1981), pp. 49–57; Goubert and Roche, *Les Français et l'Ancien Régime*, vol. II, p. 302.

8. Guy Bois, *Crise du féodalisme* (Paris, 1976), pp. 58–60. On the other hand, as Bois notes, very few villages were abandoned as a result of these losses; settlement remained stable, even as population collapsed.

of the previous century, this proved to be something of a golden age. Land was plentiful, and cheap to buy or rent; the population losses of the previous century saw to that. Taxes were relatively low, and landlords – eager to retain good tenants – were accommodating. A growing population offered profits for agricultural production, since food prices were rising.

But in the 1560s this growth slowed, and a new phase opened, one of darkening economic prospects and increasing difficulty for the peasantry. This was a drawn-out process, whose full results only became visible in the seventeenth century. Again, politics played a leading role in changing economic circumstances. In 1562 France entered a new phase of civil wars, now fought over religion. War between Catholics and Protestants continued on and off for more than thirty years, and in its last phases devastated northern France. Peace returned to most regions in the late 1590s, but the early seventeenth century brought new problems. In the 1630s France embarked on a newly ambitious international policy, which led it into full-scale war with Habsburg Spain. Taxation rose quickly, and soldiers confiscated farm goods. As late as 1640, some farming regions remained prosperous and secure, but by the mid-seventeenth century an agrarian depression hung over most of France. For the rural poor, these were terrible years. There was actual starvation in the famine of 1693–94 and during the terrible winter of 1709.

The countryside emerged from this period of difficulties just as hesitantly as it had entered. In the early eighteenth century the economic climate remained difficult for agricultural producers, but there was also cause for optimism. A more efficient government was increasingly concerning itself with improving society and controlling violence within it. As one result, for the first time the countryside enjoyed some protection from the military. Wars continued, but soldiers no longer lived freely off villagers; the government now housed them in barracks and managed to supply them without disrupting villagers' lives. The government also improved transportation within France. A handful of significant canals were built, and numerous new roads. Between 1765 and 1780, travel times between Paris and several leading provincial cities were nearly halved.[9] It became far easier for farmers to make money selling their produce. And a new era of European expansion overseas was beginning to affect economic life at home. As a result the eighteenth century – beginning in economic doldrums – became after about 1740 a period of buoyancy, and after 1763 a time of outright economic boom. Signs of prosperity could be seen across the eighteenth-century countryside. There were more village shops, with a wider array of goods. The wealthiest peasants began rebuilding their homes, seeking new forms of domestic comfort; and villagers of all classes took up new forms of consumption, as in the vogue for tobacco.[10]

9. Roche and Goubert, *Les Français et l'Ancien Régime*, vol. II, pp. 311–15.

10. Fernand Braudel, *Civilization and Capitalism, 15th–18th Century*, trans. Siân Reynolds, 3 vols (New York, 1982), vol. II, p. 68; Jonathan Dewald, *Pont-St-Pierre, 1398–1789: Lordship, Community and Capitalism in Early Modern France* (Berkeley, CA, 1987), pp. 33–4; for an important Europe-wide overview of these changes, Jan de Vries, 'Between purchasing power and the world of goods: understanding the household economy of early modern Europe', in John Brewer and Roy Porter (eds), *Consumption and the World of Goods* (London, 1993), pp. 85–132.

Until recently, French historians interpreted this alternation between good times and bad in terms of a simple, neo-Malthusian model. French agricultural technology, so their argument ran, advanced little between the fourteenth and the eighteenth centuries; and stagnant technology meant repeated demographic crises. As population rose closer to the limits set by society's productive capacities, signs of poverty became increasingly visible. Eventually, as during the fifteenth and seventeenth centuries, there would be famine, often combined with disease. Population would fall, leaving resources for the survivors and setting the foundation for a new period of growth. Only in the nineteenth century – so these historians have argued – did France free itself from this cycle.[11]

But in recent years historians have questioned the assumptions behind the neo-Malthusian model. French agriculture, they have shown, was not so stagnant as was once believed. In the later eighteenth century, it managed to feed a population 30 per cent larger than that of the late seventeenth century, and about 60 per cent larger than that of 1500 – and that population lived and ate better than its ancestors had done. Progress came in the form of steady, small improvements, rather than as an agricultural revolution. Farmers ploughed their land more often as the period advanced, and they used a wider array of implements and more horses. As a result, fields were clearer of weeds and crops grew in greater health and produced higher qualities of grain. Farmers also used more fertilizer: for the area around Paris, amounts of fertilizer increased by about 50 per cent between 1650 and 1700, and by an additional 20 per cent by 1760. The result was a substantial increase in wheat production and spectacular increases for other grains. Wheat yields increased by about 30 per cent between the later sixteenth and the later eighteenth centuries; oat yields increased by 40 per cent. In fact, despite the impressions of some contemporaries, French agriculture may have been as productive as English agriculture.[12] And facilities for storing and transporting grain also improved.[13]

Rather than reflecting the immobility of peasant agriculture, French subsistence problems reflected a complex set of market relations and political events. Warfare created periodic subsistence crises in all regions, but seventeenth-century famines

11. The standard statement of this view is that of Emmanuel Le Roy Ladurie, 'History that stands still', in his *The Mind and Method of the Historian*, trans. Siân Reynolds and Ben Reynolds (Chicago, 1981), pp. 1–27; for his use of these concepts to explicate the history of a specific region, see his study *Les Paysans de Languedoc*, 2 vols (Paris, 1966). See also Hugues Neveux, *Vie et déclin d'une structure économique: Les grains du Cambrésis, fin du XIVe-début XVIIe siècle* (Paris, 1980), and Michel Morineau, *Les Faux-semblants d'un démarrage économique: Agriculture et démographie au XVIIIe siècle* (Paris, 1971). Among French scholars, neo-Malthusianism remains highly influential: see most recently Emmanuel Le Roy Ladurie (ed.), *Paysages, paysans: l'art et la terre en Europe du Moyen Age au XXe siècle* (Paris, 1994), pp. 16, 86.

12. Jean-Marc Moriceau, 'Au Rendez-vous de la "révolution agricole" dans la France du XVIIIe sièle: A propos des régions de grande culture', *Annales: Histoire, Sciences Sociales* (January–February 1994), pp. 27–63; idem, *Les Fermiers de l'Ile de France, XVe–XVIIIe siècle* (Paris, 1994), p. 460; Robert C. Allen and Cormac Ó Gráda, 'On the road again with Arthur Young: English, Irish, and French agriculture during the Industrial Revolution', *Journal of Economic History*, 48: 1 (March 1988), pp. 93–116; Philip Hoffman, 'Land rents and agricultural productivity: the Paris Basin 1450–1789', *Journal of Economic History*, 51: 4 (December 1991), pp. 771–805. For a regional example of progress, Liana Vardi, *The Land and the Loom: Peasants and Profit in Northern France, 1680–1800* (Durham, NC, 1993), pp. 87–109.

13. Steven L. Kaplan, *Provisioning Paris: Merchants and Millers in the Grain Trade in the Eighteenth Century* (Ithaca, NY, 1984), pp. 66–79; Goubert and Roche, *Les Français et l'Ancien Régime*, vol. II, pp. 311–15.

hit most severely the region where agricultural production was most abundant, the Paris basin. Villagers there often went hungry; in a few especially terrible years, many starved. During the same years, the less efficient agriculture of the west managed to produce enough to feed a population that was just as dense.[14] Subsistence problems in the Paris basin derived from the enormous power of the urban market, which as the seventeenth century advanced drew to itself a steadily larger share of the region's production. Seventeenth-century famines resulted from the period's social changes, rather than from its immobility.[15]

PEASANTS, PROPERTY AND WORK

Rural social structures (as we will see in more detail below) did not depend primarily on ownership of the land. Villagers who owned similar acreage might have altogether different life experiences and economic positions. None the less, it remains important to determine what share of French soil the peasants owned, for access to this most basic means of production determined a variety of other village relations. As in most of early modern Europe, in France the concept of ownership itself involved complexities. In theory, most French land belonged to seigneurial lords, but real possession belonged to those who held land from the lords. Such seigneurial 'tenants' (as the law termed them) could sell their land, give it away, or leave it to their heirs, all without the lords' interference. They continued to owe the lord monetary dues and some forms of political obedience (as we shall see below), but otherwise they enjoyed the essentials of property. In much of Germany and in some other regions of early modern Europe, a clear-cut structure governed seigneurial tenures of this sort. 'Full peasants' (in the German phrase) held substantial farms; other villagers held only cottages, and worked for their landholding neighbours. But in France such clear divisions had disappeared by the late Middle Ages, a victim apparently of French peasants' commitment to egalitarian inheritance practices. Repeatedly subdivided and joined into new units, peasants' holdings in France came to include a full range of sizes and forms.[16]

During the fourteenth century, it seems, peasants dominated this form of property ownership in most parts of France.[17] But as the country recovered from its late medieval crises, peasant property became increasingly vulnerable, for mainly economic reasons. Several groups entered the market to buy peasant

---

14. Dupâquier, *La population rurale*, p. 153; on the role of war, see especially Hoffman, 'Land, rents, and agricultural productivity'.

15. This argument was developed by Jean Meuvret, *Le Problème des subsistences pendant l'époque de Louis XIV*, 6 vols (Paris, 1977–88). For summary and thoughtful reflection on Meuvret's views, George Grantham, 'Jean Meuvret and the subsistence problem in early modern France', *Journal of Economic History*, 49: 1 (March 1989), pp. 184–200; on the contrast between subsistence crisis in the plains and reasonable times in the *bocage*, Dupâquier, *La population rurale*, pp. 153–4.

16. Bloch, *French Rural History*, pp. 160–4.

17. Bois, *Crise du féodalisme*, pp. 216–18, 346–7, passim.

lands. After 1500 the number and wealth of royal officials rose, and most of them viewed land as an attractive investment; seigneurial lords as well came to understand that direct control of land might be preferable to the collection of permanently fixed feudal rents. At the same time, economic pressures encouraged villagers to sell. In an era of rising population, egalitarian inheritance divisions tended to produce holdings that were too small for economic viability. Economic uncertainties – harvest failures, the death of livestock – might force villagers to mortgage what land they held. Taxation was rising fast, and it too might require borrowing – and sooner or later debt typically led to outright loss.

Historians have charted for several French regions the decline in peasant landowning that resulted from these combined pressures. In lower Brittany, by the seventeenth century peasants owned only 11 per cent of the land; in the richest grain-growing regions near Toulouse, in the south-west, they owned about one-fifth, and south of Paris the situation was about the same. Peasant landownership survived best further from urban areas, and usually in regions where the land was poor. In the lower Auvergne, for instance, peasants still owned 61 per cent of the land in the mid-eighteenth century. Only estimates are possible for the country as a whole: they suggest that in the eighteenth century villagers owned about one-third of the land, compared to the 50 per cent held by nobles and bourgeois and the 10 per cent held by the Church. The crucial changes, it appears, came in the late sixteenth and early seventeenth centuries. The expropriation that these years produced was by no means total. Even in the mid-seventeenth century, after the wave of sales had largely ended, the French peasants retained more land than their English counterparts. But by about 1650 the difference was one of degree rather than of kind.[18] France no longer had a 'peasantry' in the form that some definitions have described – that is, agriculturists in the main independent of the marketplace, able to produce most of their basic needs from their own land.

By the mid-seventeenth century, then, the vast majority of French peasants owned less than five hectares of land, far below the minimum for survival as self-sufficient farmers;[19] and (as we will see below) only a small number had the possibility of working as large tenant farmers. How then did the majority manage to survive? For some, perhaps one-tenth of the rural population, the decline of peasant landowning meant severe poverty. These men and women survived partly by begging, partly by taking whatever short-term jobs came along. Poverty

18. Statistics from Jean Gallet, *La Seigneurie bretonne, 1450–1680: l'exemple du Vannetais* (Paris, 1983), pp. 601–3; James Collins, *Classes, Estates, and Order in Early Modern Brittany* (Cambridge, 1994), p. 64; Georges Frêche, *Toulouse et la région Midi-Pyrénées au siècle des lumières (vers 1670–1789)* (Paris, 1974), p. 153; Jean Jacquart, *La Crise rurale en Ile de France* (Paris, 1974), pp. 724–5; Abel Poitrineau, *La Vie rurale en Basse-Auvergne au XVIII siècle (1726–1789)*, 2 vols (Paris, 1965), vol. I, pp. 154–5; Emmanuel Le Roy Ladurie, 'Révoltes et contestations rurales en France de 1675 à 1788', *Annales ESC*, 29:1 (January–February 1974), pp. 6–22. For comparative overview, Eberhard Weis, 'Ergebnisse eines Vergleichs der grundherrschaftlichen Strukturen Deutschlands und Frankreichs vom 13. bis zum Ausgang des 18. Jahrhunderts', *Vierteljahrschrift für Sozial- und Wirtschaftsgeschichte*, 57: 1 (1970), pp. 1–14.

19. Pierre Goubert established the contours of this situation in a classic article, 'The French peasantry of the seventeenth century: a regional example', *Past and Present*, 10 (November 1956), pp. 55–77. Of 351 seventeenth-century villagers in the region around Beauvais, 325 owned less than two hectares of land.

at this level often required a wandering life: constantly seeking work, the very poor had only loose ties to the village community. Most peasants, however, could establish more stable lives than these. They did so by combining a complicated range of resources. Most continued to own small plots of land, and usually they rented additional plots. With these as an economic foundation, families survived by undertaking a variety of other work. Large farmers needed permanent farm servants, usually drawn from the village community; young children could be placed in these jobs, but farmers also employed mature skilled workers, who lived in the village. Several points in the agricultural year brought further, temporary work. Women and children found work every spring weeding; and the entire village could find employment during the harvest. Economic survival in these circumstances required the wage labour of the entire family. Villagers in mountainous regions might also need regularly to work away from the village; family budgets required the wages of migratory labour. On these terms, ordinary villagers could establish for themselves a solid place within village society, one that sharply distinguished them from wandering beggars.

PEASANT CLASSES

Early modern hunger made dramatically visible the fact of inequality within the countryside: in the worst years, some French peasants starved, while others had abundant resources. For just as the peasants were divided by regions, so also were they divided by class. These differences tended to widen as the period advanced, but their fundamental character underwent little change between 1400 and 1789. From the late Middle Ages until the Revolution, French peasants were divided into two groups. There were those who controlled enough land and livestock to provide for their own subsistence and to meet the additional demands that all villagers faced – to pay taxes and rents, and to buy some manufactured goods. On the other side were those who, lacking sufficient capital of this kind, needed to work at least part of the year for others, as manual labourers. All French villages were divided between these two groups, between agricultural labourers and surplus-producing farmers. The division was rarely equal, though degrees of inequality varied with time. In early fifteenth-century Normandy, about half of peasant households owned enough land to feed themselves. More commonly, as throughout the seventeenth and eighteenth centuries, agricultural labourers made up 90 per cent of the village population. These men and women had to work for wages and buy their food.[20]

Such class divisions might rest on differences in ownership of landed property, but this was not necessary or even typical. Manual labourers usually owned small plots of land within the village, and they owned their houses as well.

---

20. Bois, *Crise du féodalisme*, pp. 138ff; Goubert, 'The French peasantry in the seventeenth century', pp. 55–77; Dewald, *Pont-St-Pierre*, pp. 52–6.

Conversely, large farmers in many regions owned little more than this – they did not depend primarily on lands that they owned directly, but on land that they rented from others. They rented, of course, from those who had the most land, from nobles, the Church and the increasingly land-oriented bourgeoisie. French ruling groups had little interest in working the land themselves, an occupation that many found demeaning. They needed renters, increasingly so as the period advanced. Their holdings were expanding, and they were increasingly being drawn away from the countryside, to serve the king at court, in the army, or in the law courts. In these circumstances direct property management was a burden. Better to establish a flexible rental arrangement, usually for a term of nine years, giving the tenant a strong and direct interest in the careful management of the farm.

Not landed property, but other forms of capital divided farmers from manual labourers. To farm a substantial property required first the basic equipment – farm implements such as ploughs and harrows, which were relatively cheap, and at least one team of horses, which were very expensive. More important, owners insisted that their tenant farmers come with strong financial backing and with a reputation for skilled farming. Mistaken judgements in this matter could be costly. Tenants might fail to maintain buildings and walls, or damage the farmland itself by inadequate fertilizing or weeding. In either case, the value of the land might be damaged for years to come. Only someone with substantial financial resources could meet these demands, and usually this meant that only members of already-rich peasant families could undertake significant tenant farming. Some farmers' children might move down the social scale, to become rural labourers, but movement upward almost never took place.

To understand how the large farmers fitted into village society requires a brief examination of their economic circumstances. As an example, we may consider farmers' revenues and expenses in the Parisian basin in the years around 1600.[21] This was a region of substantial farms, with sixty to one hundred hectares of land and livestock to match: such a farm required five horses and about 100 sheep, the main source of the farm's fertilizer. In good years, the harvest of wheat and oats brought revenues of about 1,800 *livres*, and secondary activities – sales of livestock, wood, and the like – added at least 300 more. These were large sums of money, which substantially outstripped the gross incomes of most French nobles. The large farmer was indeed a substantial figure.

But with the farmer's large income went heavy expenses. One-eighth of the harvest had to be set aside as seed for next year; horses had to be fed and cared for; and servants' wages had to be paid. Alongside these basic expenses of running the farm, there were the claims of outsiders. Slightly under 10 per cent of the harvest went to the Church, as tithe payment, and the government took about as much in taxes; in most villages the large farmers carried the bulk of

---

21. The example here is taken from Jacquart, *La Crise rurale*, pp. 355ff. Cf. B. Garnier and R. Hubsher, 'Recherches sur une présentation quantifiée des revenus agricoles', *Histoire, Economie et Société*, 3:2 (1984), pp. 427–52.

royal taxation. Most important, about half of the gross harvest went to the landowner, as rent. Together, Church, state and landlord took about two-thirds of what the land produced, and their demands were inflexible as well as high. Even when harvests failed, landowners and tax collectors had to be paid.

The large farmers thus worked under extreme economic pressures, with little margin for failure. They needed to participate fully in the market for agricultural products, finding the highest prices and most advantageous outlets, and they needed to keep careful track of income and expenses. They also needed to think seriously about methods that might improve the returns from their efforts. Those who failed to do so could not long survive as farmers. Indeed, seventeenth-century conditions meant that even attentive farmers could not count on success. Taxes and rents both rose sharply in these years.

One result was an apparently inexorable decline of middling farmers, especially on the northern plains, where the economic pressures were greatest. Such figures had figured prominently in sixteenth-century villages. Employing mainly familial labour and disposing of only about twenty hectares of land, they fitted closely some stereotypical images of peasant life. But as profit margins narrowed after 1600, they became increasingly vulnerable. A single bad harvest or the need to replace a team of horses might push them into debt; further misfortunes might lead to outright bankruptcy, or at least to loss of their leases. As the middling peasants fell on hard times during the seventeenth century, farms tended to become larger and more efficient. Those tenant farmers who survived in the eighteenth century were even more commanding figures within the village than their ancestors had been. In the eighteenth-century Paris basin, thus, farmers typically had a capital of several thousand *livres* – at a time when skilled labourers earned 100–200 *livres* per year.[22]

Away from the northern plains, capitalist pressures diminished and middling farmers fared better. Partly for that reason, an alternative method of land rental survived in other regions, that of sharecropping. Under this arrangement, landowners confided their properties to tenant farmers, but along with their land they also confided the capital needed to make it fruitful: farm tools, livestock, seed. In exchange, landowners received a share of the harvest, usually at least half.[23]

Hence in early modern France sharecropping was usually associated with backwardness. It tended to prevail in the poorest regions, in the south and west of the country, where tenants could not be found who had the cash and other capital resources for more flexible arrangements. A result of backwardness, sharecropping probably also promoted backwardness. Impoverished tenants, barely making do with their diminished share of the harvest, usually enjoying scant security of tenure, could rarely improve the land they worked, or even cultivate it with proper care. In the eighteenth century, when agricultural reformers began

22. Moriceau, *Les Fermiers de l'Ile de France*, p. 870.
23. For the sharecropper's situation, Robert Forster, *The Nobility of Toulouse in the Eighteenth Century* (Baltimore, MD, 1960), pp. 56–8; idem, 'Obstacles to economic growth in eighteenth-century France', *American Historical Review*, 75: 6 (October 1970), pp. 1600–15; Steven G. Reinhardt, *Justice in the Sarladais, 1770–1790* (Baton Rouge, LA, 1991), pp. 20–5.

thinking about the matter, the prevalence of sharecropping seemed one of the scandals of French agriculture.

On the other hand, sharecropping mitigated the social inequalities that marked the more economically advanced north. Because the landowner supplied so much of the capital that farming required, sharecropping remained open to new families, and little separated sharecroppers from their neighbours within the village. In other ways too, the less developed regions of France favoured a degree of economic democracy. These regions produced a wider variety of crops than the north, and some of them could allow families to survive on small parcels of land. In mountainous and wooded regions, villages had large communal pastures, so that even impoverished families could raise some live-stock. Class divisions were sharpest in the country's most advanced regions, those whose agriculture was most capital-intensive and productive, those in which monetary relations were most widespread.

THE INDUSTRIAL COUNTRYSIDE

But another set of economic changes within the village worked to complicate these widening class divisions. In many regions, villagers enjoyed the additional economic resource of manufacturing work. By the late eighteenth century, a significant share of the French peasantry depended primarily on such sources of income, rather than on agricultural work. For that reason, peasants had more economic flexibility and larger possibilities than agriculture alone could supply.

Rural industrial production had extended across wide areas of France since the Middle Ages. In some trades, technology gave advantages to rural location. Metal-working and glass-making required large amounts of fuel, almost always wood, and hence clustered near the forests. Tanning and paper-making required water, and also produced noxious wastes that cities wanted to avoid. But above all there was the textile industry, which sought rural settings for mainly economic reasons, because labour was cheaper and working conditions freer than in the cities. Spinning and weaving could take place in the countryside, and already in the sixteenth century many rural areas depended heavily on these trades, often organized by urban merchants. Textile production dominated many villages in Flanders, Picardy, Normandy, Brittany, Maine, and in many areas of the south; by 1600, in the villages of Picardy there were far more looms than ploughs. Villagers turned willingly to such work partly because of its freedom from the demands of both Church and feudal lord. Neither tithe nor seigneurial dues were levied on rural manufacturing, in contrast to agricultural production.[24]

24. Bois, *Crise du féodalisme*, pp. 346–7; Jacques Bottin, 'Structures et mutations d'un espace protoindustriel à la fin du XVIe siècle', *Annales ESC* (July–September 1988), pp. 975–95; Collins, *Classes, Estates, and Order*, pp. 46–8; Henri Sée, *Les Classes rurales en Bretagne du XVIe siècle à la Révolution* (Paris, 1906), pp. 446ff.; Pierre Goubert, *Beauvais et le Beauvaisis de 1600 à 1730: contribution à l'histoire sociale de la France au XVII siècle*, 2 vols (Paris, 1960), vol. I, pp. 128–30.

Rural industry declined in the seventeenth century, as the entire European economy slowed and international competition became more intense. It suffered also from the state's hostility. When they thought about manufacturing, French officials envisaged urban production. This was part of a larger governmental concern for the cities, visible in its efforts to keep grain prices low and shift as much of the tax burden as possible onto the countryside. Officials viewed rural manufacturing as an infringement of urban rights and a threat to quality. Hence into the eighteenth century they continued to confiscate rural cloth production and to interfere with rural commercial networks.

But in the eighteenth century, official hostility to rural manufacturing receded, and finally in 1762 the government accorded partial freedom to rural manufacturing. Villagers had not awaited such official recognition: industry, most of it textiles, was already booming in the eighteenth-century countryside, in response to the broad upswing in the eighteenth-century economy. Near Amiens, rural weaving increased fourfold between 1690 and 1725. In Brittany, rural cloth production rose sharply after 1735, and then nearly doubled between 1767 and 1789. In lower Normandy, there was an eightfold increase in rural linen production. In villages around Saint-Quentin, in northern France, as many as two-thirds of the rural population wove fine linens in the last decades of the *ancien régime*. Such expansion appears to have characterized most of the country. In 1700 industrial and artisanal activity made up one-quarter of what France produced. By the 1780s, this share had risen to 39 per cent, roughly equivalent to the percentage of industrial activity shown in contemporary England. Since French society remained overwhelmingly rural throughout the eighteenth century, most of this increased output came from the countryside.[25] Rural industry, such statistics suggest, was not limited to a few regions. It brought a striking degree of prosperity to many eighteenth-century villages. Peasant landownership was declining, and agricultural work offered about the same possibilities that it had done for centuries. But spinning, weaving and other industrial activities brought to the village dramatically expanding possibilities.

The eighteenth century offered villagers another, still more enticing possibility: involvement in the marketing of the industry's raw materials and finished products. Urban merchants might seek to dominate some manufacturing districts, but more commonly they contracted with independent village merchants. In fact each side had an interest in such arrangements, for independent village merchants enjoyed the trust of their neighbours who produced cloth and yarn, and they took on some of the risks of the trade. In exchange, they had a chance to benefit from the profits of mercantile activity, and these might be considerable. Hence the eighteenth century saw the development of a hybrid figure, the villager who continued to own and farm land, but whose main energies were

---

25. Pierre Deyon, *Amiens, capitale provinciale. Étude sur la société urbaine au XVIIe siècle* (Paris, 1967), p. 214; Sée, *Les Classes rurales en Bretagne*, p. 449; Robert Schwartz, *Policing the Poor in Eighteenth-Century France* (Chapel Hill, NC, 1988), p. 145; see also Pierre de Saint-Jacob, *Les Paysans de la Bourgogne du Nord au dernière siècle de l'ancien régime* (Paris, 1960), p. 530, showing the rapid increase in the number of village artisans in that region. National statistics cited by Myron Gutmann, *Toward the Modern Economy: Early Industry in Europe, 1500–1800* (Philadelphia, 1988), pp. 117–20; Vardi, *The Land and the Loom*, pp. 127–202, for the interpretive questions surrounding rural industry and for close examination of how industrial regions functioned.

devoted to the cloth business. Villagers like these might run enterprises of start-ling scale and sophistication.[26]

Were villagers who took up manufacturing and merchandising of this sort still peasants? Some historians have argued that they ceased to be, that proto-industrial work detached villagers from the traditions and forms of behaviour of their ancestors, and converted them into a new kind of social being, closer to the urban industrial working class than to peasants. Such claims, however, rest on an unduly narrow conception of peasants' behaviour and ideals. Eighteenth-century merchant-weavers remained attached to their villages, even as they arranged transactions with English and German buyers. Indeed, attachment to the community formed an important business asset, allowing village merchants credit and access to goods. Rural industry allowed villagers to preserve their modes of life, rather than just challenging those modes.[27]

VILLAGERS AND LORDSHIP

In most regions of early modern France, feudal lordship provided some of the basic economic and political structures within which peasants lived. Seigneurial institutions did not weigh heavily everywhere. They were weakest in southern France, indeed non-existent in a few corners of the south. Elsewhere – notably in the west and in the wealthy province of Burgundy – they represented a heavy burden. Whatever the region, though, lordship formed the constant background to most peasants' lives.[28]

Lordship made both economic and political demands on them, though both declined over the early modern period. Over the area included within a lord-ship, its owners collected permanently fixed rents from all landholders, on the theory that the land had originally belonged to the lords, who had granted it out to peasant tenants. Lords had other economic rights. Usually they had a monopoly on milling within the village and ownership of its streams, rivers and woodlands. Many owned the markets within which peasants were required to buy and sell produce – transactions on which lords charged fees. In some regions lords could demand that villagers perform labour services, and almost everywhere they claimed a monopoly on hunting and fishing.

Lordship represented an equally important set of political constraints. All lordships included law courts, to which villagers had to bring their most basic cases, and in which they could be prosecuted for violating the lord's own rights and monopolies. A minority of lords owned more elaborate courts, the high

---

26. Vardi, *The Land and the Loom*, pp. 161–202; also Schwartz, *Policing the Poor*, p. 145; Dewald, *Pont-St-Pierre*, pp. 39–41.

27. A point originally emphasized by Peter Laslett, *The World We Have Lost* (New York, 1965), pp. 15–18.

28. For lordship's functioning, Dewald, *Pont-St-Pierre*, pp. 213–68.

justices, in which more serious matters were tried. In a few regions, lords named village mayors and officials, and everywhere they exercised a broad range of regulatory functions: supervising market prices, regulating building standards, and defending public morality, for instance by setting the hours during which taverns could be open and supervising what went on within them.

Into the mid-seventeenth century, this collection of claims and powers mattered a great deal to most French peasants. Seigneurial dues varied enormously, even within a single village, but for many peasants they represented a significant burden: in parts of Burgundy, the Auvergne and Brittany, as much as one-third of villagers' incomes. Even in regions nearer Paris, most legal business had to be carried out in the lord's courts, and milling monopolies remained vigorous. But in addition to the specific rights of lordship, there was the presence of the lord himself. His household was the largest employer in most areas, requiring numerous servants and officials, and indirectly employing tradespeople of all kinds. The lord's patronage counted more broadly: he could block or help villagers' efforts of almost any sort, including their efforts at careers outside the village. In the sixteenth and seventeenth centuries, in other words, lordship was not only a burden to villagers: it also offered opportunities.

But in most regions, the lordship withered in the later seventeenth and eighteenth centuries. In some areas, notably in Burgundy and Brittany, seigneurial dues remained a heavy burden even in 1789 – but in most areas they had lost much of their value long before, because they were fixed in cash and could not keep up with inflation. The lordship's judicial and regulatory powers suffered from the expanding power of the royal judiciary after 1660. Peasants could turn with increasing ease to urban courts, where they found better-trained and more impartial judges. Lords also spent less time in the countryside after about 1650, and this fact also reduced their influence on local life. Their households no longer dominated local economic transactions, and they no longer employed villagers as servants.[29]

Lordship's decay helps to explain the character of eighteenth-century relations between peasants and nobles. There were no significant rebellions against seigneurial authority in the eighteenth-century countryside, but neither was there respect for aristocratic authority. One historian, who examined a region in southern France, describes the situation as 'seigneur-baiting at a weekly level'. Lords in about one-quarter of the region's villages had experienced armed assaults by peasants, and about as many complained of insults and threats. Similar episodes were reported elsewhere. Villagers, it is clear, saw lordship as giving them little in exchange for its exactions. The institution had become too weak to inspire even hypocritical deference.[30]

---

29. Saint-Jacob, *Les Paysans de la Bourgogne du Nord*, pp. 116–23; Poitrineau, *La Vie rurale en Basse-Auvergne*, vol. I, pp. 344–5; Sée, *Les Classes rurales en Bretagne*, pp. 83–96; Dewald, *Pont-St-Pierre*, pp. 201–5, 251–63; Gallet, *La Seigneurie bretonne*, pp. 601–3.

30. Olwen Hufton, 'Attitudes towards authority in eighteenth-century Languedoc', *Social History*, 3: 2 (October 1978), pp. 281–302.

THE FORMS OF VILLAGE COMMUNITY

The decay of lordship was one of several forces in the early modern period that gave increasing importance to the village community in shaping peasants' lives and outlooks. French villages were in some ways poorly suited to this role, for they had only a loose legal organization. In many regions there were no village officials; decisions were made by an informal assembly of residents, often dominated by the wealthiest farmers. In contrast to parts of Germany and Switzerland, no rules blocked outsiders from village citizenship; anyone who acquired a house or holding within the village became a part of the community, and usually such membership extended even to farm servants. In contrast to England, no laws tied charity to village residence; such charity as existed functioned informally and relied on the goodwill of individuals, without reference to villagers' origins.[31]

Other forces as well weakened the cohesiveness of the village community. Village class differences created potentially large divergences of interest between the large farmers and their neighbours. The divergence became explicit in the eighteenth-century Paris basin. Especially from 1750 on, agricultural workers organized sometimes violent harvest strikes against village farmers, in pursuit of higher wages; and tensions might erupt over high grain prices, as village buyers sought to prevent farmers from sending grain to distant markets.[32] There was the fact of geographical mobility. Despite the appearance of stability, village populations might be highly mobile. Every year, about 5 per cent of villagers moved away, and most farm-labourers moved more than once in their lifetimes.[33] There was the peculiar age structure that most villages displayed. Because villagers married late, usually in their mid- or later twenties, most villages included a large number of unmarried young adults, sometimes rowdy, always imperfectly integrated into village social structures. Alongside class conflict, in other words, there was the potential within the village for divisions by age-group. Indeed, the two divisions might reinforce each other, for children of the large farmers might more easily find spouses, usually at significantly younger ages than their labourer neighbours.[34] In these circumstances, unity of belief or action was never a given. Village divisions remained powerful throughout the early modern period, and they might manifest themselves in brutal fashion. Violence arose often within the village, and often had serious results since peasants usually went armed with knives.[35]

31. For village organization and the laws surrounding it, Jean-Pierre Gutton, *La Sociabilité villageoise dans l'ancienne France* (Paris, 1979).
32. Jean-Marc Moriceau, 'Les "Baccanals" ou grèves de moissoneurs en Pays de France (seconde moitié du XVIII siècle)', in Jean Nicolas (ed.), *Mouvements populaires et conscience sociale, XVIe–XIXe siècles* (Paris, 1985), pp. 420–33; Cynthia Bouton, *The Flour War: Gender, Class, and Community in Late Ancien Régime French Society* (University Park, PA, 1993), summarizes a large literature on grain riots and explicates one of its most dramatic waves.
33. James B. Collins, 'Geographical and social mobility in early modern France', *Journal of Social History*, 24: 3 (Spring 1991), pp. 563–77.
34. Moriceau, *Les Fermiers de l'Ile de France*, pp. 152–4, 561–3.
35. Overview in Robert Muchembled, *La Violence au village (XVe XVII siècle)* (Paris, 1989).

For all this, the village retained important powers over its residents and created significant solidarities among them. Geography made some degree of solidarity inevitable. French peasants lived within small communities, usually numbering about 500 people, and in most regions houses clustered near one another. Only in western France were settlements looser, with significant numbers living in small hamlets away from the centre of the village. In such circumstances, few peasants could avoid involvement in their neighbours' lives.

The village's religious functions strengthened such involvement. Religion defined the village's boundaries, since village and parish were coterminous, and religious practice required frequent communal interactions. Villagers had to come together to make important decisions about religious life: the vestry made up of leading laymen (the *fabrique*) had responsibility for the church's material well-being, and in some cases actually hired priests for the community. Before about 1650, when the Church clamped down on such behaviour, people gossiped in the church and conducted secular business there; they danced and romanced in the cemetery. Even in the eighteenth century they usually transacted the village's secular business at the church porch, after the mass. Villagers did not always treat the church space as sacred, but it was all the more central for that very fact. The familiar treatment of sacred objects shocked some church officials, indeed led them to believe that the peasants were scarcely Christian. As evidence they could cite not only inappropriate behaviour in sacred places, but also simple absence: many sixteenth-century villagers seem to have attended church only once or twice each year.[36] But in fact the peasants seem to have had strongly Christian beliefs. Those few sources that describe village conversations suggest an obsessive interest in theological matters, and the basic Catholic rituals mattered enormously. In the sixteenth century most villagers resolutely resisted Protestant calls for religious change.[37]

But seventeenth-century Catholic reformers brought village religion into greater conformity with official religious ideas. In practice, this meant that the parish church became the increasingly exclusive focus of religious practice. Heightening the claims of religious community also required raising the stature of village priests. Through the sixteenth century, they had been an unimpressive group, poorly educated, indifferent to their duties, often simply absent. After 1600, though, reformers pushed for improvements. Clerical education rose dramatically, priests' material circumstances somewhat more slowly. In the course of the seventeenth century parish priests became solidly rooted and respected local figures, likely to remain in their offices for decades, and quite ready to push for intensified religious practice from their flocks. Communal religious life in the French village was less an inheritance from the Middle Ages – though its basic framework had been established then – than a creation of the seventeenth and early eighteenth centuries.

---

36. Alain Croix, *La Bretagne aux 16e et 17e siècles: la vie, la mort, la foi*, 2 vols (Paris, 1981), vol. II, pp. 1179–83; Timothy Tackett, *Priest and Parish in Eighteenth-Century France* (Princeton, NJ, 1977); Philip Hoffman, *Church and Community in the Diocese of Lyon, 1500–1789* (New Haven, CT, 1984); Keith Luria, *Territories of Grace: Cultural Change in the Seventeenth-Century Diocese of Grenoble* (Berkeley, CA, 1991).

37. John Bossy, 'The Counter-Reformation and the people of Catholic Europe', *Past and Present*, 47 (May 1970), pp. 51–70.

The newly reformed priests of the seventeenth and eighteenth centuries brought to their villages a complex group of messages. Intensely concerned to purify religious practices and daily morality, their preachings probably also intensified religious anxieties. As a result, like several other countries, sixteenth- and seventeenth-century France experienced a rising number of accusations of sorcery. These were typically directed against village outsiders, those who fitted least easily into the village's system of social controls: older women, who seemed a challenge to images of household organization, and shepherds, men who like-wise lived and worked at the margins of conventional village life. Probably village anxieties had always circled around figures like these. But the rise of sorcery accusations had much to do with the increasingly intense religious life that the new parish priests brought to the village. Yet French villagers never found witchcraft so frightening as did villagers in German-speaking Europe. Accusa-tions were relatively infrequent in France, and, despite the judges' use of torture to elicit confessions, individual accusations rarely grew into mass panics. The accusations themselves largely ceased after about 1700, as religious pressures lessened – and as royal judges ceased encouraging such prosecutions.[38]

In any case, the priests of the seventeenth and eighteenth centuries did not bring only anxiety to the village. They brought also a new interest in education, and thus ultimately a new degree of access to the cultural world beyond the village. In this Catholic reformers thought along lines very similar to their Protestant enemies in England and Germany: Catholics like Protestants wanted an educated laity, one that would understand its faith. Under the impetus of the Church, village schooling spread in the later seventeenth and eighteenth cen-turies. The effort was most successful in northern France. In upper Normandy, just over one-third of all men could read at the end of the seventeenth century; a century later, three-quarters could do so. Fewer than one woman in ten could read in the late seventeenth century; in 1789 the number reached about 40 per cent.[39] In the region around Toulouse, by contrast, even in 1789 only about one village in ten had a schoolmaster, and only a minority of village men could read. Here reform-minded parish priests encountered a surprising enemy: not the tradition-bound peasant, but the royal administration. 'I believe it unnecessary', wrote a high official in 1759, 'to prove at great length the uselessness of school teachers in the villages. There are forms of knowledge that ought not be given to the peasants . . . in the countryside, nothing is less necessary for the peasants than knowing how to read.'[40] Village literacy in France developed in response to local demand and to the efforts of reforming priests. In contrast to govern-mental efforts in Germany and Austria, in France the government even in the age of Enlightenment was mainly an enemy of peasant reading.[41]

38. For summary of recent research, see Robin Briggs, *Communities of Belief: Cultural and Social Tension in Early Modern France* (Oxford, 1989), esp. pp. 8–65. On the decline of sorcery and some of its social dimensions, Robert Mandrou, *Magistrats et sorciers en France au XVIIe siècle: Une analyse de psychologie historique* (Paris, 1968).

39. François Furet and Jacques Ozouf, *Lire et écrire: l'alphabétisation des français de Calvin à Jules Ferry*, 2 vols (Paris, 1977), vol. I, pp. 190–1.

40. Frêche, *Toulouse et la région Midi-Pyrénées*, pp. 411ff., quotation p. 412.

41. James Van Horn Melton, *Absolutism and the Origins of Compulsory Schooling in Prussia and Austria* (Cam-bridge, 1988), esp. pp. 171–230.

At the top of village society, in the ranks of the large tenant farmers, the Church's educational efforts produced a remarkable cultural flowering. In the mid-eighteenth-century Paris basin, a handful of large farmers received full classical educations, and most owned significant numbers of books.[42] More important, however, was the breadth of literacy within the village. By the eighteenth century, in northern France literacy cut across class divisions within the village, rather than reinforcing them. Indeed, by this point a mass publishing industry had arisen to meet the demand of ordinary rural book-buyers. In 1789 a single publisher of cheap books, one of many such figures, had an inventory of 443,069 items; publishing on this scale presupposed a large rural market for reading material. Villagers were thus more easily and quickly integrated within the larger culture.[43]

The French village was an economic as well as a cultural community, for its residents needed one another in a variety of highly practical situations. The state itself insisted on one such form of cooperation, by making taxes a collective responsibility. All individuals in the village had an interest in their neighbours' remaining solvent, for otherwise their own taxes would rise.[44] Other solidarities were more personal. Anyone who rented land or borrowed money (and eventually all villagers fell into these categories) needed co-signatories, who would guarantee his loans and his responsible use of rented property. Especially in the most mountainous parts of France, villages owned common properties, lands that all residents could use for pasturing their livestock and gathering firewood.[45] Common lands were less significant in the Paris basin, but other factors there pushed villagers toward economic cooperation. Their plots of land lay close to one another, and throughout the north fields were open, with no fences between plots. The intricate pattern of fields often required some forms of cooperation; villagers had to cross one another's land to get to their own, and the failure of one to drain his land properly might damage his neighbours'.

Along with their common properties, villages also had common economic rights and powers, above all concerning the harvest. In many villages, the decision to begin the harvest was a public and official one, taken by local officials after consultation with the principal farmers of the area. After the harvest, villagers typically had the right to pasture livestock on the stubble that the harvesters left. They might also have the right to glean, that is, to collect pieces of grain that had fallen to the ground during the harvesting process. Collective usages like these served the interests of rich and poor alike. They allowed village labourers to supplement their incomes, and to maintain more livestock than their own holdings could support; animals could be pastured on common lands and on the stubble left after the harvest. At the same time, these arrangements

42. Moriceau, *Les Fermiers de l'Ile de France*, pp. 766–7.

43. Roger Chartier, *Lectures et lecteurs dans la France d'ancien régime* (Paris, 1987), p. 249; for stress on liberating effects of village literacy, Furet and Ozouf, *Lire et écrire*, p. 358.

44. Clearly described by Hilton L. Root, *Peasants and King in Burgundy: Agrarian Foundations of French Absolutism* (Berkeley/Los Angeles/London, 1987), pp. 30–5.

45. In the mountainous sections of the Auvergne, common lands often counted for one-quarter to one-third of village territories: Poitrineau, *La Vie rurale en Basse-Auvergne*, pp. 154–5; Jacquart, *La Crise rurale*, pp. 87–90.

favoured those with the largest number of livestock, the large farmers. Likewise, collective regulation of the harvest responded to farmers' anxieties about grain theft and about ensuring orderly pasturing on the stubble.[46]

These examples suggest the complexity of the relationship between the collective life of the village and villagers' pursuit of individual self-interest. Villagers had strong ideas about economic ethics, and they relied heavily on one another. But interdependence of this kind did not end sharp calculation of economic interests. Living under severe economic pressure, villagers of all social classes needed to reconcile the pursuit of individual advantage with the benefits of collective life.

THE VILLAGE AND THE STATE

Alongside lordship and the village community, a third entity increasingly affected villagers' lives after 1500: the French state was becoming increasingly powerful and intrusive. In some measure early modern peasants everywhere confronted this problem. All lived within states that regulated larger areas of life and demanded heavier taxes. Yet the French state was uniquely burdensome, in degree if not in kind. French kings had larger international ambitions than most of their neighbours, and the French peasantry carried a higher share of their nation's tax burden than peasants elsewhere. In France neither nobles nor cities paid anything like a fair share of taxes, and correspondingly higher burdens fell on the peasants. This tax burden had already been high in the sixteenth century, but it underwent a revolutionary jump in the seventeenth, as France involved itself in the Thirty Years War. In the 1640s direct taxes were at least three times as high as they had been in the first two decades of the seventeenth century. Some reductions followed, but heavy taxation returned late in the century, to pay for Louis XIV's wars.[47]

Royal fiscal demands led to dramatic village resistance. A first rebellion came in the south-west in 1548, as the state introduced there a new tax on salt consumption; the same region rebelled again in 1594, 1624, 1636 and 1707. Parallel movements developed elsewhere in the 1630s and 1640s – in isolated regions of the south-west, and also in lower Normandy. A new wave of rebellions took place in the 1660s and 1670s, the most dramatic of them in Brittany.[48]

These movements shared important characteristics. First, they tended to arise within the underdeveloped France of the south and west; only one of the

46. Liana Vardi, 'Construing the harvest: gleaners, farmers, and officials in early modern France', *American Historical Review*, 98: 5 (December 1993), pp. 1424–47.

47. James Collins, *Fiscal Limits of Absolutism: Direct Taxation in Early Seventeenth-Century France* (Berkeley, CA, 1988), pp. 146–65. For the weight of taxation in the sixteenth century, Bois, *Crise du féodalisme*, p. 341; Jacquart, *La Crise rurale*, pp. 200–1.

48. For summary and broadly comparative interpretation of these movements, see Yves-Marie Bercé, *Revolt and Revolution in Early Modern Europe: An Essay on the History of Political Violence*, trans. Joseph Bergin (Manchester, 1987), pp. 163–7; Hugues Neveux, 'Die ideologische Dimension der französischen Bauernaufstände im 17. Jahrhundert', *Historische Zeitschrift*, 238 (1984), pp. 265–85; idem, *Les Révoltes paysannes en Europe, XIVe–XVIIe siècle* (Paris, 1997).

major movements took place in the north, and none in the Paris basin. Second, nearly all of the movements had a relatively conservative orientation. In contrast to the German rebellions of 1525, in which peasants contested basic ideas about the social order, the French rebellions had limited and self-interested goals. They were directed towards stopping the state's advance and reducing its fiscal demands, rather than to producing fundamental changes in state or society; in several instances their concern was to protect local exemptions against governmental efforts at equalizing fiscal burdens. Only in isolated instances did rebellion against the state's tax collectors lead to a wider movement against the demands of landlords and other elites. More typically, the French peasant uprisings formed part of a broad opposition to the monarchy's demands. Through 1652, French nobles and city-dwellers too expressed political disaffection, sometimes in movements of violent rebellion. The peasants were relatively modest in their aims partly because their movements did not reflect just their own interests, but rather the interests of the several groups who opposed the state's demands.[49] The rebellions of the seventeenth century demonstrated how quickly villagers could be aroused to extreme violence. But even in rebellion they showed their fundamental acceptance of the social order around them.

The great wave of French peasant rebellions weakened after 1670, and ended early in the eighteenth century. That century witnessed numerous small disorders, but nothing comparable to the events of the previous century. Rural peace resulted in part from the ferocious governmental repression of the seventeenth century, and in part from the broad prosperity brought by eighteenth-century economic expansion. But the social peace of the eighteenth-century countryside also reflected a significant change in peasants' relations with the state. Eighteenth-century peasants could feel themselves to be beneficiaries of state development, rather than its victims only, because the government's views of them had shifted. Sixteenth- and seventeenth-century administrators had been preoccupied with cities, from a well-founded belief that urban discontent would lead to political trouble. They sought to sustain urban employment by discouraging rural industry, and they kept urban food prices and taxes low, at farmers' expense. But in the eighteenth century the state's interest shifted toward the peasantry. Taxation remained high, but government now sought to spread its weight more evenly across society: it imposed significant taxes on the nobility, and it increasingly relied on indirect taxes, which drew more revenue from urban consumers. In 1762 (we have seen) it limited controls on rural industry, and a year later it reduced controls on the grain trade. Allowing farmers to sell their grain wherever prices were highest, so some officials argued, would bring prosperity and new investment to the countryside. Royal policy wavered on this issue, partly because villagers themselves were so divided. Poorer peasants suffered as much as the cities from free trade in grain. The government restored marketing controls in 1771, revoked them in 1774, and partially restored them again in 1776, after widespread grain riots in rural as well as urban districts.

49. For strong emphasis on the role of elites in mobilizing peasant rebellions, see Roland Mousnier, *Peasant Uprisings of the Seventeenth Century* (New York, 1971); for recent examination of one such movement see Collins, *Classes, Estates, and Order*, pp. 259ff., describing a complex mixture of class conflict and collusion.

But the point had been made. The state had begun to concern itself with rural interests.

The state also offered villagers more services. These might take highly dramatic form, as when state officials intervened against especially oppressive aristocrats. In 1665, thus, Louis XIV sent state officials to the mountainous and backward region of Auvergne to investigate abuses by seigneurial lords and hand out summary punishments. The effects were significant. Peasant burdens decreased, and a number of egregiously oppressive aristocrats were jailed.[50]

More important than such events, however, was the state's growing ability to offer villagers both public order and an effective apparatus for settling disputes – including disputes with social superiors. As throughout Europe, judges proliferated in early modern France, and so to a lesser degree did agents of the police. The still tiny (and often corrupt) police forces could not hope to control rural violence, but the government's legislative efforts significantly exceeded those of other European countries. For peasants this was no small matter, since their crops and livestock were highly vulnerable to theft.[51] At the same time, ordinary villagers, even those of modest means, turned regularly to the royal courts to settle their private disputes. Eighteenth-century courts and legal representation were cheap. Their expansion reinforced all peasants' ability to deal effectively with the world outside the village.[52]

The increasingly popular royal jurisdictions offered villagers something further: the use of the courts to settle essentially political conflicts with their lords. Most villages may have seemed distant indeed from the grand centres in which French judges decided fundamental questions of law. Yet villagers proved entirely capable of bringing cases to these lofty courts, whether defending what they believed to be traditional rights or challenging impositions by lords and others. Such cases can be followed from the sixteenth century on. During the eighteenth century, they became something of an epidemic in many regions. Clearly villagers were more familiar with legal remedies to their problems than many historians have supposed. They benefited as well from the tactical alliances available to them; powerful outsiders – landlords, ecclesiastical institutions, even royal officials themselves – might share an interest with villagers in securing particular decisions, even if on other matters they might be legal opponents. They benefited as well from the proliferation of impoverished lawyers in early modern France; legal representation was never hard to find, even at bargain prices. In this as in so much else, villagers could make distinctions. They knew how to ally with figures who might be enemies in other matters.[53]

50. Arlette Lebigre, *Les Grands Jours d'Auvergne: désordres et répression au XVIIe siècle* (Paris, 1976); James Lowth Goldsmith, *Les Salers et les D'Escorailles, seigneurs de Haute Auvergne, 1500–1789* (Clermont-Ferrand, 1984), pp. 155–80.

51. Iain Cameron, 'The police of eighteenth-century France', *European Studies Review*, 7: 1 (January 1977), pp. 44–75; idem, *Crime and Repression in the Auvergne and the Guyenne, 1720–1790* (Cambridge, 1981).

52. Reinhardt, *Justice in the Sarladais*, pp. 265–75; Dewald, *Pont-St-Pierre*, pp. 258–63. Julius Ruff, *Crime, Justice and Public Order in Old Regime France: The Sénéchaussées of Libourne and Bazas, 1696–1789* (London, 1984), offers a more pessimistic interpretation.

53. Le Goff, *Vannes and its Region*, p. 283; Liana Vardi, 'Peasants and the law: a village appeals to the French Royal Council', *Social History*, 13 (1988), pp. 295–313; Root, *Peasants and King in Burgundy*, pp. 155–204; Dewald, *Pont-St-Pierre*, pp. 148–51.

Peasant rebellions died out in the eighteenth century, then, partly because villagers had new and effective tools for resolving social and political conflicts. Not rebellion but litigation became villagers' preferred means for dealing with oppression. Villagers lost many such cases, but this did not diminish their enthusiasm for litigation. The geography of rural rebellion suggests that this transition in political methods had already taken place by 1600 in the Paris basin. The transition came later in more isolated regions, but by the eighteenth century this model prevailed there as well.[54]

PEASANT FAMILIES

Lordship, village and state exercised ambiguous powers over French peasants, at once offering them advantages and arousing their opposition. In legal terms the family was far weaker than these competing institutions, yet its powers were in some ways greater. Like state, village and lordship, the family helped set the limits within which villagers lived. But the family also set many of their aims in life, the most important ethical ideas guiding their decisions.

Like peasants elsewhere in Europe, at least from the mid-sixteenth century on, French peasants married late – both men and women were usually in their mid-twenties at marriage. This fact probably meant that both brought a certain degree of maturity to marriage, and that they came to the relationship as relative equals. Except in unusual circumstances, both had worked on their own before the marriage. For poorer women, indeed, such work was absolutely essential, because it allowed them to accumulate dowries, the cash and household effects that provided one of the material bases for the marriage.

Late marriage by women had another result: because it shortened their child-bearing years, it meant that they had relatively few children. French rural families usually produced only five or six infants, and many did not survive childhood. In most French regions, a quarter of all children died in their first year; another quarter died between the ages of one and ten. Despite the numbers of children born, the rural population in most periods barely reproduced itself.[55] Most of this mortality seems to have resulted from disease rather than from the direct effects of poverty. Yet even in child-rearing the division between rich and poor villagers displayed its force. In the Paris basin, the children of large tenant farmers had far better chances of surviving to adulthood than their poorer neighbours – partly because they received better nutrition, partly because their parents could provide closer attention to them.[56]

Peasants married late because of basic beliefs about how the family should function. As in most of western Europe, French peasants viewed the nuclear

---

54. Cf. D. M. G. Sutherland and T. J. A. Le Goff, 'The Revolution and the rural community in eighteenth-century Brittany', *Past and Present*, 62 (February 1974), pp. 96–119.

55. Michael W. Flinn, *The European Demographic System, 1500–1820* (Baltimore, MD, 1981), p. 33 and passim, summarizing a large body of recent research.

56. Moriceau, *Les Fermiers de l'Ile de France*, pp. 149–50.

family as the norm. There were some exceptions, notably in the south, where married children sometimes lived with their parents, or married siblings set up households together. Far more often, villagers wanted autonomous households when they married; households that included more than one married couple were very rare. For this they needed to delay marriage until they had accumulated the resources needed to rent property, or had inherited property from their parents. They could marry only when they had the resources to support an independent household. Given the importance of household autonomy, marriage could not be an emotional decision only. It marked the villagers' entry to full economic adulthood, and both men and women needed to think carefully about its economic consequences.[57] Such calculation did not eliminate all personal choice and affection from peasant marriages. But affection could work only within limits. Especially in the upper reaches of village society, where the economic stakes were highest, villagers needed to find marriage partners whose resources complemented their own.[58]

An additional fact conditioned families' decisions about marriage. In contrast to many parts of Europe, French law encouraged equality of children's financial claims on their parents. There were important exceptions, for each province had its customary laws governing inheritance. In the south-east families had more freedom to favour a single heir, and Norman law sharply limited women's rights. But in most of the country the law favoured equality among heirs, male and female alike.[59] The inheritance divisions that resulted (we have seen) contributed to the decline of peasant landowning over the early modern period, but the prospect of eventual inheritance divisions also encouraged dynamism in peasant economic life. If their children were to occupy positions comparable to their own, villagers needed to accumulate resources. Sustaining the family's position over the long term required expanding its land and other capital to the extent that circumstances allowed.[60] A similar awareness of the future affected other investments in children. Especially in the eighteenth century, villagers were ready to spend large sums of money on education, whether in the schools or in the form of apprenticeship.

In different ways, these familial strategies tended to push individuals out of the narrow sphere of village and household, and into a wider world. Among the large tenant farmers, there was the need to find vacant leaseholds for their sons as these reached adulthood; such opportunities rarely appeared in the parents' village, so most tenant farmers' sons had to look elsewhere. Poorer villagers were sent out from the home as young teenagers, to work as farm

---

57. Jean-Louis Flandrin, *Familles: parenté, maison, sexualité dans l'ancienne société*, 2nd edn (Paris, 1984), pp. 73–7.

58. For strong argument for the role of personal choice in peasant marriages, based at least on sexual attraction, see Jean-Louis Flandrin, *Les Amours paysannes (XVIe–XIXe siècles)* (Paris, 1975); for a more nuanced view, Martine Segalen, *Love and Power in the Peasant Family: Rural France in the Nineteenth Century*, trans. Sarah Matthews (Chicago, 1983), pp. 14–25.

59. Emmanuel Le Roy Ladurie, 'A system of customary law: family structures and inheritance customs in sixteenth-century France', repr. in Robert Forster and Orest Ranum (eds), *Family and Society: Selections from the Annales, Economie, Sociétés, Civilisations* (Baltimore, MD, 1976), pp. 75–103.

60. Jean-Marc Moriceau and Gilles Postel-Vinay, *Ferme, entreprise, famille: grande exploitation et changements agricoles* (Paris, 1992), p. 97; Moriceau, *Les Fermiers de l'Ile de France*, pp. 494–507.

servants or apprentices. For all classes, the need to establish autonomous households created geographical mobility.

Familial strategies also conditioned the ways in which villagers gendered their
economic lives. Together with the harsh realities of the early modern economy,
they created a relentness pressure on all household members to work, and
usually to work within the sphere of the market economy, for wages. Until their
mid-twenties, women worked as servants, accumulating the dowries that they
would need to marry. After marriage, they continued to work in the fields during
the critical periods of the agricultural year – at the harvest, and when weeding and
other forms of field work were needed. Most villagers simply could not afford
to confine women's proper role to the home. Even many who could, such as
tenant farmers' wives, in fact played an active economic role: widowed, they
commonly took over the management of their farms, and they often continued
to direct them when their children had grown.[61] Technology accommodated itself
to this weakened sexual division of labour. For the harvest, French farmers
continued to use the sickle, a small instrument easily handled by women, rather
than the scythe, which was heavy and so primarily wielded by men. This technological choice meant that men and women alike could perform even the most
physically demanding tasks of the agricultural year. Only a few tasks – notably
ploughing and hay cutting, which was performed with the scythe – were male
preserves.

All observers agreed on a further aspect of women's economic functions:
women played a prominent role in the marketplace, both buying food and mar
keting goods that their families produced. In this way also they were presumed
to be closely connected to the monetary economy. Indeed, their position probably gave them a particular sensitivity to market forces. In consequence, women
played a prominent role in food riots and in other popular upheavals during
the eighteenth century. Certainly no one found such a role surprising or inappropriate, for women and men had equal stakes in the preservation of the
household.[62]

SOME CONCLUSIONS

Like much else in French peasants' experiences, then, their familial ideals required
that they involve themselves with the world beyond the village. Faced with the
insistent pressures of inheritance division and of establishing autonomous households for each generation, villagers could not see themselves as simply preserving
inherited positions. For rich and poor villagers alike, preservation could come
only through exchange and accumulation.

---

61. Moriceau, *Les Fermiers de l'Ile de France*, pp. 313–17; Vardi, *The Land and the Loom*, pp. 65–8.
62. Cynthia Bouton, *The Flour War*, pp. 224–33; Natalie Zemon Davis, *Society and Culture in Early Modern France* (Stanford, CA, 1975), for the broader assumptions about women's participation in popular violence.

As a result, French village society had greater dynamism and more potential for development than most early modern observers recognized. There was no agricultural revolution in early modern France, but there were incremental improvements in peasant agriculture, which allowed for significant improvement in living standards. The eighteenth-century development of rural industry – not production for home use, but production organized for large-scale, often international markets – dramatically widened the countryside's productive possibilities. It improved villagers' living standards still more. Villagers were better educated and better able to cope with the wider world than historians once believed.[63]

Such successes should not conceal the dark sides of the early modern landscape. Despite its successes, the early modern countryside was also dominated by a movement of rural expropriation and by increasingly sharp class divisions among villagers. By about 1630, most northern French villagers were divided into a handful of agrarian entrepreneurs, the farmers, and a large majority of agricultural labourers. Starvation was a real threat in the seventeenth-century countryside; in the eighteenth century hunger still provoked village rioting. Social divisions were less marked in southern France, but no region escaped them altogether. Such divisions probably formed fertile ground for fear, and it was in the years of rural expropriation that village anxiety appears to have been at its highest. This was the time of sorcery accusations and of rural rebellions, many of them encouraged by rumour and fear.

Hence the importance of the cultural changes of the eighteenth century. These years brought some relaxation of village tensions, both cultural and economic. Village farmers were wealthier than ever. But the development of rural industry offered the possibility that other villagers might also establish modest fortunes. A few even managed fortunes that rivalled those of the farmers, though proto-industrial wealth almost always proved more unstable than that of the great farmers. Cultural divisions narrowed as well. Reading became a common village attainment in the eighteenth century, common to most social classes and common to men and women as well.

Such circumstances render the Revolution of 1789 an apparently paradoxical event in so far as the countryside is concerned. Why revolution, if in fact conditions were improving for most villagers, and if socio-cultural divisions were in some sense narrowing? Historians have of course long suggested answers to such paradoxes. In the mid-nineteenth century, Alexis de Tocqueville suggested that rising living conditions made the French peasants more impatient with the *ancien régime* than traditional poverty would have done. The historian and sociologist Charles Tilly suggested that the experience of rapid change in itself was disorienting to eighteenth-century peasants, creating a potentially explosive political situation. Many historians have noted the economic crises that the government's free-trade policies created, first in the early 1770s, then in the late 1780s.

---

63. Recent restatements of the opposite view, emphasizing the immiseration of the eighteenth-century countryside, include Bouton, *The Flour War*, pp. 57–9, and Schwartz, *Policing the Poor*, pp. 132–53. Cf. Le Goff, *Vannes and its Region*, pp. 293–302, for an example of modest improvement in peasants' situations in the eighteenth century.

These threatened gains peasants had made earlier in the century, and made the Crown visibly responsible for the loss.[64]

But it is possible to offer a different reading of the French countryside's place in the Revolution, and to ask how explosive the countryside actually was in 1789. There is considerable evidence for the peasantry's political excitement in 1789. Villagers looked forward eagerly to the abolition of the *ancien régime*'s tithes, hunting laws and seigneurial levies. They keenly followed events in their regions and in the capital. But few rural districts rose violently against the *ancien régime*. Many apparently spontaneous rural rebellions resulted from the directives of urban officials, rather than from local grievances. French peasants who did engage in autonomous political activity after 1789 tended to do so on the wrong side – as opponents of the Revolution, concerned with defending traditional religious practices against urban interference and irritated by the ceaseless demands of revolutionary authorities for food, money and livestock. In most regions the Revolution came to the countryside from the cities; the peasants reacted to it, sometimes positively, more often with increasing doubt or outright resistance.[65]

And indeed the world that emerged from the Revolution in some ways was less suited to their needs than the *ancien régime* had been. Many peasants acquired land during the Revolution, as the government sold off properties of the Church and some nobles. But the great beneficiaries were the principal tenant farmers, who had the resources to buy the large properties that they had rented for years before. As a result, their dominance within the village was still more absolute during the nineteenth century than it had been in previous centuries; they were now great landowners, as well as the village's principal agricultural employers.[66] At the same time, village manufacturing suffered from the Revolution. A full generation of economic uncertainty, accompanied by years of warfare, destroyed many of the commercial networks that underlay rural industry. When peace returned in 1815, international competition had become far more threatening than it had been in the eighteenth century. British industrialization was in full development, and French hopes of competing rested with establishing factories in France itself. Increasingly the nineteenth-century village found itself reduced to a mainly agricultural role. Most villagers would eventually place their economic hopes elsewhere, in migration to the cities.

---

64. Alexis de Tocqueville, *The Old Regime and the French Revolution*, trans. Stuart Gilbert (Garden City, NY, 1955); Charles Tilly, *The Vendée* (Cambridge, MA, 1964).

65. For strong statements of this view, Hilton Root, 'The case against Georges Lefebvre's peasant revolution', *History Workshop*, 28 (Autumn 1989), pp. 88–102, and Donald Sutherland, 'The Revolution in the provinces: class or counterrevolution?', in Steven G. Reinhardt and Elisabeth A. Cawthon (eds), *Essays on the French Revolution: Paris and the Provinces* (College Station, TX, 1992), pp. 116–30; for examples that illustrate the complex forces beneath 'peasant' movements during the Revolution, see also Clay Ramsay, *The Ideology of the Great Fear: The Soissonais in 1789* (Baltimore, MD, 1992), pp. 81–122, showing the range of classes mobilized and unified in 1789 and John Markoff, *The Abolition of Feudalism: Peasants, Lords and Legislators in the French Revolution* (University Park, PA, 1996).

66. Jean-Pierre Jessenne, *Pouvoir au village et Révolution: Artois 1760–1848* (Lille, 1987).

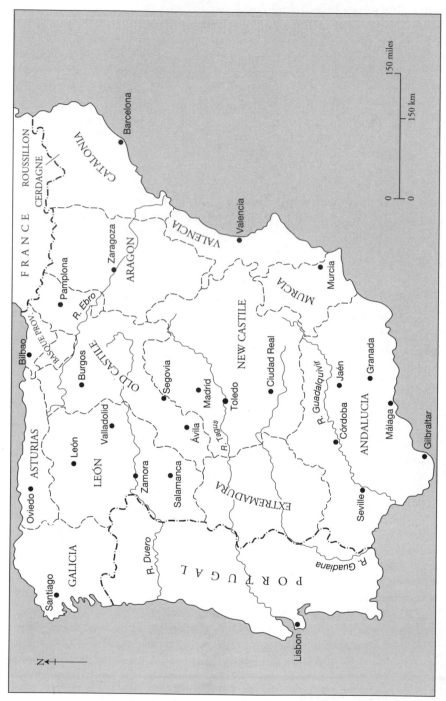

Map 3.1 Iberia

CHAPTER THREE

The Peasantries of Iberia, 1400–1800

Teófilo F. Ruiz

In Lope de Vega's rousing play, *Fuenteovejuna* (1612–14), the enraged peasants of the eponymous village murder Fernán Gómez de Guzmán, *comendador mayor* of the Order of Calatrava and their putative lord, to revenge his predatory sexual conduct and political oppression. Set during the reign of the Catholic Kings, *Fuenteovejuna* proudly upholds the individual and collective honour of the peasants. Standing as one, they resist the Crown's misguided attempts to exact punishment while pledging their unshakeable allegiance to Isabella (1474–1504) and Ferdinand (1479–1516). The sympathetic representation of Castilian and Leonese peasants – although here they are well-to-do farmers (*labradores*), genteel in their manners and concepts of honour – is frequent in Spain's Golden Age literature. Lope de Vega in this and in other plays, Calderón de la Barca in *El alcalde de Zalamea* and Cervantes in *Don Quixote*, among others, often present an exalted image of rustics, male as well as female, safeguarding their honour against the abuses of their noble masters, and doing so in ways which mimic the behaviour and elaborate codes of conduct of the highest men and women in the land. In these literary works, the innate nobility of the peasantry is evident in their deeds, not in lineage or titles.

Miguel Delibes's powerful and dark novel, *Los santos inocentes* (1981),[1] although chronologically and spatially distant from late medieval Fuenteovejuna and its western Leonese locale, offers a representation of the peasantry which is diametrically opposed to the Golden Age's benign portrait. Delibes's story takes place in a vast estate, or latifundium, in northern Castile during the Franco years. The protagonists, landless peasants, eke out a living in a miserable shack on the fringes of a rural economy. The main character is made to retrieve game for his master, as if he were a dog; his wife and children are expected to provide domestic service and menial labour in the estate's mansion and on its lands. In constant fear of eviction, they are continuously degraded and abused by their arrogant and unfeeling young master. Like *Fuenteovejuna*, *Los santos inocentes* is a tale of retribution. In the end, Zacarías, an older and half-insane member of the

I would like to thank Scarlett Freund for her comments and editorial suggestions.

1. The English title would be *The Holy Innocents*. There is a magnificent film version (1986) directed by Carlos Saura.

suffering family, kills the master to avenge the killing of his pet bird; but in this act there is no nobility or redemption, just hopelessness and death.

INTRODUCTION: TOWARDS A TYPOLOGY OF THE IBERIAN PEASANTRY

Although these two texts capture some of the flavour of peasants' lives at particular times, fiction does not always reflect historical realities. Despite their temporal and stylistic differences, these narratives of revenge none the less provide a good entry to the wide range of Iberian peasant conditions and prospects. In the period between the late Middle Ages and the eve of modernity, approximately 1400–1800, Iberia underwent dramatic changes in the construction of its political and regional identities. This transformation parallels the variegated character of its peasantries.

The shifting political fortunes of the peninsula and the long process of building the state(s) had a lasting impact on the history of the Iberian countryside and its inhabitants. In the late fourteenth century, when our story begins, Iberia was divided between several warring kingdoms. In the east, facing the Atlantic, Portugal, by the fourteenth century, had already enjoyed more than two centuries as an independent realm. Only in the period between 1580 and 1640 would it be joined to Spain; even then it was a dynastic union, and Portugal retained its traditions and its economic and social structures independent from other peninsular kingdoms. Castile, occupying most of the north, centre and south of the peninsula, was by far the largest kingdom in terms of territory and population. After 1212, Castile was the only realm to carry on the so-called Reconquest and thus to advance special hegemonic claims in Iberia. In south-eastern Spain, the Muslim enclave of Granada held on until 1492; it was to be the last refuge of Muslim power in al-Andalus. Granada's defeat and the subsequent rebellion of the *moriscos*[2] in the mountains of the Alpujarras in the second half of the sixteenth century led to their resettlement throughout Castile. There and in Aragon, the *moriscos* were to play a significant role in the agricultural life of early modern Spain. Far north in the Pyrenees lay the kingdom of Navarre, caught between its French rulers and its Spanish masters; and, on the eastern shores of Iberia, the Crown of Aragon comprised three different kingdoms or principalities: Aragon, Catalonia and Valencia. Looking eastward towards the Mediterranean, the Aragonese and Catalan possessions in Italy, and the Aegean Sea, the Crown of Aragon was a collection of linguistically, economically and politically diverse realms. Despite the assurances of history books which describe a united 'Spain', there was indeed no Spain prior to the reforms of the Bourbon kings in the eighteenth century. Until then, Iberia remained a fragmented land; a corresponding diversity marked the social and economic life of its peasantry.

2. *Moriscos* is the name given to the Muslims who remained in Spain after conversion to Christianity. In reality, most of the *moriscos*, though nominally Christian, retained their former religion, language and traditions.

To this day, of course, Spain, as opposed to its Iberian neighbour, Portugal, remains carved up into regions that are sometimes as different from each other in language, customs and topography as Spain itself is from other European countries. These political and cultural divisions, however, were not dominant factors in determining the order of peasants' lives. Far more ancient things shaped the structure of rural life: patterns of cultivation, topography, the land itself. The slow occupation of the soil in Iberia, the harvesting of its crops, was the first form of Reconquest; and it shaped the ways in which peasants organized their lives and work. How then can one define what Iberian peasants were like? There are several ways to provide a taxonomy of peasant types.

It is obvious that northern Iberia, with its abundant rain and mountains, gave rise to specific rural conditions and patterns of village settlement, and that these were different from the structures of peasant life and agricultural work found in the vast, arid and high plains (the Mesetas) of Old and New Castile. The farming and fruit-growing areas of northern Iberia also contrasted with the irrigation culture of southern Iberia (Andalusia, Algarve, Murcia and Valencia), with its concentration on wine, olive oil and silk production. Yet, even this broad geographical typology requires making room for an additional set of micro-environments, such as the transitional areas of the mountains of Burgos and the Central Sierras or the unique peculiarities of Galicia or Valencia.[3]

One way of organizing a study of the Iberian peasantry is chronologically. Reconquest and repopulation – two events which deeply shaped the history of Iberia – had an abiding impact on the character of peasant settlements. The different patterns of conquest and settlement of the Duero Valley early in the tenth century, and of Valencia and western Andalusia in the first half of the thirteenth, led to distinct forms of economic and social organization. In Valencia, to provide just a brief example, the Aragonese and Catalan conquerors retained the Muslim population on the land, albeit in semi-servile dependence. The Christian settlers soon adapted to the Moorish forms of cultivation of the *huerta* (the fabled gardens of Valencia), which consisted of smallholdings, irrigation, and communal use of water. In western Andalusia, the expulsion of the Mudejars (the Muslim inhabitants of al-Andalus) in 1264 left the land empty. After failed attempts to recreate or promote the northern Castilian pattern of smallholdings and free peasantry, the land was given to the Military Orders and to the high nobility, and divided into huge latifundia, the *cortijos* or large estates which dominate the landscape of southern Spain to this very day. This is, of course, a generalization, for in both places, Valencia and Andalusia, other forms of lordship and cultivation coexisted with the latifundia.[4]

---

3. For an excellent study of transitional areas see José Ortega Varcárcel, *La transformación de un espacio rural: Las montañas de Burgos, estudios de geografía regional* (Valladolid, 1974).

4. On irrigation and southern agriculture in general see Thomas F. Glick, *Irrigation and Society in Medieval Valencia* (Cambridge, MA, 1970), and his *Islamic and Christian Spain in the Early Middle Ages: Comparative Perspectives on Social and Cultural Formation* (Princeton, NJ, 1979). For the settlement of the south and its impact on Spanish and Latin American history see Teófilo F. Ruiz, 'Expansion et changement: la conquête de Séville et la société castillane (1248–1350)', *Annales ESC* (May–June 1979), pp. 548–65; Stanley J. and Barbara H. Stein, *The Colonial Heritage of Latin America: Essays on Economic Dependence in Perspective* (New York, 1970).

Particular historical circumstances also led to the recrudescence of serfdom in Old (northern) Catalonia from around 1000 until the successful peasant wars of the late fifteenth century, and there were similar but failed attempts to bind peasants to the soil in Castile after the Black Death. In Aragon proper, the presence of a large number of conquered *moriscos* provided abundant, docile and inexpensive labour to Christian lords. Predatory lordship, resulting from economic, political and social upheavals and the accompanying decline in feudal rents, influenced the lives of peasants in Iberia as well.

One may argue that the general framework within which the Iberian peasantry as a whole toiled remained fairly constant throughout the period under study, that is, that relationships of power between lords and peasants did not change dramatically in the centuries between 1400 and 1800. None the less, although the structures of social control and dependence were not radically altered, it is undeniable that the sixteenth century was a period of general prosperity in the countryside (especially in Castile), while the catastrophes of the succeeding century (plagues, famines, desertion of the countryside) and the recovery of the eighteenth provide a broad context in which to examine change over a period of almost four centuries.

Thus, it is against this background of decline and recovery in the Iberian countryside that the history of its peasantry must be told. Whether because of climatic changes, recurring plagues, untold violence and excessive taxation, or because of diverse patterns of settlement, population growth and decline, and often too low agricultural yields, Iberia and its peasants underwent important transformations in the period under examination in these pages. Similarly, the rise of the bourgeoisie in Iberian cities – a very uneven development – had a direct impact on the countryside and its inhabitants. As I have argued elsewhere, one cannot think of the rural world in most parts of Spain as separate from the urban world.[5] Most small towns were outgrown villages, essentially agrarian towns; and the intrusion of urban capital into the countryside dramatically transformed the conditions of land-leasing, production, land tenure and social structure within the village community.

A more traditional approach to a typology of peasants is to classify them according to their juridical status. By this I mean identifying them by whether they worked and lived in lands belonging to: 1) the Crown, or under municipal jurisdiction (known in Spanish as *realengo*, and in Portuguese as *reguengos*); 2) a lay lord (*señoríos* in Spain, *honras* in Portugal); or 3) the Church (*abadengo, coutos*). There was an additional type of lordship, one in which the peasants, in theory, could choose their lord. This type of lordship went by the name of *behetría* or, in Portuguese, *beetrias*. These categories are particularly dear to Spanish and Portuguese institutional historians, although they really provide little indication of how much money (rent) individual peasants paid, how much land they held, and under what conditions. In principle, peasants living in royal lands owed less

---

5. See Teófilo F. Ruiz, *Crisis and Continuity: Land and Town in Late Medieval Castile* (Philadelphia, PA, 1994), pp. 31–5.

dues than those under seigneurial jurisdiction, but local conditions, more often than not, determined the types of payments and tenure.

Finally, the crudest but most reliable category is one which identifies peasants by whether they owned land or not, and by how much arable they held or were able to rent from others. This strict economic division of the peasantry – with its concomitant social aspects – allows for a vision of peasant life which cuts across political and topographical differences. Whether in Castile, Portugal or the Crown of Aragon, there were peasants who owned their lands or, to be more precise, who held the usufruct of sizeable farms for the duration of their lives and their children's lives, or 'for ever', as the documents often stated. Then there were those who held a bit of land and rented additional land from others in short-term leases; and there were others with little or no land. For the latter, the only means of survival was to hire themselves out to other more prosperous farmers during the high points of the agricultural year. Access to land, enough to support oneself and one's family, separated those able to benefit from citizenship in the village community (to be a *vecino*, with rights to the common lands and pasturage) from the dispossessed who were slowly driven out of the land, and who, in time, would become a landless proletariat. In any case, what the records of contemporary census gatherers, chroniclers and writers make clear is that peasants in the Middle Ages and in the early modern period – whether or not they held land – were not conceived of as having lives or identities that were independent from their masters or their masters' domains.

In this introduction, my aim has been to provide a broad view of the different criteria according to which one may examine the history of peasants in Iberia from the late Middle Ages to the end of the *ancien régime*. In the following pages, my task is to provide a closer and more detailed view – or at least as close as space permits – of these different approaches.

DEMOGRAPHY, FAMILY STRUCTURE AND INHERITANCE

Demography

As elsewhere in western Europe, peasants, howsoever defined, constituted the overwhelming majority of the population of Iberia. Although our knowledge of the demographic resources of the peninsula is tentative, and reliable information is available only for a few localities (there is no sufficient data until the eighteenth century), historians have estimated the number of peasants in Spain to range between 75 and 80 per cent of the total population. Their percentage in Portugal, a kingdom which found its colonial, seafaring vocation by the late fifteenth century, may have been a fraction smaller.

In estimating the percentage of the peasantry as a component of the total population, however, most historians have neglected the large number of city- and town-dwellers who lived on and worked the land throughout a substantial part of the year. This was certainly the pattern in Burgos, Ávila, Segovia, and other Castilian cities in the late Middle Ages; it remains the pattern today, though in reverse fashion, when half-deserted villages fill with returning working families for the summer months (those who have migrated to the cities in search of work in the recent past), their houses reopened, their land once again tended.[6]

The ties between land and town throughout most of Iberia (and particularly in the great plains of Castile) governed patterns of settlement. Foreign travellers and ambassadors, crisscrossing the land for pleasure or at the bidding of their masters, reported again and again the peculiarities of the land: large villages separated from each other by vast empty spaces. François Bertaut, riding through Castile in 1659, reports the desolation of the countryside between Logroño and Calahorra, just before reaching the 'deserted plains of Castile'. The land was not cultivated 'except around the large cities, and one league around small cities'.[7] In whole areas of the peninsula – Castile, Aragon and parts of Andalusia – many of the towns must also be considered as partly, or in some cases fully, inhabited by peasants. In truth, of course, this varied from place to place. Seville, with its mercantile links to the New World; Lisbon, playing a similar role for Portugal; and Barcelona, with its sprawling commercial network in the Mediterranean, were cities in the proper sense of the word, but elsewhere the sharp divide between rural and urban did not exist.

In this connection, David Reher's study of the population of Cuenca, a city in New Castile with a rather large (by Castilian standards) textile industry, shows the enduring role of agriculture in what may be considered an industrial town. In 1561, at the height of textile production, almost 10 per cent of the population were classified as *jornaleros* (day-labourers engaged in rural work, though by no means exclusively). By 1752, after the decline of textile manufacturing, their number rose to 29.1 per cent of the active population, that is, of household heads.[8] Even Seville, the largest Spanish city throughout most of the period under examination, had substantial numbers of heads of household engaged in agriculture. Important Sevillian neighbourhoods, such as Triana, San Gil, San Julián and Santa Lucía, had as much as 20.7 per cent of the active population working as farmers or deriving their income from farms around the city; and Collantes de Terán, who has examined Seville's censuses with meticulous care, argues for an even larger number of peasants as a percentage of the entire population of the city.[9] What these brief examples reveal is a society which, with some rare exceptions, was essentially rural, and in which many towns served as centres for agricultural pursuits.

And yet we have made little progress. How many peasants were there after all? Estimates of the population of Iberia are, as indicated above, unreliable at best. The censuses extant for the late Middle Ages and the early modern period

6. See Ruiz, *Crisis and Continuity*, pp. 245–6; see also Ruth Behar, *Santa María del Monte: The Presence of the Past in a Spanish Village* (Princeton, NJ, 1986).

7. José García Mercadal (ed.), *Viajes de extranjeros por España y Portugal*, 3 vols (Madrid, 1952), vol. I, pp. 556, 633.

8. David Reher, *Town and Country in Pre-Industrial Spain: Cuenca, 1550–1870* (Cambridge, 1990), p. 27.

9. Antonio Collantes de Terán, *Sevilla en la baja edad media. La ciudad y sus hombres* (Seville, 1977), pp. 354–5.

Table 1: Population: Spain and Portugal, 1530–1798

Year	Spain	Year	Portugal
1530	4,698,000	1527–32	1,326,000 to 1,500,000
1591	6,632,000		
1623	6,000,000	1640	2,000,000
1717	7,500,000		
1768–69	9,308,000	1758	2,500,000
1787	10,400,000		
1797	10,541,000	1798	3,000,000

Sources: Jordi Nadal, *La población española (siglos XVI a XX)* (Barcelona, 1984); Antonio Domínguez Ortiz, *El antiguo régimen: Los Reyes Católicos y los Austria* (Madrid, 1974); A. H. de Oliveira Marques, *História de Portugal* (Lisbon, 1984), vol. II; Armando Castro, *História económica de Portugal* (Lisbon, 1981), vols II and III.

counted taxable units, i.e. hearths or *vecinos* (citizens or heads of household). Whole groups, such as the clergy or the poor, were not included in the accounts. Moreover, the coefficient which has been used by demographers fluctuates between four and five; this gives us, depending on which one is used, very different figures indeed. I, for one, favour a lower coefficient, and thus those studies which give a lower estimate of the entire population.[10]

García de Cortázar has calculated the population of all of Spain (including the Balearic islands) to have been around 5.5 million at the end of the thirteenth century and before the demographic catastrophes of the fourteenth century. Recent demographic studies estimate the population of Portugal to have numbered between 1 million and 1.2 million inhabitants at the beginning of the fifteenth century. For Spain and Portugal, the demographic ebb and tide can best be rendered as in Table 1.

Altogether Iberia had roughly less than 6.5 million inhabitants in 1400 and close to 13 million in 1797–98, of which as many as 80 per cent may have been fully or partially engaged in or dependent on agricultural work. The growth of population, however, was not even. The sixteenth century witnessed a significant increase in population, but in the seventeenth century, as a result of typhus epidemics, other illnesses and agricultural setbacks, there were dramatic population losses. By the eighteenth century, despite recurrences of typhus and other diseases, Iberia entered a phase of continuous demographic expansion which has lasted until the present.

10. In Francis Brumont, *Campo y campesinos de Castilla la Vieja en tiempos de Felipe II* (Madrid, 1984), p. 75, the average coefficient for villages in the Bureba in the late sixteenth century fluctuates between 3.3 and 4.3. Benassar's study of Valladolid's hinterland, quoted in Brumont, p. 76, gives a coefficient of 3.5 for 1567, and Pascual Madoz, the celebrated nineteenth-century geographer, estimates the coefficient at 3.5 for his own century.

Two things must be pointed out here. First, the number of peasants, as a percentage of the entire population, probably decreased by the eighteenth century. This was due to the slow process of urbanization which was part of a general trend in European society, but also to peasants fleeing the land and migrating to nearby cities or to the colonies, as they sought to escape the burdens of increased taxation, abusive lordships and the onslaught of poor crops and illness. In the plains of Castile, villages emptied out as peasants sought better opportunities elsewhere. In the area of the Alentejo (Portugal), a combination of oppressive large landholders and famines in 1596–97 and 1621–22 sent 'bands of peasants from their lands to Lisbon in search of help'.[11]

The other significant event affecting Iberian peasants was the shift which took place from centre to periphery in Spain, and from metropolis to the colonies in Portugal. From the late sixteenth century onwards, there was a substantial exodus from central Castile and Aragon – areas of dry-cereal growing and large villages – to the peripheral and coastal areas, specifically the Basque country, Catalonia and maritime Andalusia, where different crops (dairying and fruit trees in the north; olive oil and wine production in the south), agricultural techniques and climate (irrigation, frequent rain) predominated. In Spain, migration to America and to other overseas colonies had to be approved by the Crown, but this did not prevent a significant outflow of population. In Portugal, the lure of imperial possessions – of Brazil, above all – exerted its powerful spell over the population throughout the period under study. This is vividly reflected in Portuguese history books, which, after 1500, seem to lose interest in the peasantry, other social groups and internal economic conditions, and begin to focus, almost exclusively, on the history of the empire.

Family Structure

If our demographic sources are scarce and/or incomplete, the dearth is even more serious when it comes to studies of the family. Our knowledge of family structures is fragmentary at best, and even less trustworthy when dealing with peasant families. In principle, one can say that the late medieval peasant family was a nuclear or stem family, that is, a family composed of a couple and their children. An earlier period – in some parts of Iberia, as early as the tenth or eleventh centuries; in others, as late as the fourteenth – ushered in the dissolution of the extended family and the growth of 'agnaticism' (descent through male line).[12] My own studies of peasant families in northern Castile, above all in the lands of the monastery of Santa María la Real de Aguilar de Campóo

11. For some examples of depopulation (twelve villages) in the area of Segovia see Ángel García Sanz, 'La crisis del XVII en el medio rural de Castilla la Vieja, el caso de tierras de Segovia', in G. Anes Alvarez *et al.* (eds), *La economía agraria en la historia de España: Propiedad, explotación, comercialización, rentas* (Madrid, 1979), pp. 301–11; also Ángel García Sanz, *Desarrollo y crisis del antiguo régimen en Castilla la Vieja* (Madrid, 1986), pp. 82–4; for Portugal see João Lúcio d'Azevedo, *Elementos para a história económica de Portugal (séculos XII a XVII)* (Lisbon, 1967), pp. 172–3.
12. See Glick, *Islamic and Christian Spain*, pp. 137–46; José A. García de Cortázar, *La época medieval*, 2nd edn (Madrid, 1974), pp. 264–8, 422–23.

(north-central Spain) and of towns in northern Castile, show the nuclear family as the almost exclusive pattern of family organization.[13] One is forced, again, to extrapolate from Reher's work, and to hope that his figures for the eighteenth century – the earliest period in which we can undertake studies of the family with sufficient statistical data – can be transposed to the rural world in an earlier period.

In 1724, in the city of Cuenca, almost 75 per cent of all the households were organized as nuclear families, 14.1 per cent were single households, and only 5 per cent were occupied by extended families. The Cuenca countryside yielded an even larger percentage: 80.8 per cent in the eighteenth century, and 82.1 per cent in the period 1800–50. When households are examined by the occupation of the head of household, nuclear or stem families engaged in agriculture or employed as day-labourers rise to 85 per cent in 1800 and remain as high as 84 per cent in 1844.[14] There are also preliminary figures for the average size of families. Culled not only from Cuenca but from other regions as well, they fluctuate between 6.2 persons per family in the years 1680–1724 to 5.7 in the years 1730–74.[15] Nevertheless, we should not allow ourselves to be drowned by figures. Clearly, the peasant family was overwhelmingly nuclear, but there were exceptions in some regions of Iberia. In nineteenth-century central Catalonia only 52 per cent of the families were nuclear, and 45.3 per cent were considered extended families.[16] Whether these figures reflect conditions unique to a specific region or shifts in the system of family organization in the nineteenth century is hard to say. There are other exceptions. The Basque *caserío* or the *mas* in Old Catalonia (individual households surrounded by the arable and pasture lands), as opposed to the village community, suggest a modified extended family because of the necessity of farm labour.

Inheritance

The structure of the family was governed, to a certain extent, by the nature of inheritance practices. While the high nobility and even the great bourgeois families were busy creating entailments, peasants remained fairly faithful to the more egalitarian notion of partible inheritance – which in Iberia meant men and women sharing, if not always equally, in the legacy. From the fourteenth century onwards, the few extant wills of well-to-do peasants reflect the desire to divide property among all the children. The law, the *Siete partidas*, permitted the testator to favour one of the heirs, usually the first-born male, but not to the exclusion of other children. In Lorca (southern Spain) in 1710, houses and

13. Ruiz, *Crisis and Continuity*, chs 3 and 8.
14. Reher, *Town and Country*, p. 194.
15. Ibid., p. 97. Reher also provides tables on fertility and mortality which affected final family size, pp. 96, 111 and passim.
16. See Llorenç Ferrer i Alós, 'La pequeña explotación en un viñedo de la Cataluña central, siglos XIX y XX', in Pegerto Saavedra and Ramón Villares (eds), *Señores y campesinos en la península ibérica, siglos XVIII–XX*, 2 vols (Barcelona, 1991), vol. II, p. 49.

lands were shared equally among sons and daughters. A similar pattern prevailed in the region of Murcia (also southern Spain), although there are cases in which men kept the land and the women were compensated with money.[17] Such variations in partible inheritance throughout Iberia were most probably related to the diverse types of landholding and work obligations, and to the role played by women in rural work and land tenure.

The practice of partible inheritance, albeit widespread, did not preclude unusual exceptions. One of these exceptions was the inheritance system prevalent in Catalonia. Dating perhaps from the early sixteenth century, it emerged from the social and economic transformations wrought by the peasants' victory in their rebellion against servitude in the late fifteenth century. At that time, some of the newly freed peasants entered into advantageous emphyteutic (long-term) agreements which made them *de facto* owners of the land. According to Llorenç Ferrer Alós, in some areas of Catalonia in the eighteenth and nineteenth centuries the first male born (*hereu*) became the *de facto* sole heir of the family's patrimony at his father's death and, once married, the formal, legal heir. If there were no sons, the first female born (*pubilla*) inherited the undivided patrimony as well. The rest of the sons and daughters received a part of the inheritance, sometimes in cash, more often in the form of a dowry, the purchase of an apprenticeship or a job, or the sponsoring of studies. In fact, the function of the undivided property was to generate enough income to provide for a socially and familially acceptable settlement for the rest of the heirs.[18]

THE PEASANTRY: SOCIAL AND ECONOMIC STRUCTURES

In his magisterial and evocative study of the Mediterranean in the age of Philip II, Fernand Braudel describes the social structure of the peasantry in unambivalent terms: 'In Spain the traveller passing from the *secano* to the *regadíos* – from the dry to the irrigated zones – left behind a relatively free peasant to find a peasant slave.'[19] There was indeed a link between dry lands and relative freedom and between irrigation and social dependence, but the overall social and economic differences were not as clear-cut, or as simple, as Braudel argued. Although topography and history did help shape the patterns, rights

---

17. Encarna Fortes Barea and Pilar Andreu Torres, 'Mujer y sistema familiar. Algunos ejemplos de la transmisión de la propiedad en Lorca y Murcia en los siglos XVIII y XIX', in F. Chacón Jiménez *et al.* (eds), *Familia, grupos sociales y mujer en España (s. XV–XIX)* (Murcia, 1991), p. 185. See also Behar, *Santa María del Monte*, pp. 15, 83–8, 99 and passim.
18. Llorenç Ferrer i Alós, 'Familia y grupos sociales en Cataluña en los siglos XVIII y XIX', in Jiménez, *Familia, grupos sociales y mujer*, pp. 120–2.
19. Fernand Braudel, *The Mediterranean and the Mediterranean World in the Age of Philip II*, trans. S. Reynolds, 2 vols (London, 1972), vol. I, p. 75.

and autonomy of peasant lives, the many exceptions and particularities of Iberia's rural world render such categories as free and slave not very useful.[20]

Northern Iberia

From roughly the year 1000 until 1800, the areas of northern Iberia – Galicia, Asturias, Cantabria, the Basque country and Catalonia – developed their own rural practices and relations between lords and peasants. In the mountain regions, which Braudel described as areas of freedom from the imposition of state and landlords, one actually finds the reverse. Lordship, and in some cases predatory lordship, had long established itself in a wide band that extended from the Atlantic to the Mediterranean. Seigneurial power took many forms; here we can give only a brief synopsis, leaving aside the many exceptions which modify these broad categories. In Galicia, lordship, mostly ecclesiastical, weighed heavily on the peasants, and land tenure and rentals, through inheritance and subleasing, fragmented over time into progressively smaller and smaller holdings. The so-called *minifundio* – peasants working minuscule and fragmented holdings – was a feature of Galician, and in some cases Asturian, life until the Spanish government made efforts to consolidate rural property in the 1970s. This was the case of Santa María del Monte, a Leonese village studied in detail by Ruth Behar, where patterns of land fragmentation survive from medieval and early modern times into the present.

In Cantabria, we find numerous but small villages, hamlets really, where peasants engaged in a subsistence, mixed agriculture. Here, as elsewhere, the peasants worked their lands and tended their livestock under a diverse set of obligations to their lords and king. In the late Middle Ages and into the early modern period, there were few peasants without lords, and whether one paid the king, a lay lord or the Church, one was still obliged to pay. These payments varied from village to village. In 1351, a year for which we have one of the most extensive surveys of peasant dues in northern Castile, some villagers paid almost nothing, while others gave to their lords a whole range of payments in kind and money, amounting to almost half of their crop or income. Until the sixteenth century, payments, especially in the north, were still mostly in kind; mentions of some small money payments appear only from time to time. Once again, the diversity of types of payment from village to village, and within specific villages themselves, prevent any general categorization of the conditions under which the peasants worked and paid for the use of the land.[21]

---

20. Here the terms 'free' and 'freedom' do not have the meaning which they acquired after the French Revolution or as implied in political treatises of the seventeenth and eighteenth centuries. Throughout this chapter 'free' is used to denote specific peasants' rights and their mobility, that is, that they were not legally bound to the land or to their masters.

21. For use of the *Libro becerro de behetrías*, the northern Castilian 1351 survey of seigneurial rents, see Ruiz, *Crisis and Continuity*, pp. 57–64, 132–6 and passim.

The 'freedoms' enjoyed by northern Iberian peasants were in fact limited ones. Although in theory they had the right to move elsewhere, and some did in dramatic fashion – as for example the peasants of the village of Ventosa (1326), who migrated to Navarre (another kingdom) to escape noble violence[22] – peasants for the most part remained linked to their masters by fear, custom and need. Until the onset of the early modern period, they held the land on long-term or life-time leases, but that, as we shall see, would change in a later period.

In Cantabria and elsewhere in Iberia, the village was the centre of peasant life. With some exceptions, such as the Catalan *mas* or *masía* and the Basque *caserío*, we cannot in fact envisage the peasant outside the context of the village. Later on, we will revisit the life of the peasants and the village community in greater detail. For now, a look at the long tradition of village jurisdictional autonomy and rights will suffice. From 1200 onwards, the documents depict small rural councils acting as buyers, sellers and renters of property. Rural councils litigated continuously against each other, their lords and nearby towns. During these conflicts, some villages refused to pay dues to their lords. This was the case of the villagers of Matute (the Rioja), who for eleven years refused to pay dues to their lord, the monastery of the Assumption in Cañas, as a protest against the nuns' inability to protect them from noble violence.[23]

Spanish historians as well as Golden Age playwrights have always cherished the egalitarian image of the village council, where, at the ringing of bells, the 'citizens', whether *hidalgos* (petty nobles), ecclesiastics or rustics, met to argue and to make decisions affecting the life of the village. There are numerous references in the extant documents which describe such gatherings of village citizens. (*Hidalgos*, members of the lower rank of the nobility, often lived in and worked on the land, especially in northern Castile, differing little from other well-to-do peasants.) These gatherings usually took place on Sundays, inside the village church, probably after services. In some villages, such meetings still take place, or used to until a few years ago. Such was the custom in the village where my family comes from, Gallejones de Zamanzas in northern Castile, until the 1960s, and in Santa María del Monte in León.

In reality, however, village life was not as 'democratic' as depicted in Golden Age texts and in optimistic historiography. Already by the late thirteenth century, whether in some small mountain villages or in the large villages of the plain, the lords succeeded in binding peasants to the soil (Catalonia) or in exacting arbitrary and oppressive dues. As serfdom waned throughout the medieval west, in Old Catalonia it spiralled with a vengeance. At the end of the fourteenth century, as many as one-quarter of the entire population of Catalonia (and one-third of all the peasants) were serfs.[24] This is significant, since there is no evidence that the serfdom characteristic of the heartland of European feudal society was widespread or that it ever existed in other parts of Iberia.

22. Archivo histórico nacional (hereafter AHN), Clero, carpeta 1033, no. 6 (26 May 1326).
23. AHN, Clero, carpeta 1025, nos 18a, 18b, 19 (30 March 1340; 26 November 1351).
24. Jaume Vicens Vives (ed.), *Historia de España y América: Social y económica*, 2nd edn (Barcelona, 1972), vol. II, p. 215.

Indeed, most Iberian peasants were 'free', that is to say, they held lands from and paid dues, often heavy ones, to someone more powerful than they were. Yet they were not tied to the soil, nor did they pay the humiliating *chevage* or capitation fee, the grim reminder of their bondage. This is why the Catalan case is so intriguing: the servile peasants of Catalonia were able to fight a successful war against their oppressive lords and, finally, to purchase (*remença*) their freedom in the late fifteenth century.

Paul Freedman's excellent book, *The Origins of Peasant Servitude*, has already examined in detail the manner in which the lords imposed their authority over peasants, and how the peasants freed themselves. According to Freedman, from 1000 to 1300 a considerable number of peasants were enserfed in Old Catalonia, as lords violently enforced their jurisdiction and power over them. In other words, serfdom was an 'effective aspect of seignorial power'. In a period of weak royal control, the legislation of Catalonia's *corts* (parliament, assembly) legitimized lordly violence against the peasantry, as well as the lords' economic and social control of the countryside. By 1400, the lords had imposed and legalized *mal usos*,[25] and required a redemption fee (*remença*) to free their peasants. The lords also overcame unfavourable market forces and demographic decline after the Black Death; for the decline in numbers of peasants, and the consequent labour shortages and greater availability of good land, did not improve the terms of peasant tenure and work. Moreover, throughout the fifteenth century the lords enlisted lawyers, theologians and other learned people to provide moral, legal and historical (or pseudohistorical) arguments to validate serfdom. By 1462–72, with the Aragonese civil war looming in the background, the peasants, with the support of the Crown, waged a successful campaign against the nobility and their system of bondage. By 1486, the serfs of Old Catalonia had gained their freedom. These peasants, as Freedman shows, were different from the common stereotypes of serfs. Articulate and economically self-reliant, they sent ambassadors to plead their case to the royal court in far-away Naples, purchasing their freedom and defeating the nobility in pitched battle.[26]

The case of Old Catalonia is even more remarkable when one realizes that the conditions under which serfdom emerged were not very different from those which existed elsewhere in Iberia. In northern Castile, the nobility made attempts to restrict the movement of peasants shortly after the Black Death in 1350. The *fuero viejo de Castilla*, a collection of customary laws, contains provisions to that effect, but they were never successfully enforced. In Aragon, the large *morisco* population was in a state of semi-servile dependence to their Christian lords, although by law they were 'free'. Circumstances which in one area produced 'freedom' led to serfdom in another. In the end, lordly power

25. *Mals usos* included *intestia*, the lord's right to a part of the inheritance left by peasants dying without a will; *exorquia*, a 'similar levy in the event of death without direct legitimate heirs'; *cugacia*, 'confiscation of a portion of a peasant's property by reason of his wife's adultery'; *arsina*, a fine for burning one's own house or another peasant's house; *forçada*, 'payment in return for the lord's guarantee of nuptial agreements over dowry and marriage portion'. See Paul H. Freedman, *The Origins of Peasant Servitude in Medieval Catalonia* (Cambridge, 1991), p. 17.

26. Ibid.

and weak royal authority, more so in Catalonia than in Castile in this period, made all the difference.[27]

Equally striking is the subsequent development of Old Catalonia from a servile to a fairly well-to-do peasantry. From the sixteenth century onwards, a good number of peasants gained access to land by means of emphyteutic agreements (long-term or perpetual usufruct of the land). Some of these contracts led to the emergence of the *mas*, a homogeneous extension of farmland (between 100 and 200 hectares), with the household located at its centre. Through different strategies – late marriage, matrimonial alliances with female heirs (*pubilla*) – the *hereu*, heir and formal holder of the *mas*, sought to expand his patrimony. At the same time, it was not uncommon for the *hereu* to sublet portions of the *mas* to small farmers. In fact, in the region of Gerona, formerly the heartland of late medieval servitude, one-quarter of all the cultivated land was divided into more than 30,000 smallholdings and held by peasants through emphyteutic contracts in the eighteenth and nineteenth centuries.[28] Here, in this brief example, we have a perspective of the endless conflict between the consolidation of property and its fragmentation through inheritance and subletting, not just in northern Iberia but throughout most of the peninsula.

Central Iberia

Overwhelmingly in central Iberia, as in the northern regions (with the exception of servile Catalonia until 1486), the peasants held some land, ranging from sizeable farms to minuscule holdings. To have something (*algo*) was of the utmost importance, for owning or holding long-term contracts granted membership in the village community and access to the commons. From the northern mountains to southern Andalusia, from verdant Portugal in the west to the Mediterranean in the east, central Iberia was dominated by the great plains of Old and New Castile and by Aragon's plateau. On the high meseta, with little precipitation, poor soil and sparse population, the peasants lived in large villages. There, as almost everywhere else in Iberia, after 1400 an agricultural revival reclaimed the lands which had been deserted during the long crises of the previous century. This revival led to a greater specialization of what was grown, as farmers sought to market their crops. Moreover, in the great plains of central Spain, the Mesta (the guild of shepherds or the annual transhumance or movement of livestock from summer pastures in the north to winter grazing lands

27. The agency of Catalonian peasants contrasts with the relative docility of peasants elsewhere in Castile. In spite of a number of isolated acts of resistance, there was no Jacquerie, no peasant uprising in other parts of Iberia. I have offered some tentative explanations for this lack of organized peasant resistance in Castile in my 'Elite and popular culture in late fifteenth-century Castilian festivals: the case of Jaén', in Barbara A. Hanawalt and Kathryn L. Reyerson (eds), *City and Spectacle in Medieval Europe* (Minneapolis, MN, 1994), p. 310.

28. Ferrer i Alós, 'Familia y grupos sociales', 124. Also Rosa Congost, 'Enfiteusis y pequeña explotación campesina, siglos 18 y 19', in Saavedra and Villares, *Señores y campesinos en la península ibérica*, vol. I, pp. 64–8. For subdivision of vineyards see Llorenç Ferrer i Alós, 'La pequeña explotación de un viñedo de la Catalonia central, siglos 19 y 20', ibid., pp. 46ff.

in the south) shared, uncomfortably, the same geographical space. The influence of the owners of large flocks, the income which the Crown derived from the transhumance, and its signal place in the economy of Spain often made the Mesta a powerful enemy of agriculture until the modern age.

In central Castilian cities, towns and villages, a significant portion of the land was held by the village council for the benefit of all *vecinos*. These common lands consisted of pasture lands (*dehesas*) and lands which, although also reserved for grazing, were fenced and cultivated during specific times of the year (*cotos*). A great deal of the history of agriculture in the late Middle Ages and the early modern period turned on the changing relationship between common lands and the drive by members of the community and by outsiders (urban capital) to privatize common lands. This struggle, which ended in the victory of privatization, albeit the survival into the present of communal property, deeply affected the social and economic structure of the village, and of the peasantry itself.[29]

The conflict between common and private interests also disrupted the relations between urban centres and villages in the cities' hinterlands. In the late fifteenth century and throughout the sixteenth century, the municipal council of Soria, a city and region with large Mesta interests, attempted to make most of the common lands in the region available to owners of large flocks. Villages, such as Covaleda and Duruelo, sought to restrict pasture lands only to their own *vecinos*. Soria is a very good case study of the conflict between transhumance and agriculture, as villages, especially the mountain villages in the Soria region, sought to keep out transhumant flocks, while Soria's ruling oligarchs, with the support of royal officials, attempted to extend the privileges of large flock owners and their use of the commons.

In Soria, a relatively small area in the context of central Iberia, one finds a great deal of diversity. In the mountains of Soria, a substantial portion of the land was communal, and peasants owning, holding or leasing small properties constituted the dominant group numerically. On the plains, large ecclesiastical, lay and urban domains occupied most of the soil. The peasants rented land from large landowners, paying their rents mostly in kind. It was essentially a subsistence agriculture, with some specialized production of flax and saffron. But despite a period of general rural prosperity throughout most of the peninsula, the fifteenth and sixteenth centuries witnessed the progressive impoverishment of the Soria peasantry, as revealed by the peasants' inability to pay outstanding debts and their consequent loss of lands and tenure.

The wealth of Soria was in its livestock. Its flocks either travelled to Extremadura, Navarre and Aragon or circulated throughout the region of Soria, moving from one pastureland to another. There was, as with land ownership, a clear social hierarchy among flock owners. Those with large flocks came, by the sixteenth century, to play an important role in the political life of the city of Soria, and thus to wield a great deal of power in organizing and controlling the rural landscape. Below them there was a whole range of medium and small livestock owners, most of whom can also be classified as peasants, since they

29. See David Vassberg, *Land and Society in Golden Age Castile* (Cambridge, 1984), pp. 5–89 and passim.

combined their profitable livestock ownership with work in small farms, on which they raised a variety of agricultural goods.[30]

Southern Iberia

From the Algarve in southern Portugal to the Mediterranean coast, the latifundia dominated the rural world of southern Iberia. A legacy of the Christian conquest of most of Andalusia in the thirteenth century, the latifundia resulted from the failure to resettle the land according to the rural practices of the north, i.e. small farms that were cultivated by free peasants. The expulsion of the Moorish population after their rebellion in 1264 left the Crown with vast lands which had to be cultivated and defended from Muslim attacks. The first Christian settlers, granted lands in the initial *repartimientos* (distribution of lands to the victorious armies), were not quite able to adapt to the irrigation agriculture of southern Spain; nor were they always suited to the culture of the vine and olive trees. Many failed. The *huerta* of Murcia was turned to waste in less than ten years; others fled back to the north. Many of the lands were then given to the Military Orders, the magnates and the Church. The latifundia, which had Roman and Visigothic antecedents in the region, soon spread throughout western Andalusia.

This is not to say that the latifundium was the only form of organizing rural space in the south. Small landowners coexisted, especially in eastern Andalusia, with large landholders. In Lorca (in the province of Murcia), the irrigated plain was, according to Vassberg, 'largely in peasant hands and in an extremely subdivided state' into the seventeenth century. In the area of Granada, certainly after the Christians resettled the Alpujarra, the *minifundio*, or very small parcels, predominated.[31]

Similarly, the latifundia were not restricted to Andalusia. Sizeable lordships were found in Castile, in the Alentejo (Portugal), and in Aragon, where large numbers of *moriscos* endured particularly oppressive lordships. In the south, however, the size of some of these holdings and the concomitant number of peasants with little or no land, as reflected in the number of *jornaleros* (dayworkers), point to the latifundia as the dominant form of organizing agriculture and rural work.

Miguel Artola's *El latifundio: Propiedad y explotación, ss. XVIII–XX* provides an extensive analysis of and abundant data on the emergence of the latifundia in the thirteenth century, and their expansion and hegemony in succeeding centuries.[32] In western Andalusia, large landed estates, representing over 63 per cent of all cultivated land, provided work for two-thirds of the population. By the eighteenth century, the number of *jornaleros*, a truly rural proletariat, surpassed 75 per cent of the peasant population, followed by renters, who

---

30. Máximo Diago Hernando, *Soria en la baja edad media: Espacio rural y economía agraria* (Madrid, 1993), pp. 15–128.

31. Vassberg, *Land and Society*, pp. 122–5.

32. Miguel Artola *et al.*, *El latifundio: Propiedad y explotación, ss. XVIII–XX* (Madrid, 1978).

doubled the number of small proprietors. In eastern Andalusia, the number of *jornaleros*, though still significant, dropped to 50 per cent, with renters and proprietors equally comprising the other 50 per cent. The large number of salaried, landless peasants employed in the latifundia of the provinces of Córdoba, Seville and Jaén is a tell-tale sign not only of the preponderance of the large estate but of its dislocating effect on the peasant population.

PEASANT SOCIETIES: SOCIAL AND ECONOMIC CHANGE

We must now turn to a more detailed account of the peasants' occupations. How did they work the land? What did they grow? How did their lives and fortunes change over time?

We should begin with a glance at the general social and economic structure of Spain's peasantry.[33] The census of 1792 divides *labradores* (a term roughly equivalent to peasants: literally, those who plough the land, but also meaning well-to-do farmers in the late Middle Ages) into three main categories: *jornaleros*, *arrendatarios* (renters), and *propietarios* (owners). The proportions for all of Spain was: *jornaleros* 52.8 per cent, *arrendatarios* 30.6 per cent, and *propietarios* 16.5 per cent. The distribution of these three groups over the entire country, however, was very uneven. In Andalusia, the proportions were 78.2 per cent, 13.3 per cent, and 8.3 per cent respectively, while in Asturias, they became 3.1 per cent, 91.5 per cent, and 5.5 per cent.[34]

The peasants of northern Castile, whether renters or 'owners', cultivated the land in ways which harkened back to an earlier period. With few exceptions, the Roman plough — the plough of preference in the Mediterranean world – was used throughout Castile and the peninsula. This plough, far lighter than the heavy-wheeled plough of northern agriculture, was pulled by a team of oxen, sometimes by one ox. In the sixteenth century, mules began to be used in rural work in greater numbers, leading to an acrimonious debate on the advantages of one over the other. Oxen (and sometimes cows, as was the case in my family's village) were generally the animal of preference in the north, whereas mules made greater inroads in New Castile and the south.

The land was divided into two fields, following the biennial systems of field rotation (*año y vez*) common to southern lands: one field remained fallow, while the other was cultivated. With some rare exceptions, the three-field system, which revolutionized northern agriculture, never prospered in Iberia. With thin soils, a harsh climate (in the central plains) and a perpetual dearth of manure, the fallow had to be ploughed repeatedly, and, often, allowed to rest for two years. The village livestock, by which I mean the animals owned by the '*vecinos*', grazed in the arable after the harvest, and in the fallow during the year.

33. The information for Portugal is too scant, but the proportions should not have differed greatly from those of Spain.
34. Jordi Nadal, *La población española: (siglo XVI a XX)* (Barcelona, 1984), p. 102.

The arable was made up of mostly open fields – not the long straight furrows of the north, but a kind of quilt-work. At certain times of the year, close to harvest time, the arable might be fenced to keep the livestock out, whereas vineyards were almost always fenced or guarded. Most of the arable was given over to the growing of cereals. Wheat was the preferred crop, essentially because lords required most or at least half of the peasants' payments in wheat. Barley was the second most popular crop, though in some regions of Castile barley production easily surpassed that of wheat. By the sixteenth century, money payments began to replace dues in kind, but, in general, northern villages, settled in the early phases of the Reconquest, maintained full or partial payments in kind longer than the larger villages of central and New Castile. Rye was limited to areas suited by climate and topography for its growth. My own impression, however, is that the cultivation of rye, with its higher yield, was far more widespread than our sources indicate, and that it was the basic bread – the dark bread – of the poor. Oats are rarely found in rural accounts, and maize, introduced from the New World in the sixteenth century, was only slowly accepted in Galicia and in specific areas of the north.

In northern Castile, the peasants grew many other things which complemented their limited diets and incomes: legumes, some flax, vegetables in the gardens attached to their houses, and fruit trees. Everywhere, unless the climate or soil were exceedingly hostile, the peasants tended the vine for the profits it brought, for its nutritional value, for its pleasure, for gift-giving and hospitality. Monasteries also spent large sums of money on cultivating vineyards, which were not always very productive or profitable. Certain regions of Iberia – the Rioja, the region of Porto, areas of Catalonia and Andalusia – became highly specialized in the production of wine. From the thirteenth century, these regions sent their wine to other areas of Iberia and abroad. Similarly, wheat from the Tierra de Campos and the plains of Castile, and olive oil from the south fed Iberian cities and the American colonies. The mixed peasant economy also depended on livestock. A large part of the Iberian flocks did not travel in the annual transhumance, but grazed closer to home.

With the usual exceptions, there was always a dearth of agricultural tools and work animals. Rural inventories testify to the imbalance between cultivated land and the number of ploughs and oxen or mules. In a 'typical' village, the *yugero*, a man owning a plough and a team of oxen or mules who hired himself out to plough the fields in return for one-fifth of the crop, was a fixture of rural life and, often, an important man in the village social structure, as the designation of *Don* in the documents indicates. In villages with fragmented arables and insufficient ploughs or oxen, peasants either worked together or died separately. Greed fostered individualism and privatization; need encouraged communal practices.

Beyond the village stretched the woods (*monte*), which in central Spain did not mean dense forests. Since an earlier age, most of Iberia (with the exception of green Portugal and the north) had undergone a dramatic deforestation. Wood was very dear, and foreign travellers crossing Castile often complained of the absence of trees and the high price of wood.[35] In the scrawny brush nearby, and in pens behind the house, peasants raised pigs, rabbits and pigeons, garnering another source of protein for their meagre diets. Most peasants ate a simple daily fare of bread, some meat (mostly bacon) or cheese, some greens. Brumont's superb study of the Bureba gives us an average of 500 grams for the daily consumption of bread (mostly wheat, but also mixed with rye) among peasants. As for meat, the average ranged between 20 and 35 grams daily, in proportions of 50 per cent pork meat, 35 per cent mutton and 15 per cent beef. There were other items on the rural menu: cheese, poultry (usually reserved for the well-to-do), eggs, legumes, and fish, which has been consumed in large quantities in Castile from the thirteenth century to the present day. The consumption of wine, often watered down, ranged between one and two litres.[36] One must nevertheless resist the tendency to idealize the peasants' lives. These averages come from an area that was doing quite well in the sixteenth century. The diet of most peasants in Iberia was much leaner.

Throughout most of Iberia, moreover, agricultural yields were low (for wheat, a frightening yield of 2:1 is reported for the area of Ávila in the nineteenth century), and seigneurial dues and royal taxation were crushing. Working the land, especially in central Castile, was hard and often unprofitable. Brueghel's fat and prosperous peasants were not Spanish peasants, or, at least, not the immense majority of them. The image from sixteenth-century picaresque novels is one of enduring hunger. Plagues, recurring famines and droughts swept the Iberian countryside and cities well into the eighteenth century. Strategies for survival varied, a substantial number of peasants dividing their time between rural activities and artisanal pursuits. The village shoemakers, smiths, women bakers (bakers in Castile were overwhelmingly female), and small shopkeepers more often than not also worked the land and travelled to nearby towns to sell their wares and agricultural products.

If we are to speak of a 'typical' peasant, he or she would have lived in the great plains of Castile, where the largest proportion of peasants lived, and would have been mainly engaged in cereal growing. Our imaginary peasant would have held a bit of land, which he or she owned or, more likely, rented and paid dues for to a lord (royal, lay or ecclesiastical). Moreover, our peasant would have held this land 'for ever', as the documents often stated. Very often the land would not have been sufficient to support his or her family, and the peasant would have been forced to rent additional lands or to hire him or herself out at harvest or ploughing time. Until the sixteenth century, land rentals were undertaken for extended periods of time: 'for life', 'for ever', for three generations, for the life of the vine, etc. But by the onset of the modern period, rentals were restricted to shorter periods, between three and nine years, imposing further hardships on the peasantry.

---

35. García Mercadal, *Viajes de extranjeros*, vol. I, pp. 270, 702, 869, 1473, 1502 and passim.
36. Brumont, *Campo y campesinos*, pp. 202–3, see also n. 49 for diet of peasants in New Castile.

Men and women worked side by side in the fields; furthermore, women throughout most of Iberia held lands outright. In the domain of Santa María la Real, to which I have referred earlier, women represented 17 per cent of all the peasants paying rent to the monastery. In places such as Galicia and parts of Portugal – from which men often emigrated to other parts of the kingdom or abroad, leaving their families behind – women seemed until very recently to be the only ones working the fields.[37]

To proceed with our 'typical' peasant of northern and central Castile, he or she would have lived in a village. In the thirteenth and fourteenth centuries, as Iberia plunged into crisis, mountain villages may have had as little as twelve to sixteen *vecinos*, that is, a population barely reaching fifty. In the late sixteenth century, the Bureba averaged around fifty-four *vecinos* per village or an average of 200 inhabitants. In the area of Valladolid, located in the central plains of Castile, rural villages averaged as many as 157 *vecinos* or over 600 inhabitants. Even larger rural towns were found in the south.[38]

One can still see these villages along modern roads. Large stone churches, built in the heyday of the Empire, tower over the peasants' houses, also built of stone or bricks. In the north, most houses are grouped around a church and the small common where the grain was threshed. This is precisely the layout of my family's village, Gallejones de Zamanzas in northern Castile, a village which dates from the early phases of the Reconquest, and whose houses, church and patterns of cultivation (until almost everyone fled to the cities in the 1970s) are rooted in the late Middle Ages.

The Culture and Religion of the Peasants

All was not work in the fields of Iberia. The peasants lived immersed in a rich amalgam of cultural and religious practices. Illiterate for the most part until the nineteenth century, villagers none the less shared in the wider cultural world of the kingdom. Because of the proximity of most villages to towns (certainly in Castile), rural and urban worlds met in the feasts which formed part of the liturgical cycle of most towns. During Christmas, the feasts of the Epiphany, Candlemas, Carnival, Easter – above all, the feast of Corpus Christi (after the 1550s) and other religious and secular festivals – country people poured into the towns. Royal entries and the celebrations of the mighty also attracted the rustics. In Valladolid in 1428, in Jaén in the 1450s, and elsewhere throughout the peninsula, festivals enacted the hegemonic struggles between city and country for the benefit and instruction of participants as well as spectators. At such times, the peasants beheld *tableaux vivants*, attended plays, jousts and dances, and shared, albeit briefly and incompletely, in the culture of the elite and the city.[39]

---

37. See Teófilo F. Ruiz, 'Notas para el estudio de la mujer en el área de Burgos bajomedieval', in idem, *The City and the Realm: Burgos and Castile, 1080–1492* (Aldershot, 1992), ch. 4.

38. Brumont, *Campo y campesinos*, p. 76, see also n. 11. Ruiz, *Crisis and Continuity*, ch. 4.

39. See Teófilo F. Ruiz, 'Festivités, couleurs et symboles du pouvoir en Castille au XVe siècle: Les célébrations de Mai 1428', *Annales ESC* (1991), pp. 521–46; and idem, 'Elite and popular culture', pp. 296–318.

Then there were those peasants who did not travel to nearby towns, or who lived in remote villages. Their culture was a combination of religion, magic and folklore. William Christian Jr has mined Philip II's great survey of Spanish villages and towns (1575–80) for popular beliefs in the region of New Castile. His findings depict a rural world deeply embedded in a religious culture, whereby entire communities took vows to build shrines, keep collective fasts and give charity, in what amounted to deal-making bids with the saints or God. Drought, locusts, the fear of epidemics, lightning, unexpected fires and other natural disasters drove the peasants to elaborate religious observances; when in doubt about the efficacy of official rituals, they sought the remedies of travelling necromancers, conjurers and healers.

In a world of numerous priests, most villages had their own churches and sacred relics. The life of the village, especially after the Counter-Reformation, was centred around the cult of 'specialized saints': St Sebastian, St Roch (Roque), Marian cults, thaumaturgical crucifixes, powerful relics. The annual procession, the ritual meals, the activities of brotherhoods in some of the larger villages provided a sense of security and protection in a hostile world.[40]

Social and Economic Change

This world 'we have lost', to use Laslett's felicitous words, can still be seen in some corners of Iberia, where the past endures into the present. The quaint, picturesque appeal of these villages today belies the harsh realities and social conflicts which transformed the lives of peasants. The fragmented landscape of Iberian agriculture and the fairly egalitarian quality of village life in an earlier period were already under attack as early as the thirteenth century. Several developments led to social change in the late Middle Ages and in the early modern period.

First, in the fourteenth and fifteenth centuries the collapse of the Crown's and the lords' rural income – due to demographic decline (plagues, famines and wars) – led to increased violence against the peasantry, as lords sought to obtain new sources of revenue or, at least, to maintain existing ones. In what amounted to an undeclared war against the peasantry, the violence weakened the social and economic fabric of the village community and allowed for a more clear-cut discourse of difference to define rich and poor, rural and urban. If oppression led to successful rebellion in Catalonia, such was not the case elsewhere. In the rest of Iberia, peasants, according to a fourteenth-century source, were lambs, and the nobility, wolves.[41]

Second, from the thirteenth century onwards, urban capital and bourgeois investment in the countryside intruded forcefully into the rural world. City-dwellers bought property in the villages, acquired rights of *vecinaje*, bought and

---

40. See William A. Christian Jr, *Local Religion in Sixteenth-Century Spain* (Princeton, NJ, 1981).

41. See Julio Rodríguez Puértolas, *Poesía de protesta en la edad media castellana: Historia y antología* (Madrid, 1968), pp. 26–51, 207–15; also idem, *Poesía crítica y satírica del siglo XV* (Madrid, 1981), pp. 7–29.

sold rights to the commons. Entire villages were bought by powerful oligarchs and turned into contiguous estates and entailments. Although the peasants often remained on the land, they did so as short-term tenants under conditions different from the life tenancies they had enjoyed earlier, their social status and roles deeply altered. In time, urban oligarchs came to control village rural councils and to determine the political, as well as the social and economic, life of the community.

Third, within the villages themselves, some peasants achieved a great deal of success. Through purchases, inheritance and work, they consolidated and expanded their holdings, and emerged as a rural oligarchy. Social and economic differences within the village led to stratification. Throughout Iberia, a few well-to-do *labradores*, those whom Moxó describes as *campesinos hacendados*, joined with urban oligarchs to wield their power within the village. In some cases, as in the earlier example of Soria, these prosperous owners of land and flocks entered the circle of the patrician urban elites. Throughout most of Castile, Galicia, Extremadura and Andalusia, a small number of rich people, some farmers among them, confronted an immense sea of rural poverty.[42]

The long crisis of Castilian agriculture, which began with the collapse of the Spanish economy at the end of Philip II's reign and which continued, with little respite, until the end of the seventeenth century, drove a dagger into the heart of the Iberian peasantry in general and into that of Castile in particular. Wherever we turn, the sources and the historians of the period describe the impoverishment of the countryside, recurring famines, epidemics, peasants leaving their lands, turning their backs on their ancestors' way of life, and flocking to the cities in search of work or alms. Others joined the growing bands of vagabonds and bandits, a permanent feature of early modern Iberia.

The *arbitristas* (reformers of the seventeenth century) understood the maladies afflicting the peninsula. Their plans to reform Spain, some of them utterly bizarre, ranged over the whole spectrum of political, social, economic and moral renewal, but they all agreed on the sorry state of rural Spain. The eighteenth century witnessed some recovery, but by then the social fabric of the countryside had been irrevocably transformed. Political and economic differences within most villages created a divide which in some places endures until today.

Representations of the Peasantry

Here, at the end of this journey through the Iberian countryside, we must return to the questions raised at the very beginning of this chapter. How were the peasants seen, or, better yet, how were they represented in literary texts and iconographic sources? If, in Iberia, the peasants were not represented as

---

42. For evidence of increased rural poverty see Hilario Casado Alonso, *Señores, mercaderes y campesinos: La comarca de Burgos a fines de la edad media* (Valladolid, 1987), pp. 520–35; Brumont reports a different situation in the Bureba, *Campo y campesinos*, p. 195.

pejoratively as in other parts of the medieval west, this does not mean that negative depictions were scarce. In fact, what one observes is a complex mixture of positive and derogatory representations.

On the whole, the Golden Age theatre idealized the peasantry, but the peasants chosen for this idealization were the well-to-do, genteel peasants who knew how to read and write. They were Old Christians, not tainted by *converso* (Jewish or Moorish) blood, as well as prosperous *labradores*, with well-appointed houses; conversant with the political issues of the day, they always stood ready to defend their honour. Few peasants in Iberia could fulfil this role.[43] What we rarely see at all are suffering or hungry peasants.

Cervantes's representation of peasants in *Don Quixote* – Sancho Panza, Dulcinea – is more ambivalent. Not much difference remains, at the end of volume two, between noble master and peasant servant. For all his vulgarity, ignorance and frequent lapses into cowardice, Sancho displays such endearing qualities as loyalty and common sense, and a dogged instinct for survival. And although Dulcinea smells of onions and garlic, Don Quixote nevertheless glorifies her. A far more one-sided position emerged in Catalonia. As Paul Freedman has shown, specious arguments were mustered to legitimize peasant servitude. The peasants' cowardice in Carolingian times, their failure to defend Christianity against Islam, as the argument went, led them and their descendants to be justifiably tied to the soil. Peasants were cowards and thus servile – this was the prevailing view in a country where peasants had long served and continued to serve as free men in military campaigns.

From the pastoral and idealized depictions of a peasant young woman – 'the most beautiful young woman I have ever seen' – in the *Serranillas* of the Marquis de Santillana (d. 1458), to the rough and libidinous peasant women tollcollectors in Juan Ruiz's picaresque romp through the central Sierras of Castile in the early fourteenth century, to the brutal depiction of peasants as beasts by Examinis, a Catalan writer of the fifteenth century, we move through a gamut of positive and negative representations. None, however, are as savage or as callous as those of Charles V (d. 1558). Referring to his peasant soldiers – the same men who had through unceasing toil and heavy taxes contributed to the glory and maintenance of his royal domains; who had conquered him an empire across the Ocean Sea; and who were immolated on the battlefields, far away from their homes, defending causes about which they knew little – the emperor is quoted by Ambrose Paré as having asked, at the siege of Metz in 1552, whether the dying men were noble. Upon learning they were merely poor men, Charles V answered that their loss then was of no interest; for if they had been 'good' men (the implication being also of some sense) they would not have served him for a salary of six pounds.[44] Thus it was for most Iberian peasants

---

43. In many respects, these plays were as much about purity of blood and the 'innate' nobility of Old Christians as they were about the peasants themselves.

44. Quoted in Vicens Vives, *Historia de España y América*, vol. III, p. 101. There is also an anecdote, whether apocryphal or not, of a peasant who in speaking to Charles V, without knowing who he was, argued that he did not understand why he had to ruin himself paying taxes to support the emperor's foreign policies (p. 101).

throughout the period: to work and die for the benefit of the few with no rewards.

CONCLUSION

In late medieval and early modern Iberia, peasants represented the overwhelming majority of the population. With their lives, taxes and toil, the peasants supported the nobles and ecclesiastics (who were exempted from most taxes) and maintained and fought for the vainglory of the empire. Their families were usually small, nuclear families; they lived in either small hamlets or large villages. With the exception of northern Catalonia until 1486, these peasants were legally free, but paid heavy dues and, often, rents to others. Their lives were harsh, mortality was high, and their work was often unprofitable. Half the Spanish peasants were labourers, that is, people with no land or with so little land that they could not support themselves unless they hired themselves out to others. Most were poor and getting poorer, as we progress into the seventeenth century. And yet, the peasants endured and continued to endure until today. Why was this so, considering the bleak picture I have presented above? Allow me, at the end, to conclude with a personal recollection. I have a distant cousin of my father in my ancestral village, Isaías, a man in his early seventies who has never left Gallejones de Zamanzas. When asked why he had not done so, his answer was simple and direct: 'Because I cannot think of myself away from the land, because if I don't tend the land, she [land, in Spanish, is feminine] will die, I will die.' And it is this sustaining work, the love and need for the land, the miracle of growing and tending things, which gave and gives meaning and character to the lives of peasants.

BIBLIOGRAPHY

There are no books in any language dealing with the history of the peasantry in Iberia from 1400 to 1800. What we have is a vast collection of regional studies, covering a limited span of time, or short treatments of the subject in general histories of Spain or Portugal. Below is a short list of main works in English with some additional references to works in other languages.

Bisson, Thomas N., *The Medieval Crown of Aragon: A Short History* (Oxford, 1986).
Freedman, Paul H., *The Origins of Peasant Servitude in Medieval Catalonia* (Cambridge, 1991).
—— 'Cowardice, heroism and the legendary origins of Catalonia', *Past and Present*, 121 (1988), pp. 3–28.

Hamilton, Earl, *War and Prices in Spain, 1615–1800*, 2nd edn (New York, 1969).

Heer, Richard, *The Eighteenth Century Revolution in Spain* (Princeton, NJ, 1969).

—— *Rural Change and Royal Finances in Spain* (Berkeley, CA, 1989).

Klein, Julius, *The Mesta: A Study in Spanish Economic History, 1273–1836* (Cambridge, MA, 1920).

Lynch, John, *Spain Under the Habsburgs*, 2nd edn, 2 vols (New York, 1984).

MacKay, Angus, *Spain in the Middle Ages: From Frontier to Empire, 1000–1500* (London, 1977).

Ringrose, David R., *Madrid and the Spanish Economy (1560–1860)* (Berkeley, CA, 1983).

—— *Transportation and Economic Stagnation in Spain, 1750–1850* (Durham, NC, 1970).

Ruiz, Teófilo F., *Crisis and Continuity: Land and Town in Late Medieval Castile* (Philadelphia, PA, 1994).

Vassberg, David E., *Land and Society in Golden Age Castile* (Cambridge, 1984).

Some important titles in other languages:

Anes Alvarez, Gonzalo, *Las crisis agrarias en la España moderna* (Madrid, 1970).

Bennassar, Bartolomé, *Valladolid au siècle d'or: Une ville de Castille et sa campagne au XVIe siècle* (Paris, 1969).

Brumont, Francis, *Campo y campesinos de Castilla la Vieja en tiempos de Felipe II* (Madrid, 1984).

Castro, Armando, *História económica de Portugal*, Vols II and III (Lisbon, 1981, 1985).

García Sanz, Ángel, *Desarrollo y crisis del antiguo régimen en Castilla la Vieja* (Madrid, 1986).

Huetz de Lemps, Alain, *Vignobles et vins du nord-ouest de l'Espagne*, 2 vols (Bordeaux, 1967).

Saavedra, Pegerto and Villares, Ramón (eds), *Señores y campesinos en la península ibérica, siglos XVIII–XX*, 2 vols (Barcelona, 1991).

Salomon, Noël, *La campagne de Nouvelle Castille à la fin du XVIe siècle d'après les 'Relaciones Topográficas'* (Paris, 1964).

Silva, José Gential da, *Desarrollo económico, subsistencia y decadencia en España* (Madrid, 1967).

Viñas y Mey, Carmelo, *El problema de la tierra en la España de los siglos XVI–XVII* (Madrid, 1941).

Map 4.1 Italy

CHAPTER FOUR

The Peasantries of Italy, 1350–1750

S. R. Epstein

The history of late medieval and early modern Italy has generally been written either by juxtaposing distinctive and unconnected regional patterns, or by contrasting developments in the peninsula's 'south' and its 'centre-north', with the dividing line running somewhere between the regions of Tuscany, Umbria and the Marches on the one hand, and Lazio and Abruzzi on the other. From a political and institutional point of view these approaches make good sense. By the early fourteenth century at the latest, the institutional contrast between north and south was apparent to contemporaries and irreversible. By the mid-fifteenth century, when the dust began to settle after over a century of military conflict and social upheaval, five or six dominant states were in the process of emerging from the rubble. To the north, territorial states under Milanese, Venetian and Florentine leadership had established sovereignty over a motley of independent city-states and feudal lordships, while leaving many of their new subjects' prerogatives unchallenged; to the south, Sicily, Naples and the Papal States were ruled by secular or ecclesiastical monarchies, and feudal lordship was generally stronger, and the legal standing of towns weaker, than in the north.

As elsewhere in Europe, Italian political history has been told as a lengthy prelude to the birth of the nation-state with unification in 1861. Economic historians have generally adopted a similar perspective, within which Unification marks a watershed in economic policy, national market integration and the process of industrialization. They have identified the causes of the country's late industrialization in retarded unification, the persistence of 'feudal' institutions in the highly urbanized, 'bourgeois' north and in the lack of dynamic, 'bourgeois' urban societies in the agrarian and 'feudal' south. However, while paying homage to these schemes in theory, in practice most agricultural historians have dwelt rather more on regional particularities. Some general outlines are nonetheless well-established. In the first place, agriculture in the south was on the whole more specialized and commercialized than in the centre-north, where mixed cropping combining cereals and tree crops (wine, olives, fruit, nuts, mulberry leaves for silkworms) was widespread. Secondly, during the late Middle Ages wheat established itself as the townspeople's preferred food grain. The urban poor and many peasants made do with rye in central Italy and the south, and with millet in the north. From the late seventeenth century maize took over as the staple food of the urban and rural poor north of the Apennines; chestnuts remained popular in the colder and less fertile uplands. Lesser grains like barley, spelt and far were kept as animal feed and as a reserve stock against bad harvests in the better but more variable cereal crops. Typically 'Mediterranean' crops, like vines and olive trees, also began a long phase of expansion following the Black Death in response to growing consumer demand and became an increasingly important component of basic diets.

Thirdly, pastoralism underwent considerable expansion. While this was a common occurrence throughout Europe in the long period of underpopulation following the Black Death, in Tuscany, Lazio and the eastern seaboard of the state of Naples late medieval sheep transhumance became a major source of tax revenue for cash-strapped governments and took on an independent institutional life which lasted for the whole period with which we are concerned.

Although sheep transhumance was by and large alternative rather than complementary to sedentary agriculture, between 1350 and 1750 no more than a third of the country was under cultivation; between 1350 and 1500 the proportion was substantially less. The reasons were largely geographical. Nearly 70 per cent of the country rises over 500 metres above sea level; the only large alluvial plain lies in the basin of the river Po in the northern Lombardo-Venetian region. The sheer length of the peninsula means that climate varies considerably with latitude and relief. Whereas the coastal lowlands enjoy a typical Mediterranean climate, the mountainous interior is cold, well watered and often snowy; the length and intensity of the summer dry season increases as one moves southwards. But although climate constrained agricultural choices, it never determined them entirely: despite intense regional differences in soil conditions and climate, in the course of our period cropping patterns became more, rather than less, similar across the peninsula.

This chapter attempts to strike a middle path between a more strictly regional approach, which runs the risk of losing sight of the many shared features of agriculture across the peninsula, and a 'national' approach which tends to exaggerate the economic and institutional unity of the country before political unification. It is hoped that this will show the many similarities, and the occasional differences, between the southern and northern Italian peasantries under a different and possibly challenging light.

PEASANTRIES AND THE STATE

Towns and Lords: The Centre-North

Between the mid-fourteenth and the mid-sixteenth century city-states everywhere were incorporated into larger and politically more complex territorial or regional states, thereby establishing central and northern Italy's basic political framework until Unification in 1861. Historians addressing the consequences of political integration on city-states used to argue that incorporation caused a loss of control over taxation and over some strategic industries, but that the cities' fundamentally exploitative relationship with the countryside was on the whole unaffected. More recently, however, there have been attempts to distinguish more clearly between outcomes in different territorial states. Regional states were not simply a rag-bag of previously independent city-states. Their rulers recognized and at times fostered a range of institutional counterparts in the countryside which were semi-autonomous from, and frequently hostile towards, the former city-states. According to this view, the late medieval state fostered some degree of corporate pluralism by recognizing political jurisdictions and rights outside the remit of the former city-states.

This interpretation, which suggests that conditions in the countryside were less uniformly oppressive than was formerly believed, draws an important distinction between the status of the immediate urban hinterland, the *contado*, and that of the countryside beyond it, the *distretto*. In the *contado*, towns were virtually omnipotent in all major administrative, legal, fiscal and economic activities. The hinterland offered the urban elites the prestige of local office, whose costs were mostly paid by the peasantry;[1] the major law courts sat in the cities, upholding statutes that favoured citizen over peasant rights and landlord claims over tenants;[2] and the town controlled trade, manufacture and labour markets, and the distribution of taxes. The frequent portrayal of town and *contado* as locked in endless strife over fiscal, judicial and economic rights is thus not entirely misplaced. Fiscal policies in particular discriminated by social status, which in north-central Italy was a function of residence; hence, inhabitants of the dominant city, of subject cities and of the countryside were differently assessed. Whereas townspeople were mainly taxed through excise and other tariffs, and in large commercial cities like Florence, Venice and Genoa by means of interest-bearing forced loans to the state, peasants paid non-refundable poll and hearth taxes set by the ruling town. Not surprisingly, burghers strongly resented any form of taxation which required assessing their real wealth: in Republican Florence, direct taxation was attempted only twice during the early fourteenth century by two short-lived seigneurial regimes, and became associated thereafter with political 'tyranny'.[3] *Contadini* instead worried less about how taxes were collected than about the way the tax burden was distributed. They particularly disliked the fact that both the size and distribution of taxation were set by the city;[4] that assessments were very infrequently revised; and that urban property was exempt from rural taxes, with the result that land transfers

---

1. G. Chittolini and D. Willoweit (eds), *L'organizzazione del territorio in Italia e Germania: secoli XIII–XIV* (Bologna, 1994).

2. See G. Piccinni, 'I mezzadri di fronte al fisco. Primo esame della normativa senese del Quattrocento', in *Cultura e società nell'Italia medievale. Studi per Paolo Brezzi* (Rome, 1988), pp. 665–82 on Siena's regulation of sharecropping. See also below, pp. 96–7, 100–6.

3. A. Molho, 'Tre città-stato e i loro debiti pubblici. Quesiti e ipotesi sulla storia di Firenze, Genova e Venezia', in *Italia 1350–1450: tra crisi, trasformazione, sviluppo* (Pistoia, 1993), pp. 185–215.

4. Between c.1350 and 1430, the per caput tax load of the Florentine *contado* was approximately two to four times higher than in Florence itself. Cf. S. R. Epstein, 'Stato territoriale ed economia regionale nella Toscana del Quattrocento', in R. Fubini (ed.), *Instituzioni, cultura ed arte in Toscana nell'éta di Lorenzo il Magnifico*, 3 vols (Pisa, 1995), vol. I, p. 876 n. 22.

to townspeople or concessions of burgher rights to peasants (who were required by law to immigrate to towns in order to enjoy them, but did not always comply) eroded the rural tax base and caused a proportionate increase in the tax burden.[5]

The rise of territorial states did by contrast provide opportunities to renegotiate the terms of power between towns and their more distant *distretto*. Regional rulers were willing to offer some fiscal and administrative independence to feudal lordships, rural confederacies and larger rural settlements in exchange for their political and military support. While such concessions seldom involved wholesale autonomy from the city, they did help establish significant economic liberties in the countryside (such as the right to hold free markets and fairs and to engage in manufacturing outside the control of urban guilds), which would have important long-run consequences. None the less, privileged communities were more likely to be situated at a state's periphery, where petty lordships and rural communes had been able to resist earlier urban expansion and where the new territorial states were keen to counter threats of military invasion; generally less conciliatory policies prevailed where fewer independent enclaves survived from earlier periods.[6]

Both the dukes of Milan and the Venetian oligarchy granted exemptions from urban jurisdiction to rural communities which had already established a degree of autonomy during the thirteenth and fourteenth centuries. Venice may have supported peasant grievances more actively, particularly in the provinces of Brescia, Bergamo and Verona on the western border with Milan, but it always took care not to upset the local urban elites.[7] Both states pursued a generally conservative fiscal policy until the early sixteenth century, leaving tax assessments in the hands of individual cities. This was in sharp contrast with the policy of Florence. Between 1384 and 1434, the Florentine ruling class treated newly incorporated cities more like a subject hinterland than a confederacy of equals, depriving them of their own *contadi* altogether and extending Florentine fiscal jurisdiction to the entire state with the famous *Catasto* of 1424–27.[8] However, this wholesale attack on traditional prerogatives backfired, and Florence responded to several urban uprisings by quietly reverting to the old arrangements.

At the same time that Tuscany was reverting to ancient patterns of urban supremacy, Venice and Lombardy responded to major political crises (Venice's crushing defeat at Agnadello in 1509 and Milan's incorporation into the Spanish empire in 1535) by initiating a wholesale revision of existing systems of taxation. In both states, rural federations arose to negotiate the terms of assessment

---

5. In the late sixteenth-century assessment of Cremona, urban landowners paid only one-quarter of the land tax paid by the peasantry. Cf. G. Vigo, *Fisco e società nella Lombardia del Cinquecento* (Bologna, 1979), p. 27.

6. S. R. Epstein, 'Taxation and social representation in Italian territorial states', in M. Boone and W. Prevenier (eds), *Finances publiques et finances privées au bas moyen âge* (Leuven-Apeldoorn, 1996), pp. 101–15.

7. I. Pederzani, *Venezia e lo 'Stado de Terraferma'. Il governo delle comunità nel territorio bergamasco (secc. XV–XVIII)* (Milan, 1992), pp. 41–59; J. E. Law, ' "Super differentiis agitatis Venetiis inter districtuales et civitatem". Venezia, Verona e il contado nel "400"', *Archivio veneto*, 5th series, 116 (1981), pp. 5–32.

8. D. Herlihy and C. Klapisch-Zuber, *Les Toscans et leurs familles. Une étude du Catasto florentin de 1427* (Paris, 1978).

between rustics and townspeople, battling to abolish the ancient political and fiscal distinctions which sustained urban supremacy. These organizations provided rural elites with the authority and, frequently, the income from tax farming they required to consolidate local leadership, with the result that in the short run, the 'peasant oligarchies' riding the wave of sixteenth-century expansion probably gained most from fiscal reform. On the other hand, in the longer term the countryside's efforts to achieve greater freedom of action would give it a significant advantage over the more heavily regulated towns during the seventeenth-century economic downturn.[9]

Although concessions of jurisdictional rights served similar political purposes everywhere, there were some striking differences in implementation. Republican regimes like Venice (and Florence before the change of regime in the early sixteenth century) preferred to negotiate with rural communities and were generally hostile towards remaining vestiges of feudal lordship; by contrast, the dukes of Milan and lesser princes elsewhere instigated a neo-feudal revival, confirming old fiefs and establishing new ones to pay off their military followers, and instead seemed less willing to grant concessions to autonomous rural entities. Thus, for instance, after Florence became a principate under the Medici in the 1530s the practice of infeudation became a central feature of the new regime. The Tuscan example suggests that the choice of a corporatist rather than a neo-feudal strategy of alliances expressed the prevailing political culture: republicans preferred to associate with corporate groups having a modicum of popular legitimacy, while monarchists were more attuned to their military and social peers.[10]

The insurgence of feudal practices between the late fourteenth and the mid-sixteenth century was not, therefore, a purely reactionary process of 'refeudalization', but was instead part of a far wider reorganization of territorial rule.[11]

9. For Agnadello see I. Cervelli, *Machiavelli e la crisi dello stato veneziano* (Naples, 1974). For fiscal and broader institutional reforms see S. Zamperetti, 'I "sincdri dolosi". La formazione e lo sviluppo dei corpi territoriali nello stato regionale veneto tra '500 e '600', *Rivista storica italiana*, 99 (1987), pp. 269–320; G. Del Torre, *Venezia e la Terraferma dopo la Guerra di Cambrai. Fiscalità e amministrazione (1515–1530)* (Milan, 1986); L. Pezzolo, *L'oro dello Stato. Società, finanza e fisco nella Repubblica veneta del secondo '500* (Treviso, 1990); A. Rossini, *Le campagne bresciane nel Cinquecento. Territori, fisco, società* (Milan, 1994); Vigo, *Fisco e società*; A. Zappa, 'L'avvio dell' estimo generale dello Stato di Milano nell'età di Carlo V', *Società e storia*, 14 (1991), pp. 545–77. Seventeenth-century developments are discussed below, pp. 102–6.

10. G. Chittolini, 'Governo ducale e poteri locali', in *Gli Sforza a Milano e in Lombardia e i loro rapporti con gli Stati italiani ed europei (1450–1535)* (Milan, 1982), pp. 27–42; idem, 'Principe e comunità alpine in area lombarda alla fine del Medioevo', in E. Martinengo (ed.), *Le Alpi per l'Europa. Una proposta politica* (Milan, 1988), pp. 219–35; G. Pansini, 'Per una storia del feudalesimo nel Granducato di Toscana durante il periodo mediceo', *Quaderni storici*, 5 (1972), pp. 131–86; G. Gullino, 'I patrizi veneziani di fronte alla proprietà feudale (secoli XVI–XVIII). Materiali per una ricerca', *Quaderni storici*, 15 (1980), pp. 162–92; K. O. von Aretin, 'L'ordinamento feudale in Italia nel XVI e XVII secolo e le sue ripercussioni sulla politica europea. Un contributo alla storia del tardo feudalesimo in Europa', *Annali dell'Istituto storico italo-germanico in Trento*, 4 (1977), pp. 51–94. See also below, n. 11.

11. G. Chittolini, *La formazione dello Stato regionale e le istituzioni del contado. Secoli XIV e XV* (Turin, 1979), Introduction; idem, 'Signorie rurali e feudi alla fine del Medioevo', in O. Capitani *et al.*, *Comuni e signorie: istituzioni, società e lotte per l'egemonia* (Turin, 1981), pp. 659–67. Established in 1545, the duchies of Parma and Piacenza were a unique hybrid of semi-independent city-states and petty fiefdoms with a bewildering motley of competing jurisdictions. See L. Arcangeli, 'Giurisdizioni feudali e organizzazione territoriale nel Ducato di Parma (1545–1587)', in M. A. Romani (ed.), *Le Corti farnesiane di Parma e Piacenza, 1543–1622*, 2 vols

The revival was kept within strictly defined parameters. Feudatories were forced to recognize the superior authority of the state; their jurisdictional prerogatives over taxation and justice were clearly defined; they could not wage war independently. Even fiefs which remained strictly speaking autonomous, along much of the Apennines from Liguria in the north-west to Tuscany and the Marches in the centre-east, survived as *de facto* protectorates which acted as territorial buffers between larger states, provided military leaders and mercenaries, and ensured a modicum of security in areas which townsmen had neither the resources nor the ability to control. Unfortunately the inner workings of feudal lordships are still virtually unknown, so one can do little more than speculate on the nature of the relations between lords and their peasant vassals, tenants and retainers, and on the effect of lordship on peasant living conditions. It is none the less unlikely that any of these was unremittingly oppressive. A newly enfeoffed community might have to pay new dues, but any demands would have been mitigated by the ever-present threat of migration by disgruntled subjects. Additional payments had to be set in any case against the fiscal disadvantages of urban rule and the benefits of feudal paternalism: a lord with good political connections could be a powerful advocate of community interests. It is also unlikely that enfeoffment acted adversely on agriculture and trade; on the contrary, it sometimes provided a stimulus by freeing rural communities from urban monopolies. It is thus not entirely surprising that living standards in feudal or rural communal regimes were often higher than under urban rule.[12]

Lords and Towns: The South

The tendency in recent years to downplay the extent of urban power in the centre-north and to emphasize the role of rural corporate and feudal institutions has been matched by a growing recognition of the significance of southern Italian towns. Regional monographs on areas as diverse as Apulia, Sicily and Calabria convey a sense of urban vibrancy that is very much at odds with traditional renditions of the country in the lock of oppressive feudal institutions. The roots of this urban dynamism can probably be found in the later Middle Ages, when the kingdoms of Naples and Sicily experienced similar institutional developments to those of the more northerly territorial states. In both parts of Italy the goals of political integration and stability were pursued by assimilating the formerly more independent and powerful elements

(Rome, 1978), vol. I, pp. 91–121; eadem, 'Feudatari e duca negli stati farnesiani (1545–1587)', in *Il Rinascimento nelle Corti padane. Società e cultura* (Bari, 1977), pp. 77–95.

12. Chittolini, *La formazione dello stato*, pp. 263–5; S. R. Epstein, *An Island for Itself. Economic Development and Social Change in Late Medieval Sicily* (Cambridge, 1992), ch. 5; idem, 'Stato territoriale', pp. 880–3; M. A. Romani, *Nella spirale di una crisi. Popolazione, mercato e prezzi a Parma tra Cinque e Seicento* (Milan, 1975), pp. 36, 45, 141; M. Benaiteau, 'La rendita feudale nel Regno di Napoli attraverso i relevi: il Principato Ultra (1550–1806)', *Società e storia*, 3 (1980), p. 574; P. P. Viazzo, *Upland Communities. Environment, Population and Social Structure in the Alps since the Sixteenth Century* (Cambridge, 1989). See also below, pp. 86, 105.

on the one hand (the feudal aristocracy in the south, the city-states further north) and by promoting new or weaker political forces on the other (the towns under royal control in the south, rural communities and lordships in the centre-north).[13]

With the exception of L'Aquila, Messina, Naples and a few others, however, southern Italian towns never achieved the rural prerogatives of their northern peers. The southern towns' general inability to control rural resources politically, particularly food supplies, made them particularly sensitive to changes in economic circumstances, with the result that they attracted large numbers of rural immigrants when times were good and lost them just as quickly when better opportunities arose elsewhere. This demographic sensitivity was intensified by the very high rates of seasonal and permanent migration in much of the rural south. Although town governments attempted to react to demographic instability after the mid-fifteenth century by claiming greater jurisdictional rights, including authority over the villages (*casali*) in their hinterland, and by demanding fiscal and commercial privileges from the Crown in order to attract and maintain a more stable population, the effects of this political offensive are still unclear.

The absence of research on urban society in the south is all the more unfortunate because the number of peasants living in towns was so unusually high. On standard definitions of towns as centres with more than 5,000 inhabitants, southern Italy had one of the highest shares of urban population in early modern Europe, with peaks of more than 50 per cent achieved in Sicily and Terra di Bari (Apulia). While these settlements are frequently dismissed as mere 'agro-towns' which acted as temporary 'dormitories' for migrant peasants but displayed few urban features, this probably underestimates their administrative and economic sophistication, especially in the more economically developed regions of the south.[14]

More direct relations between peasants and feudal lords have attracted more attention. Seigneurialism had indisputably stronger roots in the south than in the centre-north, and the Spanish viceroys in Naples may well have deliberately supported baronial rights in order to achieve political and administrative stability.[15] In Sicily, roughly half the population lived under feudal jurisdiction; in the kingdom of Naples the proportion came closer to four fifths. Consequently, seigneurial rights provided no less than 20 per cent of total lordly income, rising in some instances to more than half. At the same time local and regional conditions displayed striking variations, ranging from Calabria, where seigneurial demands continued to rise from an already high base through to the early seventeenth century, to Terra d'Otranto and Principato, where until the 1640s

---

13. G. Galasso, *Economia e società nella Calabria del Cinquecento* (Naples, 1975), chs 2 and 4; B. Salvemini, 'Prima della Puglia. Terra di Bari e il sistema regionale in età moderna', in L. Masella and B. Salvemini (eds), *Storia d'Italia. Le regioni dall'Unità a oggi. La Puglia* (Turin, 1989), pp. 3–218; Epstein, *An Island*, esp. ch. 7; G. Muto, *Saggi sul governo dell'economia nel Mezzogiorno spagnolo* (Naples, 1992), pp. 144–7.

14. Salvemini, 'Prima della Puglia', pp. 114–15; F. Benigno, 'Assetti territoriali e ruralizzazione nella Sicilia del Seicento: note per una discussione', in Società Italiana di Demografia Storica (ed.), *La popolazione delle campagne italiane in età moderna* (Turin, 1987), pp. 56–72.

15. Muto, *Saggi sul governo*, pp. 148–52.

lords drew most of their income from commercial land rents. The weaker brand of seigneurialism in Sicily also explains why barons were able to attract immigrants to new rural settlements from the late 1580s onwards.[16]

What appear to be identical seigneurial prerogatives disguised considerable differences in practice. These differences depended to a large degree on which side of the feudal coin came uppermost, be it the patrimonial emphasis on property rights to land or the jurisdictional concern with rights of lordship over men. Whether lords tried to increase feudal dues or aimed to maximize their rent depended on a combination of factors, which included the availability of transport routes and markets, the intensity of peasant mobility, the size of fiefs and the degree of competition for labour between lords, and the presence of towns outside feudal jurisdiction; greater commercial activity, labour mobility, and feudal and urban competition generally undermined the jurisdictional aspects of seigneurialism, and tended to subject land held in fief to straightforward market pressures. In addition, the extent of seigneurial rights affected how lords responded to the seventeenth-century depression. Where strong seigneurial rights survived, exactions increased in line with population, rising sharply during the sixteenth century and tapering off after the demographic and economic downturn of the 1630s and 1640s; by contrast, lords in more commercialized regions responded to declining rents by attempting to reintroduce the exactions they had previously allowed to lapse.[17]

The Politics of Consent and Repression

Rural militias

From the late fifteenth century, Italian territorial states responded to rising military expenditure and to increasing difficulties in recruiting mercenary troops by experimenting with the use of permanent peasant militias. The example of Venice and Mantua was followed first by Florence, Lucca and Urbino, and a few decades later by the Papal States, Naples, Sicily, Savoy (Piedmont) and others. Although from a military standpoint these attempts at enlarging the military base were of little use, one not entirely unforeseen consequence was to broaden the central authorities' support in the countryside. For similar reasons, however, opposition to such experiments was intense and often posed insuperable obstacles for reform.[18]

---

16. Galasso, *Economia e società*; A. Lepre, *Terra di Lavoro nell'età moderna* (Naples, 1978); M. A. Visceglia, 'L'azienda signorile in Terra d'Otranto', *Quaderni storici*, 15 (1980), pp. 39–60; eadem, 'Rendita feudale e agricoltura in Puglia nell'età moderna (XVI–XVIII sec.)', *Società e storia*, 3 (1980), pp. 527–60; Benaiteau, 'La rendita feudale', p. 565; T. Davies, 'Village-building in Sicily: an aristocratic remedy for the crisis of the 1590s', in P. Clark (ed.), *The European Crisis of the 1590s. Essays in Comparative History* (London, 1985), pp. 191–208.

17. Benaiteau, 'La rendita feudale', p. 587; Visceglia, 'L'azienda', p. 44. The debate on 'refeudalization' is reviewed by E. Stumpo, 'La crisi del Seicento in Italia', in N. Tranfaglia and M. Firpo (eds), *La storia. I grandi problemi dal Medioevo all'Età contemporanea*, 10 vols (Turin, 1986), vol. 3/2, pp. 313–37; Muto, *Saggi sul governo*, pp. 129–56.

18. L. Pezzolo, 'Le "arme proprie" 1500–1650', *Rivista di storia economica*, 14 (1996).

Individual failures reflected each state's constitutional peculiarities. The plan for a trained peasant militia devised by Niccolò Machiavelli for the Florentine Republic in 1506 aborted because of the capital's elites' ingrained fear that the armed peasants would rise against their oppressors.[19] Ironically, the militia, which included a contingent of Florentine citizens and which was closely identified as a 'Republican' institution, was disbanded by the first Medicean regime (1512–27); Duke Cosimo de' Medici, by contrast, saw it in keeping with his policy of rebalancing relations between Florence and the provinces and reintroduced it after his return in 1530.

Venice established a trained rural militia of 10,000–12,000 men capable of being deployed outside its home territory in 1507, during the military crisis that preceded the defeat at Agnadello in 1509.[20] Venice was less fearful than Florence about arming the peasantry, and its trust was repaid after Agnadello when the peasants played a critical role in recapturing lost territory from rebel towns. Venice's problems with the militia were financial and organizational rather than political. Inducements for joining included exempting candidates from personal taxes and public labour dues on roads, canals and town walls, and paying them daily expenses during training; unfortunately the cost of all these perquisites fell on the rural communities, causing predictable resentment. The peasants' training was at best half-hearted; 'friendly brigands rather than a reliable reserve, let alone a potential shock force', they were more effective as guerrillas than as cannon fodder.[21] Venice itself took only sporadic interest in them when under severe military pressure; although active on paper during the entire sixteenth century, their first call to action after Agnadello occurred in 1615–17. Needless to say, the rulers' trust was not unstinting: peripheral areas whose devotion was uncertain were not brought into the militia system before the early seventeenth century, nor were militiamen ever employed in the increasingly determined campaign to root out rural banditry.[22]

The dukes of Savoy introduced rural militias only in the 1560s.[23] Rather than a small military contingent employed to support a core of full-time soldiers and mercenaries, however, the Piedmontese corps was meant to be a full-blown territorial army. It therefore relied for its functioning more heavily than elsewhere on the militiamen's self-interest and on a sense of commonalty between rural communities and the state. But the need to concede fiscal and legal privileges was also the project's undoing, for it threatened competing aristocratic interests which the prince was unable to ignore. In Piedmont, as elsewhere, rural militias failed because their rulers were incapable of solving a fundamental political and

19. P. Pieri, *Il Rinascimento e la crisi militare italiana*, 2nd edn (Turin, 1952), pp. 436–43; J. R. Hale, *War and Society in Renaissance Europe 1450–1620* (London, 1985), pp. 199–201.

20. M. E. Mallett and J. R. Hale, *The Military Organization of a Renaissance State. Venice c.1400 to 1617* (Cambridge, 1984), pp. 49–50, 350–66.

21. Ibid., p. 351.

22. Ibid., p. 364; L. Pezzolo, 'L'archibugio e l'aratro. Considerazioni e problemi per una storia delle milizie rurali venete nei secoli XVI e XVII', *Studi veneziani*, new series, 7 (1983), pp. 64–5, 69–70; M. Knapton, 'Il Territorio vicentino nello Stato veneto del '500 e primo '600: nuovi equilibri politici e fiscali', in G. Cracco and M. Knapton (eds), *Dentro lo 'Stado italico'. Venezia e la Terraferma fra Quattro e Seicento* (Trent, 1984), p. 110.

23. W. Barberis, *Le armi del Principe. La tradizione militare sabauda* (Turin, 1988), pp. 5–63.

ideological contradiction: between an implicitly 'Republican' institution like the militia, which presumed that military defence was in society's collective interest, and a system of power based upon inviolable differences of status between nobility, citizens and peasants and in which arms were a symbol of privilege.

Unrest and rebellion

The lack of rural uprisings in late medieval and early modern Italy on anything like the scale of Iberia, France, England and Germany is an unexplained puzzle. Although there are many recorded instances of unrest, these seldom challenged the social and political order and tended to be highly localized; the Neapolitan revolt of 1647–48 is the only known instance of a peasant rebellion turning into something akin to a national uprising.[24] More broadly based regional uprisings were more frequent between the mid-fourteenth and the mid-fifteenth century, when territorial states were being established and military and fiscal pressures were intense. A string of anti-feudal revolts broke out in Lombardy, Piedmont, Valle d'Aosta, the region of Trent and north-eastern Sicily, tapering off with the great Friulan revolt of 1511; more 'modern' tax rebellions against territorial overlords were staged by valley communities in the Lombard Alps and the Tuscan Apennines. High taxes also caused unrest among the rural subjects of Florence in 1425–27 and of Perugia in 1525, and contributed to the peasant rising of 1459 in Calabria.[25] After the first decades of the sixteenth century, however, concerted insurrections of this kind died away. Most recorded instances of unrest occurred in the feudal south, but they were very localized and did not in any sense presage the extent and intensity of the provincial uprisings of 1647–48.[26]

This remarkable acquiescence by Italian peasants has been viewed as evidence of political and economic disenfranchisement. Rural poverty in the centre-north caused by urban exploitation caused 'total resignation' among the peasantry; in Tuscany, landlord paternalism and the breakdown of community ties associated with the rise of sharecropping further weakened the capacity for collective organization. Increasing poverty and the defeat of the revolt

24. R. Villari, *La rivolta antispagnola a Napoli. Le origini 1585–1647* (Bari, 1967); A. Musi, *La rivolta di Masaniello nella scena politica barocca* (Naples, 1989), ch. 5; see also O. di Simplicio, *Le rivolte contadine in Europa* (Rome, 1986), p. 118.

25. G. Cherubini, 'Le campagne italiane dall'XI al XV secolo', in O. Capitani *et al.*, *Comuni e signorie*, pp. 417–18; Pederzani, *Venezia*, p. 64 n. 51; E. Roveda, 'Le istituzioni e la società in età visconteo-sforzesca', in *Storia di Pavia* (Pavia, 1992), vol. 3/1, pp. 73–5; E. Muir, *Mad Blood Stirring. Vendetta and Factions in Friuli during the Renaissance* (Baltimore, MD/London, 1993); Herlihy and Klapisch, *Les Toscans*, pp. 40–2; C. Cutini Zazzerini, 'Un episodio di rivolta del contado perugino del 1525', *Bollettino della Deputazione di Storia Patria per l'Umbria*, 80 (1983), pp. 153–63; Epstein, *An Island*, pp. 326–38; E. Pontieri, *La Calabria a metà del secolo XV e la rivolta di Antonio Centelles* (Naples, 1963), pp. 216–25. See also G. Cherubini (ed.), 'Protesta e rivolta contadina nell'Italia medievale', *Annali dell'Istituto 'Alcide Cervi'*, 16 (1994).

26. C. de Frede, 'Rivolte antifeudali nel Mezzogiorno d'Italia durante il Cinquecento', in *Studi in onore di Amintore Fanfani*, 5 vols (Milan, 1962), vol. V, pp. 3–42; Musi, *La rivolta di Masaniello*, ch. 5; A. Lepre, *Storia del Mezzogiorno d'Italia*, 2 vols (Naples, 1986), vol. I, pp. 285–93.

of 1647–48 in the south forced an increasingly desperate rural populace into the political dead end of 'social banditry'.[27] But whereas explanations of this kind assume that peasants could only achieve their political objectives through rebellion, it seems more reasonable to assume that revolt was an act of last resort. Under normal circumstances, peasant elites might expect to air their grievances through legitimate political channels and achieve some redress. Revolts could and did break out when adequate social and political means to filter and defuse conflict had temporarily broken down; but one cannot assume that this would be the norm. Indeed, a hankering for legal propriety often persisted even after conciliation had become impossible. The Perugian peasant rebels of 1525 sent ambassadors to the city's liege, the Pope in Rome, and referred to a recent papal edict in their attempt to have a hated hearth tax repealed. In 1647–48, peasant rebels petitioned the Spanish authorities to support their demands for institutional change; the town of Nocera even drew up a notarial act to formalize the forcible eviction of the local duke.[28]

This evidence suggests that the unusually low incidence of rural rebellions in Italy may have been a result of the peasants' better opportunities for political organization, rather than because they were unusually oppressed. The constitutional settlements achieved across the peninsula before 1500 were the outcome of protracted and far from peaceful negotiations between four principal interest groups: the ruling city's elites or the prince, the subject urban elites, the feudal lords, and the elites of autonomous rural communities and federations. From the point of view of the peasantry, the sovereign's need to accommodate so many competing interests made it possible for the first time to vent political tensions through legitimate channels which bypassed their immediate lords. A clear instance of the support this could engender among the peasantry is the rural insurrection of 1509 in support of Venice and against the latter's rebellious subject cities – which had transferred to the Imperial camp and which also happened to be the peasants' direct overlords.

Banditry

Were more isolated forms of banditry, rather than concerted communal rebellions, more typical forms of protest among the Italian peasantry? This assumption seems to underlie most studies of rural banditry, which portray it as a form of revolt just short of armed insurrection and describe it as a reaction to economic and political 'modernization'. According to this interpretation, the upsurge in banditry between the 1560s and the 1640s is the result of economic hardship among the peasantry caused by growing taxation, declining living standards and increasing social polarization, and of political distress among the

27. Di Simplicio, *Rivolte*, pp. 118–20; Cherubini, 'Le campagne italiane', p. 418; F. McArdle, *Altopascio. A Study in Tuscan Rural Society, 1587–1784* (Cambridge, 1978), p. 201.
28. Musi, *La rivolta di Masaniello*, ch. 5; Cutini Zazzerini, 'Un episodio di rivolta'.

aristocracy, whose traditional privileges were being challenged by the central-izing state.[29]

Several features of Italian banditry are at odds with this explanation. In the first place, banditry peaked between the 1570s and the 1590s and again briefly in the 1620s and 1630s, when peasant and aristocratic conditions were not unduly strained, whereas periods of more serious economic hardship experienced a degree of peace. Peasant banditry was also concentrated in the border-land zones between states, which were able better to withstand economic downturns.[30] Banditry was in any case a legal rather than an economic or socio-logical category: in principle, the bandit was not a robber, but a man tried *in absentia*, someone whom the state was unable to take to court and had outlawed (Ital. *bandito*) as a consequence.

Studies of the Papal States and the Venetian *Terraferma* do in fact suggest that the incidence of banditry may be more a measure of the state's political ineffectiveness than of criminal activities as such. The phenomenon became of serious concern a few years after the peace of Câteau-Cambrésis (1554), which ended the wars that had raged across the peninsula since the 1490s and estab-lished a stable balance of power within the peninsula. Freed from external threat, Rome and Venice trained their political ambitions inwards. With the aim of establishing unchallenged jurisdiction within their territories, they invested great effort in establishing clear political frontiers, both for its obvious political symbolism but, more especially, in order to exert greater control over virtually unregulated cross-border trade. It so happened that these peripheral areas were also where states faced the strongest challenge from near-independent feudal lordships and mountain communities.[31]

Peasant banditry seems to have been largely a consequence of this political offensive in the periphery. Lacking the military manpower and the political skills to enforce their claims, Rome and Venice resorted indiscriminately to legal bans. Relatives to the fourth degree and whole rural communities were found guilty by association; financial and other inducements were offered to spies and turn-coats.[32] Outlaws proliferated because the law could not be enforced; repression fed upon its children.

---

29. The classic statements are by E. Hobsbawm, *Bandits* (London, 1969), and F. Braudel, *The Mediterra-nean and the Mediterranean World in the Age of Philip II*, 2 vols, trans. S. Reynolds (London, 1973), vol. II, pp. 734–56. See also M. Aymard, 'Proposte per una conclusione', in G. Ortalli (ed.), *Bande armate, banditi, banditismo e repressione di giustizia negli stati europei di antico regime* (Rome, 1986), p. 510; J. Delumeau, *Vita economica e sociale di Roma nel Cinquecento*, Italian transl. (Florence, 1979), p. 144.

30. Above, n. 12.

31. I. Polverini Fosi, *La società violenta. Il banditismo dello Stato pontificio nella seconda metà del Cinquecento* (Rome, 1985); C. Povolo, 'Nella spirale della violenza. Cronologia, intensità e diffusione del banditismo nella Terraferma veneta (1550–1610)', in Ortalli, *Bande armate*, pp. 21–52; M. Cattini and M. A. Romani, 'Tra faida familiare e rivolta politica: banditi e banditismo nella montagna estense (sec. XVII)', in ibid., pp. 53–66; A. Toniolo, 'Territori indivisi. Una proposta di studio sul banditismo cinquecentesco nell'area delle partecipanze modenesi e bolognesi', in *Terre e comunità nell'Italia padana. Il caso delle partecipanze agrarie emiliane, da terre comuni a beni collettivi* (Bologna, 1983), pp. 175–85.

32. See Povolo, 'Nella spirale', pp. 37–8; M. D. Floris, 'La repressione della criminalità organizzata nella Repubblica di Genova tra Cinque e Seicento. Aspetti e cronologia della prassi legislativa', in Ortalli, *Bande armate*, pp. 87, 91.

Although judicial escalation made it virtually impossible to eradicate banditry once established, banditry also persisted because of its close association with large-scale smuggling – which had itself become a new crime in an age of increasingly definite if not definitive frontiers. Smugglers were usually organized in networks of real and fictive kin (*parentele*) which purposely straddled political borders,[33] and which had probably been established during the later Middle Ages to make it easier to pool skills, commercial information and support for expanding inter-regional and cross-mountain transhumance and trade.[34] *Parentele* structured much of their members' social and political activities, and found protection or acquiescence among local feudatories. While intermarriage and feuds between rival networks were among their most basic features, they also provided justice and settled disputes between members and with the outside world, and helped stabilize relations between the mountains and the plains.[35]

Contemporaries' and more recent views of these as the barbarous customs of a closed and archaic world are based on a misunderstanding. The state's offensive during the latter half of the sixteenth century turned mountain trade into a crime and outlawed its practitioners and feudal protectors; smugglers were transformed into robbers, and found leaders among the disaffected nobility.[36] We witness not the comforting victory of cultural modernity over archaism, but a struggle between two comparable systems of social organization and power.

THE PEASANT ECONOMY

Property Rights to Land and Tenurial Relations

Tenurial arrangements and the distribution of property underwent huge changes in the course of the early modern period. Whereas the prevailing contract in the late Middle Ages was leasehold, with rents paid mainly in kind, four centuries later rents were mostly paid in cash. Peasants owned considerably more land individually and collectively towards 1350 than 1750; landed property – particularly in the centre-north – was much more fragmented at the time of the

---

33. O. Raggio, 'Parentele, fazioni e banditi: la Val Fontanabuona tra Cinque e Seicento', in Ortalli, *Bande armate*, pp. 233–76; S. Lombardini, 'Rivolte e ribellismo contadino nel Monregalese del Seicento. Ipotesi di ricerca', *Bollettino storico-bibliografico subalpino*, 80 (1982), pp. 645–57; E. Guidoboni, 'Terre, villaggi e famiglie del Polesine di Casaglia fra XV e XVI secolo', *Società e storia*, 4 (1981), p. 828; L.Faccini, *La Lombardia fra '600 e '700. Riconversione economica e mutamenti sociali* (Milan, 1988), p. 27.

34. R. Comaschi, 'Strategie familiari, potere locale e banditi in una comunità del contado bolognese del XVI secolo', in Ortalli, *Bande armate*, p. 226.

35. Raggio, 'Parentele, fazioni'; Comaschi, 'Strategie familiari'; N. S. Davidson, 'An armed band and the local community on the Venetian Terraferma in the sixteenth century', in Ortalli, *Bande armate*, pp. 401–22; C. Povolo, 'La conflittualità nobiliare in Italia nella seconda metà del Cinquecento. Il caso della Repubblica di Venezia. Alcune ipotesi e possibili interpretazioni', *Atti dell'Istituto Veneto di Scienze Lettere ed Arti*, 151 (1992/93), p. 110.

36. Povolo, 'La conflittualità', p. 109.

Black Death. Between the mid-fourteenth and the mid-eighteenth century, there emerged an integrated system of latifundia and smallholdings in the south, and of mixed and capitalist farming in the centre-north; rural smallholders were evicted, and land was consolidated into large farms owned by townspeople and the Church.

With the exception of Lombard irrigated farming, these developments tend to be seen as posing insurmountable obstacles to economic development. Share-cropping and latifundism were employed by absentee feudal and urban land-lords to exploit tenant labour rather than to engage in capital investment and technical innovation; peasant aversion to markets put additional decisive constraints on agricultural growth. Agricultural property and tenancy rights were the paramount factors which determined a less than optimal distribution of income and a lower rate of growth than was technically feasible.[37] What evidence is there for these claims?

Property rights to land

Feudal law, which prevailed up to the late eighteenth and early nineteenth century, distinguished two categories of landownership: *dominium utile*, which conferred beneficial rights of usage and was vested in the tenant, and *dominium directum*, which included rights of disposal and of jurisdiction over the tenant and was vested in the lord. Until the early fourteenth century, the distinction was embodied in the institution of serfdom and in long-term or multi-generational leases based on customary rents; none the less, these property rights were also rapidly disappearing. Servile dues were being abandoned, to survive mainly in peripheral regions of the north; unified, 'bourgeois' property rights to land were expanding; and customary leases were being replaced with more flexible short-term contracts.[38]

While most of these developments began well before the 'shock' caused by the Black Death, the plague accelerated the pace of change. Competition for scarce and increasingly mobile labour spelled the demise of serfdom in 'core' regions;[39] demographic decline and the rise of larger, more integrated territorial states increased the rate of commercialization among survivors. Yet feudal rights remained important in several respects. Not only did seigneurial dues remain a major source of income in southern Italy, and to a lesser extent in the

---

37. The general argument was first outlined in E. Sereni, *Il capitalismo nelle campagne* (Turin, 1947); idem, *Capitalismo e mercato nazionale* (Rome, 1966); G. Giorgetti, *Contadini e proprietari nell'Italia moderna. Rapporti di produzione e contratti agrari dal secolo XVI a oggi*, 2nd edn (Turin, 1974).

38. Giorgetti, *Contadini e proprietari*, chs 2–3.

39. G. Coppola, 'Equilibri economici e trasformazioni nell' area alpina in età moderna: scarsità di risorse ed economia integrata', in G. Coppola and P. Schiera (eds), *Lo spazio alpino: area di civiltà, regione cerniera* (Naples, 1991), p. 210. See also D. Degrassi, 'L'economia del tardo medioevo', in P. Cammarosano (ed.), *Storia della società friulana. Il medioevo* (Tavagnacco, 1988), p. 295; I. Peri, *Il villanaggio in Sicilia* (Palermo, 1965); M. A. Visceglia, *Territorio feudo e potere locale. Terra d'Otranto tra Medioevo ed Età moderna* (Naples, 1988), pp. 116–17.

centre-north, even where towns established comprehensive rights of jurisdiction in competition with feudal lords, they tended to transform such rights into collective powers of lordship over the countryside.[40]

The distribution of property between peasants, feudal lords and townspeople (including Church property under the last two headings) is still rather obscure. A recent overview of early modern Naples states baldly that the proportion of feudal to non-feudal property in the kingdom cannot be quantified. On the other hand, tax surveys in the centre-north appear to show that urban property expanded almost uninterruptedly between the thirteenth century and the mid-sixteenth. By the early 1500s Florentines owned over 60 per cent of their *contado* and the inhabitants of Cremona over 57 per cent, not including the properties of the Church; similar proportions applied to the rest of the Po plain and to the Venetian *Terraferma*.[41]

That townspeople should own substantial amounts of land before the Black Death is not surprising: there were sound economic reasons both for urban immigrants to preserve their rural property and for townsmen to reinvest a share of their commercial profits in the land. But the strong growth of urban landownership after 1348–50 calls for a different explanation, which can be only partially connected with changing population levels. Between *c.*1350 and *c.*1450 the rural population declined by approximately 40–60 per cent, and urban losses were frequently larger. Urban elites benefited disproportionately from the increased land supply this provoked, because of their greater wealth and because their larger households and better organized kinship networks ensured a higher probability of survival. This difference alone in 'inheritance effects' between town and country would have caused a net transfer of land from rural to urban hands; but other factors were also at work. Land continued to accumulate, albeit at a slower rate, in urban hands when the population began to recover after the mid-fifteenth century. This suggests that the main cause of land transfers was rural hardship induced by fiscal pressure rather than demographic forces alone. In central and northern Italy, the Black Death was followed by a sharp increase in fiscal and military pressure, as princes and city-states competed for survival and territorial aggrandizement. Evidence from Florence and Brescia suggests that peasants responded to military and fiscal distress by selling their land or migrating, causing the rural tax base to shrink even further and forcing survivors into an ever-tighter fiscal vice.[42]

40. G. Chittolini and G. Coppola, 'Grand domaine et petites exploitations: quelques observations sur la version italienne de ce modèle (XIIIe–XVIIIe siècle)', in P. Gunst and T. Hoffmann (eds), *Large Estates and Smallholdings in Europe in the Middle Ages and Modern Times* (Budapest, 1982), p. 181.

41. M. A. Visceglia, 'Dislocazione territoriale e dimensione del possesso feudale nel Regno di Napoli a metà Cinquecento', in eadem (ed.), *Signori, patrizi, cavalieri in Italia centro-meridionale in età moderna e contemporanea* (Rome/Bari, 1992), pp. 31–91; Muto, *Saggi sul governo*, p. 187; G. Cherubini, 'La proprietà fondiaria nei secoli XV–XVI nella storiografia italiana', *Società e storia*, 1 (1978), pp 9–33; Arcangeli, 'Giurisdizioni feudali'.

42. D. Herlihy, 'Santa Maria Impruneta: a rural commune in the late Middle Ages', in N. Rubinstein (ed.), *Florentine Studies. Politics and Society in Renaissance Florence* (London, 1967), pp. 242–76; J. M. Ferraro, 'Proprietà terriera e potere nello stato veneziano', *Civis*, 8 (1984); D. Beltrami, *La penetrazione economica dei veneziani in Terraferma. Forze di lavoro e proprietà fondiaria nelle campagne venete dei secoli XVII e XVIII* (Venice/Rome, 1961), pp. 112–40.

Taxation was undoubtedly responsible for the slow erosion of the peasant commons. References to sales of the commons increase from the late fifteenth century, particularly in the south where both feudal and community lands were affected and where forcible enclosure by feudal lords also occurred;[43] but the best known instance of land privatization took place on the Venetian *Terraferma*. Despite frequent usurpations in the sixteenth century, the year 1647 – when Venice began a systematic sale of commons in the eastern part of its state to townsmen and, quite frequently, to wealthy peasants made good, in order to finance the war against the Ottomans – proved something of a turning-point in the dissolution of rural collective ownership.[44]

This tale of growing urban encroachment should not disguise the remarkable resilience of rural landownership. In eighteenth-century Lombardy, 54 per cent of the highlands and 70 per cent of the mountains were classed as commons; in the province of Trent the proportion rose from 22 per cent in the river plains to 70 per cent in the mountains; and commons accounted for 40–70 per cent of the Venetian state. In the south, next to commons held for local use (which survived mainly in the interior), vast tracts of land were set aside as pasture for transhumant sheep under community or state control.[45] By 1650 individual peasant ownership may also have been more widespread in the south, especially along the coasts and in mountainous areas like north-eastern Sicily and Calabria; peasant smallholding actually increased in some southern regions in the late seventeenth century, showing that ownership did not only progress in one direction.[46]

Tenurial relations

The Black Death was possibly the single most critical event for the history of Italian agriculture in our period. The late medieval demographic, social and economic 'crisis' ended a period of institutional experimentation dating back to

43. L. Chiappa Mauri, 'Riflessioni sulle campagne lombarde del Quattro-Cinquecento', *Nuova rivista storica*, 69 (1985), p. 129; Giorgetti, *Contadini e proprietari*, p. 202; Epstein, *An Island*, pp. 369–70; S. Zotta, 'Momenti e problemi di una crisi agraria in uno "Stato" feudale napoletano (1585–1615)', *Mélanges de l'École française de Rome. Moyen Âge-Temps modernes*, 90 (1978), pp. 729, 769; Benaiteau, 'Rendita feudale', p. 592; Visceglia, 'Rendita feudale', p. 555; eadem, *Territorio feudo*, p. 267; G. Poli, *Territorio e contadini nella Puglia moderna. Paesaggio agrario e strutture produttive tra XVI e XVIII secolo* (Galatina, 1990), p. 34.

44. Pederzani, *Venezia*, pp. 114–15, 196–200, 221–2, 277, 284; P. Lanaro Sartori, 'Il mondo contadino nel Cinquecento: ceti e famiglie nelle campagne veronesi', in G. Borelli (ed.), *Uomini e civiltà agraria in territorio veronese*, 2 vols (Verona, 1982), vol. I, pp. 327–8; G. Ferrari, 'La legislazione veneta sui beni comunali', *Nuovo archivio veneto*, new series, 36 (1918), pp. 5–64; D. Beltrami, *Saggio di storia dell'agricoltura nella Repubblica di Venezia durante l'età moderna* (Venice/Rome, 1955), pp. 43–8; G. Panjek, 'Beni comunali: note storiche e proposte di ricerca', in A. Tagliaferri (ed.), *Venezia e la Terraferma attraverso le relazioni dei Rettori* (Milan, 1981), pp. 371–82.

45. Coppola, 'Equilibri economici', pp. 206–9; J. A. Marino, *Pastoral Economics in the Kingdom of Naples* (Baltimore, MD/London, 1988); F. Mercurio, 'Uomini, cavallette, pecore e grano: una calamità di parte', *Società e storia*, 8 (1985), pp. 767–95; M. Caffiero, 'Usi e abusi. Comunità rurali e difesa dell'economia tradizionale nello Stato pontificio', *Passato e presente*, 24 (1990), pp. 73–93.

46. Poli, *Territorio e contadini*; Lepre, *Terra di Lavoro*, pp. 70–7; Epstein, *An Island*, ch. 5; G. Delille, *Croissance d'une société rurale. Montesarchio et la Vallée Caudine aux XVIIe et XVIIIe siècles* (Naples, 1973), pp. 128–9, 170–2, 206–7; Visceglia, 'Rendita feudale', p. 541.

the twelfth century, selected three principal tenurial arrangements, and defined the parameters of agricultural growth up to the late eighteenth century.

The most significant development in agriculture north of Rome was the reorganization of land, from highly fragmented and dispersed plots into farms averaging ten to thirty hectares. Consolidation (*appoderamento*, from *podere* = farm) produced two very different agricultural systems. In much of central Italy and several areas further north, consolidated farms turned to the multiple cropping of cereals, vines, olives, fruit trees and other labour-intensive products like flax or silk. A central purpose of this form of *appoderamento* was to establish a farm large enough to employ a family of four or five and provide for its basic needs; specialization was constrained by the overriding concern for subsistence. Mixed farming was associated with different kinds of leasehold. Share tenancy on consolidated farms (*mezzadria poderale*), which urban legislation favoured over fixed rent, was typical of Umbria, Tuscany, Emilia and the Marches.[47] Output was divided equally between landlord and tenant; the costs of seed, working livestock and tools were shared or met by the landlord, who controlled output choices and managed the sale of any surpluses. Fixed rent in kind or cash prevailed instead on the dry plains and hills of Lombardy and the Veneto, where tenants more frequently provided the working capital and were generally more independent.[48]

A quite different arrangement emerged during the fifteenth and sixteenth centuries in the irrigated plains of central Lombardy near Milan. Some of the highest rates of productivity in Europe were achieved there on consolidated farms of 50–130 hectares, which abolished the fallow outright by integrating cereal production with cattle fed on irrigated water meadows and more marginal crops like rice, flax or hemp. The farms were leased for a cash rent to rural entrepreneurs who furnished capital inputs, including the wages of seasonal migrants. The system spread gradually across much of the Po plain during the early modern period, with just a brief setback in the depths of the demographic collapse of the 1630s and 1640s.[49]

Neither the reasons for consolidating land, nor the origins of new tenants, nor the factors which determined the choice of contract are clearly understood. Consolidation has been interpreted as a way of saving on labour costs in a period of rising real wages. Since proportionately greater savings could be achieved with land-hungry crops like cereals or hay than with labour-intensive products like wine and olive oil, one would expect consolidated farms to specialize in the former and leave labour-intensive crops to be cultivated on

47. G. Piccinni, 'L'evoluzione della rendita fondiaria in Italia: 1350–1450', in *Italia 1350–1450*, p. 249; B. Campodoni, 'Proprietari, mezzadri e pigionanti in un villaggio della bassa pianura bolognese (1650–1700)', *Annali dell'Istituto 'Alcide Cervi'*, 7 (1985), p. 109.

48. See Giorgetti, *Contadini e proprietari*; Piccinni, 'L'evoluzione della rendita'; C. Poni, *Fossi e cavedagne benedicon le campagne. Studi di storia rurale* (Bologna, 1982), pp. 283–358; G. Biagioli, 'The spread of *mezzadria* in central Italy: a model of demographic and economic development', in A. Fauve-Chamoux (ed.), *Évolution agraire et croissance démographique* (Liège, 1987), pp. 139–54. For the Lombard *masseria* see below, n. 49.

49. G. Chittolini, 'La pianura irrigua lombarda fra Quattrocento e Cinquecento', *Annali dell'Istituto 'Alcide Cervi'*, 10 (1988), pp. 207–21; L. Chiappa Mauri, 'Le trasformazioni nell'area lombarda', in S. Gensini (ed.), *La Toscana nel secolo xiv. Caratteri di una civiltà regionale* (Pisa, 1988), pp. 409–32; Faccini, *La Lombardia*, ch. 6.

smallholdings. In effect, the more advanced irrigated farming in Lombardy was practised on large-scale farms, whereas the specialized vineyards and olive groves whose products were in increasing demand after the Black Death were overwhelmingly concentrated on smaller plots.[50] None the less, the fact that in much of central and northern Italy tenants of larger farms pursued a strategy of crop diversification rather than specialization suggests that labour savings were not the only purpose of consolidation.

A comparison with developments in the south casts some light on the matter. South of Tuscany, agriculture pursued the path of specialization. Grain was produced mainly on large-scale farms (*masserie, casali*) run by tenants employing seasonal wage labour, in which land alternated as arable and dry pasture for transhumant sheep. Around towns and along the coasts, by contrast, small 'Mediterranean gardens' produced labour- and capital-intensive crops such as wine, olive oil, almonds, silk and, in Sicily and Calabria, sugar cane. As a general rule the distinction between extensive and intensive land use matched that between feudal and peasant ownership. But the fault lines did not overlap entirely: Sicilian and Calabrian barons were among the first to exploit the potential of the sugar and silk industries,[51] for example, and everywhere rural elites ran their own *masserie*. Although no equivalent to the northern consolidated family farm emerged, this was not for lack of investment. On the contrary, the fact that southern Italy exported a significantly larger surplus of capital-intensive crops such as wine, oil and raw silk than the centre-north suggests that the south also invested proportionally more in them. Intercropping of grain with vines or olive trees along Umbrian, Tuscan or Venetian lines was not unknown further south, but the order of priority between the two was reversed: whereas the northern sharecropper paid more attention to the staple crop than to the cash crop, the smallholder on the Apulian coast did the opposite.[52]

It has been frequently suggested that the plague made a greater difference to agriculture in the central and northern regions than in the south. Whereas north of Rome land consolidation raised agriculture to a higher growth path, southern agriculture continued along a rut it had trodden since the twelfth century. Unable to break out of its feudal mould, it stagnated during the early modern period as a 'dependent' sector exporting surpluses to the more developed north.[53] Recent research suggests that this contrast is overdone. For Sicily, whose agriculture is often viewed as typical of southern Italian 'export-dependence', the second half of the fourteenth century marked a watershed: feudal land became more commercialized, more sophisticated credit and labour markets emerged, the domestic market became more integrated, and agricultural exports – of only marginal significance before 1350 – became a linchpin

---

50. Chiappa Mauri, 'Riflessioni', p. 127; Piccinni, 'L'evoluzione della rendita', p. 254; Poli, *Territorio e contadini*, pp. 54–6; Visceglia, *Territorio feudo*, p. 123.

51. Epstein, *An Island*, pp. 200–7, 210–22; Galasso, *Economia e società*, pp. 143–52, 174–81.

52. Faccini, *La Lombardia*, chs 6–7; Giorgetti, *Contadini e proprietari*, ch. 2; Poli, *Territorio e contadini*, p. 61.

53. R. Romano, *Tra due crisi: l'Italia del Rinascimento* (Turin, 1971), pp. 51–68; Giorgetti, *Contadini e proprietari*, pp. 72–97, 200–43; Piccinni, 'L'evoluzione della rendita', pp. 259–60, 264–6; Epstein, *An Island*, ch. 1.

of the economy. Peasants and landlords responded to changing commercial opportunities by specializing in what they could do best: smallholders in the mountainous north-east concentrated on wine, oil and silk; *massari* on the western latifundia specialized in wheat. By the second half of the fifteenth century a complex system of production had developed, in which *massari* relied upon smallholders for harvest labour, and smallholders depended upon *massari* for supplies of food grain. Similar patterns of functional integration between land- and labour-intensive agriculture emerged at the latest in the sixteenth century in other regions such as central Apulia and Neapolitan Campania. In the Tuscan and Roman Maremma and the Apulian Capitanata, by contrast, the collapse of demand for grain and depopulation associated with malarial infestations caused a proportionally greater expansion of transhumant pastoralism.[54]

Italian peasants therefore responded to the late medieval crisis either by specializing or by diversifying their output. From this perspective, the oft-remarked contrast between an 'extensive' agriculture in the south and an 'intensive' agriculture in the centre-north is misleading: in organizational and commercial terms, Lombard irrigated farming was more similar to the special-ized southern arrangements than to the self-sufficient mixed farming typical of central Italy. It is mixed farming which stands out as the exception and needs to be explained.

Specialized farming in Sicily, central Apulia, Campania and the areas of irrigated farming in the north could rely upon developed labour markets which supplied wage labour at peak periods in the agricultural cycle, and upon com-petitive product markets which redistributed output relatively efficiently. These institutional resources may have been less developed in regions where diversi-fication aimed to reduce risk by emphasizing self-sufficiency: labour was mainly supplied by the family, credit mainly by the landlord, and output was ideally consumed rather than being sold on the market. Since it seems unlikely that Tuscan or Umbrian peasants were inherently more 'risk averse' than peasants in Apulia or Sicily, it seems reasonable to suppose that they were responding to factors – such as the lack of seasonal wage labour, difficulties in gaining access to credit, or non-competitive product markets – which made specializa-tion too uncertain a path to pursue.

Households

In an essay on the family systems of pre-modern Europe, Peter Laslett de-scribed a family model and an underlying system of values which he argued were typically 'Mediterranean'. The description presumed that southern Europe (including Italy, Iberia, southern France and Greece) is a culturally homogen-eous area. Laslett's 'Mediterranean family model' displayed certain fundamental

54. Epstein, *An Island*; Salvemini, 'Prima della Puglia'; Poli, *Territorio e contadini*; G. Delille, 'L'ordine dei villaggi e l'ordine dei campi. Per uno studio antropologico del paesaggio agrario nel Regno di Napoli (secoli XV–XVIII)', in C. de Seta (ed.), *Storia d'Italia Einaudi. Annali 8: Insediamenti e territorio* (Turin, 1985), pp. 499–560; Lepre, *Terra di Lavoro*, pp. 14, 17, 21; C. Klapisch-Zuber, 'Villaggi abbandonati ed emigrazioni interne', in R. Romano and C. Vivanti (eds), *Storia d'Italia, 5. I documenti*, 2 vols (Turin, 1973), vol. I, pp. 345–9.

features: an early age at marriage for women; the absence of adolescent, pre-marital servanthood; a high proportion of multiple households containing more than two generations; and patrilocal marriage, in which the marrying son would remain in the father's household rather than setting up a new one. Richard Smith has suggested that the features identified by Laslett 'formed a constellation of variables that distinguished many Mediterranean rural societies of the later Middle Ages from England and quite possibly from other countries in northwest Europe', remarking how the comparison with England points to the existence of 'two distinctive cultural regions'. For Smith, Mediterranean rural culture displayed a preference for kin links through the male lines and a prevalence of values that were both patriarchal and placed great stress on honour and virginity at marriage.[55]

Smith's hypothesis is based on evidence from late medieval rural Tuscany, which describes a pattern of large and complex rather than nuclear households; patrilocal marriage; and a strongly patriarchal structure headed by the eldest male in the household. More recent research, however, indicates that this central Tuscan pattern was far from typical, and that there were striking differences in household structure between regions and between different rural sectors and significant change across time.

One interesting example of change over time comes from the late medieval countryside of Lucca, to the immediate north-west of the area discussed by Smith. In the early fourteenth century peasant households in this region were nuclear; they had large numbers of children who left the paternal home at marriage; male and female age at marriage was low; and up to half of wealthier peasants' property was shared out between male sons after they reached the age of twenty-five. By the mid-fifteenth century, however, peasant families had become smaller; marriage was patrilocal, and the peasant household had become extended; male age at marriage had increased; and sons could no longer claim a share of their father's property after reaching the age of twenty-five. We find a similar case in medieval Lazio, where in the tenth to twelfth centuries households were strictly nuclear and marriage was neo-local (sons left the paternal household upon marriage); by the fifteenth century, however, married sons stayed within the father's household, and after the latter's death it had become common for male heirs to continue living together and to keep the property undivided.[56]

As in late medieval Lucchesia, family structures in late medieval Lazio seem therefore to have adopted at least some of the features identified by Laslett and Smith as peculiarly 'Mediterranean', in a process which would also fit other scholars' claims that rural households in central and northern Italy became larger and more complex over time. However, this phenomenon did not apply

55. P. Laslett, 'Family and household as work group and kin group: areas of traditional Europe compared', in R. Wall, J. Robin and P. Laslett (eds), Family Forms in Historic Europe (Cambridge, 1983), pp. 513–63; R. M. Smith, 'The people of Tuscany and their families in the fifteenth century: medieval or Mediterranean?', Journal of Family History, 6 (1981), pp. 107–28.

56. F. Leverotti, 'Dalla famiglia stretta alla famiglia larga. Linee di evoluzione e tendenze della famiglia rurale lucchese (secoli XIV–XV)', Studi storici, 30 (1989), pp. 171–202; S. Carocci, 'Aspetti delle strutture familiari nel Lazio tardomedievale', Archivio della Società Romana di Storia Patria, 110 (1987), pp. 151–76.

to the entire country; by the eighteenth century the Italian countryside displayed three principal systems of household formation.[57] The first featured patrilocal and late female age at marriage and was found in the shape of the stem family in rural Lombardy, Piedmont and Liguria, and of the multiple household (including co-resident siblings) in the rest of the centre-north. The second system, based on neo-local residence and early female age at marriage, applied mainly to parts of the southern mainland and Sicily. The third system, which displayed neo-local residence and a late female age at marriage, was typical of rural Sardinia and the southern Tyrrhenian coast and also of north-central Italian cities. Within these broad patterns there was still considerable regional variation, particularly in female age at marriage and in features such as rates of celibacy and the incidence of pre-marital servanthood.[58]

These regional divergences seem to have been due in large part to differences in land tenure and associated labour markets. In the more fertile plains and hills of north-central Italy the strong correlation between *appoderamento*, under-developed labour markets and extended households responded to the need to increase labour inputs as the size of the farm expanded. In the same regions, rural labourers, small-scale tenants and landowning peasants had predominantly nuclear households.[59] On the southern Tyrrhenian coast around Naples, 'lineage'-based household structures were associated with peasant smallholders and petty artisans who grew labour-intensive tree crops requiring large but irregular inputs of labour. Along the coasts of Apulia and Abruzzi, nuclear households of highly mobile wage-labourers were associated instead with latifundia and olive groves. Geographically and economically intermediate regions displayed a combination of these features.[60]

Land, Labour and Credit Markets

Land

A strong tradition of scholarship has assumed that peasants did not treat land like any other commodity to be bought and sold on the market, but imbued it with values of family identity and prestige that were antithetical to economic maximization. In this view, peasant land transactions followed two distinct circuits:[61] a kin-based circuit, in which exchanges were restricted to relatives

---

57. F. Benigno, 'The Southern Italian family in the early modern period: a discussion of coresidential patterns', *Continuity and Change*, 1 (1989), pp. 165–94; M. Barbagli, *Sotto lo stesso tetto. Mutamenti della famiglia in Italia dal XV al XX secolo*, 2nd edn (Bologna, 1988).

58. Barbagli, *Sotto la stesso tetto*, pp. 225–34; Lanaro Sartori, 'Il mondo contadino', p. 314.

59. Poni, *Fossi e cavedagne*, pp. 283–356; A. Doveri, 'Famiglie di contadini e famiglie di pigionali del contado pisano nel secolo XVIII. Struttura ed evoluzione', *Società e storia*, 8 (1985), pp. 797–813; V. Beonio Brocchieri, 'Famiglie e mestieri nell'Alto Milanese tra '500 e '600', *Archivio storico lombardo*, 117 (1991), pp. 37–58; D. Sella, 'Profilo demografico e sociale di un comune rurale lombardo. Balsamo nel 1597', in *Studi in memoria di Luigi dal Pane* (Bologna, 1982), pp. 333–44.

60. Delille, 'L'ordine dei villaggi'.

61. This paragraph summarizes M. Cattini, *I contadini di San Felice. Metamorfosi di un mondo rurale nell'Emilia dell'età moderna* (Turin, 1984), pp. 122–40 and G. Levi, *Inheriting Power: The Story of an Exorcist*, transl. L. G. Cochrane (Chicago, 1985), ch. 3.

and prices reflected unwritten norms of 'reciprocity' rather than market values; and a market-based circuit, in which land was sold by the peasant kin to urban investors. Whereas transactions among kin were used strategically to ensure an optimal balance between land and household size, sales to 'outsiders' were merely short-term responses to financial crisis. This model implies that land could only flow *out* of the peasant sector, and is therefore closely linked with the view previously referred to that peasant ownership experienced uninterrupted decline during the early modern period.

It is hard to assess these conclusions from current studies, which are either highly localized or rely on infrequent snapshots of land distribution based on urban tax returns. Yet both aspects of the model – peasant traditionalism and the unidirectional flow of land transactions – seem overstated. This is partly because historians have been more concerned with uncovering evidence of peasant hardship and exploitation than with social and economic developments within rural society itself, and have consequently ignored most evidence of rural land acquisitions. Rural land markets were in fact more active, and the pattern of transactions between the rural and the urban sectors more complex, than this model suggests. Peasants seem to have sold *and* bought land in response to even quite rapid changes in their economic circumstances. Agricultural labourers in early modern Apulia slipped in and out of the market in expensive vine- and olive-growing 'micro-plots' with great ease, suggesting neither a strong emotional attachment to land nor a sharp distinction between short-term economic 'tactics' dictated by hardship and a long-term 'strategy' of optimization. In the centre-north, urban property expanded rapidly when rising fiscal demands on the countryside coincided with a run of bad harvests or a broader economic depression – as in the 1520s and 1530s, the 1590s, and during the central decades of the seventeenth century; at other times the balance of trade was more equal or could even be reversed. Neither can one ignore the fact that forced sales by the weaker rural strata often benefited propertied elites in the countryside equally or more than urban landlords.[62]

Land markets did not, of course, work everywhere according to identical rules. Markets faced three major constraints. The first consisted of community laws restricting or excluding sales of land to outsiders. Restrictions by urban communities were probably mostly intended to exclude buyers from rival towns,[63] but rural by-laws responded also to more legitimate worries: outsiders could disrupt communal systems of land management devised to avoid overgrazing, and when buyers were townspeople who were exempted from local taxes, any acquisition caused a net increase in the tax charges of the rural community itself. A second obstruction to the free circulation of land arose from the fact that the social and economic elites were able to avoid devolving

62. Salvemini, 'Prima della Puglia', p. 34; G. Corazzol, *Fitti e livelli a grano. Un aspetto del credito rurale nel Veneto del '500* (Milan, 1979), p. 52; Faccini, *La Lombardia*, pp. 86–90, 137–44; S. Cohn Jr, 'The movement of landed property in the *contado* of Siena: relations between city and country, 1295–1450', unpublished ms. (1984). G. Federico, 'Contadini e mercato: tattiche di sopravvivenza', *Società e storia*, 10 (1987), pp. 877–913 demonstrates the implausibility of the distinction between peasant 'tactics' and 'strategy'.

63. W. J. Connell, 'Clientelismo e Stato territoriale. Il potere fiorentino a Pistoia nel XV secolo', *Società e storia*, 14 (1991), pp. 529–30.

property outside their families through various systems of entail, male inheritance and primogeniture,[64] while the existence of seigneurial rights restricted sales of feudal land to aristocrats or to only the wealthiest commoners. Lastly, the higher tax burden borne by peasants lowered the relative price of their land compared with urban landholdings, an inbuilt bias which favoured the latter's accumulation.[65] A further and equally significant constraint was the 'feudal-communal system of land-holding',[66] which resulted in different agents (individual peasants, rural communities, feudal lords and at times the state) possessing a variety of rights over the same land.

Although it has been suggested that this system, and by implication the other restrictions outlined, was a fundamental source of economic retardation because it restrained pressures towards specialization and commercialization, it seems none the less unlikely that Italian land markets were very much less efficient than elsewhere in Europe at this time. In the most highly commercialized regions of the south, Sicily and Apulia, many traditional 'feudal-communal' constraints on land markets had already disappeared by the fifteenth century, and feudal and peasant property circulated quite freely[67] – implying that the persistence elsewhere of traditional institutions was more probably a consequence than a cause of underdevelopment.

Labour

Different agricultural systems required different kinds of labour market: specialized agriculture relied to a greater degree on seasonal wage labour than mixed cropping, which instead maximized family inputs. Although all cultivators faced shifting labour requirements during the year, specialized farmers had to cope with both fewer and larger seasonal variations than multiple croppers. Specialists were therefore more likely to maintain a small household and hire outside labour when necessary, than sustain a large family which would have lain idle for much of the year. Multiple croppers, who faced lower peaks and troughs in seasonal labour requirements, could aim to meet them instead through family labour, and thus had an incentive to maintain larger households;[68] once the system was established, they could achieve further 'smoothing' of family inputs by producing an increasing quantity of complementary seasonal crops. In other terms, one would expect to find efficient agricultural labour markets (and agricultural specialization) associated with nuclear households, and less

64. E. I. Mineo, 'Formazione delle élites urbane nella Sicilia del tardo medioevo: matrimonio e sistemi di successione', *Quaderni storici*, 30 (1995), pp. 9–42; G. Delille, *Famille et propriété dans le Royaume de Naples (XVe–XIXe siècle)* (Rome/Paris, 1985), pp. 23–85; R. Goldthwaite, *Private Wealth in Renaissance Florence. A Study of Four Families* (Princeton, NJ, 1968), p. 272.

65. Vigo, *Fisco e società*, p. 27 n. 75.

66. P. Chorley, *Oil, Silk and Enlightenment. Economic Problems in XVIIIth Century Naples* (Naples, 1965), pp. 11–13.

67. Epstein, *An Island*, pp. 344–5; Visceglia, *Territorio feudo*, p. 116; above, n. 62. Even where feudal institutions were most powerful, land could circulate quite freely. Cf. Zotta, 'Momenti e problemi', pp. 718, 729.

68. Barbagli, *Sotto lo stesso tetto*, ch. 4.

efficient ones (and less specialized agriculture) with extended households. Despite other intervening factors, this basic relationship does in fact seem to have applied, with nuclear households prevailing in the south, and extended households emerging during the later Middle Ages in the central and northern regions associated with *mezzadria poderale*.[69]

Sharecropping *poderi* were mainly unspecialized. Mixed croppers in central and northern Italy appear at first to have responded to the problem of labour shortages by employing the offspring of poor cottagers and smallholders as live-in servants; concurrently or somewhat later, Tuscan and Emilian sharecroppers began to pool resources between neighbouring farms 'to avoid using wage labour'.[70] These 'internal labour markets' were improved by the development of large property complexes (*fattorie*) which arose during the later Middle Ages to collect and redistribute produce among several dozen farms, but which from the late seventeenth century were increasingly used by landlords to intervene actively in production. At the same time the supply of seasonal wage labour from nearby cottagers seems to have increased, possibly because of the need for a more flexible labour force as *fattorie* became internally more specialized.[71] However, these developments were restrained by the landowners' practice of allocating tenants to farms with the aim of achieving an efficient balance between land and labour: if the size of the household changed following births or marriages, the tenant would be asked to move. In practice, the difficulty of finding an optimal balance between farm and family size caused high rates of peasant turnover and motivated landlords to take a close interest in their tenants' matrimonial decisions.[72]

Credit

As one would expect with such a highly commercialized and urbanized economy, rural credit was ubiquitous. Most forms of credit were already well developed before 1350. The most widespread form of rural credit was the long-term or multi-generational lease, in which tenants agreed to assart a plot and make capital investments in it in exchange for rights of usage and a nominal rate of interest (rent). This arrangement, which clearly antedates the fourteenth century, continued to be practised throughout our period, particularly for tree crops which took several years to produce a return. By the late twelfth or early thirteenth centuries one also finds more flexible short-term capital markets,

69. Ibid.; Benigno, 'The Southern Italian family'.

70. Lanaro Sartori, 'Il mondo contadino', p. 314; Sella, 'Profilo demografico', p. 339; Beonio Brocchieri, 'Famiglie e mestieri', p. 46; Poni, *Fossi e cavedagne*, p. 316.

71. S. R. Epstein, *Alle origini della fattoria toscana. L'ospedale di S. Maria della Scala di Siena e le sue terre (c.1250–c.1450)* (Florence, 1986), pp. 269–74; E. Luttazzi Gregori, 'Organizzazione e sviluppo di una fattoria nell'età moderna: Fonte a Ronco (1651–1746)', in M. Mirri (ed.), *Ricerche di storia moderna*, 2 vols (Pisa, 1976/79), vol. I, pp. 209–88; G. Giorgetti, *Capitalismo e agricoltura in Italia* (Rome, 1977), pp. 238–9; Doveri, 'Famiglie di contadini'; Poni, *Fossi e cavedagne*, p. 316.

72. Poni, *Fossi e cavedagne*, pp. 340–1; Campodoni, 'Proprietari, mezzadri', p. 118; McArdle, *Altopascio*, pp. 151–2, 164.

including the use of land as collateral for both short- and long-term loans, the lease of draught animals, and the rudiments of a market in agricultural futures (advance sales of agricultural produce); the latter allowed smaller advances to be made, often as seed or food grains rather than cash, to be repaid at the following harvest.[73] These developments were the effect both of more active land and product markets, and of the rise of powerful urban authorities which could enforce laws sanctioning distraint.

These systems were based on private bargaining. Lenders often had considerable leverage on the terms of the contract, although not primarily because they were monopolists but because they were better informed than the peasantry: rural lenders were typically village or town notaries, whose practice made them ideally situated to assess general economic conditions and potential borrowers' circumstances. For borrowers the consequences of this imbalance could be neutralized either by providing systematically cheaper loans or by improving access to market information. The first solution was attempted in central and northern regions like Lazio and the Veneto through the creation of rural pawnhouses (*Monti di pietà, Monti dei pegni*), but these institutions were probably not very effective, mainly because they excluded the use of land and the main movable goods (chattels, working animals and tools) as collateral.[74] The more sophisticated alternative, which combined the supply of credit with a system for collectively reducing risk, evolved mainly in the more commercialized regions south of Tuscany. First recorded in early fifteenth-century Sicily, the system was based on agricultural prices established through public, centralized bargaining. In *contratti alla meta* (Sicily), *alla voce, a liquidazione* (Naples) or *a signoria* (Maremma), producers were advanced working capital at an agreed price per unit of grain, cheese, olive oil, wine, silk and almonds. This price (*meta, voce*) was set after the following harvest by a committee which included creditors, debtors and public representatives. Initially these contracts were restricted to more specialized and creditworthy peasants, but during the sixteenth century they began also to include cottagers on more traditional share and fixed rent leases. Centralized bargaining lowered transaction costs and improved circulation of scarce capital in the rural sector; by drawing on producers' and buyers' future expectations, it reduced uncertainty and helped stabilize output and prices over time.[75]

73. D. Herlihy, 'Population, plague and social change in rural Pistoia, 1201–1430', *Economic History Review*, 2nd series, 18 (1965), pp. 239–40; A. Sapori, 'I mutui dei mercanti fiorentini del Trecento e l'incremento della proprietà fondiaria', in idem, *Studi di storia economica (secoli XIII–XIV–XV)*, 2 vols (Florence, 1955–67), vol. I, pp. 191–221; E. Fiumi, 'L'attività usuraria dei mercanti sangimignanesi nell'età comunale', *Archivio storico italiano*, 119 (1961), pp. 145–62; G. Pinto, *La Toscana nel tardo medio evo. Ambiente, economia rurale, società* (Florence, 1982), pp. 207–23.
74. G. Albini, 'Sulle origini dei Monti di Pietà nel dominio sforzesco', *Archivio storico lombardo*, 11th series, 2 (1985), pp. 67–112; Delumeau, *Vita economica*, p. 156; Lanaro Sartori, 'Mondo contadino', p. 330. Venice legislated on this in 1458 and 1461 in the context of pawns taken by cities in lieu of rural tax arrears. Cf. G. M. Varanini, *Comuni cittadini e stato regionale. Ricerche sulla Terraferma veneta nel Quattrocento* (Verona, 1992), pp. 125–61.
75. Epstein, *An Island*, pp. 144, 171, 205; M. Verga, 'Rapporti di produzione e gestione dei feudi nella Sicilia centro-occidentale', *Quaderni storici*, 15 (1980), pp. 120–40; Chorley, *Oil, Silk*, pp. 122, 132–3; Zotta, 'Momenti e problemi', pp. 734–6; Salvemini, 'Prima della Puglia', pp. 45, 98.

A range of solutions was thus devised to meet credit requirements for consumption and for working capital, and to a lesser extent for real estate acquisitions or improvements. Although acts of usury and exploitation did undeniably occur, credit was not simply a tool for exploiting peasant hardship by accumulating land at their expense. The records tend to overstate the proportion of debts which led to repossession, because lenders were more likely to draw up a formal contract for loans which faced a higher risk of default; a significant proportion of credit transactions took place verbally because the risk of default was low, but the terms of these arrangements can obviously not be assessed. The existence of similar rates of interest across regions, and their long-term decline,[76] indicates that rural credit markets became more competitive and efficient over time and suggests that they were not systematically biased against peasant debtors.[77]

Although individual lenders can seldom have possessed monopoly power, credit markets could be distorted by the collective powers of urban jurisdiction. The fear that a 'credit revolt' by Friulan peasants in 1533 might spread to the rest of the *Terraferma* prompted Venice to instigate a compromise between the urban elites in Udine, who upheld the rule that interest payments be made in kind at a time of rapidly rising prices, and the rural communities, who wished to repay debts in cash. Although the city of Udine and its peasants agreed (in 1563!) that payments in kind were more onerous, they disagreed on the implications: whereas the former argued that they were necessary to make the peasants work harder, the latter rebutted that they could produce more if they were left with a larger share of the seed. Further south, Naples so dominated the kingdom's credit markets before the mid-seventeenth century that serious problems arose if the flow of money from the capital was interrupted – as occurred briefly during the harvest crises of the late 1580s and 1590s, when the government's attempt to manipulate grain production in Apulia led to a walkout by local producers.[78]

The main limitation of formally constituted credit markets was the fact that they were restricted to peasants who owned substantial collateral. Landless, poor peasants must have found it hard to invest or to insure against risk by borrowing against future harvests, for the lender would have no means of compensation for default – a fact that presumably made poor peasants more reliant on locally based informal, petty credit. These difficulties may explain some of the peculiarities of central Italian sharecropping, which was dominated by propertyless tenants who under normal circumstances would not have had access to working capital. The reason why landlords were willing to advance capital under this arrangement was that they could be repaid with peasant labour at 'wages' below the market rate. Indeed, these landlords' preference

---

76. Salvemini, 'Prima della Puglia', pp. 101–2; Corazzol, *Fitti e livelli*.

77. Idem, 'Prestatori e contadini nella campagna feltrina intorno alla metà del '500', *Quaderni storici*, 9 (1974), p. 474.

78. Idem, *Fitti e livelli*, pp. 73–4 and passim; idem, 'Sulla diffusione dei livelli a frumento tra il patriziato veneziano nella seconda metà del '500', *Studi veneziani*, new series, 6 (1982), pp. 103–28; Zotta, 'Momenti e problemi', p. 783; also Chorley, *Oil, Silk*, pp. 44, 84.

for tenant over wage labour answers the question raised previously, namely why regions dominated by share tenancy were also characterized by unusually underdeveloped labour markets.[79]

Product Markets and Commercialization

The debate on the 'transition' from feudalism to capitalism in Europe is based on the German socialist Karl Kautsky's view that it was necessary to evict the peasantry from the land in order to achieve modern agricultural growth, which was a prerequisite for capitalist industrialization.[80] This claim is based on three main assumptions: first, that pre-modern agriculture was subject to economies of scale, so that larger farms run with wage labour were more efficient than peasant smallholdings; second, that pre-capitalist peasants were highly risk averse, implying that they would not innovate and increase output in the same way that capitalist tenants would; and third, that peasants aimed for 'subsistence' rather than to increase their income through 'commercialization'. Our discussion of tenurial relations and land, labour and credit markets has suggested instead that peasants responded to commercial pressures and opportunities by innovating and specializing, or alternatively by diversifying to reduce risk, on the basis of the institutionalized incentives and constraints they faced. Although the 'specializing' and the 'subsistent' peasant are obviously idealized extremes, they underline the fact that there was no such thing as 'a' peasant economy because of the considerable differences in rural incentives across space and time.

The claim about the peasantry's preference for 'subsistence' appears to be based on the prevalence in pre-capitalist rural economies of payments in kind, which are taken as evidence of a 'natural' (non market) economy. This confuses the concept of 'natural' *versus* 'monetary' economy, which applies to the means of payment in use, with that of 'subsistence' *versus* 'commercialized' economy, which applies to the nature of the economic structure.[81] The decision to pay in kind rather than money does not express a specific economic strategy: it is 'largely a matter of convenience . . . [saving] time and intermediation costs'.[82] Consequently, the presence of transactions in kind cannot be used to measure the extent of economic 'subsistence'; strictly speaking, an estimate of peasant subsistence must consider only goods produced and consumed by the same peasant household.

79. Cf. S. R. Epstein, 'Tuscans and their farms', *Rivista di storia economica*, 12 (1994), pp. 111–37.

80. R. Brenner, 'The agrarian roots of European capitalism', in T. H. Aston and C. H. E. Philpin (eds), *The Brenner Debate. Agrarian Class Structure and Economic Development in Pre-Industrial Europe* (Cambridge, 1985), pp. 213–327; I. Wallerstein, *The Modern World-System. I. Capitalist Agriculture and the Origins of the European World-Economy in the Sixteenth Century* (New York, 1974), ch. 1.

81. See e.g. R. Romano and U. Tucci (eds), *Storia d'Italia. Annali 6. Economia naturale, economia monetaria* (Turin, 1983).

82. G. Federico, 'Household budgets as a source for the study of rural economy (Italy, 1860–1940): commercialization and peasants' behaviour', in T. Pierenkemper (ed.), *Zur Ökonomik des privaten Haushalts. Haushaltsrechnungen als Quelle historischer Wirtschafts- und Sozialforschung* (Frankfurt/New York, 1991), p. 183.

The Florentine tax survey of 1424–27 can provide a rough estimate of the proportion of non-marketed output and consumption in the countryside. No more than 70 per cent of the rural population (equal to 50 per cent of the total population) had access to enough land to attempt 'self-sufficiency'. If one assumes with some exaggeration that they consumed up to 50 per cent of their net output, it follows that no more than 25 per cent of total sellable output could theoretically remain within the 'subsistence' sector.[83] These figures imply also that the oft-cited claim by the eighteenth-century Neapolitan economist Ferdinando Galiani that southern peasant households consumed no less than half their output is quite certainly wrong, not least because agriculture in many southern regions was more highly commercialized than in Tuscany.[84] It must in any case be emphasized that the Tuscan estimate is an upper limit, which assumes that virtually the only agricultural produce to reach the market was in the form of rent, and that it is highly unlikely that such a 'subsistence' economy could have sustained a rate of urbanization of 25 per cent. Both estimates in any case ignore manufactures and services produced in the countryside, which were mostly traded outside rural households, and which would further reduce estimates of the extent of the 'subsistence' sector.

It follows from the evidence discussed previously that peasant economic choice was most influenced by the institutional relations between town and country and between feudal and non-feudal lands under royal authority. These underwent the most significant changes during the late medieval and seventeenth-century 'crises'. During both periods, territorial states attacked existing fiscal, economic and jurisdictional privileges and lowered barriers to trade; the result of these two waves of 'jurisdictional integration' was to intensify commercial integration and specialization within regions of increasing size.

The late Middle Ages witnessed the expansion of territorial states in the centre-north and the consolidation of royal power in the south. The rulers' desire to broaden their political consensus generally provoked a decline of urban authority over the countryside in regions previously controlled by city-states, and greater control over feudal independence and the rise of towns under royal jurisdiction in the southern monarchies. Increased political centralization and integration weakened or abolished outright many urban and feudal controls over rural production and markets, and was followed everywhere by greater specialization within politically defined regions.[85] The most significant

83. The method of calculation follows ibid.; data on Tuscany from Herlihy and Klapisch, *Les Toscans*, p. 307.

84. F. Galiani, *Della moneta e altri scritti*, ed. A. Merola (Milan, 1963), p. 234. For Sicily, see Epstein, *An Island*, p. 282 n. 47.

85. M. Mirri, 'Formazione di una regione economica. Ipotesi sulla Toscana, sul Veneto, sulla Lombardia', *Studi veneziani*, new series, 11 (1985), pp. 47–59; P. Malanima, 'La formazione di una regione economica: la Toscana nei secoli xiii–xv', *Società e storia*, 6 (1983), pp. 229–69; M. Tangheroni, 'Il sistema economico della Toscana nel Trecento', in Gensini, *La Toscana*, pp. 41–66; Degrassi, 'L'economia del tardo medioevo', pp. 338–40, 395; Salvemini, 'Prima della Puglia', pp. 6–11, 105–8. Venice began seriously to address the issue of territorial integration only following the Treaty of Cambrai (1529), in response to a significant downturn in foreign trade; cf. Varanini, *Comuni cittadini*, pp. 163–81 and M. Knapton, 'Guerra e finanza (1381–1508)', in G. Cozzi and M. Knapton, *Storia della Repubblica di Venezia. Dalla guerra di Chioggia alla riconquista della Terraferma* (Turin, 1986), pp. 332–6 for conditions in the late fifteenth century.

developments occurred in the countryside, as peasants responded to the decline in rents and the rise in labour productivity and per caput income which followed the Black Death, by increasing output in higher-value agricultural crops (wine, olive oil, cheese, meat, plant dyes, silk) and in small-scale manufacture, and by decreasing the proportion of staple cereal crops.

Besides adequate contracts and credit markets, agricultural specialization required a flexible system of distribution that was not always at hand. Particularly where urban powers over the countryside remained strong, market institutions were not always adequate for the new needs. For example, although rural fairs expanded significantly across Italy after 1350 in response to the more specialized patterns of regional trade, fewer numbers were established where towns could enforce their monopoly over trade, as in central Italy around Florence and Perugia. By contrast, where urban jurisdiction was weak, as in southern Italy, or could be challenged effectively by rural communities, as in Lombardy and the *Veneto*, new fairs were not hindered. The same applied to the capacity of towns to control the price and distribution of grain in their hinterland. These institutional differences shaped rural responses to opportunities for increasing agrarian commercialization and specialization.[86]

Although the growth of territorial states lowered some commercial barriers between the countryside and capital cities, and gave the former some institutional autonomy, it did not fundamentally change the medieval pattern of competition through legal privilege: where urban and seigneurial claims to rural revenue did not interfere with the rulers' fiscal and economic concerns, they were generally left in place. On the other hand, the strategic importance of the grain trade for urban welfare and political stability made it a prime target for regulation. Control was strongest in the centre-north, where subject cities' prerogatives – elaborate customs systems, price controls, bans on exports and forced sales during scarcity – were tempered only slightly by the capital cities' need for larger and more distant supplies.[87] Endemic smuggling was one response to the higher transaction costs, lower sales prices and often unpredictable controls caused by market regulation.[88] With the significant exception of Rome and Naples, the grain trade was less regulated in the south, mainly because most towns lacked the requisite institutional backing, and possibly, in

86. Del Torre, *Venezia*, pp. 105–6; S. R. Epstein, 'Regional fairs, institutional innovation and economic growth in late medieval Europe', *Economic History Review*, 2nd series, 47 (1994), pp. 459–82; idem, 'Cities, regions and the late medieval crisis: Sicily and Tuscany compared', *Past and Present*, 130 (1991), pp. 3–50; idem, 'Town and country in late medieval Italy: economic and institutional aspects', *Economic History Review*, 2nd series, 46 (1993), pp. 453–77.

87. P. Macry, 'La questione annonaria negli antichi stati italiani', *Quaderni storici*, 7 (1974), pp. 236–46; A. M. Pult Quaglia, *'Per provvedere ai popoli': Il sistema annonario nella Firenze dei Medici* (Florence, 1990); Romani, *Nella spirale*, pp. 96, 104–9, 113, 115; B. Farolfi, *Strutture agrarie e crisi cittadina nel primo Cinquecento bolognese* (Bologna, 1977), p. 35; D. Zanetti, *Problemi alimentari di una economia preindustriale. Cereali a Pavia dal 1398 al 1700* (Turin, 1964), pp. 40–51; Del Torre, *Venezia*, pp. 199–201, 205–9.

88. E. Rossini and G. Zalin, *Uomini, grani e contrabbandi sul Garda tra Quattrocento e Seicento* (Verona, 1985); B. Polese, 'L'importanza della produzione cerealicola e vinicola nella formazione del reddito della Terraferma veneta dal '500 al '700', in Tagliaferri, *Venezia e la Terraferma*, pp. 383–409; Romani, *Nella spirale*, p. 63; O. Raggio, *Faide e parentele. Lo stato genovese visto dalla Fontanabuona* (Turin, 1990), pp. 136–9; G. Tocci, *Le terre traverse. Poteri e territori nei ducati di Parma e Piacenza tra Sei e Settecento* (Bologna, 1985), pp. 280–9; Chorley, *Oil, Silk*, pp. 152–3. See also above, n. 33.

the more commercialized regions, because higher agricultural productivity and better systems of distribution made intervention redundant.[89]

Advance warning of the second wave of jurisdictional reform came during the 1590s, when a series of disastrous harvests brought to an end the long economic and demographic upswing begun in the late fifteenth century, and gave 'impetus . . . to an enhanced view of government responsibilities'.[90] More proximate causes of the notorious 'seventeenth-century crisis', however, were the catastrophic epidemics of 1629–31 in the centre-north and of 1647–56 in the south. Losses of between a quarter and a third of the total population occurred at the same time as tax demands escalated, the north suffered military invasion, and the south was caught up in urban and peasant uprisings. In the short term, demographic losses and social and political upheaval caused trading networks to collapse; in Lombardy, the rural economy ground to a virtual standstill for more than a decade.[91] But in the longer run, the pressure by central authorities pursuing a sort of 'involuntary mercantilism' to abolish established fiscal and economic privileges was beneficial. The main consequence, most visible in Piedmont, Lombardy and the Veneto, was to 'ruralize' the economy: while the loss or declining significance of medieval privileges caused a sharp contraction of medium-sized cities, cheaper service and manufacturing centres in the countryside were allowed to grow.[92]

The demise of many of the jurisdictional obstacles that had survived the late medieval 'crisis' and the rise of a more entrepreneurial peasantry increased trade and territorial specialization within and between neighbouring states, particularly across the Po plain.[93] However, perhaps to an even greater degree than during the late medieval 'crisis', the speed and nature of the economic recovery was shaped by the prevailing political institutions. In the kingdom of Naples, for example, the medium-term effects of demographic collapse were far from uniformly positive. Many of the more powerful barons reacted to the decline in land rents by raising taxes on trade; the more entrepreneurial among them resorted more straightforwardly to banditry. This exacerbated the

89. M. L. Riccio, *L'evoluzione della politica annonaria a Napoli dal 1503 al 1806* (Naples, 1923); I. Fazio, *La politica del grano. Annona e controllo del territorio in Sicilia nel Settecento* (Milan, 1993); Delumeau, *Vita economica*, pp. 28, 143, 156–70.

90. N. S. Davidson, 'Northern Italy in the 1590s', in Clark, *The European crisis*, p. 170. See also P. Burke, 'Southern Italy in the 1590s: hard times or crisis?', ibid., pp. 177–90; Davies, 'Village-building'; Zotta, 'Momenti e problemi', pp. 749–51; F. Cazzola, 'Il problema annonario nella Ferrara pontificia: il legato Serra e la Congregazione dell' Abbondanza (1616–1622)', *Annali della Facoltà di Lettere e Filosofia, Università di Macerata*, 2 (1970–71), pp. 543–65.

91. Faccini, *La Lombardia*, ch. 6.

92. Ibid., pp. 19–20; R. P. Corritore, 'Il processo di "ruralizzazione" in Italia nei secoli xvii–xviii. Verso una regionalizzazione', *Rivista di storia economica*, new series, 10 (1993), pp. 353–86; S. Ciriacono, 'Vénise et ses villes. Structuration et déstructuration d'un marché régional', *Revue historique*, 276 (1986), pp. 292, 294–5, 297; Beltrami, *La penetrazione economica*, p. 5; Tocci, *Le terre traverse*; M. Verga, 'Tra Sei e Settecento: un' "età delle pre-riforme"?', *Storica*, 1 (1995), pp. 111–21.

93. Faccini, *La Lombardia*, pp. 137–44; D. Sella, *Crisis and continuity. The Economy of Spanish Lombardy in the Seventeenth Century* (Cambridge, MA., 1979), chs 6–7; P. M. Hohenberg and L. H. Lees, 'Urban decline and regional economies: Brabant, Castile, and Lombardy, 1550–1750', *Comparative Studies in Society and History*, 31 (1989), pp. 439–61; E. Sereni, *Storia del paesaggio agrario italiano* (Bari, 1961), pp. 262–4; Ciriacono, 'Vénise', pp. 294–307; G. Levi, *Centro e periferia di uno stato assoluto* (Turin, 1985), pp. 7–69; Corritore, 'Il processo', pp. 384–5 nn. 100–1.

kingdom's commercial disintegration and made it more difficult for highly commercialized, export-led economies like central Apulia's to reconvert.[94]

The sharp contraction of southern agricultural exports to the north after the mid-seventeenth century thus reflected both the north's structural transformation and a process of relative economic decline in the south. Already in the late sixteenth century, demographic stagnation in northern Italy had caused demand for southern grain to decline; previously imported commodities – silk, olive oil and wine – also began to be produced more heavily in the north.[95] The mid-seventeenth century depression and increased regional integration in the north intensified this process of 'import substitution'. In the case of silk manufacture – considered by many historians to be the harbinger of Italy's industrial revolution – the decline of urban and guild monopolies also made it easier to set up new silk mills in the Lombard, Venetian and Piedmontese countrysides.[96]

Both the late medieval and the seventeenth-century demographic crises were followed by the expansion of rural and semi-rural manufacture. Although such 'proto-industry' often arose in the more peripheral parts of the country, it was not necessarily the result of upland overpopulation or poverty; in several instances mountain peasants had already achieved higher living standards than their neighbours in the plains.[97] The fact that rapid manufacturing growth in the late seventeenth century was preceded by a similar cycle in the late fourteenth and fifteenth centuries, also suggests that the developments during the seventeenth century were less revolutionary than past theories of 'proto-industrialization' have assumed. Both phases were the consequence of a process of income and demand substitution. Population losses, specialization and the redistribution of income brought about by declining urban privilege, increased lower- and middle-class discretionary incomes and produced a relative shift in demand from staple food to cheap manufacture. Rural manufacture in central and northern Italy (little is known about developments in the south)[98] was typically situated in areas free of urban economic and fiscal control, including large boroughs lacking urban charters in the Lombard plain,[99] mountain communities in the Alpine valleys,[100] and semi-autonomous feudal lordships surviving

94. Salvemini, 'Prima della Puglia', pp. 94–9; Benaiteau, 'Rendita feudale', p. 599; Visceglia, 'Rendita feudale', pp. 546–50; Lepre, Storia, pp. 23–6, 41–2. Regional trade was recovering by the 1680s (Delille, Croissance, pp. 62, 187).

95. Galasso, Economia e società, pp. 345–53.

96. C. Poni, 'Per la storia del distretto industriale serico di Bologna (secoli XVI–XIX)', Quaderni storici, 25 (1990), pp. 93–167; S. Ciriacono, 'Échecs et réussites de la proto-industrialisation dans la Vénétie: le cas du Haut-Vicentin (XVIIᵉ–XIXᵉ siècles)', Revue d'histoire moderne et contemporaine, 32 (1985), pp. 311–23; A. Moioli, 'La deindustrializzazione della Lombardia nel secolo XVII', Archivio storico lombardo, 11th series, 3 (1986), pp. 167–203; P. Covolan, 'Famiglie e protoindustria: il caso di Racconigi tra XVII e XVIII secolo', Bollettino storico-bibliografico subalpino, 82 (1984), pp. 460–77.

97. Romani, Nella spirale, pp. 36, 45, 141; Epstein, An Island, ch. 5; Benaiteau, 'Rendita feudale', p. 574.

98. Developments after 1656 are discussed in ibid., p. 586; Marino, Pastoral economics, pp. 229–39; Lepre, Storia, vol. II, pp. 48–50; Delille, Croissance, pp. 219–20; M. Aymard, 'Commerce et consommation des draps en Sicile et en Italie méridionale (XVᵉ–XVIIIᵉ siècles)', in M. Spallanzani (ed.), Produzione commercio e consumo dei panni di lana (nei secoli XII–XVIII) (Florence, 1976), pp. 127–39.

99. Sella, Crisis and Continuity, ch. 6; G. Chittolini, '"Quasi-città". Borghi e terre in area lombarda nel tardo Medioevo', Società e storia, 13 (1990), pp. 3–26.

100. G. Zalin, 'Seguendo le relazioni dei Rettori. Manifattura e politica industriale della Lombardia Veneta', in Tagliaferri, Venezia e la Terraferma, pp. 531–46; D. Carminati Masera, 'Potere locale e stato: una

in the interstices of territorial states,[101] whose jurisdictional autonomy was extended during both periods of institutional 'crisis'; by contrast, where rural franchises were insignificant as in Tuscany, rural industry failed noticeably to emerge.[102]

'Proto-industrial' developments were not, of course, purely cyclical in nature. During the late seventeenth century the product range expanded to include silk, straw hats, cotton clothing and a larger range of metalware in addition to the cheap woollens, mixed fabrics and ironware which dominated late medieval production; there were significant technological advances between the two periods, particularly in the silk and metal industries; and both the scale of production and the number of people employed in rural manufacture were greater around 1700 than two centuries before. Yet the main source of 'proto-industrial' strength was also its most basic source of weakness, since the prerequisite of jurisdictional independence meant that industrial location was determined more by random institutional features than by factors strictly of cost. Political contingency, rather than relative production costs, determined whether a community or an entire region could 'choose' to pursue rural manufacture and overcome the main obstacle to pre-industrial agricultural progress: the long-run decline in the marginal productivity of labour.

Agricultural Productivity

Contrary to claims that Italian agriculture was impeded by institutional and cultural failings, by landlord absenteeism, exploitative contracts and peasant aversion to the market, the evidence reviewed so far has suggested that property rights, tenurial relations and credit markets were reasonably efficient and responded positively to demographic and commercial change, and that peasants did not avoid trade on principle. More serious bottlenecks to growth arose from high internal and external tariffs, which reduced competition and opportunities for specialization, and by two additional constraints on rural labour markets. The latter were caused by the lack of adequate supplies of seasonal wage labour and by urban monopolies over manufactures and services, which restricted opportunities for rural employment and exacerbated the problems caused by excess labour.

comunità biellese nel Cinque-Seicento', *Bollettino storico-bibliografico subalpino*, 82 (1984), pp. 363–89; D. Gasparini, 'Signori e contadini nella Contea di Valmareno. Secoli XVI–XVII', in G. Cozzi (ed.), *Stato società e giustizia nella Repubblica veneta (sec. XV–XVIII)*, 2 vols (Rome, 1980/85), vol. II, pp. 133–90; S. Ciriacono, 'Protoindustria, lavoro a domicilio e sviluppo economico nelle campagne venete in epoca moderna', *Quaderni storici*, 18 (1983), pp. 57–80.

101. S. Ciriacono, 'Industria rurale e strutture feudali nella Terraferma veneta tra Sei e Settecento', *Studi storici Luigi Simeoni*, 36 (1986), pp. 67–80; C. M. Belfanti, 'Dalla città alla campagna: industrie tessili a Mantova tra carestie ed epidemie (1550–1630)', *Critica storica*, 25 (1988), pp. 444–5; idem, 'Rural manufactures and rural protoindustries in the "Italy of the cities" from the sixteenth through the eighteenth century', *Continuity and Change*, 8 (1993), pp. 259–60.

102. P. Malanima, *La decadenza di un'economia cittadina. L'industria di Firenze nei secoli xvi–xviii* (Bologna, 1982) and Poni, 'Per la storia', pp. 154–5 argue that proto-industry was held back in areas of *mezzadria poderale* because sharecroppers were fully employed in agriculture; here an opposite line of causation is implied.

As elsewhere in pre-industrial Europe, Italian agriculture was characterized by high land productivity (output per hectare), indicating that farms made efficient use of available resources within the existing institutional framework, and by low labour productivity (output per person), implying that the agricultural sector was overmanned. Although the lack of reliable statistics means that the effects of low labour productivity on rural standards of living can only be surmised, a comparison between Italian and British agriculture on the eve of the First World War provides a useful benchmark. In 1909 the productivity of labour in English agriculture was 2.2 times that of Italian agricultural labour in 1911; net output per hectare in England was 0.7 times that achieved in Italy; consequently, English agricultural labourers' standard of living was roughly 1.6 times that of their Italian counterparts.[103]

Between 1350 and 1750 Italian agriculture generally became more, rather than less, labour-intensive. The land produced more, but the number of peasants living on it increased faster. Data on grain yields are difficult to interpret,[104] but prices and output per hectare suggest that the average productivity of grain farming increased significantly, despite a brief setback during the seventeenth century. Even so, although the most productive regions could match the better northern European agriculture (between sixteen and seventeen quintals per hectare was achieved at Lodi near Milan in 1771), average output in the eighteenth century was still probably closer to twelve quintals.[105]

Major capital investments in large-scale drainage and land reclamation, irrigation and land consolidation mainly in the better-watered centre-north, new settlements in late sixteenth- and seventeenth-century southern Italy, and some experimentation with new crop rotations, all played a part in these improvements.[106] New, often more labour-intensive crops were introduced. The impact of maize on rural productivity and consumption patterns in northern Italy is comparable to that of the potato in nineteenth-century northern Europe. First recorded in the Veneto in the 1560s, maize spread rapidly after the turn of the century; by the 1650s it had replaced lesser cereals in Venetian peasants' cropping patterns and was becoming a staple of the urban and rural poor. Landlords

103. P. K. O'Brien and G. Toniolo, 'The poverty of Italy and the backwardness of its agriculture before 1914', in B. M. S. Campbell and M. Overton (eds), *Land, Labour and Livestock. Historical Studies in European Agricultural Productivity* (Manchester/New York, 1991), pp. 385–409.

104. M. Aymard, 'Mesures et inteprétations de la croissance. Rendements et productivité agricole dans l'Italie moderne', *Annales ESC*, 28 (1973), pp. 475–98; A. De Maddalena, 'Rural Europe 1500–1750', in C. Cipolla (ed.), *The Fontana Economic History of Europe*, vol. 2: *The Sixteenth and Seventeenth Centuries* (London/Glasgow, 1972), pp. 342–3. Higher seeding density, which tends to lower individual seed yields, could be compensated by higher output per unit of land. Cf. P. Iradiel, *Progreso agrario, desequilibrio social y agricultura de transición. La propiedad del Colegio de España en Bolonia (siglos XIV y XV)* (Bologna, 1978), pp. 199–201; Cattini, *I contadini*, p. 118 fig. 12. Evidence of seed yields is also restricted to wheat, whose output varies more than for lesser grains.

105. Iradiel, *Progreso agrario*, pp. 199–201; G. Felloni, 'Italy', in C. Wilson and G. Parker (eds), *An Introduction to the Sources of European Economic History* (London, 1977), pp. 10–11; Aymard, 'Mesures', p. 491. English data are summarized in Campbell and Overton, *Land, Labour and Livestock*, pp. 180, 273, 279, 302–3.

106. P. Malanima, 'L'economia italiana nel Seicento', in *Storia della società italiana, XI. La Controriforma e il Seicento* (Milan, 1989), pp. 176–81; S. Ciriacono, *Acque e agricoltura. Venezia, l'Olanda e la bonifica europea in età moderna* (Milan, 1994), chs 1–2; Delumeau, *Vita economica*, pp. 154–5; Poni, *Fossi e cavedagne*, pp. 100–5; Romano, *Tra due crisi*, pp. 57–9; Davies, 'Village-building'; Verga, 'Rapporti di produzione'.

resisted it initially, apparently because they feared that the new crop would lower the commercial value of their rents or impoverish the soil, and because it was exempted from customary tithes. Northern peasants instead saw maize as a boon, since the greater outlay in labour and fertilizer was rewarded with yields two to three times those of standard grains and could be achieved on marshy land unsuited to most other crops. For reasons still unexplained the crop spread far later to central and southern Italy.[107] Less spectacular but still significant instances of agricultural intensification included the diffusion of rice, of mulberry trees for raising silkworms, and of hemp, flax, vines, olive and fruit trees. Most of these investments were made directly by the peasantry, either by sharecroppers as a means of repaying past debts, or by fixed tenants and smallholders in response to changing patterns of demand.

Although agricultural intensification in the long run lowered labour productivity and rural standards of living, landlords responded to increased land productivity by reducing the average size of tenements, or alternatively kept the land deliberately fragmented like the Venetian buyers of the commons.[108] While this course of action made perfectly good sense in the context of abundant supplies of underemployed and cheap rural labour,[109] it also contradicts the claim that peasant smallholders were the main obstacle to pre-capitalist agricultural growth.[110] In most of Italy, both landlords and peasants responded to available opportunities by intensifying their use of labour, rather than by consolidating land and employing less labour as in eighteenth-century England. Ultimately, the Italian path to agricultural development led to a dead end, for which the only solution became the nineteenth and twentieth centuries' massive flows of migration. The reason for this failure, however, was neither a lack of developed markets nor a too entrenched peasantry, but the absence of sufficient sources of non-agricultural employment for the men and women who crowded the fields.

---

107. G. Coppola, *Il mais nell'economia agricola lombarda (dal secolo XVII all'Unità)* (Bologna, 1979); G. Levi, 'Innovazione tecnica e resistenza contadina: il mais nel Piemonte del Seicento', *Quaderni storici*, 14 (1979), pp. 1092–100; M. Fassina, 'L'introduzione della coltura del mais nelle campagne venete', *Società e storia*, 15 (1982), pp. 31–59.

108. Coppola, *Il mais*, pp. 108–9; Beltrami, *La penetrazione economica*, pp. 97, 137.

109. Because peasant farms have a higher output per hectare than capitalist farms. Cf. A. Sen, 'Peasants and dualism with or without surplus labour', in idem, *Resources, Values, and Development* (Oxford, 1985), pp. 57–9.

110. Above, n. 80.

Map 5.1 Western Germany, *c.* 1500. Principalities in bold are archbishoprics, those in italic are bishoprics, all other principalities are secular

CHAPTER FIVE

The Peasantries of Western Germany, 1300–1750

Thomas Robisheaux

Close observers of Germany, whether travellers, agrarian reformers, sociologists, journalists or writers, often comment upon the vast differences between western Germany and the lands of the German east. The divide reaches back in time to the Middle Ages, and persists, in many ways, well into the late twentieth century. The line runs south along the Elbe river, through Saxony, and along the Erzgebirge Mountains and heavily forested border between Bohemia and Bavaria. East of the Elbe towns were fewer, the nobility powerful, and the peasantry weak, unable to resist an erosion of its status and a slide into bondage, dependency and poverty. West of the Elbe towns were more numerous, the nobility weaker, and the peasantry far more secure in its hold on the land. By the eighteenth century the cornerstone of the rural economy in east-Elbian Germany was the large noble estate worked by coerced and dependent peasant labour. In west-Elbia, however, the foundation of rural life was the peasant household farm, worked by the family, servants and occasionally wage-labourers.

The persistence of a strong peasantry in western Germany is also striking from a comparative perspective. When Eberhard Weis studied the region he discovered that west German peasants enjoyed security, stability and protection to a greater degree than the peasantry in neighbouring France. The peasants of Bavaria, Westphalia and other regions held 90 per cent of the land in secure tenures, the seigneurial system was held in check, and the territorial state supported the peasantry against encroachments from the nobility and the bourgeoisie.[1] One is also struck by the way that local population regimes interacted with social, economic and political structures to produce stable agrarian societies that were, at the same time, amazingly adaptable to commodity production, commerce and wage labour without dislodging the peasantry from the land. Regions varied considerably from each other, of course, and similarities with other peasantries are evident. But the security, stability and long-term protection

---

1. Eberhard Weis, 'Ergebnisse eines Vergleichs der grundherrschaftlichen Strukturen Deutschlands und Frankreichs vom 13. bis zum Ausgang des 18. Jahrhunderts', *Vierteljahrschrift für Sozial und Wirtschaftsgeschichte*, 57 (1970), pp. 1–14.

of the peasantry in western Germany still stands out from a comparative European perspective. What made this development possible?

LAND, RESOURCES AND PRODUCTIVITY

Geography accounts for some of the distinctive advantages of western Germany's peasantries. The lands of western Germany were rich agricultural lands, and, especially along the river Rhine and in south-west Germany, could support relatively dense rural populations. The fertile soils of the North European plain stretch across the northern part of the region before opening into the plains of the Low Countries and northern France. The long course of the river Rhine, and the rivers and valleys that formed the Rhine basin, set the region apart from the Low Countries and the highland areas of Alsace and Lorraine in the west. To the east the river Elbe formed another boundary: west of it were the fertile soils of Westphalia and north-west Germany east of the river were the thinner soils of Brandenburg, Mecklenburg, Pomerania and eastern Saxony, lands that supported smaller populations. To the east and south mountains and the Upper Rhine separated the region from Bohemia, Tirol and Switzerland. The first regions of Germany cleared for cultivation in the Middle Ages were known as the old German lands. By the thirteenth century their peasant populations supported the densest concentrations of towns in the German Empire and provided colonists that settled new German lands east of the Elbe.

Within this large region contemporaries distinguished the more densely populated lands of Upper Germany (southern Germany) from the more thinly populated regions of Lower Germany (northern and north-western Germany). Highland regions – the Eifel, Hunsrück, the rough hill country of Hesse, Franconia and Thuringia – divided the north from the south. In the early modern period the advantages of land, climate and transportation lay largely in the south. The river Rhine not only provided rich lowland areas for agriculture but also stimulated trade, commerce and the growth of cities. The rivers Danube and Main did as well. Naturally small subregions varied considerably from each other. Franconia, Swabia and the Upper Rhine had denser rural populations than did the thinly settled highland areas of the Alps, the Black Forest, the Odenwald, the Frankenwald and the Bavarian Alps. Northern and north-western Germany along the Rhine, the Weser and the Elbe were also favourable for agriculture and trade. The highland regions of the interior – the Hunsrück, the Eifel, and the highland regions of the Hessian Wetterau and Vogelsberg, for example – had poorer soils and were more inaccessible to trade and communication.

Despite these regional variations, one type of village settlement predominated throughout the entire region: the compact village (see Map 5.2). Most of these villages were founded as agriculture and population expanded

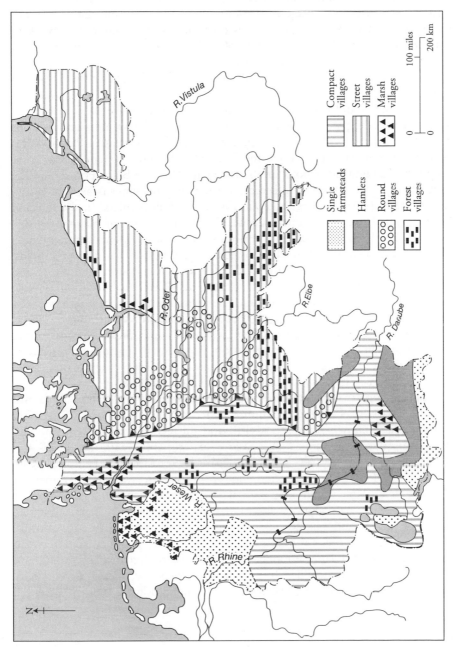

Map 5.2 Types of village settlement in Germany

between 1000 and 1300. Wilhelm Abel estimates that Germany had 171,000 villages in 1300. Of these about 46,000 were abandoned between 1300 and 1500 as population contracted in the wake of the Black Death and migrations to the cities.[2] Few new village settlements were added during the early modern period so that the rural population continued to live within a network of settlements that was largely fixed by 1500. When lands from abandoned villages were brought under the plough again in the late fifteenth and sixteenth centuries, the peasants who worked them resided in villages or towns farther away.[3]

Houses, barns and other buildings clustered at the centre of the compact village. Surrounding the village were the individual fields, common lands, woods and pastures. Large villages had a parish church in the centre. Planting was coordinated and regulated in a three-field crop rotation system. There were exceptions. In highland regions of the Bavarian Alps, the Black Forest, and the rugged hilly areas of Swabia and western Franconia peasant farms were sometimes more dispersed across the countryside in small hamlets. In the lowland plains of north-western Germany one also finds individual farmsteads dispersed across the landscape. The farmhouses and barns opened onto a courtyard and were surrounded by dependencies (small houses for workers), fields, orchards and woods. In the moors of East Friesland and along the Weser and Elbe one could find long finger-like settlements stretched out along a single lane. The fields disappeared out behind the farms to the village borders in the distance. For most peasants, however, everyday life revolved around the interactions created by the compact village with its shared public spaces, parish church, cooperative work routines, common management of land and resources, gossip at the well, the tavern, mill or kitchen. These daily interactions lent a strong communal character to peasant society and politics.[4]

Underpinning the village was a largely subsistence-oriented peasant economy. Like other parts of Europe, agriculture rested on the application of farming techniques well known since the twelfth and thirteenth centuries, and no significant improvements came until peasants experimented with new crops and crop-rotations in the mid- to late eighteenth century. Over the centuries peasants had developed seed varieties and crop rotation systems that maximized crop yields while minimizing the risk of losses. In general, this meant that peasants cultivated hardy and reliable cereal strains of spelt, rye, oats and barley instead of riskier and higher yield cereal varieties. In the sixteenth century seed–yield ratios for rye, a rough indicator of productivity, fluctuated between 1:3 and 1:6, harvests large enough for a farm to feed a peasant family and perhaps leave a small surplus.[5] In bad years surpluses vanished. Productivity also depended upon keeping livestock and draught animals, animals essential

2. Wilhelm Abel, *Geschichte der deutschen Landwirtschaft vom frühen Mittelalter bis zum 19. Jahrhundert* (*Deutsche Agrargeschichte*, vol. 2) (Stuttgart, 1962), p. 103.

3. Abel, *Geschichte der deutschen Landwirtschaft*, pp. 142–5.

4. For a brief introduction to the issues and the literature on the German peasant commune see Heide Wunder, *Die bäuerliche Gemeinde in Deutschland* (Göttingen, 1986).

5. B. H. Slicher van Bath, *Yield Ratios, 810–1820* (A. A. G. Bijdragen, 10) (Wageningen, 1963), p. 75.

not just for pulling ploughs but also for providing manure. Agriculture therefore depended on a fine balance of resources, and when the balance was upset, when animals were lost due to war, disease or crisis, productivity fell, and hunger and famine resulted.

One should not assume that peasants instinctively resisted agricultural innovation. Innovation depended, however, upon the development of market relationships, capital for investment, commercial instruments, stable prices, and an efficient infrastructure that made it possible to take economic risks. These conditions did not develop in most parts of western Germany before the eighteenth century, but in areas close to cities and market towns some commercially oriented agriculture was possible. In the late fourteenth and fifteenth centuries, as the prices for meat and dairy products rose, some peasants responded by turning fields or wastelands into pasture, and raised cattle. Other regions turned to the cultivation of specialized crops. In the Rhineland fruit orchards, market gardening and viticulture developed close to urban centres. The Upper Rhine became well known for its apples, cherries and vegetables. Viticulture spread, becoming an integral part of peasant production all along the Rhine, Alsace, the Neckar and Main valleys, and even in some places further north. As textile production spread in parts of southern and central Germany flax became an important cash crop. Other specialized crops included rape, anise, safflower, and hops for the expanding brewing industry. Around the large Rhenish cities peasants adopted fertilizing and crop rotation systems pioneered in the Low Countries and an intensive market-gardening economy developed. In some parts of north-western Germany seed–yield ratios rose to 1:6 and even 1:8 by the eighteenth century.[6] Farther from the centres of commerce, however, grain production continued to predominate. The equilibrium between population, land and technology could be broken through, in other words, but the breakthrough had less to do with inadequate technology than it did with capital investment, income distribution, market systems, crops and field systems.

The persistence of the common field system has sometimes been cited as an obstacle to agrarian development. To a certain extent it was. Common field systems had evolved over the course of centuries and by the late Middle Ages they were sustained by village custom and law. Village ordinances available after the fifteenth century laid out precisely how fields were to be worked, what crops were to be grown, where cattle were to graze, and how the woods or other communal resources were to be used. The scattering of fields also served to insure against loss. The farming of small strips of land scattered over the village lands may have been inefficient in some ways, but low yields or losses in one field might be balanced by gains in another. These old and tested field systems, finely attuned to local conditions and supported by custom, were the backbone of the village economy. Given the precarious balance of resources that the peasant economy depended upon, custom emphasized the management of resources for the common good and not use for private gain. Upstarts

6. Jan de Vries, *The Economy of Europe in an Age of Crisis, 1600–1750* (Cambridge, 1976), pp. 35–6.

who challenged this balance, who encroached on lands or challenged the allocation of resources, whether they were lords, outsiders or neighbours, could provoke resistance and even rebellion. At the heart of the Twelve Articles, the political programme of Upper Swabian peasants during the Peasants' War of 1525, peasants reasserted their demands for control over common lands, waters, meadows, fields and woods.[7] Behind the defence of communal resources was a prevailing moral idea of common use (*Gemeiner Nutz*): resources were to be used for the common good of the community, not for private gain.[8] And yet field systems could be adapted quickly to new commercial opportunities, as the villagers of the Württemberg village of Neckarhausen did in the eighteenth century.[9]

The west German peasant economies, while subsistence-oriented, were therefore responsive to local conditions, and must be understood within the context of regional economic development. The most market-oriented economies developed in regions with an expanding economic infrastructure around cities. In Upper Swabia ties with Augsburg, Ulm, Ravensburg and Memmingen and the textile trade led to peasant involvement in flax production and the putting-out system. Similarly complex town–country relationships developed in the mining areas of the Upper Palatinate and Saxony in the fifteenth and sixteenth centuries. Market relations within the Breisgau region around 1500 were also tied to commercial and political links with nearby Freiburg.[10] In Westphalia the peasant economy developed close ties with the North Atlantic colonial economies after 1650.[11] By the eighteenth century commercial ties were pervasive and complex, and peasants had adapted property exchanges, kinship, marriage and work routines in complex ways to this new commercial environment.

POPULATION

Regulating access to the land and scarce resources was a central feature of the peasant societies of west Germany. This was primarily achieved through a self-regulating population regime. Lack of detailed demographic data before 1650 makes it difficult to determine exactly when and how this system became

---

7. Peter Blickle, *The Revolution of 1525: The German Peasants' War from a New Perspective*, trans. Thomas A. Brady Jr and H. C. Erik Midelfort (Baltimore, MD, 1977), pp. 195–201.

8. See Winfried Schulze, 'Vom Gemeinnutz zum Eigennutz: Über den Normenwandel in der ständischen Gesellschaft der frühen Neuzeit', *Historische Zeitschrift*, 243 (1986), pp. 591–622.

9. David Sabean, *Property, Production, and Family in Neckarhausen, 1700–1870* (Cambridge Studies in Social and Cultural Anthropology, 73) (Cambridge, 1990), pp. 355–70.

10. Tom Scott, *Freiburg and the Breisgau: Town-Country Relations in the Age of Reformation and Peasants' War* (Oxford, 1986); and 'Economic conflict and co-operation on the Upper Rhine, 1450–1600', in E. I. Kouri and Tom Scott (eds), *Politics and Society in Reformation Europe: Essays for Sir Geoffrey Elton on his Sixty-Fifth Birthday* (London, 1987), pp. 210–31.

11. See Jürgen Schlumbohm, *Lebensläufe, Familien, Höfe: Die Bauern und Heuerleute des Osnabrückischen Kirchspiels Belm in proto-industrieller Zeit, 1650–1860* (Veröffentlichungen des Max-Planck-Instituts für Geschichte, 110) (Göttingen, 1994).

established in different regions, but indirect evidence suggests that it was in place in most regions by the end of the sixteenth century. The system primarily involved controls on marriage: an imposed period of dependent service for young people, a postponement of marriage beyond sexual maturity for most women and men, and requirements that couples have economic resources to establish a new household. When periodic mortality crises occurred, the local reserve of marriageable young people could marry, establish a household, and then begin to replace the losses through new births.[12]

The population of western Germany conformed to the broad pattern of population expansion, contraction and recovery now documented for most of western Europe in the early modern period. Population losses in central and southern Germany during the seventeenth century, however, tended to be larger than in most other parts of Europe. The replacement of these heavy losses was a slow process, and full recovery occurred only in the early eighteenth century. By 1750 areas of mixed agriculture and rural industry in the Rhineland, the Upper Rhine region, Württemberg and parts of central Germany were growing again, and fast becoming the most densely populated regions in the German lands.[13]

A period of long and sustained population growth began in the second and third quarters of the fifteenth century. The trend seems first to have begun in Upper Germany, and then followed in northern and central Germany. In the monastic lands of Upper Swabia indirect evidence of pressures on the land and communal resources appears by the 1450s.[14] Reports of poverty, landlessness and the splintering of landholdings might also have indicated a burgeoning population, although the rate of growth, population density, and the strains on local resources cannot be clearly determined.[15] By the 1540s and 1550s sustained population growth was also occurring in Saxony and Thuringia. Growth rates varied from region to region, averaging perhaps 0.7 per cent per year for the whole of the sixteenth century. In places like rural Hohenlohe population growth might have reached as much as 3 per cent per year.[16] After 1560, however, the rates of growth slowed and became more erratic as famines and epidemics became more common, but overall expansion continued up to the 1620s in most regions. Looking at rural population around 1600, densities increased as one moved from north to south.[17] By 1634 rural areas in

12. See Jürgen Schlumbohm, 'Sozialstruktur und Fortpflanzung bei der ländlichen Bevölkerung Deutschlands im 18. und 19. Jahrhundert', in V. Eckart (ed.), *Fortpflanzung: Natur und Kultur im Wechselspiel* (Frankfurt am Main, 1992), pp. 322–46.

13. For a survey of German population in the early modern period and a discussion of the relevant demographic theories and literature, see Christian Pfister, *Bevölkerungsgeschichte und historische Demographie 1500–1800* (Munich, 1994), pp. 8–24, 73–81.

14. David W. Sabean, *Landbesitz und Gesellschaft am Vorabend des Bauernkriegs: eine Studie der sozialen Verhältnisse im südlichen Oberschwaben in den Jahren vor 1525* (Quellen und Forschungen zur Agrargeschichte, 26) (Stuttgart, 1972).

15. Blickle, *The Revolution of 1525*, pp. 76–8.

16. Thomas Robisheaux, *Rural Society and the Search for Order in Early Modern Germany* (Cambridge, 1989), pp. 70–1.

17. Fritz Koerner, 'Die Bevölkerungszahl und -dichte in Mitteleuropa zum Beginn der Neuzeit', *Forschungen und Fortschritte*, 33 (1959), pp. 325–31.

Württemberg and the western Black Forest had a population density of fifty per square kilometre, densities comparable to the heavily populated Netherlands and northern Italy.[18]

One of the central features of the demographic regime was the periodic mortality crisis. After 1560 crises came frequently, and probably with greater losses, than in the early sixteenth century. Crops failed repeatedly in Franconia between 1570 and 1576, and high death rates and begging were widely reported.[19] The 1590s were also a decade of crisis. Local populations recovered from these crises quickly, however, typically through an increase in marriages and births in the years following a crisis. In Upper Hesse, for example, the large numbers of deaths recorded in the parish registers for 1598 were followed by several years of increased numbers of marriages and baptisms.[20]

The onset of the Thirty Years War in 1618, and the famines, devastating epidemics of plague and other diseases, and the dislocations that came with them triggered catastrophic population losses in many regions during the 1620s, 1630s and 1640s. The upheavals and reversals varied considerably from region to region, however. Franconia, Hesse, Bavaria, the Rhineland-Palatinate and Württemberg, for example, lost between 30 and 50 per cent of their entire populations.[21] By contrast the population in the western Black Forest, Westphalia and the Rhineland remained relatively stable. Scholars generally agree that plague and other epidemic diseases account for the largest losses during the 1620s and 1630s.[22] What distinguishes the mortality crises of this period from sixteenth-century crises was their scale, and the failure of the recovery mechanisms to work in the customary ways. Hard-hit communities failed to make up losses quickly. In Hesse and Bavaria, where the mortality crises of the 1630s have been closely studied, unusually high numbers of infant and childhood mortality rates were reported, as well as far fewer marriages in the years following steep losses in the population. As a result, fewer births occurred following the crises than had been the case in the sixteenth century.[23] Recovery was delayed by a generation, and population did not return to its pre-war levels until the early eighteenth century. In regions close to the frontiers with France, the Mosel Valley, the Palatinate and Alsace, recovery was delayed even longer due to the French wars between the 1670s and 1690s. But in a region like Lower Saxony, which suffered few losses during the wars, recovery was already evident by the 1670s.[24] Migration also helped replace some population losses in Saxony, the

18. Pfister, *Bevölkerungsgeschichte und historische Demographie*, p. 13.

19. Rudolf Endres, 'Zur wirtschaftlichen und sozialen Lage Frankens vor dem Dreißigjährigen Krieg', *Jahrbuch für fränkische Landesforschung*, 28 (1968), p. 35.

20. John C. Theibault, *German Villages in Crisis: Rural Life in Hesse-Kassel and the Thirty Years War, 1580–1720* (Atlantic Highlands, NJ, 1995), pp. 109–10.

21. Günther Franz, *Der Dreißigjährige Krieg und das deutsche Volk: Untersuchungen zur Bevölkerungs- und Agrargeschichte* (Quellen und Forschungen zur Agrargeschichte, 7), 3rd edn (Stuttgart, 1962), pp. 42–7.

22. See Manfred Vasold, 'Die deutschen Bevölkerungsverluste während des Dreißigjährigen Krieges', *Zeitschrift für bayerische Landesgeschichte*, 56 (1993), pp. 147–60.

23. Theibault, *German Villages in Crisis*, pp. 166–74; and Rudolf Schlögl, *Bauern, Krieg und Staat: Oberbayerische Bauernwirtschaft und frühmoderner Staat im 17. Jahrhundert* (Veröffentlichungen des Max-Planck-Instituts für Geschichte, 89) (Göttingen, 1988), pp. 70–81.

24. Pfister, *Bevölkerungsgeschichte und historische Demographie*, p. 18.

Palatinate, Franconia and Württemberg. By the middle of the eighteenth century population was growing once again, and continued into the early nineteenth century.

The mechanism controlling population was a system of late marriage and related social controls on young people. These mechanisms were first introduced effectively in Germany's cities and towns in the late fifteenth and early sixteenth centuries, and then extended to the countryside. Through religious reforms, new state controls over marriage, and peasants' own efforts to control marriage and inheritance, effective sets of controls were gradually introduced. By the seventeenth century in Bavaria a young couple could marry only when an appropriate amount of wealth was committed to establish a new independent household. The result was a high age at first marriage. Women tended to marry in their mid-twenties, men even later.[25] In some regions the age at first marriage continued to climb into the eighteenth century. Because of high mortality rates second marriages were common, although widows commonly found it more difficult to remarry than did widowers. One other feature of this demographic regime was a low rate of illegitimate births. Several factors worked together to make this so: a late age of menses for women (between sixteen and eighteen years), and state and social controls over sexuality and reproduction. When state controls relaxed after the mid-eighteenth century, illegitimacy tended to rise.[26]

Religion and the catastrophic population losses of the seventeenth century also influenced local fertility and mortality rates. Mortality rates in west Germany were generally comparable to many parts of France, Spain and Italy: they were highest for infants and children. Up to 50 per cent of all children died before they reached the age of fifteen. These aggregate statistics, however, mask significant local variations. While studying the population history of two villages, Hesel in East Friesland and Gabelbach in Bavaria, Arthur Imhof discovered widely differing mortality and fertility rates at the local level. Infants in Hesel had a much higher survival rate than they did in Gabelbach. In Gabelbach the infant mortality rate was 34 per cent. In Hesel it was only 13 per cent. Pointing to Gabelbach's terrible population losses during the Thirty Years War, Imhof argues that the peasants of Gabelbach may have been traumatized, and parents consequently developed more tolerance of high infant mortality rates.[27] Hesel, in contrast, never experienced the trauma of catastrophic losses. Religious attitudes apparently contributed to different attitudes toward death as well. Imhof speculates that Protestantism might have taught parents to care more for their children, while Catholic beliefs and practices regarding infant death made it easier for Catholic parents to accept high infant mortality rates.[28] Mothers in Catholic Gabelbach nursed their children for only

25. John Knodel, *Demographic Behaviour in the Past: A Study of Fourteen German Village Populations in the Eighteenth and Nineteenth Centuries* (Cambridge Studies in Population, Economy and Society in Past Time, 6) (Cambridge, 1988), pp. 121–30.

26. Knodel, *Demographic Behaviour in the Past*, pp. 192–7.

27. Arthur E. Imhof, *Die verlorenen Welten: Alltagsbewältigung durch unsere Vorfahren – und weshalb wir uns heute so schwer damit tun . . .* (Munich, 1984), pp. 106–7.

28. Ibid., pp. 107–14, 159–69.

a year and they experienced shorter birth intervals than did mothers in Protestant Hesel. The longer nursing periods and longer birth intervals therefore contributed to higher survival rates of infants in Protestant Hesel.

Rural populations also experienced a great deal of mobility and migration, although the actual patterns are difficult to identify, let alone quantify, before the nineteenth century. Since the founding of towns in the Middle Ages, villages provided a steady stream of migrants to nearby towns and cities, and this pattern continued unabated into the early modern period. In the eighteenth century the towns of Brunswick and Wolfenbüttel drew up to two-thirds of their immigrants from villages within a six kilometre radius. Immigration fell off in direct proportion to the distance from the town.[29] Religious attitudes also shaped migration. The Catholic cities of Cologne and Koblenz attracted hardly any immigrants at all from the Protestant villages in their immediate vicinity. Instead immigration came from Catholic communities farther away. Religion also influenced the vast movements of refugees and settlers during and after the Thirty Years War. After 1650 Swiss and Austrian Protestants, for example, resettled Protestant Württemberg and parts of Franconia. Protestant peasants expelled from Catholic Bohemia resettled in Lutheran Saxony.

ECONOMY

Population movements were obviously related to changes in the agrarian economy. In 1935 Wilhelm Abel discovered that population and agriculture in medieval and early modern Germany moved in closely related cycles of advance and decline. The medieval cycle, he argued, began around 1000 and, after three centuries of almost uninterrupted advance, came to an end around 1350. After a decline between 1350 and 1450 the agrarian economy recovered, advanced throughout the sixteenth century, and reached a peak, depending on the region, during the second quarter of the seventeenth century. A serious reversal of the agrarian economy occurred during and after the Thirty Years War, but by the late seventeenth century a recovery and a new advance had begun. Before the eighteenth century the agrarian population and economy simply could not break through these Malthusian limits.[30]

The theory appears to account for the central feature of the early modern rural economy: the persistence of subsistence-oriented peasant agriculture. And yet changes in the peasant economy cannot be explained using a simple neo-Malthusian model of change. Regional and local economies were far too differentiated, the mixture of market- and subsistence-oriented agriculture far too complex, to be explained with monocausal theories of change. Population

29. Pfister, *Bevölkerungsgeschichte und historische Demographie*, pp. 45–6.

30. Wilhelm Abel, *Agrarkrisen und Agrarkonjunktur: Eine Geschichte der Land- und Ernährungswirtschaft Mitteleuropas seit dem hohen Mittelalter*, 2nd edn (Hamburg, 1966). The argument also informs his other major works, such as *Geschichte der deutschen Landwirtschaft*, and *Massenarmut und Hungerkrisen im vorindustriellen Europa: Versuch einer Synopsis* (Hamburg, 1974).

movements, recent studies have shown, were not the only driving mechanisms of the village economy. Other factors must also be considered: land tenure, the burden of taxes, rents and dues, relationships with the state, infrastructure, transportation, rural industry, proximity to urban markets, and class, household and family structures. Despite these debates over general explanations of agrarian change, case studies have consistently supported Abel's general finding for the early modern period: a broad agrarian advance in the sixteenth century followed by contraction and recovery in the seventeenth and eighteenth centuries.

Several factors made western Germany's peasantry well placed to benefit from the agrarian advance of the fifteenth century. First, population losses were never as severe in western Germany as they were in the east-Elbian German lands. The west could therefore recover and advance more quickly than the east. Peasantries in the western regions also benefited from close proximity to the centres of commerce in central and southern Germany. Upper Germany – especially the Upper Rhine region, Upper Swabia and Franconia – and the mining and commercial regions of Saxony and Thuringia were naturally positioned to benefit from the commercial expansion that centred on the cities of south Germany.

The development of heritable land tenure also gave west German peasants secure control over the land and its devolution. By the fifteenth century peasants were successfully contesting land tenure customs and laws that favoured landlords, systems in which land reverted to the lord after the death of the tenant. They were replaced by heritable land tenure. In Franconia the turning-point came around 1400.[31] In other lands the transition took place later, often after resistance, negotiations and sometimes rebellion. Direct control over the devolution of land gave peasants broader control over the products of the land, bolstered the peasant family as the central unit of agricultural production, and made property rights and inheritance the pivotal issues in peasant family life. Peasants made other gains at the expense of lords. Seigneurial rents and many dues became fixed, and servile relationships loosened, thereby making some seigneurial revenues less important as a source of income for lords in the early modern period. Lords tried to renew serfdom as a means of binding peasants to the land, and securing access to peasant resources, in south-west Germany during the fifteenth century, but these efforts eventually failed.[32] In addition, depopulation made land available for internal colonization, a dynamic process that made an expanding middling peasantry possible. Finally, peasants near towns and cities were favoured with the opportunity to produce specialized cash crops or to develop rural craft industries. All of these conditions combined to strengthen the middling peasantry and their role in agricultural and rural industrial production. Landlords may have continued to shape the economy through the collection of seigneurial rents, dues and services, but they would

31. Hildegard Weiss, 'Das Agrarwesen vom Spätmittelalter bis zum Ende des 18. Jahrhunderts', in Max Spindler (ed.), *Handbuch der Bayerischen Geschichte*, vol. 3: *Franken, Schwaben, Oberpfalz bis zum Ausgang des 18. Jahrhunderts* (Munich, 1971), pt 1, pp. 460–1.
32. Blickle, *The Revolution of 1525*, pp. 68–76; and Saarbrücker Arbeitsgruppe, 'Die spätmittelalterliche Leibeigenschaft in Oberschwaben', *Zeitschrift für Agrargeschichte und Agrarsoziologie*, 22 (1974), pp. 9–33.

never again play a central role in direct agricultural production in the German west.

The first phase of the agrarian expansion between 1450 and 1560 was linked directly to population growth. Population growth increased the demand for land and food, and this in turn increased prices for grain and other agricultural commodities. Peasants cleared land that had gone out of production after 1350 or transformed pastures back into fields. The best evidence for the beginning of this agrarian advance comes from southern Germany. A sizeable middling peasantry led the recovery, clearing new lands, repairing and enlarging old farms, employing labourers and producing surpluses of grain to feed the growing population. Communal pastures, woods and waters came under pressure, provoking disputes over access to these resources. In parts of Upper Swabia lords divided up common lands, settled new tenants on them and aggressively collected the new rents, dues, tithes and other services that they owed. Along the Upper Rhine market gardening and viticulture flourished. In the County of Hohenlohe more households appeared on the rent rolls in the decades after 1500, the most evident changes coming in the expansion of viticulture and the large number of small peasants devoted to winegrowing.[33] The picture for central and northern Germany is incomplete, but population growth and an agrarian advance were also general trends by 1550.[34] The rural economy often had close ties to mining in these regions. In the mining districts of Saxony and Thuringia peasants supplemented incomes from agriculture with work in the mines and in related transportation and service activities.[35] Because of population pressure and higher demands for food, grain prices, which had fallen steadily in the late fourteenth and early fifteenth centuries, levelled off in most cities by the second quarter of the century, and then began a steady advance. The price of grain rose slowly after 1500, then steeply in the 1520s and 1550s. By 1560 overall prices of agricultural products had increased – doubled or tripled in some cities compared to 1500.[36]

How to characterize the changes in regions of traditional subsistence agriculture is a difficult issue. Certainly no structural changes took place. Agricultural production remained an activity organized primarily by the peasant household. Seigneurial rents, dues and obligations remained largely unchanged, although in parts of southern Germany seigneurial burdens sparked unrest and rebellion. Some important changes did occur, however. First, new land was won and brought under the plough. Along the North Sea coast, in East Friesland and in the moors of north-west Germany, peasants used the technologies of the Dutch in erecting dykes and winning new land from the swamps and the sea. Abel estimates that about 40,000 hectares of new land were cleared for agriculture in this way in the sixteenth century.[37] In some parts of the northern

33. Robisheaux, *Rural Society and the Search for Order*, pp. 26–8.

34. Karlheinz Blaschke, *Bevölkerungsgeschichte von Sachsen bis zur industriellen Revolution* (Weimar, 1967), pp. 144–9.

35. Peter Kriedte, *Peasants, Landlords and Merchant Capitalists: Europe and the World Economy, 1500–1800* (Cambridge, 1980), pp. 36–8.

36. Abel, *Geschichte der deutschen Landwirtschaft*, pp. 168–71.

37. Abel, *Agrarkrisen*, p. 109.

Rhineland new techniques of intensive agriculture were introduced around cities, and improvements in productivity resulted. In similar ways industrial crops such as flax and hemp, and dye plants like woad, were more widely cultivated, signs both of the spread of the rural textile industry and also more complex commercial ties of peasants with the market economy. A similar trend towards deeper ties with the market economy accompanied the expansion of viticulture.[38] Because of these new opportunities for wage labour and cash income, and the new pressures to pay taxes in cash, the numbers of peasants with market-related activities grew substantially, making many more peasants subject to the ups and downs of the commercial economy.

A key feature of this agrarian advance was therefore the deepening dependency of peasant households on the market economy. The innovative production unit here was not the large consolidated farm, as it was in France or England, but the medium-sized peasant household. The stability of the land market and land tenure supported the peasantry in this regard, and would continue to do so until the agrarian reforms of the early nineteenth century. Most land continued to pass within the network of peasant kin.[39] When territorial states began to codify inheritance laws, transactions became more orderly and publicly scrutinized.[40] In some regions open markets in land began to appear in the sixteenth century, but they had a limited influence in shaping landholding patterns. In the northern Rhineland the trend went farther than anywhere else in Germany, but territorial lords and princes strongly resisted the trend and limited its spread.[41] Because of the legal restrictions on land, townsmen had few opportunities to acquire rural property at the expense of the peasantry. The seizure of Church lands by the state also failed to encourage the development of free markets in land since territorial princes tended to incorporate these properties into their own seigneurial holdings, thereby becoming the dominant seigneurial lords within their territories.

Inheritance customs therefore had decisive consequences on the shape of local peasant societies and economies. In regions where impartible inheritance prevailed, where farms were passed down intact from one generation to the next, a relatively wealthy peasant elite emerged. With grain prices rising, wages declining and seigneurial obligations fixed, these elites were well positioned to prosper during the sixteenth century. These village elites dominated many of the communities of north-western Germany, scattered parts of Hesse, Franconia, the Hohenlohe plain, the Black Forest and some parts of Bavaria. In regions of partible inheritance, however, the middling peasantries could not easily survive. As lands were divided, each generation of landholders held smaller and smaller plots of land. Smallholdings multiplied, and often outnumbered middling and

38. See Friedrich-Wilhelm Henning, *Handbuch der Wirtschafts- und Sozialgeschichte Deutschlands*, vol. 1: *Deutsche Wirtschafts- und Sozialgeschichte im Mittelalter und in der frühen Neuzeit* (Paderborn, 1991), pp. 670–706.

39. For a general survey of the distribution of different inheritance customs in Germany see Barthel Huppertz, *Räume und Schichten bäuerlicher Kulturformen in Deutschland: Ein Beitrag zur deutschen Bauerngeschichte* (Bonn, 1939).

40. David Sabean, *Power in the Blood: Popular Culture and Village Discourse in Early Modern Germany* (Cambridge, 1984), pp. 6–8.

41. Henning, *Handbuch*, pp. 691–2.

sizeable peasant farms by 1600.[42] In Württemberg and Franconia partible inheritance created a large population of impoverished smallholders.

Regardless of how peasants divided up the land, agrarian expansion slowed after 1560. While it continued in most areas into the early seventeenth century, signs of stagnation and crisis multiplied. The famines and epidemics of the 1570s were the worst of the sixteenth century. By the 1590s population growth had stalled in some regions. After 1600 crises became more serious, leading in some regions to a collapse in agricultural production, losses in population and a reversal of long-term secular trends. Why did these economic troubles mount after 1560? And why did some regions fare better than others? Most current answers to these questions focus on the strains within the rural economy as it failed to develop and the population continued to grow. Population was simply outstripping the economy's ability to sustain it. But was it?

A neo-Malthusian argument provides a plausible first answer to the question. Land was indeed in short supply after 1560. Villagers still brought new lands under cultivation, but they tended to be marginal lands where agricultural productivity was low. Reflecting the limits on productivity and mounting pressures on the food supplies, grain prices rose even faster than they had in the first half of the sixteenth century. Land rents skyrocketed. Peasant incomes fell as landlords reaped windfall profits. All of these problems, the argument goes, contributed to the worsening subsistence crises. In regions of traditional peasant agriculture these were ominous signs of an economy no longer able to meet the minimal needs of villagers.[43]

A simple neo-Malthusian view of the crises, however, has a number of shortcomings. The theory assumes that the subsistence crises of this period were caused by crises of production while, in fact, many of the crises originated in the distribution system. In regions with a more developed infrastructure the shortages of food were far less severe. The elaborate international grain trade that had developed in north-western Europe, for example, cushioned the north-western part of the Empire from serious famines and food shortages. The effect of market relationships was no less significant in the interior of Germany. Along the Upper Rhine many local village economies had become intricately tied together into a regional network of markets more elaborate than in the Middle Ages. Even as economic growth slowed, the villages of this region continued to diversify into small craft production; the more diversified rural economy cushioned them somewhat from the ups and downs of any single trade.[44]

Many regions were also no longer engaged simply in agricultural production. Rural industry had spread, and linked peasants to commercial and industrial cycles in subtle ways. In areas of rural industry the troubles of the late sixteenth

---

42. See the case study of two regions of north-western Germany by Lutz K. Berkner, 'Inheritance, land tenure and peasant family structure: a German regional comparison', in Jack Goody, Joan Thirsk and E. P. Thompson (eds), *Family and Inheritance: Rural Society in Western Europe, 1200–1800* (Cambridge, 1976), pp. 71–95.

43. Robisheaux, *Rural Society and the Search for Order*, pp. 153–67.

44. Scott, 'Economic conflict and co-operation on the Upper Rhine.'

century may therefore have reflected cyclical problems of commerce and manufacturing. In southern Germany the crises of the late sixteenth century were also signs of a stagnating textile industry as competition from other regions increased. Regions of rural industry were particularly vulnerable during subsistence crises.[45] In other words, many village economies depended on local artisan production on a much broader scale than the late Middle Ages. The economic troubles of these village economies often had as much to do with local commercial cycles as they did with the problems of traditional agriculture.

Interestingly, the crises of the 1570s, 1580s and 1590s could have been much worse than they in fact were. Why? German authorities were willing and able to distribute bread or grain in times of shortage, or to administer prices and regulate markets. These policies were often designed to head off public disorders or rebellion, but broader institutional protection of the poor and hungry often effectively countered local shortages of food.[46] These policies may have been self-serving, and they obviously failed to keep prices down in the long term, but they made subsistence crises less severe than they otherwise would have been.

The problems of the seventeenth century were different. By the middle third of the seventeenth century the agrarian advance had come to an end. Population, wages and prices reversed their sixteenth-century trends. In the wake of the population decline grain prices fell and wages rose. The origins of these reversals were complex, and have given rise to controversy and dispute. In general scholars now question simple explanations centring on the Thirty Years War. Did the war bring on the crises? Or did the roots of the crises lie in the social and economic changes of the sixteenth century? Signs of crisis mounted alarmingly between 1590 and 1620: slowed population growth, massive rural impoverishment, a mounting burden of taxes and peasant indebtedness, exhaustion of marginal soils, mounting mortality crises due to malnutrition and difficulties in distributing food supplies, and a stagnation in the south German urban economies. Given these problems, some scholars argue that had the war not intervened agrarian reform would have been unavoidable. The crises of the seventeenth century, in other words, may have postponed significant agrarian reform until the eighteenth century.[47]

While acknowledging the sixteenth-century roots of these seventeenth-century troubles, one cannot deny that the Thirty Years War itself made the crises far worse than they would otherwise have been. The movements of troops and battles were not the primary causes of the dislocations. The trigger for the collapse of agriculture was usually fiscal: crushing burdens of war taxes

45. For a challenging view about the relationship of the peasant economy and population in areas of rural industry see Peter Kriedte, Hans Medick and Jürgen Schlumbohm, *Industrialization before Industrialization: Rural Industry in the Genesis of Capitalism* (Cambridge, 1981); and their recent rethinking of their positions in 'Sozialgeschichte in der Erweiterung – Proto-Industrialisierung in der Verengung? Demographie, Sozialstruktur, moderne Hausindustrie: Eine Zwischenbilanz der Proto-Industrialisierungs-Forschung', *Geschichte und Gesellschaft*, 18 (1992), pp. 70–87, 231–55.

46. Heinrich Bechtel, *Wirtschaftsgeschichte Deutschlands vom Beginn des 16. bis zum Ende des 18. Jahrhunderts* (Munich, 1952), pp. 219–22; and Robisheaux, *Rural Society and the Search for Order*, pp. 167–73.

47. Schlögl, *Bauern, Krieg und Staat*, p. 367.

were imposed that drained away resources from the rural economy. Heavy population losses from the plague and other diseases then disrupted agricultural work and caused labour shortages. Regions experienced these dislocations to different degrees. North-west Germany, including Westphalia, Friesland, the northern Rhineland and Lower Saxony, experienced hardly any serious dislocations during the war. Elsewhere, however, in Hesse, the Rhineland Palatinate, Franconia, Württemberg and Bavaria the agrarian crises were wrenching.[48] These regions suffered burdens of taxes and other exactions that stripped peasant households of grain reserves, horses, oxen and other resources, driving most into poverty and heavy debt. In these regions thousands of peasants fled their villages, their ability to bear the burdens exhausted. In Hesse, for example, structural weaknesses in the agrarian economy combined with calamitous population losses and a crushing burden of taxes to bring on the most traumatic agrarian crisis in the region's history.[49]

After the war two very different periods of economic development can be distinguished from each other. Between 1650 and 1720 a slow recovery occurred. Many scholars see in this era a new paternalistic role for the territorial state in supporting the peasantry. Government policies protected the middling and large peasant households as a tax base for the state. A seigneurial reaction was thereby averted, and the peasantry stabilized precisely at the time that weakened peasantries in east-Elbian Germany were reduced in status by the nobility. The small north-west German principalities have been held up as models of this policy, but similar trends were evident in the policies of states in central and southern Germany as well.[50] With state protection also came regular taxation. The peasantry's difficulty in adjusting to this regular burden of state taxation hampered economic recovery. In Württemberg, for example, the transition from periodic state exactions to regular taxation pushed smallholders to engage in more commercial activities, adjustments that took decades to work through. Agriculture remained the mainstay of production in the villages, but large numbers of artisans and smallholders remained on the land and continued to combine small-scale subsistence agriculture with wage labour and craft production.[51] The entrance of peasants into broader participation in the market economy was evident almost everywhere in western Germany.[52]

By 1720 a second stage in the recovery cycle had begun. One can detect the signs not only of a broad agrarian advance but also widespread economic diversification. Agrarian prices recovered after 1720, rose steadily, and provided incentives for peasants to extend agricultural production. Land was put back into production that might otherwise have laid waste. Around 1750 new experiments with the techniques of intensive agriculture began.[53] Broader participation in market relationships and economic specialization accompanied this advance.

48. See Robisheaux, *Rural Society and the Search for Order*, pp. 201–26; and Schlögl, *Bauern, Krieg und Staat*.
49. Theibault, *German Villages in Crisis*, pp. 165–92.
50. For the general context of these state policies see Henning, *Handbuch*, pp. 786–92.
51. Sabean, *Power in the Blood*, pp. 8–12.
52. Robisheaux, *Rural Society and the Search for Order*, pp. 247–54.
53. See, for example, Alfred G. Straub, *Das badische Oberland im 18. Jahrhundert: Die Transformation einer bäuerlichen Gesellschaft vor der Industrialisierung* (Husum, 1977).

Württemberg once again illustrates the trend. After 1720 small commodity production spread widely, peasants producing a wide variety of manufactured goods and developing closer market relations with the numerous small towns of the duchy. Some villages specialized in particular types of craft production or even in one stage of the production process for a commodity. Property changed hands rapidly, responding to new strategies by families adapting to commercial changes. Work routines and even the circulation of material and capital goods changed. Once again agricultural holdings in partible regions fissured. The disjunctions in wealth were not as severe as in the sixteenth century, however, and almost all classes of peasants were involved in a variety of market relationships.[54] In north-western Germany market ties with the Atlantic economy reached far into the countryside, stimulating an even larger involvement in textile production than before. In areas near Osnabrück, for example, most households became involved in weaving for the market, although their involvement in manufacturing did not challenge the social structure of the region.[55]

SOCIETY

West German agrarian societies reflected the norms of a broader society dominated by the nobility and based on rank and status. In its simplest and most idealized expression, society was ordered into separate, corporately conceived Estates, in which the peasantry naturally ranked below the nobility and the clergy. These were hierarchical norms largely imposed from above, and enforced by law, but they also were woven into popular consciousness as well. Rank, status, hierarchy and honour guided not only the social behaviour of the nobility, the clergy and townspeople but also peasants as well. Despite the ups and downs of the rural economy, these norms remained intact throughout the early modern period. Only in the late eighteenth century would the norms of a society of Estates begin to be challenged.

Stability and continuity should not be confused with rigidity and inflexibility, however. By the sixteenth century sections of the peasant population were surprisingly mobile and increasingly stratified, with broad and complex relations to market towns, elites and communities beyond the village. After 1450, as population grew and the economy became more complex, stratification by wealth and occupation increased. The divisions between the landed 'full peasant' (*Bauer*) and middling and poor smallholders widened into the early seventeenth century.[56] One of the striking trends by the middle of the sixteenth century was therefore the emergence of wealthy peasant elites, substantial

54. Sabean, *Property, Production, and Family in Neckarhausen, 1700–1870*.
55. Schlumbohm, *Lebensläufe, Familien, Höfe*.
56. Henning, *Handbuch*, pp. 701–4; and Willi A. Boelcke, 'Wandlungen der dörflichen Sozialstruktur während Mittelalter und Neuzeit', in Heinz Haushofer and Willi A. Boelcke (eds), *Wege und Forschungen der Agrargeschichte* (Frankfurt am Main, 1967), pp. 80–103.

propertyholders, many of them producing for the market. They often dominated village politics, and sometimes developed close ties with elites in the state and Church. One reason for their emergence was strictly economic: the agrarian advance enabled substantial peasants to prosper when land became scarce and grain prices soared. These farmers, tenant farmers and small entrepreneurs worked farms large enough to produce surpluses for the market and thereby benefited from ties with a commercial and cultural world beyond the village. Many of these families intermarried, developing marriage strategies that circulated large farms within a virtually closed caste of families.[57] Within the village these householders held full rights within the village commune, and sat on the village assembly. Their numbers tended not to increase, but their dominance of village wealth and property was overwhelming.[58]

One cannot always discern how the polarization of wealth affected the tenor of social relationships in the village in the sixteenth century. At times the gaps in wealth and security created tensions. At other times they became the basis for patron–client relationships and stable relationships of dependency and loyalty. Middling peasant households, for example, exhibited complex behaviour by the late sixteenth century. Their relative numbers remained the same in 1600 as in 1500, but they declined as a percentage of the population as the numbers of cottagers, rural artisans and labourers steadily grew. The heads of these households sat on the village communal assembly, shared in common village resources, sometimes sold surpluses on the market in good years, and, in times of rural unrest, made common cause with peasant elites. Their lands, however, rarely provided sufficient reserves after a harvest or a famine, and they often supplemented their incomes through wage labour and craftwork. Often they became indebted to lords and creditors. Winegrowers in southwestern Germany, for example, were particularly vulnerable as export markets declined and wages fell.

The polarization of social life in the sixteenth century is more evident when one looks at the groups at the bottom of the social hierarchy: the smallholders, cottagers, labourers and the landless poor. In contrast to other parts of western Europe, no large landless rural proletariat emerged in the German west. Heritable land tenure made it possible for even impoverished peasants to cling to a few tiny strips of land. Still, by any measure, rural poverty grew substantially in the sixteenth century. These groups have always been difficult to study and defy easy categorization. They did not form a uniform class. Smallholders and cottagers might naturally be included in this group, but occupationally it could be extraordinarily diverse, and include winegrowers, cobblers, tailors, barrelmakers, potters and carpenters. Women were often disproportionately represented in this group. Upon the death of a husband, peasant women often lost income and status, and could become involved in struggles over the family's patrimony.[59]

57. Imhof, *Die verlorenen Welten*, pp. 151–4.
58. Robisheaux, *Rural Society and the Search for Order*, pp. 84–91.
59. Heide Wunder, *'Er is die Sonn', sie ist der Mond:' Frauen in der frühen Neuzeit* (Munich, 1992), pp. 51–6.

Village social relationships were complicated when groups and individuals became enmeshed within broader relationships of dependency with institutions, social groups and elites from beyond the village. The plight of the poor in the German County of Hohenlohe illustrates what was a problem common to many rural regions. Lacking the means to produce their own food, the poor found their fortunes fluctuating unpredictably as wages and prices went up and down. In times of food shortage they were the first to feel the disruptive effects of high prices for bread and grain and tried to mobilize local institutions or the government to protect them.[60] The spread of rural industry reinforced this dependency on the market economy. Poor relief and charity, while better organized by the late sixteenth century, tended to stigmatize the poor and accentuated social gaps within the village. Social polarization lessened following the population decline of the mid-seventeenth century, and, when growth occurred again in the eighteenth century, stability was maintained through social controls centred on the household.

The cornerstone of the peasant community was the household and family. In some regards west German peasant households shared features with the north-west European model of the household and marriage. Beginning in the fifteenth century, however, and accelerating with the Reformation and state reforms in the sixteenth century, the territorial state adopted laws and practices that both idealized the 'whole house' (das ganze Haus) as a domestic unit and established it as the basis of taxation. For these reasons the peasant household and family were at the centre of state efforts to discipline the rural population.[61] The breakup of most seigneurial estates worked directly by lords and the establishment of heritable land tenure in the fifteenth century also encouraged the state to focus its attentions on the peasant household. Not only was agricultural labour now being mobilized increasingly within the household and family, but kinship ties became the pathways by which peasant property was controlled and passed down. For peasants, too, the household and family had a primacy in that they structured gender roles and generational relationships. Property and emotion, and even identity, were inseparably linked to each other through the family and household.[62] The household and family were therefore not private institutions in the modern sense, but institutions subject to state and Church regulation for fiscal as well as for social and moral purposes.

Demographically speaking, west German peasant households shared the features of the north-west European domestic household. Its size was small: four to five individuals based primarily, although not exclusively, on nuclear families. Servants and other dependants were counted as part of the household. Household structures also played central roles in creating and reproducing social inequality. Cases from three different regions illustrate a range of possibilities.

60. Robisheaux, *Rural Society and the Search for Order*, pp. 153–62.

61. On the household and family in general see Richard van Dülmen, *Kultur und Alltag in der Frühen Neuzeit*, vol. 1: *Das Haus und seine Menschen 16.–18. Jahrhundert* (Munich, 1990); and the cogent arguments of Wunder, *'Er is die Sonn', sie ist der Mond'*, pp. 57–88.

62. See Hans Medick and David Warren Sabean (eds), *Interest and Emotion: Essays on the Study of Family and Kinship* (Cambridge, 1984).

In the Schwalm region of Hesse, household structures and marriage patterns separated villagers into three classes: a tiny elite of families holding large farms, and larger but separate classes of middling and poor families. The elite was strictly endogamous. One can trace out marriage strategies between these elite peasant families that took several generations to complete.[63] In north-western Germany a different type of social system developed involving the interdependence of large and small households. An elite of peasants controlled most of the land, and passed on these large farms to heirs who could not legally split them apart. Their households were huge: eight or ten or more individuals, including children, servants and other dependants. These households were closely linked in turn through ties of clientage to smaller nuclear households of smallholders and labourers living nearby. The interlocking relationship of these two types of households − one large and complex, the other small, simple and nuclear − reproduced social inequality in each generation, but in a way that also guaranteed social stability over time.[64] A third case from Württemberg shows that household and kin relations were not necessarily simpler in regions of small nuclear households and partible inheritance. In Neckarhausen kinship functioned in extremely complex and changeable ways to shape property relationships, labour and the circulation of material goods.[65]

In all of these cases marriage formed the central domestic bond, and between the sixteenth and eighteenth centuries peasant marriages were more tightly controlled and publicly regulated than in the Middle Ages. The Protestant Reformation provided one impetus in this direction. When territories embraced Protestantism, marriage was secularized, new marriage laws drawn up, and marriage disputes came under the jurisdiction of secular marriage courts.[66] In addition, property requirements had to be met before a couple could marry and set up a new household. These tight controls contributed to the demographic behaviour we have already discussed: a rising age at first marriage, enforced celibacy and domestic service for young men and women, and low illegitimacy rates.[67] Population pressure on property and inheritance provided another incentive for the state to regulate marriage. Inheritance laws were codified and by the eighteenth century inheritances and other property exchanges were subject to intrusive state laws and reviews. Legal instruments of exchange − wills, inheritance settlements and retirement contracts − became common. Gender relationships were judged according to the norm of the 'well ordered' household. Women should be married, and those who were not under the formal authority of a husband, father or master were easily suspected of 'disorderliness'.[68]

63. Imhof, *Die verlorenen Welten*, pp. 136−54.

64. Schlumbohm, *Lebensläufe, Familien, Höfe*, pp. 615−18.

65. Sabean, *Property, Production, and Family in Neckarhausen*.

66. For a recent general perspective see Joel Harrington, *Reordering Marriage and Society in Reformation Germany* (Cambridge, 1995).

67. Pfister, *Bevölkerungsgeschichte und historische Demographie*, pp. 24−32.

68. See especially Lyndal Roper, *The Holy Household: Women and Morals in Reformation Augsburg* (Oxford, 1989).

Even with this emphasis on structure and hierarchy in peasant society, mobility was an integral part of everyday life in the village. Migrations from the country-side to the city were well established since the Middle Ages, as we have seen, and helped towns to make up for the population losses due to surpluses of deaths over births. Most local migration involved young men and women seeking wage labour or domestic service.

As a consequence of local mobility, economic diversification and the growth of the state, peasant communities were often forced to interact with outsiders who took up residence in the village. Outsiders were distinguished in several different ways. Some of them – state and seigneurial officials, commercial middle-men and the clergy – tended to open the village to broader institutions of authority and the regional market economy. These groups derived authority, power and prestige from their relationships beyond the village, and adopted the classic role of the 'broker' between the little world of the peasants and the larger world of the town and the court. Their roles within and beyond the village were therefore complex and ambiguous. Shopkeepers, pedlars, millers, innkeepers and artisans connected the community with nearby towns and mar-kets, but they were also often blamed for unfair marketing practices, hoarding and high prices.[69] A village headman (a *Schultheiß* or *Grebe*) might exercise author-ity and responsibilities on behalf of the state or lord, but he generally came from the village itself and had ties of kinship, friendship and interest within the village. By the eighteenth century the balance in these relationships tipped decisively in favour of the state. After the Reformation the clergy were also looked upon as outsiders even though they played central roles in the religious lives of villagers. In Protestant Germany pastors tended to become a separate and self-reproducing caste. Parish pastors were university-educated and owed their appointments to the territorial Church. Rarely did they have local kin ties within the parish.

Many peasant women also went through phases of life as outsiders within the village, perhaps as a domestic servant or as a wife drawn from a nearby village. Acceptance into the family, the circle of village women and the broader community proceeded in stages, and failure to integrate often resulted in ostra-cism and conflict. Exclusion might occur in many ways, beginning with a break-down in gift-giving and exchanges of food, labour and gossip, and escalating, in extreme cases, to suspicions of witchcraft. The witch was, above all, an out-sider feared for her powers over food, children, animals, life and property.[70]

Small rural communities of Jews, protected by princes, also existed and they were set apart as outsiders on the basis of their religious faith and customs. In all of these cases outsiders served multiple functions: they subordinated the community to the state, the Church and the market, and tied it to other villages and even to other faiths. Peasants also used them to establish the boundaries of the local community.

69. Robisheaux, *Rural Society and the Search for Order*, pp. 162–7.
70. Wunder, *'Er is die Sonn', sie ist der Mond'*, pp. 191–203.

Peasant women were central in all of the social and economic changes of the early modern period. Domestic and public spaces in the village were marked out by gender with women gathering in kitchens, wells and the marketplace. Through their talk women frequently influenced the honour and reputation of individuals, and the degree of acceptance within the community. The importance of property and inheritance in peasant families also meant that a woman's dowry was essential in assuming proprietorship of a farm or establishing an independent household.[71] Where clear evidence has been turned up about property transactions, as in Neckarhausen, women appear as shrewd calculators and managers of property in their own and their families' interests. Customs varied greatly but in some areas women exercised considerable control over their dowries while married or assumed pivotal roles in disposing of property as widows. A widow's decisions about remarriage and the disposal of the patrimony directly affected the fortunes of everyone with a claim to an inheritance.[72] In areas where rural industry developed, women played a key part as wage-labourers, and accumulated money for their own dowries.[73] The concentration of property in the hands of village men, however, made women dependent on male kinsmen for much of their lives and they were therefore more vulnerable when it changed hands or the wealth was dissipated.

Women were also perceived as symbols of order and disorder. This was partly the result of the Reformation with its ideology about women as pious and obedient wives and the new state ideology of the household and marriage as cornerstones of public order. One example of this fact involves the growing number of prosecutions of women for illegitimacy, infanticide and witchcraft after 1560. In each of these categories women were singled out for discipline and punishment far more often than men. When these efforts to discipline village women overlapped or coincided with village customary beliefs and practices – as they did with charivaris – the result was less tolerance for disorderly women. Groups of women gathered on occasion at a spinning bee or during the lying-in following childbirth. Campaigns to close down spinning bees occurred repeatedly during the early modern period, the authorities fearing the implications of women without male authority, but they largely failed.[74] A woman's speech was listened to carefully, both for the social information it communicated and as an indicator of honour and shame, obedience or disobedience.

LORDSHIP AND THE STATE

The persistence of a middling and smallholding peasantry, coupled with heritable land tenure, a weak lower nobility, and state protection of the peasantry,

---

71. Ibid., pp. 225–9.
72. Robisheaux, *Rural Society and the Search for Order*, pp. 133–6.
73. Merry Wiesner, *Women and Gender in Early Modern Europe* (Cambridge, 1993), pp. 82–114; and Wunder, *'Er is die Sonn', sie ist der Mond'*, pp. 89–117.
74. Ibid., pp. 26–9.

meant that west German peasants enjoyed more security and protection in their relationships with lords and the state than peasants in most other regions of Europe. Generalizing about state–lord–peasant relationships is hazardous, however, because authority was fragmented, and seigneurial jurisdictions frequently overlapped and conflicted. Regional and local variation was extreme in the Holy Roman Empire. To complicate the picture, territorial princes incorporated seigneurial institutions, rights and jurisdictions into the institutions of the state, thereby fusing the older powers of lordship with the new powers of the state. Friedrich Lütge has tried to classify these patterns into six regional patterns of lordship for Germany, but the only clear distinction that he draws is between east and west.[75] East of the Elbe lords established a *Gutswirtschaft*: large noble estates worked by peasants held in personal bondage to the lord. West of the Elbe lords retreated from direct cultivation of the land and established *Grundherrschaft*: land was leased out to peasants who enjoyed broad use rights over the land in return for payments of rents, dues and services.

Three general points must be kept in mind in studying lordship or *Herrschaft* in western Germany. First, *Herrschaft* expressed institutional and, in some cases, personal relationships of authority over specific people, lands, incomes and jurisdictions. Peasants might have one lord with rights over the land and its resources, another for personal bondage (serfdom), and a third for justice. Lordship could be exercised not only by the nobility, but also by princes, ecclesiastical institutions, towns and other corporations. Second, *Herrschaft* involved *reciprocal* relationships between peasants and their lords or state authorities. The lord's right to demand rents, dues, services and taxes was balanced by the peasant's right to protection (*Schutz und Schirm*). In this regard the burdens of lords and, to a surprising extent, those of the state as well, were subject to change, fluctuation and renegotiation, and are difficult to quantify. Authority was legitimate in peasants' eyes so long as it provided 'protection' and this meant that seigneurial and state institutions were often responsive to peasant demands and expectations. Finally, peasants shared in the formal and informal processes of domination. Simple dualistic models of lord–peasant relationships that focus only on the politics of domination and obedience, or of resistance, therefore obscure the important ways in which villagers were complicit in the institutions and relationships of authority.[76]

While these points were valid throughout the early modern period, one can detect significant changes beginning around 1550. Before this time seigneurialism was still dynamic and flexible, changing and adapting to new economic and social circumstances, and often provoking peasant resistance. After the middle decades of the sixteenth century, seigneurial institutions stabilized. Indeed they tended to become entrenched. The state then slowly intruded systematically into lord–peasant relationships. The process advanced at different rates in

75. Friedrich Lütge, *Geschichte der deutschen Agrarverfassung vom frühen Mittelalter bis zum 19. Jahrhundert* (*Deutsche Agrargeschichte*, 3) (Stuttgart, 1963), p. 101.

76. For a useful introduction to the concept see 'Herrschaft', in Otto Brunner, Werner Conze and Reinhart Koselleck (eds), *Geschichtliche Grundbegriffe: Historisches Lexikon zur politisch-sozialen Sprache in Deutschland* (Stuttgart, 1982), vol. 3, pp. 1–102.

different lands until, in the wake of the Thirty Years War, peasants were firmly subordinated to the burdens of the territorial state and its institutions, and seigneurialism declined.

Following the weakening of seigneurial institutions in the late fourteenth and early fifteenth century, a long period began in which lordship was 'territorialized', that is, lords and princes adjusted the institutions of lordship to concentrate their various authorities into progressively more compact territorial domains. The trend was never completed. Rights of dominion remained fragmented and overlapping in many areas, and were frequently disputed right down to the end of the Empire in 1806. Still, between 1450 and 1525 peasants felt the pressure of the efforts at consolidation, and the attempts to expand seigneurial incomes, rights and dues that went with it. In south-west Germany, a region of extreme political fragmentation, ecclesiastical and secular lords rounded off their lands, acquired judicial rights over their tenants (*Gerichtsherrschaft*), and raised, if possible, rents, dues and fines.[77] The most aggressive lords settled new tenants on peasant communal lands, engrossed village woods, pastures and waters, and even used serfdom to restrict peasant mobility and control property. Similar trends were at work in Franconia and Thuringia. In each case lords tried to improve the administration of their lands and increase incomes. In places where the early territorial state began to emerge, in Bavaria, Württemberg, Hesse, and the prince-bishoprics of Mainz, Würzburg and Bamberg, occasional taxes were levied.[78] All of these conditions contributed to the tensions between peasants and their lords that exploded in the Peasants' War of 1525.

After 1525 the attempts to undermine peasant rights were not renewed. Instead the dominant long-term tendency was for the territorial state to acquire progressively more access to peasant resources. This trend continued into the eighteenth century. One important way this occurred was through taxation. Over the course of the sixteenth century the peasantry was subject to periodic taxes, usually to support the Holy Roman Empire and the wars against the Turks. These fell unevenly across the Empire, the smaller patrimonial states being less able to protect themselves from the levies than the larger territorial states. By the 1590s taxes had became almost a yearly burden, and peasants frequently fell into arrears in meeting them.[79] Assessing the combined burden of feudal rents, dues and the new state taxes is exceedingly difficult, for the burden varied greatly from village to village, and fell unevenly across different strata of peasants. In Hohenlohe, for example, the peasant elite met their assessments well, but the middling peasantry, smallholders and rural poor often could not. The overall amounts were also not as important as the way that the levies were collected. Local officials often relaxed the collection efforts when

77. Blickle, *The Revolution of 1525*, pp. 44–9.

78. Ibid., pp. 29–44.

79. Winfried Schulze, *Deutsche Geschichte im 16. Jahrhundert 1500–1618* (Frankfurt am Main, 1987), pp. 220–2; and his detailed study of imperial taxes, *Reich und Türkengefahr im späten 16. Jahrhundert: Studien zu der politischen und gesellschaftlichen Auswirkungen einer äußeren Bedrohung* (Munich, 1978).

the peasant economy declined or resistance stiffened. The actual burden therefore fluctuated, depending on the harvests.[80]

Accompanying the state's growing fiscal demands were new powers to police peasant social, moral and religious behaviour. The Reformation and the formation of Germany's confessional states had profound social and political consequences in the countryside. When the rulers of Hesse and Württemberg introduced the Reformation, for example, the state secularized Church properties and acquired seigneurial authority over the peasants on these lands. Seigneurial institutions and incomes, including rents, tithes, dues, and fines imposed by seigneurial courts, were therefore incorporated into the institutions of the state. Princes who owed obedience only to the Holy Roman Empire also claimed the rights to administer higher justice in their territories. State courts also acquired an authority above the local seigneurial courts. Church jurisdictions over marriage and moral behaviour fell to the state as well. In Catholic regions, such as Bavaria, the Church remained prominent as a landlord, but the secular rulers were one of the largest landholders in the land, and for peasants the exactions and powers of the state merged almost seamlessly into those of the seigneur.[81] While most German states remained small in geographical size, the combination of all of these different authorities made state authority formidable and potentially overwhelming at the local level.

The territorial state, in other words, evolved as a set of institutions, rights and governing powers that overlay, but did not supplant, seigneurial institutions. While the state extended its authority in the sixteenth century, the nobility and the independent ecclesiastical corporations maintained themselves through their seigneurial rights over the land and by means of increasing incomes that came through the clearing of new allodial lands, revenues from forest management, and other rents and dues. In regions where the nobility and the Church remained strong, a balance was worked out between the prince and the Estates.[82]

In the middle decades of the seventeenth century, however, the scales tipped irrevocably in favour of the territorial state. The shift occurred for several reasons. The nobility in central and southern Germany had weakened, mostly as a consequence of debts incurred during the Thirty Years War. Many seigneurial lands were sold off or permanently alienated to the territorial state. Rural incomes also declined as a consequence of the long depression in agrarian prices. Noble incomes never fully recovered to their pre-war levels, and many nobles were forced to seek employment in the service of the states.[83] Finally, the territorial state firmly established regular taxation on peasant households at this time. The Thirty Years War had accelerated the process of extending state authority by forcing peasants to accept a regular burden of war taxes. Towards the end of the war the German states simply incorporated the institutional

---

80. Robisheaux, *Rural Society and the Search for Order*, pp. 176–86, 191–7.
81. See R. Po-Chia Hsia, *Social Discipline in the Reformation: Central Europe 1550–1750* (London, 1989).
82. Schulze, *Deutsche Geschichte im 16. Jahrhundert*, pp. 204–20; and Walter Achilles, *Landwirtschaft in der frühen Neuzeit* (Munich, 1991), pp. 35–41.
83. For the general trend see Henning, *Handbuch*, 807–17.

innovations developed to meet the urgent circumstances of the war. The territorial tax replaced the war tax. The development of the so-called 'peasant protection policies' (*Bauernschutzpolitik*) was therefore a fiscal necessity for the state.[84] Peasant farms provided the state with its tax base and were therefore protected by law. It was forbidden to break them up or alienate them to the nobility.

Some quantitative measurements of the combined burden of seigneurial rents and dues and state taxes on the peasantry are available for the eighteenth century, and they confirm the impression that the territorial state had superseded the lord in extracting resources from the peasantry. From among all the exactions on the peasantry in north-western Germany roughly 60 per cent went to the state. The nobility received only 30 per cent, and the rest fell to the Church and schools. How heavy was the burden on peasant income? F.-W. Henning calculates that after reductions for feudal rents in Brunswick, the state extracted between 23 and 26 per cent of the peasant income. In Hanover the burdens were comparable.[85]

PEASANT POLITICS

Next to the family and household and the seigneurie, the village commune assumed the most important role in governing the public life of west Germany's peasants. Indeed the lands of Switzerland and 'old Germany', especially southern and central Germany, developed the strongest peasant communal traditions in all of early modern Europe. For this reason the communal tradition stands at the centre of our understanding of peasant politics. What role did the commune play in organizing everyday life or resistance and rebellion? What political values did the commune instil in villagers?

By the late Middle Ages most villages had strong self-governing institutions. These institutions managed the rotation of crops, regulated agricultural work and governed access to communal lands and other resources. At the centre of the village's institutions was the communal assembly. Only full propertyholders had the right to sit in the assembly, and it was the assembly that drew up and enforced the ordinances, selected officials, and sometimes negotiated with lords or their stewards over seigneurial obligations.[86] Village courts punished peasants who violated communal ordinances. In south-west Germany many villages even tended and managed the local parish church. When seigneurial institutions weakened after 1350, communal institutions assumed even broader latitude in governing their internal affairs. Many villages extended their control over local resources as manors were broken up. Little used or contested lands then fell to the village commune. In a number of regions peasant communes

---

84. Achilles, *Landwirtschaft in der frühen Neuzeit*, pp. 39–40; and Franz, *Der Dreißigjährige Krieg*, pp. 91–4.
85. Achilles, *Landwirtschaft in der frühen Neuzeit*, p. 35.
86. Peter Blickle, *Deutsche Untertanen: Ein Widerspruch* (Munich, 1981).

successfully contested lords for control of pastures, fields, woods and streams between 1400 and 1500. With control over the land came the legal and jurisdictional rights over them.[87] Heritable land tenure bolstered this resurgence of communal authority by providing the village with a strong middling peasantry in firm control of the land.

The large number of peasant rebellions from this period can only be understood against this background of a widening communal movement. The geography of the revolts supports this interpretation. The revolts clustered in the regions with the strongest communal traditions: south-western Germany and Franconia.[88] North-western Germany, a region with different settlement patterns and weaker communal traditions, experienced far less unrest. Most of the revolts were directed against seigneurial lords. Peasants usually demanded that lords end serfdom and other restrictions on their mobility, and that labour services, arbitrary fines and judicial punishments be moderated as well. Many protested against the unjust acquisition of communal fields, pastures, woods and waters. In a representative case tenants of the Upper Swabian monastery of Ochsenhausen protested at the extension of serfdom and the land tenure system between 1496 and 1502. The conflict ended in a treaty that established heritable land tenure.[89]

The dynamics of these revolts were shaped by communal loyalties. In virtually every case the commune was the institution that mobilized peasants, presented grievances, and negotiated settlements or organized violent resistance. In the presentation of grievances one sees peasants' understanding of *Herrschaft* as a reciprocal relationship at work. Villagers never understood these demands as innovations or progressive reforms. Appeals were couched instead in the language of local or customary law. The rural disturbances associated with the Drummer of Niklashausen in Franconia had religious overtones, but this was the exception and not the rule in these revolts.[90] The result was that rebellions were restricted to small areas, i.e. to the area where the local law applied. The Bundschuh risings along the Upper Rhine in 1502 and 1513 and the Poor Conrad Rebellion in Württemberg in 1514 were the largest rebellions, but they did not spill over into neighbouring territories. These late medieval revolts represented part of the background for the German Peasants' War of 1525.

The Peasants' War stands out as certainly the largest, and arguably the most well organized mass peasant movement in modern European history. In light of recent research it is no longer convincing to view the revolt as a rebellion against the emerging early modern state or as a part of an 'early bourgeois revolution' in Germany.[91] Neither view satisfactorily explains the complexity of

---

87. See Wunder, *Die bäuerliche Gemeinde*, pp. 61–79.

88. Peter Blickle, 'Peasant revolts in the German Empire in the late Middle Ages', *Social History*, 4 (1979), pp. 223–39.

89. David Sabean, 'Probleme der deutschen Agrarverfassung zu Beginn des 16. Jahrhunderts: Oberschwaben als Beispiel', in Peter Blickle (ed.), *Revolte und Revolution in Europa: Referate und Protokolle des Internationalen Symposiums zur Erinnerung an den Bauernkrieg 1525* (Munich, 1975), pp. 132–50.

90. Richard Wunderli, *Peasant Fires: The Drummer of Niklashausen* (Bloomington, IN, 1992).

91. Two works that embodied these older views of the rebellion are: Günther Franz, *Der deutsche Bauernkrieg*, 12th edn (Darmstadt, 1984); and Adolf Laube, Max Steinmetz and Günter Vogler, *Illustrierte Geschichte der*

the regional revolts that made up the rebellion as they are understood today. While no consensus interpretation has emerged to replace these older views, the most challenging recent view has been put forward by Peter Blickle. Blickle locates the roots of the rebellion in an 'agrarian crisis' of the late Middle Ages. In his view the revolt was no ordinary peasant revolt but a 'revolution of the common man', that is, a political revolution – and not a blind peasant fury – that struck at the foundations of seigneurial and state authority.[92] Its leaders sought to replace the old order with a new federal, cooperative and communal political order. In contrast to earlier views Blickle also argues for the Peasants' War as an extension of the Reformation. Rebels overcame the limits of appeals to local and customary law by rallying around godly law as the basis of their programmes, thus invoking the powerful evangelical teachings of Luther and Zwingli and attempting to establish a communal Reformation at the local level.[93] In other words, peasants aimed not simply at combating seigneurial burdens but formulated political programmes that, had they been implemented, would have established a more egalitarian political, social and religious order. Aspects of Blickle's arguments remain unconvincing, but his synthesis points to the vitality of the peasant communal tradition, its widespread appeal, and its power to mobilize German peasants to achieve political, economic and religious goals.[94]

Did 1525 mark a watershed in lord–peasant relationships? The evidence that it did is not clear. The revolt certainly marked no obvious turning-point in the structures of authority: lordship remained a reciprocal relationship between lords and peasants, an exchange of loyalty and resources for protection and support. The legal status of peasants also remained unchanged; beyond the retributions immediately after the rebellion was put down no seigneurial re-action took hold. After 1525 the balance in agrarian relationships may have shifted slowly in favour of the territorial state, but peasants continued to expect protection and support from their lords and rulers.[95]

Lord–peasant relationships, however, were not as prone to break down and lead to rebellion after 1525. The epicentres of rural unrest in central Europe shifted away from south-west and central Germany to Switzerland, Austria and east-Elbian Germany. In a recent study of 125 peasant rebellions in the Old German Empire and Switzerland between 1300 and 1789, Peter Bierbauer notes

---

deutschen frühbürgerlichen Revolution (Berlin, 1974). The massive literature on the Peasants' War has only been partially catalogued. For bibliographical guides see Ulrich Thomas, *Bibliographie zum deutschen Bauernkrieg und seiner Zeit: Veröffentlichungen seit 1974* (Stuttgart, 1977); Peter Bierbauer, 'Kommentierte Auswahlbibliographie', in Horst Buszello, Peter Blickle and Rudolf Endres (eds), *Der deutsche Bauernkrieg* (Paderborn, 1991), pp. 353–95; and the recent bibliographical comments in Peter Blickle, *Die Revolution von 1525*, 3rd edn (Munich, 1993), pp. 298–320, 341–54. For a recent compilation of documents in English see Tom Scott and Bob Scribner (eds), *The German Peasants' War: A History in Documents* (Atlantic Highlands, NJ, 1991).

92. Blickle, *The Revolution of 1525*.

93. Peter Blickle, *Communal Reformation: The Quest for Salvation in Sixteenth-Century Germany*, trans. Thomas Dunlap (Atlantic Highlands, NJ, 1992).

94. For one such critical perspective see Tom Scott, 'The Peasants' War: a historiographical review', *Historical Journal*, 23 (1979), pp. 693–720, 953–74.

95. For long-term perspectives see Blickle, *Deutsche Untertanen*, pp. 112–36; and Wunder, *Die bäuerliche Gemeinde*, pp. 80–113.

that only ten took place in western Germany after 1525, most of them in south-western Germany.[96] Bavaria, for example, experienced several rebellions (the Haag rebellion in 1596, the Upper Bavarian Revolt of 1633–34, and the Bavarian Peasant Rising of 1705). Most of the other risings took place in the small territories and lordships in an arc of fragmented lands stretching from Upper Swabia across the Outer Austrian lands and the Black Forest to the Upper Rhine. The most protracted rebellions were the three Saltpetre Wars (1725–27, 1738 and 1743–45) which took place in the splintered County of Hauenstein in the Black Forest. No significant rebellions occurred in north-western Germany, the Rhineland and Franconia in this period.

The decline in the number of rebellions did not mean that peasants became more passive or that the reciprocal relationships between lords and peasants went into decline. Peasants continued to share in the practices and institutions of *Herrschaft* that were an integral part of the territorial political order. Several new patterns distinguish peasant politics in this era from the late Middle Ages and the Peasants' War. First, resistance to taxes and other exactions tended to become channelled into the courts and other legal institutions.[97] This trend followed on the successful establishment of the imperial court system, territorial state courts, and the state's efforts to integrate peasant households more firmly into the seigneurial and state hierarchy of authority. New tax registers and surveys of peasant property made it possible for state officials to collect revenues, record tax assessments, payments and debts, and to administer peasant petitions for protection and support. Peasants were drawn into these processes as individuals, families and special groups, or corporately as villages or districts.[98] The give-and-take of peasant politics therefore did not disappear after 1525: it became part of the everyday negotiation of obedience and protection. In parts of southern Germany peasants even participated in the government formally by sitting in territorial assemblies.[99] Many tensions that built up and led to rebellion before 1525 were now defused, negotiated and regulated in an intensive, even routinized and legalistic fashion by 1600.

In addition, territorial states made heads of households the cornerstones of public political and moral order. In effect they became extensions of state authority at the lowest level. This trend partly followed the Reformation with its emphasis on the 'whole house' as the cornerstone of a godly social order. Housefathers were idealized as the representatives of public order. In practical terms, peasant elders were given more legal authority over young people,

96. Peter Bierbauer, 'Die deutsche Forschung im europäischen Vergleich', in Peter Blickle, Peter Bierbauer and Claudia Ulbrich (eds), *Aufruhr und Empörung? Studien zum bäuerlichen Widerstand im Alten Reich* (Munich, 1980), pp. 1–68. Bierbauer's list, however, is far from complete.

97. See Winfried Schulze, 'Die veränderte Bedeutung sozialer Konflikte im 16. und 17. Jahrhundert', in Hans-Ulrich Wehler (ed.), *Der deutsche Bauernkrieg, 1524–26 (Geschichte und Gesellschaft*, Sonderheft 1) (Göttingen, 1975), pp. 277–302.

98. See Winfried Schulze, *Bäuerlicher Widerstand und feudale Herrschaft in der frühen Neuzeit* (Stuttgart/Bad Cannstatt, 1980), and the case of Hohenlohe in Robisheaux, *Rural Society and the Search for Order*, pp. 167–73, 194–7.

99. Peter Blickle, *Landschaften im Alten Reich: Die staatliche Funktion des gemeinen Mannes in Oberdeutschland* (Munich, 1973).

domestic servants and labourers. The patriarchal household established gendered norms of order for men and women.[100] In the small hierarchical world of the household wives were both subordinates to their husbands and co-rulers with them over children and servants. Heads of households, parents and village authorities were therefore made complicit with secular and spiritual authorities in policing sexual and marital behaviour within the village. Peasants did not necessarily resist these new moral laws because the diffusion of state authority and power often enabled peasants to turn social disciplining to their own purposes.[101] Close ties with district officials, for example, could secure favours in return, such as relief from taxes, loans, grain supplies during a famine, or help in a legal dispute. The steps by which the state was drawn into the domination of village affairs were by no means one-sided. By the middle decades of the seventeenth century a watershed was passed, however. After the Thirty Years War the village and the peasant household were more tightly subordinated to territorial state authority than in the sixteenth century.

Peasant rebellions, when they did break out, must be understood within a broad field of politics at the local level. One sees this principle at work in conflicts as seemingly different as the violent Bavarian peasant rebellion of 1632–34 and the protracted litigation which peasants pursued against their lords in the imperial courts of south-west Germany. What general features did resistance show after 1525? First, resistance was most often directed against the rising burden of taxes levied by the early modern state. While the fusion of seigneurial institutions with the territorial state meant that resistance could break out against labour services or other seigneurial burdens, the 'tax revolt' tended to supplant the revolt against seigneurial burdens typical of the late Middle Ages.[102] Second, passive resistance, bargaining and litigation assumed important roles in peasant political strategies. Rebellions broke out only when negotiation or litigation failed to defuse tensions; they were the last stage in a long and complicated process.[103] Third, conflicts tended to be channelled into courts, commissions of arbitration, and other legal institutions. Seventeenth- and eighteenth-century peasants were keenly aware of the laws, their legal rights and legal procedures open to them. An imperial decree of 1654 made the subjects of small territorial states responsible for imperial taxes, but it also guaranteed legal recourse within the imperial courts. Some disputes went on for decades and conflict became routine.[104] Peasants rarely appealed to religion

100. See Thomas Robisheaux, 'Peasants and pastors: rural youth control and the Reformation in Hohenlohe, 1540–1680', *Social History*, 6 (1981), pp. 281–300.

101. For several intriguing cases of peasants and the politics of domination see Sabean, *Power in the Blood*.

102. Schulze, *Bäuerlicher Widerstand*.

103. Ibid., pp. 86–114; and Peter Blickle, 'Auf dem Weg zu einem Modell der bäuerlichen Rebellion – Zusammenfassung', in Blickle, Bierbrauer and Ulbrich, *Aufruhr und Empörung?*, pp. 298–308.

104. See, for example, the general comments of Werner Troßbach, 'Bauernbewegungen in deutschen Kleinterritorien zwischen 1648 und 1789', in Winfried Schulze (ed.), *Aufstände, Revolten, Prozesse: Beiträge zu bäuerlichen Widerstandsbewegungen im frühneuzeitlichen Europa* (Geschichte und Gesellschaft, Bochumer Historische Studien, 27) (Stuttgart, 1983), pp. 234–5; and the cases he has studied in Hesse, *Bauernbewegungen im Wetterau-Vogelsberg-Gebiet, 1648–1806: Fallstudien zum bäuerlichen Widerstand im Alten Reich* (Quellen und Forschungen zur hessischen Geschichte, 52) (Darmstadt, 1985); and 'Widerstand als Normalfall: Bauernunruhen in der Grafschaft Sayn-Wittgenstein-Wittgenstein 1696–1806', *Westfälische Zeitschrift*, 135 (1985), pp. 25–111.

to justify their demands. The Peasants' War had been an exception. After the early Reformation, mainstream Protestantism lost its radicalizing potential among peasants.[105] Appeals were grounded in the language of local and territorial law and justice. Finally, the dynamics of peasant movements became more complex as village unity was increasingly difficult to sustain. The commune was still a source of solidarity, but movements splintered often into factions. The Saltpetre Wars, for example, deteriorated into a virtual civil war among the peasants of the Black Forest.[106]

Other types of communal disorders also occasionally broke the peace of the village. Some disturbances arose as part of an effort to enforce communal social and economic norms. The village was a moral community, and, on occasion, certain groups or members from the entire commune banded together to discipline neighbours who threatened those norms. Disorders in which villagers protested violations of marital and sexual norms were common. The charivari and the local witch-hunt – both of them more common after 1560 – shared in common the defence of communal norms about marriage and the proper role of women. Many witch prosecutions, for example, originated within the village, and involved villagers denouncing women who violated social norms or who were thought to use power in terrifying ways.[107] Witchcraft was, after all, women's work for evil purposes. In other disorders women themselves might band together to demonstrate loudly against a neighbour violating marital norms.[108] A last type of communal disorder involved protests over food shortages, unfair prices and marketing practices. This type of disturbance assumed the operation of a moral economy and became more important as market relationships broadened in the late sixteenth and seventeenth centuries.[109]

CONCLUSION

Surveying the peasantries of western Germany in the middle of the eighteenth century, one could hardly conclude that they were in decline. The demographic regime, patriarchal household and family structures, the economy, weakened seigneurial institutions and state protection combined at the village level to create strong, socially disciplined and commercially oriented peasantries. To be sure, the variations from region to region, and even from village to village, were extraordinary. Overall, however, the structures of authority and the legacy of village communalism interacted to place the peasantry in secure control of the

---

105. Klaus Gerteis, 'Regionale Bauernrevolten zwischen Bauernkrieg und französischer Revolution', *Zeitschrift für historische Forschung*, 6 (1979), pp. 37–62.
106. David Luebke, *His Majesty's Rebels: Communities, Factions and Rural Revolt in the Black Forest, 1725–1745* (Ithaca, NY, 1997).
107. Wunder, '*Er ist die Sonn', sie ist der Mond*', pp. 191–203.
108. Ibid., pp. 227–9.
109. Thomas Robisheaux, 'Peasant unrest and the moral economy in the German southwest, 1560–1620', *Archiv für Reformationsgeschichte*, 77 (1987), pp. 174–86.

land. A renewal of seigneurial authority would have been almost impossible by 1750.

Even more important, the growth of regional market economies had not dislodged large numbers of peasants from the land or created a large landless proletariat. English- or French-style agrarian capitalism had no footholds in western Germany. One finds instead mixtures of peasant capitalism, household commodity production, subsistence agriculture and rural industry within a broadening commercial economy that defy simple sociological models. Even where rural industry and craft production spread widely in the German country-side, and wage labour and commerce had become common, workers were still peasants farming small parcels of land. When Enlightenment reformers dis-cussed agricultural reform in western Germany they therefore placed their hopes not in the nobility or large estates worked by wage-labourers, but in the peasantry and the efficiently managed peasant farm. It was not the peasant who was endangered but the noble and clerical seigneur, and the history of agrarian reform in this part of Germany would bear that out in the early nineteenth century.

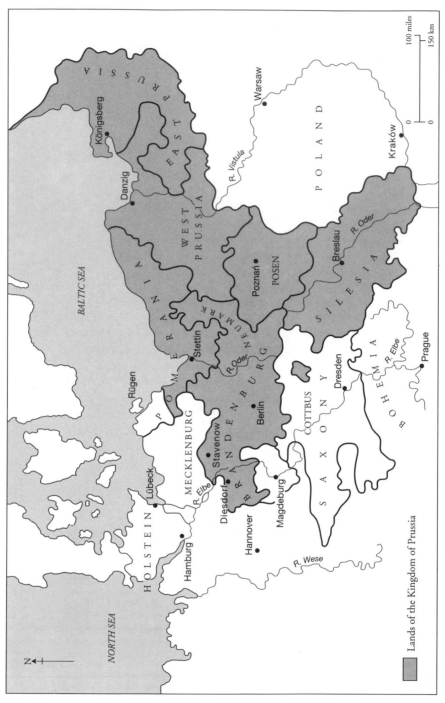

Map 6.1 The Prussian region in 1793

Village Life in East-Elbian Germany and Poland, 1400–1800: Subjection, Self-Defence, Survival

William W. Hagen

HISTORIOGRAPHICAL TRADITION: THE VIEW FROM THE MANOR HOUSE

The story that these pages examine figures in popular and scholarly tradition as one of coercion and injustice: the imposition upon the villagers of north-eastern Germany and the Polish lands, at about the time when Columbus first sailed, of a centuries-long subjection, even as their counterparts in western Europe shook off medieval bondage; and the transformation of their noble landlords from benevolent or benign neighbours into harsh or tyrannical masters.[1] Its reflection can be found in the verses of an anonymous Polish poet of the early seventeenth century, 'The Peasant's Lament Over the Nobility':

1. The notes accompanying this essay are not exhaustive. Literature in German and Polish is cited below. In English, see Hans Rosenberg, 'The rise of the Junkers in Brandenburg-Prussia, 1410–1653', *American Historical Review* [hereafter: *AHR*], 49 (1943), pp. 1–22, 228–42; F. L. Carsten, *The Origins of Prussia* (Oxford, 1954) and idem, *A History of the Prussian Junkers* (Aldershot, 1989); Edgar Melton, 'The Prussian Junkers, 1600–1786', in H. M. Scott (ed.), *The European Nobilities in the Seventeenth and Eighteenth Centuries*, vol. II: *Northern, Central, and Eastern Europe* (London, 1995), pp. 71–109; Robert I. Frost, 'The nobility of Poland-Lithuania, 1569–1795', ibid., pp. 183–222; Stefan Kieniewicz et al., *History of Poland* (Warsaw, 1968), chs 5–12; Stefan Kieniewicz, *The Emancipation of the Polish Peasantry* (Chicago, 1969); Andrzej Kaminski, 'Neo-serfdom in Poland-Lithuania', *Slavic Review*, 34 (1975), pp. 253–68; Leonid Żytkowicz, 'Trends of agrarian economy in Poland, Bohemia and Hungary from the middle of the fifteenth to the middle of the seventeenth century', in Antoni Mączak et al. (eds), *East-Central Europe in Transition: From the Fourteenth to the Seventeenth Century* (Cambridge, 1985), pp. 59–83; Jacek Kochanowicz, 'The Polish economy and the evolution of dependency', in Daniel Chirot (ed.), *The Origins of Economic Backwardness in Eastern Europe. Economics and Politics from the Middle Ages until the Early Twentieth Century* (Berkeley, CA, 1989), pp. 92–130; Jerome Blum, 'The rise of serfdom in eastern Europe', *AHR*, 42 (1957), pp. 807–36; Arcadius Kahan, 'Notes on serfdom in western and eastern Europe', *Journal of Economic History*, 33 (1973), pp. 86–99. For critiques of world-system and other neo-Marxist approaches to early modern developments in east-Elbian Europe, see Kochanowicz, 'Polish economy'; Jerzy Topolski, 'Continuity and discontinuity in the development of the feudal system in eastern Europe (Xth to XVIIth centuries)', *Journal of European Economic History*, 10 (1981), pp. 373–400; Edgar Melton, '*Gutsherrschaft* in East Elbian Germany and Livonia, 1500–1800: a critique of the model', *Central European History* [hereafter: *CEH*], 21 (1988), pp. 315–49; William W. Hagen, 'Capitalism and the countryside in early modern Europe: interpretations, models, debates', *Agricultural History*, 62 (1988), pp. 13–47. On the landlord–village relationship in Brandenburg, see idem, 'How mighty the Junkers? Peasant rents and

Our lords are a great woe to us,
they fleece us almost like sheep.
You can never sit in peace,
unless maybe you forget the bad things
over a mug of beer.

Pay your rents, the watchman's fees, the tribute –
chickens for using the meadows;
I don't know anymore what all we don't owe:
wheat, acorns, hops and nuts –
we stuff the sacks for the landlords.

Friend! Neighbour! They're bearing down harder,
every year they raise the labour services,
now we have to work in pairs.
But, of course, the fine lords still know how
to adorn themselves.

It's not enough that you work yourself into a sweat,
the bailiff is busy with his cane.
But just go to complain, his lordship will thunder at you:
'Get out, you thief, what are you snivelling about!'[2]

Framing the charge in the language of liberal modernity, Hans Rosenberg sternly wrote in 1978 that the east-Elbian German landlords gained their ends at the cost of 'the legal and social degradation, political emasculation, moral crippling, and destruction of the chances of self-determination of the subject villagers'.[3]

Nor did the abolition of the early modern manorial regime and the villagers' legal disabilities in the nineteenth century undo the damage. The aristocratic large estates, worked by subservient labourers, survived in both eastern Germany and Poland until the aftermath of the Second World War, when expropriation, plunder and Communist land reform finally destroyed them. The persistence into the twentieth century in both countries of an agrarian sector dominated by conservative large landowners figures pervasively in explanations of the failure of liberal democracy to take root there.

seigneurial profits in sixteenth-century Brandenburg', *Past and Present*, 108 (1985), pp. 80–116; 'Seventeenth-century crisis in Brandenburg: the Thirty Years' War, the destabilization of serfdom, and the rise of absolutism', *AHR*, 94 (1989), pp. 302–35; 'The Junkers' faithless servants: peasant insubordination and the breakdown of serfdom in Brandenburg-Prussia, 1763–1811', in Richard Evans and W. R. Lee (eds), *The German Peasantry. Conflict and Community in Rural Society from the Eighteenth to the Twentieth Centuries* (London, 1986), pp. 71–101; and 'Working for the Junker: the standard of living of manorial laborers in Brandenburg, 1584–1810', *Journal of Modern History*, 58 (1986), pp. 143–58.

2. 'Lament chłopski na pany,' quoted in Jerzy Topolski, 'Rozwój folwarku pańszczyźnianego (1453–1655)', in Władysław Rusiński (ed.), *Dzieje wsi wielkopolskiej* (Poznań, 1959), p. 47.

3. Hans Rosenberg, 'Die Ausprägung der Junkerherrschaft in Brandenburg-Preußen, 1410–1618', in idem, *Machteliten und Wirtschaftskonjunkturen. Studien zur neueren deutschen Sozial- und Wirtschaftsgeschichte* (Göttingen, 1978), p. 82. On Rosenberg's heavy impact on German historiography, see William W. Hagen, 'Descent of the *Sonderweg*: Hans Rosenberg's History of Old-Regime Prussia', *CEH*, 24 (1991), pp. 24–50.

This chapter will show that the regime of commercialized manorialism that rose to predominance in sixteenth-century Poland and east-Elbian Germany did indeed impose heavy burdens on its village subjects. Yet it does not advance historical knowledge, whether of early modern or modern Europe, to exaggerate the landlords' powers, as the historical literature has very strongly tended to do. One of the costs of this approach is to disable the villagers as historical subjects. Another is to reduce the social and political history of central Europe to the expression and institutional embodiment of aristocratic interest alone. The result is a one-eyed view.

It is striking that, while enormous scholarly effort has gone into researching the regime of early modern manorialism in Poland and east-Elbian Germany, the history of the villagers themselves remains largely unwritten. They figure as the landlords' labour force, paying feudal rents in fieldwork, tribute-grain and cash for their village land-tenures or house-leases. In recent years, historians have taken an interest in their efforts to resist seigneurial exploitation. But to an overwhelming degree their role in the historical literature is that of the legally subordinated, hard-pressed and largely passive economic subject – *homo oeconomicus subditus*.

Interpreting the Rise of the Manorial System in Early Modern East-Elbian Germany

A virtue of the literature is its broad view of the system of commercialized large-estate agriculture worked by subject villagers in east-Elbian central Europe – or, in shorthand, the east-Elbian manorial system – from its origins in the fifteenth century to its abolition in the nineteenth. This approach reached its first culmination in the influential work of Georg Friedrich Knapp, notably his paradigm-setting book of 1887, *The Peasant Emancipation and the Origin of the Rural Labourers in the Older Parts of Prussia.*[4] Like Max Weber and other late nineteenth-century scholars, Knapp sought to explain the strength in his day of the east-Elbian landlords and the misery of their agricultural labourers through a historical analysis of the large-estate system. Knapp's work, reinforced by his many able students, conveyed an interpretation subsequently embraced and refined in the standard literature, and familiarized in English through the works of Hans Rosenberg and F. L. Carsten. This approach, because of its critical stance toward the expansion of the landed nobility's powers over the villages, may be called the liberal critique. Since its interpretive predominance is still largely intact, a summary of its essential propositions will be useful, the more so as its empirical strength persists, except in certain respects that will be duly considered. The limitations of the liberal critique lie less in what it emphasizes than in what it screens out.

4. Georg Friedrich Knapp, *Die Bauernbefreiung und der Ursprung der Landarbeiter in den älteren Theilen Preußens*, 2 vols (Leipzig, 1887). On Knapp, and the entire tradition of German scholarship on noble landlordism in the east-Elbian lands, see the valuable work of Heinrich Kaak, *Die Gutsherrschaft. Theoriegeschichtliche Untersuchungen zum Agrarwesen im ostelbischen Raum* (Berlin, 1991).

Knapp and his followers argued that, in the medieval German colonization from the twelfth to the fourteenth century of the previously Slavic east-Elbian lands, the village farmers were settled (or, in the case of the pre-existing Slavic cultivators, resettled) on extremely good terms, as personally free, hereditary possessors of sizeable farms owing moderate, fixed rents to their overlords, whether princely, ecclesiastical or noble. But, as the political position of the German rulers in the east weakened, the nobility usurped, partly or wholly, their powers of taxation and jurisdiction over the villages. When, later still, the eastern nobility lost their functions as feudal warriors and, likewise, in consequence of the Protestant Reformation, their access to comfortable ecclesiastical livings, they turned to large-scale farming. In the sixteenth century, they widened their previously modest familial manor farms into broad estate demesnes, aiming to produce surpluses for sale on the urban markets of Europe where, because of the sixteenth-century 'price revolution', agricultural commodity values were rising rapidly.

The east-Elbian landlords gained the additional acreage they needed by more or less high-handed enclosure into their demesnes of lands belonging to their village subjects. The all-important labour needed to work the now-extensive domanial fields they obtained by imposing upon the surviving village farmers heavy, hitherto unknown, weekly labour-rents, carried out by the fullholding farmers with their own teams of horses or oxen, or rendered in manual labour by the villagers whose smaller holdings did not allow the maintenance of draught animals sufficient for work at the manor.

In this way, the landed nobility, who unselfconsciously bore the late medieval and Renaissance name of Junkers, ceased to be their village subjects' protective neighbours, but became their exploitative overlords instead. Attaining predominance in the assemblies of the Estates in their several principalities – in Schleswig-Holstein, Mecklenburg, Brandenburg, Pomerania, Silesia, Lusatia and the eastern Baltic duchy of Prussia – the nobility forced the fiscally weak rulers to ratify laws blocking the subject farmers' previous easy sale of their holdings and departure from the villages. Other laws anchored the weekly labour services the landlords were imposing on their subjects who, should they attempt to flee, could now be recovered by their masters and forcibly returned. The landlords strengthened the powers of their seigneurial courts, which heard in the first instance all cases involving their village subjects, by pressing the territorial princes to restrict or abolish the villagers' right of appeal against seigneurial decisions to the higher courts.

The east-Elbian rulers found approval of such legislation easier since they themselves were the masters of numerous large estates, in the form of the Crown lands, whose extent had mushroomed through the secularization of Church lands in the Protestant Reformation. Thus they too were, on a large scale, Junker landlords, with subject villages of their own. As for the nobility themselves, the Reformation added to their already robust powers patronage rights over the churches in their bailiwicks, ensuring that the villagers' pastors would keep their eyes cocked for signals from the manor house.

The rise of the manorial system spelled disaster for the towns of German east-Elbia, above all because the Junkers broke urban monopolies on beer and spirits production as well as on the grain trade. Instead, the nobility forced the products of their breweries and distilleries on their subject villages, while selling their export-destined grain surpluses directly to Baltic or western European wholesalers, cutting out the local middlemen. Town growth faltered, and with it the capacity to resist Junker political predominance, as well as the ability to absorb significant numbers of immigrants, whether legal or runaway, from the oppressed villages.

In seventeenth-century Brandenburg-Prussia, the devastation wrought by the Thirty Years War and other military crises raised a regime of militarized princely absolutism from the smoking ashes. The landlords bartered support for the new political order, which from their viewpoint had the defect of requiring payment by their village subjects of heavy new state taxes, in exchange for princely concession to them of more despotic seigneurial powers in the countryside. In other regions, such as Mecklenburg, where rulers failed to gain mastery over the noble Estates, the landlords availed themselves cost-free of similar expanded authority. Consequently, everywhere in German east-Elbia the late seventeenth and eighteenth centuries witnessed the high noon of Junker domination of the villages and the darkest night of their rural subjects' legal degradation, material impoverishment and cultural despair.

At this point, the Knapp school looked to the absolutist monarchy of Brandenburg-Prussia, for it seemed that only a powerful and efficient government could have enacted the reforms necessary to curb noble exploitation of the countryside. In his zeal to strengthen the fisc and expand the army, Frederick William 1 (r.1713–40) aimed to improve the countryman's lot, raising his productivity and so also his taxable potential. The enlightened autocracy of Frederick II (r 1740–86) took steps to abolish hereditary subjection in the villages, widen the rural commoners' access to the royal appellate courts, limit noble enclosure of village land, reduce labour services and register the villagers' manorial obligations in legally enforceable contracts, as well as to eliminate communal three-field agriculture by separation of manorial from village land and by adoption of fallow-free rotations on individualized landholdings of landlord and subject farmer alike.

Unlike his predecessors, who had hailed the Prussian monarchy's enlightened policies, Knapp found the Prussian absolutists' efforts more successful in concept than execution, principally because of the opposition of the corporate nobility and their spokesmen within the bureaucracy, if not – as later, more hard-boiled historians held – because the Hohenzollern rulers themselves esteemed the nobility's interests above those of the common people. Similarly, when after Napoleon's crushing defeat of Prussia in 1806 an era of state-initiated liberal restructuring began in earnest, the nobility's conservative opposition steered the all-important agrarian reform onto tracks which ensured their own survival on highly favourable terms. The villagers' legal disabilities disappeared, but the fullholders among them gained in freehold the family farms they cultivated only upon surrender of one-third or one-half of their arable to the landlords in compensation for the cessation of all feudal rent payments, including the well-hated labour services.

As for the small-scale village farmers, whose rent had been exacted in manual labour, in most cases their claims to freehold tenures in the course of the 'peasant emancipation' of 1807–16 were denied. The landlords were now free to evict them and enclose their holdings into the estate demesnes. Often, the evicted smallholders had no choice but to accept resettlement as full-time manorial workers on small, seigneurially owned cottage holdings. Thus they joined the ranks of the legally free rural labourers whose worsening poverty created the glaring social problem in the agrarian east that inspired Knapp and others to investigate the history of east-Elbian manorialism. For other small-holders who avoided eviction, the Revolution of 1848 brought them a belated right to freeholds against monetary payments funnelled by the state to the land-lords. While many exercised this right, and so entered alongside the previously emancipated largeholders the new class of free village farmers in nineteenth-century east-Elbia, the weightier outcome of the conservatively biased reforms was to expand the Junker estates greatly and create for their unhindered exploitation on the now free labour market a large class of landless workers.

Such, in broad strokes, is the liberal analysis of the rise of the Junker estates in German east-Elbia, which with varying accents remains today the dominant interpretation of the subject in west German and Anglo-American scholarship. Its principal flaw is its relegation of the history of the villagers themselves, and their efforts to ward off seigneurial and state-orchestrated onslaughts, to the invisible wings of the historical stage. Correspondingly, it greatly overestimates the Junkers' capacity to exercise their untrammelled will, while misinterpreting their aims and achievements at a number of points. It continues nevertheless to frame scholarly debate, in part through the analytical vocabulary it introduced into use, even when, as regularly occurs in the Anglo-American literature, its terminology is misunderstood or mistranslated.

The Knapp school emphasized a basic dualism in German agrarian his-tory and society. *West* (and south-west) of the Elbe river there had prevailed from the High Middle Ages a regime that Knapp and like-minded scholars termed *Grundherrschaft*. This concept translates into English as 'lordship over land', and was meant to convey the concept of seigneurial authority – princely, ecclesiastical, and especially noble – over subject villagers, establishing the basis for lordly claims to rents payable by the villagers. Since the exercise of such lordship did not entail the maintenance of large-scale seigneurial demesne farms, its economic benefits were confined to receipt of the villagers' rents in cash or kind. *Grundherrschaft* thus amounted to the feudal landlordism that predomin-ated in western Europe following the liquidation of early medieval manorialism after the eleventh century.[5]

The agrarian constitution *east* of the Elbe Knapp termed *Gutsherrschaft*, or 'manorial lordship' (from *Gut*, here meaning a large estate). This form of

5. An excellent recent survey of medieval developments is offered by Werner Rösener, *Peasants in the Middle Ages* (Urbana, IL, 1992 [German original: 1985]).

seigneurialism prompted the landlords to claim from their subjects, not only rents in cash and kind, but above all labour services, which were essential to the functioning of the demesne farms from which the lordships drew their principal incomes. The sway of such lordship encompassed the villages from which it drew labour services, and its very existence presupposed the establishment of a large-scale domanial economy run from the manor house. Typically *Gutsherrschaft* rested upon the lordship's possession also of judicial lordship (*Gerichtsherrschaft*), whether legally acquired or usurped from the feudal ruler. In those cases where manorial lordships succeeded in fastening strict personal serfdom (*Leibeigenschaft*) upon their subject villagers, the manorial lords (*Gutsherren*), apart from being simultaneously judicial lords (*Gerichtsherren*), were also lords disposing of the persons of their enserfed villagers (*Leibherren*). But in east-Elbia this last term was a rarely encountered import from the west. It was instead in scattered regions in west and south Germany that lordship over subjects' persons (*Leibherrschaft*) had survived as a separate form of authority, distinct from lordship over lands or judicial lordship.[6]

A third essential term in Knapp's vocabulary was *Gutswirtschaft*, not to be confused with *Gutsherrschaft*. It translates simply as 'manorial (or domanial) economy', and refers to agricultural production based on large demesne farms worked by compulsory labour services of subject villagers. *Gutswirtschaft* was the economic expression and objective of *Gutsherrschaft*. 'Manorial lordship' (*Gutsherrschaft*), rather than being the opposite of 'lordship over land' (*Grundherrschaft*), was instead a particular form of it. The former arose out of the latter, which – as seigneurialism – was an almost universal condition in medieval and early modern Europe, as the adage 'no land without a lord' (*nulle terre sans seigneur*) signalled.[7]

Manorial lordship was a much more powerful form of noble authority over subject villagers than a noble landlordism contenting itself with the levying of rents in cash or kind. Manorial lordship reduced the villages to appendages of the domanial economy. The manorial courts dominated the village communes, judging the individual villagers as economic subjects of the manor as well as in their private lives. Where personal serfdom prevailed, manorial lordship extended to full-scale control over the villagers' lands and farmsteads, and over their rights of marriage and inheritance as well.

In the Knapp school's eyes, the history of German east-Elbia from the late Middle Ages presented the unhappy spectacle of the rise of an ever more powerful manorial lordship. An originally benign *Grundherrschaft* yielded to a *Gutsherrschaft* in the service of a manorial economy or *Gutswirtschaft* to which the independence, dignity and prosperity of the village farmers and cottagers were subordinated and sacrificed. Nineteenth-century liberalism failed to right these

---

6. On these matters, see the classic works, developing the Knapp tradition, of Friedrich Lütge, *Geschichte der deutschen Agrarverfassung* (Stuttgart, 1963) and Günther Franz, *Geschichte des deutschen Bauernstandes* (Stuttgart, 1970), as well as Peter Blickle, *Deutsche Untertanen: Ein Widerspruch* (Munich, 1981).

7. Accordingly, as Kaak suggests, the alternative in *economic* terms to *Gutsherrschaft* would be *Zinsherrschaft*, or 'lordship based on money rents' (*Zins*), including also natural rents in grain or livestock. In the latter mode, the labour services central to 'manorial lordship' would figure only marginally or not at all. Kaak, *Gutsherrschaft*, pp. 429ff.

wrongs. Instead, the manorial economy survived in modern dress, with anti-democratic effects of the worst kind.

The villagers themselves, in this interpretation, figure primarily as victims. Many of them were evicted from their farms to make way for the enlarged seigneurial demesnes of the sixteenth century or, after the ravages of seventeenth-century war, never recovered their familial holdings, which the large estates engrossed or rented to new tenants on degraded legal terms. The landed villagers' unmarried children were forced into compulsory, ill-paid labour as servants on the manor or, if they lived as landless cottagers or lodgers in the villages, were subject to miserly wage statutes promulgated in the Junkers' interest. Often their house rents required unpaid manorial service, especially from women. Where, as in Brandenburg-Prussia, heavy state taxes converged with seigneurial rent, the few shreds of comfort the villagers had salvaged before the Thirty Years War vanished. The common folk trudged through the final century and a half of the manorial system in bone-grinding poverty, ever more of their children unable even to aspire to a life of threadbare self-sufficiency as members of landholding households, but condemned instead to the ranks of the ill-housed landless. The benevolence of individual estate-owners or state-demesne managers could at best diminish the pain of such an existence. Nor could villagers easily exchange it for the opportunities and risks of urban life. Release from seigneurial subjection, even if legally possible, might be costly, while the lack of village artisan workshops and schooling left most rural youth no alternative but to work in agriculture.

Since its formulation, the liberal critique has gained strength by the addition, pioneered by Wilhelm Abel, of a dimension of quantitative economic history. The development of the manorial system has been successfully embedded in a framework of fluctuating market opportunities, slowly evolving agrarian technology, and shifts in the interrelationships of land, labour and capital. Identification of the demographically driven long-range cycles in the western and central European pre-industrial economy established, in the concept of the 'late medieval crisis' of the fourteenth and fifteenth centuries, the socio-economic matrix out of which the east-Elbian manorial system emerged. This work discovered that, at their origins, the expanded noble demesne farms arose less through enclosure of settled village farmland than through absorption of village land abandoned through late medieval depopulation. Likewise, econometric analysis of the robust growth cycle of the 'long sixteenth century' (c.1480–1620) clarified the conditions under which the manorial system grew to thriving maturity before succumbing to the ravages of the 'crisis of the seventeenth century'.[8]

This work reinforced, rather than challenged, the Knapp school's narrative. The economic history literature has paid some attention to the village farmers in their capacity as market producers and manorial labourers, but it has not

8. See Wilhelm Abel, *Agrarkrisen und Agrarkonjunktur: Eine Geschichte der Land- und Ernährungswirtschaft Mitteleuropas seit dem hohen Mittelalter*, 3rd edn (Hamburg, 1978), and idem, *Die Wüstungen des ausgehenden Mittelalters* (Stuttgart, 1976). Cf. Peter Kriedte, *Spätfeudalismus und Handelskapital. Grundlinien der europäischen Wirtschaftsgeschichte vom 16. bis zum Ausgang des 18. Jahrhunderts* (Göttingen, 1980) [English translation 1983].

attempted to track their long-term rents or household standards of living. Such work perhaps appeared unpromising, given that the broad picture of the villagers' plight seemed already known, and that piecing together such patterns at the micro-level was arduous work from patchy sources.[9]

After 1949, an alternative to the liberal critique emerged in the massive Marxist-Leninist literature which scholars in the German Democratic Republic published during the forty years of its existence. Yet upon closer inspection it is clear that the effect of this work was primarily to reformulate the basic narrative of the Knapp school in the language of Marxism, and so to attempt to validate the Marxist analytical method as such, rather than to replace the dominant western interpretation. Friedrich Engels himself had, in the late nineteenth century, analysed the rise of the Junkers as the consequence in the sixteenth century of the successful imposition upon their village subjects of the 'second serfdom' – the first serfdom having been that of the early medieval western European manorial system that slowly withered away after the eleventh century. But in this, as in other respects, there was little the Marxist-Leninist history of east-Elbian manorialism could add to the story of seigneurial exploitation which the liberals had already told. Scholars in the GDR argued that the Junker economy needed to be understood as a component of the capitalist mode of production burgeoning within the 'late feudalism' of early modern Europe. They argued that absolutism was a political system reinforcing seigneurial exploitation of the villages with the power of a militarized state that, in most respects, was but an executive committee of the nobility. Accordingly, they took an acid view of the efforts of eighteenth-century enlightened absolutists and early nineteenth-century liberal reformers to 'emancipate' the subject villagers from the estate-owners' grasp. Yet, none of these perspectives was foreign to the Knapp school's analysis, especially in the more stringent, anti-Junker and anti-Hohenzollern forms it assumed after the First World War.

It is true that GDR scholars emphasized the class struggle between landlords and villagers as liberal historians rarely did. But, in the absence in early modern east-Elbian Germany of great 'peasant wars', such as that in south and west Germany of 1525, it remained only to speak of 'the lower forms of the class struggle', attaining at most the dimensions of local rent strikes and occasional attendant violence. Moreover, the fundamental importance to the constitution and maintenance of the feudal mode of production which Marx had assigned to 'extra-economic coercion', exerted by political elites against the subordinate classes and especially the tributary villagers, established a theoretical roadblock preventing GDR scholars from ascribing to such subaltern resistance any real power to better the lot of those engaging in it, or to bring about structural changes leading to the demise of the manorial system itself.

9. See Friedrich Wilhelm Henning, *Dienste und Abgaben der Bauern im 18. Jahrhundert* (Stuttgart, 1969), and the economic history literature cited in Hagen, 'Working for the Junker' and 'Capitalism and the countryside'. Cf. idem, 'Der bäuerliche Lebensstandard unter brandenburgischer Gutsherrschaft im 18. Jahrhundert. Die Dörfer der Herrschaft Stavenow in vergleichender Sicht', in Jan Peters (ed.), *Gutsherrschaft als soziales Modell. Vergleichende Betrachtungen zur Funktionsweise frühneuzeitlicher Agrargesellschaften* (Munich, 1995), pp. 179–96.

One consequence of this perspective was that, despite its partisanship for the labouring classes, GDR scholarship neglected the study of incomes and consumption standards among the subject villagers, just as it rarely ventured into the realm of family structure and popular culture. In the end, it produced, not a new interpretation of early modern east-Elbian manorialism, but a Marxist-Leninist version of the older story. Buttressed by much valuable empirical research, it reinforced the liberal stress on top-down processes initiated by or on behalf of the landed nobility at the expense of the villages and towns.[10]

Modelling Manorialism in Early Modern Poland

In no central or eastern European land did noble landlordism and village subjection hold more untrammelled sway than in the Polish Commonwealth, nor in the historical literature is any other such system more notorious for its abuses and impoverishing effects upon the common people. Because its militarized and absolutist neighbours carved up the decadent Polish state among themselves in the three partitions of 1772, 1793 and 1795, spectacularly wiping a vast and venerable aristocratic monarchy off the map, judgement of the manorial system has long been tied to the part it played in the demise of a once robust and expansive country. During the partition era (1795–1918), the vital importance to Polish nationalism of the nobility and noble-born intelligentsia lent the issue of the gentry-dominated pre-partition agrarian system a political significance more urgent still than the debates in Germany over the Junkers' past. And, since the mobilization of the villagers was crucial to the nationalist movement, the memory of their suffering under the old regime was an extremely delicate matter.

In the inter-war years, the social and economic historian Jan Rutkowski (1886–1949) developed an analysis of early modern Polish manorialism, contrasted with other central and eastern European agrarian systems, that acquired in Polish scholarship a paradigmatic status similar to the Knapp school's in Germany.[11] The German-Polish comparison was never far from Rutkowski's thoughts, particularly since German influences played a decisive part at several

---

10. Works of synthesis characteristic of GDR scholarship are Joachim Herrmann *et al.*, *Deutsche Geschichte in 10 Kapiteln* (Berlin, 1988), esp. ch. 4, and Günter Vogler and Klaus Vetter, *Preußen. Von den Anfängen bis zur Reichsgründung* (Berlin, 1979). On GDR historiography on east-Elbian agrarian society and economy, see Kaak, *Gutsherrschaft*, chs 5–6. The GDR literature on east-Elbian peasant resistance is of considerable empirical value. For references to it, as well as for a reconceptualization of the problem, see Jan Peters, 'Eigensinn und Widerstand im Alltag. Abwehrverhalten ostelbischer Bauern unter Refeudalisierungdruck', *Jahrbuch für Wirtschaftsgeschichte* [hereafter: *JbfWg*], (1991/2), pp. 85–103.

11. See Rutkowski's book-length essay of 1921, 'Poddaństwo włościan w XVIII wieku w Polsce i niektórych krajach Europy', in idem, *Wieś europejska późnego feudalizmu (XVI–XVIII w.)* (Warsaw, 1986), pp. 25–215. This is a collection, edited by Jerzy Topolski, of some of Rutkowski's principal articles. The essay here cited is an exceptionally knowledgeable comparative study of peasant subjection in eighteenth-century Poland, Germany and France. On Rutkowski's career and accomplishments, see Topolski's introduction, pp. 5–24, and his book, *O nowy model historii. Jan Rutkowski (1886–1949)* (Warsaw, 1986). See also Rutkowski's general economic history of Poland, *Historia gospodarcza Polski*, vol. I: *Czasy przedrozbiorowe*, 3rd edn (Poznań, 1947), a valuable work available in French translation as *Histoire économique de la Pologne avant les partages* (Paris, 1927). Important too is his substantial essay, 'Le régime agraire en Pologne au XVIIIe siècle', *Revue d'Histoire Économique et Sociale*, 14–15 (1926–27), pp. 473–505, 66–103.

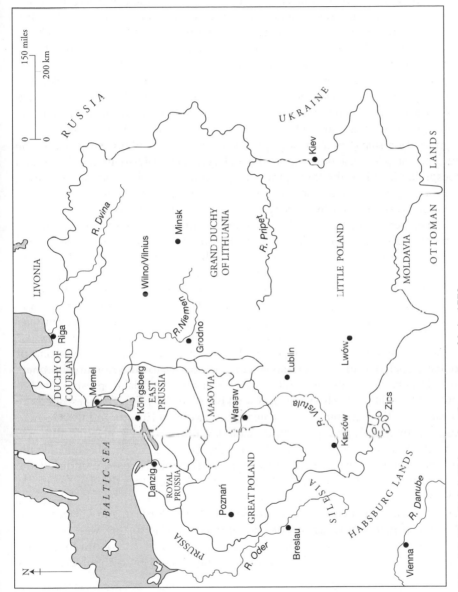

Map 6.2 The Polish-Lithuanian Commonwealth in 1772

points in Polish agrarian development. In the thirteenth and fourteenth centuries, the reception of the German law (*ius Theutonicus*) fundamentally restructured the Polish countryside. In part this refers to the penetration into the Polish lands of the German colonization movement, in which entirely new settlements, of Germans but also of Poles, were founded on the same good terms for village farmers as obtained further west in German east-Elbia. But in part it refers to the replacement by the Polish Crown, Church and nobility of pre-existing Polish Slavic legal and economic arrangements in the already settled countryside (and towns) with the basic institutions of medieval western Europe in their German forms: the village of hereditary farmers (*Erbpächter*), mainly fullholders (*Hufenbauern*) but including also landed cottagers (*Kossäten*, *Gärtner*); the village commune, based on the three-field system of arable cultivation, governed by a mayor (*Schulze*), mayoral court, and aldermen (*Schöffen*); the seigneurial lordship (*Grundherrschaft*), possessing demesne land for self-provisioning but confining its exactions upon the villagers primarily to money rents and dues in kind; and, in the towns, the self-governing and self-adjudicating council, representing the semi-autonomous merchant and artisan guilds.

Controversy, fuelled by scarcity of evidence, still envelops the question of the character of the pre-existing agrarian constitution which German-law settlement and resettlement eclipsed. It seems that prior village farm tenures had been precarious, whether because of Polish custom or because the reception in eleventh- and twelfth-century Poland of western European seigneurial immunities facilitated the enserfment of the villagers. In any case, the German-law tenures – entailing property ownership, freedom of movement and full access to the courts – were far superior, but did not everywhere prevail over the villagers' earlier disabilities, especially not in central and eastern Poland.[12]

Nevertheless, the post-German law, late medieval era in Poland was one of robust population growth and advancing prosperity for the nobility, burghers and villagers alike. This was still more the case since Poland, presumably because of its still relatively sparse and weakly urbanized population, escaped the torments of the bubonic plague which struck western Europe and the German lands in the mid-fourteenth century, with severe recurrences into the fifteenth century. Poland, by contrast, though sporadically singed by war, benefited in the fifteenth century from great victories over the Teutonic Knights, securing it the lands at the Vistula mouth with Danzig (Gdańsk) and other thriving towns. At the same time, Polish expansion south-eastwards into the Ukraine, begun a century earlier, opened new frontiers for noble landlordism and villagers who abandoned marginal lands or objectionable conditions further west.

Against this background, Rutkowski's explanation of the boom in the sixteenth century of expanded demesne farming worked by compulsory labour

12. On medieval Poland and the reception of German law, see Benedykt Zientara, Antoni Mączak *et al.*, *Dzieje gospodarcze Polski do roku 1939* (Warsaw, 1988), chs 2–3, and Zientara's '*Melioratio terrae*: the thirteenth-century breakthrough in Polish history', in J. F. Federowicz (ed.), *A Republic of Nobles. Studies in Polish History to 1864* (Cambridge, 1982), pp. 28–48. Cf. Piotr Gorecki, '*Viator* to *Ascriptitius*: rural economy, lordship, and the origins of serfdom in medieval Poland', *Slavic Review*, 42 (1983), pp. 14–35, and Richard C. Hoffmann, *Land, Liberties, and Lordship in a Late Medieval Countryside. Agrarian Structures and Change in the Duchy of Wrocław* (Philadelphia, 1989), parts 2–3.

retains its persuasiveness. The tendency of the older German literature, with its focus on 'manorial lordship' (*Gutsherrschaft*), was to emphasize the coercive political powers of the east-Elbian nobility in the rise of early modern manorialism, assigning to economic incentives a secondary – if not negligible – role. To Rutkowski, as to other Polish scholars after him, the crucial development was the *convergence* of increasingly strong seigneurial authority over the villages with access to new and highly profitable grain markets in western Europe (and, secondarily, to reinvigorated home markets). As Rutkowski showed, pointing to Sicily and the German North Sea coast, export opportunities in the absence of the villagers' legal subjection to seigneurial authority did not produce a system of manorialism such as emerged in east-Elbia. But, as a look at Russia revealed, neither did subjection of the villages produce this result in the absence of strong market incentives. The nobility needed to perceive their advantage in organizing large-scale demesne production to gain profitable access to foreign markets (as the Polish landlords did via Danzig), *and* to possess the authority to extract new and greatly increased labour services from their village subjects.[13]

The Polish nobility were even more successful than their counterparts in German east-Elbia in fastening their control, as the mightiest of the Estates of the realm, upon the princely power. By 1572 the kings of Poland had been reduced to elective status, while the relatively very numerous class of the nobility (*szlachta*) governed the land through a gentry parliament (*sejm*) whose class-bound republicanism eventually deadlocked the central government. Power devolved to the seigneurial bailiwick to a far greater extent even than in the aristocratic German quasi-republics of Schleswig-Holstein, Mecklenburg or Pomerania. Such a thorough-going 'manorial lordship' arose in Poland that Rutkowski and others saw small point in debating, as scholars interested in German agrarian dualism did, its relation to other types of lordship. Instead, the prime concept in the Polish literature became the 'system of manorialism with compulsory labour' (*system folwarczno-pańszczyzniany*, where *folwark* [from the German *Vorwerk*] denotes a demesne farm and *pańszczyzna* the unpaid manorial service of the subject villagers). Anchoring the system was peasant subjection, or *poddaństwo*, a term linguistically equivalent to the German *Untertänigkeit*, inasmuch as both derive from 'subject' (*poddany*, *Untertan* [Latin *subditus*]).

While in east-Elbian Germany gradations of subjection remained important, in Poland the term *poddaństwo* came by the eighteenth century at the latest to convey a meaning equivalent to English 'serfdom'; to its adjectival form the words 'free' (*wolny*) or 'loose' (*luźny*) were routinely opposed. Rutkowski observed that seigneurial authority over the villages grew so strong that monarchy-wide legislation concerning landlord–village relations and the villagers' subjection ceased early in the sixteenth century to define local conditions, if it ever had before. Polish manorialism developed as a highly decentralized manifestation of customary law, governed by seigneurial courts beyond which after 1518 the

---

13. See, apart from Rutkowski's works cited above, his 'Geneza ustroju folwarczno-pańszczyźnianego w Europie środkowej od końca średniowiecza', in idem, *Wieś europejska*, pp. 216–24.

subjects of the nobility could not appeal to royal adjudication and which until 1768 exercised in law, if rarely in practice, powers of capital punishment.[14]

By the eighteenth century, the Polish villagers' subjection was a hereditary personal attribute that extended beyond occupants of village farms to all rural groups, from unhoused workers to millers and estate officials (though legally free persons were found in all ranks). Extension of subjection to landless persons opened the way to sale of villagers apart from the landholdings they occupied, reducing them to near-slavery. This was a boundary sometimes crossed, although the mass of village subjects never experienced removal through sale to new lordships. For them, manorial lordship meant land tenure by indeterminate leasehold (*dzierżawa bezterminowa*), hereditary by custom but not by law and exposing them to the risk – doubtless sometimes realized – of being transferred at the manor's will from their paternal holding to a less desirable one. The manor hired the landless among them as workers or servants at low statutory wages. None could marry or otherwise leave the lordship without seigneurial permission, seemingly often denied. Unless they could claim free status, all were liable to legally unlimited demands for unpaid labour service, though in practice this varied with custom and with the capacity of households to maintain a labour surplus in excess of that needed for their own survival and reproduction.

Such was Polish serfdom, properly so called because it inhered in the manor's disposition over the persons of its subjects (*Leibeigenschaft*), as opposed to the liabilities entailed by occupancy of subject farms in those areas of east-Elbian Germany where milder forms of subjection prevailed. If we set aside for later discussion the ambiguities of the German situation, the question arises why the legal and tenurial rights of the Polish villagers should have deteriorated more drastically than those of their east-Elbian German counterparts. In both cases the starting point for the rise of early modern manorialism and its attendant village subjection was the situation defined by high medieval German-law settlement. This had conferred strong rights, not to say freedom itself, upon the rural common people.

To this question Rutkowski had no clear answer. Its resolution called for a more exact understanding of the step-by-step rise of the large estates than surviving records seemed to allow. But Rutkowski, like many other Polish scholars,

---

14. In the late eighteenth century, two-thirds of the subject villagers lived under the legal jurisdiction of the nobility, while the rest lived in roughly equal measure under the Church and the Crown. Rutkowski, 'Poddaństwo włościan', p. 60. In 1578 the *sąd referendarski* was established as a royal court of appeals from decisions of the manor-courts on the Crown estates, but governmental leasing of these estates to noble tenant-farmers, and the alienation into the hands of the magnate nobility of provincial governorships and the Crown lands attached to them, greatly weakened the royal government's ability to protect its village subjects. Ibid., p. 160. See also Andrzej Wyczański, *Wieś polskiego odrodzenia* (Warsaw, 1969), p. 173. On the villagers' legal status in general, see also Zientara and Mączak, *Dzieje gospodarcze*, pp. 136ff., 154ff.; Andrzej Wyczański, *Polska Rzeczą Pospolitą Szlachecką*, 2nd edn (Warsaw, 1991), pp. 39ff.; Edward Trzyna, 'Wtorne Poddaństwo', in Stefan Inglot *et al.*, *Historia chłopów polskich*, vol. I: *Do upadku rzeczypospolitej szlacheckiej* (n. p., 1970), pp. 309ff. The last important monarchy-wide legislation concerning the terms of peasant subjection in Poland to which the literature customarily refers were the decrees of the diets of Bydgoszcz and Toruń in 1520–21, fixing as the minimum level of the landed villagers' weekly manorial service, in the absence of higher local norms, of one day weekly. Wyczański, *Wieś*, p. 147.

was more interested in the manorial system's connection to the eighteenth-century partitions. Here the bloodlettings Poland repeatedly suffered between the mid-seventeenth century and 1772 must be remembered. This succession of disasters registered the defeat of Renaissance Poland's answer, in the form of the decentralized, cavalry-armed, gentry-dominated parliamentary monarchy, to the challenge of early modern state-building. It likewise witnessed the impoverishment, alongside the repeatedly plundered common people in town and village alike, of the lesser nobility, while the magnate aristocracy, long a powerful presence in the country, rose during the seventeenth century to primacy.

In putting their ravaged estates back into operation, the Polish nobility frequently replaced vanished fullholding peasants with halfholders or cottagers, sparing themselves the cost of rebuilding and equipping the larger farms with livestock and other working capital. Often they took advantage of the desertion of their villages to seize the best of their vanished subjects' farmland for themselves. The result, emphasized by Rutkowski, was an eighteenth-century village farmer class with smaller holdings on poorer soils than before 1648, but with labour rents driven up by the impossibility of fully repopulating the Polish villages before the late eighteenth century. The Polish towns, deprived of the custom of once robust villages, fell into deep decadence. Thus was the tax-base of the state perforated with weakness.

How, in such extremity, could the reform-minded nobility rejuvenate the Commonwealth and ward off the partitions? Rutkowski, like others unwilling to succumb to historical inevitabilism, thought that the impediment to reform lay in the deficient will of the self-satisfied conservative aristocracy, corrupted by foreign blandishments and bribes. In itself, the existence of the manorial system could not explain Poland's misfortunes, for clearly variations of the same system underlay the absolutist musculature of the country's militarized and bureaucratized tormentors.[15]

After 1949, Polish Marxist historiography received Rutkowski's legacy respectfully. His concept of Polish manorialism, and of the declining welfare of the subject villagers under its sway, found confirmation and deepening in the massive scholarship devoted after the war to pre-partition Poland. It was consistent with Polish tradition (and with Lenin's emphasis on intra-class polarization) to treat the rise of the magnate aristocracy, at the gentry's and poor nobility's expense, as the crucial social and political dynamic of the old Commonwealth. But the impoverishment of the villagers, and the long decline after the 1640s of grain exports to the west, taken together with the dissolution of the state amid foreign conquest, challengingly posed the question of the 'transition from feudalism to capitalism' in its Polish form.[16]

15. Rutkowski, 'Poddaństwo włościan', pp. 191ff.; idem, 'Gospodarcze podłoże rozbiorów Polski', in *Wieś europejska*, pp. 375–86.

16. In the synthetic literature on early modern Polish rural society, the closest approximation to the Marxist-Leninist paradigm is offered in the above-cited compendious works, not without their merits, edited by Inglot, *Historia chłopów polskich*, and (for a regional example) by Rusiński, *Dzieje wsi wielkopolskiej*. For a recent critique of interpretations stressing the triumph of the magnate class, see Frost's above-cited 'Nobility of Poland-Lithuania'.

Undoubtedly the most interesting, though not the most orthodox response came from the economic historian Witold Kula, whose *Economic Theory of the Feudal System: Towards a Model of the Polish Economy 1500–1800* (1962) presented an analysis of Polish manorialism driven by export opportunities offering Polish large landowners uniquely favourable terms of trade across a period of 300 years. The *szlachta* landlords cashed in on such opportunities through piece-meal incorporation of the villagers' land into their demesnes and a corresponding rising exploitation of unpaid village labour. The de-urbanizing effects of this process meant that, when after 1772 the noble exporters gradually lost forever their western markets, there was no home base from which capitalist development through agricultural modernization and industrialization could proceed. In nineteenth-century Poland, once the partition governments had imposed 'peasant emancipation', capitalist estate agriculture developed thanks principally to the abundant cheap labour of the liberated landless or smallhold-ing villagers, while industrialization depended largely on infusions of non-Polish capital. This outcome hardly looked like the robust triumph of the bourgeoisie.[17]

Kula's emphasis on the manorial system's dependence on export markets provoked challenges. It was objected that in the sixteenth century domestic demand was equally important, while after 1750 population recovery helped revitalize home markets and so opened the road to domestic growth, as well as to the liquidation of village subjection, which an abundant labour supply rendered superfluous. Many villagers in the sixteenth century, and again in the eighteenth, possessed a greater degree of personal freedom and material well-being than the Rutkowski–Kula script allowed. Still, no one rejected the fun-damental story of the villagers' long-term degradation, especially since civil war and foreign aggression unquestionably rained great destruction on the land after 1648.[18]

THE VIEW FROM THE VILLAGE

German and Polish historiography on early modern manorialism have much in common. Both concentrate on the landed nobility. Princely power figures as a

---

17. Witold Kula, *An Economic Theory of the Feudal System. Towards a Model of the Polish Economy 1500–1800* (London, 1976 [Polish original: 1962]). On Kula and his legacy, see Jacek Kochanowicz, 'Czy tylko historia gospodarcza? Jubileusz Witolda Kuli', *Kronika Warszawy*, 1 (1985), pp. 129–46, and idem, 'La Théorie Économique . . . Après Vingt Ans', *Acta Poloniae Historica*, 56 (1987), pp. 197–211. Kochanowicz develops the interpretive tradition founded by Kula in his above-cited 'Polish economy' as well as in 'L'Exploitation paysanne en Pologne à la charnière des XVIIIe et XIXe siècles. Théorie, Histoire, Historiographie', *Acta Poloniae Historica*, 57 (1988), pp. 203–37, and in *Spór o teorię gospodarki chłopskiej. Gospodarstwo chłopskie w teorii ekonomii i w historii gospodarczej* (Warsaw, 1992), ch. IV ('Gospodarstwo chłopskie w epoce przedprzemysłowej').

18. For modifications of Kula's framework, see the above-cited works by Kochanowicz; for challenges to it, see the above-cited works by Andrzej Wyczański as well as Jerzy Topolski, 'The manorial-serf economy in central and eastern Europe in the 16th and 17th centuries', *Agricultural History*, 48 (1974), pp. 341–52; idem, 'Sixteenth-century Poland and the turning point in European economic development', in Federowicz, *A Republic of Nobles*, pp. 70–90, and Topolski's above-cited 'Continuity and discontinuity'.

more or less ineffectual brake on the estate-owners' aggressive pursuit of their private self-interest, while the village farmers and labourers play, mostly passively, the injured parties. Clerics and other members of the learned class were complicitous in the villagers' misfortunes. Merchants and artisans viewed them in impotence or indifference. No doubt, the structural development of the early modern east-Elbian nobility, and their relation as a class to state power, are important themes. But the rural commoners' history is more than the negative reflection of the Junker and *szlachta* landlords' ascent.

To gain a village-level perspective, the material well-being of the nobility's subjects should not be inferred from the disabilities of their legal status. Instead, their condition must be understood, in the case of landholding farmers, in terms of the *rents* burdening their holdings and, in the case of labourers, in terms of their *real wages*. This requires the long-term tracking of rents and wages, a task the German and Polish literature alike has left incomplete at best, as well as the empirical reconstruction of the productive powers and consumption patterns of the village household.

The social world of the villagers possessed autonomy, despite the efforts of landlords, clergy and state to mould and regiment it. The country people's aspirations and accomplishments were kinship-bound, so that the analysis of household and family life looms large. The tools of historical demography are useful, especially to balance health and longevity against disease and mortality. To piece together from sources transcending demographic data – that is, from probate, judicial and seigneurial records – multi-generational histories of individual households offer more nuanced insights than population analysis alone can provide, but this is difficult to accomplish for periods before the later seventeenth century. Still, much about social and communal life emerges from the records concerning both individual fates and collective actions which are abundantly housed in judicial archives. These sources allow more study of the interplay between communal and individual identity than has yet occurred. The promise of such work has been realized in recent social and cultural ethnographies of the east-Elbian countryside, as well as in studies of gender issues. The investigation of village resistance to higher authority, whether confined within judicialized boundaries or expressed in collective or individual insubordination and violence, has yielded valuable results, but can also be carried farther.[19]

The pages below do not suffice to discuss all such work. Instead, they examine early modern manorialism from the villagers' perspective, especially that of the families of large and small farmers among them, who until the late

---

19. See the works, inspired variously by social and cultural anthropology and gender analysis, of Karl-S. Kramer and Ulrich Wilkens, *Volksleben in einem holsteinischen Gutsbezirk* (Neumünster, 1979); Jan Peters, Hartmut Harnisch and Lieselott Enders (eds), *Märkische Bauerntagebücher des 18. und 19. Jahrhunderts. Selbstzeugnisse von Milchviehbauern aus Neuholland* (Weimar, 1989); Silke Göttsch, *'Alle für einen Mann . . .' Leibeigene und Widerständigkeit in Schleswig-Holstein im 18. Jahrhundert* (Neumünster, 1991); Ulrike Gleixner, *'Das Mensch' und 'der Kerl'. Die Konstruktion von Geschlecht in Unzuchtsverfahren der Frühen Neuzeit (1700–1760)* (Frankfurt am Main, 1994); and the collection of articles edited by Peters, *Gutsherrschaft als soziales Modell*. See also the social and cultural analysis offered in Lieselott Enders, *Die Uckermark. Geschichte einer kurmärkischen Landschaft vom 12. bis zum 18. Jahrhundert* (Weimar, 1992).

eighteenth century composed the great majority of rural society. The aim is to grasp the strengths and weaknesses of the villagers' position in the successive stages of the manorial system both in east-Elbian Germany and Poland. It is premature to offer macro-level models, even within these spheres of central and eastern European agrarian society. The argument instead proceeds by discussion of localities that are strongly bathed in empirical light. Such settings are not necessarily exemplary, though in some respects they may be. But any more all-encompassing interpretations will need to account for the conditions they reveal, as well as for other more or less widespread characteristics which they do not exhibit. Rural history has always revelled in local diversity and particularity, but uniqueness is easily exaggerated. Human circumstances vary by degrees, and are always open to comparison.

The Villagers in the Late Middle Ages

Recent research upholds the long-established view that medieval villagers in east-Elbian Europe who were settled – or whose pre-existing settlements were reorganized – under the provisions of the German law enjoyed, though within a system of seigneurialism, strong personal and tenurial rights. The fullholders possessed, according to soil fertility, one or two hides (*Hufen* or *łany*) of arable land – the hide usually at seventeen hectares (or 42.5 acres) – along with shares of the village meadows and woods. Rents, at the moment of settlement, were fixed, while labour services on the modest and uncommercialized home farms of the local lordship were minimal – a few days annually of ploughing, some work in the seigneurial harvests, some road and other construction work, some haulage to nearby towns.[20]

This is the backdrop the English-language literature customarily hangs out to the Junkers' and Polish *szlachta*'s imposition in the late fifteenth and early sixteenth century of the regime of manorialism with its heavy labour rents. But the picture is incomplete in two ways. In the high medieval period following the German-law settlement movement, population growth, monetary depreciation, and mounting pressures on princely and seigneurial incomes pushed rents upward. Then, in the fourteenth and fifteenth centuries, eastern Germany suffered demographic catastrophe followed by considerable political violence. The resulting depopulation and falling agricultural commodity prices dragged village rents down. Although Poland was spared a western-style crisis, regional warfare and frontier expansion to the south-east seem to have worked also toward a late medieval reduction of the charges in rent and taxes weighing

---

20. In Polish the hide was also known as *ślad* or *włóka*. On the positive quality of German-law settlement, see Enders, *Uckermark*, pp. 60ff.; Hoffmann, *Land, Liberties, and Lordship*; Benedykt Zientara, 'Rozkwit feudalizmu (XIII–XV w.)', in Zientara and Mączak, *Dzieje gospodarcze*, pp. 79–134; and Zientara, '*Melioratio terrae*'. For a dissenting view, see Hartmut Harnisch, 'Die Landgemeinde im ostelbischen Gebiet (mit Schwerpunkt Brandenburg)', in Peter Blickle (ed.), *Landgemeinde und Stadtgemeinde in Mitteleuropa. Ein struktureller Vergleich* (Munich, 1991), pp. 309–32. For a persuasive rebuttal of Harnisch's argument, see Lieselott Enders, 'Die Landgemeinde in Brandenburg. Grundzüge ihrer Funktion und Wirkungsweise vom 13. bis zum 18. Jahrhundert', *Blätter für deutsche Landesgeschichte*, 129 (1993), pp. 195–256.

upon the village farm. In other words, before early modern manorialism bestrode the stage, rural society had passed through a centuries-long development distancing it greatly from the pristine dawn of the east-Elbian German-law movement.

In Brandenburg, for example, post-colonization levies in the early thirteenth century on the typical fullholding of two hides of land amounted to seigneurial rent in cash equivalent to the market value of a few bushels of rye or barley, together with the tithe, soon to be translated from an ecclesiastical to a princely income, and a sporadic tax (the *Bede*). But in 1279–82, the margrave gained his vassals' assent to a permanent *Bede*, calculated as a 10 per cent surcharge on a rent and tithe burden by then reckoned at twenty-four bushels per hide, which amounted to a very sizeable share of a village farm's grain surplus. Yet, in the following decades, in the midst of monetary devaluation and intermittent civil war, the exactions from the village farm rose higher still, while the beleaguered margraves pawned or otherwise surrendered to the noble landlords the incomes from the tithe and the princely tax.

In the mid-fourteenth century bubonic plague struck a society already suffering from relative overpopulation and low agricultural productivity. The Brandenburg land census of 1375 reveals that the burden of rents and taxes had recently begun to reverse its ascent, as village farmers left their holdings uncultivated and abandoned (*wüst*) because of death, or movement to more fertile holdings now available, or flight to avoid a virulent 'feudal gangsterism' that raged long into the fifteenth century. A study of farm rents in forty-one Brandenburg villages that remained under cultivation at the time of the successive censuses of 1375, 1450 and 1480 shows that the sum of all levies, measured in bushels of rye, fell absolutely from 1375 to 1450 by 29 per cent. Even allowing for the imposition in 1450 of a new tax on village holdings, rents in 1480 stood 17 per cent lower than a century before. It strengthened the advantage that village farmers derived from this trend that seigneurial rents had fallen faster than grain prices.[21]

A similar pattern emerges from a recent study of central Silesia, a land whose early medieval Polish character was in the late Middle Ages slowly yielding to Germanization under the impact of immigration and socio-cultural influences from the west following the introduction of the *ius Theutonicus*.[22] Further east, in the heartlands of the Polish Commonwealth, the population escaped the waves of plague that swept toward but did not engulf Silesia, just as it also avoided the civil war ravaging north-eastern Germany and Silesia as well. In the Polish heartlands population growth from the mid-fourteenth century to the late sixteenth century was extremely robust, averaging 3.8 per cent yearly over this long period.[23] Not surprisingly, a recent analysis of village rents and taxes in the central region of Mazovia identifies late medieval developments in Poland differing considerably from the Silesian and Brandenburg pattern. In general, German-law villages in Poland housed farms smaller than those in east-Elbian Germany: among fullholders, one hide rather than two hides of land. This

21. Hagen, 'How mighty the Junkers?', pp. 85–93.
22. Hoffmann, *Land, Liberties, and Lordship*, pp. 127, 213, 297, 323ff.
23. Zientara and Mączak, *Dzieje gospodarcze*, pp. 138–9.

difference may derive in part, as Polish historians' estimates of village farm surpluses suggest, from higher soil fertility in Poland than in north Germany.[24] But it also seems plausible to suppose that Poland's escape from the Black Death and its subsequent rapid population increase, coupled with widespread adoption of the German law in a form permitting (though not requiring) partible inheritance, had the effect of reducing the average size of village farms in comparison with east-Elbian German conditions, where ecological considerations buttressed impartible inheritance practices. In Mazovia, at the end of the fifteenth century, the very numerous halfholdings – or farms with but a half-hide (about twenty acres) of arable – probably overshadowed larger holdings. Abandoned farms were not uncommon, but they had mostly been absorbed by the demesne farms of the crown, Church and multitudinous nobility. In most villages, seigneurial rents were payable in bushels of grain. The average levy per hide in 132 villages was nearly ten bushels, though payable in oats, commonly reckoned at half the value of bread-grains. Money rents (*czynsz*) per hide averaged thirty-six Prague *groszy*, the common coin of the day. This payment had risen, to offset devaluation, from twelve *groszy* in the mid-fourteenth century. Accompanying these charges were a tax of nine *groszy* per hide and the tithe on crops, collected *in natura*.

Mazovian villagers had been, since 1421, subject to seigneurial claims to one day of weekly manorial service, and in 1500 perhaps one-third of them were performing this work, or hiring farm servants in their stead. The example of numerous villages which had monetized their tithe and labour service obligations shows that, on average, commutation of labour services cost the farmer thirty-three *groszy* per hide, or about the same sum the average cultivator paid in cash in seigneurial rent.[25] Apart from pointing to the economic significance at this early date of weekly labour service, these data suggest altogether that late medieval Polish rents were, in contrast to east-Elbian Germany, comparatively high. This was, presumably, largely because no population collapse on the western European model had occurred in Poland, where the fifteenth century was one of eastward colonization, urban development and, after the Commonwealth in 1466 had secured its conquest of Royal Prussia with Danzig from the Teutonic Knights, expanding timber and grain exports via the Baltic to western Europe.[26]

High farm rents in cash and kind could signal good farm incomes, just as low rents could signify poverty. If the villagers' material well-being is to be judged, evidence on the movement of rent must be paired with information on household property-holding and consumption patterns. In the sixteenth

---

24. Hubert Wajs, *Powinności feudalne chłopów na Mazowszu od XIV do początku XVI wieku (w dobrach monarszych i kościelnych)* (Warsaw, 1986), pp. 46ff.; on village farm yields, see Leonid Żytkowicz, 'Okres gospodarki folwarczno-pańszczyźnianej (XVI–XVIII w.)', in Inglot, *Historia chłopów polskich*, pp. 257–83.

25. Mazovian data from Wajs, *Powinności feudalne*, pp. 46ff., 75ff., and 153ff. Seigneurial demands on village labour in Mazovia, the stronghold of a numerous smallholding nobility, were likely to have been heavier than elsewhere in Poland.

26. Zientara and Mączak, *Dzieje gospodarcze*, pp. 135ff.; Marian Małowist, 'Constitutional trends and social developments in central Europe, the Baltic countries, and the Polish-Lithuanian Commonwealth', in Jarosław Pelenski (ed.), *State and Society in Europe from the Fifteenth to the Eighteenth Century* (Warsaw, 1981), pp. 71ff.

century, the proliferation of seigneurial courts administered by officials trained in the Roman law produced written records, often gathered together in protocol books, of household inventories and inheritance settlements. Some of these, from the late sixteenth and early seventeenth centuries, have survived, but have not yet been employed to draw the fine-grained picture of household kinship and property relations which the denser documentation of the late seventeeth and eighteenth centuries, including parish registers, allows. For earlier periods, the historian confronts much patchier princely and seigneurial records.

From east-Elbian Germany the records of the prosperous nunnery of Diesdorf, in the Brandenburg Altmark on the west bank of the Elbe, throw some light on the servants employed at the convent's home farms and on the farmers inhabiting its thirty-three subject villages in the middle and late fifteenth century. Most of the villagers cultivated fullholdings of two hides. Their tenures were hereditary leaseholds (*Erbpacht*), allowing them to buy and sell whole farms among themselves. At the moment of sale, a symbolic bough would be exchanged from seller to buyer, who paid for the two barrels of beer drunk by the transacting parties and their neighbours. The convent took its share as a usually modest entry-fine levied on the buyer. The seller might continue to live on the farmstead in separate retirement quarters (*das Altenteil*), as was customary when generational transfers occurred. The convent did not require its farmers to secure substitutes before they quit their holdings, but in the absence of buyers it would itself acquire the farms for future resale. Keen on fully occupied villages, the convent recognized the claims of heirs to farms as late as ten – or even thirty – years after their parents' death.[27]

The farmers in this cloth-producing region, like the convent, kept good numbers of sheep. Wearing swords and spurs, they rode their saddled horses (unless, as easily happened, these were plundered by local knightly highwaymen). In the periodic court sessions at the convent, the village mayors sat as jurors, and only if they could not agree on the customary law did the convent administrator (*Probst*) or his bailiff (*Vogt*) take command.

The farmers' grain rents, their principal burden, had by the late fifteenth century fallen significantly since the census of 1375. Money rents, remnants of privatized taxation, were low, although current taxes in the form of single levies were sporadically heavy. Manorial labour service, apart from haulage, amounted to a few days annually of ploughing and harvest work. Occasionally feudal violence engulfed the region. In 1467 the convent noted of one village's rent obligations that 'they give nothing this year, because the Duke of Saxony took everything they had'. Still, Diesdorf's historian thought the farmers were 'favourably situated'.[28] Among the convent's steadily employed housed servants at its two demesne farms, there were foremen (*Hofmeister*) and mistresses of the female workers (*Meyerschen*) who also supervised the dairy work. There were

27. Gottfried Wentz, *Das Wirtschaftsleben des altmärkischen Klosters Diesdorf im ausgehenden Mittelalter* (Berlin, 1922), passim. On the late medieval Altmark, see also Evamaria Engel, 'Lehnbürger, Bauern und Feudalherren in der Altmark um 1375', in eadem and Benedykt Zientara, *Feudalstruktur, Lehnbürgertum und Fernhandel im spätmittelalterlichen Brandenburg* (Weimar, 1967), pp. 37–191.

28. Wentz, *Wirtschaftsleben*, pp. 55, 102.

numerous herders, wagon drivers, stablemen, and ploughmen with teams of horses and oxen. On occasion, the mounted servants would be supplied by the convent with swords and spurs for their boots. A numerous group of rural artisans and occasional wage-workers lived as landed cottagers in the villages near the demesne farms.

In the sixteenth century Diesdorf was secularized and converted to large-scale demesne farming based on its subject farmers' heavy new unpaid weekly labour services. But, like other east-Elbian German lordships, entry into the age of early modern manorialism did not change it unrecognizably. In that transition very many late medieval arrangements remained the same or changed only slowly: the subject villagers' farms, though now burdened by new labour rents; the manorial workforce; the administrative structure of the lordship itself.

The Villagers and the Rise of Commercialized Manorialism in the Sixteenth Century

Controversy and speculation are rife on how precisely the new manorialism arose, and how the weekly labour services were imposed upon the villagers. It was long held that the process cannot be satisfactorily reconstructed. So far as Brandenburg is concerned, such pessimism is unjustifiable. The seigneurial power to extract weekly labour services from subject villagers existed long before market opportunities, in the late fifteenth and early sixteenth centuries, convinced the noble landlords, and administrators of princely and ecclesiastical lordships, that consolidation of demesne land into large farms worked by unpaid village labour was a feasible strategy for reversing the late medieval decline of feudal incomes. Everywhere in sixteenth-century Europe the nobility turned to entrepreneurialism, especially in commercialized agriculture.[29]

In east-Elbia, where the most profitable form of large-scale farming was cereal-crop cultivation, the propertied nobility were rich in land but poor in

29. In the German literature, no consensus on the emergence of early modern manorialism has formed. Kaak's *Gutsherrschaft* surveys established interpretive positions. For a micro-level reconstruction of the process in the electorate of Brandenburg, see Hagen, 'How mighty the Junkers?'. Cf. Peter-Michael Hahn, *Struktur und Funktion des brandenburgischen Adels im 16. Jahrhundert* (Berlin, 1979). See also Marian Małowist, 'Über die Frage der Handelspolitik des Adels in den Ostseeländern im 15. und 16. Jahrhundert', *Hansische Geschichtsblätter*, 75 (1957), pp. 29–47; Hartmut Harnisch, 'Grundherrschaft oder Gutsherrschaft. Zu den wirtschaftlichen Grundlagen des niederen Adels in Norddeutschland zwischen spätmittelalterlicher Agrarkrise und Dreißigjährigem Krieg', in Rudolf Endres (ed.), *Adel in der Frühneuzeit. Ein regionaler Vergleich* (Cologne, 1991), pp. 73–98. On East Prussia, see Gustav Aubin, *Zur Geschichte des gutsherrlich-bäuerlichen Verhältnisses in Ostpreußen von der Gründung des Ordensstaates bis zur Steinschen Reform* (Leipzig, 1910); Heide Wunder, 'Zur Mentalität aufständischer Bauern. Möglichkeiten der Zusammenarbeit von Geschichtswissenschaft und Anthropologie, dargestellt am Beispiel des Samländischen Bauernaufstandes von 1525', in Hans-Ulrich Wehler (ed.), *Der Deutsche Bauernkrieg 1524–1526* (Göttingen, 1975), pp. 9–37; Michael North, 'Untersuchungen zur adligen Gutswirtschaft im Herzogtum Preußen des 16. Jahrhunderts', *Vierteljahrschrift für Sozial- und Wirtschaftsgeschichte*, 70 (1983), pp. 1–20. On Poland, see (apart from Rutkowski's above-cited works) Leonid Żytkowicz's argument in Inglot, *Historia chłopów polskich*, pp. 247ff., as well as Żytkowicz, 'Trends of agrarian economy', pp. 60–8; Topolski, 'The manorial-serf economy', pp. 341–52, and 'Sixteenth-century Poland', passim; Małowist, 'Constitutional trends', passim; Witold Kula, 'Money and the serfs in eighteenth century Poland', in E. J. Hobsbawm *et al.* (eds), *Peasants in History. Essays in Honor of Daniel Thorner* (Calcutta, 1980), pp. 31–2; and Kochanowicz, 'Polish economy', pp. 95–104.

capital to invest in plough and draught teams and in wage labour to work them. Arable farming required year-round, if intermittent labour. The rural common people, understandably, preferred cultivation of their own holdings to the life of wage-labourers living in rented housing at the manor or on the farmsteads of their village neighbours. Farm rents in the lordships' villages had fallen to low levels by the late fifteenth century, while the earnings on villagers' crop and livestock sales were starting to rise. In the lordships' eyes, village rent increases were beginning to appear justifiable. Urban markets were improving, especially further west. They could be reached by river traffic, although land transport, if paid for at free market rates, was uneconomic. But if such haulage, along with the field work of ploughing, harrowing and harvesting, were translated into unpaid labour extracted as rent, large-scale commercialized demesne farming could be made to pay a steady and – as the long sixteenth century proved – rising profit.

Could the landlords have imposed the burden and risk of such commercialized farming on their villagers, leasing out their demesne land in its entirety and collecting in return rising money rents from now more numerous subjects? Such an arrangement calls to mind on a smaller scale the landlord–tenant farmer system emerging simultaneously in England. In that case, the east-Elbian nobility would have been obliged to share the profits of the long-range grain trade on distant markets with their subject farmers and with the urban merchants to whom the villagers would have sold their crops. The abandoned village farms in east-Elbian Germany, combined with the seigneurial demesnes, comprised a large mass of land. To settle it fully at satisfactorily high rents would have taken long years.

Instead, the landlords organized compact demesne farms and compelled their village subjects, alongside a minimal corps of paid workers, to cultivate and harvest them, and to transport the threshed grain to market or port towns. They exercised their powers as jurisdictional lords (*Gerichtsherren*) to extract unpaid construction work from their subjects, so as to raise the buildings, including even manor houses, necessary to the country gentleman's life. The new regime did not dispossess the landed villagers. Not until the late sixteenth century did forced purchases by the nobility of subject farms lead to a limited degree of expansion of demesne land at the villages' expense.[30]

From the sixteenth-century villagers' point of view, the rise of commercialized manorialism represented less a loss of legal rights and status than a menacing, potentially deadly, rent increase. In 1484 the first of many statutes limiting the landed villagers' freedom of movement, and the terms on which manorial servants were hired, emerged from the noble-dominated Brandenburg Estates. But before the Thirty Years War, except in north-eastern and south-eastern enclaves of the land, such limits – the defining marks of subjection (*Untertänigkeit*)

---

30. On the question of seigneurial enclosures of village land, see Hagen, 'Seventeenth-century crisis', pp. 310–11; Siegfried Korth, 'Die Entstehung und Entwicklung des ostdeutschen Großgrundbesitzes', *Jahrbuch der Albertus-Universität zu Königsberg/Pr.*, 3 (1953), pp. 148–70; Enders, *Uckermark*, pp. 172ff.; Topolski, 'Rozwój folwarku pańszczyźnianego', pp. 52ff.; Wyczański, *Polska*, pp. 17ff.; Żytkowicz, 'Okres', pp. 247ff.

– were treated in law as attributes of village farms under seigneurial authority, rather than as inherent in the subject farmers' persons. The disabilities they entailed could be exchanged for the liberty of a rural commoner on condition the subject farm were sold to a competent successor-farmer. But most farm-owning villagers preferred to stand their ground, defending their claims to the fruits of their labours as best they could, rather than to abandon their patrimonies for the life of a landless worker.[31]

The crucial task was to hold the new weekly labour services within manageable bounds. Often the landlords imposed these services step by step, presenting their claims first as 'requests' and later as customary 'rights'. In other cases, the new demesne farms were constructed in a flurry of heavy manorial services that were later regularized at a fixed weekly rate, with or without food and drink and varying sometimes by season, including extra labour in the harvests and a limited degree of long-distance haulage. In some cases the subject villagers in Brandenburg, in return for shouldering the much-resented manorial services, bargained down the level of seigneurial grain rents. Although these had fallen since the High Middle Ages, they usually still represented significant charges well worth reducing, whereas money rents generally declined to vestigial importance.[32]

By the eve of the Thirty Years War, most of the fullholders in Brandenburg, as elsewhere in German east-Elbia, rendered two or three days of weekly domanial labour with a team of horses or oxen. Frequently they sent sons or hired hands to perform this work (thereby themselves evading the seigneurial field bailiff's abuse). They bore the cost of such unrecompensed manpower, as they did of the teams. They had to accept that an unmarried son or daughter whose labour was not essential to the household economy might be conscripted for a term of three years (or more) as a compulsory manorial servant, in exchange for room, board, clothing and footwear, and a meagre wage in cash (*Gesindezwangsdienst*). Still, the subject farmers' rents in grain and cash rarely stood so high as to prevent them from profiting through sales of their surpluses from ascending commodity prices. They too, though more modestly than their landlords, cashed in on the long sixteenth century. They had not lost their right as members of village communes, recognized in law as collective legal personalities, to sue their lordships at law for tolerable conditions of manorial service. These were the principal reasons why they neither fled their holdings in large numbers (losing the capital and profits they embodied) nor rebelled *en masse* against the new regime. Over the course of 150 years manorialism rose steadily, like a flooding river, but it never wholly swamped the villages.

If in Brandenburg conditions for the subject farmers were endurable, elsewhere in German east-Elbia harsher forms of seigneurial exploitation emerged. In Schleswig-Holstein, Mecklenburg and Pomerania – weakly governed lands on the Baltic coast facing extremely favourable export markets – legislation in

31. Still fundamental on questions of legal status in Brandenburg is Friedrich Grossmann, *Über die gutsherrlich-bäuerlichen Rechtsverhältnisse in der Mark Brandenburg vom 16. bis 18. Jahrhundert* (Leipzig, 1890), esp. chs 3–4. Of comparable importance for the Uckermark region is Enders, *Uckermark*, esp. ch. III.
32. See Hagen, 'How mighty the Junkers?', pp. 97–108; Enders, *Uckermark*, pp. 161–81.

the late sixteenth and early seventeenth centuries gradually undermined the villagers' hereditary tenures, converting them into leaseholds cancellable at landlordly will (*Laßgüter*). This removed all impediments to the enclosure of subject farms into the seigneurial demesne. By claiming in Roman-law terms that, since the subject villagers were not freeholders (*emphyteutae*), they must be mere tenants at will (*coloni*), tied to the soil (*ad glebam adscriptus*) if not actually slaves (*homini proprii*), the landlords' jurists laid the legal foundation for personal serfdom (*Leibeigenschaft*).[33]

The most important practical implication of these changes in law was the confinement of the villagers as individuals within the seigneurial jurisdiction, whether they held land or not. It was now possible to dispossess them of their farms, and yet to retain them in the lordship as labourers. But it is unlikely that extensive use was made of such powers before the depopulation of the Thirty Years War triggered a fierce competition among landlords for subject farmers and manorial workers. It seems that their pre-war effect was mainly to facilitate some enclosure of village farmland into the seigneurial demesne. It was essential to leave enough subject farmers on the land to supply the manorial service without which the noble estates would themselves have to bear the heavy costs in labour and draught teams necessary for their operation.

While there is evidence that, on the eve of the seventeenth-century wars, some of the landed villagers in east-Elbian Germany were faltering under the burden of labour rents, research also suggests that many others lived in tolerable material sufficiency, even in the more precarious legal conditions of the Baltic littoral. Livestock holdings, a crucial measure of capital accumulation in the villages, were frequently strong. Occasionally villagers appear among the investors in urban funded debts, a form of bank deposit. Loss of village land through enclosure is difficult to track, but the Brandenburg census of 1624, surveying the 734 villages of the Mittelmark district (a large part of the entire electorate), found that 80 per cent of the village arable land, as defined for purposes of taxation, remained in the villagers' possession. Here the nobility succeeded after 1575 in engrossing 7 per cent of their subjects' land, while they held 13 per cent from earlier times, having appropriated it after its abandonment in the late medieval crisis. Altogether, the Brandenburg villages (including those under urban jurisdiction) possessed about 60 per cent of the countryside, while the remainder comprised in roughly equal measure the demesne and forest land of the nobility and the princely household.[34]

Among the 16,271 rural householders counted by the Mittelmark census of 1624, 46 per cent were fullholding farmers (*Bauern*), while 33 per cent were landed smallholders (*Kossäten*), many cultivating as much as one hide of land. Cottagers, possessing garden land alone, comprised only 5 per cent of village householders, while the remaining 16 per cent were shepherds and other

33. Friedrich Mager, *Geschichte des Bauerntums und der Bodenkultur im Lande Mecklenburg* (Berlin, 1955), pp. 92–7 and 63–107, passim. See also Enders, *Uckermark*, pp. 191ff.; Kaak, *Gutsherrschaft*, pp. 122ff., 247ff.

34. See Hagen, 'How mighty the Junkers?', pp. 107–8, and 'Seventeenth-century crisis', pp. 310–11; Enders, *Uckermark*, pp. 172–5; Kaak, *Gutsherrschaft*, pp. 253ff.; Johannes Schultze, *Die Mark Brandenburg*, vol. 5 (Berlin, 1969), p. 173.

herders, millers, smiths and fishermen. These figures screen out the unhoused workers and itinerant poor, but they show that the rise of commercialized manorialism did not undermine the pre-existing German east-Elbian village structure based on large and medium-sized farms.[35]

In Poland, the sixteenth-century subject farms supplying compulsory labour to the *szlachta*'s expanded manors were smaller than their German counterparts. A picture of village conditions in a still early stage of the new regime emerges from the survey of 1564–65 of the Crown villages and estates in the governorship (*województwo*) of Poznań, in western Poland. In thirty-eight villages, there were 625 landholding farmers (*kmiecie*), but on average each cultivated only seven-tenths of a hide (here called *ślad*), or about twelve hectares (thirty acres). Among them, 34 per cent worked holdings of one full hide, while 60 per cent held but a half-hide. Swelling the ranks of the smallholders, there were 168 'gardeners' or cottagers (*ogrodnicy, zagrodnicy*) tilling mini-farms and otherwise working for wages.[36]

The fullholders' rents in cash and kind were low by comparison with those of the late fifteenth-century Mazovian farmers discussed above. Leaving aside taxes (moderate charges showing no tendency to rise) and the tithe (a fixed rate), rents per hide in 1564–65 amounted on average to forty-four *groszy* in cash and, in seigneurial tribute grain, to about four bushels of oats.[37] The corresponding Mazovian rents were fifty-six *groszy* and ten bushels of oats. But while only a minority of Mazovian farmers had rendered (at most) one day of weekly manorial service, in the Poznań governorship the fullholders in a majority of the twenty-six villages whose manorial services the census specified were obliged to supply labour with a team to the manor whenever commanded to do so. Opposed to these cases of unlimited labour services, there were a few villages with fixed quotas of two or three days weekly. Since the fourteen Crown demesne farms cultivated by these villages were still not large – each one encompassing on average only about eleven hides – unlimited services probably came closer in practice to two or three than to five or six days of weekly labour. But the liability to more crushing labour services remained.

This evidence does not prove that villagers in central and western Poland bargained down their seigneurial rents in cash and tribute grain in exchange for heavier manorial service. But they suggest that such trade-offs might have occurred. The Poznanian farmers' payments in cash and kind to the manor house were certainly minimal, so that most of their farm surplus – after tithe and taxes – remained in their own hands. Jerzy Topolski found that, in 150

---

35. The 1624 cadastre was published in Grossmann, *Über die gutsherrlich-bäuerlichen Rechtsverhältnisse*, pp. 109–38. See table IX, p. 138.

36. Computations from Andrzej Tomczak *et al.* (eds), *Lustracja Województw Wielkopolskich i Kujawskich 1564–1565*, Część I (Bydgoszcz, 1961), pp. 124–210.

37. The quantity of approximately four bushels derives from the average payment of 1.6 *ćwiertnie*, a measure equal in 1659 to two bushels (that is, to two *korce wielkopolskie*). The Polish bushel, though very variable, in this case approximated to the Brandenburg bushel. See the metrological table in Czesława Ohryzko-Włodarska (ed.), *Lustracja Województw Wielkopolskich i Kujawskich 1659–1665*, Część I, p. XXXVII. On metrological questions in early modern Poland and generally, see Witold Kula, *Measures and Men* (Princeton, NJ, 1986 [Polish original: 1970]).

villages under the jurisdiction of the archbishops of Gniezno, most of them strung across western and central Poland, the average farmer held, in 1554, thirteen head of horses and cattle of all types – a respectable number for predominantly medium-sized holdings. The Polish literature, like the German, suggests that, where farms did not shrink to the point at which no marketable surplus remained, they maintained a tolerable level of material well-being before the mid-seventeenth-century deluge of invasion and devastation washed over them.[38]

Against the grain of earlier Polish historiography, Andrzej Wyczański has argued that, despite the Polish villagers' loss in 1518 of appellate rights against their seigneurial lordships, they retained, both individually and communally, the prerogatives of legal personality at the local level. They continued to engage in property transactions of all sorts, and in other judicial business as well. Goaded by seigneurial abuse and dispossession, they took flight more readily than villagers in east-Elbian Germany. They could normally be sure of finding protection, often on the property of a greater nobleman than their previous lordship, so that, instead of being returned as refractory subjects to the bailiwick they had fled, the new landlord would settle privately with the former landlord to retain the absconded subject. Some villagers fled alone, others with family and possessions, circumstances taken into account in such negotiations (which suggest the idea of involuntary sale). Although most flights occurred within a short radius, the drift of village deserters and legal settlers south-east toward the Ukraine and east and north into the former Lithuanian lands of the Commonwealth ensured that places were available in many villages of the old heartlands for new subject farmers and labourers.[39]

The two centuries before the mid-seventeenth century were the golden age of the pre-partition Polish Commonwealth. Despite evidence that, to counteract falling profits, the nobility began at the end of the sixteenth century to engross village farmland and intensify unpaid manorial service, a picture roughly comparable to that drawn by the literature on east-Elbian Germany prior to the Thirty Years War is discernible. Although signs of crisis were on hand, as the homespun poem introducing this essay testified, the fullholding villagers' farms permitted household reproduction and consumption at levels above bare subsistence. The rural common people's diet was adequate or even good. Their clothing, though cut from coarse materials, displayed the same styles as the townspeople's and nobility's. Their housing was, at its best, decent, while their livestock holdings were often strong enough to withstand the rigours of manorial service and the claims upon them of heirs' marriage portions. The

---

38. Topolski, 'Rozwój folwarku pańszczyźniancgo', pp. 56ff. But Topolski also found that, in 1603, the average number of horses and cattle on such holdings had fallen by 20 per cent since 1554, while in 1617 it was 36 per cent lower than in 1554. Ibid., p. 57. See also Topolski, 'Continuity and discontinuity', pp. 394ff.; Wyczański, *Wieś*, pp. 151ff.; and Zientara and Mączak, *Dzieje gospodarcze*, pp. 148ff.

39. Wyczański, *Polska*, pp. 39–43; idem, *Wieś*, pp. 134ff., 177ff. On flight from the villages and other forms of resistance, see Józef Leszczyński, 'Walka chłopów z uciskiem i wyzyskiem feudalnym (XVI–XVIII w.)', in Inglot, *Historia chłopów polskich*, pp. 398ff., and Jacek Kochanowicz, 'Between submission and violence: peasant resistance in the Polish manorial economy of the eighteenth century', in Forrest D. Colburn (ed.), *Everyday Forms of Peasant Resistance* (London, 1989), pp. 34–63.

access of village children to urban trades and education was better then than in the eighteenth century.[40]

The Villagers in the Seventeenth-Century Crisis

The seventeenth-century wars, prolonged in Poland into the early eighteenth century, cut deep wounds in the central European rural world. Although modern scholars exaggerated the resulting population losses, wherever the armies penetrated, death through violence, hunger and epidemics stalked the countryside. Many villagers survived through flight, but at the cost of impoverishment and homelessness following abandonment of the farmstead. Masses of villages burned to the ground. Many still stood abandoned decades after the wars ended, their fields overgrown and, often, home to wolfpacks that had appeared after the fighting started.

A consequence of the wars that has only recently received due attention was the widespread collapse of seigneurial authority in the villages. As the noble landlords – along with ecclesiastical and state domain administrators – failed in their self-legitimating obligation to protect their subjects from harm and hunger, the villagers took to their own devices. They stopped paying rents and taxes, and abandoned manorial service; they moved from one short-term leasehold to another, depending on the drift of war; they drove the price of wage labour through the ineffectual ceilings of the frequently readjusted wage statutes. When peace returned, they contracted with their old or with new landlords to rebuild and occupy the abandoned farms, provided they were granted a period of freedom – commonly six years – from rents and taxes. A practice maddening to the landlords was the desertion by some such settlers of their holdings after the free years had passed, so as to seek out another lordship which would sign them on anew as unencumbered colonists.[41]

The landlords reacted with an aggression born of their own ruin and loss of authority. In German east-Elbia, they pressed government authorities to ratify and generalize the doctrines of personal serfdom that had been seeping into the area before 1618, but whose future strength was then still unpredictable. New servile legislation proliferated in the mid- and late seventeenth century. In Poland, such laws were unnecessary, since the seigneurial courts had since 1518 possessed full discretionary authority over the subject villagers' tenurial rights and duties. Here the rigours of serfdom developed by stages from local usages. But undoubtedly Polish landlords adopted more stringent practices in the post-1648 period.

The new laws authorized landlords to recover farmers who had fled during the wars, so that they could be compelled again to cultivate their ancestral

---

40. See the computation of the improving terms of domestic trade for Polish village farmers in the sixteenth century in Andrzej Wyczański, 'Czy chłopu było źle w Polsce XVI wieku?', *Kwartalnik Historyczny*, 85 (1978), pp. 633–7, and 627–41, passim; Wyczański, *Wieś*, pp. 151–69; Topolski, 'Rozwój folwarku pańszczyźnianego', p. 56ff.

41. Hagen, 'Seventeenth-century crisis', pp. 314ff. To judge from the standard literature, this subject still awaits treatment in the Polish context.

holding or other lands assigned to them. They also aimed to sweep aside the subject farmers' pre-existing tenurial rights, which when good had allowed sale of holdings and departure from the lordship. It sought to override pre-existing rents and labour services, which had varied with the strength of tenurial rights (although in practice many weak tenures had rendered only moderate dues and services). The landlords wished to hold their subjects within the seigneurial bailiwick, whether they occupied landholdings or not, and to have a free hand in moving them from one farm to another, which in some cases allowed expansion of the manorial demesne onto more fertile, formerly village soils. They aimed to evade earlier limits on the compulsory service of unmarried manorial farm-workers, and to extend the term of duty indefinitely.[42]

This seigneurial offensive rightly looms large in the literature. Yet its efficacy is questionable. From the villagers' perspective, the crippling obstacle to effective resistance to landlordly aggression was the life-threatening poverty to which war and its scourges had so often reduced them. In this condition, many had little choice but to bow to seigneurial power, so as to gain the foothold of a farmstead, even at the cost of personal subjection, tenurial insecurity and heavy feudal rents. Polish court records of the seventeenth and eighteenth centuries register numerous cases of submission to hereditary serfdom (*poddaństwo*) on the part of legally free individuals. Mostly these were marriages by men into subject households, entailing their subordination and that of their future children to seigneurial authority. For such people, the freedom of the open road must have seemed illusory.

Legislation on serfdom permitted landlords to hunt down absconded subjects, but there were limits to this tactic, set by the revenge which desperate and embittered subjects could take on the lordships through theft, mutilation of livestock, or arson. The long-prevailing post-war labour shortages meant that flight to less demanding landlords remained a strong option, especially since the police powers even of such a burgeoning absolutist regime as Brandenburg-Prussia were from the villagers' viewpoint gratifyingly inadequate. Under these circumstances, it behoved the estate-owners to offer reasonable terms to new subjects settling in their villages. These included *de jure* or *de facto* hereditability of the farms they would rebuild, seigneurial provision of construction timber, and moderate labour services following the initial free years.

It was also common, and of long-lasting importance, that the landlords frequently found themselves obliged to supply their new tenants with essential farm equipment, tools, furniture, and a basic contingent of livestock (typically four horses, a cow, a sow and a few sheep). This 'iron stock' (German: *Hofwehr*, Polish: *załoga*) reified the seigneurial claim to ownership of the holding, and was exempt from inheritance settlements among the villagers. The frequency of this arrangement testified to the villagers' post-war penury, and unmistakably

---

42. Ibid., pp. 324ff.; Grossmann, *Über die gutsherrlich-bäuerlichen Rechtsverhältnisse*, ch. 4; Kaak, *Gutsherrschaft*, pp. 327ff.; Enders, *Uckermark*, pp. 336ff.; Rutkowski, *Historia gospodarcza*, pp. 250ff.; Zientara and Mączak, *Dzieje gospodarcze*, ch. 5; Trzyna, 'Wtórne Poddaństwo', pp. 363ff.; Wyczański, *Polska*, pp. 290ff.; Władysław Rusiński, 'W dobie upadku gospodarczego (1655–1793)', in Rusiński, *Dzieje wsi wielkopolskiej*, pp. 69ff.; Kochanowicz, 'Polish economy', pp. 103ff.

signalled the decline in their earlier strong property rights. But it entailed costs to the landlords, not only at the start, but later, when expired livestock – especially draught teams – needed replacement, or when the subject farmers' houses needed renovation. Because many lordships were mired in debt, such renewal of their subjects' working capital was highly unwelcome to them, so that in many villages housing grew shabby and ramshackle and the horses used in manorial service old and feeble. This was a reason, especially among the lesser nobility, for the inferior productivity, by comparison with sixteenth-century standards, of eighteenth-century estate agriculture.[43]

While the literature emphasizes the harsh legal subjection of post-1648 villages, the spread of manorial production based on seigneurial draught teams and permanently employed manorial servants, whether freely or compulsorily recruited, tells a somewhat different story. These comparatively self-enclosed manorial systems figure in German historiography as *Eigenwirtschaften*, in opposition to 'partial' manorial economies depending mainly on the landed villagers' unpaid weekly labour ('*Teilbetriebe*'). While they existed earlier wherever domanial production lacked sufficient subject farmers, the manor based on wage labour (for even compulsorily recruited workers commanded a wage) proliferated in the post-war decades when the village farms were still unoccupied or under reconstruction. In Brandenburg, it was not until the early eighteenth century that the landlords could abandon such more or less self-sufficient production and compel their subjects to reshoulder the pre-war burdens. Even then, it was sometimes impossible to rescind fully concessions on labour services granted in the resettlement period.[44]

In Mecklenburg and the north-eastern Brandenburg district of the Uckermark, draconian post-war servile legislation impeded repopulation. In Mecklenburg the number of farmers shrank drastically to those who survived the Thirty Years War and whose landlords could reassemble them as a village labour force. Outsiders did not enter the land seeking colonists' holdings, while many Mecklenburgers fled to regions where better tenures were available (as in neighbouring Brandenburg). The remaining farmers' holdings grew quite large (four or six hides), with sizeable households of family members and resident servants, and with large livestock holdings to perform the heavy daily labour services with two or more servants. Many *Eigenwirtschaften* arose, especially when in the eighteenth century crop rotations which reduced or eliminated fallowing and increased fodder production were adopted on the nobility's demesne farms. The profitability of this change, and the reduction it entailed in grain-crop cultivation, enabled many estate-owners to dispense altogether with the old regime of unpaid manorial service. Instead, especially in the late eighteenth century, numerous largeholding subject farms were enclosed into the estate demesnes, while their occupants were reduced to cottagers living from wage

43. Hagen, 'Seventeenth-century crisis', pp. 324ff.; Wyczański, *Polska*, pp. 293–303.
44. See the evidence and literature cited in Hagen, 'Seventeeth-century crisis', pp. 321ff. For additional instances of *Eigenwirtschaften*, see Renate Schilling, *Schwedisch-Pommern um 1700. Studien zur Agrarstruktur eines Territoriums extremer Gutsherrschaft* (Weimar, 1989).

labour on the estates, working alongside the increasing number of permanently employed wage-labourers housed at the manors.[45]

In the Uckermark, the Prussian regime conceded the nobility's juridically flimsy claim that personal serfdom (*Leibeigenschaft*) was locally customary. Armed with this ruling, the Uckermark Junkers depressed many an unfortunate among their surviving villagers into semi-bondage. Yet, as in Mecklenburg, the existence of strict serfdom impeded repopulation. The estate-owners began settling unoccupied farms with personally free, short-term leaseholders (*Pachtbauern*). Such farmers, working on contracts of three or six years, owned their own livestock and equipment, and often paid substantial sums for their leases. Lacking heritable tenures and liable to punitive non-renewal of their contracts, they did not trouble their lordships with the lawsuits over rents and services which communities of subject but hereditary farmholders in Brandenburg frequently initiated. As the villages gradually replenished their ranks, the logic of holding labour immobile by juridical means weakened. After the mid-eighteenth century, legal references to serfdom yielded to the language of subject status (*Untertänigkeit*), while the number of personally free leaseholders and labourers came to predominate.

As in Mecklenburg, abandonment in the Uckermark of three-field agriculture in favour of new rotations encouraged a move away from the regime of manorial service toward self-sufficient estates worked by wage labour. For the subject farmers, and often for the short-term leaseholders as well, this meant payment of a fee commuting the labour-service obligation into cash (*Dienstgeld*, or 'service money'). The Uckermark thus offers a good illustration of the linkage between labour shortages, weak capitalization of estates, poor markets, and personal serfdom. When these conditions of the long post-war depression yielded to economic growth in the demographically reinvigorated eighteenth century, with its rising commodity prices and opportunities for technological improvement in agriculture, the utility to the estate-owners of personal serfdom, never very great, lost its strength. But, as in Mecklenburg, the lasting legacy of strict serfdom was the disappearance, or drastic reduction, of hereditary tenures among the farm-holding villagers.[46]

In Poland, the wounds of war never altogether healed before 1772.[47] Although there were some prosperous moments in the century after 1648, the landlords' export markets in the west were far less absorbent and profitable than they had been earlier. Only the magnate producers, who could expand their volume of production, kept a secure foothold on foreign exchanges. But, like their lesser colleagues, they found it increasingly advisable to process their grain crops into beer and liquor to sell to their subjects at the seigneurial tavern. The

---

45. Mager, *Geschichte des Bauerntums*, pp. 141ff.; Kaak, *Gutsherrschaft*, pp. 134ff., 257ff.

46. Hartmut Harnisch, *Die Herrschaft Boitzenburg* (Weimar, 1968), pp. 138ff.; Enders, *Uckermark*, pp. 451ff., 504ff.

47. For recent estimates of post-1648 population losses in Poland, see Zientara and Mączak, *Dzieje gospodarcze*, pp. 233ff.; Wyczański, *Polska*, pp. 290ff.; Kochanowicz, *Spór o teorię*, p. 118; Irena Gieysztorowa, *Wstęp do demografii staropolskiej* (Warsaw, 1976), pp. 189–90. Gieysztorowa's book, equipped with a detailed summary in French, is the principal general study of early modern Polish demography.

landlords' alcohol monopoly (*propinacja*), sometimes underpinned by truck-system payments to workers, loomed ever larger on the credit side of their ledgers, though its effects on the villages were often deadly.[48]

Post-war depopulation was locally extreme, while decapitalization among the middle and lesser gentry impeded the resettlement of their villages, given the need to equip them with housing and livestock. As a result, many Polish estates found it necessary, in the absence of full villages, to move temporarily to the more self-sufficient *Eigenwirtschaft* mode of operation. When the subject farms were resettled, it was often as inexpensive smallholdings. For the larger-scale subject farmers (*kmiecie*) the seventeenth-century crisis spelled a permanent and severe diminution of their ranks. In some regions of the country, particularly in the west and north, the nobility began settling foreign colonists in their villages. In heavily taxed Brandenburg-Prussia, as elsewhere in German east-Elbia, many responded to this opportunity, arriving in Poland to carve out medium or large farms as personally free hereditary leaseholders, often paying (alongside fixed money rents) commutation fees instead of rendering manorial service. Since many of the first such settlers had been recruited from the Low Countries to reclaim swampy land, the free colonists in general were often called 'Hollanders' (*olędrzy*), though most were German, and some were Poles.

This wave of settlement assumed quite large proportions, creating in the neighbourhood of the Polish villagers, living in personal serfdom, a growing body of free farmers. Rapid population growth in the late eighteenth and early nineteenth centuries, accelerated by potato cultivation, reduced the significance of legal subjection. Landlords could find the labourers and tenant farmers they needed, whether free or not, while the villagers' mobility and income opportunities were now constrained less by seigneurial coercion than by competition among themselves for work.

The Villagers in the Eighteenth Century

As numerous travellers reported, the passage across east-Elbian Germany into Poland marked a steady deterioration of material conditions. The villages grew more ramshackle, the towns sleepier and more agrarianized. Among the common people, the comfortable minority shrank in number while the ranks of the miserable swelled.[49] Yet the study of village living standards and well-being across this broad terrain has only begun. Certainly it mattered whether a villager lived under the mighty kings of Prussia or the feeble kings of Poland. In Prussia, military interest ruled that landlords should not evict their subject farmers (whose sons served in the army) and engross their land into the domanial economy. Neither should they crush their villages under seigneurial rent, for it

48. See Jerzy Lukowski, *Liberty's Folly. The Polish-Lithuanian Commonwealth in the Eighteenth Century, 1697–1795* (London, 1991), chs 2–3, and Kula, *Economic Theory*, ch. 4. Cf. also Antoni Mączak, 'Money and society in Poland and Lithuania in the 16th and 17th centuries', *Journal of European Economic History*, 5 (1976), pp. 69–104.

49. Larry Wolff, *Inventing Eastern Europe. The Map of Civilization on the Mind of the Enlightenment* (Stanford, CA, 1994), passim.

was the middling and large farmers whose taxes were the fiscal linchpin of the absolutist system.

The rulers of Prussia maintained a network of state army granaries that stabilized the domestic economy by driving up low prices through purchases and pulling down high prices through sales. The royal domanial estates, leased to middle-class tenant farmers, encompassed a large portion of the country-side, and exhibited progressive techniques that many private estates emulated. Villagers with hereditary tenures could and often did collectively resist their lordships' demands through court action.[50]

These circumstances helped preserve the largeholding farmers as a class. For this protection – or '*Bauernschutz*' – the villagers paid a price, not only in the taxes and conscription weighing upon them, but also in the laws sanctioning their lordships' compulsory recruitment of their unmarried and supernumerary sons and daughters as manorial labourers. Nor should the interests of the villages be identified too narrowly with those of the landholding farmers. Population growth during the High Middle Ages, the sixteenth century, and the late eighteenth and early nineteenth century expanded the ranks of the lower village strata – the cottagers with marginal landholdings and the nearly or wholly landless – much more rapidly than those of the half- and fullholders. The long-run tendency in German east-Elbia, and especially in Brandenburg-Prussia, was toward polarization between the proportionally ever-smaller class of self-sufficient farmers and the growing numbers of those who depended more or less vitally on wage labour.[51]

Neither can the Brandenburg-Prussian heartlands stand for all of German east-Elbia. In Schleswig-Holstein, Mecklenburg, Swedish Pomerania and in Lusatia, severe forms of personal dependency prevailed, tenurial rights were flimsy and rents heavy. Within the Prussian borders, the regions of relatively strong village rights – the Brandenburg Altmark and Mittelmark, the Magdeburg district, middle and lower Silesia – contrasted with areas of weak rights in the Uckermark, the New Mark to the east of the Oder river, Prussian Pomerania east of the Oder mouth, and Upper Silesia. The countryside in far-flung East Prussia exhibited a complex mix of legally secure and insecure villagers.[52]

---

50. Gustavo Corni, 'Absolutistische Agrarpolitik und Agrargesellschaft in Preußen', *Zeitschrift für historische Forschung*, 13 (1986), pp. 285–313. On the villagers' access to the appellate courts, see Hagen, 'Junkers' faithless servants', passim.

51. Yet, compared with Europe west of the Elbe, the relative size of the self-sufficient farmer class in north-eastern Germany (with such regional exceptions as Mecklenburg) was large. On growth of the land-less classes, see Jan Peters, 'Ostelbische Landarmut – Sozialökonomisches über landlose und landarme Agrarproduzenten im Spätfeudalismus', *JbfWg*, 5 (1970), pp. 97–126; Hartmut Harnisch, 'Bevölkerung und Wirtschaft. Über die Zusammenhänge zwischen sozialökonomischer und demographischer Entwicklung im Spatfeudalismus', *JbfWg*, 10 (1975), pp. 57–87; Hagen, 'Working for the Junker', passim. Rutkowski argued that the Prussian landlords, in return for acceptance of state policy protecting the existence of the relatively large farms of their village subjects, won state acquiescence in a hard-line policy toward wage labour, evident in the salience in Prussia of compulsory manorial service (*Gesindezwangsdienst*). In Poland such compulsory service on the part of the sons and daughters of the landed villagers was largely unknown, since the heavy labours of the subject farmers sufficed to meet the landlords' needs. See Rutkowski, *Poddaństwo włościan*, pp. 201–2.

52. On eighteenth-century East Prussia, see Aubin, *Zur Geschichte des gutsherrlich-bäuerlichen Verhältnisses*, and Henning, *Dienste und Abgaben*.

Yet precisely where the law sanctioned strict serfdom, increasingly large populations of legally free villagers arose. The lines separating the free from the subject farmers began to blur, especially where, as (at the government's encouragement) in Brandenburg-Prussia, commutation payments increasingly eclipsed the inefficient and contentious weekly labour services, the prime burden of subjection.[53]

As for Poland, personal subjection and the diminution of holdings characteristic of manorialism's end-phase coexisted regionally with larger but backward subject farms in the east and with large, market-integrated, prosperous holdings cultivated by freemen (olędrzy, gburzy) in the west and north, including the hinterland of Danzig. A harsh regime of labour services imposed upon middle and small subject farms predominated in the Polish heartland but, except for the tithe, little remained by the eighteenth century of seigneurial rents in cash or kind, or of taxes with any bite. The small scale of subject farms, and the low levels of money rents and taxes, meant that pressure upon them to commercialize their surpluses was weak. Many more subject farmers in Poland than in Germany lived within an economy of self-sufficiency and minimal market dealings.[54]

There were also differences in mentality embedded in religion and popular culture in Catholic Poland and overwhelmingly Protestant eastern Germany. Yet it is a question whether, at the level of household structure, life trajectories and material culture, the social experience of east-Elbian German and Polish villagers did not encompass more common than disparate elements. A resolution of this problem lies beyond present horizons, but a step forward can be taken by considering, at the conclusion of this essay, the villagers' condition in two eighteenth-century lordships, one German and the other Polish.

The Subject Farmers Under the Stavenow Lordship

The manor farms and villages comprising the seigneurial jurisdiction of Stavenow lay in north-western Brandenburg.[55] In the late eighteenth century, the arable land of the lordship's four demesne farms spanned 1,400 acres (560 hectares), while in seven villages the proprietors, of the von Kleist lineage, commanded three days of unpaid weekly labour with teams from each of sixty fullholding subject farms (*Hüfnerhöfe*), most of them with two hides of land, and three days

---

53. See Harnisch, *Boitzenburg*, and idem, 'Bäuerliche Ökonomie und Mentalität unter den Bedingungen der ostelbischen Gutsherrschaft in den letzten Jahrzehnten vor Beginn der Agrarreformen', *JbfWg*, 24:3 (1989), pp. 87–108. Landlords' inclination to accept commutation payments rose as population growth drove the price of free wage labour down.

54. Witold Kula, 'The seigneury and the peasant family in eighteenth-century Poland', in Robert Forster and Orest Ranum (eds), *Family and Society. Selections from the Annales* (Baltimore, MD, 1976), pp. 192–203; idem, 'Money and the serfs', passim; see also, apart from his other works cited above, Jacek Kochanowski, 'The Polish peasant family as an economic unit', in Richard Wall *et al.*, *Family Forms in Historic Europe* (Cambridge, 1983), pp. 153–66. Cf. Wyczański, *Polska*, pp. 292–3, 301–3.

55. This discussion is based upon Hagen, 'Der bäuerliche Lebensstandard', as well as idem, 'Seventeenth-century crisis', 'Junkers' faithless servants', and 'Working for the Junker', cited above.

of manual labour from each of the twenty-five landed cottagers (*Kossäten*), most of them with one hide. In 1763 there were eight households of rent-paying day-labourers (*Kätner*), living in cottages with gardens. They were employed mainly by the Stavenow lordship, but worked at other manors and seasonally for the village farmers as well. Their numbers doubled by the early nineteenth century, at which time the Kleists were also maintaining at their manor farms a steadily employed body of fifty-four estate officials and labourers, all earning room, board and wages.

The compulsorily recruited manorial servants were the unmarried sons and daughters of the fullholding farmers, living in workers' quarters and fed at a common table. The freely recruited were older, mostly married workers, living in manorial cottages of their own and receiving from the lordship annual grain stores and other food provisions, along with firewood, grazing rights and cash wages. In the villages there were small numbers of independently housed millers, smiths, tavernkeepers, linenweavers and livestock herders. But there was no proto-industrial proletariat and not even many lodgers (*Einlieger*) among the fullholders, whose dwelling space was mostly reserved for the proprietors' kin, including retired elders, and hired hands, often also relatives.

This was a village society dominated by middle-sized farms meant to be self-sufficient after payment of rent and taxes. Most of these holdings housed families that had rebuilt them, with seigneurial materials and inventories, from the ashes of the Thirty Years War. The lordship did not dispute its farmers' here-ditary tenures, even if the iron stock and the farms themselves were inalienable and reassignable to new occupants in case of abandonment or incompetent management. Otherwise the farm's assets belonged to its inhabitants, who redistributed them among themselves according to law and custom upon the death of their elders and upon the occasion of their own marriages.

By farm-size, tenurial right and rent burdens, the Stavenow farmers were typical cultivators in German east-Elbia, even though there were many others with larger or smaller holdings. The Stavenowers' legal disabilities were neither crushing nor trivial. Non-inheriting children who had served their terms of compulsory service at the manor could leave the jurisdiction as free individuals, though often they only married into subject households in nearby lordships. Many such outmigrants had never been called upon to work at the Stavenow manor. Upon succeeding to the proprietorship of a village farm, the new house-hold head swore an oath of subjection, though without losing access to the royal courts. The landless were 'protected subjects' (*Schutzuntertanen*), liable to an annual fee equivalent to a week or two of day-labourers' wages.[56]

The subject farmers paid weighty tribute into the state's coffers. All able-bodied sons were recruited into the army, where they underwent basic training before being furloughed back to the villages. They were then free to work as fortune dictated, but might be recalled to active duty at any time. Only the soldier who acquired a fullholding could be sure of permission to marry and

---

56. The landless were also free to migrate out of the Stavenow bailiwick though – and in this the landed villagers were no different – if they did so upon receiving an inheritance, they surrendered one-sixth of it to the seigneurial court (that is, to the lordship) as a departure fine.

discharge from the reserves, though as a farmer he now paid the direct taxes financing the steely apparatus of absolutism. Yet the heaviest levy of seigneurial rent weighed upon the farm household's labour, rather than its crops or market earnings. At Stavenow, seigneurial rents in cash and kind together with state taxes together equalled only about one-third of the average cash value in the 1730s of the typical fullholder's grain surplus (although this was not fully monetized, but largely consumed in the household).[57]

In the years 1721–71 the average Stavenow fullholding, excluding young animals, counted five work horses, about five cattle, three to four pigs, and seven sheep. In these years, their value nearly doubled (to ninety-eight talers [*Reichstaler*]). One taler amounted to the weekly wage in cash of a rural day-labourer, or half the weekly earnings of a skilled worker in the towns.[58] Average farm debt also doubled, but was offset threefold by the livestock values. The value of the marriage portion paid out of farm capital to grown children rose from ten to twenty-two talers, excluding the costs of the wedding celebrations. The dowry of a young bride from a fullholder's household, including the inherited marriage portion as well as her own savings (but leaving aside the value of her bridal gown and other clothing and linen), rose from thirty-two to forty-five talers. The bridegrooms, because men's wages were higher, brought more still into their new households.

The lordship periodically appraised the subject farmers' houses and farm buildings. In 1727, among seventy-one dwelling houses, typically of fairly large dimensions and constructed with timber frames, 70 per cent were 'good' or 'new', 13 per cent were 'average', and the rest were 'bad' or 'very bad'. Thus, in 1727, 83 per cent of the houses appeared to the seigneurial appraisers in good or normal condition. Around 1771 this figure still amounted to 66 per cent. The evidence on manorial workers' diets is fuller than on the farmers', but it is clear that both groups usually ate ample portions of bread grains and vegetables, with perhaps more meat than the literature would suggest, along with herring, fresh and dried fruit, cheese, and strong and weak beer. There are no signs of eighteenth-century famine, though the central European harvest failures of 1770–72 left scars, as did earlier bad harvests or epidemics (1709–10, 1718–19), and war years (1756–63).

Post-mortem inventories show that, in their prime, the Stavenow farmers, and especially their wives, possessed large quantities of clothing and personal linen, sometimes of fair value. Household furniture included various chests and cupboards, while beds and bedding often represented good sums. The elderly's possessions were fewer, but in most farmers' households the retired proprietor and his wife lived in separate quarters on the farmstead and received from their successors fixed annual provisions of bread grains, along with fire-wood, minor grazing rights, the harvest of fruit trees, and their own garden plots. These retirement portions (*das Altenteil*) were the coveted reward of

---

57. The household also took in untaxed earnings from the sale of livestock, garden and orchard products.
58. Account needs to be taken of the devaluation of the Prussian currency by one-sixth in 1750.

decades-long toil. The records of the seigneurial court at Stavenow show that, in five-sixths of the court-ratified retirement contracts, the elders received customary provisions.[59]

The median age of fullholders at the moment of their first marriage and assumption of farm proprietorship was twenty-six, and on average twenty-eight. Women married a few years younger. The typical fullholder's career lasted twenty-one years, though 38 per cent persevered longer than twenty-five (and up to forty-seven) years. Women's high mortality in childbirth confined the average marriage to sixteen years, so that the typical farmer remarried at least once. Yet one-third of seventy-five eighteenth-century marriages lasted twenty years or more, while one-tenth reached thirty years and beyond. The average appraisal found 3.6 children in the household. The data are scattered for farm servants, but a fullholding usually employed at least one hired hand, since the two mature workers a fullholder needed could rarely be simultaneously recruited from among his children. If it housed two retirees and two hired hands, a farmstead could number as many as ten people.

Farm proprietorship passed, in four of five cases, from parents to children or stepchildren. Only one in ten successions entailed seigneurial intervention, which normally resulted in the recruitment of the nearest eligible kin. In seven of ten cases, fullholders' heirs married fullholders' children. As for life expectancy, data on farmers alone need assembling, but among 618 eighteenth-century cases from all social categories in several Stavenow villages, among adults of both sexes who lived to age thirty-nine or longer, 20 per cent subsequently died in their forties, 20 per cent in their fifties, 33 per cent in their sixties, and 27 per cent at age seventy or older. Put differently, half of all people thirty-nine and older died between forty and sixty-three years of age, while the other half died after age sixty-three.[60]

After 1763, the Stavenow villages waged an embittered, decades-long struggle against the lordship's efforts to raise labour services and other feudal rents. At considerable expense, they took their case to the appellate court in Berlin, meanwhile staging local rent strikes and aiming sporadic, low-grade violence against seigneurial officials. Government mediation satisfied neither side, but the lordship's maximal claims went unfulfilled. To take advantage of steeply rising grain prices, seigneurial managers invested in additional draught teams and hired more free wage-labourers. In this way, the manorial economy grew less dependent on compulsory labour.

When after 1806 the Prussian government enacted liberal reforms, it proved easier than expected to gain the landlords' assent to the emancipation of their subjects. As members of the widespread class of hereditary but technically non-proprietarial farmers (*erbliche Laßbauern*), the Stavenowers' compensation payments to their former landlords were sizeable. Yet they survived to become

59. In the remaining cases the court imposed restrictions because of economic difficulties facing the new proprietors at the time of the farm transfer.

60. Of course, these demographic figures would look much worse if the heavy child mortality of the period were included in the reckoning.

medium or small-scale freeholders in the dawning age of free-market capitalist agriculture. Though not a triumph, it was a feat they owed largely to their own resourcefulness to have endured as well as they did three centuries of Junker lordship.[61]

The Subject Farmers on the Raczyński Estates

Properties of magnate families loomed large on the Polish landscape. In western Poland, the Raczyński lineage commanded a landed fortune, and in 1756–57 part of it was set aside as a widow's portion. It encompassed one manorial seat and ten demesne farms, worked by subject farmers in fifteen villages. Apart from the income from these sources, the widow Raczyńska drew rents from three proprietary small towns and from eleven 'German villages' (*wsie niemieckie*), that is, recent settlements of free colonists.[62]

The survey of 1756–57 treated the subject villages, inhabited by Poles, differently than it did the 'German villages'. A notation of rents per type of 'German' farmer sufficed, though sometimes the appraisers named the proprietor (occasionally dignified as *gospodarz*, meaning 'householder' or 'farmer'). In the Polish villages, the estate officials listed the inhabitants of each household, including children, servants and lodgers. They recorded the condition of their housing and draught animals, and the personal status – 'subject' or 'free' – of the household head. Neither money rents nor tribute grain figured here, nor did the surveyors describe the individual Polish villagers' labour obligations. Instead, there was but one entry concerning the manorial service, entitled 'obligations of the fullholders [*kmiecie*] in this and other properties':

They work the whole year with oxen from Sunday to Sunday, and from St Wojciech's Day [23 April] to St Martin's [11 November] they add one manual worker daily. Each fullholder gives six capons yearly and 60 eggs. The halfholders [*półślednicy*] work three days weekly with oxen and do three days of weekly manual work. The cottagers [*chałupnicy*] serve as they serve everywhere. The gardeners [*zagrodnicy*] send one person daily for manual labour.[63]

---

61. On the eighteenth-century end-phase and nineteenth-century liquidation of Prussian neo-manorialism, see Kaak, *Gutsherrschaft*, pp. 64ff., 396ff.; Hartmut Harnisch, 'Vom Oktoberedikt des Jahres 1807 zur Deklaration von 1816. Problematik und Charakter der preußischen Agrargesetzgebung zwischen 1807 und 1816', *JbfWg*, Sonderband (1978), pp. 232–93 and *Kapitalistische Agrarreform und industrielle Revolution* (Weimar, 1984). See also the literature cited in Hagen, 'The Junkers' faithless servants' and idem, 'The German peasantry in the nineteenth and early twentieth century: market integration, populist politics, votes for Hitler', *Peasant Studies*, 14 (1987), pp. 273–91, as well as Edgar Melton, 'The decline of Prussian *Gutsherrschaft* and the rise of the Junker as rural patron, 1750–1806', *German History*, 12 (1994), pp. 286–307.

62. This section is based upon an analysis of the Raczyński survey of 1756–57 reproduced in Janusz Deresiewicz (ed.), *Materiały do dziejów chłopa wielkopolskiego w drugiej połowie XVIII wieku*, vol. I: *Województwo poznańskie* (Wrocław, 1956), pp. 19–83.

63. Ibid., pp. 60–1.

The halfholders and landed cottagers comprised the big majority of the landed villagers. While they were partly free to cultivate their own farms, they were basically a labour force at the manorial officials' service, living in seigneurially owned housing and working with oxen and horses mostly supplied from the manor.

At Stavenow, estate appraisals ranged over a middle ground, noting the condition of the subject farms' iron stock and housing, but focusing mainly on the fixed dues and labour services each type of holding rendered, and ignoring the internal composition of the subject household. In this case, it was principally the holding (or *Hof*) which was of value to the lordship, while in the Polish case it was the subjects themselves.

In the fifteen subject villages, the survey recorded 1,341 people living in 294 households. As the first column in Table 1 shows, there were six basic household types: fullholding farmers (*kmiecie*), comprising about one in forty households; halfholders (*półślednicy* or *półrolnicy*), comprising about one-fifth; cottagers with very small arable holdings (*chałupnicy*), amounting to nearly one-quarter; cottagers with gardens (*komornicy*), representing one-tenth; lodgers renting or granted quarters in a farmer's household (*komornicy*), amounting to almost one-eighth; and separately housed manorial servants and employees, accounting for almost one-third of all households. Since the number of resident children and servants varied by household type, while lodgers were scattered among the farmers' households, the distribution of the entire population by household exhibited different proportions, as the second column shows.

In these, as in most other Polish villages, the social and economic centre of gravity rested among the middle-sized farmers and the smallholding cottagers. The few households of fullholders (*kmiecie*) were well-supplied with servants and with children, the older of whom they could afford to keep at home, even in a married state, rather than sending them out to work as farm servants, as the poorer households did. Likewise, the fullholders kept relatively good stables of horses and oxen, although they mostly belonged to the manor.[64] These were the Polish counterparts to the dominant class of subject farmers at Stavenow.

The Raczyński survey says nothing about elders living in retirement. The Polish pattern was rather for the farmers to remain as household heads until their death, relying as they grew older and weaker upon their grown children, who were often married and living with their families in the parental household, awaiting the moment when they would assume its management. Such arrangements seem to have prevailed not only among the fullholders but also among the numerous halfholders (*półrolnicy* or *półślednicy*), whose households – with four children, one servant, and on average one lodger – were

64. Among the fullholders, 4.4 of their 5.6 oxen were owned and supplied by the manor, 2.5 of their 3.6 horses. If the class of village farmers proper on the Raczyński estates is defined as the sum of *kmiecie*, *półrolnicy* and *chałupnicy*, the ratio of large and medium-sized farmers to smallholders is 50:50. Rutkowski's figures for 17,375 tenures in the years 1750–52 yield an analogous ratio of approximately 60:40. His data derived mainly from Crown estates, where largeholders' tenures were somewhat more secure than under noble jurisdictions. 'Régime agraire', pt II, p. 84.

Table 2: Population by household type in fifteen service villages in western Poland, 1756–1757

| | Household type | | Population by household type | | Children/ hsehld (avr.) | Servants/ hsehld (avr.) | Total hsehld size (avr.) | Horses (avr.) | Oxen (avr.) | Housing | | |
	No.	%	No.	%	No.	No.	No.	No.	No.	good No.	fair No.	bad No.
1. kmiecie	8	2.7	77	5.8	4.4	2.0	9.6	3.6	5.6	2	2	4
2. półrolnicy	58	19.7	478	35.6	3.9	1.1	8.2	2.5	3.5	20	6	30
3. chałupnicy	67	22.8	380	28.3	2.9	0.3	5.7	1.3	2.2	22	10	29
4. komornicy	31	10.6	151	11.3	2.3	-0-	4.9	-0-	-0-	3	14	13
5. lodgers	38	12.9	–^	–^	1.7	-0-	2.8	-0-	-0-	–	–	–
6. manorial employees	92	31.3	255	19.0	2.5	-0-	2.8	-0-	-0-	18	5	20
Total	294	100.0	1341	100.0	2.4+ 2.9++	1.1* 0.8+++	5.2^^	2.5*	3.8*	65= 33%	37= 19%	96= 48%

Source: Janusz Deresiewicz (ed.), Materiały do dziejów chłopa wielkopolskiego w drugiej połowie XVIII wieku. Tom I. Województwo poznańskie (Wrocław, 1956), pp. 19–83.

^ Lodgers distributed among categories 1–3.
+ Average among all households.
* Average among categories 1–3.
^^ Including lodgers.
++ Average among parents with children.
+++ Average number of servants unrelated by kinship to household head.

184

sizeable for farms in the twenty-acre range. They kept, on average, six horses and oxen, also mostly in seigneurial ownership. With these draught animals, whose pasturage was perhaps meagre, the halfholders met the lordship's requirements for ploughing, harrowing and hauling. In the peak seasons, they were summoned daily to the manor farms. It was essential that enough hands remain in the household to work the holding's own land and earn extra income through occasional wage labour.[65]

The many cottagers with small arable holdings (*chałupnicy*) held a pair of oxen and a horse or two, half of these animals their own. They kept on average three children at home, while only one in three hired a servant or housed a lodger. Their obligation in the high season was to supply the manor with one or two manual workers on a daily basis. Their lesser colleagues, the cottagers with garden land only (housed *komornicy*), had still smaller households and kept no draught animals. They owed a few days of unpaid weekly manual service, often provided by women, and otherwise lived from wage labour. About half of these mostly poverty-blighted cottagers were widows or women whose husbands had absconded. The lodgers (unhoused *komornicy*) comprised even more women (86 per cent) than did the landless cottagers, but in part this followed from the customary definition of the group as essentially female. One-third were married with children, mostly farm servants' wives. A quarter of them were married without children, probably women with elderly or disabled husbands. Over 40 per cent were women living alone with children.

Finally, the manorial employees and servants comprised a variegated group. Some labourers at the demesne farms lived in the villages as lodgers, and were registered as such. In this group were counted, among others, manorial officials, such as bailiffs, scribes and foresters (22 per cent); seigneurial shepherds (16 per cent), who often possessed some property in the form of the fifth part of the flocks they tended; artisans and tavernkeepers (19 per cent), also a not wholly penurious group; and domanial ploughmen and male and female farmworkers (19 per cent). A majority of these employees were married, living more or less decently in separate dwellings with their families.

Fewer than half (48 per cent) of the manorial employees lived in personal subjection; the majority were free from compulsory labour and impediments to moving elsewhere. The seigneurial surveyors did not record the legal status of the lodgers, perhaps because they represented a doubtful asset. Among the other villagers, rates of personal subjection were extremely high, ranging from 85 per cent of the landless cottagers to 100 per cent of the halfholders. In these villages only a few had absconded: five were farmers' children, two were

---

65. See Kula, 'The seigneury and the peasant family'; Kochanowicz, 'The Polish peasant family', pp. 153–63; as well as the valuable study, based on Mazovian sources, by Andrzej Woźniak, 'Małżeństwa chłopskie w XVIII-wiecznej wsi pańszczyźnianej', *Etnografia Polska*, 22 (1978), pp. 133–57, and 23 (1979), pp. 153–74. The family sizes in the Raczyński villages in western Poland reported in the text above considerably exceed Woźniak's figures (pp. 158–60) for Mazovian villages. The same is true in relation to Kochanowicz's eighteenth-century data on family sizes in southern Polish villages (pp. 155–61). The difference would seem to reflect the larger size and, perhaps, greater material welfare of farms in Great Poland in contrast to those in central and southern Poland.

husbands of women registered as lodgers, and one was a farmer who had deserted his wife and children.[66]

Some of the lordship's inhabitants voluntarily surrendered their freedom, such as Jakub Kinowski, a domanial scribe, 'who subjected himself *officiose* so as to marry his wife in the village here'.[67] In other cases, the villagers claimed free status, but long residency created a presumption of subjection. As the surveyors wrote of a watchman and his wife, 'they claim not to be subjects [*niepoddani*], and yet they have lived here for years'. But in the same village they accepted a smallholder's assertion that 'he and his wife and children are freely contracted and not subjects [*niepoddani, kontraktowi*], and they have their own farm inventory'.[68]

In the absence of seigneurial court records inventorying the subject villagers' possessions, measures of the villagers' individual well-being are at present scarce. Among 188 appraised houses, 51 per cent were found to be bad, very bad, or dangerous, requiring major repairs or complete rebuilding; only 35 per cent were rated in new or good condition, while the rest (14 per cent) were average.

The maintenance of the subject farm at a tolerable level of material welfare depended on the size and age-composition of the household's labour force. Young children and incapacitated elders were liabilities, especially to the newly married couple taking possession of a farm. If such a couple could recruit brothers or sisters or other near-relations to join the household as farm servants, and if the elders could perform useful labour, the chances were fair that the household would manage until the farmer's own children could work for him as servants or otherwise contribute to the income of the household. But if such a young couple were obliged to clothe and feed non-kin servants, and maintain sickly elders and young children as well, their household could easily sink into misery at the first bad harvest.[69]

Several instances of relative well-being among the subject villagers under the Raczyński lordship support this view. The halfholder and forester Jędrzej occupied a house with a good thatched roof, a timbered living room, and entry-hall and bedroom constructed of lumber. Its foundations needed repair, as did his stable. One barn was good, the other was old. He kept four oxen and three horses, all belonging to himself. With his wife he had three daughters, of whom two had been put into service (*rozporządzone*) outside the house. The third daughter and her husband served in the household as servants while

---

66. In one case, a halfholding farmer had married one daughter to a freeman and outsider. The lordship approved this on condition that the father would bring another young women into his household as a worker, which he had not yet done; the farmer had a second daughter who, 'having been insubordinate' in her service to the lordship, 'absconded'. This left the household with a third daughter, identified as 'the studious Anna (*Scholastyka Anna*)'. Deresiewicz, *Materiały*, p. 42.

67. Ibid., p. 30.

68. Ibid., pp. 38–9.

69. Woźniak, 'Małżeństwa', passim. Cf. also Kula, *Economic Theory*, pp. 72ff., and 'The seigneury and the peasant family', passim. Rutkowski held that landlords were likely to make concessions on labour services to very young household heads (and that in general they respected the villagers' inheritance claims on the paternal farm): *Historia gospodarcza*, p. 270. According to Woźniak 'Małżeństwa', p. 138, the lesser gentry frequently moved their subject farmers from one holding to another. The Raczyński inventory makes no references to such practices.

raising their two small children. Here there were no incapacitated elders, nor were the children a great burden on the four adults.[70]

There was the halfholder Tomasz and his wife, of whose house, barn and stable the surveyors wrote that 'all buildings are in good array'. One of their daughters had married and moved away, but the remaining two daughters and two sons lived at home 'working for their parents as servants'. Tomasz could claim as his own four oxen and two horses. The halfholder's widow Janowa occupied with her ten children a dwelling house described as old and bad, although her outbuildings were good. The surveyors noted that 'she runs the farm' with her three oldest sons, together with the hired servant-girl Barbara. The widow had two manorial oxen as well as three of her own, together with four horses, two her own.[71]

In another case, a halfholder's widow managed the farm with her married son and his wife, together with a younger unmarried son. But the household also counted an unmarried servant-girl and a married farm servant with four children and a wife, who as a lodger was obliged to perform unpaid weekly lodgers' service (komorne) at the manor. There was the fullholder Wojciech, whose dwelling was 'properly good' (należycie dobra), with outbuildings 'in good array'. With his wife Regina he had three children, including a son married to a fullholder's daughter. His other children lived at home. Wojciech kept six manorial oxen and four manorial horses, and employed two male farm servants, both seigneurial subjects.[72]

By contrast, among many bleak pictures recorded by the surveyors, there was the cottager's holding of a certain Zdzymaj, 'who has absconded'. The dwelling house was good, but the outbuildings bad. 'The woman' – Zdzymaj's abandoned wife – 'manages for herself', though she had no livestock, having traded her last animal for food. Living with her was the lodger Mateusz, with two children and a wife who performed the lodger's service. 'This Mateusz neither serves nor does anything else', probably because of illness. The house-mistress's sister also lived with her, together with two daughters who served at the manor in their mother's place.[73] Seemingly, the absence of able-bodied men doomed the women to an impoverishment that probably grew only worse.

As for judgements on the communal well-being of these villages, the appraisers remarked of the inhabitants of Sycyno:

the whole village says that they perform labour services beyond the measure of their obligation for the tenant farmer [that is, for the nobleman leasing the Sycyno demesne farm from the Raczyński lordship]. The cottagers say that, from time to time, they haven't got enough land for bread, and that to help the people His Honour tenant farmer Zabłocki gave them, according to their need, bread and barley seed, and for that reason they are this year suffering great oppression [wielkiego ucisku].[74]

70. Deresiewicz, Materiały, p. 25.
71. Ibid., p. 46.
72. Ibid., pp. 46, 54.
73. Ibid., p. 28.
74. Ibid., p. 43.

Of the principal manor farm at Wyszyna, the surveyors concluded that, on average, winter sowings (usually of rye) would only yield 'one grain', that is, that average crops would only double the seed sown. From the villagers' land at Wyszyna, except for two communal fields, 'no benefit can be expected, because the harvests there have been very weak. It will be necessary to support the people, both with seed grain and with bread.' At the settlement of Prosna, however, the manorial harvests were 'as they should be' (*obrzędnie*) and, except for three enfeebled farmers, the manor would not need to provide from its own harvests for the villagers. Around Grylewo cultivation was 'as it should be', as also at Sycyno and the town of Szamocin, but at Stobnica it was 'bad' (*licho*).[75]

The survey offers some evidence that manorial servants, especially those who were married and separately housed, kept household livestock and received adequate food provisions from the manor. In the 'German villages', references were rare to ruined householders who had absconded or who could not pay their considerable money rents. They were largely free of labour services, although some replaced the commutation fees with two or three days of weekly work. While their material circumstances remain unclear, the regime of cash rents points to greater well-being than in the Polish villages. Their condition was, in all likelihood, closer to that of the Stavenow farmers.

Poverty was widespread among the Polish villagers, but survival at some tolerable level of material welfare was possible. Conditions on the Raczyński estates, in themselves ambiguous, cannot be generalized, and it will be long before a picture claiming representativeness for the pre-partition Commonwealth can be drawn. The evidence presented here suggests that, depending on the human and livestock resources of the farmstead, sufficiency could be attained. Unfortunately, the Polish Commonwealth could not guarantee the villages' security, which easily yielded to plunder and impoverishment in times of foreign invasion and civil war.

The toll on the common people of the proverbial 'Polish anarchy', understood as governmental weakness, should be rated higher – in contrast to the impoverishing effect (real though it was) of seigneurial exploitation – than the historical literature generally allows. For many twentieth-century Polish historians, it has been easier to condemn the landlords' fleecing of their subjects than to accept that the impotence and bankruptcy of the state ruined the land and its inhabitants.

CONCLUSION

The historical literature has viewed the agrarian world of east-Elbian Germany and Poland through the eyes of the landed gentry. Both through their ancient

75. Ibid., p. 80.

legitimate authority and their powers of extra-economic coercion, they worked their will upon the villages, successfully carrying out the seigneurial counter-revolution of the long sixteenth century. Yet, as this essay has argued, their triumph was imperfect, both in the period before the crisis of the seventeenth century and in the end-phase of commercialized manorialism. The subject farmers stubbornly defended their labour power and farm surpluses, whether in negotiations with the lordships exchanging natural rents for manorial service, or in striking terms for the resettlement of an abandoned or devastated holding, or through the smallest possible exertion expended in work at the manor, or rent-strikes and lawsuits, or other forms of resistance and the pursuit of minor advantages in the long tug-of-war they fought with their lordships.

From this angle, the differences in the situation and development of the Polish villages, by contrast with those in east-Elbian Germany, appear to be great in degree but smaller in kind. While the access of most subject farmers in Brandenburg-Prussia to the princely courts gave them a powerful weapon of self-defence that most Polish (and other east-Elbian German) villagers lacked, in other respects variations in legal condition from west to east were perhaps less important. The villagers were all primarily interested in leading the life of small or medium farmers, consuming the products of their labours, selling their surpluses on local markets, and fulfilling their expectations of the life-cycle as village custom defined and culturally legitimized it. All struggled to minimize the burden upon them of seigneurial rent. All could be driven by misfortune and despair into illegal flight. The towns were not closed to them, but it was difficult to take much with them in the way of start-up capital, whether human or material, for an urban career.

This essay has stressed the importance of judging the villagers' condition by the rents they paid their lordships, by the taxes and tithes extracted from them, and by their material circumstances, as reflected in housing, accumulated property and working capital, diet, longevity, and other such measures. It can in some cases be shown that, by these standards, the villagers experienced better and worse times under the centuries-long manorial regime. The conjuncture of the moment must be understood before judgements on well-being or misery are rendered. The exogenous impact upon the rural common people of state-building or state-breakdown processes, and of the fiscal burdens and wartime toll they entailed, must also be justly weighed, without resorting to the reductive tactic of interpreting all developments in the political sphere as reflections of the interests of the landed nobility. The history of these central European villages steered not toward ineluctable, structurally determined outcomes, but rather traced a course defined, in each land, by the multi-sided rivalry of manor, village, Crown and town. In the end the villages, though battered and bruised, survived the contest.

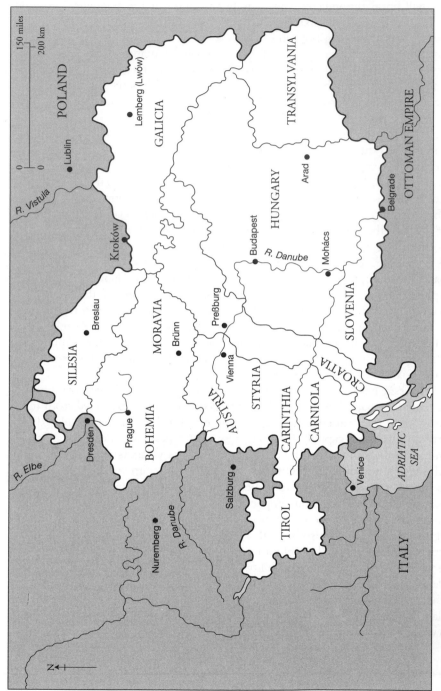

Map 7.1 The lands of the Austrian Empire

CHAPTER SEVEN

Peasantries Under the Austrian Empire, 1300–1800

Hermann Rebel

One of the advantages that the study of peasant societies offers to historical social science is that it makes clear there are no rural village entities that constitute a stable and originating stage of human development from which later commercial and industrial forms evolved and on which these latter continue to depend in some way. This essay is intended, in part, to show that the 'immemorial' appearance of such historically old agricultural societies as those in the Austrian, Bohemian and Hungarian mountains and floodplains can deceive us about the 'authentically' or 'originally' rural qualities of a region's culture.

The modern Austrian Republic is the core remnant of a much larger region whose boundaries and hierarchical arrangements once constituted an 'empire' that escapes easy historical identification[1] and whose rural population – over 50 per cent of the total as late as the beginning of this century and owning about 70 per cent of the arable land during the eighteenth century and 94 per cent by the early twentieth century[2] – has been too diverse to fit easily into separate sectors of social categories such as peasants or artisans. One of the best recent social history texts, Ernst Bruckmüller's *Sozialgeschichte Österreichs*,[3] offers a masterful synthesis of many researchers' findings, including much material on various Austrian rural populations, and yet by scrupulously confining itself almost exclusively to the area of modern Austria it misses an important ingredient in the story, namely that the peasant experience in the Austrian core states is not fully explicable without a context that includes peasantries from the wider historical 'empire'.

Another recent survey, Charles Ingrao's ambitious *The Habsburg Monarchy, 1618–1815*, purports to offer such a wider perspective. At the outset he even invokes an 'Austrian empire', one that then appears, however, as founded merely in the integration of disparate, centripetal territories by the Habsburgs'

---

1. C. Maier, 'Whose Mitteleuropa? Central Europe between memory and obsolescence', in G. Bischof and A. Pelinka (eds), *Austria in the New Europe* (New Brunswick/London, 1993); interesting in this regard as well is M. Mitterauer, 'Die Anfänge österreichischer Geschichte als Problem', *Österreich in Geschichte und Literatur*, 6 (1962).

2. R. Sandgruber, *Österreichische Agrarstatistik, 1750–1918* (Vienna, 1978), pp. 222, 30, 230.

3. (Vienna, 1985).

famous 'dynastic diplomacy'.[4] This conflation of dynasty, monarchy and region may appear appropriate to the period Ingrao surveys, but it also reveals his approach's association with a current ideological redefinition of 'empires' as endlessly flexible and optimizing constructions organized by managerial and capital-accumulating central powers merely to respond to successive crises.[5] Significant distinctions within and between the social formations that constituted the Habsburg monarchy and its integrating dynasties[6] are not at issue in such an approach. The ostensibly miserable lives of the subaltern appear as irritating intrusions into such a story and Ingrao remains content to describe once again 'the peasantry' – with Bohemians and Hungarians alternating as general indicators – perpetually suffering worsening conditions of forced labour under so-called second serfdom until relief arrived by way of cameralist and humanitarian reforms during the second half of the eighteenth century. This is an old model of imperial social relations[7] in which peasantries are fated to appear as third parties caught between provincial and central authorities, destined to suffer combined oppressions when the powerful are at peace and destabilized and drawn into war when they are not. In such a view, peasants appear as a social 'sector' but their differences, alliances, conflicts and motivations stand outside the historical processes that are perceived to matter.

Looking further back along the traditions of diplomatic intelligence, however, we can find a subtle and useful perspective on what kind of entity the old Austrian empire was. Otto von Bismarck, in his recollections, recounts his counsel to the Prussian prince and military staff against continuing the war with Austria in the late spring of 1866. He saw the Austrian empire as an unconquerable region stretching from 'Tirol to the Bukovina', unassimilable not only because the swamps of Hungary would defeat Prussian armies already threatened by cholera but also because it represented a historically evolved and fragile association of peoples. He saw the Habsburgs not as creators but as beneficiaries of an order they did not fully control and whose tribute-producing self-organization could collapse under the pressures of further destabilization and conquest.[8] 'Peasants' were not explicitly a part of Bismarck's vision, to be sure, but the Austrian empire's social order that he respected as the disparate

4. (Cambridge, 1994), pp. 1–2 and passim.

5. E. Jones, *The European Miracle* (Cambridge, 1987); J. Komlos, *Nutrition and Economic Development in the Eighteenth Century Habsburg Monarchy* (Princeton, NJ, 1991); for the beginnings of a critique of this perspective see J. M. Blaut, *The Colonizer's Model of the World* (New York, 1993) and H. Rebel, 'The Austrian model for world development: a neoclassical excitation', *East Central Europe*, 19: 1 (1992).

6. Cf. A. Lhotsky, 'Was heißt "Haus Österreich"?', in his *Aufsätze und Vorträge* (Munich, 1970); V. Press, 'The Habsburg lands: the Holy Roman Empire', in T. Brady, H. Oberman and J. Tracy (eds), *Handbook of European History, 1400–1600*, vol. I (Leiden, 1994). It is understood that 'Austrian empire' does not here refer to the official renaming of 1804.

7. G. Ostrogorsky, *History of the Byzantine State* (New Brunswick, NJ, 1957 [1940]); S. N. Eisenstadt, 'Introduction' to idem, (ed.), *The Decline of Empires* (Englewood Cliffs, NJ, 1967).

8. O. von Bismarck, *Gedanken und Erinnerungen* (Munich, 1961), pp. 300–13. Bismarck understood that he had placed the Habsburgs' state into his bankers' hands for receivership and that the interest payments the latter would extract from the loans forced on the defeated Austrians depended on the unbroken continuation of the empire as a tribute-producing formation. Cf. W. Treue 'Die Finanzierung der Kriege 1864–1871 durch die deutschen Länder', *Vierteljahrschrift für Sozial- und Wirtschaftsgeschichte*, 75: 1 (1988), pp. 3–4 and passim.

and yet indivisible, unconquerable and yet potentially destructible source of wealth was the result of centuries of corporate-territorial formation in which peasants' economies and social cultures were inextricably entwined.

The Austrian empire's social construction was as old as the late Classical period's commercial political economies built on the specific convergence between Alpine mountain passes, connecting Italy and the Balkans to the inner continent, and the Danube, connecting south-western Europe to the Black Sea and beyond. Although there had been farmer-fishermen in the rivers' floodplains and along the Alpine lakes since at least neolithic times, the central economic pursuits had never been in agriculture but in salt as well as in base and precious metals mining and in the related refining, manufacturing, monetary and weapons industries, commerce and trade that had long been (and to a considerable extent still are) the Austrian core territories' sources of relative economic and political independence. The agriculturists, from the outset, appeared in supporting roles and only moved to the foreground with the alleged 'modernization' of the empire under the Habsburg state beginning in the sixteenth century. They were never a part of the organization of Austrian dynastic-aristocratic and other corporate entities that took shape around the interlocking commercial and extractive-industrial economies within the shifting boundaries of the Alpine-Danubian 'empire'.[9]

Even though farmers and cottager-artisans had by 1300 organized themselves into communal house owners' associations to manage their commons and, individually and collectively, to enter into relations with members of the constituted territorial corporations, they remained, with notable exceptions, unincorporated at the territorial (*Landschaft*) level. They did not have much to bargain with. They were rent-payers in a market in which property-owning corporations saw agricultural land-clearing enterprise as a relatively high-risk and low-return investment. As early as the tenth century there is evidence that the Austrian empire's core commercial regions did not depend on locally produced foodstuffs but lived on food imports from Bohemia and from the import-transit trade in Hungarian cattle.[10] Moreover, much of the region's military, extractive and industrial labour was not recruited locally but immigrated from the German empire and from peripheral areas to the south and east. One of the aspects of Austrian peasant politics to bear in mind in the narrative below is the peasantries' persistent efforts to step up to a place in the territorial-corporative order and yet, at the same time, to expand and defend their innately limited local economies and corporatively subaltern forms of 'house' and 'commune' authority against erosion by their landlords as well as by their own dispossessed and by migrant outsiders. The oldest social division in the Austrian empire is that between members of families and institutions that have territorial corporate status and those without, i.e. between corporate magisterial authorities (later: *Obrigkeiten*) and everyone

9. The classic introduction to the constitutional foundations of the Austrian provinces is O. Brunner, *Land and Lordship* (Philadelphia, 1992 [German edn 1965]); G. W. Sante and A. G. Ploetz Verlag (eds), *Geschichte der deutschen Länder. Territorien-Ploetz* (Würzburg, 1964); A. Hoffmann, 'Grundlagen der Agrarstruktur der Monarchie', in idem (ed.), *Österreich-Ungarn als Agrarstaat* (Vienna, 1978).

10. A. Hoffmann, *Wirtschaftsgeschichte des Landes Oberösterreich* (Salzburg, 1952), pp. 77, 72–4.

else, who are then 'subjects' (later: *Untertanen*) to one or several of the former groups. Peasants and their families' house communities were the social core of the Austrian empire's subject population living an always 'marginal' and occasionally devastating history of boom and bust cycles within the empire's relatively secondary and limited agricultural sectors. Their experience holds one key to disclosing the processes of this region's production of an especially conflict-ridden version of modernity, to comprehending its simultaneous unconquerability and always-threatening collapse.

PEASANTRIES: ANALYTICAL MODELS AND THE AUSTRIAN EXPERIENCE

Austrian-German usage has its equivalent to the ambivalent English 'peasant' in the word *Bauer* (pl. *Bauern*). One finds it used variously – sometimes appearing in its pre-modern forms as *Paur* or *Bawer* – in royal proclamations, legal and managerial documents, broadsides, songs, court records, scholarly and popular writings from the Middle Ages to the present and often in ways far more ambiguous than and even subversive of the 'original' sense of the old high German expression that designated any member of a rural house community. We find antiquarian writers who describe at length Austrian traditional diets as typical *Bauernessen*, but then go on to reveal that such diets did not in fact consist only of locally produced grains served as bread and porridge but often contained more exotic foods from Hungary and Italy. Indeed, while some 'peasants', fully in step with the commercial-cosmopolitan quality of the Austrian empire, enjoyed such supra-regional diets, we find that it was the live-in hired labourers (*Gesinde*) for whom special fields were set aside to grow combinations of inferior grains for the kind of porridge that supposedly was the peasant staple.[11]

A noteworthy ambiguity also appears in the current Austrian designation *Nebenerwerbsbauer* for someone who literally makes a 'peasant-living-on-the-side'. It is not unusual to find, for example, seasonal articles placed in Austrian rural papers by local officers of the 'Peasant League' (*Bauernbund*) reminding *Nebenerwerbsbauern* to register their wives who are managing the farm with their industrial employers' social insurance so that the wives do not lose their benefits while the husbands are seasonally unemployed.[12] This raises questions about who exactly is the 'peasant' here and what is her relationship to the 'industrial' partner in the family's 'agricultural enterprise' (*Landwirtschaft*)? And why does she run the risk of being uninsured if her industrial partner does not register her under his insurance plan? Does it mean that what is recognized as a 'peasant' household is in fact split internally both by economic sector and gender

---

11. W. Huditz, 'Vom österreichischen Bauernessen einst und jetzt', *Österreichische Zeitschrift für Volkskunde*, new series, 24: 1 (1970); A. Hoffmann, 'Österreichs alte Landkultur und ihre Grundlagen', *Oberösterreichische Heimatblätter*, 4 (1950).

12. E. Lengauer, 'Wichtig für Nebenerwerbsbauern!', *Oberösterreichische Landwirtschaftszeitung*, 30 January 1985.

in ways that align clearly less privileged women with the purportedly 'backward' and 'premodern' peasant sector? From a historical perspective it opens questions concerning the extent to which women's work can be and has been systematically misrecognized in analyses of Austrian and other 'peasantries'.[13] Moreover, it requires historical analysts to consider to what extent this splitting of the 'peasant' enterprise and family into hierarchical and possibly conflicting occupational sectors is a matter of the decay and passing away in the face of the alleged 'modernization' of a once-stable and dominant historical 'peasant culture'[14] or whether it appears as an updated replaying of historical social forms peculiar to the Austrian peasants' particular social world whose complexity is thus both recalled and repressed in language about *Bauern*.

During the past decade there has appeared a series of memoirs written or narrated by Austrian rural servant women and men, midwives, cottagers' children, Alpine dairy farmers, migrant labourers and others.[15] The question with which such texts challenge historians is whether these are memories of a peasant past that is irretrievably gone or whether they are evidence of an endless process of memory work in so-called 'everyday life' in which everyone participates to keep alive perpetually and repetitiously re-enacted past moments whose continuing presence is denied by discourses about progress and modernity. One of the most striking and often repeated memories concerns the punitive, violent tenor of life in rural families and communities, an everyday, normal violence that is particularly visited on children and women. For several of the memoirists (and their editors) such violence is in some bygone 'peasant' past, but any reading of the current provincial press reveals this to be far from true.

In this essay, 'peasant' does not designate a social or economic type but a highly flexible and always risky option that can exist in the interstices of all historical political economies where self-sustaining – which can often be nothing more than self-exploiting – rural families find 'farming' to be one of several realistic means to pursue a life that appears to offer sufficient material as well as spiritual satisfactions. For the Austrian case, this requires our abandoning the persistent description of peasants from this region as 'serfs'.[16] Leaving aside

---

13. J. Ehmer, 'Die Stellung der Frau in der Familie – vom feudal-ständischen zum bürgerlichen Patriarchalismus', in E. Weinzierl and K. Stadler (eds), *Justiz und Zeitgeschichte*, vol. 3, (Salzburg, 1977); G. Roth, *Im tiefen Österreich* (Frankfurt am Main, 1990), pp. 95–7 and passim; H. Rebel, 'Peasants against the state in the body of Anna Maria Wagner', *Journal of Historical Sociology*, 6: 1 (1993). In this connection one finds C. Delphy's concept of 'housework' particularly stimulating; see her *Close to Home* (London, 1984). For 'misrecognition' see P. Bourdieu and L. J. D. Wacquant, *An Invitation to Reflexive Sociology* (Chicago, 1992), p. 168.

14. Cf. Bruckmüller, *Sozialgeschichte*, p. 527 and idem, *Nation Österreich* (Vienna, 1984), p. 197.

15. Compare M. Mitterauer's preface to the first book in the series, M. Gremel, *Mit neun Jahren im Dienst* (Vienna, 1991 [1983]) to that by C. Hämmerle for M. Horner, *Aus dem Leben einer Hebamme* (Vienna, 1985); other notable recent titles include N. Orthmayr (ed.), *Knechte* (Vienna, 1992) and M. Gremel's sequel *Vom Land zur Stadt* (Vienna, 1991).

16. C. A. Macartney, *The Habsburg Empire 1790–1918* (New York, 1969), pp. 61–2, (mistakenly) tried to restrict usage of the term to designate the condition of peasant dependence he understood as *Leibeigenschaft*; 'serfdom' seems intrinsic to a vision that sees peasants as a transitional historical type, cf. W. Rösener, *The Peasantry of Europe* (Oxford, 1994) or, worse, as an indistinguishable human mass, Ingrao, *Monarchy*, pp. 25, 42; a suggestive departure is J. Bak, 'Serfs and serfdom: words and things', *Review of the Fernand Braudel Institute*, 4: 1 (1980).

the nineteenth-century liberal-propagandistic grounds for this usage as well as its association with Marxist notions of a 'second serfdom', one may say that it simply performs the same screening function as *Bauer* but with a memory trace that points us away from the fundamental legal and social character of Austrian peasants, who could be but were not primarily distinguished as being 'servile'.

Bauer, throughout the centuries under discussion here, was always a formal role function that designated in civil and public law the incumbent chief of the private law domain that was a legally established farm (*Bauernhof*) ranging from two to three whole 'hides' (*Hufen*) down to a quarter hide.[17] Those with holdings below this level were cottagers and smallholders (*Häusler*, in Bohemia *Chalupner*) who, until the late eighteenth century, did not share in the obligations or in the communal rights and privileges of the 'housed' peasant tenants. Indeed, as a sub-peasant class of householders they were closer to the truly subaltern 'unhoused' lodgers and servants, and stood always on the threshold of further downward social mobility into this class of people whose increasingly servile labour sustained the peasant enterprises but who were left socially adrift and in constant danger of the personal disasters of unemployment and incarceration.

Although, as a legal class, the incumbent heads of peasant houses never managed to join the evolving complexes of territorial (*Landschaft*) corporations, they nevertheless enjoyed a 'dominion' analogous to that of the corporate lords by acting as heads of legally empowered house administrations. However conditionally they held their tenures, they were 'free' under a theoretically universal 'house peace' (*Hausfrieden*) which it was their duty to their lords as well as to the houses' inhabitants to uphold in return for enjoying the immunities of their status. Their quasi-judicial authority replicated, ideologically if not in fact, within the peasant house community the corporative social contract binding together the empire's social formation as a whole.[18] The Austrian peasant house was, paradoxically, the fundamental unit in the legal-social order and yet it was also 'below' and outside that order in the sense that how it organized itself internally, privately, was of no concern as long as public order was maintained. The inner life of the peasant house was, throughout the long period examined in this essay, 'outside the law' and could therefore become, for those who had to live under 'the peasant's' exclusive authority, a place of oppression and even terror. This latter clearly surfaces in Austrian rural traditions which still find ritual expression in processions, during early December, by masked bands posing

17. A *Hufe* could vary in size from ten to forty-five acres depending on the circumstances of its 'origin' in the land clearing and development process during the early and High Middle Ages. It included buildings as well as land, could claim specific descriptions of rights and duties and was intended to provide for a *familia* that could consist of various combinations of blood- and role-kin living on the premises. Land without living and production buildings was relatively rare until the seventeenth century and was called *ledig* and was cultivated and 'traded' outside the farm complex. Hoffmann's estimates of actual medieval and early modern Austrian farm sizes range from a large estate farm (*Meierhof*) of about 135 acres through a full farm (*Hof*) of about 75 acres, to small farms (*Halbhof*, *Lehen*) from 50 to 20 acres, to a cottage (*Sölde*) around 12 acres and a small garden house (*Häusel*) with five. *Wirtschaftsgeschichte*, p. 32.

18. Brunner, *Land*, pp. 211–13 and passim.

as werewolves and as 'the wild hunt' to invade select families' houses to steal the kitchen table which the family members in turn have to defend with force.[19]

The housed peasants, especially those community leaders with large farms, experienced daily the perks of miniature lordship authorized by the official languages of 'house' and 'family' in which always lurked a sufficient allusion to 'dynasty' to draw them into identifying, for the most part, with the evolving aristocratic ethic of 'house management'. On the other hand, the same seductive 'identity' formation educated the peasantry into recognizing when aristocratic corporate and estate management interfered with and imposed exploitive choices on the peasants' subaltern corporate interests. This could spark, as we will see, political initiatives and resistances across a wide spectrum of issues.

For the purpose at hand of modelling a 'peasant option', such peasant politics suggest an approach whose focus is not on the 'feudal' or other typological and possibly transitional character of such actions, but rather on the complexity of the contingencies faced by, and the various rational qualities demanded of, successful peasant incumbents. Towards this end there appeared in the social scientific literature that sought to typify peasants some very useful contributions in the proposals by Foster, Popkin, Scott and a host of others, about the diverse and relative rationalities and values orientations of both historical and contemporary peasantries. Without necessarily agreeing, one learns a great deal from these debates about what might be specifically peasant propensities for 'behaviour toward risk' and one gains a better appreciation of the complexities of the different kinds of rationality required by the peasant option.[20] They remain of fundamental importance for our approach.

Eric Wolf's *Peasants*[21] is something of a summary of, as well as a new departure from, these debates. His central arguments are organized around a discussion of the various 'funds' peasant families and communities must produce and manage not only to feed themselves and replace their productive capacity from year to year but to be able to perform the economic, social, ceremonial and other combined cultural tasks that were required of and advantageous to them in their respective historical environments. Wolf moves the debate beyond whether peasants were naturally conservative, values-rational, safety-oriented investors of their land and labour or whether they tended to be risk-taking, market-rational maximizers, by showing that to coordinate strategies for balancing their private familial with their communal needs they had to be both – and that they engaged in a special 'peasant rationality' only in so far as this appeared in terms of agricultural and village contingencies that could vary greatly in proportion to the manner and complexity of their internal and external articulations with both local and wider markets.

19. O. Koenig, *Klaubauf – Krampus – Nikolaus; Maskenbrauch in Tirol und Salzburg* (Vienna, 1983).

20. J. Potter, M. Diaz and G. Foster (eds), *Peasant Society* (Boston, MA, 1967) contains Foster's 'Limited good', E. Wolf's 'Closed corporate peasant communities' and F. Friedman's classic 'The world of *La Miseria*'; also T. Shanin (ed.), *Peasants and Peasant Societies* (Oxford, 1987), especially S. Ortiz, 'Peasant culture, peasant economy'; D. McCloskey, 'English open fields as behavior toward risk', in P. Uselding (ed.), *Research in Economic History* (Greenwich, CT, 1976) and his updated 'The open fields of England: rent, risk and the rate of interest, 1300–1815', in D. Galenson (ed.), *Markets in History* (Cambridge, 1989).

21. (Englewood Cliffs, NJ, 1966).

Fundamental to Wolf's model is a consideration of issues of cultural ecology and this has found explicit, but only partial resonance among the best analysts of Austrian peasantries. Michael Mitterauer has produced a considerable body of work on Austrian peasant 'ecotypes . . . understood as regionally dominant economic styles . . . originating in adaptations to natural environmental conditions'[22] in which he follows, by a method of family reconstitution, the highly differentiated movements of people into and out of peasant families and enterprises, and discloses for early modern rural Austria family strategies analogous to what Richard Wall, writing in a similar vein but about a nineteenth-century English context, terms the 'adaptive family economy'.[23] This approach of observing trends in family formation, the life-cycles of domestic groups, responses to changing economic options, etc., especially as it has been pursued by the faculty and students at the Institute for Economic and Social History at the University of Vienna and by such other researchers as P. Viazzo,[24] has undermined some traditional taxonomies of Austrian peasants, eliminating among other axioms the seemingly obvious correlation of impartible inheritance with large farm sizes and of partibility with regions of smallholdings. Detailed empirical and statistical work suggests that there were many significant deviations from allegedly ideal types of the large peasant family enterprise and it has revealed that the Alpine-Danubian range of resource and labour options, however conditioned by natural circumstances, was relatively broad and that the demographic-familial dimensions of the Austrian peasants' strategic and tactical options changed over time in response to the influences of industrial-capitalist development.[25]

Such applications of an 'ecotype' model have vastly increased our sensitivity to the varieties of the Austrian peasant experience and put family choices and demographics at the centre of the peasants' many-sided calculus. They do not, however, carry out the larger cultural ecology project of which this research is only a part. The latter brings only biological-economic considerations to a systems-theoretic modernization framework with the result that specific peasant societies, however more 'ecologically diverse' they now appear, are reduced to mere instances of a single transitional social type, all moving at different speeds and by different paths toward absorption by capitalist modernity which is destined to neutralize virtually all ecologically grounded, social, gendered and other differences of labour and family formation.[26]

---

22. M. Mitterauer, 'Formen ländlicher Familienwirtschaft. Historische Ökotypen und familiale Arbeitsorganisation im österreichischen Raum', in J. Ehmer and M. Mitterauer (eds), *Familienstruktur und Arbeitsorganisation in ländlichen Gesellschaften* (Vienna, 1986), p. 188; idem, 'Ländliche Familienformen in ihrer Abhängigkeit von natürlicher Umwelt und lokaler Ökonomie', in his *Historisch-Anthropologische Familienforschung* (Vienna, 1990).

23. 'Work, welfare and the family: an illustration of the adaptive family economy' in L. Bonfield *et al.* (eds), *The World We Have Gained* (Oxford, 1986).

24. 'Illegitimacy and the European marriage pattern: comparative evidence from the Alpine area', in Bonfield, *World We Have Gained*; idem, *Upland Communities* (Cambridge, 1989).

25. Mitterauer, 'Familienwirtschaft'; J. Ehmer, *Heiratsverhalten, Sozialstruktur und ökonomischer Wandel* (Göttingen, 1991) puts Austrian demographic-familial forms and behaviours, with an extensive focus on peasants and rural labouring classes, in an English and Prussian comparative framework.

26. See the editors' introduction 'Zur Einführung: Familienstruktur und Arbeitsorganisation in ländlichen Gesellschaften', in Ehmer and Mitterauer, *Familienstruktur*, pp. 10–11; also Mitterauer, 'Familienformen', pp. 142–3 and passim.

Wolf's reworking of Julian Steward's ideas about cultural ecology sought to avoid a narrowly naturalistic environmentalism and the biologistic dangers that he perceived in the 'new evolutionism' of post-Second World War American anthropology. He stressed, instead, that 'culture is not an organism' but 'a body of materials – material, social and ideal forms – to which new material may be added and old material may be lost'.[27] For Wolf, 'cultures' decide what will be 'environment' or 'resource' and do so along historical trajectories by means of variously remembered, reinvented and repeated forms that are constantly rearticulating in response to opportunities and pressures both from within and from the larger economic and political environments. These latter go beyond the idealized, economic-technological growth trends of theoretically 'free' commodity and labour markets that neoclassical analysts choose to perceive. Wolf's peasants live, instead, in economies where secular swings in intertwined and highly contingent markets determine economic options; where agricultural economies can both industrialize and deindustrialize in no particular order of sequence and without necessarily following a 'modernization' direction; where the peasant economy is part of local corporate and business as well as of distant financial sectors; and where the state is in all cases a significant part of the cultural ecology in the sense that it can support or deny 'natural' ecological adaptions according to the interests and passions of those who inhabit various parts of its apparatus. Finally, there is in Wolf's model an explicit modification if not outright rejection of the Durkheimian interest in cultural ecology as a dimension of social cohesion when he suggests that our evaluation of cultural systems has to approach a kind of cost-benefit accounting in which the distribution of the costs of keeping order are measured against the distribution of benefits. In Wolf's alternative, the 'performance' of a culture measured in terms of its capacity to overcome oppressive repetitions-without-change – i.e. without the accumulation of more 'freedom' – remains a central object for analytical concern since this performance is itself part of the historical experience of any cultural ecology.[28]

Wolf, working with John Cole,[29] tested his model on two linguistically and ethnically distinct peasantries whose villages are neighbours, whose landholdings commingle in the same Alpine valley complexes and whose histories were intertwined since the earliest medieval settlements accompanying the corporate organization of the transit trade in the Val di Non, a contested Tirolean border zone of the Austrian empire that has been under Italian rule since 1919. Villagers in predominantly German-speaking St Felix and Romance-speaking Trett faced identical ecologies that limited their farm sizes, the number

27. E. Wolf, *Anthropology* (New York, 1974), pp. 30, 55 and passim; idem, 'The study of evolution', in S. Tax, (ed.), *Horizons of Anthropology* (New York, 1964) and R. Murphy, 'Julian Steward', in S. Silverman (ed.), *Totems and Teachers* (New York, 1981), esp. pp. 193–7.

28. Wolf, 'Evolution', pp. 114–15; idem, *Anthropology*, pp. 66–7, 94–7.

29. *The Hidden Frontier: Ecology and Ethnicity in an Alpine Valley* (New York, 1974); cf. E. Wolf, 'Ownership and political ecology', *Anthropological Quarterly*, 45: 3 (1972) and J. Cole, 'Cultural adaptation in the eastern Alps', *Anthropological Quarterly*, 45: 3 (1972); also S. Silverman, 'Agricultural organization, social structure and values in Italy: amoral familism reconsidered', *American Anthropologist*, 70: 2 (1968).

of children they could support, the pasture margins they could expand into and so on, and yet they experienced completely different histories and built different families and communities. The dominant German imperial powers in these valleys had been successive Bavarian, Tirolean and Habsburg dynasts against whom the Romance-speaking rural communes put up a relatively successful resistance by rallying around urban centres to keep intact certain of their communal and familial, that is to say, 'private' practices. The German-speaking peasant communities, on the other hand, were increasingly enrolled in the public service of successive dynastic-corporate states against whom the Romance-speakers could only resist by discounting their 'peasant' occupations and forming, wherever they could, urban social or occupational linkages. The German peasants appear historically in closed corporate families and communities whose privileged heads and heirs enlisted the resources of their holdings, including their families, into sustaining viable large peasant farms that were charged, ideologically, with representing the allegedly central institutions and values of a German-speaking empire. Their Romance-speaking neighbours, cast as a historically defeated underclass, pursued their contacts with local and distant urban centres to weave complex occupational, kin and migrant networks with which they could meet their obligations to the imperial authorities and yet retain considerable communal and familial independence against both the state and against the staunchly settled German hierarchs next door.

The central irony at the heart of such patterns of ethnic class division among peasantries in the Austrian empire concerns the different qualities of life of neighbouring and outwardly similar communities. Both peasantries had to face a natural ecological limitation in that their communities could support only about half of their offspring, with the rest having to go elsewhere. The way they handled this problem reveals a great deal about them. The Romance-speaking peasantry depended on partible inheritance patterns whereby those who had to leave the family farm retained a material interest in it equal to those who remained behind to manage the assemblage of parcellized holdings. This arrangement, although no doubt subject to structural weaknesses and personality conflicts, offered multiple options to a wide circle of family members in a resilient kin-partnership alliance system. The German communities, on the other hand, representing the victorious imperial enterprise and increasingly identifying state-driven impartible inheritance with 'German custom', more effectively resisted pressures to parcellize holdings but did so at the cost of expelling children, identified for whatever reason as unsustainable, into out-migration and servile labour. This made for an isolated, defensive, tense and divided peasant idyll in which absolute exclusion and certain downward mobility (and worse) for some poisoned the relations of all. For Cole and Wolf, it is such divergent and conflict-ridden peasant cultural formations that fuelled much of the ethnic and nationalist 'identity' politics that finally tore the Austrian empire apart. It is one of the intentions of this essay to test their model against the broad sweep of peasant history in the Austrian empire as a whole.

MEDIEVAL 'CRISES' AND PEASANT COMMUNES, 1300–1500

The medieval Austrian empire's commercial development depended to a great extent on the relative strength, before 1450, of Christian-European control of the Levant trade through Venice, Pisa and Genoa, tapped for Austria by such trading towns as Judenburg in Styria. The Italian linkage provided a modest to poor environment for development of the Austrian economy. The north Italians preferred to connect with the Champagne fairs and the Flemish markets beyond, English and Norman merchants brought Northern Italy and Sicily into the Atlantic orbit, while Marseilles and the Savoyards' passes became the favoured European links to the Mediterranean. Vienna, astride the Danube valley, was reduced to a tribute centre 'protecting' the modest commerce that moved between the German empire and the Hungarian-Slavic regions.[30] By 1300, the fundamental structures of a settled peasant society had appeared precisely because the conservative tribute orientation of dynastic, corporate and military investments further marginalized the Austrian economy as a whole. The exclusive use by privileged corporations of key Alpine passes to Italy, the channelling of trade toward mandated roadways that were advantageous to tribute and not to market rates of return, and the heavy tolls and restrictions imposed on trade between the German duchies and Hungary all curbed the expansion of Austrian markets. Not only were Austrians cut out of the western European cloth trade by the mid-fifteenth century, but the volume of imports of such foodstuffs as Bohemian farm produce and Hungarian cattle also greatly diminished.[31]

The upshot was an intensification of mixed farming production in the Austrian duchies as well as in Styria.[32] It also forced a decline in nomadic cattle pastoralism in Hungary and a turn toward more settled farming there. Hungary, it must be remembered, suffered from more or less severe export controls vis-à-vis the other parts of the Austrian empire so that more burdened forms of peasant enterprise developed there in the more restrictive framework of aristocratic-corporate and military powers that could circumvent these limitations by negotiation or force. The peasant settlers in the German core states gathered in locally self-determining and relatively 'free' corporative forms based on the houses of market, parish, and magisterial-judicial communities, all organized under the legal jurisdictions of individual member-families of the territorial Estates or of the royal dynasty. In areas where the majority of the peasants were Hungarian or Slavic there also developed local corporate forms comparable to

30. P. Curtin, *Cross-Cultural Trade in World History* (Cambridge, 1984), pp. 115–19; R.-H. Bautier, *The Economic Development of Medieval Europe* (New York, 1971), pp. 65–8, 96–107.

31. Hoffmann, 'Die geschichtlichen Grundlagen der österreichischen Wirtschafts- und Sozialstruktur', in *150 Jahre Sparkassen in Österreich* (Vienna, 1972), p. 6; idem, *Wirtschaftsgeschichte* pp. 60–3, 72–3. From this perspective one could argue that the increasing Islamic pressure on Hungary and Inner Austria (Styria, Carinthia etc.) was an attempt to break through the stranglehold the Austrian empire had on the overland trade between south-eastern and western Europe.

32. Basic descriptions and details of Austrian peasant economies in the Middle Ages may be found in F. Tremel, *Wirtschafts- und Sozialgeschichte Österreichs* (Vienna, 1969), pp. 42–77 and passim.

those of the German-speaking peasantry. We will consider below whether their collective bargaining power was less and whether the legal obligations under which they held tenure on their farms were both quantitatively and qualitatively more oppressive.

To approach these questions we examine, first, the rural economy's experience with the expanding mining industries in Tirol and elsewhere in the empire during the fourteenth and fifteenth centuries and, second, the specifically 'Austrian' experience with the demographic crisis known, after Le Roy Ladurie, as the 'Malthusian Renaissance' and with the related crises of deflationary rural markets after 1300 and their reinflation after 1450 (Wilhelm Abel's 'price scissors'). In the fourteenth century, the German-Austrian peasantries, freed from Hungarian and other competition, found a growing market when the boom in the iron mines and steel manufactories of northern Italy and southern Germany spilled over into the Austrian empire, particularly to Styria, Carinthia and Carniola. The banking houses of Nuremberg and Augsburg and the Habsburg court invested in these mining centres as well as in the silver and copper mines in Tirol and in the salt mines around Hallein and Hallstatt in the *Salzkammergut*, the Austrian Habsburgs' treasury's salt monopoly district. Elsewhere, Bohemian silver mining attracted investment and rural support communities, as did iron mining in Hungarian Slovakia and in Silesia. The miners' contracts with the landowners were in some respects analogous to those of the peasants in that the corporate landowners and the royal authorities were content to collect tribute from miner-cottagers who organized production and earned precisely assessed shares of the product for their labours of discovery and extraction with the rest going to the landowners, shareholders and tribute authorities. Unlike peasants, however, miners formed a trans-regional occupational culture, were organized in self-governing communities incorporated under royal authority and led social lives in which individual house-authority was secondary to fraternal companies organized around parish endowments and communal charities.[33]

The economic impact of late medieval mining on the agricultural sectors was considerable and gave the Austrian regions' experience of the European-wide crisis of population loss and declining agricultural incomes during the fourteenth and fifteenth centuries a special cast. Property inventories (*Urbare*) of the Upper Austrian monastery Kremsmünster contain evidence about the first abandonment of settled farms (*Wüstungen*) in 1299, long before the plagues that allegedly caused population decline swept through Europe in the 1340s. Other regions within the empire – eastern Lower Austria and the Burgenland region, areas north of the Danube and to the south-west of Linz, eastern Styria – also experienced such early abandonments and depopulations which were certainly worsened by the Black Death and its episodic recurrences in the region from

33. Agricola, *De Re Metallica*, trans. H. C. and L. H. Hoover (New York, 1950), pp. 89–100; J. Gimpel, *The Medieval Machine* (New York, 1977), pp. 59–74, 93–9; W. Stark, *Ursprung und Aufstieg des landeswirtschaftlichen Großbetriebs in den böhmischen Ländern* (Brno, 1934), pp. 23–6, Bautier, *Economic Development*, pp. 220–5; Bruckmüller, *Sozialgeschichte*, pp. 162–6; also still interesting is R. Ehrenberg, *Capital and Finance in the Age of the Renaissance* (Fairfield, NJ, 1985 [1928]), pp. 134–5.

the 1380s through 1411 and 1521.[34] It appears increasingly likely that the onset of epidemic diseases was preceded by an economic destabilization resulting from the technological and commercial revolutions of the High Middle Ages initiating market-driven abandonments of select areas of recently developed farm lands that were not competitive in an increasingly deflationary agricultural commodities market. The late medieval decline in prices and profit crisis forced ecclesiastical, aristocratic and urban corporations to restructure their enterprises in ways that put pressure on labour and on the social stability (and fertility controls) of certain areas, resulting in turn in a growing marginal population ready to be hit hard by disease and famine.

The latter occurred in Austrian areas as deflationary price trends forced producers to cut back even as periodic harvest failures between 1310 and 1320, locusts in 1338–40 followed by years of heavy snows and flooding affected specific Austrian and surrounding markets with market shortages and inflationary spikes. Abel has drawn up comparative spreadsheet tables to show how fourteenth-century harvests affected incomes by farm size. Small farms, caught between too little product during bad harvests and too low prices after good harvests, were bound to fail; middling enterprises suffered under exceptionally good and exceptionally bad harvests; large holdings did least well under exceptionally good harvest and deflationary price conditions but held the finally decisive competitive advantage when, during bad years, they enjoyed high rates of return while both other groups suffered losses.[35]

The Austrian peasantries' experiences during the late medieval crisis bear out Abel's model. It was in many respects a very profitable time, especially, but not only, for an emerging class of peasant farmers who were able to draw abandoned holdings into their own to secure a greater market share in grain production and to pasture cattle. The mining centres, populated mostly by immigrants from Germany, grew precisely in time to save the region from the worst aspects of the late medieval deflation. The demand generated by urbanizing mining enclaves for support industries and consumer-oriented crafts and services in turn generated employment opportunities for those who had to supplement or abandon their farming enterprises. Not only did this minimize the region's population losses due to famine and outmigration, but agricultural prices were also kept from falling too steeply by rising wages in mining, industrial and craft employments that increased in both absolute and relative terms until the second half of the fifteenth century, when the 'price scissors' began to cut the other way as wages fell and prices rose again. By this time, there had been shakeouts among both the landowning corporate authorities and the peasant householders who had both learned to deploy similar options and strategies during the deflationary century and confronted the reinflation with restructured communal-administrative forms that, after 1500, increasingly

---

34. Bruckmüller, *Sozialgeschichte*, pp. 134–5.

35. *Agricultural Fluctuations in Europe* (New York, 1980), pp. 10–13 and ch. 2; A. Pribram, *Geschichte der Preise und Löhne in Österreich* (Vienna, 1938) is still indispensable. For the later periods see Sandgruber, *Agrarstatistik*; idem, *Die Anfänge der Konsumgesellschaft* (Vienna, 1982); idem, 'Agrarkrisen und Agrarkonjunkturen', *Beiträge zur historischen Sozialkunde*, 1: 2 (1971), pp. 28–31.

had to take the actions of the royal dynastic state into their 'ecological' accounts as well.

The strong negotiating position of those peasant farmers who were able to engross and diversify their farms was reflected in the appearance of many local and even some translocal peasant legal challenges in the courts, of political movements, refusals to pay tributes or render labour services, and outright rebellions. These manifestations in the Austrian empire, in Salzburg, Tirol, the German stem duchies, Bohemia and Hungary were the eastern end of a broad sweep of peasant resistance running from the Rhineland through southern Germany and Switzerland to south-eastern Europe (with the exception of Bavaria) and through northern Germany as well. Peter Blickle's comparative overview of this movement stresses that peasants were resistant in regions where their communes (*Gemeinden*) were sufficiently well developed to give them some sort of corporate standing and the resources to resist. Peasant communalism throughout central and eastern Europe has to be a key concern, but his view of the uprisings as the work of someone he calls the *gemeiner Mann* (the 'common', i.e. 'communal', man) remains unsatisfying for a number of reasons, not least of which is the insufficient analysis of the peasants' complex motives and of the outcomes they were constrained to accept.[36] Although he tries to incorporate the view that the revolts were driven by the agrarian demographic and business crises of the late Middle Ages, his is finally only a modification of the social-romantic perspective of Günther Franz's still much-cited work concerning the historical implications of the peasants' alleged goal of a patriarchal-communal empire under a single German emperor.[37] Ascribing such a problematical 'higher' political vision to late medieval peasant politics distracts from appreciating the peasantries' differential creations and exercises of economic and social options and of their political education in this period.

The Austrian regions' peasant movements were influenced differently by the opening of the wage-price scissors at the beginning of the period and by their closing after about 1450. The implicit threat of farm abandonment and the territorial corporations' and landlords' income crisis in the fourteenth century set the stage at the outset for a general increase in the peasants' freedoms, in their ability to form communal and, in rare cases, territorial corporations, to negotiate binding contracts and treaties, to appeal to territorial Estates or royal authorities for arbitration in lawsuits concerning cash or labour tribute increases or the landlords' appropriation of the commons, and to defend successfully (in their most lasting and perhaps tragic achievement) the private disposition

---

36. Blickle, best known for his encyclopaedic studies of the territorial-legal constructions of the German regions, has continued to develop *Gemeinde* as both a 'historical' and analytical concept; see his 'Social protest and reformation theology', in K. von Greyerz (ed.), *Religion, Politics and Social Protest* (London, 1984), and now his edited volume *Landgemeinde und Stadtgemeinde in Mitteleuropa* (Munich, 1991); also relevant for the present essay is his 'Peasant revolts in the German empire in the late Middle Ages', *Social History*, 4: 2 (1979).

37. *Der deutsche Bauernkrieg* (Munich, 1943 [1933]); an enduring 'classic' of National Socialist historiography, now in its 12th edition; cf. H. Rosenberg, *Probleme der deutschen Sozialgeschichte* (Frankfurt am Main, 1969); W. Schulze, *Deutsche Geschichtswissenschaft seit 1945* (Munich, 1993), pp. 34–5 and passim.

of the labour resources and inheritance funds of their families and house communities. After the 1450s, with the resumption of population growth, the return to full capacity in land use, and the growing alliance among factions of dynastic courtiers, financiers and administrative departments to exploit the ruling houses' rural properties, the peasantries' bargaining power diminished in the struggle to defend, often unsuccessfully, the gains of the earlier period against renewed pressures from corporate landlords and treasury (*Hofkammer*) officials.

The Vorarlberg peasant communes bargained for and achieved territorial incorporation during the late fourteenth century. The peasants of Tirol in 1404 obtained constitutional documentation fixing their and their landlords' mutual rights and obligations. During the following decades they sided with royal forces against the nobility, taking a page no doubt from the latter's exploitation at the same time of the ruling dynasties' internal troubles, to acquire territorial corporate status for their communes organized around independent administrative-judicial districts (*Gerichte*). In Bohemia, the Hussites' rank-and-file were for the most part peasants who liberated and reorganized their parish corporations and restructured villages and markets under the rule of local councils of urban and peasant householders. With the unreliable help of aristocratic mercenaries and innovations in military tactics (war-wagons to form *ad hoc* defensive perimeters on the battlefield) they were able to create for a time an 'independent' Bohemia during the 1420s and even managed to export their organizational practices and religious convictions into the Austrian duchies to the south and into Silesia. Their movement fell apart in a factional civil war that saw the re-establishment of royal authority by 1436 and the erosion of the peasants' gains under Habsburg rule in the sixteenth century, culminating in the defeat at White Mountain in 1620.[38] In Upper Austria, the peasant communities at the outset rebelled almost exclusively against increases in ecclesiastical tribute extraction authorized by papal decree. Even though their movements both before and after 1450 were often brutally defeated and did not gain them territorial corporate status, their persistent politicization during the sixteenth and seventeenth centuries earned them considerable economic and social independence within the constraints of the Habsburgs' tribute state, to the point that their 'condition' became the model for late eighteenth-century reformers' ideal peasant society.[39] In the remaining German and Inner Austrian provinces, peasant communes achieved similar self-rule under territorial corporate Estates' jurisdictions. In Hungary, finally, a substantial number of the peasantry, often themselves claiming military-noble lineage, formed alliances with the nobility and merchants during the early fifteenth century in large market towns (*oppida*) where they attained

38. J. Hoensch, *Geschichte Böhmens* (Munich, 1992), pp. 135–53; for a not insurmountable critique of the 'peasant' qualities of the Hussite movement see F. Graus, 'The crisis of the Middle Ages and the Hussites', in S. Ozment (ed.), *The Reformation in Medieval Perspective* (Chicago, 1971); idem 'The late medieval peasant wars in the context of social crisis', *Journal of Peasant Studies*, 3: 1 (1975); F. Seibt, *Revolutionen in Europa* (Munich, 1984); in some views, the Hussites weakened peasants' economies and strengthened the landlords, Rösener, *Peasantry*, pp. 106–7.

39. H. Rebel, *Peasant Classes: The Bureaucratization of Property and Family Relations under Early Habsburg Absolutism, 1511–1636* (Princeton, NJ, 1983); cf. F. A. von Raab, *Unterricht über die Verwandlung der k.k. böhmischen Domänen in Bauerngüter* (Vienna, 1777).

virtual independence as tenants under the judicial authority of the privileged towns and regions and engaged in livestock raising and marketing for export.[40] The remainder, indeed the majority, of the peasantry (*jobagiones*) appeared in village communes regulated by a royal decree (1351) imposing uniform legal and communal rules that were similar to those in the other parts of the Austrian empire, except that, as early as the fourteenth century, their landlords could exercise judicial dominion to extract labour tribute from them.

By 1450, the peasantries in the Austrian empire had, both in conflict and cooperation with their landlords and territorial authorities, largely dismantled the remnants of the feudal, personal relationships of the early Middle Ages and had become 'free' within a territorially organized system of dynastic-corporate landlordship. They had achieved membership in self-administering communal corporations, the freedom to own, inherit and transfer leaseholds, and they were free to leave with their 'movable' wealth after satifying their obligations to landlords and communes. Their subordination was not a matter of feudal and individual vassalage but took the form of a collective 'hereditary subject' (*Erbuntertan*) status in which their landlords were also their judicial overlords, making them in effect 'subject-citizens' of estate-managing dynastic corporations, organized by magisterial districts (*Ämter*) in which the tenured were not only farmers but also made up the lowest tier of administrative officers grouped in village or regional-communal organizations. In a world without civil law for the unincorporated, the tenured peasants occupied a genuinely liminal position in the sense that they stood between, on one hand, the private-law world of their houses where they were autocratic rulers empowered to enforce obedience even by inflicting physical violence and, on the other, the public-law realm of estate administration where they were responsible for their communities' obedience to the ban on unauthorized violence. Their public performances were governed by administrative rules (*Weistümer, Taidinge*)[41] that, beginning in the second half of the fifteenth century, could only be altered unilaterally by the estate authorities.

By 1500, after a second period of crushed rebellions in Salzburg (1463, 1478, 1495), Upper Austria (1489), and Inner Austria between 1471 and 1492, the peasantries of the Austrian empire settled down to developing the new, albeit limited, combinations of economic, legal and social options at their disposal. Three areas of this adaption give insight into the sophistication and complexity of their project. First, in the area of legal reform, they were able to negotiate the elimination of private and personal contracts of fealty (*Leibeigenschaft*) from the permissible forms of peasant–landlord relationships. This strengthened their communal political solidarity because *Leibeigenschaft* had been the lords'

40. J. Bak, 'Quincentennial of the birth of György Székely Dósza (a report on the state of research)', *East Central Europe*, 1: 2 (1974), pp. 155–6; idem, 'Entstehung eines einheitlichen Hörigenstandes in Ungarn', unpublished conference paper, Department of History, University of British Columbia, Vancouver, 1981; F. Erdei, 'Peasant society', *Peasant Studies Newsletter*, 4: 2 (1975).

41. Österreichische Akademie der Wissenschaften (ed.), *Österreichische Weistümer* (Vienna, 1870–1968); Brunner, *Lordship*, chs 3–5; H. Feigl, 'Von der mündlichen Rechtsweisung zur Aufzeichnung: die Entstehung der Weistümer und verwandter Quellen', in P. Classen (ed.), *Recht und Schrift im Mittelalter* (Sigmaringen, 1978), Rebel, *Classes*, pp. 150–6 and passim.

means of using personal contracts to undermine communities by placing into their midst heads of houses whose personally privileged relationship with the corporate authorities placed them outside the shared obligations and rules.[42] To make their arguments about conditions of tenure, the peasant communes, while certainly expressing both 'divine' and 'old' law sentiments, adapted readily to such Roman law innovations as emphyteutic tenure by which the tenant acquired a long-term lease contract and in return guaranteed not to reduce the capital value of the leasehold. The peasants' invocations of different currents and traditions of law corresponded to the unsettled state of law itself in which all traditions were in play. When tenants invoked the 'old law', in many cases successfully, this was not an empty conservatism but an appeal to specific customary law found in repeatedly edited and published collections of legal practice (the various *Spiegel*) in which earlier receptions of the Roman law already intertwined with German-Imperial and even Slavic traditions. Its regulation of family membership, succession and inheritance made this 'old law' particularly useful for the peasants' struggle to retain control of family property and labour.[43]

A second area in which peasants successfully defined and expanded new communal assets and options was in their parish institutions, particularly in turning the ecclesiastical corporate privileges of local churches to their personal and collective advantage. The models for this were in the Alpine miners' formation of parish guilds (*Zechen*)[44] and in the Hussites' call for extending to the laity the sacrament of the cup, including, not coincidentally, ecclesiastical privileges in the wine trade. The most significant endeavours in this area concerned the formation of parish trust funds (*Stiftungen*) for purposes of church upkeep and improvements, celebrations, masses, burials, and various kinds of social welfare. Not only do these developments reveal waxing and waning surplus wealth and piety in the peasant communes, but also the latter's desire to imitate the political economy of the aristocratic corporations and to obtain for themselves the advantages of quasi-public 'benevolent' trust funds which could do double duty as a local source of lending capital. Their considerable success in this regard played a significant role in their personal and communal finances until the mid-eighteenth century.[45]

Finally, it is the different outcomes of this period's battles between and among corporate, state and peasant householders for shares of rural labour resources that shape the two ethnic communal forms of the Austrian peasantries.

42. The best study is still H. Rabe's much neglected *Das Problem Leibeigenschaft* (Wiesbaden, 1977); for a south German case from the eighteenth century in which *Leibeigenschaft* is used in a successful political-legal attack on peasant communal solidarity see A. Suter, '*Troublen' im Fürstbistum Basel, (1726–1740)* (Göttingen, 1985).

43. H. Wunder ' "Old Law" and "Divine Law" in the German Peasant War', *Journal of Peasant Studies*, 3: 1 (1975); G. Strauss, *Law, Resistance and the State: The Opposition to Roman Law in Reformation Germany* (Princeton, NJ, 1986).

44. K.-H. Ludwig, 'Miners, pastors and the peasant war in Upper Austria', in J. Bak and G. Benecke (eds), *Religion and Rural Revolt* (Manchester/Dover, NH, 1984).

45. H. Feigl, 'Entwicklung und Auswirkungen des Patronatsrechtes in Niederösterreich', *Jahrbuch des Vereins für Landeskunde*, new series, 43 (1977), pp. 88–90; A. Zauner, *Vöcklabruck und der Attergau* (Vienna, 1971), pp. 569–71 and passim.

The serious battles for the control of labour do not take place until the later sixteenth and the seventeenth centuries, but the switches for two developmental tracks, one pointing toward a 'Germanic' core without labour tributes and the other to a 'non-German' fringe where such impositions became the central institution of the rural economy, were set by 1500. The two main areas of contention concerned, first, the extent to which landlords could reach directly into the peasants' households and command specific 'surplus' labourers (*Gesinde*: servants, children) and, second, the kinds of labour and the number of days of labour tributes that could be negotiated as part of the conditions of tenure. We will return to the first of these in the next section and focus here on the terms and economic implications of the second.

Alone the etymologies of the several words – *Frondienst, Scharwerk, Werchart, Robot* etc. – used in the Austrian and German empires for labour services contradict any sense that there were innately 'Germanic' or 'Slavic' types of such service that can account for their historical divergence by a prior ethnic division. Large areas in the Bohemian-Hungarian territories, united under the Lithuanian-Polish Jagiełłons in the 1480s and, in effect, handed to the Habsburgs to defend against Turkish seizure after 1526, indeed evolved, by the early eighteenth century, into virtual forced-labour zones while at the same time such services had largely disappeared or been commuted to release-fees (i.e. periodic cash tributes in place of actual labour) in the rest of the Austrian empire. However, ever since the Austrian empire, including the Bohemian-Hungarian territories, had come under Carolingian institutional and legal influence, there had existed basically two kinds of labour service, one in which landlord and peasant 'negotiated' the specific terms and one in which those representing royal authority could requisition households for such labour as was arguably necessary for the public good. It is of some significance that this second requirement was left open-ended as to amounts and times of work and that even those who held various feudal immunities could not claim exemption from it; moreover, it is this second category of service that became, after 1450, the primary legal ground for increasing labour-tribute extraction from tenants.[46] There was then, paradoxically, intrinsic to the *Franco-German* tradition a power to command labour unconditionally, one that could or could not be invoked, depending on the ruling authorities' intentions concerning this or that tenantry. In Bohemia, as early as the thirteenth century, it was German colonists who displaced prior contracts without labour services with ones that included them, and we can observe that the trend toward increasing these services in 'Slavic' Bohemia provoked resistance during the fifteenth century.[47] At the same time, in the German-speaking Austrian territories the commutation of labour services to release-fees was already under way on some ecclesiastical estates by 1300, with considerable pressure from the peasantry throughout the fifteenth century to

46. Bruckmüller, *Sozialgeschichte*, p. 58; the classic archival work on Austrian labour services is still G. Grüll, *Die Robot in Oberösterreich* (Linz, 1952).
47. Stark, *Ursprung*, pp. 13–14.

get rid of even these. It is no surprise that these labour-exempt tenants them-selves appear, at about the same time, to have begun to extract labour services from those independent labourers and artisans who did not have 'housed' status in the peasant communes but occupied cottages or rooms in the villages. A labour-tribute regime came to be concealed below the threshold of corpor-ate and communal authority in a realm of private law, without regulations, other than what the market and the 'community' tolerated from time to time, governing the commanding and exploitation of labour.[48] Hungary's experience with labour service, finally, is similar to that of Bohemia in that here too such earlier medieval services (also called *robot*) that had fallen into desuetude during the period of declining prices were revived again by the late fifteenth century and sharply increased as the ruling Magyar nobility sought to increase its market share in agricultural products to take advantage of rebounding prices. Labour tributes aside, the Hungarian peasantry's copyholding tenants (*jobbágy*) had temporarily regained their freedom to move in 1547 and resembled in many aspects the other peasantries of the Austrian empire even during the turmoils of the sixteenth and seventeenth centuries.[49]

To appreciate these developments, we need to be clear on the implications of labour tribute for peasants' households. Contrary to a persistent tendency to perceive labour services and rents as interchangeable,[50] in the present essay labour services appear as a form of tribute. For the households subject to their (however 'negotiated') imposition, they cannot be a market-rational choice because they diminish the 'wage' that donors of labour can earn on their farms in direct proportion to the landlords' increased demand for labour.[51] Where, by 1500, the 'German' peasantries, although also subject to increasing cash tribute exactions, were free to dispose of their households' labour according to their relationship to the existing markets as producers, the peasantries of the Slavic, Pannonian, Inner Austrian and Alpine fringes were placed at one remove, indeed, in an inversely rational (and therefore, arguably, colonialized) relationship to the market, as they had to retain labour not for their own but for their lords' market production calculus. The devolution of this difference plays a significant role in the ill-fated social and political history of the region as a whole.[52]

48. Bruckmüller, *Sozialgeschichte*, p. 141.

49. Bak, 'Entstehung', pp. 4–7, 12–13; A. Janos, *The Politics of Backwardness in Hungary, 1825–1945* (Princeton, NJ, 1982), pp. 26–34.

50. Cf. Bak, 'Entstehung', pp. 5–6; H. Knittler, 'Zwischen Ost und West: Niederösterreichs adelige Grundherrschaften 1550–1750', *Österreichische Zeitschrift für Geschichtswissenschaften*, 4: 2 (1993), pp. 195, 201 and passim. Cf. F. Lütge, *Deutsche Sozial- und Wirtschaftsgeschichte* (Berlin, 1962), p. 121.

51. R. Rosdolski, 'The distribution of the agrarian product in feudalism', *Journal of Economic History*, 11 (1951); H. Rebel, 'The Prussian *Junker* and their peasants: articulations with kinship of a tribute-taking class', in R. Rapp and J. Schneider (eds), *Articulating Hidden Histories* (Berkeley, CA, 1994); for discussions of 'tribute' see F. C. Lane, 'The role of governments in economic growth in early modern times', *Journal of Economic History*, 35 (1975); E. Wolf, *Europe and the People Without History* (Berkeley, CA, 1982), and H. Rebel, 'Cultural hegemony and class experience: a critical reading of recent ethnological-historical approaches', *American Ethnologist*, 16 (1989) explore articulations of tribute forms with other modes of production.

52. Cole and Wolf, *Frontier*, pp. 168–75 and passim.

PEASANT ADAPTIONS TO CORPORATE AND IMPERIAL
RESTRUCTURING, 1500–1700

The period of rising agrarian prices from the 1450s through the 1620s prompted corporate and royal treasury entrepreneurs into diverse responses which prompted, in turn, adaptive counter-measures and adjustments among the various peasantries of the empire. It is to the lasting credit of Robert Brenner[53] that he reasserted (against persistent arguments seeking to biologize cultural-historical processes) the historical indeterminacy of the relationships among social classes, demographic-commercial trends and strategic adaptions. However, almost in contradiction of his own argument about similar trends allowing different adaptions, he denies that the same general rise in grain prices could have driven the very different developments of eastern and western European aristocratic corporate and economic organization. His assumption that in the west it was peasant communal resistance that prevented aristocrats from increasing their landholdings, labour extractions and domain farm production, whereas in the east they could thus innovate against less well organized peasants, does not pay enough attention to the different strategies which aristocratic and mercantile investors could marshal to profit from inflationary markets without necessarily becoming direct producers.

Almost nowhere in the Austrian empire were market-responsive, short-term leases an option, but this still left two strategies with different advantages in different markets. Having 'tamed' the peasantry during the early sixteenth century with communalist concessions as well as with military force, rentier-landlords could, to offset the inflationary devaluation of rents, impose new and greater transaction fees of all kinds and convert 'feudal' services into fees. With such cash tributes, consortia of aristocrats and merchants entered the local markets as monopsonic buyers of their peasants' surplus grains and exploited their relatively higher market share to get the best prices in regional and distant markets. The trade-off for the peasants in this model was their acceptance of the risks of production in return for having most of the arable land at their disposal (peasant-controlled land is, in Austrian usage, 'rustical') and for managing their communal labour and inheritance accounts in private but with documents and records issued and enforced by their landlords' magistracies. The relative efficiency of this strategic choice tends at the outset to be high in that, compared to a labour-appropriating regime, peasant farmers paid considerably higher percentages of their incomes in tributes and yet retained higher profits because of higher productivity and flexible labour management.[54]

53. 'Agrarian class structure and economic development in pre-industrial Europe', *Past and Present*, 70 (1976); much of the ensuing debate is reproduced in T. H. Aston and C. H. E. Philpin (eds), *The Brenner Debate* (Cambridge, 1985).

54. See the interesting calculations by F. W. Henning, *Dienste und Abgaben der Bauern im 18. Jahrhundert* (Stuttgart, 1969).

From this perspective, the second alternative of putting labour-tribute peasantries to work on the corporate landowners' farms ('dominical' land)[55] was at best a second choice at any time, but one that in certain places and times could appear, to the dominant investors, as the best available option. Particularly in areas such as Hungary and Bohemia where the export trade was largely in the hands of foreign trading companies[56] and rural market and communal life had been stunted under regimes of judicial terror, landlords acquired a controlling market share by entering directly into agricultural production. They seized and consolidated the most productive farms into large plantations and progressively converted the remaining tenancies from rental into labour-tribute (*robot*) contracts. A secondary benefit to the landlords occurred when labour obligations did not cover specific labour needs[57] and they could tap a secondary labour market whose wage levels were depressed by the general conditions of labour in a *robot* economy. From a world market perspective, the forces driving the expansion after 1500 of the Bohemian-Hungarian labour-service enterprises were not only the commercial connections to western Europe but also the prices in *domestic* markets inflated by the wars on the Austrian-Ottoman frontiers during the sixteenth and seventeenth centuries.[58] This important shift in perspective changes our outlook on the crisis of this system when, by 1700, the Ottoman tide had turned and these areas, knitted more tightly into the Habsburgs' victori ous construction of an autarkic tribute empire, went into recession.

One of the conditions of being competitive in the inflationary markets of the sixteenth century was to be able to adjust labour forces precisely to the changing demands of the interlocking agricultural and business cycles. To succeed, enterprises had to escape the rotation cycle and calendar of the commons and be able to respond to increasingly smaller margins for maintaining surplus labour by gaining greater freedom to expel and reabsorb workers as the markets seemed to demand. The optimum model for such competition emerged in the adjacent south German states. This involved landowning corporations of 'urbanized' rural aristocracies who balanced their rural estates' labour accounts by mobilizing urban guilds toward putting-out industries, mostly in textiles, so that these could absorb and give off labour as the agricultural sector required.[59] Urban centres like Augsburg or entire territories like Bavaria, with a large proportion of parcellized landholdings and small but commercially

55. The German term to describe landlords' direct economic exploitation of their farms (*Meierhöfe*), whether by wage or service labour, is *Gutswirtschaft*; the merging of landlordship (*Grundherrschaft*) with judicial rights over tenants results in *Gutsherrschaft*, which may or may not include the practice of *Gutswirtschaft*.

56. Such commercial underdevelopment persisted through the eighteenth century. See A. Klima, 'English merchant capital in Bohemia in the eighteenth century', *Economic History Review*, 12 (1959/60).

57. Knittler, 'Ost und West', pp. 211–12.

58. Z. Pach, 'Sixteenth-century Hungary: commercial activity and market production by the nobles', in P. Burke (ed.), *Economy and Society in Early Modern Europe* (New York, 1972) and 'Labour control on the Hungarian landlords' demesnes in the 16th and 17th centuries', in P. Gunst and T. Hoffmann (eds), *Grand domaine et petites exploitations en Europe au moyen age et dans les temps modernes* (Budapest, 1982); also A. Klima, 'Agrarian class structure and economic development in pre-industrial Bohemia', in Aston and Philpin, *Brenner Debate*.

59. M. Paas, *Population Change, Labor Supply and Agriculture in Augsburg, 1480–1618* (New York, 1981).

active 'proto-industrial' towns,[60] held advantages that the Austrian territories could scarcely match. Austria's provincial aristocratic corporations' refusal to collaborate with urban elites forestalled any political and commercial mergers of urban and rural nobilities, particularly in the Bohemian and other 'border' territories, and ensured that the Austrian empire's competitive disadvantages in European trade would worsen.[61] In some of the trading towns such as Linz and Bruck an der Mur there were incipient developments along the lines of the Augsburg model but these died in their regions' economic crises at the end of the seventeenth century.

Not only were landowning corporations restructuring to adapt to new market opportunities, but the ruling Habsburg dynasty emerged in the early sixteenth century as an active participant in this process and affected the peasants' political-economic environment in no small measure. Historians have tended to pay attention to the Habsburgs' later interventions in rural economic and social relations for the ostensible purpose of securing the empire's future material and soldiers by 'protecting the peasants' (*Bauernschutz*),[62] a notion explicitly voiced in 1680 as rationale for Leopold I's regulation of *robot* in 1680. However, the ruling dynasty's involvement in peasant protection may be found considerably earlier and in a different, though not unrelated, context.

Beginning under Maximilian I in the early sixteenth century, the royal treasury (*Hofkammer*) settled on two strategies to modernize its operations and to take on a public financial character. First, it reconsolidated royal salt-mining regalia in the area between Ischl and Hallstatt and administered this *Salzkammergut* directly not only to profit from the salt monopolies but also to create a centre for the region's rural economy to stimulate tribute-producing domestic trade between 'salt-free' Bohemia and the Upper Austrian alps. Second, and more important, the treasury began to raise loans by pawning, in a crude form of 'public debt', royal incomes and estates which were held and managed for profit by the Crown's creditors – mostly aristocratic-dynastic corporations – for contractually fixed periods of time. In this way almost all of the peasants on royal estates came under lien administrations[63] (*Pfandherrschaften*) whose terms of emphyteutic tenure, stipulating the undiminished return of the pawned property, required periodic interventions by *Hofkammer* officials to guard royal interests by 'protecting' peasants against possibly destructive exploitations. When between a third and a half of a landlord's incomes derived from Crown peasants administered under the *Kammer*'s rules, then, if only for the sake of administrative uniformity and efficiency, those rules became by the mid-seventeenth century a standard for the subject population generally.

---

60. E. Schremmer, 'Agrarverfassung und Wirtschaftsstruktur', *Zeitschrift für Agrargeschichte und Agrarsoziologie*, 20 (1972).

61. Hoffmann, *Wirtschaftsgeschichte*, pp. 161–2; Hoesch, *Geschichte Böhmens*, pp. 178–9; O. Pickl, 'Die bürgerlichen Vermögen steirischer Städte und Märkte im 16. Jahrhundert', *Innerösterreich*, 3 (Graz, 1968).

62. W. Schulze, *Landesdefension und Staatsbildung* (Vienna, 1973), pp. 191–2.

63. In early modern Upper Austria, of almost 11,000 treasury farms only 800–1200 were under direct royal administration. The rest were in the hands of lien administrators. Rebel, *Classes*, pp. 27–8. The term 'lien administration' is awkward, to be sure, but it is the legally most accurate rendering of *Pfandherrschaft* the author has found.

Many of the peasant protests and uprisings of the sixteenth and seventeenth centuries turned around issues of lien administration and allowed royal authorities to develop a consistent policy toward the various peasant subjects. Tirolean peasants rose in 1523 against the new emperor Ferdinand I's *Pfandherren*. In Upper Austria, in the period 1511–14, several thousand peasant rebels successfully fought against the innovations and sharp practices of Wolfgang von Polheim, a Viennese courtier, business entrepreneur and lien administrator, and were pacified in the course of the sixteenth century by the intervention of royal commissars acting as mediators. In Carniola, there were rebellions against lien administrators beginning in 1484 with the major uprising of 1515 starting with the murder of a *Pfandherr*. The German peasant wars of 1525 that spilled into Tirol, Salzburg, Upper Austria, and portions of Styria included persistent demands for the abolition of lien administration. One of the primary objectives of the great Upper Austrian peasant war of 1626 was to get rid of the territorial *Pfandherr*, Maximilian of Bavaria.[64]

Involved in all of these and other protests, the Crown increasingly moved toward advancing its interests by arbitrating publicly negotiated rules to govern private contracts between landlords and peasant communes and householders. In 1527 it was mandated that the leasehold terms of all tenancies be fixed and recorded in registers (*Gültbücher*). After uprisings in Lower and Upper Austria in 1594–97 against increased labour and cash tributes and against attempts by estate managers to appropriate labour directly from peasant householders (*Gesindezwang*), Emperor Rudolph II's 'Interim Resolution' (1597) limited several of the tribute innovations and reaffirmed the peasantries' rights to control their communities' labour. This not only strengthened the peasant householders' capacity to produce the cash tributes that were the landlords' chief source for profits in these regions, but it also channelled the peasants' desire for territorial corporate status into the construction of a new corpus of public law rulings and precedents that, in the long run, weakened the patrimonial courts controlled by members of the territorial corporations and expanded royal authority. After the defeat of the last uprisings against this new system in the 1620s and 1630s in Upper Austria and Styria, peasant communes began to lose control over their parish churches, education and trust funds to the Counter-Reformation Church and state.

The victorious Crown could by mid-century throw its weight behind peasants or landlords depending on the *Hofkammer*'s perceived interest. Leopold I's *Tractatus de iuribus incorporalibus* (1679) summarized the administrative law that emerged from this period of peasant war and politics with a codification of the still unincorporated and communally much weakened peasantry's relations to their landlords. In Hungary's constitution of 1689, the so-called *Einrichtungswerk*, the Crown curbed aristocratic mergers of judicial and administrative jurisdictions and, for a time, even strengthened the political position of the peasantry. This

---

64. Zauner, *Vöcklabruck*; Bruckmüller, *Sozialgeschichte*, pp. 186–214; G. Grüll, *Bauer, Herr und Landesfürst* (Linz, 1963); idem, *Der Bauer im Lande ob der Enns am Ausgang des 16. Jahrhunderts* (Linz, 1969); E. Zöllner (ed.), *Revolutionäre Bewegungen in Österreich* (Vienna, 1981) and F. Dörrer (ed.), *Die Bauernkriege und Michael Gaismair* (Innsbruck, 1982); Rebel, *Classes*, pp. 3–20 and passim.

adsorption of the peasants' private law arrangements on a rising surface of public law was accompanied by expressions of pious good intentions toward the peasants but took care, with the exception of Hungary, to enhance the landlords' ruling place in the sharing of the state's administrative power and left openings for further royal actions along these lines during the eighteenth century.[65]

Recent scholarship has tended to emphasize the negotiated, contractual qualities of the early modern peasant, landlord and state arrangements, but such an implicit denial of the violence accompanying these processes diminishes our sense of their historical weight considerably. The terrible scenes of public execution-by-torture, red-hot crowns of iron burned into the skulls of the Hungarian peasant leader György Dósza in 1514 and of the Slovene leader Matija Gubec in 1573, the 'dicing' at Frankenburg in 1625, the dismemberment of Martin Laimbauer in Linz in 1636 before the eyes of his child who was about to experience the same fate, all enter popular historical memories in images, commemorations, songs and stories. Sometimes, later, they become sources for some romantic nationalism but in their own time they were part of a general knowledge, always present below the surface of normal social awareness, about what visitations of state-terror were permissible to override oppositions against the changes and increases in tribute extraction that were at the heart of the ruling dynasties' new system of public and private corporate finances. The authorities' reconstitution of resistant peasant communities with 'decommunalizing'[66] rituals of judicial murder is a buried legacy whose historical recreations and paths remain to be explored.

Pfandherrschaft gained influence among the corporate landlords because it enabled and eventually required yet another heightening of the level of competition among them. From their headquarters in Vienna, the leading corporate families of the empire maintained their position at court (where deals were negotiated and made) by transferring and managing, in addition to their own properties, royal liens in all territories of the empire.[67] They became an absentee nobility who increasingly dealt with peasants as abstractions, with tenancies appearing as impartible tribute-producing units in accounting and inventory ledgers that now allow historians detailed insights into the workings of enterprises at all levels. The late Alfred Hoffmann, one of the first to explore these sources extensively, coined the term *Wirtschaftsherrschaft*[68] ('economic lordship') to describe the diversified entrepreneurial activities and incomes of landlords in the German Danubian provinces. He noted that their incomes derived from an acquisition of judicial and market rights, the purchasing and territorial consolidation of rent- and tribute-producing farms, parish church rights, tithes, etc. and from engaging directly in such more capital-intensive production as

65. A. Tautscher, *Wirtschaftsgeschichte Österreichs* (Berlin, 1974), pp. 262, 333, 706–7.

66. E. Bruckmüller, 'Die Strafmaßnahmen nach den bäuerlichen Erhebungen des 15. bis 17. Jahrhunderts', in E. Zöllner (ed.), *Wellen der Verfolgung in der österreichischen Geschichte* (Vienna, 1986), pp. 113–15.

67. The devolution of this property-managing cosmopolitanism appears in the lists of property owners with more than 5,000 hectares in 1913 in Sandgruber, *Agrarstatistik*, pp. 234–40.

68. *Wirtschaftsgeschichte*, pp. 98–99; idem, 'Die Grundherrschaft als Unternehmen' *Zeitschrift für Agrargeschichte und Agrarsoziologie*, 6 (1958); G. Grüll, *Weinberg. Die Entstehungsgeschichte einer Wirtschaftsherrschaft* (Graz, 1955); Rebel, *Classes*, ch. 2 and passim.

viticulture, fish ponds, brewing, saw-mills, etc. using their own unique combinations of *robot* and wage labour.[69] The new revenue structure of this kind of enterprise combined rents, transaction fees, conversion fees (including various *robotgelder*), the ordinary and extraordinary taxes the Estates negotiated with the Crown, and, finally, the incomes from estate enterprises. A key aspect of this new landlord economy was that often the overall profit was smaller than any one of these incomes, so that each of them, with the exception of low and still declining rents, was essential for the success of the whole.[70] It was a by no means secure corporate economy to which the peasants had to adjust and its crises during the eighteenth century increasingly become theirs as well.

Aspects of *Wirtschaftsherrschaft* appear, with different emphases and modifications, in all the 'Austrian' territories, including those where we find *robot*-based *Gutswirtschaft*.[71] In some regions of Lower Austria, for example, the finer we adjust our empirical focus, the more intermingled the cash- and labour-tribute enterprises appear.[72] The result was that the mix of peasant options and resistances was never fully contained by regional or ethnic divergences as such but always by the shifting market choices of the landlords who found that for some specific locales and some kinds of production, a labour-tribute producing class of farmers bound by migration and military restrictions, which were only enforceable in a territorial framework, seemed a necessity. The more oppressive and, for the peasantry, economically irrational option of becoming a labour-tribute producer was for most of the empire's peasants, including some communities in Bohemia and Hungary, not a uniform threat but a continuing source of economic and political pressure and made the relative freedom of the cash-tribute producers, increasingly associated with German communities, appear as an intrinsically privileging distinction, despite the relatively high social costs this adaption imposed on family and communal life.

Recent archival findings by this and other researchers allow a suggestive outline of the inner workings of such cash-tribute producing households during the seventeenth and eighteenth centuries.[73] By the mid-seventeenth century, we

---

69. Rebel, *Classes*, pp. 130–7; Knittler, 'Ost und West', p. 213 and idem, 'Gewerblicher Eigenbetrieb und frühneuzeitliche Grundherrschaft am Beispiel des Waldviertels', *Mitteilungen des Instituts für österreichische Geschichtsforschung*, 92 (1984).

70. Rebel, *Classes*, pp. 134–5.

71. A. Spiesz, 'Die neuzeitliche Agrarentwicklung der Tschechoslovakei: Gutswirtschaft oder Wirtschaftsherrschaft?' *Zeitschrift für bayerische Landesgeschichte*, 32 (1969); W. Stark, 'Die Abhängigkeitsverhältnisse der gutsherrlichen Bauern Böhmens im 17. und 18. Jahrhundert', *Jahrbücher für Nationalökonomik und Statistik*, 164 (1952); Tremel, *Sozialgeschichte*, pp. 242–5; Schremmer, 'Agrarverfassung'. The work of Pach and others outlines very similar developments in Hungary. The legal, administrative and commercial restrictions imposed on Hungarian landlords after the reconquest allowed peasants more administrative freedom than was usual and made the formation of Hungarian *Wirtschaftsherrschaften* more difficult.

72. Knittler, 'Ost und West', passim; and indeed this is the Cole/Wolf model as well. Judging that areas where the highest *robot* demands were made (usually up to and beyond the two to three days a week that was the 'norm' officially accepted by Leopold I's *Robotordnung* of 1680) were also the areas where it was most prevalent, we find that besides Bohemia and Hungary, such areas included and overlapped with regions in Moravia, Lower Austria and Inner Austria as well.

73. The early seventeenth-century quantitative materials receive extensive treatment in Rebel, *Classes*, passim; later data are drawn from similar research done in 1984–85, 1988 and 1991 for a book in progress with the working title 'Family Formations, Disinheritance and the Progress of a Social Pathology in Provincial Austria, 1649–1948'.

can observe a gradient of economic and social differentiation, with considerable wealth and the acquisition of privileged farms and houses going to an emergent elite of agriculturists who had specialized as teamsters, millers and innkeepers. Rural weavers and peasants who had diversified their households with textile, metal, wood or other industrial occupations were clearly improving themselves beyond a numerically well-represented rural middle class engaged simply in mixed farming. Below that there were both relatively poor and wealthy cottagers and lodgers, several of whom had diversified into craft or specialized wage labour, and below them were servants and day-labourers, of whom several had managed to retain an inheritance portion or a small piece of unencumbered land.

By around 1700, this nearly Bell-curved early seventeenth-century economic and social profile with 31 per cent in the bottom third, 61 per cent in the middle and 9 per cent at the top had begun to flatten considerably with the proportion of the poor at 53 per cent in the bottom third, 29 per cent in the middle third and 18 per cent in the top group. The occupational foundations of this changing wealth distribution were also shifting. The very poor have all but ceased to appear because, besides an occasional record of an outstanding inheritance debt, there was nothing to inventory. Almost everyone in the lower and middling groups who had a house engaged increasingly in some aspect of textile-related industrial diversification, while weavers had, significantly, all but disappeared. Wealthier peasants, on the other hand, were 'deindustrializing' and returning to more intensive grain and livestock operations, while teamsters and innkeepers, still the peasant elite, were hitting harder times, with a sharp decline in long-distance trade balanced by only a slow increase in domestic military and civilian transport that benefited teamsters more than it did innkeepers.

Incumbent farmers and their designated heirs had devised strategic adaptions to the cash-tribute extracting environments in which they found themselves. They engaged, whenever possible, in *inter vivos* inheritance, both to benefit the 'retiring' elders (*Auszügler*), who emerged as a class of petty money lenders, and to avoid the *post-mortem* inventorying of the full household for the allocation of residual inheritance portions as well as the landlords' 10 per cent tribute (*Freigeld*). Recent scholarship is demonstrating that the class of residual heirs – the 'dispossessed', who in social romantic histories still move through a liminal 'youth stage' of servant labour before they rejoin peasant society proper by marrying back into property-ownership – were expelled from their home farms at a relatively young age (often as early as seven to nine years old) and began servant careers with one- to two-year labour contracts[74] which in time took them out of their home communities to increasingly distant places where they could make no welfare or inheritance claims. By 1700, it was common for

---

74. M. Mitterauer's household reconstitution studies demonstrate the short-term labour circulation of the *Gesinde*; cf. his articles 'Familienwirtschaft' and 'Gesindeleben im Alpenraum', in his *Familienforschung*; J. Ehmer, *Heiratsverhalten*, ends the 'youth stage' romance once and for all; idem, 'The "Life Stairs". Ageing, generational relations and small commodity production in central Europe', in T. Hareven (ed.), *Ageing and Generational Relations over the Life Course* (Berlin, 1995) reflects on the cultural pressure the young put on older incumbents in such a system.

estate administrations to require heir-incumbents to pay the residual portions that had been assessed into accounts managed in trust by those administrations. This signified not only a loss of control over family affairs for the incumbents, but also weakened the chances for the dispossessed to claim their portions as their trust funds disappeared in successive private corporate and public fiscal crises.

The inventories reveal also the exhaustion, by 1700, of the strategic advantage gained by some cash-tribute producers who had earlier added a proto-industrial diversification to their household economies. Before we can compare their industrial experience to that of the labour-tribute producing peasantries, we need to be clear about the world-market framework. The almost universal dependence of the Austrian empire's peasant sectors on putting-out industries (*Verlagsindustrien*) also meant a dependence on trade outside the empire. The peasants of the German core territories were almost completely dependent on textile putters-out based in neighbouring Bavaria, the Inner Austrian peasantries depended on metal and textile industrial links with northern Italy and the Adriatic, while those of Bohemia and Hungary looked outward to capital and markets as far away as Leipzig, Hamburg and the Baltic. The Hungarian peasantry, struggling to convert the roll-back of Turkish power to their own economic and political advantage, were defeated by Habsburg military power in protracted peasant–gentry uprisings in 1683–99 and 1707–15. The severe tariff impositions that followed after 1756 separated Hungary's economy once again from the rest of the Austrian empire and left its agricultural sector isolated, without an industrial sector to manage rural labour efficiently, and consequently relatively uncompetitive. As we will see in the next section, Hungary's experience in this regard was indicative of a trend in eighteenth-century Habsburg trade policies generally that put pressure on the viability of the 'proto-industrial' sectors necessary everywhere in the empire.

Pending household inventory and accounts investigations to reveal the inner workings of the labour-tribute peasantries' economies, we know enough to say that their household management took place in a framework comparable to the cash tribute producers. Since they also controlled their inheritance dispositions we also find there attempts at forming a class of *Auszügler* and battles over the control of inheritance trust funds.[75] In the area of labour arrangements the labour-tribute peasants necessarily developed in an entirely different, but still also comparable, direction. While the cash-tribute producers remained competitive by taking in or expelling labour as the market demanded, the labour-tribute peasantries remained in the economically derationalized labour-market position of having to sustain in their household economies the labour necessary for the tribute services they were required to render for, in effect, competing landlords' production. Unlike the cash-tribute producers, who kept hired labour through slack moments with a weak industrial addition to their individual farm economies, the labour-tribute producers did not sever relations with their dispossessed but rather kept them in the neighbourhood as a cottager class that

75. Stark, 'Abhängigkeitsverhältnisse', pp. 349–50, 443–5.

took over and converted into even smallholdings farms for which no *robot*-service tenants could be found. There they sustained themselves with proto-industrial, mostly textile, production and were available for *robot* labour either through their families, the peasant community or through the labour obligations (including 'spinning *robot*') they owed to landlords directly.[76] Bohemian cottage-based proto-industrialization followed the Bavarian model, and by the eighteenth century actually outproduced and undersold the limited in-house industries of the cash-tribute peasants in the Austrian core areas.[77]

If we compare family and communal relations, labour-tribute producers ironically did not have to make the cash-tribute producers' difficult choices about expelling surplus family labour, thereby undermining emotional ties of family and community. Instead, they prized and maintained family networks and mutual obligations to manage better the conflicting labour needs of landlord and peasant economies. The second irony is that it is in the resistances of the Bohemian peasants against this system – not so much in their rebellions from the 1670s through the 1690s against statutory labour service rules, but rather in their attitude of rejection, after the mid-seventeenth century, of the 'security' of heritable, lifetime leases and the related tribute and family burdens[78] – that we have an emerging, albeit short-lived, market rationality appearing among the peasantries of this region, a higher quality of economic rationality than even that yet to be displayed by the 'enlightened' bureaucrats and aristocratic model farmers in the next century.

PEASANTS IN THE CAMERAL POLICE STATE, 1700–1800

The Europe-wide trough in grain prices that bottomed out in the 1690s was followed by an accelerating rising trend during the eighteenth century. The Austrian peasantries benefited, but not at the higher English, French or German market rates,[79] and the empire's rural sectors remained generally depressed throughout the century. Cash-tribute peasants particularly could not benefit from comparatively stagnant wages because they remained stuck in a house economy of lodgers' tribute-labour and of live-in servants on annual contracts.[80] There was enough economic energy, however, for an upswing in parish church activities after the 1680s, centred especially on Counter-Reformation votive art and on revived liturgical-year pageants with a vital and distinctively 'peasant baroque' style of decorative design and costume.[81] Much of this village renaissance focused (and depended) on parish guilds to administer various trust funds for benevolent

76. Stark, 'Ursprung', pp. 31–47 and 'Abhängigkeitsverhältnisse', passim.
77. Hoffmann, *Wirtschaftsgeschichte*, pp. 184–5, 190, 193–5; the Bavarian model, decribed as the 'territorialization of the trades (*Gewerbe*)', appears in Schremmer 'Agrarverfassung', pp. 62–3 and passim.
78. Stark, 'Ursprung', p. 56 and passim.
79. Abel, *Fluctuations*, p. 199, also pp. 160, 197.
80. Hoffmann, *Agrarstaat*, pp. 24–5.
81. Max Kislinger, *Alte Bauernherrlichkeit* (Linz, 1957).

activities and it is significant that we find guilds that were in serious financial trouble by mid-century. There is evidence that some rural householders could still become as wealthy as well-off citizens of market towns. Georg Grüll points to the 1721 inventory of an *Auszügler* from a wealthy region south of Linz[82] whose outstanding loans alone amounted to 18, 403 fl,[83] a very large sum, considering that the average total inventory value for *Auszügler* who still engaged in money lending in this period was about 800 fl and declining.[84]

There is a further irony when we consider that the weakening eighteenth-century peasant sector coincided with the moral upgrading of peasantries in the imperial values and status systems. In Atlantic Europe, the period's renewed 'enlightened' interest in agriculture sought a better integration of a wide spectrum of commercialized agricultural assets into growing financial markets and paid little or no attention to rural cultivators themselves.[85] In central and eastern Europe, cameralist officials sought to broaden and tighten their grip on rural communal assets behind a smoke-screen of neostoic discourses about individual discipline, self-sacrificial service and universal 'bliss'.[86] The incumbent heads of peasant farms, perceived to be managing order and tribute-producing 'firms', became both the subject and object of so-called 'housefather writing' (*Hausvaterliteratur*), produced by academics and bureaucrats, some of whom had dabbled in military and business entrepreneurship. This literature, drawing on classical and neoclassical models of a so-called 'good economy of the whole house' (*oikos*), emphasized householders' psychological, self-disciplining capacities that, in turn, authorized heads of peasant households to overcome any moral hesitations they might have felt in the exercise of their own police obligations, including the selection for disinheritance and expulsion of certain of their children for the sake of maintaining the ongoing integrity of their houses' tribute-producing capacities.[87] By mid-century, J. H. G. Justi, self-proclaimed 'universal Cameralist' and one of the founders of Empress Maria Theresia's

82. *Bauernhaus und Meierhof* (Linz, 1975), pp. 275, 272–3.

83. The silver *gulden* (fl) was the main currency and accounting unit in the Austrian empire during the seventeenth and eighteenth centuries.

84. This last is from my analysis of household inventories from the Upper Austrian estate Aistersheim at the Oberösterreichisches Landesarchiv in Linz.

85. F. Huggett, *The Land Question and European Society since 1650* (London, 1975) is still a good comparative introduction. The care taken in the construction of the London financial markets to provide a viable niche for rural real estate bonds is outlined in H. Roseveare, *The Financial Revolution* (London, 1991). There were no such developments in the Austrian empire.

86. H. Matis (ed.), *Von der Glückseligkeit des Staates* (Berlin, 1981); cf. J. Gagliardo, 'Moralism, rural ideology and the German peasant in the late eighteenth century', *Agricultural History*, 42: 2 (1968); for an interesting study of the failure of German intellectuals and reformers to implement the English model even in a place one would expect to be more amenable, see O. Ulbricht, *Englische Landwirtschaft in Kurhannover in der zweiten Hälfte des 18. Jahrhunderts* (Berlin, 1980).

87. The classical historical views on all this are G. Oestreich, *Neostoicism and the Early Modern State* (Cambridge, 1982); O. Brunner, 'Das "ganze Haus" und die alteuropäische "Ökonomik" ', in his *Neue Wege der Verfassungs- und Sozialgeschichte* (Göttingen, 1968) and idem, *Adeliges Landleben und europäischer Geist* (Salzburg, 1949); for a solid critique of Brunner, D. Nicholas, 'New paths of social history and old paths of social romanticism', *Journal of Social History*, 3: 3 (1970); for another approach entirely see H. Rebel, 'Reimagining the *oikos*: Austrian cameralism in its social formation', in J. O'Brien and W. Roseberry (eds), *Golden Ages, Dark Ages: Imagining the Past in Anthropology and History* (Berkeley, CA, 1991); Schulze, *Geschichtswissenschaft*, pp. 205, 209–10, 290 and passim offers a disturbing perspective.

academy for state officials, proposed to reward state officeholders, among whom peasant householders stood on the lowest rung, according to their ability to discipline their private houses 'according to the main characteristics of [their] public person'.[88] This was a prescription for the distribution of social costs within peasant households and, specifically, for absorbing and managing privately the hardships implicit in the cameralists' tribute-oriented foreign and domestic trade projects.

There is a persistent tradition in Austrian historiography that tries to portray the cameralists as economic liberals anticipating Adam Smith,[89] but this ignores their corporate statism and the tribute production that was their primary objective. What these latter concerns meant for Austria's peasantries becomes apparent when we examine an early cameralist presentation concerning state export subsidies in linens that one of the leading administrators and writers, J. W. Hörnigk, made to the Upper Austrian Estates in 1677.[90] Complaining that the province's linen trade with Italy was declining because 'foreign' capitalists were dealing with peasant producers directly, he advocated that outsiders be excluded from the linen trade altogether. Instead, a quota of the peasants' linen product was to be purchased by an Austrian corporation with a foreign trade monopoly which would guarantee the 'traditional' price (about twice what was then current) for the export linen, leaving the rest to be traded and to find its price in the monarchy's domestic and local 'free' markets. The trading monopoly would be underwritten by a treasury subscription fund, to which the Estates were invited to contribute, to cover initial guaranteed payments and give the corporation a better bargaining position in foreign markets. Despite the Estates' protests against this subversion of an existing free market and their predictions of financial ruin, such and similar schemes appear to have been followed with some but not all of the predicted results.

Peasant producers suffered in several ways in such a system. While they were indeed 'free' to compete in a closed imperial market to gain tenure on a limited number of privileged houses that could engage in price-guaranteed commercial production for corporate and monopoly-controlled export markets, the majority of peasant producers, now effectively excluded from export markets, were forced into regional competition with other peasantries in the empire. The result was that the family and communal alliances, described above, between labour-tribute peasantries and cottage industries in Silesia, Bohemia, Moravia, Lower Austria and elsewhere outproduced, undersold and destabilized their neighbours' cash-tribute enterprises depending on limited in-house industries to manage their labour calculations. At the same time, import and market access restrictions against foreign firms broke the fragile and volatile circulatory capital and commodities markets, essential to efficient putting-out industries,[91] that had connected western Austrian peasantries to successful rural industrial regions in Bavaria, and producers in Silesia, Bohemia and Hungary

88. J. H. G. Justi, *Staatswirthschaft* (Leipzig, 1758), vol. 1, p. 108.
89. A. Brusatti, *Betrachtungen zur Wirtschafts- und Sozialgeschichte* (Berlin, 1979), p. 111.
90. Hoffmann, *Wirtschaftsgeschichte* pp. 187–9.
91. Cf. J. de Vries, *The Economy of Europe in the Age of Crisis, 1600–1750* (Cambridge, 1976), p. 102.

to northern markets in Leipzig and Hamburg. The labour policies enforced by the Imperial Trades Edict of 1731 and by the Commerce Directory during the second half of the eighteenth century not only prevented industrial trades from organizing beyond local communities but also systematically eliminated guilds and other associations from export-oriented industries, which in turn severely reduced guild and parish trust and welfare funds that had been a significant sector in the peasant communities' social economies.[92] Hungarian peasants' connections to industrial development were severely limited with the prohibitive tariffs of 1756 and the transit duty regulations of 1775. Finally, the prices of agricultural goods, determined by 'free' markets confined within the imperial trade zone, inevitably remained low compared to western Europe inflationary markets. Low prices in turn depressed wages in the export industrial sectors and benefited only the limited export monopolies who could compete better in foreign markets.[93] Peasant housefathers, on the other hand, had to manage, within their families, the contradictions of a system that increasingly depended ideologically and administratively on the peasant households that its commercial policies were rendering uncompetitive and impossible.

We have already pointed to the evidence concerning declining levels of wealth and economic activity in the eighteenth-century inventories that qualifies current claims concerning improving rural 'living standards' in the period.[94] To this we can add that the foreign trade connections of peasant teamsters and innkeepers evident in seventeenth-century inventories' credit listings disappeared completely during the eighteenth century.[95] The inventories also furnish evidence of absolutely declining numbers of residual heirs and the complete disappearance of those children from prior marriages who, during the seventeenth century, had been listed even though they were not entitled to a portion. It appears that the Austrian cash-tribute producing peasants were driven, during the eighteenth century, toward expelling prospective residual heirs at an accelerating rate to remain competitive and, failing that, to abandoning peasant tenure altogether. The declining opportunities for employment in these areas are reflected in the relatively stagnant population growth at the end of the eighteenth century, contrasting significantly with a relative population boom in labour-tribute areas in Bohemia and Lower Austria, as well as in Tirol where the 'German' peasant areas contributed only 8 per cent growth to an overall 26 per cent growth in the period 1790–1850.[96] The combined peasant/industrial communities in the labour-tribute areas (as well as some specialized agricultural areas such as the wine region of Lower Austria) continued to be able to absorb population while the cash-tribute producing areas generally could not. The greater economic pressure

92. Hoffmann, *Wirtschaftsgeschichte*, p. 520.

93. Idem, *Bauernland Oberösterreich* (Linz, 1974), p. 105.

94. R. Sandgruber, 'Marktökonomie und Agrarrevolution', in A. Drabek *et al.* (eds), *Ungarn und Österreich unter Maria Theresia und Joseph II.* (Vienna, 1982), pp. 132–3, 141–2; cf. Hoffmann, *Wirtschaftsgeschichte*, pp. 318–19.

95. Rebel, *Classes*, pp. 210, 214–15.

96. Bruckmüller, *Sozialgeschichte*, p. 287; K. Klein, 'Die Bevölkerung Österreichs vom Beginn des 16. bis zur Mitte des 18. Jahrhunderts', in H. Helczmanovszky (ed.), *Beiträge zur Bevölkerungs- und Sozialgeschichte Österreichs* (Vienna, 1973).

on the latter was accompanied by an increase in the appearance of significant numbers of unemployed vagrants and criminal gangs as early as the late 1720s and 1730s. These latter, appearing as a particularly dangerous symptom of a number of severe economic, taxation and military problems, sparked a broad-spectrum reform effort, identified with Maria Theresia and her son Joseph II, especially after the state authorities recognized that Austria's defeat in the war of the Austrian Succession (1740–48) had resulted in part from failures in revenue productivity and economic organization.

The restructuring of public and private institutions begun by Maria Theresia's new Directory for Public Administration and Royal Finances in 1749 was not merely reactive, however, but also sought to find positive opportunities for asserting the authority of the Crown over that of the territorial political corporations in governing the administratively united Austrian and Bohemian territories. It is significant that at the outset Hungary remained under the administration of the still 'private' dynastic *Hofkammer* and that its peasantries, exempt from these reforms, were prompted to rebellion against exploitation by their courtier-landlords during the 1750s.[97] The ensuing forty years of often confusing and unenforceable reform initiatives, retractions, overlaps, contradictions, advances and retreats[98] burdened the peasantries of the empire as a whole with a full panoply of interventionist state institutions whose primary intention was to squeeze out more revenues by replacing the patrimonial and territorial-corporative administration of the rural population with state agencies creating and shaping new 'public' sectors in finance, defence, civil law, criminal justice and trade.

Rural reforms began with surveys and reassessments of fixed properties and rural tribute units to 'rectify' tax-base data (*Fassionen*).[99] They distinguished 'rustical' from 'dominical' lands in terms of their different yield ratios in order to impose military and other 'contributions' on both peasants and, for the first time, corporate landlords. To be sure, the 'dominical' lands of the latter were taxed at half the rate of the peasants' 'rustical' cultivation and there was no way to prevent landlords from extracting their share from their subject populations. There is no need here to chart the variable successes and failures of such tax-base and cadastral surveys as they became almost immediately obsolete and were repeated, with different objectives and languages each time, between the 1780s and the 1880s.[100]

---

97. G. Ember 'Der österreichische Staatsrat und Ungarn in den 1760er Jahren', and H. Haselsteiner, 'Wehrverfassung und personelle Heeresergänzung in Ungarn', in Drabek *et al.*, *Ungarn*.

98. The heroic recent effort in P. Dickson, *Finance and Government under Maria Theresia, 1740–1780*, 2 vols (Oxford, 1987) to untangle portions of this thicket is much appreciated but has to be consulted cautiously.

99. In Upper Austria this increased the number of known taxable houses by 43 per cent from the last tax census in 1527/44. G. Grüll, 'Die Herrschaftsschichtungen in Österreich ob der Enns 1750', *Mitteilungen des oberösterreichischen Landesarchivs*, 5 (1957), p. 317.

100. Sandgruber, *Agrarstatistik*, pp. 29–34; R. Rosdolski, *Die Grosse Steuer- und Agrarreform Josefs II.*, (Warsaw, 1961), chs 4, 5; the failures of and historical experiences with these obsessive cameralist quests for taxonomies of peasant types, land qualities, etc. 'on the ground' will probably never be captured better than in the nightmarish adventures of Kafka's government land-surveyor K. in *The Castle* (1926). For a more recent fiction that captures Austrian peasantry further along the same historical and literary trajectories see K. Hoffer, *Bei den Bieresch* (Frankfurt, 1986).

Even before the breakthrough of taxing 'dominical' incomes, the Theresian reformers had begun to permit peasant subjects to buy their freedom from their landlords' patrimonial judicial and political administrations. They did not thus cease to be subjects but became subject to the Crown; it was not until the Civil Law of 1811 that peasants became citizens and then only those who held tenure on a house, with those 'inside' the house still fully subject to the heads' private law. In the period 1751–70, the lords' exclusive controls of local markets were dismantled by, among other things, the termination of their monopsonic rights in local agricultural commodity markets – while at the same time and in full accord with cameralist trade policy these rights were increased and enforced on behalf of entrepreneurs who ran 'factory' monopolies for putting-out industries in export goods. Also beginning in 1749, territorial administration was increasingly taken out of the Estates' governing committees' hands and given to court-appointed governorships (*Gubernia*) at the territorial level and to regional district offices (*Kreisämter*) and to the new 'German' regiments' recruiting area commanders below that, all of whom began to develop alternative bodies of rules, regulations and courts to rival and displace patrimonial jurisdictions. The final abolition of *Leibeigenschaft* in 1781 further reduced the legal power of the landlords to maintain strategic and legally privileged relationships with select peasant-agents in the subject community. Some of the corporate landlords, especially in the cash-tribute areas, tried to avoid being hit hard by all of these measures (which diminished the state tributes and transaction fees they once controlled) by obtaining offices in the growing state apparatus. From examinations of estate accounts and of the landlords' enterprises in cash-tribute areas it is clear that their rural economies were in trouble.[101] Those landlords, on the other hand, who cultivated their own lands with low-overhead *robot* labour and enjoyed a lower tax rate and larger market share than the 'individualized' peasant producers in the cash-tribute regions, who were their main competitors in the internally 'free' Austrian-Bohemian markets, were in a much more advantageous market position.[102]

From this perspective, Joseph II's peasant 'liberation' takes on a different appearance from the progressive liberal episode which it is still often made out to be. Joseph's physiocrat reform ideology was a suitable ally to cameralism's closed trade empire and together they ensured that the – by then centuries-old – practical insights that tenant farm production was not competitive without an industrial sector to optimize agriculture's narrow labour margins and that this industrial sector was not in turn viable without being in competitive touch with the larger world market, were completely lost. Joseph's reforms were driven, moreover, by practical political, military and treasury objectives. As early as 1761[103] he proposed to do away with *robot* in a scheme that was echoed three

101. Grüll, *Weinberg*; Knittler, 'Eigenbetrieb'; E. Wangerman noted the end of the aristocratic building boom after 1763. *The Austrian Achievement* (New York, 1973), p. 127.

102. Rosdolski, *Agrarreform*, pp. 59–60.

103. In a memorandum cited in W. Wright, *Serf, Seigneur and Sovereign* (Minneapolis, 1966), p. 43. Wright's exposition of the arguments is worth consulting, ch. 4 and passim. His reading of the reforms differs from the arguments presented here.

years later by the royal war council (*Hofkriegsrat*) who saw a greater potential for drafting recruits from a cash-tribute peasant society. The Josephinian military plan was to create a uniform class of cash-tribute producing peasant subjects under direct state jurisdiction. They would be entitled to keep 70 per cent of their product and render 17 per cent to their landlords (who were reduced thereby to passive rentiers) and 13 per cent to the state. It was to assign these portions that Josephinian authorities conducted their cadastral surveys. The key to the system was the military which would, in an analogue to the Prussian experience,[104] absorb and give off labour as agricultural production required, thereby solving the rural labour problem without dependence on industry. For former labour-tribute areas, Josephinian administrators planned to terminate the parcellization of land to cut back on the cottage-based putting-out system whose competition had been undermining the cash-tribute, 'German' peasants. The numbers of these latter were to be augmented by immigrants from German areas to settle reconstituted, impartible manorial farms in Bohemia and elsewhere as hereditary, long-term leaseholders.

The experimental abolition of *robot*, by 1777, on over twenty royal estates in Bohemia under the direction of a plan proposed and administered by Franz Anton Raab,[105] a member of the Commerce Commission, revealed the full intentions of the so-called reform and provoked opposition from across the social spectrum, from landlords, commercial interests and even the peasants. These protests were not, as Wright and others have argued, grounded in mere conservatism but represented rather a reaction against the further loss of market responsiveness for these regions under the plan's reactionary provisions for long-term hereditary leases and fixed distribution of income in which the landlords and commercial interests would in effect lose labour services and demesne farms while the treasury collected not mortgageable *robot* abolition fees but perpetual release-fee payments that were periodically renegotiable. It was on this last point that the peasants' opposition focused in particular. There were a number of uprisings in Bohemia in the 1770s and 1780s directed against lords' ongoing increases and enforcements of *robot*. These movements' primary purpose was not conversion of labour service to a cash tribute but its outright abolition and, indeed, the abandonment of the tribute system altogether. In 1784 one Upper Austrian estate using *robot* labour experienced a violent strike that lasted three years until its administrators finally required the regional *Kreisamt* and military authorities to crush the strike and to enforce the *robot*. The apparent irony of anti-*robot* state authorities enforcing labour-service extractions is diminished when we observe that private and public authorities had to cooperate in order to defend the principle of tribute itself against the *robot*-peasants' challenge.[106]

---

104. Still best understood in O. Büsch's neglected *Militärsystem und Sozialleben im alten Preußen* (Berlin, 1962).

105. Raab, *Unterricht*, passim explicitly rejects short-term leases and labour-service as not desirable for a cameral state that wants settled peasants committed to a steady production of cash tributes (see footnote 39).

106. Grüll, *Herr*, pp. 206–14; H. Feigl, 'Ein neues Geschichtsbild über das Wirken Maria Theresias und Josephs II. auf dem Gebiet der Landwirtschaft und der ländlichen Sozialstruktur?', in idem (ed.), *Die Auswirkungen der theresianisch-josephinischen Reformen auf die Landwirtschaft und die ländliche Sozialstruktur Niederösterreichs* (Vienna, 1982); also H. Hofbauer and A. Komlosy, *Das andere Österreich* (Vienna, 1987), pp. 78–86.

Joseph II's brother and successor, Leopold II, was a skilled administrator trained in the dynasty's Tuscan estate management and fiscal traditions which had been one source for Maria Theresia's original reform course.[107] He terminated Joseph's impossible tax scheme, returned the collection of taxes and tributes to the patrimonial authorities, he re-empowered some of the Estates' committees and added peasant representatives, and he did not force abolition of *robot*. On the other hand, he kept intact the policy of supporting long-term leases for cash-tribute peasant tenants and continued Church and welfare reforms that further weakened the peasants' parish organizations. Leopold's successor, Francis I, ruling with a long-lived dead hand (Macartney's phrase), allowed the cameralist-Josephinist ideology's influence to continue to grow, against some opposition from law faculty and commercial groups, well into the nineteenth century with no appreciable change in the imbalance and direction of forces in the countryside.[108] The self-consuming and destructive competition between the two peasant sectors within the region lived on in exhaustion at least until the second half of the nineteenth century. By then the *robot* option had disappeared and the cash-tribute form was radically modernized by the reforms that followed the 1848 uprisings. Impartible tenure was abolished by law in 1868 but lived on as a cultural ideal, an ideological rallying point for the declining empire's 'German tradition'.

One of the main protagonists that has emerged from this history has been the labour-tribute form and its paradoxical unfolding from being the 'identifying' oppression of colonialized Hungarian and Slavic peasantries to becoming the motor behind a dynamic economic and social adaption that outperformed – without requiring disruptive severances of family connections – an economically and systemically unviable cash-tribute sector which was nevertheless held up as the ruling German social ideal by the imperial corporate and state authorities. The more mobile, skilled and socially connected non-German labourers from the labour-tribute producing communities contrasted with and appeared as a competitive threat to the socially disconnected and dispossessed children emerging from the 'free' but involuted, self-exploiting cash-tribute peasant houses and cottages, particularly when the former became free to move from their fringe areas and appeared as migrant or seasonal labour in the mining and manufacturing industries of the core Alpine and Danubian regions. The next step is to write a history that understands, finally, how recurrent Austrian episodes of destructive terrorism against ethnically identifiable 'foreigners' are the ongoing resonances of the early modern peasantries' experiences.

---

107. H. Mikoletzky, *Kaiser Franz I. Stephan und der Ursprung des Habsburg-Lothringischen Familienvermögens* (Munich, 1961); Macartney, *Empire*, ch. 3.

108. Thus H. Weitensfelder, *Interessen und Konflikte in der Frühindustrialisierung* (Frankfurt am Main, 1991) tells a recognizable story about, among other things, how trade restrictions continued to 'underdevelop' rural communities in Vorarlberg during the first half of the nineteenth century.

Map 8.1 Russia. 1: Russian Heartland; 2: Russian North; 3: Black-Soil Steppe-
Forest; 4: Middle Volga; 5: Left-Bank Ukraine; 6: Right-Bank Ukraine; 7: Belorussia

CHAPTER EIGHT

The Russian Peasantries, 1450–1860

Edgar Melton

Since Semevskii's classic studies, most subsequent historians of the Russian peasantry have echoed one major theme – the unbridled exploitation of the rural population.[1] There is much truth in this, but the Russian peasantry was much too large, too varied, and too protean to fit such a generalization. Some groups, to be sure, endured particular hardships, such as the serfs on labour services during the last century of serfdom. This group, however, accounted for less than a quarter of the peasant population by the 1850s, and other groups, including the many serfs who paid quitrent in place of labour services, often lived as well as, if not better than, their counterparts in western Europe. The present essay attempts a more balanced picture of the Russian peasants, one that accounts for the geographical and social diversity of rural life in Russia, and its evolution over four centuries.

Writing about a large peasant population inhabiting a vast territory for more than four centuries requires, at the start, at least a few definitions and clarifications. The geographical focus here is on the lands of European Russia inhabited by East Slavs; while geographers may differ over definitions of *European* Russia, the treatment here deals primarily with the territories lying between the Ural Mountains and the present-day eastern boundaries of Lithuania, Poland, Slovakia and Romania.

The primary focus is on the Russian peasants in three major regions. First, there is the heartland, the geo-political core of the Russian state as it emerged in the sixteenth century. The heartland includes the large territories around Moscow, Novgorod, and Pskov. The second region, the north, includes the territories lying north of the heartland in a vast but thinly settled region between the upper Volga and the White Sea. Both the heartland and the north were settled by Russian populations in the course of a long period beginning in the mid-thirteenth century. Taken together, these two territories – roughly three million square kilometres – embraced most of the lands of the Russian state as it existed in the mid-sixteenth century. The black-soil forest-steppe

---

1. V. V. Semevskii, *Krest'iane v tsarstvovanie imperatritsy Ekateriny II*, 2 vols (St Petersburg, 1881–1901); also his *Krest'ianskii vopros v Rossii v xviii i pervoi polovine xix v.*, 2 vols (St Petersburg, 1888).

region was settled later, in the late sixteenth and seventeenth centuries, and added another million square kilometres to the Russian state. It lies south and south-east of the heartland, in a large territory between the Ukraine, in the west, and the Ural mountains and middle Volga, in the east.

In addition to the primary focus on the Russian peasants, this chapter also includes the Ukrainians and Belorussians. This somewhat complicates the narrative, since the Ukraine and Belorussia belonged, through much of our period, to Poland-Lithuania, and only became part of the Russian state in the period from 1667 to 1795. This essay devotes special attention to them for several reasons: first, because their history differs considerably from that of the Russian peasants, and second, because their geographical position, on Russia's western borderlands, gives them particular importance in Russian history.

The western borderlands aside, agricultural conditions varied greatly in the three major regions of Russia proper. The far north (north from latitude 58/ 55° N) belongs to a vast belt of coniferous forest stretching west from Finland to Kamchatka, in Eastern Siberia. This belt, known as the *taiga*, is generally unsuitable for cereal cultivation, but further to the south (although still in the northern region), cereal cultivation becomes a much better proposition beginning with the mixed-forest zone (deciduous and non-deciduous) which begins along a line running (roughly) from St Petersburg east to Viatka. The mixed-forest zone embraces both the lower part of the north and virtually all of the heartland.

The basic characteristic of the mixed-forest zone is its severe climate and relatively poor soil. The climate, marked by high precipitation and a short growing season (120–50 days per year), has greatly influenced the quality of the soil. There are not enough hot days during the year to evaporate the water in the top soil, and this ground water leaches much of the organic and mineral content out of the top soil, sinking it into the subsoil below. In short, the land is not rich, generally yielding only marginal harvests unless well-fertilized.[2]

Despite the low fertility of the soil in the heartland and near north, the low population density, averaging only four people per square kilometre in 1550, made for an abundance of arable and forest that to some degree compensated for the harsh climate and poor soil. Thus, by 1450, the peasants in the mixed-forest zone of the heartland and north had developed a resilient, if not exactly flourishing, agricultural economy centred on stockbreeding and the cultivation of rye, oats and flax. By the late fifteenth century, the three-field system dominated, although it long continued to coexist with less intensive cropping systems.

Whatever the shortcomings of agriculture in the mixed-forest zone, it was sufficient to support a general demographic and economic expansion of the late fifteenth and early sixteenth centuries. In the region around Novgorod, normal yields for rye, the major crop, averaged 4:1, about the same as in Schleswig-Holstein and Brandenburg-Prussia.[3] In the central regions of the

2. For geographical factors in Russian history, Carsten Goehrke, 'Die geographischen Gegebenheiten Rußlands in ihrem historischen Beziehungsgeflecht', in Klaus Zernack *et al.* (eds), *Handbuch der Geschichte Rußlands* (Stuttgart, 1981–), vol. I/1, pp. 9–72.

3. A. L. Shapiro, *Russkoe krest'ianstvo pered zakreposhcheneniem (xiv–xvi vv.)* (St Petersburg, 1987), pp. 20–2.

heartland, around Moscow, it was generally lower, averaging only 3:1, while yields for oats, the other major crop, were also low everywhere, averaging only 3:1.

The black-soil forest-steppe, marked by fertile plains dotted with islands of deciduous forests, is much better suited for agriculture. High summer temperatures dry much of the accumulated moisture in the soil, which enables it to retain its high organic and mineral content. And while this also created occasional droughts (twice per decade, on average), it generally yielded excellent grain harvests, averaging 5:1 in the late eighteenth and early nineteenth centuries. Russian settlement of the black-soil forest-steppe began late, however, and the region does not figure significantly in this narrative until the late seventeenth century.

PERIODIZATION

The period covered here has four distinct phases. The first period, 1460–1580, marked the consolidation of the Russian state in the heartland and north, and was accompanied by more or less steady economic and demographic expansion. The second phase, 1580–1649, was one of initial political disaster and demographic crisis that culminated in the Time of Troubles (1598–1613). A slow recovery – political, as well as economic and demographic – marked the last three decades of this period. The primary characteristics of the third period, 1650–1750, are colonization and settlement of the black-soil steppe-forest, the rise of serfdom, and the consolidation of the absolutist state. In the fourth period, 1750–1860, we see the emergence of a regional division of labour between the heartland (dominated by trade and rural industry), and the black-soil forest-steppe (dominated by market-oriented demesne farming based on serf labour). During this period, the state and nobility increased their exploitation of the peasantry as never before. At the same time, however, this was also the golden age of the peasant commune, in which communal self-government reached the high point of its power.

PHASE 1: 1450–1580

The 1450s provide a useful starting point for several reasons. First, in that decade began the final phase in Muscovy's consolidation of her political dominance over the Russian heartland and the north. The late fifteenth century was also significant for the other major East Slav populations – the Ukrainians and Belorussians. The Ukrainian principalities (Volhynia and Kiev) became vassal states of the Grand Duchy of Lithuania, of which Belorussia already comprised the major part. The Belorussians inhabited the central and eastern lands of the Lithuanian state, while the Ukrainian population inhabited the newly acquired regions in the south, around Kiev, and in the Volhynian and Podolian lands of the north-western Ukraine.

In the mid-fifteenth century, the Russian population began to recover from successive devastations wrought by the Black Death, which had reached their height in the first half of the fifteenth century.[4] The demographic and economic recovery that followed saw not only the resettling of deserted villages, but also the creation of many new settlements.

The rural population in this period fell into four major groups: the *chernososhnye*, or peasants on 'black lands', meaning those living on lands belonging to and under the authority of the Muscovite state; the *dvortsovye* peasants, living on lands belonging to the household of the Muscovite grand prince; the peasants under ecclesiastical landlords; and, finally, those under noble landowners. In the course of the sixteenth century, the proportion of peasants living under noble landowners grew rapidly, while the *chernososhnye* peasants, those living on state lands, almost disappeared as a category. Later data, from the census of 1678, shows that noble landowners had nearly 60 per cent of the peasants, followed by the Church with 18 per cent, the state with about 12 per cent, and the tsar's household with 10 per cent.

The dominant family type in this period was similar to that in western and central Europe, that is, the 'simple' family made up of the married couple and their children.[5] In sixteenth-century Russia, as in many parts of Europe, the farmstead was the basic assessment unit for rents, although it often corresponded only in theory to a typical farmstead. In the Novgorod region, occupying the north-western part of the heartland, the farmstead assessment unit, the *obzha*, typically contained about forty acres of land, in which the sown area might vary between 5 and 19 acres. In the central heartland, around Moscow, the farmstead assessment unit was the *vyt'* (50–65 acres), although most peasant farms were much smaller, ranging between 25 and 40 acres.[6]

Average farmsteads in sixteenth-century Russia were much smaller than the typical farmsteads in Brandenburg or East Prussia, which averaged two *Hufen* (over eighty acres). One reason why peasant farmsteads in Russia were so much smaller than in east-Elbian Germany was the lower productivity of Russian peasants. Based on later studies that assume a yield ratio of 4:1, a peasant household in East Prussia (five members) had the productive capacity to work forty to fifty acres of arable without resorting to hired labour, while a peasant household in Russia (six members) had a maximum capacity of only thirty acres.[7]

At the same time, however, it is important to remember that the rural economy in Russia was probably much less oriented to cereal cultivation than in

---

4. Carsten Goehrke, *Die Wüstungen in der Moskauer Rus'. Studien zur Siedlungs-, Bevölkerungs- und Sozialgeschichte* (Wiesbaden, 1968), pp. 76–8.

5. Ibid., p. 143.

6. R. E. F. Smith, *Peasant Farming in Muscovy* (Cambridge, 1977), pp. 84–5, and V. I. Buganov *et al.* (eds), *Istoriia krest'ianstva SSSR s drevneishikh vremen do velikoi oktiabr'skoi sotsialisticheskoi revoliutsii*, 5 vols (Moscow, 1987–), vol. II, pp. 248–61.

7. For East Prussia, F. W. Henning, *Dienste und Abgaben der Bauern im 18. Jahrhundert* (Stuttgart, 1969), pp. 130–1; for Russia, Shapiro, *Russkoe krest'ianstvo*, p. 58.

east-Elbia. In the Russian heartland, cereal cultivation was only one, and not always the most important, part of the household economy. Forests and streams supported a diverse range of activities including fishing, beekeeping and hunting, while salt production was of major importance in the north. In the heartland, moreover, rural production of linen and canvas was already emerging, although peasants produced it more as a rent in kind than as a commodity for the market.[8]

Soviet historians have constructed a model of a typical peasant farmstead in the Pskov region (north-western part of the heartland) in the early sixteenth century. Assuming a yield ratio of 4:1 for rye, a household of five, working a farmstead with thirty acres of arable, had a yearly income the equivalent of over 300 kopecks (in money of the time), of which half went for their own consumption needs, 20 per cent for seed, and another 20 per cent for seigneurial rents. This left about 10 per cent – enough for taxes and other expenditures, but not enough for significant capital accumulation.[9]

Above the farmstead stood the peasant commune, which was not centred on the village, but rather on the *volost'*, which usually encompassed a group of villages. It is quite likely that this form of organization existed throughout the Russian heartland in the fifteenth century, but it is only for the 'black' (state) lands in northern Russia that we have detailed studies. The *volost'* commune in northern Russia typically contained twenty to thirty villages, and was often coterminous with the church parish. In the sixteenth century, when most villages were still very small (three households), it is not surprising that the state tried to organize them into larger fiscal and administrative units. Land use was probably the most complex task carried out by the *volost'* commune, and the meadows and woodlands belonging to a given village were jointly held and regulated by the farmsteaders of that village. Each household within the village enjoyed hereditary rights on its arable, but this was not the right to a specific, discrete parcel of land, but rather the right to a certain share of village land in accordance with the documented holdings of that household. Thus, the village might periodically repartition land among its households, but a family with an original deed to one *vyt'* would receive a share twice as large as a household whose original deed was for only half a *vyt'*. Above the village commune, *volost'* officials administered and regulated access to the larger tracts of land within the *volost'*, including parish church lands, forests, roads linking the villages, large lakes, and, often, salt works. It also had responsibility for settling new households on vacant farmsteads.[10] At this level, the *volost'* officials also carried out most administrative, judicial and policing tasks in their territory. The officials were peasants elected by the *skhod*, or *volost'* assembly. These officials and their titles varied from one *volost'* to the next, but usually included the headman (*starosta*), the treasurer (*tseloval'nik*) and the elders who sat on the *volost'* court. In addition to electing its officials, the assembly also had responsibility for

8. Buganov, *et al.*, *Istoriia krest'ianstva*, vol. II, p. 330.
9. A. L. Shapiro (ed.), *Agrarnaia istoriia severo-zapada Rossii, xvi veka* (St Petersburg, 1974), p. 91.
10. Ibid., p. 274.

assessing each household for its share of state and local taxes. These were not broad popular assemblies, and *volost'* self-government tended to be more oligarchic than democratic. Participation was limited, rarely including more than half the householders in the *volost'*, and they, in turn, usually elected their officials from the 'best' (richest) households.[11]

Until the mid-sixteenth century, *volost'* officials were responsible to the provincial governor appointed by the grand prince. Beginning in 1539, however, the Muscovite government, in an attempt to suppress growing banditry in the northern provinces, began to vest communes there with increasing power and autonomy, making them (or at least their officials) responsible only to the central administration in Moscow. Reforms carried out by Ivan IV in the period 1556–61 broadened these measures, eliminating some provincial governors altogether, while expanding the fiscal and judicial prerogatives of the communes.[12]

The role of the commune also expanded in the heartland in this period, although it is unlikely that communes there enjoyed the same degree of local power and autonomy as their northern counterparts. Much of the heartland was in the hands of private landowners, either lay nobles or ecclesiastical foundations, and the presence of these authorities, or their representatives, may have limited the scope of communal self-government. This notwithstanding, communes in the heartland functioned the same way as in the north, with assemblies that elected communal officials and allocated rents and taxes.[13]

Historians continue to debate the complex question of seigneurial rents and dues in this period. The main issue here is the degree to which we can talk of a 'second serfdom' in Russia similar to that in Poland and east-Elbian Germany. We will deal with this question in more detail in the next section, limiting discussion here to some general points. First, it has been possible to trace the evolution of seigneurial rents for only certain types of estates: monastery landholdings in the lands around Moscow, and noble estates in the north-west, around Novgorod and Pskov. Secondly, demesne farming, based on compulsory labour services, existed only on a relatively small scale throughout most of the sixteenth and seventeenth centuries.

The estate records of the Tsarevo-Konstantinov monastery for the late fifteenth and early sixteenth century show that a peasant on a farmstead of five *desiatinas* (13.5 acres) had to cultivate one *desiatina* (2.7 acres) of monastery demesne. In other words, labour services for the landlord took about one-sixth of his labour. Demesne farming was somewhat more developed in the north-west, around Novgorod, Pskov and Tver. When Ivan III annexed Novgorod to Muscovy in the late fifteenth century, he confiscated roughly three million acres of land, dividing it into estates that he then gave out to his nobles under conditional tenure (*pomestye*) that was theoretically dependent on the recipient's continued participation in the feudal levies called in time of war or military

11. Ibid., pp. 141–3.
12. Ibid., p. 275.
13. L. V. Danilova, *Sel'skaia obshchina v srednevekovoi Rusi* (Moscow, 1984), p. 206.

emergency. In contrast to the monasteries of the Moscow region, the service nobles seem to have taken a more aggressive approach to expanding their demesne arable. This was especially the case in Bezhetskaia district, near Tver, where demesne lands occupied a quarter of the land under cultivation. This had less impact on peasant obligations than might initially appear, however. In Bezhetskaia district, demesne arable averaged less than three acres per peasant household, and actually much less, since slaves provided 80 per cent of the agricultural labour on these lands.[14]

Slavery in Russia existed on two levels. At the higher level, slaves played an important role in the military and administrative retinues of the ruler and his aristocracy, a role perhaps similar to that of the ministerials, the unfree nobility in medieval Germany. By the mid-sixteenth century, however, this group was apparently diminishing through assimilation into the free nobility. At the lower level, many nobles kept household and agricultural slaves, and although part of this stratum had received their own land allotments in the course of the late fifteenth and sixteenth centuries, they remained slaves (*kholopy*). In the late six-teenth century, new categories of non-hereditary slaves also appeared – prim arily as the result of debt servitude.[15] Judging from north-west Russia, slaves probably accounted for only 7–8 per cent of the Russian population in the sixteenth and seventeenth centuries.[16] Moreover, slave labour seems to have been largely absent on Church estates, and despite its impressive role on sei-gneurial estates in certain districts, like Bezhetskaia, slaves probably accounted for less than 10 per cent of the agricultural labour force.[17]

Future research will doubtless fill many of the existing gaps in our know-ledge of seigneurial rents and dues in this period, but it is unlikely to revise Jerome Blum's conclusion that 'throughout the sixteenth and seventeenth cen-turies *obrok* in cash and kind remained the predominant type of peasant obliga-tion'.[18] Even in Bezhetskaia district, demesne farming accounted for only half of seigneurial revenues, while in other areas the percentage was much smaller, averaging only a fifth, while rents in cash and kind made up the remaining 80 per cent.[19]

Although regional variations within the heartland make it difficult to generalize about the relative importance of each kind of rent, rents in kind – mostly grain – still played the dominant role in the sixteenth century. In most of the north-west, they accounted for approximately half of the peasants' rents to their land-lords. On court lands around Moscow, and in the north, they often accounted for much more, often comprising 75–90 per cent of the peasants' rents.[20]

14. Shapiro, *Agrarnaia istoriia . . . xvi veka*, pp. 280–5.

15. Buganov *et al.*, *Istoriia krest'ianstva*, vol. II, p. 271.

16. According to the best estimate, they were less than 10 per cent of the population. Richard Hellie, *Slavery in Russia, 1450–1725* (Chicago, 1982), pp. 679–89.

17. According to Hellie's estimate, they accounted for only 5 per cent of the labour services performed on seigneurial estates. Ibid., p. 685.

18. Jerome Blum, *Lord and Peasant in Russia from the Ninth to the Nineteenth Century* (Princeton, NJ, 1961), p. 225.

19. Ibid., p. 285.

20. Shapiro, *Russkoe krest'ianstvo*, p. 92, n. 33.

While rents and dues did not substantially increase in this period, taxes increased dramatically, at least in the period 1550–80. Again, our best sources come from the Novgorod region, where the real tax burden nearly doubled. This greatly increased the total of rent and taxes imposed on the peasants, which had claimed only 25–30 per cent of the income of a 'typical' peasant household in 1550. By 1580, it claimed half or more of the household's income, largely because of this increase in taxes.[21]

PHASE 2: 1580–1649

This period has drawn much attention from agrarian historians, largely for two reasons: first, because of the demographic crisis of the period 1580–1620, and second, because of the gradual development of serfdom, which culminated in the Law Code of 1649. Without denying either the severity of the former, or the long-term importance of the latter, the historical picture of these developments needs to be modified, if not totally revised.

The sources clearly reveal a process of demographic decline after 1550, especially in the north-western regions of the heartland. Outbreaks of typhus and famine began in the 1560s, and may have taken a million lives between 1580 and 1620.[22] In addition, however, the demographic crisis deepened and spread as the result of internal political and financial collapse brought on by the Livonian War (1558–82). This war, the most ambitious of Ivan the Terrible's expansion policies, required large expenditures that placed ruinous tax burdens on the peasantry. As tax burdens on the peasant household doubled, the hard-pressed peasants in the heartland apparently fled to the black-soil forest-steppe beyond Muscovy's southern frontier.[23] By the 1580s, when the first phase of the crisis reached its high point, between 65 and 95 per cent of the farmsteads in the heartland apparently stood deserted. In the centre of the heartland, as well as in certain parts of the north, the sources also suggest high levels of depopulation.[24]

This standard interpretation also sees a second wave of demographic crisis connected with the Time of Troubles (1598–1613). Beginning with a famine that gripped the heartland between 1601 and 1603, the crisis intensified as civil war, peasant uprisings and foreign intervention devastated the Russian heartland. At its height, between 1610 and 1620, the depopulation in many regions exceeded even the disastrous levels of the 1580s, and it was only the last decades of the seventeenth century that saw a return to the population levels of 1500.[25] In the territories around Novgorod, for example, the tax registers for

---

21. Ibid., pp. 106–7.
22. Goehrke, *Wüstungen*, pp. 170–2.
23. Shapiro, *Agrarnaia istoriia . . . xvi veka*, pp. 24–6.
24. Goehrke, *Wüstungen*, pp. 113–14.
25. V. D. Nazarov, 'Krest'ianstvo Rossii v xvi–seredine xvii v.', in Z. B. Udaltsova *et al.* (eds), *Istoriia krest'ianstva v Evrope. Epokha feodalizma*, 3 vols (Moscow, 1985–88), vol. II, p. 422.

1500 had placed the population at 396,000; according to the cadastre of 1582, however, it had sunk to 95,000, and then to 42,000 by 1620. Although the next sixty years saw a more or less steady recovery, the population in 1678—247,000 – still fell well short of the levels of 1500.[26]

So much for the standard picture, and indeed there is no denying that this was a period of deep crisis, one of the darkest in Russian history. At the same time, however, scholars have greatly exaggerated the demographic dimensions of the crisis. The main sources for it come from the land registers of the late sixteenth and early seventeenth centuries, which were compiled from periodic visitations by government clerks. Although the Muscovite government ordered their clerks to visit each village, this was obviously impossible, and the clerks often depended for their information largely on the 'sworn' testimony of *volost'* elders, whose interest it was to exaggerate the economic and demographic ruin as much as possible. Muscovite officials were also notorious for their corruption and venality, and bribery certainly played a role here, since paying off the clerk to understate the population was an excellent investment that paid off in lower tax assessments.[27]

The main problem is that cadastres and land registers have limited value, unless it is possible to corroborate them from other sources. There are other problems, as well. Thus, for example, migration from the heartland to the forest-steppe seems to have come *after*, and not during, the crisis years 1580—1620. How could the heartland, with its population supposedly reduced by a half or more, send large numbers of colonists south without further reducing its own population?

There is also evidence based on the internal market, where salt production and consumption played a major role in the economy of seventeenth-century Russia. Sources are fragmentary, but an important study by Paul Bushkovitch suggests that salt production, if it did not increase absolutely, certainly did not reflect a catastrophic fall in population. Indeed, judging from evidence for Vologda (the north) and Kaluga (the heartland), the market for salt may even have grown in these areas during the period 1580–1630, although it may have declined precipitously in north-west Russia.[28]

Again, this is not to deny the deep crisis that took place in these years, but simply to caution against exaggerating its demographic and economic dimensions. A crisis there certainly was, but it was a less a demographic collapse than a crisis of authority that reflected the limited capacity of the Muscovite state to tax its peasants. The tax unit in the Muscovite state was the *sokha*, which, depending on the quality of land, varied from 800 to 1,600 acres. Thus, unlike rents and dues, which used the 'typical' farmstead (*vyt'* or *obzha*) as the assessment unit, taxes used large and cumbersome units of land that offered little chance of exactitude. The tax reforms of Ivan the Terrible had compensated for this cumbersome system in two ways. First, they converted into cash all

26. A. L. Shapiro (ed.), *Agrarnaia istoriia severo-zapada Rossii xvii veka. Naselenie, zemlevladenie, zemlepol'zovanie* (St Petersburg, 1989), p. 11.
27. For a critique of the land registers, see ibid., pp. 12–19.
28. Paul Bushkovitch, *The Merchants of Moscow, 1580–1650* (Cambridge, 1980), pp. 127–50.

duties and taxes that the peasants owed to the state. Second, they placed responsibility for tax collection in the hands of *volost'* or other officials chosen from the local peasantry.

Initially, the results were impressive, and the amount of taxes that the peasants in the Novgorod region paid into the treasury apparently increased more than sixteen times![29] This growth in fiscal power was deceptive, however, for two reasons. First, it rested on the agricultural productivity of the heartland and the north, which was, as we have already seen, very limited.[30] Second, the growth in fiscal power rested on the cooperation of communal authorities, who were naturally more sensitive to the complaints of their fellow villagers than to the fiscal needs of the state. Initially, this may have functioned quite well, but the protracted war over Livonia changed this. Rising fiscal demands confronted a tax collection system that was almost totally in the hands of locally elected peasants who probably feared their own neighbours much more than they did the infrequent visits of state officials who were also corrupt and bribable. In short, the communal officials charged with tax assessment and collection probably stopped complying, and covered their passive resistance by exaggerating the population losses in their villages. The tax lists compiled in this period reflect these distortions, which have been perpetuated in the historical literature.

But distorted and exaggerated as it was, the crisis was still real, and the social and political collapse culminating in the Time of Troubles had a strong impact on the economic life of the rural population in the heartland. One of the most vivid results was the rapid growth of a landless or semi-landless population (*bobyli*) since the mid-sixteenth century. The *bobyli* were a legal and fiscal category of rural dwellers who did not occupy a farmstead, did not belong to the village commune, and paid only a nominal tax to the state. Some engaged in trade or rural crafts with considerable gain, but most seem to have been poor peasants who had given up their farmsteads and become farm-workers in order to avoid paying high taxes and rents.[31] A relatively small social stratum in 1550, the *bobyli* grew quickly as the crisis deepened. In the period 1580–1620, for example, the number of *bobyli* in the Novgorod region increased nearly sixfold, to more than a quarter of the total population.[32] In the centre, they were even more numerous, accounting for roughly 40 per cent of the rural population there.[33]

It is likely that many so-called *bobyli* continued to hold farmsteads, simply posing as landless workers in order to avoid taxes. The Thirty Years War had similar effects in seventeenth-century Bavaria, where many peasants became cottars and agricultural workers whose mobility enabled them to stay one step ahead of the census-takers.[34] We also see the growth of the landless and semi-landless population in Brandenburg during the Thirty Years War. There, as also

29. Nazarov, 'Krest'ianstvo', p. 433.
30. Ibid., p. 424.
31. Goehrke, *Wüstungen*, pp. 230–1.
32. Shapiro, *Agrarnaia istoriia . . . xvii veka*, p. 18.
33. Goehrke, *Wüstungen*, pp. 231–2.
34. Rudolf Schlögl, *Bauern, Krieg, und Staat. Oberbayrische Bauernwirtschaft und frühmoderner Staat im 17. Jahrhundert* (Göttingen, 1988), p. 241.

(apparently) in the Muscovite heartland, the rural population proved unable or unwilling to take on the responsibilities of a farmstead, and opted instead for the status of a cottager or, more often, a farm-worker. This was a logical reaction to war and political instability, since a farmstead becomes a liability in unsettled times, when a passing military unit could wipe out years of accumulated investment in land and livestock, leaving in its wake only more taxes and rents. At the same time, the population decline created a growing demand for farm-workers, who were able to negotiate favourable terms for their labour.[35]

This leads us to another point, namely that periods of crisis do not necessarily imply a decline in the market economy. As Wilhelm Abel has shown for late medieval Europe, such crises often create new economic opportunities for the rural population.[36] Thus, for example, the period 1580–1650 saw a rapid growth of Russian trade, internal as well as foreign. Grain production may have fallen, but stock-breeding expanded, based on the evidence from Archangel, in the north, then the major outlet for Russian exports to western Europe. In the crisis period, between 1580 and 1620, the ship traffic at Archangel (mostly Dutch) nearly tripled, with cattle products (tallow and leather) providing the most important Russian exports.[37]

The Evolution of Russian Serfdom

It is important to remember that Russian serfdom belongs in the larger context of agrarian developments throughout eastern Europe in the sixteenth and seventeenth centuries. These developments varied in degree from one region to another, but all lands east of the Elbe river and the Bohemian *massif* shared several common characteristics in the early modern period. First was the growth and consolidation of seigneurial control over the rural populations on their lands. Second was the use of this control to increase seigneurial revenues by setting up large, market-oriented demesnes for which the subject peasants had to supply most of the labour, whether their own or that of their hired hands.[38]

These agrarian developments, sometimes called the 'second serfdom', or 'neo-serfdom', first began in Poland in the late fifteenth century, emerging later in Livonia, east-Elbian Germany and Russia. For over a century, scholars have advanced various explanations to account for this phenomenon, although the reasons are still unclear.[39] The discussion here does not pretend to answer the 'whys' of this problem, focusing instead on the two most prominent components

35. Edgar Melton, 'The decline of Prussian *Gutsherrschaft* and the rise of the Junker as rural patron, 1750–1806', *German History*, 12: 3 (1994), p. 340.

36. Wilhelm Abel, *Strukturen und Krisen der spätmittelalterlichen Wirtschaft* (Quellen und Forschungen zur Agrargeschichte, xxxii) (Stuttgart, 1980), pp. 130–2.

37. Bushkovitch, *Merchants of Moscow*, pp. 44–9.

38. For a discussion of this process in Poland, east Germany and Livonia, Edgar Melton, '*Gutsherrschaft*, in East Elbian Germany and Livonia, 1500–1800: a critique of the model', *Central European History*, 21 (1988), pp. 315–49.

39. The most detailed and extensive discussion of these theories and the best general bibliography is the recent study by Heinrich Kaak, *Die Gutsherrschaft* (Berlin, 1991).

of serfdom – seigneurial control, on the one hand, and market-oriented demesne farming, on the other.

The evolution of seigneurial control in the sixteenth and early seventeenth centuries suffers from a lack of concrete evidence other than the legislation aimed at restricting and (later) prohibiting peasant movement. For Russia, we see the first general restrictions in the Law Code of 1497, which permitted peasants to move *only* during a two-week period after the harvest around St George's Day (in the autumn: 26 November), and *only* upon paying a moderate fine to their lord.[40] Subsequent legal changes did not come for nearly a century, when in 1580 Ivan IV, obviously reacting to widespread peasant flight, temporarily forbade peasants to move. Many such 'forbidden years' followed, including every year after 1603, until the Law Code of 1649 bound the peasant and his family to the land of the lord, who had the right to force their return if they ran away from his estate. It also gave the lord jurisdiction over his peasants in all cases except theft, robbery and homicide, which were the preserve of the state.[41] Henceforth, the seigneur's peasants were part of his household, and therefore subject to his will.[42]

The Law Code of 1649 was a major turning-point in relations between the noble and his peasants. Up to this point, the law had defined the peasants' legal status according to the size and type of farmsteads they occupied. The Law Code of 1649 changed this by binding not only the head of household, but all his family and farmhands, to the lord and his heirs, thus eliminating much of the legal distinction between peasant and slave, and between peasant and cottar (*bobyl'*). The Law Code did not completely merge slaves with peasants, a transformation that required additional legislation in the late seventeenth and first half of the eighteenth century. In 1680 those slaves living in their own households had to pay the same taxes as peasants, and when in 1719 the state subjected all peasant, cottar and slave males to the poll tax (*podushnaia podat'*), it more or less completed the legal merging of the three categories. In 1724 additional legislation further increased the servile status of all who stood under seigneurial control by requiring seigneurial permission for them to leave the estate. Another law introduced in 1731 prohibited seigneurial peasants from signing legal contracts without their lord's permission.[43]

The reality, of course, was often quite different, and legal restrictions imposed on peasant movement initially proved only partially successful. In Russia, as everywhere in east central Europe during the late sixteenth and early seventeenth centuries, peasant flight was a mass phenomenon that no state or local

40. Some historians, such as Jerome Blum, have assumed that the tax was so heavy as to be prohibitive, but, as A. L. Shapiro has recently pointed out, the amount was well within the reach of a typical peasant household. Blum, *Lord and Peasant*, p. 249. Shapiro, *Russkoe krest'ianstvo*, p. 210.

41. Richard Hellie (ed. and trans.), *The Muscovite Law Code (Ulozhenie) of 1649*, 2 vols (Irvine, CA, 1988–89), vol. I, arts 1–2.

42. C. Zajtzeff, 'Das Rechtsbewusstsein der russischen leibeigenen Bauern', *Jahrbücher für Kultur und Geschichte der Slaven*, 10 (1934), pp. 424–5.

43. V. A. Aleksandrov, 'Rossiiskoe krest'ianstvo v seredine xvii–seredine xix v.', in Udal'tsova *et al.*, *Istoriia krest'ianstva v Evrope*, vol. III, pp. 316–22.

ruling class could effectively control.[44] Also, legal restrictions on peasant movement could only be effective if landowners cooperated in enforcing them. This often proved impossible, however, since there was a severe shortage of rural labour, which made more for competition than for cooperation within the ruling elite. Thus, in the seventeenth and eighteenth centuries, the great landlords became notorious for luring peasants away from smaller estates.[45] To further complicate the picture, the state also competed with its own elite for scarce manpower, and laws suspending the peasants' right to leave their landlords could have little effect if, as periodically happened, the government hindered the return of fugitive peasants who had entered military service on the southern frontier.[46]

Despite these qualifications, the Law Code of 1649 initiated a more rigorous enforcement of restrictions on peasant movement, and led to the forcible return of thousands of fugitive peasants during the next two decades.[47] One group of runaways, apprehended in 1652, had lived first by hiring themselves out as farm-labourers, then as stable hands for a dragoon regiment, later as tenants on a monastery estate, and had not been caught until after they had entered frontier military service.[48]

Enforcement of the restrictions, however, was erratic, and despite the law, which bound the peasants to their lords 'forever', the government, in practice, was still more interested in securing its southern frontier than it was in recovering fugitive peasants.[49] Service on the southern steppe-forest frontier thus continued to absorb, at least temporarily, most of the fugitive population. Indeed, despite the flood of settlers, the census data show a decline of the peasant population in many frontier regions. The rural population did not actually decline: they simply exchanged the formal status of taxable peasants for that of petty military servitors (*sluzhilye liudi po priboru*).[50]

If restrictions on peasant movement were slow to take effect, demesne farming, the other component of Russian serfdom, also developed quite slowly, and though it had long existed in the Russian heartland (especially on monastery lands), it did not reach levels comparable to Poland and east-Elbian Germany until the second half of the eighteenth century. As we have already seen, labour services on the lands of the Tsarevo-Konstantinov monastery (central Russia) required peasants to work one acre of demesne arable for every five of

44. See, for example, the fine article by William W. Hagen, 'Seventeenth-century crisis in Brandenburg: the Thirty Years War, the destabilization of serfdom, and the rise of absolutism', *American Historical Review*, 94 (April 1989), p. 317.

45. A. I. Petrikeev, *Krupnoe krepostnoe khoziaistvo xvii* (St Petersburg, 1967), pp. 172–3.

46. A. A. Novosel'skii, 'Rasprostranenie krepostnicheskogo zemlevladeniia v iuzhnykh uezdakh Moskovskogo gosudarstva v xvii v.', *Istoricheskie zapiski*, 4 (1938), p. 29.

47. A. G. Mankov, *Razvitie krepostnogo prava v Rossii vo vtoroi polovine xvii v.* (Moscow, 1962), pp. 126–7.

48. A. A. Novosel'skii, 'Vol'nye i perekhozhie liudi iuzhnykh uezdov', in V. K. Tatsunskii (ed.), *Materialy po istorii sel'skogo khoziaistva i krest'ianstva SSSR* (Moscow, 1962), pp. 64–5.

49. Jack Culpepper, *The Legislative Origins of Peasant Bondage in Muscovy* (Forschungen zur osteuropäischen Geschichte, xiii), (Berlin, 1969), p. 209.

50. I. N. Miklashevskii, *K istorii khoziaistvennogo byta Moskovskogo gosudarstva*, 3 vols (Moscow, 1895), vol. 1, *Zaselenie i sel'skoe khoziaistvo iuzhnoi Ukrainy xvii v.*, p. 201.

their own, which translates into labour services of roughly one day per week. This was light compared to Poland, where peasants on lands belonging to the archbishop of Krakow already owed three to five days per week by the mid-fifteenth century.[51]

Unlike Poland, moreover, demesne farming did not expand rapidly in the sixteenth century. The problem may have been simply the lack of major grain markets. Even the Joseph-Volokolamsk monastery, which lay in the Moscow region, and had relatively strong ties to the urban grain market in Moscow, marketed less than a fifth of its total grain production.[52] Here again, the comparison with Poland is useful. A typical estate in mid-sixteenth-century Poland marketed between 50 and 70 per cent of its grain production.[53] Whatever their reasons, Russian estate-owners in the late sixteenth and early seventeenth centuries were generally slow to develop their agriculture beyond the level of manorial self-sufficiency, and few undertook an aggressive transition to market-oriented demesne farming. As we shall see, the large-scale shift to market-oriented demesnes did not take place until the second half of the eighteenth century.

Belorussia

War and depopulation, the driving forces behind the agrarian crises of east central Europe, generally spared Belorussia during this period, although they returned with a special vengeance in the second half of the seventeenth century. The mid-sixteenth century not only witnessed the complete integration of the kingdoms of Poland and Lithuania into one Commonwealth, but also saw the culmination of another process – one in which the Lithuanian nobility and the Catholic prelates had gained control of 70 per cent of all the land in Lithuania and Belorussia. For the Belorussian peasants, who numbered roughly two and a half million, this had meant a steady increase of seigneurial domination, especially by the great Lithuanian magnates. These last, numbering only twenty families (Radziwiłł, Sapieha, etc.), controlled a quarter of all the peasant households in Belorussia.[54] Thanks, moreover, to the Lithuanian Statutes of 1566 and 1588, seigneurs in Lithuania and Belorussia enjoyed unchallenged authority (in theory at least) over peasants who had lived on their lands for more than ten years.[55] It is still not entirely clear, however, what this meant in reality. Studies of the Belorussian peasantry are relatively few, and most have relied heavily on a theoretical model inferred from (supposed) Polish agrarian developments. This model emphasizes the role of Baltic grain exports in creating

---

51. Melton, '*Gutsherrschaft*', p. 321.

52. Wolfgang Kuttler, 'Zum Verhältnis von Spätfeudalismus und Genesis des Kapitalismus. Wesen und Auswirkungen der Gutsherrschaft und Leibeigenschaft in Livland und Rußland im 16. Jahrhundert', in Peter Hoffmann and Heinz Lemke (eds), *Genesis und Entwicklung des Kapitalismus in Rußland*, (Berlin, 1973), p. 80.

53. A. Wyczański, 'L'économie du domaine nobiliare moyen 1500–1580', *Annales: Économies, Sociétés, Civilisations*, 18 (1963), pp. 84–5.

54. Buganov, *et al.*, *Istoriia krest'ianstva*, vol. III, p. 588.

55. Ibid, vol. II, pp. 293–4.

economic incentives for the nobility to subject their peasants to compulsory labour services on their market-oriented demesnes in the sixteenth century.[56]

One problem is that the model relies far too much on the role of Baltic grain exports as an explanatory factor. Even in the Polish heartland, grain exports in the sixteenth century accounted for less than 3 per cent of the total grain harvest, while the role of the internal market was apparently much greater, accounting for at least 10 per cent.[57] In Belorussia, estate-owners participated even less in the Baltic grain trade, even though Belorussia lay astride three river networks (the Bug, Nieman and Western Dvina) connecting her to the Baltic. Although north-eastern Belorussia served as Riga's primary commercial hinterland, it did not play a role in grain exports. In fact, Riga's grain exports, not unimportant in the sixteenth century, were already in decline by 1580, and accounted for only 10 per cent of the value of her exports in the seventeenth century. Even then, the grain came from Livonia, and not from Belorussia.[58]

The most important of Riga's exports – and the primary exports produced in Belorussia – were hemp and hempseed, which together accounted for nearly half the value of Riga's export trade in the seventeenth century. This is significant, since hemp belonged not to the seigneurial (demesne) economy, but rather to the productive sphere of the peasant farmstead.[59] This does much to explain the apparently favourable position of the Belorussian peasants, especially in the eastern parts, during this period. A sampling of nearly 4,000 Belorussian farmsteads on seigneurial estates in the late sixteenth century shows that more than a third paid only cash rents and performed no labour services, while many others commuted at least part of their seigneurial dues into cash payments.[60] This was also true of the immense Crown estates in Belorussia and Lithuania (over a thousand villages), where many (probably most) peasants were able to commute their labour services to cash quitrents.[61] In the eastern parts of Belorussia, which produced much of the hemp exported through Riga, most estate-owners had commuted labour services to cash rents, but required their peasants to sell them their hemp at lower prices. The estate-owners than resold it to merchants, or shipped it to Riga on their own accounts.[62]

Some other regions also escaped the demesne system, with its compulsory labour services. Samogitia (north-western Lithuania) lay in the Nieman basin, less than a hundred miles from the Baltic port of Klaipeda, but neither

56. Witold Kula, *An Economic Theory of the Feudal System: Towards a Model of the Polish Economy 1500–1800* (London, 1976).

57. Robert I. Frost, 'The nobility of Poland-Lithuania, 1569–1795', in H. M. Scott (ed.), *The European Nobilities in the Seventeenth and Eighteenth Centuries*, 2 vols (London, 1995), vol. II: *Northern, Central, and Eastern Europe*, p. 200.

58. V. V. Doroshenko, *Torgovlia i kupechestvo Rigi v xvii veke* (Riga, 1985), p. 142. This superb study of Riga's trade and merchants encompasses far more than the title suggests.

59. Ibid., p. 126.

60. B. Z. Kopysskii, 'Khoziaistvo Belorusskogo krest'ianina v kontse xvi-pervoi polovine xvii veka', *Istoriia SSSR*, 2 (1984), p. 151.

61. D. L. Pokhilevich, 'Kapitalisticheskie zigzagi v istorii feodal'nogo pomest'ia', in V. K. Iatsunskii (ed.), *Voprosy istorii sel'skogo khoziaistva krest'ianstva i revoliutsionnogo dvizheniia v Rossii* (Moscow, 1961), p. 47.

62. M. B. Topolska, 'Peculiarities of the economic structure of eastern White Russia in 16th–18th c.', *Studia Historiae Oeconomicae*, 6 (1969).

serfdom nor the demesne system were significant there. Flax cultivation provided the basis of the peasant economy there; its marketing was in the hands of the larger peasant proprietors, who paid quitrent to their seigneurs, and often employed numerous farmhands.[63]

Another factor in the peasants' relatively favourable conditions in this period was the scarcity of labour. Belorussia, like all the borderlands between Poland-Lithuania and Muscovy, was sparsely populated, which placed peasant labour at a premium. In addition, the competition for labour provided numerous opportunities for peasants who wanted to flee their landlords. So scarce was labour, in fact, that local authorities were reluctant to carry out death penalties imposed on peasants for serious crimes, often commuting them to hereditary serfdom. This happened in 1596, for example, when a free peasant was sentenced to death for helping three serfs escape from one estate-owner and settle on another's estate. Instead of putting the convicted man to death, the court made him a serf of the estate-owner whose serfs he had helped escape.[64]

The situation was not uniform, however, and if the demesne economy based on labour services was largely absent in north-eastern Belorussia, it dominated the countryside in south-west Belorussia, around Brest, Grodno and Pinsk. Moreover, in the period 1533–65, a series of agrarian 'reforms' helped pave the way for the spread of demesne farming. Bona Sforza, the Italian wife of Sigismund I of Poland, had initiated these reforms on her own lands in Lithuania and Belorussia in 1533, and Sigismund's successor, Sigismund Augustus (r.1548–72), extended them on all Crown lands in the period 1557–64. Many of the Lithuanian magnates then followed suit on their own estates.

The reforms introduced a new farmstead unit that was to function as the assessment basis for taxes and seigneurial rents and dues. Modelled on the *Hufe*, this farmstead unit, the *wloka*, was fifty-four acres, and became the basic farmstead in Lithuania and Belorussia. The reform also attempted, with some success, to rationalize the physical layout of estate villages, and to consolidate all demesne lands belonging to a given estate. The reform also established peasant obligations in accordance with the size of their farmstead. Thus, a peasant holding an entire *wloka* on good land belonging to a Crown estate owed the monetary equivalent of 106 Polish *groschen*, most of which the Crown peasants paid in cash. A peasant holding a *wloka* of good land on a seigneurial estate had to cultivate 7.5 acres of seigneurial demesne (two days of labour services per week), plus owing rents in cash that varied according to the landowner.[65]

In the second half of the sixteenth century, full farmsteads in Belorussia had livestock inventories reflect the relatively large scale of peasant farming. Nearly half (46 per cent) of the full farmsteads had two or more work teams.[66] Peasant

63. Buganov, *et al.*, *Istoriia krest'ianstva*, vol. II, pp. 292–3.

64. M. A. Iuchas, 'O dobrovol'nom perekhode vol'nykh liudei v krepostnye v Litve xvi–xviii vv.', *Ezhegodnik po agrarnoi istorii vostochnoi Evropy 1968* (St Petersburg, 1972), p. 108.

65. Buganov *et al.*, *Istoriia krest'ianstva*, vol. II, pp. 296–303.

66. D. L. Pokhilevich, 'Biudzhet krest'ian Belorussii i Litvy v xvi v.', *Istoriia SSSR*, 1 (1972), p. 148.

households in Belorussia were also large; those occupying a full farmstead had an average of ten to twelve members, six of them working-age adults.[67] This does not mean that they were all family members, or that large, multiple-generation families were typical in Belorussia. Indeed, the estate inventories do not distinguish between family members and live-in hired hands, and it is likely that the latter account for the large households. This was typical for large farmsteads throughout much of east central Europe.[68] In Little Poland at the end of the sixteenth century, 50 per cent of the peasant farms employed hired labour.[69]

In any case, the occupants of a full farmstead in Belorussia certainly needed plenty of workers, since working the farmstead required 1,583 workdays (one person working one day), of which the female adults provided roughly half. In addition, there were usually labour services owed the seigneur. In Lithuania and Belorussia, the peasant could apparently commute these labour services by paying a quitrent, but if he performed the labour services, they required 134 workdays per year, bringing the total to 1,717 workdays.[70] This was not, of course, a heavy labour service burden, since it claimed only 8 per cent of the total workdays, but if we assume that most of this work, say 1,200 workdays, had to be performed by adults *during the growing season* (roughly 200 days in Belorussia), a household with six adult workers (hired and/or family members) would have just barely sufficed.

In the mid-sixteenth century, administrators on Polish-Lithuanian Crown domains assumed an average yield of 5:1 for the major cereals (rye, oats and barley). Given such yields, a full peasant household would have earned enough to pay its expenses as well as commute its labour services to quitrent.[71] This does not take into consideration peasant earnings from hemp, which make the picture more favourable, although it may have also added to the labour inputs.[72]

This estimate may, however, be misleading for several reasons. First, as already noted, it is not clear that peasant farmsteads in sixteenth-century Belorussia had to furnish labour services. In his classic study Werner Conze argued that labour services did not come until the seventeenth century. Second, full peasant farmsteads were the exception. Conze, for example, found that the actual farmsteads were usually much smaller than a *włoka*, with most of them varying from 20 to 35 acres.[73] Many peasants may have refused to accept such large farmsteads because the seigneurial obligations attached to them had

67. Ibid., p. 151.
68. Melton, '*Gutsherrschaft*', pp. 328–49.
69. Frost, 'Nobility of Poland-Lithuania', p. 201.
70. Pokhilevich, 'Biudzhet', p. 153.
71. Ibid., p. 148.
72. From the peasants' standpoint, hemp had the advantage of being a pure cash crop that they could cultivate in small garden plots, one that brought a cash return six times higher than grain. Moreover, though it was labour-intensive, requiring 158 workdays per year per acre (roughly five times the labour per acre of grain), nearly 70 per cent of the work could be done by women. Edgar Melton, 'Serfdom and the peasant economy in Russia, 1780–1861', unpublished doctoral thesis, Columbia University (University Microfilms, Ann Arbor, MI, 1985), pp. 151–3.
73. Werner Conze, *Agrarverfassung und Bevölkerung in Litauen und Weißrußland* (Leipzig, 1940), pp. 127–9.

become too high. This is what happened when Polish landowners tried to introduce the *włoka* reform in the Ukrainian lands east of the Dniepr (left-bank Ukraine).

Ukraine

The history of the Ukraine and its rural population is inextricably bound with that of the cossacks, whose frequent uprisings made the late sixteenth and seventeenth centuries a turbulent epoch. The fact that the only interlude of relative calm (1638–48) bore the name 'golden peace' suggests the violence of the other decades in this period. In the fifteenth century, most of the Ukraine was a sparsely populated, or even totally unsettled, steppe frontier contested by Poland, Lithuania and the Crimean Tatars. The only organized principalities there were centred in Kiev, on the Dniepr, and in north-western Ukraine (Galicia, Podolia and Volhynia). By the late fifteenth century, Galicia and Podolia belonged to Poland, Volhynia and Kiev to Lithuania, but these lands were regularly ravaged and occupied by Turkish and Tatar forces, and the population remained very sparse.

In the early sixteenth century, landowners in Western Podolia and Volhynia began attempts to impose a Polish-style serfdom on the peasants there, restricting their right to move, while demanding compulsory labour services on demesne lands. This provoked massive peasant flight to the south-east, into the vast, unsettled frontier lands between the Dniester and Dniepr basins. Other rural groups, fugitive peasants from Poland, Lithuania, Belorussia and Moldavia, also trickled into the region. Free 'cossack' communities emerged, who lived by exploiting the natural abundance of fish, furs, honey and cattle.

Landowners in Volhynia and Podolia naturally tried to secure the return of their runaways, but with little success, since the Polish government had embarked on a new policy aimed at securing their territories by encouraging military settlement of the frontier lands between the Dniester and middle Dniepr. To this end, Polish and Lithuanian aristocrats were placed in charge of vast territories in the region, and they, in turn, sent their agents to Volhynia and Podolia to recruit more settlers. At the same time, they raised military regiments from the cossack communities to provide personal retinues and border detachments for security against Tatar and Turkish raids.

Cossacks in military service enjoyed exemption from taxes and rents, but the others were treated as peasants, subject to labour services and rents on Crown or private lands. In the 1530s the Polish authorities in the Ukraine also mobilized the cossacks to build a network of fortified settlements (*sechi*) on the islands and tributaries of the lower Dniepr, and these settlements became the basis for the 'cossack republic' known as the *Zaporozhskaia Sech'*. The *Sech'* was a primitive hybrid, a combination of mercenary army and extended peasant commune. Although it embraced a relatively small part of the cossack population in the Ukraine, it became the core of subsequent cossack rebellions that mobilized substantial parts of the rural population.

These uprisings began in the 1590s and reached a high point with the famous rebellion led by Bogdan Kmel'nitskii (1648–52). The rebellions fed primarily on cossack grievances against Polish policies in the new provinces in the Ukraine. After the Union of Lublin in 1569, there was a new influx of Polish-Lithuanian magnates, sent to govern the new Ukrainian counties. These border magnates brought their own retinues of petty nobles, and by the late sixteenth century the Ukraine had become a Polish colony, swarming with rapacious freebooters from all classes. To make matters worse, the Polish Crown had frequently recruited cossack auxilliaries during times of war. These troops received immunity from taxes and seigneurial exactions, but once peace returned most of them were demobilized and found themselves treated as subject peasants. Many fled to the *Zaporozhskaia Sech'*, where they became the core of resistance to Polish authority.

Outside the *Sech'*, the cossack nobility, the so-called registered cossacks, who had the right to own landed estates, also found themselves subject to the pretensions and demands of the Polish magnates who governed there, especially during peacetime. Cossack nobles wanted to force out the Polish nobility in order to acquire more landed property and increase their authority over the cossack rank-and-file. To this end, they proved adept at mobilizing rank-and-file discontent against the Polish nobility. The Union of Brest (1596), which imposed Catholic doctrine and Papal supremacy on the Orthodox populations of the Commonwealth, may have created another powerful grievance among the cossacks.

Despite this discontent, Polish authorities were able to crush the cossack rebellions of 1590–91, 1595 and 1635–38. In 1648, however, the revolt led by Bogdan Khmel'nitskii, one of the most prominent members of the cossack nobility, proved different. Sparked by a feud between Khmel'nitskii and one of the border magnates, the rebellion of 1648 inaugurated a new period of violence and instability that lasted through much of the late seventeenth century, and purged much of the region of its Polish landowning class.[74]

PHASE 3: 1650–1750

The century discussed in this section is crucial in a number of ways. First, it marks the rise of Russia's imperial fortunes, beginning with acquisition of left-bank Ukraine and Siberia in the late seventeenth century, and continuing through the Northern Wars of the early eighteenth century. It also marks the consolidation of the 'peasant state', the effective harnessing of the rural population to the tasks of supplying money, labour and military manpower to the state and

---

74. On Ukrainian society see Carsten Kumke, *Führer und Geführte bei den Zaporogen. Struktur und Geschichte kosakischer Verbände im polnisch-litauischen Grenzland 1550–1648* (Berlin 1993); on the Khmel'nitskii rebellion see Dmitry Zlepko, *Der große Kosakenaufstand 1648 gegen die polnische Herrschaft* (Munich, 1980).

its elite.[75] A number of developments supported this consolidation. First, the peasant population (not counting Belorussia, Ukraine or the Baltic provinces) nearly doubled, from nine million in 1678 to sixteen million by 1762.[76] We must also take into account the growth of serfdom, settlement of the black-soil steppe, and, finally, the fiscal reforms of Peter the Great, including the introduction of a census (1719), the capitation tax, and conscription.

As we have already seen, the *Ulozhenie*, the Law Code of 1649, provided the legal basis for serfdom, and subsequent legislation in the late seventeenth and early eighteenth centuries rounded it out. We have also seen, however, that reality was more recalcitrant. Massive peasant flight proved difficult to control, and continued on a large scale throughout the serf period. The anarchic state of affairs during the Regency of Sophia (1682–89), and the grim preoccupation with national survival during the Northern Wars with Sweden (1700–21), may have distracted the government and its elite from taking effective measures (if such existed) against such flight. True, the Law Code of 1649 had done away with the previous statute of limitations on the return of fugitive peasants, but the actual apprehension and return of fugitives was still the private concern of the landlord, and thus an expensive and protracted affair.

Even the government's renewed attention to this problem in the 1720s, and draconian legislation aimed at curbing peasant flight, met with only partial success. According to decrees issued in 1721, communal officials who harboured runaway peasants faced flogging and galley servitude, while landlords caught with runaways risked heavy fines and confiscation of their estates. Enforcing such measures, however, often proved impossible simply because the government lacked the necessary manpower. In 1724, for example, there was only one regiment of dragoons guarding Russia's western borders, a force completely inadequate to restrain the armed masses of runaway peasants, who sometimes fought pitched battles with the dragoons. The situation there was so serious that the Ruling Senate even considered sending an entire army to the western borders just to halt the flood of runaways.[77]

Another problem was that peasant flight, despite landowners' constant complaints, had its positive side, at least from the government's standpoint. Most peasant flight was from districts in the heartland where conditions for agriculture were poor, and indeed the primary reason given by those who were later apprehended and questioned was not serfdom itself, but simply impoverishment.[78] Resettlement under better conditions often turned impoverished fugitives into taxpayers, while if forcibly returned, they would revert to their previous poverty and the government would forfeit their taxes. Moreover, even

75. On Russia as a 'peasant state', Edgar Melton, 'Household economies and communal conflicts on a Russian serf estate, 1800–1817', *Journal of Social History*, 26 (Winter, 1993), pp. 560–4.

76. Population figures taken from Ia. E. Vodarskii, *Naselenie Rossii v kontse xvii–nachale xviii veka* (Moscow, 1977), p. 192, table 44; and V. M. Kabuzan, *Izmeneniia v razmeshchenii naseleniia Rossii v xviii-pervoi polovine xix v.* (Moscow, 1971), p. 87.

77. E. V. Anisimov, *Podatnaia reforma Petra I. Vvedenie podushnoi podati v Rossii 1719–1728* (St Petersburg, 1982), pp. 116–34.

78. N. V. Kozlova, *Pobegi krest'ian v Rossii v pervoi treti xviii veka* (Moscow, 1983), pp. 58–9.

when the government tried to return runaways, the latter often managed to escape *en route*, vanishing into the forests.

The situation may have improved somewhat in the second quarter of the eighteenth century, after Peter's tax reform (1719) had imposed a poll tax on all male peasants. The government now had to curb peasant flight to protect its tax base. In 1745 it forced Polish authorities in right-bank Ukraine to return more than ten thousand peasants who had fled Russian territories.[79] Such successes, however, could not compensate for the large number of runaways, which totalled more than 327,000 in the period 1727–41.[80]

The constant recourse to flight – one of the most common forms of peasant resistence – probably helped keep down the growth of seigneurial dues and rents in this period. Demesne farming generally remained at a much lower level of development than in Poland or Brandenburg-Prussia and even seems to have declined on Church estates in the heartland. One reason for this may have been the lack of additional land, a circumstance aggravated by the *Ulozhenie* of 1649, which deprived Church landlords of the right to acquire new lands.[81] Thus, while most Church peasants continued to perform some labour services, these obligations declined, while cash rents became increasingly important. In the middle and late seventeenth century, peasant communities on Church estates began to supplement their allotments by collectively renting additional land from their ecclesiastical landlords.[82] The peasants needed the land, and instead of accepting more allotment land (which would have increased their labour services), they found it more advantageous to rent it for cash. The monasteries also gained, since, with short-term leases of one to five years, they were able to retain long-term control of the land.[83]

Demesne farming *did* enjoy a vigorous expansion on Church lands in some regions of the north, such as the district of Vologda. There, on estates belonging to the archbishop of Vologda, demesne arable more than doubled, growing from 1,100 to nearly 2,400 acres between 1670 and 1715.[84] A very similar pattern prevailed on the neighbouring estates of Spaso-Prilutsk monastery, and in both cases expansion of demesne meant heavier labour services per peasant household. In the 1670s the peasant household there had to work an average of 3.5 acres of demesne arable, but by 1715 the burden had grown to 9.5 acres.[85] The typical peasant farmstead there had twelve acres of arable, which means that labour services on the demesne may have claimed nearly half of the household's labour, at least during the agricultural season, when labour services probably exceeded three days per week. Again, however, Church lands in Vologda offer

---

79. Buganov *et al.*, *Istoriia krest'ianstva*, vol. III, p. 580.

80. Kozlova, *Pobegi krest'ian*, p. 145.

81. Aleksandrov, 'Rossiiskoe krest'ianstvo', p. 322.

82. N. A. Gorskaia, *Monastyrskie krest'iane tsentral'noi Rossii v xvii veke* (Moscow, 1977), pp. 120–206, 318–25.

83. L. N. Vdovina, *Krest'ianskaia obshchina i monastyr' v Tsentral'noi Rossii v pervoi polovine xvii v.* (Moscow, 1988), p. 142.

84. E. N. Baklanova, *Krest'ianskii dvor i obshchina na Russkom Severe* (Moscow, 1976), p. 95.

85. Ibid., pp. 98–9.

one of the exceptional cases where demesne farming in late seventeenth- and early eighteenth-century Russia reached a level similar to Poland and east-Elbian Germany.

On lay estates in the heartland, demesne farming became much more wide-spread, as is clear from the massive study by the Soviet historian Iu. Tikhonov, who focused on central Russia in two consecutive periods: 1649–79 and 1680–1725. Throughout both these periods, demesne farming was widespread, and in the period 1680–1725 it existed on 90 per cent of all the estates in Tikhonov's sample, most of which had shifted completely to demesne farming and had no other kinds of rent.[86]

While labour services became much more widespread, they still remained comparatively light, however. Thus, on the vast majority of estates that Tikhonov studied, each male peasant worked an average of only one acre of demesne arable during the period 1650–79; the following period, 1680–1725, actually saw a decline, to only four-fifths of an acre![87] Very few seigneurial estates in the heartland relied solely on cash quitrents, but on those that did, the value of the quitrents (expressed in the currency in 1700) declined even more, from ninety-one *kopecks* per male peasant (1650–79) to forty-seven (1680–1725).[88]

Settlement of the Steppe-Forest Zone

One of the most important – and most neglected – developments in this period was the settlement of the black-soil steppe-forest lands. Although it began in the sixteenth century, settlement did not become significant until the 1630s, with the return of stability after the Time of Troubles. Tatar raiding expeditions, seeking captives to ransom or sell into slavery, had long posed a major obstacle to expansion into these fertile lands, and so, in the period 1636–53, the Muscovite government constructed an ambitious system of garrisons, outposts and watchtowers to defend colonists on the frontier. Construction and manning of this system, the most important part of which was the western stretch known as the Belgorod Line, created heavy demands for manpower that encouraged the social as well as geographical mobility of runaway peas-ants. Many who fled the heartland ended up enlisting in military service on the Belgorod Line, receiving small land-grants in exchange. Noble landowners in central Russia complained of this, submitting petitions to the government claim-ing that they had runaway peasants in service on the steppe frontier, but it was not in the interest of the military commanders there to cooperate.[89]

86. Iu. Tikhonov, *Pomeshchich'i krest'iane v Rossii. Feodal'naia renta v xvii–nachale xviii v.* (Moscow, 1974), pp. 291–6.

87. Ibid., p. 294, table 58.

88. Ibid., p. 298, table 60.

89. A. A. Novosel'skii, 'Kollektivnye dvorianskie chelobitnye o syske beglykh krest'ian i kholopov vo vtoroi polovine xvii v.', in N. I. Pavlenko (ed.), *Dvorianstvo i krepostnoi stroi Rossii xvi–xviii vv.*, (Moscow, 1975), pp. 303–43.

Not only Russian peasants settled on the Belgorod Line. In the 1630s many Ukrainians fled the cossack rebellion and ensuing Polish reprisals, moving into the nearby Russian steppe frontier, where they enlisted in military service on the Belgorod Line. This relative trickle of Ukrainian settlers became a flood after the Kmel'nitskii uprising in 1648, as thousands of Ukrainian peasants and cossacks poured into Muscovite territory to escape the bloodletting.[90] Establishment of the semi-autonomous Hetmanate, under Muscovite protection, in the Ukrainian territories east of the Dniepr (1654), did not halt Ukrainian settlement on the Belgorod Line. Turkish and Tatar invasions of the Ukrainian lands west of the Dniepr (right-bank Ukraine) in the 1660s also fed the stream of Ukrainian settlers pouring into Muscovite territory. Eager to encourage this, the government offered Ukrainian settlers their 'traditional' privileges: exemption from all taxes, freedom from customs duties, and the right to distill and sell liquor.

By the 1680s, a more sedentary agricultural society was beginning to replace the wild frontier lands of the steppe-forest. The peasant population alone numbered well over half a million people, and by 1720 the number would be twice that. Initially, the peasants who settled there described themselves as 'free wandering people', and insisted on maintaining that status. If they settled on monastery or seigneurial lands, it was often on contractual terms that bound them to work only for a specific period of time, after which they remained free to move.[91]

In addition to the peasants, however, there were also another 130,000 males in frontier service, most of them recruited from the peasantry. These had settled in fortified villages where they held collective land-grants in exchange for frontier service.[92] Indeed, the Muscovite government had made collective land-grants precisely because they had the advantage of concentrating the recipients in defensible settlements.[93] The recipients received equal or unequal shares of land, depending on their rank or status. To a greater or lesser degree, most enjoyed the status of petty nobles, and were initially exempt from taxation. Some actually held peasants, and a few managed to establish a foothold in the hereditary estate-owning nobility. Most, however, had land-grants that were little more than large farmsteads ranging from forty to 125 acres, and thus became known as *odnodvortsy*, meaning 'single farmsteaders', and their military settlements functioned as village communes.[94]

Many Ukrainian and cossack settlers lived in military settlements on a very similar basis, and indeed petty nobilities such as these were not at all unusual in the borderlands of eastern Europe. Two such groups existed in the Habsburg

90. D. M. Bagalei, *Ocherki iz istorii kolonizatsii i byta stepnoi okrainy moskovskogo gosudarstva* (Moscow, 1887), pp. 387–91; also, A. N. Aranovich, 'Pereselenie Ukraintsev v Rossii nakanune osvoboditel'noi voiny 1648–1654', *Vossoedinenie Ukrainy s Rossii* (Moscow, 1954), pp. 81–7.

91. A. A. Novosel'skii, 'Vol'nye i perekhozhie liudi iuznykh uezdov', in Iatsunskii, *Materialy po istorii sel'skogo khoziaistva i krest'ianstva SSSR*, pp. 64–5.

92. Vodarskii, *Naselenie Rossii*, pp. 105–6, 225–7.

93. V. M. Vazhinskii, *Zemlevladenie i skladyvanie obshcheny odnodvortsev v xvii v.* (Moscow, 1977), pp. 60–1.

94. N. A. Blagoveshchinskii, *Chetvertnoe pravo* (Moscow, 1890), p. 500 and passim.

lands: the *hajdú* (*haiduks*), who performed military service in north-eastern Hungary along the Turkish frontier, and the *Székely*, who had a similar function in eastern Transylvania.[95]

Initially, the black-soil steppe was more military than agricultural, and was actually dependent on grain imports from the heartland until the late seventeenth century. After 1680, however, the influx of noble estate-owners began to transform it into the granary of eighteenth-century Russia. Ever mindful of the chronic turmoil between cossacks and Polish nobles in the Ukraine, the Muscovite government had tried initially to keep its powerful nobility from setting up large estates in the frontier districts. But the death of Tsar Fyodor, in 1682, unleashed a savage round of factional strife within the Muscovite aristocracy, and first Sophia (regent 1682–89), and then her opponent and half-brother Peter the Great, had to woo allies among the aristocratic families at court. Thus, during Sophia's regency the government quietly permitted Muscovite landowners to establish latifundia in the black-soil steppe. Peter was more generous, and handed out immense land-grants there to favourites such as Count Golovkin and Prince Menshikov. When the latter fell into disgrace and had his estates confiscated in 1727, his lands in the steppe region had a total population of nearly 60,000, including both Russian serfs and free Ukrainian settlers.[96]

This influx of latifundists from the heartland transformed the structure of the black-soil steppe-forest. Eager to populate their new estates with a labour force, they offered temporary immunity from rents, often for as long as five to six years. Such concessions, plus the promise of a large farmstead with fertile land, attracted Russian and Ukrainian peasants, as well as urban craftsmen, who set up shop in the larger estate villages.[97] In 1700 there were already nearly 500 large estates (those having at least fifty serf households) in the black-soil region; by 1737 the number of large estates had more than doubled, numbering more than a thousand.[98]

This did not initially bring demesne farming. None of the peasants, for example, on Count Golovkin's vast steppe estates were performing labour services in the 1740s.[99] Demesne farming was also absent on Menshikov's steppe estates, as well as on those belonging to Count Sheremetev, the wealthiest landowner in Russia.[100] At the same time, however, the influx of great and middle landowners hastened the transformation of the black-soil steppe into a sedentary agricultural economy. This was one of the most important developments in

95. Peter Schimert, 'The Hungarian nobility in the seventeenth and eighteenth centuries', in Scott, *The European Nobilities*, vol. II, pp. 161–4.
96. S. M. Troitskii, 'Raionirovanie form feodal'noi renty v Rossii v pervoi chetverti xviii v.', *Ezhegodnik po agrarnoi istorii vostochnoi Evropy 1968*, pp. 116–19.
97. L. I. Petrova, 'Nadelennost' zemlei i skotom krest'ian kurskoi votchiny v xviii–xix vv.', *Ezhegodnik po agrarnoi istorii vostochnoi Evropy 1964* (Minsk, 1966), p. 383.
98. Vodarskii, *Naselenie Rossii*, p. 169.
99. P. K. Alefirenko, 'Krest'ianskoe khoziaistvo grafa M. G. Golovkina', in N. M. Druzhinin (ed.), *Materialy po istorii sel'skogo khoziaistva i krest'ianstva*, vol. v (Moscow, 1961), p. 137.
100. K. Shchepetov, *Krepostnoe pravo v votchinakh Sheremetevykh* (Moscow, 1947), pp. 285–7.

Russian history, because it provided Russia with a new fund of arable land with a fertility that made its cultivation twice as productive as in the heartland.[101]

While the full implications of this would not become clear until the second half of the eighteenth century, other developments, tied to the reforms of Peter the Great, would have a more immediate impact on the peasant population. Two components of the Petrine reforms are especially important here: the imposition of the poll tax, and the introduction of military conscription. As we have already seen, the *sokha*, the basic assessment unit for taxing the rural population in the sixteenth century, was very cumbersome, not least because it was based not on units of production (the household or the individual), but on large aggregate units of arable land. This changed in the second half of the seventeenth century, and in 1679 the peasant household became the basic unit for all direct taxes, with the cadastre of 1678 providing most of the necessary information. This, however, created another problem. As long as the household was the basis of taxation (as well as rents), peasants could evade or lessen their obligations by leaving their own lands and taking employment as farm-labourers in the households of more prosperous peasants. This lessened the number of tax units, while also making it difficult for estate-owners to maintain their labour supply. Peasants who chafed under seigneurial exactions and state taxes could lessen them by doubling up in one household.[102]

The problem reached a crisis point during the reign of Peter the Great. In 1708, at the height of the Northern War with Sweden, Peter ordered a new cadastre, hoping that it would lead to new tax revenues. Instead, it showed that the number of peasant households had declined by a fifth since 1678. Peter and his advisors therefore decided to undertake a census, as the first step toward imposing a capitation tax on all male souls. The first census, taken in the period 1719–23, evoked considerable resistance on the part of the rural population, but census-taking became increasingly effective, and had profound implications for the rural population. By imposing the same poll tax on virtually all non-noble males, the state equalized the fiscal status of numerous groups of the rural population, and facilitated their gradual amalgamation into two major groups, seigneurial peasants (serfs) and state peasants. It also provided an effective means for drawing the rural population more securely into the web of state obligations; armed with its census data, the state could easily determine how much tax a village owed simply by multiplying the males listed in the village by the head tax (initially seventy-four *kopecks* per male). Estate-owners soon followed suit, using census data as the basis for calculating the quitrents and labour services their peasants owed. The census also provided the state with an effective basis for conscription, which became a constant – and dreaded – feature of

---

101. The most reliable crop yields in the heartland for the early eighteenth century, the records of the Donsk monastery, show average yields of 3:1, while the most reliable study of the black-soil region shows yields of 6:1. A. E. Chekunova, 'Urozhainost' zernovykh kul'tur v monastyrskom khoziaistve pervoi chetverti xviii v.', *Problemy agrarnoi istorii*, 2 vols (Minsk, 1978), vol. I, pp. 36–45. For the black-soil steppe, Steven Hoch, *Serfdom and Social Control in Russia: Petrovskoe, a Village in Tambov* (Chicago, 1986), p. 29.

102. A. L. Shapiro, 'Perekhod ot povytnoi k povenechnoi sisteme oblozheniia krest'ian vladel'cheskimi povinnostiami', *Ezhegodnik po agrarnoi istorii vostochnoi Evropy 1960* (Kiev, 1962), pp. 207–17.

village life. In the period 1724–1825, there were ninety conscription levies, which may have taken as much as 8 per cent of the male population.[103]

Perhaps the most important result of the census and tax reform, however, was to strengthen immensely the role of the commune in Russian society. While both state and seigneurial authorities used the census to determine the aggregate taxes and rents and obligations owed by each commune, they also made each commune collectively responsible for them. In effect, they left it to the communal authorities to decide *how* these obligations would be distributed within the community. In practice, this often made the commune an 'encapsulated political unit', in which peasants competed for favourable treatment from the communal authorities. We will deal with this later in a section devoted specifically to the peasant commune.

Belorussia and the Ukraine

For the peasants in Belorussia, the crucial events in this period were the Northern Wars (1655–60 and 1700–21), which severely damaged the rural population and its agriculture. A population decline had already begun in 1648, as the peasant war sparked by Kmel'nitskii in the Ukraine had caught fire in Belorussia as well. Thousands of Belorussian peasants had risen against Polish rule, and the grisly aftermath – hundreds of peasants quartered or impaled on pikes stuck along country roads – had led to the mass flight of terrorized survivors. Famine and pestilence followed in 1650, and the Muscovite and Swedish armies that invaded Belorussia in the mid-1650s found a rural population that was already dangerously depleted.[104] By 1670, more than half the farmsteads in Belorussia were deserted, and after only partial recovery, half the farmsteads were once again empty by 1720, and were not fully reoccupied until the 1770s.[105] During these wars, large-scale requisition of cattle and grain had destroyed many peasants' productive capacity and they were unable to maintain their farmsteads. Some fled to the Ukraine, while many others became landless agricultural labourers or sharecroppers on seigneurial estates.

Faced with the diminished productive capacity of their peasants, most landlords had no choice but to commute their peasants' labour services to quitrents. By 1700, demesne farming and labour services had almost completely disappeared on Crown estates.[106] On seigneurial estates the situation depended on local circumstances, but there also we see a decline in labour services in favour of quitrents and (for those landlords who could afford it) hired labour.[107]

In much of the Ukraine, the Khmel'nitskii revolt had exterminated or driven out Polish landlords, especially in left-bank Ukraine east of the Dniepr, and in

---

103. Aleksandrov, *Sel'skaia obshchina*, p. 245, n. 13; on conditions in the eighteenth-century army, see Elise K. Wirtschaftler, *From Serf to Russian Soldier* (Princeton, NJ, 1990).

104. V. I. Meleshko, *Ocherki agrarnoi istorii vostochnoi Belorusi vtoroi polovina xvii–xviii v.* (Minsk, 1975), pp. 15–19.

105. Buganov *et al.*, *Istoriia krest'ianstva*, vol. III, p. 591.

106. V. I. Meleshko, 'Sotsial'no-ekonomicheskoe polozhenie krest'ian v kricheskom starostve v kontse xvii–pervoi polovine xviii v.', *Ezhegodnik po agrarnoi istorii vostochnoi Evropy 1968*, pp. 94–102.

107. Ibid., p. 594.

right-bank Ukraine between the Dniepr and the Bug rivers. This delayed the spread of serfdom into the Ukraine until the second half of the eighteenth century.

Little Russia, the Ukrainian lands east of the Dniepr river (left-bank Ukraine), had been more or less under Russian control since 1686. There, cossack military settlers lived on lands organized as semi-autonomous territorial regiments, each administered by regimental officers and lower officials, the latter elected by the cossack rank-and-file. In the late seventeenth century, the majority of these were personally free, enjoying 'traditional' privileges that included the right to produce and sell distilled spirits, and exemption from all taxes. Most of these cossacks, however, enjoyed only customary rights to their lands, which belonged to the regiment as a whole.

The *Starshina*, the senior officers who formed much of the ruling elite in each regimental territory, were on their way to becoming a landed gentry, since the regiment provided them with estates for their upkeep. Having rid the land of Polish estate-owners, the *Starshina* were nevertheless careful not to repeal the Lithuanian Statutes of 1566 and 1588, which had provided the legal basis for serfdom in Lithuania and the Ukraine, and in the 1730s the cossack *Starshina* finally gained recognition of their seigneurial rights over the rank-and-file cossacks settled on their lands.[108] They also made repeated attempts to curb the constant movement of the rural population, although this initially had little effect in a frontier society where most of the rural population was rootless. Indeed, by the middle of the eighteenth century, there were approximately 115,000 rural households in left-bank Ukraine, of which 80 per cent were landless farm-workers.[109]

In right-bank Ukraine, the Khmel'nitskii rebellion had exterminated or driven out Polish estate-owners from the south-eastern Ukraine between the Bug and Dniepr basins. It had not destroyed the great estates in the north-western Ukraine (Volhynia and Western Podolia), but attempts by Polish estate-owners to resurrect demesne farming there remained limited by peasant flight to the south-east, into the core area of Khmel'nitskii's cossack movement. There, despite the formal reassertion of Polish political authority, and the return of the great landowners in the early eighteenth century, the rural population continued to rebel against any attempts at imposing seigneurial rents. In order to attract and retain peasants on their estates, landowners had to provide them with cattle and inventory, along with four to six rent-free years to be followed by very light quitrents in cash.[110]

Another problem was the *haidamak* movement, which began in the Ukraine in the 1620s. The term *haidamak* was probably derived from the *hajdú*, the military settlers on the Turkish frontier in north-eastern Hungary. Like the cossacks and *odnodvortsy*, the *hajdú* included marginal social elements of all kinds,

108. V. A. Miakotin, *Ocherki sotsial'noi istorii Ukrainy v xvii–xviii vv.*, 2 vols (Prague, 1924), vol. I, pp. 85–96, 117–18.
109. Buganov, *et al.*, *Istoriia krest'ianstva*, vol. III, p. 573.
110. V. A. Markina, *Krest'iane pravoberezhnoi Ukrainy konets xvii–60 gody xviii v.* (Kiev, 1971), p. 20.

and the word *hajdú* was often synonymous with bandit.[111] Some historians have portrayed the *haidamak* movement as a revolt of the rural masses against Polish landlords, and the *haidamaks* doubtless qualify for inclusion among Hobsbawm's 'primitive rebels'. Yet their 'political' activities consisted almost entirely of murdering or terrorizing Jews and Polish landowners, activities they financed by rustling cattle on the great estates. Not until 1768 did the *haidamaks* appeal to the peasants to rise up against their lords.[112]

PHASE 4: 1750–1861

During this period, the peasant population (excluding Belorussia, Ukraine and the Baltic provinces) doubled again, from sixteen million in 1762 to thirty-two million in 1857. There were also major shifts in the structure of this rural population. In 1762, 55 per cent of the peasants were serfs, belonging to seigneurial landowners. Only a quarter of the peasant population were state peasants, and the remainder lived on lands belonging to the court or to ecclesiastical landlords. By 1857, only 40 per cent of the peasants were serfs, while more than half were under state jurisdiction. The spectacular growth of the latter had various origins. In 1763 Catherine the Great secularized ecclesiastical lands, placing the peasants on them under state jurisdiction, and thus greatly adding to the number and proportion of the latter. At the same time, a substantial part of the serf population purchased their freedom, was manumitted, fled, or found some other means of changing its status.[113] Peasant flight remained an important source of social and geographical mobility, especially since the government encouraged settlement of the south-east borderlands, even though it conflicted with its continuing support for serfdom. During the first half of the nineteenth century, an estimated 600,000 people migrated to the North Caucasus alone. Many of them were fugitive peasants who believed, or claimed to believe, that migration to this region did not require official authorization.[114] In any case, the serf population grew more slowly than the peasant population as a whole, increasing from 8.8 million in 1762 to only thirteen million by 1857.[115]

Historians once viewed the late eighteenth and early nineteenth centuries as the golden age of the Russian nobility and the nadir of the peasants' fortunes. This may hold true for serfs on *barshchina*, but the latter, which made up 55 per cent of the serfs, accounted for just slightly more than a fifth of the peasant

111. Schimert, 'The Hungarian nobility', p. 161.

112. Markina, *Krest'iane*, pp. 166–8.

113. Steven L. Hoch and Wilson R. Augustine, 'The tax censuses and the decline of the serf population in Imperial Russia', *Slavic Review*, 38 (1979), pp. 403–25.

114. See the fine study by David Moon, *Russian Peasants and Tsarist Legislation on the Eve of Reform: Interaction between Peasants and Officialdom, 1825–1855* (Basingstoke, 1992), pp. 23–61.

115. Kabuzan, *Razmeshchenie*, pp. 89, 171.

population as a whole by the 1850s.[116] Conditions for the state peasants, all of whom paid *obrok*, varied considerably in the early nineteenth century, since *obrok* averaged less than 10 per cent of the peasants' income in the richer provinces (mostly the heartland, with its crafts and rural industries), while it reached 20 per cent in some of the poorer provinces.[117] But despite these variations, the *obrok* and tax burdens paid by state peasants were comparatively light, and even declined in the nineteenth century. Thus, in the period 1797–1859 the average tax and *obrok* burden (excluding local taxes) paid by state peasants declined from 4.1 to only 3.4 silver rubles per male soul.[118]

Rent and tax burdens for serfs on *obrok* also decreased, at least for the second half of the eighteenth century.[119] In the first half of the nineteenth century, however, *obrok* burdens generally rose, especially in the heartland, although the rise was generally moderate. According to averages taken from three large estates in the heartland, *obrok* grew from 5.5 to 7.3 silver rubles between the late eighteenth century and the 1830s.[120] There were other estates where it was higher, but it is difficult to assess the relative weight of cash rents on the peasant economy. Many serfs on *obrok* earned substantial cash incomes, so that an *obrok* exceeding twenty silver rubles per male might take less than 5 per cent of household income.[121]

In any case, the most important development affecting the Russian peasantry in this period was not serfdom *per se*, but rather the emergence of a regional division of labour and production based on two large and complementary regions: the newly settled black-soil steppe and middle Volga (which functioned increasingly as the granary of Russia), and the non-black-soil region of the heartland, which, while retaining its agrarian character, emerged as the cradle of Russian capitalism, a dynamic network of proto-industrial and commercial villages.

The previous period, which had seen the settlement of the black-soil steppe and the foundation of large estates, had laid the foundations for this regional division of labour. As we have seen, the heartland was never particularly hospitable to cereal cultivation, although for centuries the rural population there had no alternative but to produce their own food. There were, of course, local grain markets in the seventeenth and early eighteenth centuries, and considerable variations could coexist even within single districts, where there might be localities with a marketable grain surplus alongside those with chronic deficits.

116. It is difficult to compute the proportion of serfs on *barshchina* and *obrok* because many serfs had mixed obligations that combined both forms. The figure of 55 per cent includes all peasants with any *barshchina*, even though many of these performed only minimal labour services. See Blum, *Lord and Peasant*, pp. 394–400, and Fedorov, *Pomeshchich'i krest'iane*, pp. 246–9.

117. Blum, *Lord and Peasant*, pp. 485–7.

118. Buganov *et al.*, *Istoriia krest'ianstva*, vol. III, p. 366, table 1. Values for 1797, expressed in paper rubles, have been converted to silver rubles. A paper ruble in 1797 was worth only 74 per cent of its silver counterpart.

119. Arcadius Kahan, 'The costs of "westernization" in Russia: the gentry and the economy in the eighteenth century', in Michael Cherniavsky (ed.), *The Structure of Russian History* (New York, 1970), p. 233.

120. Melton, 'Enlightened seigniorialism', p. 678.

121. Idem, 'Proto-industrialization, serf agriculture, and agrarian social structure: two estates in nineteenth-century Russia', *Past and Present*, 115 (1987), p. 91.

The overall grain picture, however, was generally unfavourable in the heartland, and by the mid-eighteenth century the region as a whole faced major grain deficits. In some provinces, like Moscow and Vladimir, local grain production apparently satisfied less than half the requirements of the rural population there.[122]

By 1760, the need for grain in the heartland proved a positive force, since it created both a demand and a rise in grain prices that lasted for the next half-century.[123] The fertile grain-producing regions of the black-soil steppe-forest began shipping large quantities of grain to the heartland.[124] This was in part the cause, and in part the effect, of two other developments that transformed the Russian agrarian economy. First, there was the expansion of demesne farming, which took place throughout Russia, but was particularly pronounced in the black-soil steppe.[125] Indeed, evidence from the plentiful estate records of this period shows that expansion of demesne arable continued well into the first half of the nineteenth century. A typical case was Prince Bariatinskii's estate in Kursk province, where demesne arable increased from 5,500 acres in 1800 to more than 9,000 acres by 1815.[126]

We will have more to say later about the impact of demesne expansion on the peasants who had to work these demesnes. Here, it is useful to look at the development of the agrarian economy in the heartland. There, freed from the iron necessity of producing all their own subsistence needs, many peasants in the non-black-soil region were able to move to a more diversified economy in which cereal cultivation usually remained, but became increasingly subordinate to petty trade, craft production, or various forms of wage labour.

Of course, rural trade and industry were not new developments in the Russian heartland. In the sixteenth century, salt production and iron mining were both tied closely, though not exclusively, to the village economy, and in the seventeenth century market-oriented rural crafts had emerged in significant concentrations in at least 400 villages in the heartland around Moscow and Vladimir.[127] The same period also saw the formation of a large stratum of trading peasants operating in the same region, and a recent study has identified at least 700 of them operating in the late seventeenth and early eighteenth century. Some dealt in local or regional trade that was often connected with the craft villages mentioned above, but as many as a third dealt in long-distance trade with the lower Volga and Astrakhan.[128]

Rural trade and industry were not, of course, unique to Russia, but, compared to central and western Europe, they played a special role in Russia, if

122. V. A. Fedorov, *Pomeshchich'i krest'iane tsentral'no-promyshlennogo raiona kontsa xviii–pervoi poloviny xix v.* (Moscow, 1974), pp. 56–8.

123. B. Mironov, 'Revoliutsiia tsen v Rossii v xviii veke', *Voprosy istorii*, 11 (1971), pp. 49–61.

124. I. D. Koval'chenko, 'O roli tovarnosti zemledeliia v Rossii v pervoi polovine xix v.', *Ezhegodnik po agrarnoi istorii vostochnoi Evropy 1963* (Vilnius, 1964), p. 74.

125. L. V. Milov, 'O roli perelozhnykh zemel' v russkom zemledelii vtoroi poloviny xviii v.', *Ezhegodnik po agrarnoi istoriia vostochnoi Evropy 1961* (Riga, 1963), pp. 279–87.

126. Petrova, 'Nadelennost' zemlei i skotom', p. 375.

127. Melton, 'Proto-industrialization', p. 74.

128. V. P. Tarlovskaia, *Torgovlia Rossii perioda pozdnego feodalizma (Torgovye krest'iane vo vtoroi polovine xvii–nachale xviii v.)* (Moscow, 1988), pp. 72–132.

only because the urban population, only 5 per cent of the total by 1800, was so small. At least one historian has argued that the Russian economy and society in this period were fundamentally different from that of central and western Europe. The latter were marked by a profound split between town and country that was largely absent in Russia, where the division of labour was not between town and country, but between villages that specialized in trade and manufacturing, and those that specialized in agriculture.[129]

The increased availability of grain from the black-soil steppe-forest was thus accompanied by a massive shift to rural industry in the heartland. This apparently took place in the middle decades of the eighteenth century, and resulted in a fundamental transformation of the agrarian structure. In the heartland, large numbers of landowners liquidated or reduced their own demesnes, and commuted their peasants' labour services into payment of cash quitrents. At the beginning of the eighteenth century, less than 20 per cent of the seigneurial peasants in the heartland had paid cash rents, but by the 1780s this had grown to more than 60 per cent.[130]

For Russia, this was a change on the same scale as the decline of serfdom and commutation of labour services in late medieval Europe. Many peasants drastically curtailed their agricultural activities, a trend that alarmed some estate-owners. One, describing a journey along the upper Volga in 1747, wrote that: 'I saw not a single field that was entirely cultivated . . . the strips were sown by half or even less, and even where sown, rare was the field that one would consider of even average quality. Most would not even produce enough for seed.'[131]

Such extremes, of course, did not exist everywhere in the non-black soil region, and it is important not to exaggerate the level of non-agricultural production. In almost every province in the heartland, there remained islands of demesne farming, where the majority of peasants performed labour services. But even with such caveats, the rapid expansion of rural trade and industry in the Russian heartland after 1750 was one of the most important developments in the peasant village.

By the late eighteenth century, there were at least three major networks of rural industry in Russia: the Moscow textile region, the Vladimir-Kostroma textile region, and the tanning and metal-working region in Nizhnii Novgorod. Taken together, they included hundreds of villages. Thus, for example, the cutlery industry in Pavlovo included in its network at least 120 villages and more than 7,000 peasants.[132]

These networks were, moreover, only the cutting edge of a much larger market economy that had sliced deeply into the provinces of the heartland by

129. Otto Brunner, 'Europäisches und russisches Bürgertum', in idem., *Neue Wege der Verfassungs- und Sozialgeschichte*, 2nd edn (Göttingen, 1968), pp. 226–32.

130. Melton, 'Proto-industrialization', p. 76.

131. L. V. Milov and A. Chistozvonov, 'Les propriétaires fonciers et les paysannes de Russie aux xvii et xviii siècles', in Peter Gunst and Tamás Hoffmann (eds), *Large Estates and Small Holdings in Europe in the Middle Ages and Modern Times* (Budapest, 1982), p. 354.

132. See the pioneering study by Klaus Gestwa, *Proto-Industrialisierung in Rußland. Das Baumwollgewerbe in Ivanova und das Kleineisengewerbe in Pavlova 1741–1932* (forthcoming). I am grateful to Dr Gestwa for sending me a draft of this important study.

the late eighteenth century. Rural industry and trade resonated throughout the heartland, creating demands for raw materials, foodstuffs, and most of all for transport. The latter was one of the most labour-intensive sectors in the rural economy, mobilizing the seasonal labour of thousands of peasants.

Our main concern here, however, is not with the Russian economy as a whole, but with the very different types of peasant communities that grew out of these developments. Thanks to Steven Hoch's rich study of Petrovskoe, a village on the Gagarin estate in the province of Tambov, we now have a detailed picture of peasant life on a labour-service estate in the black-soil steppe-forest (see p. 251, n. 101). Hoch's study is especially valuable because his conclusions are consistent with what we know about the black-soil region as a whole. Most peasants in Petrovskoe lived in large, multi-generational households averaging eight to nine family members. Their dwellings, primitive log cabins without floorboards or windows, were heated by brick stoves vented through a simple hole in the wall. Adjacent to the cabins were the outbuildings used for threshing, drying and storing the grain, and a garden for growing vegetables and hemp.

In the first quarter of the nineteenth century, an average household of eight members had about twelve *desiatinas* (thirty-two acres) of arable land, which it cultivated in open fields in which its neighbours' lands, as well as the demesne lands of the seigneur, were intermingled. In addition to working its own lands, the household also had to work a roughly equal amount of seigneurial arable using its own horses. Under the three-field rotation, roughly a third of the arable lay fallow in any given year, so the average household actually cultivated a total of approximately forty acres per year, half for itself and half for the estate-owner. Communal repartitions took place rarely, perhaps once every twenty years, but the commune frequently readjusted allotments in accordance with the household's changing labour capacity, and the greater the tax and labour-service burdens carried by the household, the more arable it received for its own use. Each household also had access to hayfields, meadows and forest, which helped support its livestock inventory, which for the average household included four horses and three cows.

Because of the short growing season (five to six months compared to eight to nine months in western Europe), the agricultural work calendar was much more intense, much of it concentrated in a six-week period from mid-July to late August. During this time, labour-service obligations on seigneurial lands inevitably competed with the household's need to cultivate its own holdings, and normally only the large households with strong labour capacities could satisfy both.

Within the household, there was generally a well-defined division of labour, and while men and women shared in harvesting the grain, men usually did the ploughing, harrowing, hay-cutting and threshing, while women tended the garden, raked the hay, sheaved the grain and carried it to the threshing floor.

Agricultural techniques were primitive, but the black-soil steppe was fertile. During the first half of the nineteenth century, crop yields in Petrovskoe averaged 6:1 for rye and 5:1 for buckwheat and oats, yields very similar to those in France and Germany at this time. Excluding oats, which probably went to the horses, an average harvest provided the household with a daily ration of two pounds of rye and buckwheat per person. This, combined with the household's production of milk and vegetables, provided a diet that may have been adequate, although it was markedly inferior to the diet of farm-labourers in early nineteenth-century Brandenburg. The latter lived in brick dwellings, and ate 50 per cent more grain, in addition to large amounts of cheese, milk, butter and beer.[133]

In bad years, mostly crop failures followed by epidemics, the peasants of Petrovskoe suffered terribly. Thus, during the subsistence crises of 1821–22, 1833–34 and 1848–49 the peasants were dependent on rations from their estate-owner which, however, provided them with less than 40 per cent of their normal food intake. Malnutrition, combined with disease, took a heavy toll of lives, especially among infants and children.

The peasants of Petrovskoe had regular, but very limited, ties to the market economy. Forced to expend much of their labour capacity on their allotments and the lands of the seigneur, they had limited surplus capacity for additional production. They were able to earn the small amounts of money needed for taxes and communal assessments by carting their landlord's grain to the market during the winter months, and may have earned additional money from the sale of hemp. In any case, however, there were few, if any, opportunities for capital accumulation, and this, coupled with social and demographic forces operating within the community, maintained an egalitarian distribution of wealth between the households.

The most striking feature of life in Petrovskoe was the crucial role of the large, patriarchal household. In the late eighteenth and first half of the nineteenth century, this type of household dominated the black-soil steppe-forest, where the average family had from eight to ten members.[134] Such households had the advantage of assuring a high and constant labour capacity necessary especially during the peak season when peasants had to work seigneurial lands as well as their own allotments. Basically, the large household sought to maintain the labour capacity of two adult couples. This was done by enforcing early and universal marriage, in which the married sons, along with their families, had to remain in their parents' household. Households might therefore become extremely large, especially if there were three or more married sons living under the same roof. When the household patriarch died or retired, however, his sons, with married children of their own, had sufficient labour capacity to establish new households, thus beginning a new cycle.

This also reinforced a high fertility rate, although demographic growth in Petrovskoe retained a distinctively pre-industrial cast, in which high mortality rates kept the population in check. Life expectancy in Petrovskoe averaged only twenty-seven years, and nearly half the population died before the age of five.

Another characteristic of life in Petrovskoe was the frequent use of corporal punishment as a means of controlling the serf labour force. Indeed, a quarter

133. William Hagen, 'Working for the Junker: the standard of living of manorial laborers in Brandenburg, 1584–1810', *Journal of Modern History*, 58 (March, 1986), p. 154.
134. V. A. Aleksandrov, *Obychnoe pravo krepostnoi derevni Rossii* (Moscow, 1984), p. 57.

of the adult males of Petrovskoe were punished at least once a year, usually by floggings administered for negligent performance of labour services to the seigneur, or for thefts of estate property. Chronic offenders might get tougher treatment, and the commune routinely got rid of peasants it viewed as socially undesirable by sending them off to fill the yearly conscription levies.

Life on an *obrok* estate in the heartland was very different, as we can see from the case of Baki, a large estate in Kostroma province.[135] Unlike egalitarian Petrovskoe, property differentiation was relatively advanced in Baki, where sixteen wealthy or prosperous serf entrepreneurs, several of them with thousands of rubles in capital, dominated the commune. Below them were the backbone of the commune, the middle-level peasants who accounted for 60 per cent of the households. Below them were the poor, who accounted for another 30 per cent of the households. The relatively advanced degree of property differentiation makes it difficult to generalize about living standards in Baki, but housing, at least for the middle and better-off peasants, was clearly better than in Petrovskoe. Baki peasants lived in two-storey dwellings built from planks, rather than logs, with the household occupying the second storey (with wooden floor) while the ground floor functioned as a cattle shed.

There were also great differences in family structure, economy and the seigneurial regime. Large households were rare in Baki, and while the average household had only five to six members, poorer households averaged only 3.6 members. The key to the peasant economy in Baki was its diversity, and for most peasants economic survival depended largely on their ability to combine subsistence farming with at least two or more sources of cash income. The primary source of cash income was timber, taken illegally from the vast forests of the estate and adjoining court lands.

Timber-cutting in the winter was also part of the slash-and-burn cultivation on which the peasants depended. After cutting a stand of timber, the peasants burned the tree-roots in the forest clearing, creating a layer of ash that mixed with the soil to provide extremely good crop yields. The small livestock holdings (middle peasants averaged only one to two horses and two to three cows per household) could not possibly provide enough fertilizer to bring more than marginal crop yields on the peasants' regular allotments, but slash-and-burn clearings gave yields of 10:1 or even better over a three-year planting. After three years, the clearings, known as *kuligy*, lost much of their fertility, but the peasants often cleared new *kuligy* every winter, thus maintaining more than one at a time. Indeed, many households in the Vetluga region had six to nine *kuligy* at any one time.[136] It is not surprising, then, that peasants attached more importance to their slash-and-burn clearings than to their allotments, and indeed the only land disputes in Baki were over the slash-and-burn clearings, which the peasants treated as their own, buying, selling or even gambling them away.

---

135. The following account of Baki is taken from Melton, 'Household economies and communal conflicts', pp. 559–85.

136. L. P. Gorlanov, 'Krest'ianskie dvizheniia v udel'noi derevne tsentral'nogo promyshlennogo raiona v 1797–1863', in N. V. Voskresenskaia (ed.), *Krest'ianstvo tsentral'nogo promyshlennogo raiona: istoriia, istoriografiia, istochniki* (Kalinin, 1982), pp. 15–16.

According to a government study of one Vetluga estate located very close to Baki, timber-cutting and its by-products brought its inhabitants an average of 270,000 paper rubles per year in the period from 1820 to 1825. This was an average of 350 paper rubles per male soul, a huge income by peasant standards.[137] It is likely that the timber economy brought the Baki peasants a similar per capita income, and even though household income in Baki was inequitably distributed, middle peasants with three males may well have earned 700 rubles a year from timber alone. In addition, most households, at least the middle peasants, supplemented this with additional cash earnings from crafts or petty trades. Their wives and daughters often ran food stalls at the weekly market, which brought in additional income. The lower stratum of middle peasants hired themselves out as barge-workers for the timber dealers on the estate. Thus, annual cash earnings of middle-peasant households may have been as high as 800 paper rubles, and were certainly more than enough to pay the quitrents, taxes and assessments that together made up the cash obligations the peasants owed to seigneur, state and commune. In 1812, for example, the entire commune (2,000 males living in over 600 households) paid cash obligations that totalled over 45,000 paper rubles, including *obrok*, taxes and local assessments. Unfortunately, we do not know the actual breakdown per household, but if a middle household with three males paid roughly a hundred rubles per year, it clearly had a large disposable income.

Most of the peasants in Baki, then, were prosperous in comparison to their counterparts on Petrovskoe. Their diversified economies, for example, provided protection against both crop failure and market downturns. In a bad harvest year, they could purchase grain, while surviving years of low cash earnings by living off their farm. Significantly, there is no evidence of subsistence crises in Baki during the first third of the nineteenth century.

The poorer peasants of Baki may not have gone hungry, but they certainly did not share the prosperity of their better-off neighbours. The most obvious cause of their poverty was lack of sufficient labour capacity for a diversified household economy. The poor households averaged less than two adults, male or female, a circumstance that in itself largely precluded a diversified household economy. Only a third of the poor households were able to maintain the combination of farming, woodcutting and off-farm occupation that characterized the middle peasants. Nearly half of the poor were virtually landless, working as seasonal labourers or servants for their more prosperous neighbours, and a few were beggars.

In Baki, as in Petrovskoe, the odds of life depended on the size of the household, but unlike Petrovskoe, there were no systematic attempts to force the peasants to live in large or even medium households. This illustrates vividly the difference between serf life on a *barshchina* estate in the black-soil steppe, and an *obrok* estate in the heartland. The need for labour control on *barshchina*

---

137. This income data was the result of an official study undertaken to investigate the causes of a bloody uprising on the estate in 1826, which cost the lives of eleven peasants. The apparent reason for the uprising was the seigneur's attempt to get a larger share of this income by raising quitrent to a much higher level. V. A. Fedorov, *Krest'ianskoe dvizhenie v tsentral'noi Rossii 1800–1860* (Moscow, 1980), pp. 56–8.

estates dictated a highly regimented life in which there was little room for social or economic autonomy. On *obrok* estates, however, there was no demesne economy and thus no need for labour control. Indeed, many peasants on *obrok* normally required a great deal of autonomy in order to earn the cash to pay their quitrents, often leaving the village for long periods of off-farm labour.

The long periods spent away from the village probably encouraged independence from patriarchal authority, while also making it possible to earn a livelihood. Thus, even if larger households were more 'rational', the social and economic framework on *obrok* estates encouraged the peasants' tendency to form small, independent households. Throughout the heartland, peasant households were smallest on *obrok* estates with well-developed trade and rural industry.

The Peasant Commune

The form and structure of communal life varied throughout Russia, but the discussion here focuses on the so-called repartitional land commune, which dominated in the heartland and the black-soil steppe-forest. The rise in the sixteenth century of communal officials charged with the apportionment and collection of taxes, suggests that the commune as we know it was largely the creation of the state.[138] Communal repartition of land, for example, apparently first appeared after the introduction of the poll tax, in 1719. Communes began to apportion land to families according to the number of taxable male souls per household, and new repartitions took place in response to changes brought on by a new census. Initially, the commune seems to have been extremely rigorous in its control of land, stopping short only at the peasants' individual garden plots. The shares allotted each household were confirmed by majority vote and individual appeals for readjustments were rarely successful.[139] After 1750, however, communal control and regulation of land somewhat diminished, largely because it increasingly conflicted with the growing sense of household property. As long as the household continued to render its share of communal obligations (taxes, rents, etc.), it increasingly viewed its allotment as heritable and even alienable, as long as the land transfer remained within the commune. Ambitious peasants who wanted to increase their landholdings preferred to acquire them privately, through purchase, rent, or even outright seizure.[140]

Despite its diminishing control over land use, the intensification of serfdom and the growing power of the state actually enhanced the power of the commune. Neither the Russian state nor its landowning elite was able to maintain a bureaucracy capable of administering the population at the village or parish

138. P. A. Kolesnikov, 'Osnovnye etapy razvitiia severnoi obshchiny', *Ezhegodnik po agrarnoi istorii. Problemy istorii russkoi obshchiny* (Vologda, 1976), p. 14. Gerd Spittler, 'Staat und Klientelstruktur in Entwicklungsländern. Zum Problem der politischen Organisation von Bauern', *Europäisches Archiv für Soziologie*, 18 (1977), pp. 75–6.

139. L. N. Vdovina, *Krest'ianskaia obshchina i monastyr' v tsentral'noi Rossii v pervoi polovine xviii v.* (Moscow, 1988), pp. 68–76.

140. L. S. Prokof'eva, *Krest'ianskaia obshchina v Rossii vo vtoroi polovine xviii–pervoi polovine xix veka* (St Petersburg, 1981), pp. 54–128.

level, and bureaucratic supervision, to the degree that it existed at all, ended at the level of the district town, where the land captain and a tiny military force (often invalids) 'administered' rural districts of 40,000–60,000 inhabitants.

Below the district level, most governance was in the hands of the commune and its elected officials. For peasants under the jurisdiction of the state, or those belonging to the imperial court (appanage peasants), the *volost'* was the basic administrative unit, and the villages within the *volost'* normally elected the *volost'* authorities.[141]

Russian estate-owners had legal jurisdiction over their serfs, but they were usually absent from their estates, and even when they hired estate managers, local governance usually remained in communal hands.[142] Depending on the size of the estate, the commune might embrace a village, or only part of a village. Most serfs, however, lived on large estates with many villages, and in such cases, all the villages on a single estate were normally organized into one commune, with elected *vybornye* (literally, selectmen) representing each village.[143]

August von Haxthausen, the first serious student of the Russian commune, visited numerous communes in the 1840s and was deeply impressed with communal government, which, in his view, made every commune a 'free republic'.[144] This, however, was an idealized view that was often, if not always, at odds with the reality of communal life. The role of the Russian commune offers a prime illustration of what Gerd Spittler calls the 'peasant state', a state whose existence depends on its peasant population to supply the revenue, labour, rents and conscripts that support the ruler and his civil/military elite.[145] At the beginning of the nineteenth century, peasants made up more than 90 per cent of the taxable population, and provided, in addition, virtually all the cash rents and labour dues that comprised the main income of the landed elite. They also provided all rural services in Russia, including tax assessment and collection, road and bridge repair, rural mail delivery, troop quartering and logistic support, and data collection. They also contributed the overwhelming majority of conscripts, through a selection process carried out by the communes themselves, which also had to kit out each recruit.

As we have already seen, the higher authorities decided the per capita burden of taxes, rents and other obligations, and then used their census data to determine the aggregate for each commune. But they then left it to the

141. The properties belonging to the imperial court provided financial support for the various members of the imperial family. Originally, the peasants living on these properties were known simply as court peasants (*dvortsovye krest'iane*), and numbered about 750,000 people of both sexes in the 1720s. In 1797 the Emperor Paul placed all court properties and the peasants living on them under the supervision of the newly created Department of the Appanage (*Udel*) and the peasants became known as appanage peasants. Blum, *Lord and Peasant*, pp. 493–4.

142. Peter Kolchin contrasts the 'absentee mentality' of Russian serf owners with the intense paternalism of southern planters in his magisterial work, *Unfree Labor: American Slavery and Russian Serfdom* (Cambridge, MA, 1987).

143. The top 5 per cent of Russian landowners (those with more than 500 male serfs each), owned 55 per cent of all the serfs in Russia. Melton, 'Enlightened seigniorialism', p. 681.

144. August von Haxthausen, *Studies on the Interior of Russia*, ed. and with an Introduction by S. Frederick Starr (Chicago, 1972), pp. 71–2.

145. Gerd Spittler, *Verwaltung in einem afrikanischen Bauernstaat: Das koloniale Französisch-Westafrika, 1919–1939* (Wiesbaden, 1981), p. 13.

communal authorities, especially the communal headman (*burmistr*) and the clerk (*zemskii*), to distribute these *within* the commune. The headman was the communal executive, representing the commune with higher authorities, hearing his neighbours' complaints, and acting as judge in trials and disputes. He was theoretically subject to the communal assembly (*mirskoi skhod*), to which each household sent a representative, but large assemblies were cumbersome and unruly and even when they took place, poor peasants were often excluded. Most meetings included only the selectmen or elders from each village, which in practice weakened the assembly's checks on their communal officials.[146]

The communal clerk was often more powerful than the headman because his command of reading and writing made him the crucial link between the literate world of the higher authorities and the preliterate world of his fellow villagers. His power, however, depended less on facilitating than on impeding the flow of information, since it was control of information that enabled him to control the commune. The higher authorities (state and seigneur) had formal power over the commune, but they had little knowledge of local conditions, and therefore depended largely on the clerk. Few of the peasants were literate, so they also depended on the clerk, who thus remained in control of written information passed down from higher authorities, as well as the reports sent from the commune to the seigneur.

The power of communal officials varied, of course. In state peasant communes, there were probably few effective checks on the *volost'* officials, while communal officials may have been less powerful on *barshchina* estates, where the need to maximize the peasants' labour capacity forced estate managers to intervene actively in communal affairs. On seigneurial estates where the peasants were on *obrok*, the reality lay somewhere in between. On many *obrok* estates, there were also estate managers who could check the abuses of communal officials and limit the clerks' control over information. But on many other *obrok* estates, the managers were unable or unwilling to control the communal officials, especially since many estate-owners had a visceral distrust of estate managers and discouraged them from meddling in communal affairs.[147]

For many seigneurs and their managers, *obrok* communes were hard to control because they were dominated by the wealthy peasants. In the early nineteenth century, for example, the clerk of the Baki commune was married to the daughter of one of the richest serfs in the commune, and this kinship provided the core of a faction that used its control to dispense patronage, especially in the divisive issue of recruit selection. So powerful was this faction that it was able to secure the dismissal of a conscientious estate manager who tried to reform communal government.[148] Such abuses were not unusual, and communal officials, especially the clerks, were notorious for their corruption and bribe-taking.

The power of communal officials also had a profound effect on the peasants' mentality and behaviour. From the standpoint of the individual peasant,

146. Melton, 'Household economies', pp. 563–4.
147. Idem, 'Enlightened seigniorialism', pp. 684–5.
148. Idem, 'Household economies', pp. 569–78.

increases in taxes or rents were less important than his relationship to the communal authorities, since it was the latter who would determine his share of the increase. If he belonged to their patronage network, he could expect favourable treatment; if not, he would probably bear an inordinate share of the burden.[149] In practice, then, the commune was a political arena in which the peasants constantly jockeyed for favourable position with the communal authorities. This did not, however, necessarily undermine the peasants' capacity for collective action, as we shall see in the next section.

COLLECTIVE FORMS OF PEASANT RESISTANCE TO HIGHER AUTHORITY

The most vivid forms of resistance, the so-called peasant wars of the seventeenth and eighteenth centuries, probably had less impact on rural conditions than the frequent, but isolated, riots and uprisings in individual communes. In any event, the greatest of the peasant wars, the revolts led by Stenka Razin (1667–71) and Emelian Pugachev (1773–75), began not with the peasantry, but with the cossacks on the south-eastern frontier, in the regions of the Don and southern Urals. There, a turbulent population of cossacks, fugitive peasants and nomadic tribespeople provided a volatile mix of social antagonisms and political resentments fuelled by threats to local autonomy. Only later, as the insurgent forces moved from the periphery toward the heartland, did rebellion spread to the peasant populations of the Urals and middle Volga, where it fed on popular resentments against the growth of serfdom and the abuses of state officials.[150] The threat to established authority was very real, and the state had to mobilize large armies to crush the insurgents and restore order.

If such peasant wars were extremely rare, riots (*bunty*) and uprisings (*volneniia*) were relatively frequent occurrences. For the period 1801–60, Soviet historians have counted more than 2,700 rural uprisings, a conservative figure that includes mainly those that were serious enough to report to the provincial governors. The most striking aspect of these uprisings is their increasing frequency – from an average of less than twenty per year in the first decade of the nineteenth century, to more than a hundred per year in the 1850s.[151]

In most uprisings and riots, the peasants involved had specific grievances, often against estate managers or communal officials, but also against the seigneur, even if they consciously tried to avoid the *appearance* of a direct challenge to the latter's authority. Grievances often stemmed from the attempts of a new estate-owner to impose higher rents, or to replace quitrents with labour services, but

---

149. Ibid., p. 562.
150. For the Stenka Razin revolt, Buganov *et al.*, *Istoriia krest'ianstva*, vol. III, pp. 193–202; for Pugachev, Dorothea Peters, *Politische und gesellschaftliche Vorstellungen in der Aufstandsbewegung unter Pugachev (1773–1775)* (Berlin, 1973), pp. 43–171.
151. Buganov *et al.*, *Istoriia krest'ianstva*, vol. III, pp. 418–19.

might also stem from the peasants' real, or feigned, misunderstanding of tsarist legislation. During the Crimean War, for example, a number of peasant riots stemmed from the belief that the tsar had decreed that peasants volunteering for the state militia would be freed from serfdom. In some cases, when officials refused to allow the would-be volunteers to enlist, the latter believed that the officials were in collusion with estate-owners to obstruct the tsar's will.[152]

Village uprisings often began with a communal petition to the estate-owner. Since the latter was usually absent, delivery of the petition often took several months, giving peasant resentments plenty of time to fester. Some estate-owners punished peasants who submitted petitions, although most were probably anxious to avoid the cost and disruption of a riot, and were inclined to take seriously their peasants' complaints. The problem was that, as absentee landlords, they could not know the real issues, and often misunderstood the peasants' intentions. This was the case with a peasant riot that broke out in Baki in 1836, ostensibly over the estate manager's project to build a saw-mill. The estate-owner, Prince Lieven, had approved the project, and clearly underestimated the peasants' resistance to it. This is understandable, since resistance to the project seems to have served primarily as a pretext for a riot organized by a rival faction to overthrow the communal faction that was then in power.[153] And indeed, though the peasants always had legitimate grievances, the issues at stake in peasant riots were often pretexts for factional struggles within the commune.

CONCLUSION

The underlying reasons for the agrarian reforms of the mid-nineteenth century, especially the abolition of serfdom in 1861, lie beyond the scope of this chapter. It is enough to say that the usual explanations for the abolition of serfdom – its 'backwardness', its immorality, the fear of peasant uprisings, and the personal convictions of Tsar Alexander II – all fall short of the mark.[154] In any case, this chapter has suggested that serfdom was only part of a much larger dilemma posed by the very existence of the peasant state: could a state whose existence depended on the aggregate authority, cooperation and fiscal capacity of thousands of communal officials, carry out the tasks of a great power in the modern world? Maxim Gorky, who of all Russians posed this question most thoughtfully, was pessimistic, and Russian history in the twentieth century has not proved him wrong.[155]

152. Moon, *Russian Peasants*, pp. 114–64.
153. This incident receives detailed treatment in my forthcoming book on the Baki commune.
154. See David Saunders's thoughtful comments in his *Russia and the Age of Reaction and Reform, 1801–1881* (London, 1992), pp. 135–44. See also David Moon, 'Reassessing Russian serfdom', *European History Quarterly*, 26 (1996), pp. 483–526.
155. Maxim Gorky, 'On the Russian peasant', in R. E. F. Smith (ed.), *The Russian Peasant 1920 and 1984* (London, 1985).

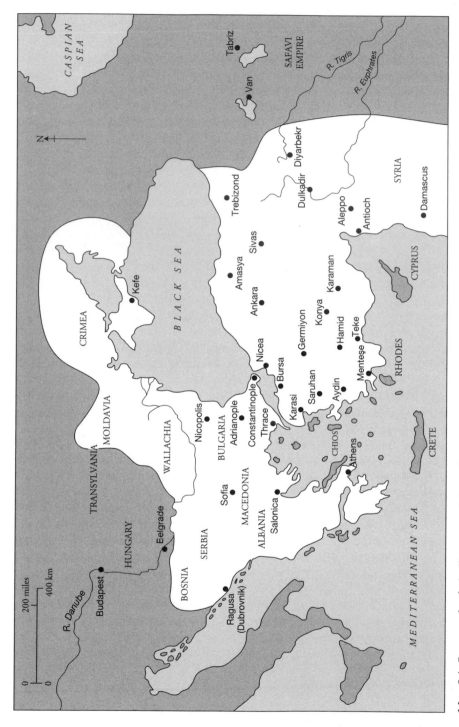

Map 9.1 Ottoman lands in Europe and Anatolia

CHAPTER NINE

The Ottoman Peasantries, c.1360—c.1860

Fikret Adanır

Modern historiography on the Ottoman empire has developed on the one hand along lines reflecting western economic, political and cultural predominance and on the other in answer to the needs of a robust nationalism that in time permeated all spheres of cultural and political life in the successor states. In this process the peasantry, which formed the overwhelming majority of the emerging national societies, has often been the object of a historiographic mystification, since the new regimes — whether colonial, European-sponsored or national — sought legitimation not least in a projection of the Ottoman past as a period of foreign occupation (the proverbial 'Turkish yoke') that had brought socio-economic and cultural decline along with degradation of the peasant masses to a state of *de facto* servility. Conversely, there have been and still are distinct tendencies in the Republic of Turkey towards the idealization of the Ottoman centuries as a 'golden age' of independent peasantries.[1]

Empirical research on Ottoman rural life is of a rather recent date. The paradigm represented since 1929 by the French periodical *Annales* can be considered a first impulse towards a more systematic and more comparative approach to the history of peasantries of the Ottoman empire.[2] Fernand Braudel's impressive demonstration of the unity of the Mediterranean world of the sixteenth century, irrespective of political, religious and cultural demarcation lines, enhanced the importance of quantitative methods for historical research.[3] In

---

1. For critical evaluations see Rifa'at 'Ali Abou-El-Haj, 'The social uses of the past: recent Arab historiography of Ottoman rule', *International Journal of Middle East Studies*, 14 (1982), pp. 185–201; Suraiya Faroqhi, 'Agriculture and rural life in the Ottoman empire (ca 1500–1878)', *New Perspectives on Turkey*, 1 (1987), pp. 3–34; Halil Berktay, 'The search for the peasant in western and Turkish history/historiography', in Halil Berktay and Suraiya Faroqhi (eds), *New Approaches to State and Peasant in Ottoman History* (London, 1992), pp. 109–84; Maria Todorova, 'Bulgarian historical writing on the Ottoman empire', *New Perspectives on Turkey*, 12 (1995), pp. 97–118. Literature on the 'Ottoman decline' paradigm in Fikret Adanır, 'Der Zerfall des Osmanischen Reiches', in Alexander Demandt (ed.), *Das Ende der Weltreiche. Von den Persern bis zur Sowjetunion* (Munich, 1997), pp. 108–28, 242–51.

2. Traian Stoianovich, 'Social history: perspective of the Annales paradigm', *Review. A Journal of the Fernand Braudel Center for the Study of Economics, Historical Systems and Civilisations*, 1:3/4, (1978), pp. 19–48; Halil İnalcık, 'Impact of the *Annales* school on Ottoman studies and new findings', ibid., pp. 69–96.

3. Fernand Braudel, *The Mediterranean and the Mediterranean World*, (New York/Cambridge/Philadelphia, 1972).

a programmatic article making direct reference to Braudel's work, the Turkish historian Ömer Lûtfi Barkan proposed the initiation of a new phase in the study of Ottoman history: the rich source material preserved in the Turkish archives should be made the object of systematic, quantitative and comparative inquiry. He predicted that such research would support the concept of the Ottoman empire as an 'entité géographique ou type de civilisation répondant en somme à l'histoire d'une grande partie de la civilisation méditerranéenne ou proche-orientale'.[4]

Barkan and his followers succeeded in raising the study of the late medieval and early modern history of south-eastern Europe and the Near East to a new level. New were above all the types of source material utilized, such as poll-tax registers, cadastral surveys or court records, whereas the traditional historiography had shown a distinct preference for sources of a narrative character.[5] Historians in individual Balkan countries responded positively to the new trend. From the 1950s on an impressive number of editions of sources pertaining to the Ottoman period of Balkan history have appeared, stimulating research in the demographic, urban and agrarian history of the Ottoman period.[6] Not least, the Marxist insistence on the theory of succeeding social formations – slavery, feudalism, absolutism, socialism – necessitated a reinterpretation of the Ottoman past, for even though the romantic concept of a 'national renaissance' was not given up, it was recognized that the emergence of the social forces which accomplished and supported such a revival had to be explained. This could be done best by investigating the evolution of agricultural life.

In the early post-Second World War era, Marxist historiography posited first the mass expropriation of Balkan peasantries by the eighteenth century, followed by the emergence of commercialized agriculture based on paid labour.[7] Western research, in particular, soon modified this picture; not only was it now asserted that the peasants had remained owners of their plots, but also that the absence of mass peasant expropriation was indicative of the underdeveloped

4. Ömer Lûtfi Barkan, 'Essai sur les données statistiques des registres de recensement dans l'Empire ottoman aux XVe et XVIe siècles', *Journal of Economic and Social History of the Orient*, 1 (1957), pp. 9–36, here at p. 10.

5. The importance of Ottoman sources for the study of Balkan history is discussed in Andreas Tietze, 'The Balkans and Ottoman sources – Ottoman sources and the Balkans', in Henrik Birnbaum and Speros Vryonis, Jr (eds), *Aspects of the Balkans, Continuity and Change* (The Hague/Paris, 1972), pp. 285–97, and Bistra Cvetkova, 'Les *tahrir defterleri* comme sources pour l'histoire de la Bulgarie et des pays balkaniques', *Revue des Etudes Sud-Est Européennes*, 16 (1978), pp. 91–104.

6. See among others Branislav Djurdjev, *Turska vlast u Crnoj Gori u XVI i XVII veku. Prilog jednog nerešenot pitanju iz naše istorije* (Sarajevo, 1953); Hazim Šabanović, *Bosanski pašalik. Postanak i upravna podjela* (Sarajevo, 1959); Nicoară Beldiceanu, *Recherche sur la ville ottomane au XVe siècle. Etude et actes* (Paris, 1973); idem, *Le timar dans l'Etat ottoman (début XIVe–début XVIe siècle)* (Wiesbaden, 1980); Bistra A. Cvetkova, *Les institutions ottomanes en Europe* (Wiesbaden, 1978); Nikolai Todorov, *Balkanskiiat grad, XV–XIX vek* (Sofia, 1972) [in English as *The Balkan City, 1400–1900*, Seattle, WA/London, 1983]; idem and A. Velkov, *Situation démographique de la Péninsule balkanique (fin du XVe s.–début du XVIe s.)* (Sofia, 1988); Olga Zirojević, *Tursko vojno uredjenje u Srbiji (1459–1683)* (Belgrade, 1974); Aleksandar Stoianovski, *Gradovite na Makedoniia od kraiot na XIV do XVII vek. Demografski prouchuvania* (Skopje, 1981); Vasiles Demetriades, *Topografia tes Thessalonikes kata ten epoche tes Tourkokratias 1430–1912* (Thessaloniki, 1983).

7. See, for example, Hristo Gandev, *Zarazhdane na kapitalisticheski otnosheniia v chiflishkoto stopanstvo na severozapadna Bulgarija prez XVIII v.* (Sofia, 1962); Hristo Hristov, *Agrarniiat vupros v bulgarskata natsionalna revolutsiia* (Sofia, 1976).

status of south-eastern Europe under Ottoman rule.[8] The subject intermingled with the intense discussion over the issue of peripheralization of backward areas on a global scale. *Dependencia* theories that purported to explain structural underdevelopment flourished in the 1960s and 1970s. Thus, some students of Immanuel Wallerstein, focusing on the dependent incorporation of the Ottoman empire into the world economy, highlighted the lack of feudalism as a significant factor.[9] In this connection, they stressed the non-hereditary character of benefices, the absence of subinfeudation and patrimonial jurisdiction, the state control of craftsmen, as well as the regulation of supply and demand within the framework of a 'command economy'. Such a system was bound to foster an agricultural sector characterized by small peasant holdings.[10]

The research of the last decades reveals a growing awareness on the part of historians of the inherent limitations of the source materials preserved in state archives. These are seen as reflecting the standpoint of the ruling elites, whereas an approach more conducive to fathoming the political potential of pre-modern rural societies would accentuate better the regional perspectives. The first results of research in this direction are encouraging: in the field of historical demography the old idea that the Slavic extended family (*zadruga*) was widespread in the Balkans has been challenged.[11] Similarly, the image of an economically modest and politically passive peasantry has been replaced by that of a rural population that was fully conscious of the resources at its disposal, often demanding justice successfully against iniquities.[12] Also the relationships

8. Bruce McGowan, *Economic Life in Ottoman Europe. Taxation, Trade and the Struggle for Land, 1600–1800* (Cambridge/Paris, 1981); idem, 'The study of land and agriculture in the Ottoman provinces within the context of an expanding world economy in the 17th and 18th centuries', *International Journal of Turkish Studies*, 2:1 (1981), pp. 57–63; Halil İnalcık, 'The emergence of big farms, *çiftliks*: state, landlords and tenants', in J.-L. Bacqué-Grammont and P. Dumont (eds), *Contributions à l'histoire économique et sociale de l'Empire ottoman* (Louvain, 1983), pp. 105–26; Gilles Veinstein, 'On the *çiftlik* debate', in Çağlar Keyder and Faruk Tabak (eds), *Landholding and Commercial Agriculture in the Middle East* (Albany, NY, 1991) pp. 35–53.

9. Huri İslamoğlu and Çağlar Keyder, 'Agenda for Ottoman history', *Review. A Journal of the Fernand Braudel Center for the Study of Economics, Historical Systems and Civilisations*, 1: 1 (1977), pp. 31–55; Immanuel Wallerstein and Reşat Kasaba, 'Incorporation into the world-economy: change in the structure of the Ottoman empire, 1750–1839', in J. L. Bacqué-Grammont and P. Dumont (eds.), *Economie et société dans l'Empire ottoman* (Paris, 1983), pp. 335–54; Huri İslamoğlu-İnan (ed.), *Ottoman Empire and the World Economy* (Cambridge/New York, 1987); Reşat Kasaba, *The Ottoman Empire and the World Economy – The Nineteenth Century* (Albany, NY, 1988).

10. Huri İslamoğlu-İnan, 'Les paysans, le marché et l'état en Anatolie au XVIe siècle', *Annales. ESC* (1988), 1025–43. For a critique of this position see Halil Berktay, 'The feudalism debate: the Turkish end – is 'tax-vs.-rent' necessarily the product and sign of modal difference?', *Journal of Peasant Studies* (1987), pp. 291–333, and Berktay and Faroqhi, *New Approaches to State and Peasant in Ottoman History*. On the 'command economy' in the Ottoman Balkans see John R. Lampe and Marvin R. Jackson, *Balkan Economic History, 1550–1950. From Imperial Borderlands to Developing Nations* (Bloomington, IN, 1982).

11. Maria N. Todorova, 'Myth-making in European family history: the zadruga revisited', *East European Politics and Societies*, 4: 1 (Winter 1990), pp. 30–76; eadem, *Balkan Family Structure and the European Pattern. Demographic Developments in Ottoman Bulgaria* (Washington DC, 1993).

12. Hans Georg Majer et al. (eds), *Das osmanische 'Registerbuch der Beschwerden' (Şikâyet defteri) vom Jahre 1675. Österreichische Nationalbibliothek Cod. mixt. 683*, vol. I (Vienna, 1984); Suraiya Faroqhi, 'Political initiatives "from the bottom up" in the sixteenth- and seventeenth-century Ottoman empire: some evidence for their existence', in Hans Georg Majer (ed.), *Osmanistische Studien zur Wirtschafts- und Sozialgeschichte. In memoriam Vančo Boškov* (Wiesbaden, 1986), pp. 24–33; Karen Barkey, 'The use of court records in the reconstruction of village networks: a comparative perspective', *International Journal of Comparative Sociology*, 32 (1991), pp. 699–715; Amy Singer, *Palestinian Peasants and Ottoman Officials. Rural Administration around Sixteenth-Century Jerusalem* (Cambridge, 1994).

between the Christian subjects and the Muslim rulers appear in a new light, when personal records left by subjects are consulted instead of the often superficial accounts by European travellers.[13] Yet, despite such progress, it can be maintained that the social history of the Ottoman peasantries is still in its rudiments.

The present essay draws upon research representing various traditions. It starts from three general assumptions: (i) that there was a remarkable degree of continuity from pre-Ottoman to Ottoman rule in respect of landholding regulations, services and taxes; (ii) that the legal status and the real situation of the peasantry showed significant regional dissimilarities and remained at the same time open to continuous change – for better or worse – during the period covered in this study; (iii) that despite all vicissitudes the empire left to its successor states more or less independent peasantries – a fact that formed a dominant trait of the emerging national economies well into the twentieth century.

The area under consideration stretches from the Danube Basin to the Fertile Crescent, encompassing the core provinces of the empire – the Balkan Peninsula, the western and central parts of Anatolia – and sometimes by way of comparison parts of historical Syria. The periodization differentiates between the following more or less distinct phases: (i) agriculture and settlement in the late medieval period; (ii) peasantries in an expanding empire of the fifteenth and sixteenth centuries; (iii) taxfarmers, brigands and sharecroppers: rural life in the grip of provincial elites in the seventeenth and eighteenth centuries; (iv) peasantries and agriculture at the end of the Ottoman *ancien régime*: the first half of the nineteenth century.

AGRICULTURE AND SETTLEMENT IN THE LATE MEDIEVAL PERIOD

Ottoman territories in the Balkans and Asia Minor have a characteristic in common: they are predominantly mountainous or hilly, which somehow limits the amount of land available for agriculture. As one historian has rightly observed, Bosnia and Hercegovina alone would cover, if 'ironed out', a surface as large as Europe.[14] The Dinaric range stretching from Slovenia over Bosnia-Hercegovina to Montenegro and Albania is a karstic massif quite hostile to human settlement. Montenegro, the 'Black Mountain', where the Dinaric Alps reach their climax, is perhaps the agriculturally poorest region of the whole peninsula. The neighbouring territory to the east, the so-called Sandžak, and the woodlands (Šumadija) extending further north towards Belgrade, can hardly be counted as good farming lands either. The mountainous country continues

13. Johannes Strauss, 'Ottoman rule experienced and remembered. Remarks on some local Greek chronicles of the *Turkokratia*', in F. Adanır and S. Faroqhi (eds), *Ottoman Empire in Historiographic Discussion* (forthcoming).
14. John V. A. Fine Jr, *The Early Medieval Balkans. A Critical Survey from the 6th to the Late 12th Century* (Ann Arbor, MI, 1983), p. 1.

southwards into Greece, forming the system of the Pindos as a divide between Epiros and Thessaly. A little east of the Vardar and Morava valleys, which form a north–south axis through Macedonia connecting the Pannonian basin with the Aegean, the southerly extensions of the Transylvanian Alps command the scene: the Balkan range proper (Stari Planina) separates Danubian Bulgaria from Thrace, which in turn is cut off from the Aegean by the considerable heights of the Rhodopes. On the other side of the Straits, Asia Minor with its average altitude of more than 1,130 metres is a rugged land block as impressive as the Balkan Peninsula.

Although they are peninsulas surrounded by water on three sides, both the Balkans and Anatolia are effectively shielded from maritime influences, a fact that also has negative consequences for agriculture in the flatlands. Thus the Anatolian interior forms a zone of continental climate with typically hot and dry summers and extremely cold and rather dry winters, despite the almost subtropical location of the country at latitudes similar to those of Italy between Rome and Sicily.[15] The central plateau around Konya, renowned as the granary of modern Turkey, receives less than 300 mm of rainfall annually, a value considered as the minimum for cereal cultivation in the Near East.[16] A similarly pronounced continental climate is the distinctive feature also of the Balkan interior where meagre annual rainfall causes serious droughts.[17] Thessaly, for example, cut off from western winds by the surrounding mountains, has a steppe character with low rainfalls 'characterized by marked irregularity from one year to another'.[18] The plains of Salonika, Seres and Skopje, too, are locations with low amounts of rainfall; thus the area of Macedonia used productively at the beginning of the twentieth century – including also pasturelands – amounted to barely 20 per cent of the total.[19]

Viewed from the angle of historical geography, however, the plains seem to have presented actually more problems than the hills and mountains, as Fernand Braudel was to observe in respect of the Mediterranean basin of the sixteenth century. He drew attention to three basic problems in the plains: frequent flooding, malaria, and the lack of fresh water. A solution to these problems was a prerequisite for productive cultivation everywhere.[20] In the Balkans and Anatolia, the alluvial plains were especially notorious. Formed as late as the Roman period, by the sixth century they were already getting rapidly swampy – a process that was partly due to a dramatic decrease in population and partly to the fact that the newcomers were of a different cultural background and thus unfamiliar with the traditional methods of drainage and irrigation.[21] As a result, even the

---

15. Wolf-Dieter Hütteroth, *Türkei* (*Wissenschaftliche Länderkunden*, 21) (Darmstadt, 1982) pp. 20f.

16. Ibid., p. 111.

17. Lampe and Jackson, *Balkan Economic History*, p. 4.

18. Richard I. Lawless, 'The economy and landscapes of Thessaly during Ottoman rule', in Francis W. Carter (ed.), *An Historical Geography of the Balkans* (London, 1977), pp. 505–6.

19. *Makedoniia kako prirodna i ekonomska tselina*, ed. Institut za natsionalna istoriia (Skopje, 1978), pp. 60, 108, 172. Cf. also Jacques Ancel, *La Macédoine. Son évolution contemporaine* (Paris, 1930), p. 53.

20. Braudel, *The Mediterranean and the Mediterranean World*, pp. 60–85.

21. J. L. Bintliff, 'New approaches to human geography. Prehistoric Greece: a case study', in Carter, *An Historical Geography of the Balkans*, p. 71.

highland basins began to deteriorate into large tracts of marshes, and ever more peasants saw themselves confronted with the choice of either perishing on these unhealthy, although fertile flatlands or trying to survive on healthy, but obviously sterile mountains.[22] Consequently, livestock husbandry became increasingly important, necessitating a semi-nomadic way of life at the expense of field-crops production, a development that was well under way before Turcoman nomads appeared in the eastern marks of the Byzantine empire.

It is generally accepted that the Turkification of Asia Minor was, at least during its earlier phases, also a process of nomadization of rural life.[23] Nomadism seems, however, at first to have been restricted to the Anatolian plateau itself, the disease-ridden coastal plains being avoided also by the newcomers.[24] An interesting aspect of this development was the close relationship – sometimes outright solidarity – between the semi-nomadic indigenous populations and the Turcomans.[25] But soon a sedentarization process set in; the nomads' winter quarters in protected sites of the plateau grew into new villages, and during the fourteenth and fifteenth centuries, when the settled agricultural population emerged as the dominant factor in the western half of Asia Minor, a 'peasant-nomad dichotomy began to crystallize'.[26] The rise of the Ottoman dynasty in the early fourteenth century took place within such a framework. Originally perhaps a nomadic tribe, the Ottomans displayed almost from the start a keen interest in the sedentarization of the nomads, actively supporting the crop-producing peasantry against pastoral groups.[27] But at the same time the Ottomans remained concerned with ensuring the precarious loyalty of tribal elements, the total alienation of which would not have been conducive to the interests of an expanding state.

This ambivalence was an important trait of early Ottoman rule in the Balkans, too, where the presence of strong nomadic groups not least as a military factor had to be reckoned with. Under the pressure of Slavic invasions since the sixth century, indigenous Romanized populations had moved into less accessible areas where they were able to preserve – or to develop – tribal organizations

22. Johannes Koder, *Der Lebensraum der Byzantiner. Historisch-geographischer Abriß ihres mittelalterlichen Staates im östlichen Mittelmeerraum* (Darmstadt, 1984), pp. 55–6. Jacques Ancel commented on the situation of Macedonian peasants at the beginning of the twentieth century as follows: 'là où il est fertile, le pays est malsain, et il est sain aux endroits stériles'. *La Macédoine*, p. 71.

23. Speros Vryonis Jr, *The Decline of Medieval Hellenism in Asia Minor and the Process of Islamization from the Eleventh through the Fifteenth Century* (Berkeley/Los Angeles/London, 1971), passim.

24. Xavier de Planhol, 'Geography, politics and nomadism in Anatolia', *International Social Science Journal*, 11 (1959), p. 526.

25. Keith Hopwood, 'Peoples, territories, and states: the formation of the Beğliks of pre-Ottoman Turkey', in Caesar E. Farah (ed.), *Decision Making in the Ottoman Empire* (Kirksville, MO, 1993), p. 131. Cf. also Anthony Bryer, 'Greeks and Türkmens. The Pontic exception', *Dumbarton Oaks Papers*, 29 (1975), pp. 113–49.

26. De Planhol, 'Peoples, territories, and states', p. 526. Compare also Keith R. Hopwood, 'Nomads or bandits? The pastoralist/sedentarist interface in Anatolia', in Anthony Bryer and Michael Ursinus (eds), *Manzikert to Lepanto. The Byzantine World and the Turks 1071–1571. Papers Given at the Nineteenth Spring Symposium of Byzantine Studies, Birmingham, March 1985* (Amsterdam, 1991).

27. See Rudi Paul Lindner, *Nomads and Ottomans in Medieval Anatolia* (Bloomington, IN, 1983), passim. The term tribe is to be understood rather in its political meaning, that is, not so much in the sense of a group the identity of which is based primarily on a shared lineage. See idem, 'What was a nomadic tribe?', *Comparative Studies in Society and History*, 24 (1982), pp. 689–711.

and cultures. The extant sources refer to these groups as 'Vlach'.[28] The question of their ethnic origins remains a disputed issue.[29] What deserves attention
in our context is that the term 'Vlach' acquired in time a socio-professional
connotation as well. It designated all those groups which had a distinct legal
status on the basis of *ius valachicum* and differed from the peasant society at
large by their practice of transhumance, that is, the seasonal movement of
livestock and herders between mountain and lowland pastures.[30] In time about
a dozen regions came to be referred to as 'Valachia', such as an Old Valachia
(Stari Vlach) between Montenegro and Serbia, an Upper Valachia in Epiros, a
Magna Valachia or Valachia Maior in Thessaly, a Valachia Minor in Aetolia
and Acarnania, a Valachia north of the Balkan range (Danubian Bulgaria), a
Rhodope Valachia, a White Valachia (modern Wallachia in Romania), a Black
Valachia (Moldavia), another Valachia Minor (Oltenia) and so on.[31] In cooperation with other – mostly Turkic – nomadic peoples, such as the Cumans, the
Pechenegs, or the Tatars, the Vlach groups played an increasingly important
role in the military and political life of the peninsula. Thus it has been argued
that the establishment of the Second Bulgarian Tsardom (1187–1393) was
actually a product of Vlacho-Cuman cooperation.[32]

Another pastoral group as important as the Vlachs was the Albanians, who
apppear in the sources – as nomads and mercenaries – from the middle of the
eleventh century.[33] At the beginning of the fourteenth century, Albanian clans
can be seen emigrating into Thessaly.[34] In 1382 the King of Aragon allowed
them to settle in Attica, and after 1394 they began to arrive in the territory of
the Despotate of Mistra.[35] Since the beginning of the fifteenth century, Venetian
authorities were eager to attract Albanians as settlers for their island colony of

---

28. For an overview see Petre Ş. Năsturel, 'Vlacho-Balcanica', *Byzantinisch-Neugriechische Jahrbücher*, 22 (1977–84), pp. 221–48.

29. For a discussion of historiographic controversies see Tom J. Winnifrith, *The Vlachs: The History of a Balkan People* (London, 1987), pp. 41–52, and idem, 'The Vlachs of the Balkans: a rural minority which never achieved ethnic identity', in David Howell (ed.), *Roots of Rural Ethnic Mobilisation* (Comparative Studies on Governments and Non-Dominant Ethnic Groups in Europe 1850–1940, vol. 7) (Aldershot/New York, 1993), pp. 277–303.

30. M. Gyóni, 'La transhumance des Vlaques balkaniques au Moyen Age', *Byzantinoslavica*, 12 (1951), pp. 29–42; Vasil Marinov, 'Ethnographische Charakteristik der Transhumanz in den Ländern der Balkanhalb-insel', in Association Internationale des Etudes Sud-Est Européennes, *Actes du premier congrès international des études balkaniques et sud-est européennes*, vol. VII (Sofia, 1971), pp. 535–48; Nicolae Dunăre, 'Typologie des traditionellen Hirtenlebens im karpato-balkanischen Raum', *Zeitschrift für Balkanologie*, 11: 2 (1975), pp. 5–39.

31. Traian Stoianovich, *Balkan Worlds. The First and Last Europe* (Armonk, NY/London, 1994), p. 127.

32. This gave rise to a controversial discussion. See among others Petur Mutafchiev, 'Proizchodut na Asenovtsi', *Makedonski pregled*, 4: 4 (1928), pp. 1–42; V. N. Zlatarski, 'Potekloto na Petra i Aseniia, vodatsite na vustanieto v 1185 g., *Spisanie na BAN*, 45 (1933), pp. 8–48; Robert L. Wolff, 'The "second Bulgarian empire". Its origin and history to 1204', *Speculum*, 24 (1949), pp. 167–206; Dimitur Angelov, 'Potekloto na Asenevtsi i etnicheskiiat charakter na osnovanata ot tiach durzhava', *Istoricheski Pregled*, 3 (1947), pp. 374–83; Plamen Pavlov, 'Za roliata na Kumanite v bulgarskata voenna istoriia (1186–1241 g.)', *Voennoistoricheski Sbornik*, 6 (1990), pp. 14–23.

33. Georg Stadtmüller, *Forschungen zur albanischen Frühgeschichte*, 2nd edn (Wiesbaden, 2nd edn, 1966), pp. 160–73. Compare also Alain Ducellier, 'Les Albanais du XIe au XIIIe siècle: nomades ou sedentaires?', *Byzantinische Forschungen*, 7 (1979), pp. 23–36.

34. Johannes Koder and Friedrich Hild, *Hellas und Thessalia* (Vienna, 1976), p. 74.

35. Dionysios A. Zakythinos, *Le Despotat grec de Morée*, vol. II: *Vie et institutions* (Athens, 1953), pp. 30–2.

Euboea which was experiencing a catastrophic population decrease.[36] Indeed, the Albanian 'expansion' had to do with a demographic decline that at that time was felt practically everywhere.[37] The feudal lords who needed labour, but who appreciated also the military talents of the newcomers, were prepared to grant them a status comparable to that of the Vlachs.[38] But just like the Vlachs, the Albanian herders were seldom welcome to the indigenous populations. It seems that the uncontrolled seasonal wanderings of the transhumant groups exacerbated further the process of desertion in the flatlands of the Balkan Peninsula.[39]

These developments were accompanied by a deterioration of the social status of the peasantry as well. The evolution of the *pronoia* since the twelfth century from a strictly service-oriented system of military fiefs to a system of hereditary estates in the hands of the monasteries, the Church and the court aristocracy – all furnished with wide-ranging immunities – had rendered the cultivators, the *paroikoi*, more and more dependent peasants attached to the soil.[40] Apart from paying taxes, they were the labour force which worked on the domains of the (mostly monastic) landlords. In Serbia, for instance, where the same system was adopted, Stefan Dušan's famous Land Code burdened the peasants, in addition to the annual payment of a fixed sum called the 'tsar's *perper*', with labour services of two days per week. Moreover, they had to 'mow senna' one day per annum and do another day's work in vineyards, not to mention the delivery of one-tenth of the harvest and various other local dues and services.[41] It has been calculated that approximately one-third of the working capacity of the peasant families and their animals was claimed by the feudal lords.[42] Under such pressures, peasant holdings could not prosper, many people got dispersed, whole villages became deserted, and the countryside began to offer a 'bleak picture of decline'.[43]

The Ottoman conquest since the middle of the fourteenth century – the first Ottoman base on the European side of the Dardanelles was established in 1354 – was spearheaded by *akıncı* bands who raided the frontier zones in the

36. Alfred Philippson, *Die griechischen Landschaften*, vol. I, pt 2: *Das östliche Mittelgriechenland und die Insel Euboea, nebst einem Anhang: Beiträge zur historischen Landeskunde des östlichen Mittelgriechenlands und Euboeas*, von Ernst Kirsten (Frankfurt am Main, 1951), p. 635; Johannes Koder, *Negroponte. Untersuchungen zur Topographie und Siedlungsgeschichte der Insel Euboia während der Zeit der Venezianerherrschaft* (Vienna, 1973), p. 172.

37. Angelika E. Laiou-Thomadakis, *Peasant Society in the Late Byzantine Empire. A Social and Demographic Study* (Princeton, NJ, 1977), pp. 223–66.

38. Tax obligations of the Albanians in the Peloponnese were comparable to those of the Vlachs. See Zakythinos, *Le Despotat*, II, pp. 33f.

39. See, for example, Božidar Ferjančić, *Tesalija u XIII i XIV veku* (Belgrade, 1974), pp. 198–205.

40. Peter Charanis, 'The monastic properties and the state in the Byzantine empire', *Dumbarton Oaks Papers*, 4 (1948), pp. 53–118; Georgije Ostrogorski, *Pronija. Prilog istoriji feudalizma u Vizantiji i u južnoslovenskim zemljama* (Belgrade, 1951), pp. 61–105, 127–50; Donald M. Nicol, *The Last Centuries of Byzantium 1261–1453* (London, 1972), passim.

41. See Nikola Radojčić (ed.), *Zakonik Cara Stefana Dušana 1349 i 1354* (Belgrade, 1960), p. 56.

42. Miloš Blagojević, *Zemljoradnje u srednovekovnoj Srbiji* (Belgrade, 1973), ch. 5, pp. 337–412. Compare also Michael L. Boyd, 'The evolution of agrarian institutions: the case of medieval and Ottoman Serbia', *Explorations in Economic History*, 28 (1991), pp. 36–53.

43. Laiou-Thomadakis, *Peasant Society*, pp. 221–2.

fashion of modern 'shock-troops'. These raids caused much new devastation in the countryside, especially along the main routes of invasion through the plains of Thrace, Macedonia and Thessaly. But in the light of the above analysis, it would hardly be warranted to ascribe the depopulation of these plains to the Ottoman conquest alone, as has been done sometimes.[44] Similarly, the line of interpretation which associates the Ottoman advance in the Balkans with *gaza*, the Islamic Holy War, is questionable.[45] As opponents of this thesis have convincingly pointed out, early Ottoman rulers pursued 'a pragmatic policy of political and military aggrandizement' rather than a Holy War.[46] More significant in this connection is the fact that many *akıncı* were of Turcoman origin and that the Ottoman advance was actually accompanied by an influx of nomads into the lowlands of Rumelia (the Ottoman term for the Balkans). The newcomers, who sometimes were deported with the object either of getting rid of an unruly element from Anatolia or of furthering the repopulation of deserted areas, were organized in the fifteenth century as *yürük*, a semi-military category resembling that of the Vlach under *ius valachicum*.[47] Thus it can be presumed that Turcomans in the Balkans, as stock raisers practising transhumance, shared certain values and interests with similar social groups, such as the Vlachs and Albanians. At any rate, it is known that some Vlachs of Thessaly were incorporated into the Ottoman military system quite early and that Albanians in the Peloponnese cooperated with the Ottomans in the fifteenth century.[48] Under these conditions not only could the military conquest of the Balkans be carried on successfully, but also some strategically important regions of the peninsula, such as Thrace, north-eastern Bulgaria, and the lowlands of Macedonia and Thessaly, acquired a predominantly Turkish character.[49]

44. See, for example, A. E. Vacalopoulos, 'La retraite des populations grecques vers des régions éloignées et montagneuses pendant la domination turque', *Balkan Studies*, 4 (1963), pp. 265–76, or Christo Gandev, *Bulgarskata narodnost prez XV vek. Demografsko i etnografsko izsledvane* (Sofia, 1972), passim.

45. This thesis, which was propounded most effectively by Paul Wittek, *The Rise of the Ottoman Empire* (London, 1938), still carries great authority as evidenced by the work of the leading Ottomanist, Halil İnalcık, 'The Ottoman state: economy and society, 1300–1600', in idem and Donald Quataert (eds), *An Economic and Social History of the Ottoman Empire 1300–1914* (Cambridge, 1994), pp. 9–409, here pp. 11ff.

46. Ronald C. Jennings, 'Some thoughts on the gazi-thesis', *Wiener Zeitschrift zur Kunde des Morgenlandes*, 76 (1986), p. 158. See further Rudi Paul Lindner, 'Stimulus and justification in early Ottoman history', *Greek Orthodox Theological Review*, 27 (1982), pp. 207–24; Colin Imber, 'Ideals and legitimation in early Ottoman history', in Metin Kunt and Christine Woodhead (eds), *Süleyman the Magnificent and His Age. The Ottoman Empire in the Early Modern World* (London/New York, 1995), pp. 138–53.

47. Ömer Lûtfi Barkan, 'Osmanlı İmparatorluğunda bir iskân ve kolonizasyon metodu olarak sürgünler', *İktisat Fakültesi Mecmuası*, 11 (1949–50), pp. 524–69, and 13 (1953–54), pp. 209–37; Halil İnalcık, 'Ottoman methods of conquest', *Studia Islamica*, 2 (1954), pp. 122–5; M. Tayyib Gökbilgin, *Rumeli'de Yürükler, Tatarlar ve Evlâd-ı Fâtihan* (Istanbul, 1957), pp. 9–53.

48. Nicoară Beldiceanu, 'Les Roumains à la bataille d'Ankara', *Südost-Forschungen*, 14 (1955), pp. 441–50; Zakythinos, *Le Despotat*, II, p. 34.

49. İlhan Şahin, Feridun M. Emecen and Yusuf Halaçoğlu, 'Turkish settlements in Rumelia (Bulgaria) in the 15th and 16th centuries: town and village population', in Kemal H. Karpat (ed.), *The Turks of Bulgaria: The History, Culture and Political Fate of a Minority* (Istanbul, 1990), pp. 23–40; Machiel Kiel, 'Anatolia transplanted? Patterns of demographic, religious and ethnic changes in the district of Tozluk (N.E. Bulgaria) 1479–1873', *Anatolia*, 17 (1991), pp. 1–29; idem, 'La diffusion de l'Islam dans les campagnes bulgares à l'époque ottomane (XVe–XIXe siècles). Colonisation et conversion', in Daniel Panzac (ed.), *Les Balkans à l'époque ottomane (Revue du Monde Musulman et de la Méditerranée*, 66 (1992/4)), pp. 39–53.

PEASANTRIES IN AN EXPANDING EMPIRE: THE FIFTEENTH AND SIXTEENTH CENTURIES

Status and Taxation

Our knowledge of rural life in the early Ottoman period is based chiefly on the codes of regulations issued for individual provinces (*liva kanunnameleri*), records of taxation surveys (*tapu tahrir defterleri*) and registers of kadi courts (*kadi sicilleri*). The provincial *kanunnames* were compiled with the object of itemizing tax rates, delineating the modes of tax collection by *timar* (fief) holders, stipulating land tenure, transfer and inheritance, and fixing the various franchises and liabilities.[50] More often than not, a conquered territory was left – for a transitional period varying from a couple of years to decades – in the hands of the indigenous lords who might by some feudal arrangement be loosely bound to the Ottoman ruler. But gradually the *timar* system was introduced in most places, meaning direct subjection to central authority, a development that was accompanied by the registration of property, revenue and population of the respective regions.[51] In the process, all arable land including the domains of the former lords and some monastic property was declared *miri (dominium eminens)*, the revenues of which were awarded as grants in lieu of salary or other recompense to members of the Ottoman ruling class, military personnel, administrators, judges and members of the ruling house.[52] Depending on the amount of annual income, these grants were divided into *has*, *zeamet* and *timar*. Holders of a *has*, the largest revenue grant under the *timar* system, were mostly provincial governors, i.e. *beylerbeys* and *sancakbeys*, and, of course, the ruler and the members of his household. Holders of a *zeamet*, a more modest revenue grant, were usually the beys of smaller sanjaks or similar officers of the standing army. Incumbent

---

50. For a selection of *kanunname*s concerning agriculture see Ömer Lûtfi Barkan, *XV ve XVI'ncı asırlarda Osmanlı İmparatorluğunda ziraî ekonominin hukukî ve malî esasları*, I: *Kanunlar* (Istanbul, 1943). A more comprehensive edition is that by Ahmed Akgündüz, *Osmanlı kanunnâmeleri ve hukukî tahlilleri*, vols 1–9 (Istanbul, 1990–96). See also Heath W. Lowry, 'The Ottoman liva kanunnames contained in the defter-i hakani', *Osmanlı Araştırmaları*, 2 (1981), pp. 43–74. On the relationship between the secular *kanun* and the religious *shari'a* see Halil İnalcık, 'Suleiman the Lawgiver and Ottoman law', *Archivum Ottomanicum*, 1 (1969), pp. 105–38, and Richard C. Repp, 'Qānūn and Sharī'a in the Ottoman context', in Aziz Al-Azmeh (ed.), *Islamic Law: Social and Historical Contexts* (London, 1988), pp. 124–45.

51. Halil İnalcık, 'Ottoman methods of conquest', *Studia Islamica*, 2 (1954), pp. 103–29; Ömer Lûtfi Barkan, 'Research on the Ottoman fiscal surveys', in Michael A. Cook (ed.), *Studies in the Economic History of the Middle East* (London, 1970), pp. 163–71; Bistra Cvetkova, 'Early Ottoman *tahrir defters* as a source for studies on the history of Bulgaria and the Balkans', *Archivum Ottomanicum*, 8 (1983), pp. 133–214; Irène Beldiceanu-Steinherr and Nicoară Beldiceanu, 'Règlement ottoman concernant le recensement (première moitié du XVIe siècle)', *Südost-Forschungen*, 37 (1978), pp. 1–40, and idem, 'Ottoman fiscal surveys as a source for social and economic history', in Huri İslamoğlu-İnan, *State and Peasant in the Ottoman Empire: Agrarian Power and Regional Economic Development in Ottoman Anatolia during the Sixteenth Century* (Leiden, 1994), ch. 2, pp. 22–55. For critical assessments as regards the value of these documents as historical sources see Gyula Káldy-Nagy, 'Der Quellenwert der Tahrir Defterleri für die osmanische Wirtschaftsgeschichte', in Majer, *Osmanistische Studien zur Wirtschafts- und Sozialgeschichte*, pp. 76–83; Heath W. Lowry, 'The Ottoman tahrir defterleri as a source for social and economic history: pitfalls and limitations', in idem, *Studies in Defterology. Ottoman Society in the Fifteenth and Sixteenth Centuries* (Istanbul, 1992), pp. 3–18.

52. On the *miri* system see İnalcık, 'The Ottoman state: economy and society', pp. 103–19.

on both categories was to furnish warriors, the exact number of whom was supposed to be proportionate to the size of the revenue. The predominantly military character of the system becomes even more conspicuous when one looks at the holders of the much smaller *timar* fiefs called 'horsemen' (*sipahi*), who partook in military campaigns personally and were expected to live on their holdings in times of peace.

On the basis of an extant budget of the empire from the second decade of the sixteenth century, it has been calculated that 51 per cent of the total revenue was accrued from the sultan's *has*-domains, 12 per cent from the *vakıf* and *mülk* lands, and 37 per cent from the lands granted as fiefs to the military personnel. Of these 37 per cent granted to the military, about 19 per cent were in the possession of provincial governors, i.e. *sancakbeys* and *beylerbeys*, and only about 18 per cent in the hands of the *sipahis*.[53]

Apart from these lands under the control of the military and other servants of the state, there existed private property (*mülk*) and property dedicated in perpetuity whose revenues supported a religous or charitable purpose (*vakıf*). In addition to large estates owned by the conquering leaders of the fourteenth century, private estates could emerge on account of the rulers' 'generosity', as when they transferred property to their relatives, friends and slaves as a kind of special gift. Such property was then usually converted into a religious foundation and was thereby excluded from the *timar* system.[54] The *mülk* and *vakıf* property, as well as most of the *has*-domains, were usually worked as fiscal units (*mukataa*) in accordance with the system of tax farming (*iltizam*).[55] A *mukataa* was usually granted for a period varying from one to twelve years. The tax-farmer (*mültezim*) appeared in this connection as a risk taker, an entrepreneur, who as the highest bidder in a public auction was delegated the right to collect taxes. The state (or private deed holders) kept the right to give notice at any time on such tax-farming contracts and to grant the revenue source to another bidder, should that person undertake to collect more taxes.[56]

Under these conditions, a feudal aristocracy, comparable to that in Europe, could not establish itself in the Ottoman empire. The socio-political unrest which shook up Anatolia and the Balkans for two decades following the Ottoman defeat against Timur in 1402, and in which strong feudal interests

53. Ömer Lûfi Barkan, 'H. 933–934 (M. 1527–1528) mali yılına ait bir bütçe örneği', *İktisat Fakültesi Mecmuası*, 15 (1953), pp. 251–329, and Yavuz Cezar, *Osmanlı maliyesinde bunalım ve değişim dönemi* (Istanbul 1986), pp. 36–40.

54. Ömer Lûtfi Barkan, 'Türk-İslam hukuku tatbikatının Osmanlı İmparatorluğu'nda aldığı şekiller: Mülk topraklar ve sultanların temlik hakkı', *Hukuk Fakültesi Mecmuası*, 7 (1941), pp. 157–76; idem, 'Osmanlı İmparatorluğunda bir iskân ve kolonizasyon metodu olarak vakıflar ve temlikler', *Vakıflar Dergisi*, 2 (1942), pp. 279–386.

55. M. Tayyib Gökbilgin, *XV–XVI. asırlarda Edirne ve Paşa livası. Vakıflar – mülkler -mukataalar* (Istanbul, 1952). On the institution of *iltizam* see also Bistra A. Cvetkova, 'Recherches sur le système d'affermage (*iltizam*) dans l'Empire ottoman au cours du XVIe–XVIIe s. par rapport aux contrées bulgares', *Rocznik orientalistyczny*, 27: 2 (1964), pp. 111–32.

56. Linda T. Darling, *Revenue-Raising and Legitimacy. Tax Collection and Finance Administration in the Ottoman Empire 1560–1660* (Leiden/New York/Cologne, 1996), pp. 123ff.; Murat Çizakça, *A Comparative Evolution of Business Partnerships: The Islamic World and Europe, with Specific Reference to the Ottoman Archives* (Leiden/New York/Cologne, 1996), pp. 140f.

joined occasionally with nomadic, anti-feudal forces in popular uprisings against the state, culminated in a victory of the central government.[57] Sultan Mehmed II (1451–81), in particular, aimed at consolidating the power of the ruling family as opposed to other established groups.[58] It was during his rule that the palace bureaucracy actually rose to power, its beginnings dating back to the rule of Murad I (1359–89). At that time the state had begun to train selected Christian children and prisoners of war for bureaucratic service in the palace and to create a new army (*yeni çeri,* Janissaries) under the direct command of the sultan.[59] Parallel to this development, many renegades were appointed to high offices in the government. Naturally this uprooted elite was absolutely loyal to the sultan. As 'slaves of the Porte' (*kapıkule*) they were in their own interest supporters of centralism.

These arrangements did not mean that pre-Ottoman social structures were totally destroyed to be substituted by a novel order. On the contrary, there is unanimity of opinion that Ottoman rule displayed a remarkable degree of flexibility and pragmatism in dealing with political factors in the countryside. In the Balkans, for instance, some members of the former elite were granted *timar* fiefs of varying sizes, thus becoming affiliated to the ruling military class (*askeri*) of the new empire. (By the middle of the sixteenth century most of these converted to Islam.[60]) In certain parts of Anatolia (e.g. Rum Vilayeti), pre-Ottoman Muslim groups – contrary to the *miri* principle – continued to hold ownership rights to the land under the so-called *malikane-divani* system and could thus lay claim to the agricultural surplus on practically equal terms with the central authority well into the sixteenteenth century.[61] Yet the basic tenet of the new regime was that those who were assigned revenue in form of a *timar* fief, or were entitled to rent on the basis of their property rights, could determine neither the conditions of the actual production processes nor the amount of their rents themselves.[62] Significantly, they did not enjoy personal

57. The revolt of Sheikh Bedreddin (1416) has been characterized as 'perhaps the most significant, albeit failed, revolutionary movement in Ottoman history'. See Cemal Kafadar, *Between Two Worlds. The Construction of the Ottoman State* (Berkeley/Los Angeles/London, 1995), p. 143. Cf. further Nedim Filipović, *Prints Musa i Sheih Bedreddin* (Sarajevo, 1971), and Ernst Werner, *Die Geburt einer Großmacht: Die Osmanen (1300–1401). Ein Beitrag zur Genesis des türkischen Feudalismus,* 4th edn (Berlin 1985), pp. 217–33.

58. See Bistra A. Cvetkova, 'Sur certaines réformes du régime foncier au temps de Mehmet II', *Journal of Economic and Social History of the Orient,* 6 (1963), pp. 104–20.

59. Cf. Speros Vryonis, Jr, 'Seljuk gulams and Ottoman devshirmes', *Der Islam,* 41 (1965), pp. 224–52; Vassilis Demetriades, 'Some thoughts on the origins of the *devşirme*', in Elizabeth Zachariadou (ed.), *The Ottoman Emirate (1300–1389)* (Rethymnon, 1993), pp. 23–34.

60. The interesting subject of a Christian fief-holding cavalry in a Muslim state has been discussed by several historians. See Halil İnalcık, 'Timariotes chrétiens en Albanie au XVe siècle d'après un registre de timar ottoman', *Mitteilungen des Österreichischen Staatsarchivs,* 4 (1951), pp. 118–38; idem, 'Stefan Duşan'dan Osmanlı İmparatorluğuna. XV. asırda Rumeli'de hıristiyan sipahiler ve menşeleri', in *Fuad Köprülü Armağanı* (Istanbul, 1953), repr. in idem, *Osmanlı İmparatorluğu. Toplum ve Ekonomi* (Istanbul, 1993), pp. 67–108; Bistra Cvetkova, 'Novye dannye o hristianakh-spahiiakh na Balkanskom poluostrove v period turetskogo gospodstva', *Vizantiiski vremennik,* 13 (1958), pp. 184–97; Aleksandar Stojanovski, 'Kon prashanieto za hristiianite-spahii vo Makedoniia', *Glasnik na Instituta za natsionalna istoriia* 4: 1/2 (1960), pp. 304–16; Nicoară Beldiceanu, 'Timariotes chrétiens en Thessalie (1454/55)', *Südost-Forschungen,* 44 (1985), pp. 45–81.

61. Ömer Lûtfi Barkan, 'Türk-İslam hukuku tatbikatının Osmanlı İmparatorluğunda aldığı şekiller, I: Malikane-divani sistemi', *Türk Hukuk ve İktisat Tarihi Mecmuası,* 1 (1939), pp. 119–85. See also Margaret L. Venzke, 'Aleppo's mālikāne-dīvānī system', *Journal of the American Oriental Society,* 106 (1986), pp. 451–69.

62. İslamoğlu-İnan, *State and Peasant in the Ottoman Empire,* pp. 68f.

jurisdiction over the peasants working the land either, every subject in the realm being principally equal before the *kadi* who was alone entrusted with dispensing justice according to both Sultanic and Islamic law.[63]

In this framework, the peasants constituted the most important segment of the taxpaying 'subjects' (*reaya*, literally 'flock'), in contradistinction to the tax-free class of the *askeri*. The *kanunnames* and other sources make it clear that the peasants disposed over buildings (houses, shops, sheds, etc.), vineyards and orchards as freehold property (*mülk*) with the corresponding rights of free usage, alienation and bequest.[64] But the peasants possessed their arable plots, pastures or meadows, which fell under the category of *miri*, in the form of a perpetual lease (*tapu*). The *tapu* document, while granting the rights of usufruct in return for the payment of a sum called *resm-i tapu*, implied at the same time a certain degree of subjugation and dependency.[65] On the one hand, the peasant was entitled to organize production independently. He even could transfer the usufruct of his land to another peasant, bequeath it to his son, and, where he did not have a male successor, his wife, daughter and brother had the right of pre-emption. On the other hand, the *tapu* contract burdened the peasant not only with rendering tithes from produce in kind but also with certain personal obligations towards the supreme owner of the land (state) or the person (*timariot* or tax-farmer) representing it. First of all, the peasant was obliged to cultivate his farm (*reaya çiftlik*) without interruption. Thus, he was not permitted to let the land lie fallow for longer than three years without reason.[66] Secondly, the land could not be sold, donated or mortgaged. Interestingly, it was not even permitted to plant wine or fruit trees or erect buildings on it, since this would amount to modifying its *miri* status.[67] Thirdly, the *reaya* peasants were not allowed to abandon their *çiftliks* freely in order to settle elsewhere, unless the loss in revenue accruing to the *timar* holder was compensated by the payment of a special 'farm breaker's tax' (*çiftbozan resmi*) of eighty *akçe* upwards.[68] Even though this rule does not seem to have been enforced systematically and it was apparently rather easy – especially for unmarried men – to become artisans or traders in towns, it was nevertheless legally feasible to fetch back dispersed peasants

63. For a discussion of the subject in a comparative perspective see Haim Gerber, *State, Society and Law in Islam: Ottoman Law in Comparative Perspective* (Albany, NY, 1994). The dual role of an Ottoman kadi is stressed by İlber Ortaylı, *Hukuk ve idare adamı olarak Osmanlı Devleti'nde kadı* (Ankara, 1994).

64. Barkan, 'Türk-İslam hukuku tatbikatının Osmanlı İmpratorluğu'nda aldığı şekiller, pp. 157–76.

65. For a systematic treatment of the term *tapu* and its meaning in the context of the timar system see İnalcık, 'The Ottoman state: economy and society', pp. 108–14.

66. Cf. Selami Pulaha and Yaşar Yücel (eds), *Le Code (kânûnnâme) de Selim Ier (1512–1520) et certains autres lois de la deuxième moitié du XVIe siècle / I. Selim kânûnnâmesi (1512–1520) ve XVI. yüzyılın ikinci yarısının kimi kanunları* (Ankara, 1988), p. 24.

67. See Colin Imber, 'The status of orchards and fruit-trees in Ottoman law', *Tarih Dergisi*, 12 (1981–82), pp. 763–74.

68. See McGowan, *Economic Life in Ottoman Europe*, p. 53. According to the *liva kanunname* of Vidin, a Muslim peasant giving up agriculture had to pay 6 *akçe* as recompense for the tithes and 20 *akçe* for the *resm-i çift*; if he was a Christian, he had to pay 62 *akçe* for the tithes and 25 *akçe* for ispence. But at any rate he was free to abandon agriculture in order to pursue a different trade. See Bistra A. Cvetkova, 'Actes concernant la vie économique de villes et ports balkaniques aux XVe et XVIe siècles', *Revue d'études islamiques*, 40 (1972), p. 356.

within a period of ten years.[69] That peasant mobility or flight was a widespread phenomenon can be construed from the draconian threats that the sultans sometimes pronounced, as when in 1476 a collector of poll-tax in southern Macedonia was ordered to claim one half of the revenue losses from the *timar* holders themselves and the other half from the peasants remaining on the spot. The tax collector was also instructed to report the names of the fugitives so that the sultan could send an agent to search for them and, once found, deport them to Anatolia and get their sons drafted into the Janissary Corps.[70]

For the peasant's farmstead, the so-called '*reaya çiftlik*', served to a large extent as the basis of the assessment and redistribution of taxes, services and dues. Already the term '*çift*', meaning a pair of oxen yoked to a plow, signals the antiquity of the fiscal institution in question: just like the respective terms in some European languages (e.g. *Joch*, yoke), here too we have to do with a rendition of the Latin *jugum* or the Greek *zeugarion*, in other words, with a remarkable instance of continuity.[71] The size of a *reaya çiftlik* varied, according to the quality of the soil, from 60 to 150 *dönüms*, that is, roughly from six to fifteen hectares.[72] For a full *çiftlik* a Muslim 'household' (*hane*) had to render the 'farm tax' (*resm-i çift*). This being a tax levied strictly on land and not a personal tax, even a member of the ruling elite was not exempted from it if he held land originally cultivated by a peasant family, whereas a peasant who abandoned agriculture would no longer be liable.[73] The amount due differed from region to region, reflecting the different conditions under which the respective area had been integrated into the Ottoman system. In the Balkans in the second half of the fifteenth century, 22 *akçe* was the most common rate (33 *akçe* being equivalent to a Venetian ducat).[74] Later on, rate deviation between regions increased, and especially in Anatolia higher rates were demanded, in the eastern sancaks 50 *akçe* becoming the norm.[75] In Divriği, for example, the *resm-i çift* amounted to 50 *akçe*, whereas in southern

69. Pulaha and Yücel, *Le Code (kânûnnâme) de Selim Ier*, p. 42. But Mustafa Ali writing in 1581 complained that although ever more peasants were flooding into urban centres, the *kanun* which forbade such practice had never been applied. See Andreas Tietze (ed.), *Mustafā 'Alī's Counsel for Sultans of 1581*, pt 1 (Vienna, 1979), p. 57. For a stronger accentuation of the peasant attachment to soil under the *çiftbozan* regulations see Aleksandar Matkovski, *Kreposnishtvoto vo Makedoniia vo vreme na turskoto vladeenye* (Skopje, 1978), passim.

70. Robert Anhegger and Halil İnalcık (eds), *Ḳānūnnāme-i sulṭānī ber mūceb-i 'örf-i 'osmānī. II. Mehmed ve II. Bayezid devirlerine ait yasaḳnāme ve ḳānūnnāmeler* (Ankara, 1956), p. 76; Nicoară Beldiceanu, *Les actes des premiers sultans conservés dans les manuscrits turcs de la Bibl. nationale à Paris*, I: *Actes de Mehmed II et de Bayezid II du ms. fonds turc ancien 39* (Paris, 1960), p. 149; Akgündüz, *Osmanlı kanunnâmeleri ve hukukî tahlilleri*, p. 509.

71. Halil İnalcık uses the term 'çift' unequivocally in the sense of Byzantine 'zeugarion'. See 'The Ottoman state: economy and society', pp. 143ff. Nicoară Beldiceanu and Petre Ş. Năsturel conclude, however, that the term is of Persian origin and was utilized in pre-Ottoman Turcoman states as well. Cf. 'Droits sur la terre de labour dans les Balkans et en Anatolie à l'époque ottomane (XIVe–XVIe siècles)', *Südost-Forschungen*, 50 (1991), pp. 61–118.

72. Barkan, *XV ve XVInci asırlarda Osmanlı İmparatorluğunda ziraî ekonominin hukukî ve malî esasları*, I: *Kanunlar*, index: *çiftlik*. See also Table no. II in Beldiceanu and Năsturel, 'Droits sur la terre de labour', p. 74, and Table I:33 in İnalcık, 'The Ottoman state: economy and society', p. 147.

73. Pulaha and Yücel, *Le Code (kânûnnâme) de Selim Ier*, pp. 21, 46.

74. For the rate of the *akçe* vis-à-vis the Venetian ducat in this period see Beldiceanu and Năsturel, 'Droits sur la terre de labour', p. 82f.

75. Zeki Arıkan, '1518 (924) tarihli Çemişgezek livası kanunnâmesi', *Tarih Dergisi*, 34 (1983/84), pp. 116–18; İsmet Miroğlu, *Kemah Sancağı ve Erzincan Kazası (1520–1566)* (Ankara, 1990), p. 179; Behset Karaca, '1518 (H.924) tarihli tahrir defterine göre Kiğı sancağı', in *Prof. Dr. Bayram Kodaman'a Armağan* (Samsun, 1993),

Syria it was not levied at all.[76] A 'half-çiftlik' (nim-çift), charged with 25 akçe, was the smallest unit for a peasant family, those cultivating less land being considered officially as 'poor'.[77] A married peasant possessing less than half a çiftlik (ekinli bennâk) paid 18 akçe and those with no land at all (caba bennâk) 12 akçe.[78] Especially with a view to the last category, some authors speak of the bennâk as a personal tax levied irrespective of cultivation of land. Indeed, the kanunname for Harput of 1566 designated the bennâk as baş hakkı, a 'poll tax'.[79] A similar lump sum of 6 akçe was levied on unmarried Muslim men if employed outside their family under the title of 'bachelor's tax' (resm-i mücerred).[80]

Non-Muslim married males with a minimum income of 300 akçe paid, in lieu of the resm-i çift, a personal tax called ispence. A virtual poll tax, the ispence (along with some categories of the resm-i çift) seems to have represented the cash equivalent of labour services which the peasantry had had to render in pre-Ottoman times.[81] Again, the amount due differed from region to region. In most parts of the Balkans the ispence meant the payment of 25 akçe.[82] A lower amount (20 akçe) is registered for the Albanians in the Peloponnese, but apparently 50 akçe were demanded from each head of household in the sancak of Gyula.[83] It seems that in Hungary generally ispence was replaced by a household tax under the name of resm-i kapu, which amounted to 50 akçe for adult males.[84] As for Anatolia, in the sancak of Kemah in the east Christian heads of households paid, varying according to their economic situation, from 10 to 50 akçe in the early sixteenth century,[85] whereas the non-Muslim reaya in the Cilician Plain (Çukurova) during the same period had to pay, again under the title of an 'household tax' (resm-i hâne), as much as 132 akçe annually.[86] Also widows (bîve) paid 6 akçe.[87]

Non-Muslim adult males were burdened with an extra poll tax called cizye, usually one gold piece or its equivalent in silver coins (60–70 akçe in the period

p. 149. See also the table illustrating regional and periodical variations in the rates of the resm-i çift in Halil İnalcık, 'Osmanlılarda raiyyet rüsûmu', Belleten, 23 (1959), pp. 575–610, repr. in idem, Osmanlı İmparatorluğu. Toplum ve ekonomi üzerinde arşiv çalışmaları, incelemeler (Istanbul, 1993), p. 40.

76. Zeki Arıkan, 'XVI. yüzyılda Divriği', in X. Türk Tarih Kongresi (Ankara, 1994), pp. 2407f.; Singer, Palestinian Peasants and Ottoman Officials, p. 48.

77. İnalcık, 'The Ottoman state: economy and society', p. 148.

78. Arıkan, 'XVI. yüzyılda Divriği', pp. 2407f.

79. Mehmet Ali Ünal, XVI. Yüzyılda Harput Sancağı (1518–1566) (Ankara, 1989), p. 130.

80. İsmet Mıroğlu, Kemah Sancağı ve Erzincan Kazası (1520–1566) (Ankara, 1990), p. 180.

81. According to Halil İnalcık, ispence was a veritable kulluk vergisi, a tax symbolizing serfdom. See Hicrî 835 tarihli sûret-i defter-i sancak-i Arvanid (Ankara, 1954), pp. xxiif., and 'Osmanlılarda raiyyet rüsûmu', pp. 36–37. Cf. also Dušanka Bojanić-Lukač, 'De la nature et de l'origine de l'ispendje', Wiener Zeitschrift für die Kunde des Morgenlandes, 68 (1976), pp. 9–30.

82. See Friedrich Kraelitz-Greifenhorst (ed.), 'Kânûnnâme Sultan Mehmeds des Eroberers. Die ältesten osmanischen Straf- und Finanzgesetze', Mitteilungen zur osmanischen Geschichte, 1 (1921/22), p. 28.

83. N. Beldiceanu and I. Beldiceanu-Steinherr, 'Recherches sur la Morée (1461–1512)', Südost-Forschungen, 39 (1980), pp. 37–8; Bruce McGowan, 'Food supply and taxation on the Middle Danube (1568–1579)', Archivum Ottomanicum, 1 (1969), p. 175.

84. Gyula Kaldy-Nagy, Kanuni devri Budin tahrir defteri (1546–1562) (Ankara, 1971), p. 1.

85. Mıroğlu, Kemah Sancağı ve Erzincan Kazası (1520–1566), p. 182.

86. Yusuf Halaçoğlu, 'Tapu-Tahrîr defterlerine göre XVI. yüzyılın ilk yarısında Sis (=Kozan) sancağı', Tarih Dergisi, 32 (1979), p. 881.

87. İnalcık, 'Osmanlılarda raiyyet rüsûmu', p. 58.

1520–70).[88] Exempted from the *cizye* were, apart from women and children, ill and elderly persons, disabled people, the poor, and the clergymen.[89] In most parts of the Balkans, the *cizye* was actually levied until the end of the seventeenth century as a household or hearth tax.[90] In Hungary, in imitation of the pre-Ottoman usage, it was called *resm-i filuri*, which indicated the payment of one Hungarian florin or its equivalent in *akçe* per household; for example, a *resm-i filuri* of 70 *akçe* was taken from each household in the sancak of Srem annually.[91] In Palestine, too, the *cizye* was collected per household, not per person, 60–70 *akçe* being the average rate during the sixteenth century.[92] Further taxes paid in cash were the marriage tax (*resm-i arûs*), 60 *akçe* for a marrying girl and 30 for a widow,[93] as well as the sheep tax (*resm-i ağnam*), one *akçe* for every three sheep at the time of Mehmed II, and afterwards one *akçe* for two sheep.[94]

The agricultural tithes in kind represented the most widespread form of taxation under Ottoman rule. Not only traditional field products such as cereals were subject to tithe but also some typical 'cash crops' such as cotton and flax and even products of specialized economic pursuit such as honey or even silkworm cocoons and raw silk.[95] Consequently, tithes represented a most substantial portion of the income of the ruling elite. According to one calculation, 20.75 per cent of the total revenue in Euboea, 32.67 per cent in Macedonia and 33.44 per cent in the Peloponnese during the second half of the fifteenth century originated from this source.[96] Other calculations indicate significantly higher percentages; thus in 1461 the value of the tithes levied on field crops in an urban centre such as Corinth amounted to 72.78 per cent of the total revenue,[97] and in respect to several Anatolian districts during the first decades of the sixteenth century, a 52 per cent share of the tithes on average has been established.[98]

As was the case with other taxes, the ratio of the tithe, too, showed regional differentiation, seldom falling, however, to the nominal level of a 'tenth' of the produce, the amounts actually taken increasing from one-tenth upwards.[99] In the

88. İnalcık, 'The Ottoman state: economy and society', p. 68.

89. Hamid Hadžibegić, *Glavarina u Osmanskoj državi* (Sarajevo, 1966), pp. 13–20.

90. See Elena Grozdanova, 'Za danuchnata edinitsa hane v demografskite prouchvaniia', *Istoricheski pregled*, 3 (1972), pp. 81–91; Machiel Kiel, 'Remarks on the administration of the poll tax (*cizye*) in the Ottoman Balkans and value of poll tax registers (*cizye defterleri*) for demographic research', *Etudes balkaniques*, 4 (1990), pp. 70–104; Darling, *Revenue-Raising and Legitimacy*, pp. 82–7.

91. Ömer Lûtfi Barkan, '894 (1488/1489) yılı cizyesinin tahsilâtına âit muhasebe bilânçoları', *Belgeler*, 1 (1964), p. 6; Bruce McGowan (ed.), *Sirem Sancağı mufassal tahrir defteri* (Ankara, 1983), p. 1.

92. Singer, *Palestinian Peasants and Ottoman Officials*, p. 55.

93. Arıkan, '1518 (924) tarihli Çemişgezek livası kanunnâmesi', pp. 116–18. Cf. also Pulaha and Yücel, *Le Code (kânûnnâme) de Selim Ier*, p. 41, and Halaçoğlu, 'Tapu-Tahrir defterlerine', p. 881.

94. Hamid Hadžibegić, 'Porez na sitnu stoku i korišćenje ispaša, *Prilozi za orijentalni filologiju*', 8–9 (1958–59), pp. 63–109.

95. Nicoară Beldiceanu and Irène Beldiceanu-Steinherr, 'Corinthe et sa région en 1461 d'après le registre TT 10', *Südost-Forschungen*, 45 (1986), p. 38.

96. Evangelia Balta, *L'Eubée à la fin du XVe siècle: Economie et population. Les registres de l'année 1474* (Athens, 1989), p. 87.

97. Beldiceanu and Beldiceanu-Steinherr, 'Corinthe et sa région en 1461', p. 39.

98. Lûtfi Güçer, *XVI.–XVII. asırlarda Osmanlı İmparatorluğunda hububat meselesi ve hububattan alınan vergiler* (Istanbul, 1964), pp. 62f.

99. Barkan, *XV ve XVInci asırlarda Osmanlı İmparatorluğunda ziraî ekonominin hukukî ve malî esasları*, I: *Kanunlar*, pp. 24, 167, 193f., 205, 235, 289.

sancak of Kemah in eastern Anatolia, Christian subjects had to give one-fifth of the produce. However, a differential system obtained in the case of the Muslim population of the same area: the urban Muslim households owning gardens and vineyards delivered a 'genuine' tithe of one-tenth, whereas the Muslims in the countryside were expected to deliver one-seventh of the produce of their vineyards, gardens and cotton fields, and one-fifth of the produce of their lands sown with cereals.[100] The region of Çemişgezek in the south-east, which had known similar conditions, experienced some sort of a social levelling in this regard, with Muslims and non-Muslims paying equal tithes at the ratio of one-fifth by 1541.[101] In the case of some valuable crops such as rice, the cultivation of which required substantial investments of capital, one half of the produce was regularly demanded in the name of tithe.[102] Only in a few regions such as Palestine were the tithes levied in cash.[103]

A totally different category were the so-called *avarız* taxes, partly extraordinary obligations decreed by the sultan especially in times of war, partly customary dues levied for the purposes of the provincial government. In both cases, Muslims and non-Muslims were equally liable. Collected in the early sixteenth century irregularly, at intervals of several years, these levies assumed in the course of the seventeenth century the character of annual direct taxes.[104] Their assessment and redistribution took place within a system of nominal 'tax houses' (*avarız haneleri*), each unit of which consisted of three to four, according to some estimations even up to fifteen, actual households.[105] The obligations involved were a) *nüzül*, the delivery of barley and flour for the army at designated stations; b) *sürsat*, the provisioning of the army during campaigns with flour, bread, barley, meat, butter, honey, hay and the like; c) *iştira*, the procurement by state agents of, and, by implication, the obligation of the peasantry to sell, grain for military purposes at prices fixed often under the market value.[106] Since it was difficult to transport grain over long distances, sometimes a cash sum in lieu of the *nüzül* was levied, which was then referred to as *avarız akçesi*.[107] Likewise, oarsmen's service in the galleys of the navy during the frequent campaigns of the sixteenth and seventeenth centuries – an especially onerous task for the peasantry – was early converted into a cash payment called *kürekçi bedeli*.[108] In order to protect the peasantry from over-taxation, the various *avarız* levies were meant to be

100. Miroğlu, *Kemah Sancağı ve Erzincan Kazası*, p. 189.
101. Arıkan, '1518 (924) tarihli Çemişgezek livası kanunnâmesi', p. 109.
102. Halaçoğlu, 'Tapu-Tahrîr defterlerine', p. 882.
103. Singer, *Palestinian Peasants and Ottoman Officials*, p. 53.
104. Bistra Cvetkova, *Izvunredni danutsi i durzhavni povinnosti v bulgarskite zemi pod turska vlast* (Sofia, 1958); Avdo Sućeska, 'Promjene u sistemu izvanrednog oporezivanju u Turskoj u XVII vijeku i pojava nameta tekâlif-i şâkka', *Prilozi za orijentalni filologiju*, 10–11 (1960–61), pp. 75–112; idem, 'Die Entwicklung der Besteuerung durch *Avâriz-i dîvânîye* und die *Tekâlîf-i örfîye* im Osmanischen Reich während des 17. und 18. Jahrhunderts', *Südost-Forschungen*, 27 (1968), pp. 89–130.
105. Cf. McGowan, *Economic Life in Ottoman Europe*, p. 106. For a definition of the term *avarız hane* in the Ottoman *kanun* tradition see M. Akif Erdoğdu, 'Karaman Vilâyeti kanunnâmeleri', *Ankara Üniversitesi Osmanlı Tarihi Araştırma ve Uygulama Merkezi Dergisi*, 4 (1993), p. 490.
106. See Güçer, *XVI.–XVII. asırlarda Osmanlı İmparatorluğunda hububat meselesi ve hububattan alınan vergiler*, pp. 69–135.
107. McGowan, *Economic Life in Ottoman Europe*, pp. 106f.
108. Mustafa Akdağ, *Celâlî isyânları (1550–1603)* (Ankara 1963), pp. 33f.

mutually exclusive, although numerous petitions by taxpayers complaining about the abuses indicate that this rule was not strictly observed.[109]

The exemption from the *avarız* was a principal form of granting privileges during the earlier centuries of Ottoman rule, and the Islamic charitable foundations (*vakıf*) played an important role in this context. Members of the ruling elite of the expanding empire were granted agricultural property – mostly deserted lands – as freehold in recognition of their services, but, no doubt, also in the expectation of an augmented revenue, once the 'revivification' by means of sedenterizing nomads, inducing peasants from outside to move in as new settlers, or even engaging servile labour, was successful. Income from such estates was usually dedicated in perpetuity for pious purposes, which served also common interests such as supporting public kitchens, hospices, schools, bridges, caravanserais, and the like.[110] Rural *vakıfs* enjoyed a certain degree of administrative and fiscal autonomy and were thus able to 'protect' their peasants. The sources indicate that once a village was integrated into a *vakıf*, the number of its inhabitants tended to rise.[111]

The exemption from the extraordinary levies did not, however, always mean an alleviation of the tax load of the peasantry. For example, the status of the rice cultivator (*çeltükcü reaya*), which brought with it a compensation in the form of freedom from the *avarız*, was hardly a coveted one.[112] Those peasants who functioned as horse breeders, bridge-builders, miners, tar extractors, salters, charcoal burners or producers of gunpowder, oil and grease – to name most common 'privileged' occupations – fared presumably hardly better than the rice cultivators. There were 'exempted' (*muaf reaya*) groups with semi-military duties, who guarded mountain passes (villages with *derbendci* status), served as 'warriors' (*voynuk*) in the Ottoman army or policed the countryside (the *martolos* service).[113] Along with the pastoral Turcoman and Vlach groups, Gypsies, too, had auxiliary functions for the military, enjoying therefore exemption from the *avarız* taxes.[114] Altogether one-third of the non-Muslim population in the Balkan Peninsula seems to have belonged to a *muaf* category as late as the first half of the seventeenth century. This proportion in some districts reached spectacular

109. Darling, *Revenue-Raising and Legitimacy*, p. 263.

110. Ömer Lûtfi Barkan, 'Türk-İslam hukuku tatbikatının Osmanlı İmpratorluğunda aldığı şekiller: Mülk topraklar ve sultanların temlik hakkı', *Hukuk Fakültesi Mecmuası*, 7 (1941), pp. 157–76; idem, 'Osmanlı İmparatorluğunun toprak vakıflarının idari malî muhtariyeti meselesi', *Türk Hukuk Tarihi Dergisi*, 1 (1941–42), pp. 11–25; idem, 'Osmanlı İmparatorluğunda bir iskân ve kolonizasyon metodu olarak vakıflar ve temlikler', *Vakıflar Dergisi*, 2 (1942), pp. 279–386; idem and Ekrem H. Ayverdi, *İstanbul vakıfları tahrîr defteri. 953 (1546) târîhli* (Istanbul, 1970), especially pp. xvi–xix; İnalcık, 'The Ottoman state: economy and society', pp. 120–31, 167–71.

111. Evangelia Balta, *Les vakifs de Serrès et de sa région (XVe et XVIe s.)* (Athens, 1995), pp. 59–68.

112. For the organization of the production, and the special fiscal system applied, in rice cultivation see Nicoară Beldiceanu and Irène Beldiceanu-Steinherr, 'Riziculture dans l'Empire ottoman (XVe–XVIe siècle)', *Turcica*, 9–10 (1978), pp. 9–28; Halil İnalcık, 'Rice cultivation and the *çeltükci-re'âyâ* system in the Ottoman empire', *Turcica*, 14 (1982), pp. 69–141; Margaret L. Venzke, 'Rice cultivation in the plain of Antioch in the 16th century. The Ottoman fiscal practice', *Archivum Ottomanicum*, 12 (1987–92), pp. 175–276.

113. Milan Vasić, *Martolosi u jugoslovenskim zemljama pod turskom vladavinom* (Sarajevo, 1967); Aleksandar Stojanovski, *Dervendzhistvoto vo Makedoniia* (Skopje, 1974); Yavuz Ercan, *Osmanlı İmparatorluğunda Bulgarlar ve Voynuklar* (Ankara, 1989).

114. M. Tayyib Gökbilgin, 'Çingeneler', in *İslâm Ansiklopedisi*, vol. III, pp. 420–6.

dimensions; in Sofia, for example, 31 per cent of the households enjoyed some degree of exemption from state taxes, in Radomir it was 45 per cent, in Kustendil 46, Varna 49.97, Demirhisar 51, Zihna 55.3, Kratovo 58.6, Salonika 68.2, Drama 78.7, and Siderokapsa 90 per cent respectively.[115]

Settlement, Agriculture, Population

The above summary may explain to a large extent why the Ottoman agrarian system as crystallized since the second half of the fifteenth century found a high degree of acceptance in most regions of the empire. Above all, the abolition of most labour services and the conversion of the remaining ones into cash payments were arguments in support of the new regime, which appeared to promise 'freedom from servitude'. Thus, in a frontier province such as Bosnia, the Ottomans were able to compete successfully with their rivals, Christian magnates on the other side of the border, for the favour of Croatian peasants. By 1551, the magnates felt compelled to ask King Ferdinand to emancipate the peasantry, since the Turks had declared their peasants free and many Croatians had already fled in that direction; indeed, in 1556, some 70,000 peasants left the Habsburg territories for Ottoman Bosnia.[116]

Research on the agrarian relations of the period from a regional perspective corroborates that the prevailing conditions were generally conducive to growth. Reconstruction of the existing urban centres, the establishment of new ones, the needs of a large and frequently campaigning army, and the opportunities to export to Italy and other Mediterranean countries were strong incentives to extend the arable. The frequency with which the term *mezraa* is utilized in the provincial surveys, denoting arable but uninhabited land usually in the vicinity of a village, can serve as a good gauge for agricultural expansion.[117] In the late medieval period, such lands were mostly pasture grounds for the flocks of nomads. In the registers from the second half of the fifteenth century onwards, however, they begin to appear also as cultivated spots, inhabited by Yürük or Vlach herdsmen. By the sixteenth century, many of them developed into fully-fledged villages. An internal colonization of this type can be observed not only in the Balkans but also in Anatolia.[118] In Syria, finally, the sixteenth-century

115. Elena Grozdanova, 'Bevölkerungskategorien mit Sonderpflichten und Sonderstatus – nach unveröffentlichten osmanisch-türkischen Dokumenten der Orient-Abteilung der Nationalbibliothek', in Majer, *Osmanistische Studien zur Wirtschafts- und Sozialgeschichte*, p. 63.

116. See Nedim Filipović, 'Pogled na osmanski feudalizam (s posebnim obzirom na agrarne odnose)', *Godišnjak Istoriskog Društva Bosne i Hercegovine*, 4 (1952), pp. 67–8. See also Gökbilgin, *XV–XVI. asırlarda Edirne ve Paşa livası*, pp. 161ff.

117. Fikret Adanır, '*Mezra'a*: Zu einem Problem der Siedlungs- und Agrargeschichte Südosteuropas im ausgehenden Mittelalter und in der Frühen Neuzeit', in Ralph Melville *et al.* (eds), *Deutschland und Europa in der Neuzeit. Festschrift für Karl Otmar Freiherr von Aretin* (Stuttgart, 1988), pt 1, pp. 193–204; idem, 'Tradition and rural change in southeastern Europe during Ottoman rule', in Daniel Chirot (ed.), *The Origins of Backwardness in Eastern Europe* (Berkeley/Los Angeles, 1989), pp. 137–9.

118. Wolf-Dieter Hütteroth, *Ländliche Siedlungen im südlichen Inneranatolien in den letzten vierhundert Jahren* (Göttingen, 1968), pp. 163–208.

expansion of settlement went 'almost as far to the south as around 1960, after the first post-war boom of Syrian agriculture'.[119]

Most of the new lands beyond the bounds of old villages brought under the plough during this period can be characterized as 'marginal' in the sense that labour-intensive forms of cultivation were not very practicable, not least because of security considerations and insufficient means of transport. The extension of the arable resulted therefore in an agriculture even more dependent on wheat and barley, although other grains such as oats or millet, and vetch were also sown in small quantities. In particular, the semi-arid Anatolian plateau became a region of cereals grown in monoculture.[120] Similar tendencies could be observed elsewhere, for example, on the Middle Danube where the sedentarization of Vlach herders led to a spectacular increase in grain production.[121] However, the new cultivators on the fertile *chernozem* soils along the Danube continued to give high priority to livestock raising, while older settlements in the hilly country stuck to practising a more variegated and labour-intensive economy including viticulture.[122] In Anatolia, too, where the borderline between nomadism and settled life was not sharply defined, it was quite easy to abandon tillage on the marginal lands in order to revert to old practices.[123]

Exceptions were perhaps the case where extension of the arable aimed primarily at the production of rice or a commercial crop such as cotton. Rice was grown in many places in smaller quantities since the fourteenth century, but in the sixteenth century it enjoyed some sort of state promotion, having already secured a prestigious position in the cuisine of the rich.[124] The demand was high and the supply scant, so that prominent members of the elite invested capital in rice paddies established on reclaimed lands in river valleys or coastal plains. Beypazarı near Ankara, Boyabat near Sinop, the plain of Çukurova in Cilicia and the plain of Antioch became known as regions of rice cultivation.[125] In the Balkans, it was the Maritsa valley in Thrace which became the chief centre of production. Thus, the Austrian envoy to the Porte who travelled through

119. Idem, 'Settlement desertion in the Gezira between the 16th and 19th century', in Thomas Philipp (ed.), *The Syrian Land in the 18th and 19th Century. The Common and the Specific in the Historical Experience* (Stuttgart, 1992), p. 286. See also Wolf-Dieter Hütteroth and Kemal Abdulfattah, *Historical Geography of Palestine, Transjordan and Southern Syria in the Late 16th Century* (Erlangen, 1977), passim.

120. Huri İslamoğlu and Suraiya Faroqhi, 'Crop patterns and agricultural production trends', *Review. A Journal of the Fernand Braudel Center for the Study of Economics, Historical Systems and Civilisations*, 2: 3 (1979), pp. 401–36.

121. Bruce McGowan, 'The Middle Danube *cul-de-sac*', in H. İslamoğlu-İnan (ed.), *The Ottoman Empire and the World-Economy* (Cambridge, 1987), pp. 170–7.

122. Cf. McGowan, *Sirem Sancağı mufassal tahrir defteri*, pp. lxxf.

123. Hütteroth, *Ländliche Siedlungen*, pp. 211–15. Cf. also Suraiya Faroqhi, 'Rural society in Anatolia and the Balkans during the sixteenth century', *Turcica*, 11 (1979), pp. 110–15. On the importance of cereal grains and the role the *mezraa* type of lands played as the demand increased or decreased, see Margaret L. Venzke, 'The question of declining cereals' production in the sixteenth century: a sounding on the problem-solving capacity of the Ottoman cadastres', in *Festschrift for Tibor Halasi-Kun, Journal of Turkish Studies*, 8 (1984), pp. 251–64.

124. See Suraiya Faroqhi, *Kultur und Alltag im Osmanischen Reich. Vom Mittelalter bis zum Anfang des 20. Jahrhunderts* (Munich, 1995), p. 231.

125. Faroqhi, *Kultur und Alltag*, p. 231; Mustafa Soysal, *Die Siedlungs- und Landschaftsentwicklung der Çukurova. Mit besonderer Berücksichtigung der Yüregir-Ebene* (Erlangen, 1976), pp. 17f. For a short history of rice in the Middle East, see Venzke, 'Rice cultivation in the plain of Antioch', pp. 179–89.

this area in the summer of 1608 commented on the beautiful rice fields in the plain round Philippopolis.[126] But rice was already being cultivated in the fifteenth century in places such as Seres, Drama, Komotini, Verria, Menlik, among many others.[127] In Thessaly 8.23 per cent of the tithes paid by the inhabitants of the town of Fener were made up of this crop.[128] It is no surprise, therefore, that rice fields appeared frequently among the rural property of charitable foundations.[129]

Cotton, too, a fibrous crop known in Asia Minor since antiquity, was expanding during the sixteenth century. One-fifth of the arable surface of the Çukurova, a traditional reserve of Turcoman nomads, was devoted to its cultivation.[130] In the Aegean coastal regions, likewise winter quarters of nomadic groups, cotton growing advanced even more spectacularly. In the district of Manisa, where out of 195 villages 74 were registered as uninhabited, but as being cultivated by people from outside, that is by semi-nomadic Yürüks, cotton was after cereals the most important crop.[131] Cotton production in the Aegean reached its peak during the eighteenth century.[132] In the Syrian economy, it had long played an important role.[133] In Palestine, for example, in the Akka plain and the lower parts of Galilee, it was the chief crop during the sixteenth century.[134] As for the Balkans, cotton appears in the sources of this period as a product subject to tithe and was grown chiefly in the flatlands of Macedonia and Thessaly.[135]

It seems that a more diversified crop pattern, coupled with a higher level of mobility on the part of inhabitants, was characteristic of areas which could at the same time boast a remarkable degree of settlement continuity. Comparative research on the medieval Byzantine Matzouka in Pontic Anatolia, on the one hand, and the Ottoman Maçuka of the sixteenth century, on the other, allows illuminating conclusions in this regard.[136] The settlement pattern, even the names of the villages, remained unchanged. The socio-economic conditions continued

126. Karl Nehring, *Adam Freiherrn zu Herbersteins Gesandtschaftsreise nach Konstantinopel* (Munich, 1983), p. 118.

127. M. Tayyib Gökbilgin, *XV–XVI. asırlarda Edirne ve Paşa livası. Vakıflar – mülkler -mukataalar* (Istanbul, 1952), pp. 137–40.

128. Nicoară Beldiceanu and Petre Ş. Năsturel, 'La Thessalie entre 1454/55 et 1506', *Byzantion*, 53 (1983), p. 137.

129. Klaus Schwarz and Hars Kurio, *Die Stiftungen des osmanischen Großwesirs Koğa Sinān Pascha (gest. 1596) in Uzunğaova/Bulgarien* (Berlin, 1983), pp. 18–22. Cf. also Halil İnalcik, 'Capital formation in the Ottoman empire', *Journal of Economic History*, 19 (1969), pp. 133f.

130. Soysal, *Die Siedlungs- und Landschaftsentwicklung der Çukurova*, pp. 34f.

131. Emecen, *XVI. asırda Manisa kazası*, pp. 121–3, 236, 250–5. Cf. also Suraiya Faroqhi, 'Notes on the production of cotton and cotton cloth in XVIth and XVIIth century Anatolia', *Journal of European Economic History*, 8 (1979), pp. 405–17.

132. Necmi Ülker, 'The rise of Izmir, 1688–1740' (PhD, University of Michigan, 1974), pp. 110–16; Elena Frangakis-Syrett, 'The trade of cotton and cloth in İzmir: from the second half of the eighteenth century to the early nineteenth century', in Keyder and Tabak, *Landholding and Commercial Agriculture*, pp. 97–111.

133. See Eliyahu Ashtor, 'The Venetian cotton trade in Syria in the Later Middle Ages', *Studi Medievali*, 17 (1976), pp. 675–715.

134. Hütteroth and Abdulfattah, *Historical Geography of Palestine, Transjordan and Southern Syria*, pp. 84f.

135. Balta, *Les Vakıfs de Serrès*, pp. 217, 221, 228; Beldiceanu and Năsturel, 'La Thessalie entre 1454/55 et 1506', p. 139.

136. Cf. Anthony Bryer, 'Rural society in Matzouka', in Anthony Bryer and Heath W. Lowry (eds), *Continuity and Change in Late Byzantine and Early Ottoman Society* (Birmingham/Washington, DC, 1986), pp. 53–95; Heath W. Lowry, 'Privilege and property in Ottoman Maçuka in the opening decades of the Tourkokratia: 1461–1553', ibid., pp. 97–128; Ronald Jennings, 'The society and economy of Maçuka in the Ottoman judicial registers of Trabzon, 1560–1640', ibid., pp. 129–54.

to be favourable. Although situated in a mountainous region, the district had more arable than could be cultivated. The peasants were mobile; along with agriculture, some of them mastered artisanal skills which they practised not only in the neighbouring urban centre Trabzon but also in the imperial capital Istanbul. Agriculture was not dependent on cereals alone; as important were the products of orchards, hazelnut and olive groves, vineyards, beehives and pastures. Although geographically an isolated region, the people of Maçuka seemed 'very much part of a cash society; everything in the society had its cash value'.[137] The relations between the agents of the state and the peasants of Maçuka were by no means free of conflicts, but 'taxes could not be taken by force, so anyone who claimed the right to any tax revenues had to call on the court if some villagers did not pay fully and adequately. Villagers, in turn, could summon to court, or have summoned there, any tax collector whom they believed had not treated them properly.'[138]

Similar developments could be observed in Chalkidiki where most of the land belonged to the monasteries of Athos.[139] Once Chalkidiki came under Ottoman rule, the Islamic *vakıfs* began to penetrate the area, several new villages emerging in the process, while Christian monastic property, too, continued to grow. A substantial portion of the peasantry was granted the status of *muaf*, enjoying exemptions from most of the state taxes, and instead of natural tithes many paid a lump sum in cash which was decidedly more advantageous. Apart from field cultivation and livestock raising, mining (saltpetre and silver), burning of charcoal and extraction of salt from the sea were important occupations of the population.

These conditions may appear to be specific to Chalkidiki and therefore not suitable to be generalized for the rest of the Balkans in this period.[140] But recent research in the history of other regions of the empire seem to confirm the basic tendencies. At least structurally, the Aegean coastal belt and especially the Archipelago had much in common with the situation in Chalkidiki. For example, the population of the island of Imbros was exempt from the poll tax, the *ispence* and the tithe, the cultivators paying only a fixed sum proportional to the surface of land they worked, and in Thasos only 50 *akçes* were required under the title of *resm-i çift* in lieu of the tithe.[141] The inhabitants of Limnos were mostly sheep raisers, the *tahrir* of 1489 recording 24,509 sheep on the island, the tax rate amounting to the annual payment of one *akçe* per head of animal, as was arranged between the Christian peasants themselves and the Ottoman tax-collectors.[142] The island of Chios, enjoying a high degree of autonomy under

137. Jennings, 'Society and Economy', p. 154.
138. Ibid., p. 142.
139. Vasilis Dimitriades, 'Ottoman Chalkidiki: an area in transition', in Bryer and Lowry, *Continuity and Change*, pp. 39–50.
140. Ibid., p. 40.
141. A. E. Vacalopoulos, *The Greek Nation, 1453–1669. The Cultural and Economic Background of Modern Greek Society* (New Brunswick, NJ, 1976), pp. 18–20.
142. Nicoară Beldiceanu, 'Structures socio-économiques à Lemnos à la fin du XVe siècle', *Turcica*, 15 (1983), pp. 247–66; cf. also Heath W. Lowry, 'The island of Limnos: a case study on the continuity of Byzantine forms under Ottoman rule', in Bryer and Lowry, *Continuity and Change*, pp. 235–59.

Ottoman rule since 1566, specialized in the production of mastic, along with citrus fruits, almonds, wine and other cash crops.[143] In these areas, cereals surely continued to be the dominant crops, but olives, fruits, vegetables and vines played an ever larger role. Viticulture served as supplier not only of grapes, raisins, wine and vinegar, but also of *pekmez*, the grape syrup which was an important substitute for sugar. Finally, a diversified agriculture of this type was highly conducive to the development of a cash economy, and the fact that a high percentage of taxes was levied in cash proved in the long run a strong inducement to seek the market.[144]

Such factors may also explain the remarkable peasant mobility that can easily be gathered from the extant documents. When peasants turned to growing cash crops, as was for example the case in the village of Radilofo in Eastern Macedonia,[145] a parallel tendency to abandon agriculture in order to pursue a different trade in a town has been observed as an equally important development from the early sixteenth century. This is rather surprising since the average tax-load per urban household was often higher than that in the countryside; in other words, migration could hardly have been motivated by hopes of avoiding high taxation.[146] Indeed, it seems to be connected with new economic opportunities in cities that exercised a strong attraction on the rural populace – a phenomenon that was perceived by some critical members of the elite as a threat to the very foundations of the Ottoman social order:

The low-class yokels . . . in Constantinople, Bursa, and in well-guarded Adrianople, the working people known under the name of *manav*, have quitted their homeland and paternal roof where they were registered subjects (*ra'īyet*) and children of subjects on royal crown-lands or on the fiefs (*tīmār*) of *sipāhīs* and *za'īms* in the villages and rural regions of the prosperous lands [of the Empire], have come to learn various trades and different skills, and have become completely settled and occupied with daily increasing gain. The lowliest ones of them who are the back-carrying porters, the men that roast chestnuts and sell them, and the brokers on the flea-market, make at least a hundred gold pieces every year, and most of them more. Of course, their *sipāhīs* do not benefit of them nor do they contribute a penny, or pay something in compensation of the *ra'āyā*-dues.[147]

A certain dynamism in village life and the attractiveness of urban centres in terms of economic opportunities were connected not least with a spectacular

143. Hedda Reindl-Kiel and Machiel Kiel, 'Kaugummi für den Sultan. Ein Beitrag zur Wirtschaftsgeschichte der Insel Chios im 17. Jahrhundert', *Osmanlı Araştırmaları*, 11 (1991), pp. 181–214.

144. Spyros I. Asdrachas, 'Aux Balkans du XVe siècle: producteurs directs et marché', *Etudes balkaniques*, 3 (1970), pp. 36–69.

145. Heath W. Lowry, 'Changes in fifteenth-century Ottoman peasant taxation: the case study of Radilofo', in Bryer and Lowry, *Continuity and Change*, pp. 23–35.

146. Evangelia Balta, 'Rural and urban population in the Sancak of Euripos in the early 16th century', *Archeion Euboikôn Meletôn*, 29 (1990–91), pp. 55–185, here at p. 87.

147. Tietze, *Mustafa 'Alī's Counsel for Sultans of 1581*, p. 57. On Mustafa Ali see Cornell Fleischer, *Bureaucrat and Intellectual in the Ottoman Empire. The Historian Mustafa Ali (1541–1600)* (Princeton, NJ, 1986). The question of social prejudice implied by this type of literature is discussed in Rifa'at 'Ali Abou-El-Haj, 'The Ottoman *Nasihatname* as a discourse over "morality" ', *Revue d'Histoire Maghrebine*, 47–8 (1987 = Mélanges Robert Mantran), pp. 17–30.

growth of population from the second half of the fifteenth century onwards. The rural population of Attica, for example, grew during the period 1506–70 between 1.04 and 4.20 per cent annually, and more and more peasants felt compelled to indulge in the cultivation of supplementary crops such as cotton and flax or to start viticulture in areas where it was until then unknown.[148] The demographic upswing was apparently a general phenomenon, at least until the last quarter of the sixteenth century.[149] In the process, good agricultural land became scarce in most places, leading eventually to a kind of population pressure that is believed to have stood behind the widespread phenomenon of postponed marriages during the last decades of the century. According to one estimate, the ratio of bachelors to adult males rose in some parts of Anatolia from approximately 3 per cent at the end of the fifteenth to 48 per cent at the end of the sixteenth century.[150]

As has been described earlier, the extension of the arable into the marginal lands was a rather successful mode of tackling the food problem. Another answer to the new situation was the intensification of land utilization by the introduction of leguminous crops such as lentils and broad beans, the cultivation of which had a fertilizing effect on the soil.[151] Yet another event in this regard was rural craft production, in the main weaving and spinning of woollen textiles, which flourished parallel to the increase in cotton cultivation, but particularly in sheep-farming.[152] Since the immigration of Iberian Jews (1492), the pastoral economy had received new impetus. Salonika, which was now a predominantly Jewish city, developed into the foremost textile production centre in the whole Mediterranean basin. Approximately 60,000 cloths produced per annum presupposed the supply of raw wool of almost four million sheep in that period. Indeed, a much higher number of sheep must have existed, since substantial amounts of wool were consumed by peasant families themselves, while a yearly quota was exported to Ragusa and Italy, not to speak of huge quantities of lamb and mutton needed to feed a population that did not like pork. Under such conditions it was no wonder that wool prices soared, and sheep-farming began to dominate agriculture.[153]

To sum up, migration, especially of the village youth, was the work of a whole set of intertwined factors that ended with creating serious problems for urban life

---

148. Balta, 'Rural and urban population in the Sancak of Euripos in the early 16th century', pp. 92, 97.

149. See Barkan, 'Essai sur les données statistiques des registres de recensement dans l'Empire ottoman aux XVe et XVIe siècles', pp. 26–31; Josiah C. Russell, 'Late medieval Balkan and Asia Minor population', *Journal of Economic and Social History of the Orient*, 3 (1960), pp. 265–74; Leila Erder and Suraiya Faroqhi, 'Population rise and fall in Anatolia, 1550–1620', *Middle Eastern Studies*, 15 (1979), pp. 322–45.

150. See Michael A. Cook, *Population Pressure in Rural Anatolia, 1450–1600* (London, 1972), pp. 25–7. Cook's findings have been corroborated by further research. Thus the number of households in the district of Manisa in western Anatolia increased between 1531 and 1575 only by 40.14 per cent, whereas that of bachelors by 238 per cent. See Emecen, *XVI. asırda Manisa kazası*, p. 125. A similar development has been observed with respect to south-eastern Anatolia, see Ünal, *XVI. Yüzyılda Harput Sancağı*, p. 131.

151. İslamoğlu-İnan, *State and Peasant*, pp. 152f.

152. Ibid., pp. 167–71.

153. Questions of supply and demand in the Ottoman wool economy as well as the effects of flourishing sheep-farming on the traditional agriculture are discussed by Benjamin Braude, 'Community and conflict in the economy of the Ottoman Balkans, 1500–1650' (PhD, Harvard University, 1977), pp. 40–8.

as well. It is generally recognized that population growth in the towns surpassed by far that of the rural areas.[154] But until the last quarter of the sixteenth century, the supply of staples seems to have remained at a sufficient level. In fact, the mid-century had even seen a boom in wheat exports to Italy.[155] But later on it became increasingly difficult to supply Anatolian towns with provisions, even though a high percentage of the inhabitants was engaged in agriculture.[156] The problem had, of course, an entirely different magnitude when the object was to supply a huge city like Istanbul.[157] The Ottoman state resorted here to the time-honoured method of pre-emptive purchases within a geographically feasible and therefore limited area of supply, encompassing mainly the Bulgarian Black Sea shore, the northern coast of the Aegean, and the eastern shores of the Sea of Marmara.[158] Later on, in the eighteenth century, Danubian principalities, too, were added to the granaries of the imperial capital.[159] The long-term trend has been characterized by a distinguished historian of the region as prejudicial to the countryside. The ruling elite showed itself deeply 'committed to a policy of urbanization'.

Confronted by the problems of a vast territorial state, the Ottoman government instituted a system of command-economic relationships that were designed to favor the capital, its provincial cities, its armed forces and centers of administration, the pastoral populations that complemented its war arm, and Muslims and other partisans of the imperial enterprise . . . As the Ottoman urban system became more urban during the sixteenth, seventeenth, and eighteenth centuries, therefore, it became more 'nongenerative' or 'parasitic,' with an ever greater imbalance of wealth between towns and cultivators.[160]

154. See Metodije Sokoloski, 'Le développement de quelques villes dans le sud des Balkans aux XVe et XVIe siècles', *Balkanica*, 1 (Belgrade, 1970), pp. 81–106; Ronald C. Jennings, 'Urban population in Anatolia in the sixteenth century: a study of Kayseri, Karaman, Amasya, Trabzon, and Erzurum', *International Journal of Middle Eastern Studies*, 7 (1976), pp. 21–57; Aleksandar Stojanovski, *Gradovite na Makedoniia od kraloi na XIV do XVII vek. Demografski prouchuvaniia* (Skopje, 1981); Peter K. Doorn, 'Population and settlements in central Greece: computer analysis of Ottoman registers of the fifteenth and sixteenth centuries', in P. Denley, S. Folgelvik and C. Harvey (eds), *History and Computing*, vol. II (Manchester, 1989), pp. 193–208; Machiel Kiel, 'Central Greece in the Suleymanic age. Preliminary notes on population growth, economic expansion and its influence on the spread of Greek Christian culture', in Gilles Veinstein (ed.), *Soliman le Magnifique et son temps* (Paris, 1993), pp. 399–424.

155. Maurice Aymard, *Venise, Raguse et le commerce du blé pendant la seconde moitié du XVIe siècle* (Paris, 1966), pp. 125ff.

156. The system of urban food supply is described in Suraiya Faroqhi, *Towns and Townsmen of Ottoman Anatolia. Trade, Crafts, and Food Production in an Urban Setting, 1520–1650* (Cambridge, 1984), pp. 194–266.

157. See the years of famine between 1578 and 1637 in Güçer, *XVI–XVII asırlarda Osmanlı İmparatorluğunda hububat meselesi ve hububattan alınan vergiler*, pp. 8f.

158. On the system of provisioning Istanbul see Lûtfi Güçer, 'XVI. yüzyıl sonlarında Osmanlı İmparatorluğu dahilinde hububat ticaretinin tebi olduğu kayıtlar', *İktisat Fakültesi Mecmuası*, 13 (1951–52), pp. 79–98; Robert Mantran, *Istanbul dans la seconde moitié du XVIIe siècle: Essai d'histoire institutionelle, économique et sociale* (Paris, 1962), pp. 181–213; Suraiya Faroqhi, 'İstanbul'un iaşesi ve Tekirdağ-Rodosçuk limanı (16.–17. yüzyıllar)', *ODTÜ Gelişme Dergisi 1979–80 Özel Sayısı*, pp. 139–54.

159. Marie Mathilde Alexandrescu-Dersca Bulgaru, 'Contribution à l'étude de l'approvisionnement en blé de Constantinople au XVIIIe siècle', *Studia et Acta Orientalia*, 1 (Bucharest, 1957), pp. 13–37; eadem, 'L'approvisionnement d'Istanbul par les principautés roumaines au XVIIIe siècle. Commerce ou réquisition?', in Daniel Panzac (ed.), *Les Balkans à l'époque ottomane, Revue du Monde Musulman et de la Méditerranée*, 66 (1992/4), pp. 73–8.

160. Stoianovich, *Balkan Worlds*, p. 195.

TAX-FARMERS, BRIGANDS AND SHARECROPPERS: RURAL LIFE IN THE SEVENTEENTH AND EIGHTEENTH CENTURIES

From Sipahi to Tax-Farmer

The late sixteenth century portended a period of crisis and profound change. To begin with, rural society was troubled by shifts in climate that affected production negatively.[161] But not only the peasantry experienced hardships; the holders of *timars*, the *sipahis*, also found themselves confronted with grave problems. As the Islamic year 1000 (1591 AD) approached, a mixture of apocalyptic expectations and cyclical pessimism took hold of imaginations.[162] Not even the period of demographic upswing during the earlier part of the century had brought affluence to the lower echelons of the military class, since the population growth and the increase in the number of taxpayers had not meant a commensurate augmentation of revenue.[163] Moreover, the Ottoman currency, the *akçe*, had lost approximately 50 per cent of its silver content from 1451 to 1574, while retaining its nominal value, the basis of assessment of *timar* revenues. And this inflationary development became uncontrollable once American silver reached the Levantine markets in the 1580s; the *akçe*'s weight within a decade was halved once more. The subsequent 'price revolution' reached its climax at the turn of the seventeenth century. Its consequences were quite devastating, especially for groups with 'fixed incomes' such as the majority of the timariots.[164]

Not surprisingly, therefore, the *sipahis'* interest in attending to their military duties waned. It was also obvious that as cavalrymen they were becoming rapidly obsolete. For horsemen were no longer really a match for contemporary European infantries who were equipped with muskets. Moreover, this was a period of military campaigns protracted into tedious and costly siege operations, the outcome of which was determined above all by the employment of specialists such as miners or sappers.[165] As for war booty, it was increasingly a thing of the glorious past. Continual warfare against Shiite Persia in the east (1578–90) and

---

161. For a careful discussion of the question of whether climatic conditions should be considered as an important cause of social unrest during the early modern period, see William J. Griswold, 'Climatic change: a possible factor in the social unrest of seventeenth century Anatolia', in H. W. Lowry and D. Quatacrt (eds), *Essays in Honor of Andreas Tietze* (Istanbul/Washington, DC, 1993), pp. 37–57.

162. Erika Glassen, 'Krisenbewußtsein und Heilserwartung in der islamischen Welt zu Beginn der Neuzeit', in U. Haarmann and P. Bachmann (eds), *Die islamische Welt zwischen Mittelalter und Neuzeit. Festschrift für Hans Robert Roemer* (Beirut, 1979), pp. 167–79; Cornell Fleischer, 'Royal authority, dynastic cyclism, and "Ibn Khaldûnism" in sixteenth-century Ottoman letters', in Bruce B. Lawrence (ed.), *Ibn Khaldun and Islamic Ideology* (Leiden, 1984), pp. 46–68.

163. Cf. Spyros Asdrachas, 'Sociétés rurales balkaniques aux XVe et XVIe siècles: Mouvements de la population et des revenus', *Etudes balkaniques*, 13: 2 (1977), pp. 49–66.

164. Halil Sahillioğlu, 'The role of international monetary and metal movements in Ottoman monetary history, 1300–1700', in J. F. Richards (ed.), *Precious Metals in the Later Medieval and Early Modern Worlds* (Durham, NC, 1983), pp. 269–304; Ömer Lûtfi Barkan, 'Les mouvements des prix en Turquie entre 1490 et 1655', in *Histoire économique du monde méditerranéen 1450–1650. Mélanges en l'honneur de Fernand Braudel*, vol. I (Toulouse, 1973), pp. 65–79, and idem, 'The price revolution of the sixteenth century: a turning point in the economic history of the Near East', *International Journal of Middle East Studies*, 6 (1975), pp. 3–28.

165. Caroline Finkel, *The Administration of Warfare: The Ottoman Military Campaigns in Hungary, 1593–1606* (Vienna, 1988).

the Catholic Habsburgs (1593–1606) in the west – sometimes on both fronts simultaneously – was a heavy drain on the *sipahis*' morale, especially since their minds were never free of anxiety concerning affairs on the home front.[166] Thus, more and more *sipahis* simply remained at home, perhaps engaging some peasants to serve as their substitutes.[167] The central state, on the other hand, in dire need of ever more infantry troops, first tried to raise the number of the janissaries, but soon opted likewise for a more economical solution: the *ad hoc* recruitment of underemployed youth for military purposes, mostly in the retinue of provincial governors. In this way, large groups of mercenaries of peasant origin, known under various names such as *levend, sekban, sarıca* or *gönüllü*, came into being, whose chief aspiration was to achieve integration into the established military order. Meanwhile, however, their payment was dependent upon the availability of funds at the disposition of governors who did not hesitate to introduce new local levies to that end. But normally the peasant-soldiers were stood down as soon as the campaigning season was over, or, when kept, they were allowed – if not expected – to roam about and live off the land.[168]

These developments, which were reciprocally related to the economic and socio-political change that was already under way, had a destabilizing effect on rural society. Understandably, villagers resented visits by military leaders and their retinues. The latter reacted by forming marauding bands, joined by wandering *suhtegân* (students of medressehs mostly of peasant stock) and often by some malcontent *sipahis*. Public order, especially in Anatolia, collapsed completely. *Sipahis*, peasants, students and dissatisfied local rulers revolted, with *levends* and *sekbans*, who rallied around some leader, making up the mass of the rebels. The settled peasantry suffered most; the climax of these *celâli*-revolts between 1603 and 1610, usually referred to as the 'great flight' (*büyük kaçgunluk*), saw the depopulation of wide stretches of land in Anatolia. Many villagers either fled to the towns or withdrew to mountainous, remote areas where they established new settlements; some joined the swelling number of peasant-soldiers or tried their fortune in outright banditry.[169]

Uncultivated peasant lands were appropriated partly by provincial governors, partly by janissaries, who had been garrisoned in provincial centres since the middle of the sixteenth century.[170] But also civilian groups with an urban

---

166. Irène Beldiceanu-Steinherr and Jean-Louis Bacqué-Grammont, 'A propos de quelques causes de malaises sociaux en Anatolie Centrale aux XVIe et XVIIe siècles', *Archivum Ottomanicum*, 7 (1982), pp. 71–115, especially pp. 71–81.

167. Vera Mutafchieva and Strashimir Dimitrov, *Sur l'état du système des timars des XVIIe–XVIIIe ss.* (Sofia, 1968), pp. 21ff.

168. Mustafa Cezar, *Osmanlı tarihinde levendler* (Istanbul, 1965), passim; Halil İnalcık, 'The socio-political effects of the diffusion of fire-arms in the Middle East', in V. J. Parry and M. E. Yapp (eds), *War, Technology and Society in the Middle East* (London, 1975), pp. 195–217; İnalcık, 'Military and fiscal transformation in the Ottoman empire, 1600–1700', *Archivum Ottomanicum*, 6 (1980), pp. 283–337.

169. Mustafa Akdağ, *Celâli isyanları (1550–1603)* (Ankara, 1963); William J. Griswold, *The Great Anatolian Rebellion, 1000–1020/1591–1611* (Berlin, 1983); Karen Barkey, *Bandits and Bureaucrats: The Peculiar Route of Ottoman State Centralization* (Ithaca, NY, 1994), pp. 141–88.

170. Suraiya Faroqhi, 'Land transfer, land disputes and *askeri* holdings in Ankara (1592–1600)', in Robert Mantran (ed.), *Mémorial Ömer Lütfi Barkan* (Paris, 1980), pp. 87–99; Jean-Paul Pascual, 'The Janissaries and the Damascus countryside at the beginning of the seventeeth century according to the archives of the city's military tribunal', in Tarif Khalidi (ed.), *Land Tenure and Social Transformation in the Middle East* (Beirut, 1984), pp. 357–69.

background, who had distinguished themselves as organizers of local militias during the time of troubles, showed an interest in land. As tax-farmers and moneylenders they had an intimate knowledge of the countryside and had – to a certain extent – even gained the esteem of the peasantry whom they had tried to protect both against the marauding bands and the arbitrary acts of the officials. Under the leadership of the local *kadis*, these 'notables' (*ayan*) represented an emerging elite that was bent on acting as intermediaries between rural society and the central government.[171]

No doubt, the complex process of dissolution of the *timar* system as the dominant form of distribution of the revenue had long set in.[172] It was being gradually replaced by the *mukataa* system, i.e. tax-farming which had long been in use on larger benefices. But now *mukataa* was promoted as an institution in order 'to centralize and maximize revenue', as well as 'to monetarize the tax system' – a development that entailed several disadvantages from the point of view of the taxpayer.[173] For 'over-exploitation of the tax source, extortion, and lack of long-term investment were the inevitable undesirable effects of this practice', since tax-farmers could never be sure of the duration of their tenure.[174] Equally detrimental was the escalating application of the so-called *maktu'* method, i.e. tax assessment not on an individual basis as in the traditional *timar* system but on the village community as a whole in a fixed lump sum. The villagers were expected to undertake a collective liability *vis-à-vis* the tax-collecting agent of the state. Indeed, drawn up in response to the increasing mobility of the taxpaying subjects, the new system seemed, as one historian rightly pointed out, totally 'divorced from the idea of a settled peasantry'.[175] Payment of a fixed lump sum would, of course, theoretically be advantageous to a peasant community in times of population growth, but in the case of a decreasing population it meant a heavier tax-load on the individual peasant, and the population in the Ottoman Balkans most probably decreased – about 25 per cent according to one estimate – during the first decades of the seventeenth century.[176]

Despite efforts to reorganize the provincial administration,[177] and a rather successful centralization of the revenue-extraction systems, Ottoman government remained hard-pressed for resources for most of the seventeenth century. Thus,

171. On the emergence of the *ayans* see Avdo Sućeska, *Ajani. Prilog izuchavaniu lokalne vlasti u nashim zemljama za vriieme Turaka* (Sarajevo, 1965); idem, 'Bedeutung und Entwicklung des Begriffes A'yân im Osmanischen Reich', *Südost-Forschungen*, 25 (1966), pp. 3–26; Kemal H. Karpat, 'Some historical and methodological considerations concerning social stratification in the Middle East', in C. A. O. van Nieuwenhuijze (ed.), *Commoners, Climbers and Notables* (Leiden, 1977), pp. 83–101; Yücel Özkaya, *Osmanlı İmparatorluğunda âyânlık* (Ankara, 1977).

172. Douglas Howard, 'The Ottoman timar system and its transformation, 1563–1656' (PhD, University of Indiana, 1987).

173. Darling, *Revenue-Raising and Legitimacy*, pp. 122f.

174. Çizakça, *A Comparative Evolution of Business Partnerships*, p. 141.

175. Molly Greene, 'An Islamic experiment? Ottoman land policy on Crete', *Mediterranean Historical Review*, 11 (1996), p. 71.

176. See McGowan, *Economic Life in Ottoman Europe*, pp. 86f. For a more cautious and critical assessment in this regard see Maria N. Todorova, 'Was there a demographic crisis in the Ottoman empire in the seventeenth century?', *Etudes balkaniques*, 2 (1988), pp. 55–63. For a discussion of the question of advantages and disadvantages of the *maktu'* system see Darling, *Revenue-Raising and Legitimacy*, pp. 104f.

177. Cf. İ. Metin Kunt, *Sancaktan eyalete. 1550–1650 arasında Osmanlı ümerası ve il idaresi* (Istanbul, 1978), passim.

the annual budgets of the empire continued to show a growing deficit.[178] Towards the end of the century, financial necessity compelled the government to initiate two new reforms with wide-reaching consequences. First, the traditional method of poll-tax collection on a household basis was replaced in 1691 by calculation on the basis of the number of adult non-Muslim male individuals. The result was a spectacular augmentation of revenue, although the system was not immediately applied in many parts of the Balkans during the ongoing war with the Holy League out of consideration for the susceptibilities of the Christian subjects.[179] Secondly, the system of tax-farming was restructured in 1695 in a way that made life-term tax-farming a reality. This new system came to be known as *malikane mukataa*. The entrepreneur who made a bid for a life-lease tax-farm had to undertake to make annual payments to the treasury in addition to a large lump sum paid at the beginning that served as a kind of surety. As long as the conditions of the contract were observed, the *malikane* enjoyed full immunity from state intervention – with the exception that the *kadi* remained responsible for the spheres of public administration and the judiciary. On the death of the tax-farmer, the *malikane* was supposed to be resold at a public auction, but in reality the inheritors had enjoyed preferential rights of bidding. Although it was allowed to sell a *malikane*, such action was rather discouraged by the fisc which levied in this case a special tax equal to 10 per cent of the original downpayment (after 1735). It was expected that the tax-farmer would invest in his *malikane* in order to enhance its productivity and profitability.[180]

The introduction of the *malikane* system brought relief to Ottoman finances. Moreover, the empire enjoyed during most of the eighteenth century a sustained economic and demographic upswing. Until the period of catastrophic wars beginning in the 1760s, the state itself participated actively in the economic growth. Between 1717 and 1760, large manufactures as state enterprises emerged, which gave a boost to the production of textiles, printed cotton cloths, silk, paper, glass, porcelain, tobacco, and various dyes. The islands of Chios and Crete developed in this period to become important exporters of silk and cotton textiles. The latter island also experienced an upswing in olive oil production and the soap industry. The Sofia-Samokov area in Bulgaria saw a spectacular expansion of the iron industry, the active ironworks numbering about 80 in the 1720s, and quite a few furnaces being added in the following decades. Indeed, the *kadi* of Samokov was to plead for a halt to issuing permits for new furnaces because of the advanced stage of deforestation of his district.[181]

---

178. See the table in Mehmet Genç, 'Osmanlı maliyesinde malikâne sistemi', in O. Okyar and Ü. Nalbantoğlu (eds), *Türkiye iktisat tarihi semineri (8–10 Haziran 1973)* (Ankara, 1975), p. 236.

179. See McGowan, *Economic Life in Ottoman Europe*, pp. 80–2. In nominal terms, poll-tax revenue more than doubled in the next century. Cf. Darling, *Revenue-Raising and Legitimacy*, p. 240.

180. Genç, 'Osmanlı maliyesinde malikâne sistemi', pp. 236–40; Çizakça, *A Comparative Evolution of Business Partnerships*, pp. 159f., 164. For an emphatically positive assessment of the malikane system see Ariel Salzmann, 'An ancien regime revisited: "privatization" and political economy in the eighteenth-century Ottoman empire', *Society and Politics*, 21 (1993), pp. 393–423, and eadem, 'Measures of empire: tax farmers and the Ottoman ancien régime, 1695–1807' (PhD, Columbia University, 1995).

181. On the interrelationship of state, war and economy see Mehmet Genç, 'A comparative study of the life term farming data and the volume of commercial and industrial activities in the Ottoman empire during

297

The general economic recovery since the early eighteenth century was also accompanied by an upsurge in commercial activity. The traditional arteries of Levant trade through the Mediterranean were supplemented after 1718 by continental trade routes through the Danubian basin and further south along the valleys of Morava and Vardar.[182] Obviously, behind textile manufacturing stood cotton cultivation, and behind soap production the olive economy.[183] New crops such as maize and tobacco, too, found a ready acceptance in the countryside.[184] The government ban on the export of cereals, a familiar aspect of trade during the seventeenth century, practically disappeared, giving a new impetus to grain cultivation, especially in coastal areas of Greece.[185] Thus, a recent study of Patras in the eighteenth century has shown that wheat, currants, cotton and tobacco were grown as commercial crops primarily for export. Similary, the production of silk, wool, wax, leather, juniper berries and fruit had export as its object. The authors of the study have ascertained an increase in the number of settlements as 'a result of long-term expansion in economic activity and a related growth in the population of the district as a whole'. This process was accompanied by land colonization 'stimulated by the demand mediated through the port of Patras' and affecting 'the more distant, higher and marginal land, as well as the neighbouring plains'.[186]

Çiftliks and Commercial Agriculture

The emergence of an increasingly export-oriented agriculture in the Ottoman empire has been associated with the *çiftlik* formation. In contrast to the traditional term of the Ottoman *timar* system (*reaya çiftlik*), the *çiftlik* of the eighteenth century was a sizeable farm devoted to production for a distant market. The peasants who cultivated the land could not claim any rights of ownership over the arable, nor was the former *timar* holder in a position to do so. The

the second half of the 18th century', in N. Todorov (ed.), *La Révolution industrielle dans le sud-est européen – XIXe siècle* (Sofia, 1977), pp. 242–79; Genç, 'Osmanlı ekonomisi ve savaş', *Yapıt*, 49: 4 (April–May 1984), pp. 52–61, and 50: 5 (July 1984), pp. 86–93; Genç, 'Entreprises d'état et attitude politique dans l'industrie ottomane au XVIIIe siècle', in J. Thobie and J.-L. Bacqué-Grammont (eds), *L'Accession de la Turquie à la civilisation industrielle. Facteurs internes et externes. Actes du Colloque d'Istanbul, 2–4 décembre 1985* (Istanbul, 1987), pp. 5–12; Genç, 'L'économie ottomane et la guerre au XVIIIe siècle', *Turcica*, 27 (1995), pp. 177–96.

182. Nicholas Svoronos, *Le commerce de Salonique au XVIIIe siècle* (Paris, 1956), pp. 180–5 and passim; A. E. Vacalopoulos, *History of Macedonia 1354–1833* (Salonika, 1973), pp. 387–425; Virzhiniia Paskaleva, *Sredna Evropa i zemite po dolniia Dunav prez XVIII–XIX v. (Sotsialno-ikonomicheski aspekti)* (Sofia, 1986), pp. 50–79.

183. On the 'political economy' of olive oil' and and the interrelationship of 'soap, class, and state', see Beshara Doumani, *Rediscovering Palestine. Merchants and Peasants in Jabal Nablus, 1700–1900* (Berkeley/Los Angeles/London, 1995), pp. 131–81 and 182–231 respectively.

184. Traian Stoianovich, 'Le mais dans les Balkans', *Annales ESC*, 21 (1966), pp. 1026–40; Aleksandar Matkovski, 'Auftreten und Ausbreitung des Tabaks auf der Balkanhalbinsel', *Südost-Forschungen*, 28 (1969), pp. 48–93; Lawless, 'The economy and landscapes of Thessaly during Ottoman rule', p. 519.

185. Spyros I. Asdrachas, 'Marchés et prix du blé en Grèce au XVIIIe siècle', *Südost-Forschungen*, 31 (1972), pp. 178–209.

186. Malcolm Wagstaff and Elena Frangakis-Syrett, 'The port of Patras in the second Ottoman period. Economy, demography and settlements, c.1700–1830', in Panzac, *Les Balkans à l'époque ottomane*, pp. 89–91.

owner of the land was a new type of entrepreneur, generally referred to as *çiftlik sahibi*.[187]

Viewed merely as a category of private property, but sometimes having a specific settlement status distinct from that of a village, references to *çiftliks* are already frequent in the documents of the sixteenth century. It seems that some influential men of that period claimed ownership of land usually on locations known as *mezraa*. Often a water mill, a sheep ranch or an orchard of a few fruit trees was registered as *çiftlik*.[188] In regions where the *timar* system had never been introduced and the economy was characterized by extensive animal husbandry, private property of this type was even more common. For example, research on the history of the Pontic steppes has shown that some districts along the lower Dniester (Akkerman, Kili and Bender) had a surprisingly high concentration of *çiftliks* – each with a few persons registered on them – already in the sixteenth century. Owners were mostly persons of a military status.[189] Even in Danubian Bulgaria, where the *timar* system was in application, *çiftliks* of these dimensions are quite common, without, however, being at all typical of rural society there.[190]

References to *çiftliks* increase in the documents stemming from the early seventeenth century. Since it was also the time of the *celâlî* rebellions, a theory broaching the forcible expropriation of the peasants by powerful social groups has found broad acceptance.[191] Later on, it was the attention shown to this theory within both Marxist and Balkan nationalist historiography that helped it retain credibility.[192] However, the conditions under which such expropriation might have taken place remained open to discussion.

A highly plausible explanation has highlighted the importance of peasant indebtedness as a factor of the destabilization of the Ottoman land regime in the seventeenth and eighteenth centuries. The inflation of the late sixteenth century followed by a considerable fall in population and in grain prices in the next century, coupled with the negative aspects of tax-farming especially when it was applied on a basis of collective liability, forced the peasants in the Balkans as well as in Anatolia to borrow money in order to fulfil their tax obligations. Interest rates were quite usurious, reaching sometimes 60 per cent. Many peasants were compelled to take a mortgage on their houses, gardens and fields, or they had to sell their crops before the harvest only to buy their own produce again in winter at higher prices. Innumerable peasant households were ruined in this way. Thus,

187. Cf. McGowan, *Economic Life in Ottoman Europe*, p. 122.
188. See the many references in McGowan, *Sirem Sancağı mufassal tahrir defteri*.
189. Gilles Veinstein, 'Colonisation et régime foncier dans l'Empire ottoman: le cas des steppes du nord de la Mer Noire au XVIe siècle', in M. Balard (ed.), *Etat et colonisation au Moyen Age et à la Renaissance* (Lyon, 1989), pp. 425–39.
190. Cf. Vera P. Mutafchieva, 'Kum vuprosa za chiflitsite v Osmanskata imperiia prez XIV–XVII v.', *Istoricheski pregled*, 14: 1 (1958), pp. 34–57.
191. See, for example, Akdağ, *Celâlî isyanları*, pp. 37–44.
192. Cf. Fikret Adanır, 'Zum Verhältnis von Agrarstruktur und nationaler Bewegung in Makedonien 1878–1908', in R. Melville and H.-J. Schröder (eds), *Der Berliner Kongreß von 1878. Die Politik der Großmächte und die Probleme der Modernisierung in Südosteuropa in der zweiten Hälfte des 19. Jahrhunderts* (Wiesbaden, 1982), pp. 445–61; Adanır, 'The Macedonian question: the socio-economic reality and problems of its historiographic interpretation', *International Journal of Turkish Studies*, 3: 1 (Winter 1984–85), pp. 43–64.

titular dispossession, as opposed to physical dispossession, leaves the cultivator in place but generally imposes new and harsher conditions upon him. The most general and effective instrument in producing this effect (where outright coercion is not practicable) is to initiate a debt cycle by lending to the cultivator, then threatening him with breach of contract and bringing him more or less totally under control.[193]

Consequently, powerful groups appeared who usurped the land and converted it into private estates, i.e. *çiftliks*. The attempts of the government to stop usury and the rural exodus by decree were futile.[194] Similar situations obtained in the Arab provinces of the empire. In Damascus, for example, 'new power groups came to the fore dominating, among other things, the real estate market and financial dealings in the countryside', whereby 'credit and moneylending constituted major aspects of urban-rural relations'. Among property sellers, villagers represented a high percentage which could be explained 'also by the collective debts they contracted and their inability to repay them'.[195]

However convincing these results may be, the state of research does not yet allow a conclusive judgement in this regard. On the contrary, there are equally plausible explanations which focus on the question of labour, investigating whether the new landowning groups had at their disposal peasants to work their estates and whether these estates were important for their roles within the socio-political context. Thus, ongoing research on land-credit relations in the Macedonian district of Kara Ferye (modern Verria) in the first half of the seventeenth century shows that peasant indebtedness was indeed widespread, about 80 per cent of the villages appearing as (collective) debtors at least once during that period. Money lending was practised both by individuals and pious foundations, the latter playing a slightly greater role and the average interest charged being 20 and 15 per cent respectively. But the question whether the indebtedness of the peasantry had effected a change in landholding patterns is easily answered by pointing out that cash *vakıfs* did not show interest in land or gaining control over peasants. They were not even interested in getting their principal back, provided that yearly interest was paid regularly. Neither could individual creditors easily force debtors in distress to sell out to them at a low price. The law required that such land be sold by auction. At any rate, although 12 per cent of land sales during the period 1621 to 1652 were transacted on account of debts, only in a few cases was the buyer also the creditor.[196]

193. McGowan, *Economic Life in Ottoman Europe*, p. 66.

194. Mustafa Akdağ, *Türkiye'nin iktisadî ve içtimaî tarihi*, vol. II (Istanbul, 1974), pp. 249–59. Cf. also Avdo Sućeska, 'O nastanku čifluka u našim zemljama', *Godišnjak društva istoričara Bosne i Hercegovine*, 15 (1965), pp. 37–57, here pp. 39–41.

195. Abdul-Karim Rafeq, 'City and countryside in a traditional setting. The case of Damascus in the first quarter of the eighteenth century', in Philipp, *The Syrian Land in the 18th and 19th Century*, pp. 295–332.

196. Eleni Gara, 'Indebtedness of peasants and its impact on agrarian relations – the case of the Kara Ferye district in Macedonia in the 17th century', paper presented to the VII. International Congress on the Economic and Social History of the Ottoman Empire (1300–1920), Heidelberg, 25–29 July 1995. I am grateful to the author for permitting me to use her manuscript.

The eighteenth century can be seen as the culmination of the *çiftlik* economy in Ottoman Europe. It was also the period in which the *ayans* as the new provincial elite consolidated their power. Especially after the outbreak of the Russo-Ottoman war in 1768, the Porte considered it opportune to charge the *ayans* officially with the administration of the rural districts (*kaza*). They thus took over part of the duties which had formerly belonged to the *kadi*, such as allocating and collecting the taxes, ensuring public law and order, preventing smuggling, maintaining a postal service, levying troops, provisioning supplies for the army, and the like. Until 1779, the election of the *ayan* had to be confirmed by the provincial governor; afterwards the Sublime Porte, the Ottoman government, took over this procedure.[197] In the process the provincial governors were degraded practically to officials with only representative functions. During this time a few *ayan* families evolved to become quasi-rulers of entire provinces. This development reached its climax when, in a time of domestic power struggles, the ruler of Rusçuk, Alemdar Mustafa Pasha, marched with his troops to the capital and enthroned Mahmud II (1808–39) as sultan.[198] Mustafa Pasha, now himself Grand Vizier, hoped to reconcile the conflicting interests of the various groups within the ruling elite by way of consultations in an 'advisory assembly'. For this purpose the prominent *ayans*, the provincial governors, leading notables and magnates were invited to the capital. The result of the consultations was an 'alliance pact' (*sened-i ittifak*) in which the central government and the *ayans* agreed to respect their mutual rights and privileges. This amounted to an official sanctioning of the *ayans'* standing within provincial society.[199]

In short, from the last decades of the eighteenth century the Ottoman empire experienced something like an *ayan* feudalism. Especially when the so-called *kırcali* revolts broke out in the Balkans and spread quickly during the chaos of the war against Russia and Austria (1787–92), the weakness of the central government was visible to all.[200] The heavy defeat in this war discredited the Ottoman government further. In this general atmosphere of turmoil, many inhabitants of the mountain villages sought refuge in the cities. Others found shelter with powerful landowners in the valleys, accepting the status of sharecroppers.

In the light of the above analysis it becomes clear that the rule of *ayans* should coincide with the heyday of the *çiftlik* economy. An overview of agrarian relations in that period shows that *çiftliks* were indeed widespread in some provinces in the Balkans. First among these was Bosnia. This frontier province had a privileged status within the empire. Muslim military lords and the *ayans* were able to establish almost absolute control over land. This was facilitated partly by the fact that frequent wars forced Christian peasants to flee to nearby

197. Vera P. Mutafchieva, 'L'institution de l'ayanlik pendant les dernières décennies du XVIIIe siècle', *Etudes balkaniques*, 2–3 (1965), p. 236.

198. On the rise of Alemdar Mustafa see A. F. Miller, *Mustafa pasha Bairaktar. Ottomanskaia imperiia v nachale XIX stoletiia* (Moscow, 1947), pp. 119ff.

199. An analysis of the *sened-i ittifak* in Halil İnalcık, 'Sened-i İttifak ve Gülhane Hatt-ı Hümâyûnu', *Belleten*, 28 (1964), pp. 603–22.

200. On the *kırcali* period see Vera P. Mutafchieva, *Kurdzhaliisko vreme* (Sofia, 1977).

Venetian or Austrian territories. When they returned, they found their parcels occupied by strange sharecroppers and were thus forced to accept sharecropping conditions themselves. In addition, the Ottoman government actively discouraged the sale of property, especially *miri* land, to non-Muslims in Balkan frontier zones.[201] Somewhat similar conditions obtained in the region of Vidin in north-western Bulgaria which was notorious on account of its special regime of *gospodarlık*, a combination of pre-Ottoman feudal usages with the system of *malikane*, life-lease tax-farm. Again, since Vidin was part of the Ottoman military frontier, the Christian peasantry had no chance of acquiring agricultural land. As late as the early nineteenth century, the peasants of Vidin, who, of course, paid their regular taxes to the treasury, were obliged to work for two months on the land of the *agha*, i.e. *gospodar*, to deliver him significant amounts of grains as well as offering him 'in conformity with the ancient custom' various personal presents.[202]

A regime of *gospodarlık* could be found also in the district of Kustendil in north-western Bulgaria. Recent research shows that despite 'feudal' obligations towards the *agha*, the peasants under *gospodarlık* did not fare much worse than the independent peasantry. It is true that they had to pay in compensation for rent (i) a fixed amount of grain, (ii) free labour services on the *agha*'s *çiftlik*, (iii) gifts of wood, charcoal, butter, cheese, meat, etc., and (iv) sometimes a certain amount of money. Nevertheless, what the peasants paid to the *gospodar* did not surpass 5 per cent of their total income. As state taxes they had to pay the tithe (10 per cent of the produce); *emlâk* (0.4 per cent of the value of buildings); 3 per cent on income earned through crafts not related to agriculture; and 27–28 *guruş* as military exemption tax (*bedel-i askeriye*).[203]

Serbian agriculture in the late eighteenth century had totally different structures. With approximately ten persons per square kilometre, the so-called Pashalik of Belgrade was an underpopulated country. Only a tiny portion of the land, some hilly areas, was under cultivation, while the flatlands and valleys were covered by dense forests. Agriculture served the basic needs of a self-sufficient society. Animal breeding, especially the breeding of pigs, was more important than corn growing.[204] The towns were few and populated predominately by Muslims and other non-Serbian groups. Trade and crafts, with the exception of the rural pig trade, were controlled by non-Serbs. The peasantry enjoyed a high degree of self-rule. The administrative system of the country was based on a virtual federation of autonomous villages in which the heads of extended families (*zadruga*) elected their own *kmet* (headmen), and the village headmen elected the district primate (*knez*). The assessment and collection of taxes were privileges of the village headmen, who acted also as rural magistrates. Further-

201. Nedim Filipović, 'Odžakluk timari u Bosni i Hercegovini', *Prilozi za orijentalni filologiju*, 5 (1954–55), pp. 251–74; Yuzo Nagata, *Materials on the Bosnian Notables* (Tokyo, 1979); Srećko M. Džaja, *Konfessionalität und Nationalität Bosniens und der Herzegowina: Voremanzipatorische Phase 1463 bis 1804* (Munich, 1984), pp. 43–101.
202. Halil İnalcık, *Tanzimat ve Bulgar meselesi* (Ankara, 1943), pp. 83–107.
203. Slavka Draganova, *Kiustendilski region 1864–1919. Etnodemografsko i sotsialnoikonomichesko izsledvane* (Sofia, 1996).
204. Olga Srdanović-Barać, *Srpska agrarna revolucija i poljoprivreda od Kočine krajine do kraja prve vlade kneza Miloša (1788–1839)* (Belgrade, 1980), pp. 30–2.

more, the Serbs had the right to carry arms and to partake freely in trade with Habsburg lands.[205]

In the Peloponnese, too, we find autonomous structures. People elected their administrative councils, and the *ayans* were here not Muslims but Greeks. The power base of the Peloponnese provincial elite was, as in the case of Muslims, real estate, but not necessarily *miri* land cultivated by the peasantry. Thus, Panayot Benakis, the primate of Kalamata in the eighteenth century, owned mostly buildings, gardens, vineyards or olive orchards.[206] Even though by 1790 some *çiftliks* were also included among his property, this does not modify the general picture of a typical Ottoman *ayan* whose primary concerns lay elsewhere. One historian has rightly pointed out that the

significance of both Turkish lords and Greek primates as landowners per se was less than has generally been assumed. Both these elite groups derived their power and wealth more from administration, tax collection, and usury, than from outright ownership or direct exploitation of land. For under the peculiar Turkish system of shared rights in land, and given the universal practice of tax farming, the receipt of taxes and other dues was a property right. The extensive estates of powerful lords and archons, therefore, consisted not of farms which they would operate themselves, but rather of claims upon virtually every type of income which villagers produced, paid as rents, taxes, interest, and other exactions.[207]

This judgement reiterates in many ways conclusions drawn in respect of other parts of the Ottoman empire. Regarding the *çiftlik* agriculture in western Anatolia it has been concluded that the shortage of labour forced the estate-owners to convert their lands into cattle ranches.[208] The leading *ayan* of the region owed his wealth to financial operations as moneylender and tax-farmer.[209]

Forms of Peasant Protest

Peasants and Petitioners

Peasant resistance has often been equated with peasant revolt.[210] It took a long while before the insight prevailed that the 'resistance of the peasantry is . . . often most effective when it follows the path of least resistance'.[211] With respect

205. Stevan Pavlowitch, 'Society in Serbia, 1791–1830', in R. Clogg (ed.), *Balkan Society in the Age of Greek Independence* (Totowa, NJ, 1981), pp. 137–56, here p. 138.

206. Gilles Veinstein, 'Le patrimoine foncier de Panayote Bénakis, *kocabaşı* de Kalamata', *Journal of Turkish Studies*, 11 (1987), pp. 211–33.

207. William W. McGrew, *Land and Revolution in Modern Greece, 1800–1881: The Transition in the Tenure and Exploitation of Land from Ottoman Rule to Independence* (Kent, OH, 1985), p. 38.

208. İnalcık, *The Emergence of Big Farms*, p. 118.

209. Ibid., p. 124. See also Gilles Veinstein, '"Ayân" de la région d'Izmir et commerce du Levant (deuxième moitié du XVIII siècle)', *Revue de l'Occident musulman et de la Méditerranée*, 20 (1975), pp. 131–47.

210. Cf. Peter Bierbrauer, 'Bäuerliche Revolten im Alten Reich. Ein Forschungsbericht', in P. Blickle (ed.), *Aufruhr und Empörung? Studien zum bäuerlichen Widerstand im Alten Reich* (Munich, 1980), pp. 1–68.

211. James C. Scott, 'Resistance without protest and without organization: peasant opposition to the Islamic zakat and the Christian tithe', *Comparative Studies in Society and History*, 29 (1987), pp. 417–52, here at p. 423.

to Ottoman Europe, the historiography has been preoccupied with the armed resistance of the subject Christian peoples against the despotic rule of Muslim conquerors. The focus was on the heroic deeds of Balkan outlaws who opposed Turkish rule such as the haiduks and the klephts.[212] Empirical research on the basis of regional documentation, however, has revealed that spectacular violence on the part of a settled peasantry was rather rare. No wonder, for such action would have been at best irrational, if not altogether lethal, for the peasants themselves. Ottoman peasants were individuals who acted in a political space and, more often than not, consciously. Thus, in a study on sixteenth-century Palestine it has been shown that even routine administrative measures 'were adjusted through a continual process of negotiation and compromise', whereby peasants demonstrated great determination to 'moderate, postpone, or even try to cancel payments due'. In this struggle, the *kadis* stood the test 'as the local arbiters of justice'. Peasants regularly appealed to them 'against the iniquities or offences of the *sipahis*, janissaries, and others'.[213]

Just as the *kadi* was able to convey to the peasantry the feeling that they had a chance for a fair trial, so the sultan was very keen to generate and preserve the image of a just ruler. Indeed, 'the Ottoman political system rested on the premise that anyone, man or woman, might turn to the ruler to ask for a redress of grievances'.[214] During the *celâlî* rebellions, when the peasantry suffered perhaps more from the oppression by provincial governors, a 'justice decree' (*adaletname*) issued by Ahmed I in 1609 condemned openly the abuses of government officials. The style and content of such documents encouraged the people to make use of the political instrument of complaint.[215] Perhaps the most effective weapon in the hands of the peasants was the threat to flee. Especially in periods of population decline, as was the case in the seventeenth century, the ruling elite was certainly willing to go a long way to meet the demands of a resolute peasantry.[216]

Haiduks and Klephts

But, of course, there was also genuine social banditry. The term 'haiduk' itself reveals the social background of these outlaws. Originally it denoted cattle-drivers in Hungary.[217] About the middle of the sixteenth century, the word began

---

212. See Fikret Adanır, 'Bemerkungen zum Heiduckenproblem bei Jireček und in der modernen bulgarischen Historiographie', *Mitteilungen des Bulgarischen Forschungsinstituts in Österreich*, 3 (1980), pp. 73–95; idem, 'Heiduckentum und osmanische Herrschaft. Sozialgeschichtliche Aspekte der Diskussion um das frühneuzeitliche Räuberwesen in Südosteuropa', *Südost-Forschungen*, 41 (1982), pp. 43–116.

213. Singer, *Palestinian Peasants and Ottoman Officials*, pp. 120–3.

214. Suraiya Faroqhi, 'Political activity among Ottoman taxpayers and the problem of Sultanic legitimation (1570–1650)', *Journal of the Economic and Social History of the Orient*, 35 (1992), p. 2.

215. Ibid., p. 10; Hans Georg Majer (ed.), *Das osmanische 'Registerbuch der Beschwerden' (Şikâyet defteri) vom Jahre 1675. Österreichische Nationalbibliothek Cod. mixt. 683*, vol. I (Vienna, 1984). On 'justice decrees' see Halil İnalcık, 'Adâletnâmeler', *Belgeler*, 2: 3–4 (1965), pp. 49–165.

216. Cf. Aleksandar Matkovski, *Otporot vo Makedoniia vo vremeto na turskoto vladeenie*, vol. I: *Pasivniot otpor* (Skopje, 1983).

217. See István Rácz, *A hajdúk a XVII. században* (Debrecen, 1969), pp. 10–24; Mária Ivanics, 'Anmerkungen zur Etymologie hajdú "Heiduck" ', *Acta Orientalia Academiae Scientiarum Hungaricae*, 48 (1995), pp. 391–403.

to designate auxiliary military forces composed of peasants who had been dislocated during the wars.[218] Unwilling or unable to return to a settled agrarian way of life, these peasant-soldiers were an internal socio-political problem for the House of Habsburg as well as the Hungarian Estates, until they were granted a privileged status by István Bocskai, Prince of Transylvania, as reward for their services during the war against the Habsburg dynasty between 1604 and 1606.[219] At that time, the term 'haiduk' began to be applied to mercenaries of Balkan origin in Moldavia and Wallachia as well.[220] Especially during wars between the Habsburgs and the Ottomans, such haiduk detachments would cross the Danube and raid Ottoman territory.[221]

Peasant-soldiers, like haiduks, revolted whenever their 'privileges' were in jeopardy, not for the sake of any anti-feudal goal. Military life, duties and rights helped develop a military consciousness.[222] The history of the Austrian military border in the course of the sixteenth, seventeenth and eighteenth centuries corroborates this thesis. The *Grenzer* served the House of Habsburg loyally on all battlefields of Europe. The moment, however, the Vienna government attempted to return them to their former peasant status, discontent mounted; from 1695 on rebellion was endemic along the frontier.[223] In the first half of the eighteenth century, especially in the Vojvodina, where the terrain was particularly suitable for haiduk activity, 'public security hardly existed; no one felt safe from the hayduks who attacked churches, monasteries, state and local officials, and invaded villages in the daytime, striking even larger urban centres, such as Karlovci and Vrsac'.[224]

The brief outline of developments in the Austrian empire helps us to understand the developments in the Ottoman Balkans as well. The Ottoman border organization, the *serhad*, actually served as the model for the *Militärgrenze*. From the beginning, the Ottomans enlisted, as shown earlier in this chapter, the services of certain social strata of the local population for military or internal security purposes. Pastoral groups with Vlach status as well as Turcoman Yürüks played a key role in this system. Organized into various military or semi-military categories such as *martolos*, *voynuk* and *derbendci*, Christian Vlachs, Serbs, Bulgars, Albanians and Greeks not only guarded the southern bank of the

218. Ference Szakály, 'Das Bauerntum und die Kämpfe gegen die Türken bzw. gegen Habsburg in Ungarn im 16.–17. Jahrhundert', in G. Heckenast (ed.), *Aus der Geschichte der ostmitteleuropäischen Bauernbewegungen im 16.–17. Jahrhundert* (Budapest, 1977), p. 254.

219. Rácz, *A hajdúk*, pp. 46–91.

220. During the rule of Prince Matei Bassarab in the second quarter of the seventeenth century, there were more than 20,000 mercenaries in Wallachia: Slavs from lands south of the Danube, Cossacks, Ukrainians, Tatars, Poles and Hungarian haiduks. Cf. Lajos Demény, 'Die Rolle des Soldatenelementes in den Volksbewegungen des 17. Jahrhunderts. Der Charakter des Sejmen-Aufstandes in der Walachei im Jahre 1655', in Heckenast, *Aus der Geschichte des ostmitteleuropäischen Bauernbewegungen*, p. 94.

221. See M. Berindei, M. Kalus-Martin and G. Veinstein, 'Actes de Murad III sur la région de Vidin et remarques sur les qanun ottomans', *Südost-Forschungen*, 35 (1976), doc. no. X, pp. 58–60.

222. Cf. Szakály, 'Das Bauerntum und die Kämpfe gegen die Türken', pp. 251–66.

223. Ibid., p. 366; Wayne S. Vucinich, 'Serbian military tradition', in B. K. Király and G. E. Rothenberg (eds), *War and Society in East Central Europe*, vol. I (New York, 1979), p. 287. Cf. also Catherine Wendy Bracewell, *The Uskoks of Senj: Piracy, Banditry, and Holy War in the Sixteenth-Century Adriatic* (Ithaca, NY/London, 1992).

224. Ibid., p. 288.

Danube against raids from Valachia and Transylvania, but were also responsible for the safety of important overland routes throughout the Balkans. As such, their main duty was to chase and fight bandits, the haiduks and klephts.

Just as the Ottomans could rely on the loyalty of their subjects irrespective of religious or ethnic affiliation, so the bandits, too, had no reason to differentiate on these grounds: anyone could become their victim. Ragusan sources of the seventeenth century are full of accounts of Christian 'haiduzi' who attacked 'una carauana di mercantie' and murdered 'un mercante christiano'.[225] A certain Fra Bernardina, a 'missionario in Servia', laments in 1666 the fact that the peasants around Skopje were suffering more from the exactions of the haiduks than under the burden of Ottoman taxes.[226]

Discontent began to spread among privileged military groups in the Ottoman Balkans by the end of the sixteenth century, when the empire was experiencing a process of intense socio-economic and political transformation. The same factors which eventually rendered the *sipahis* obsolete as a military force affected other military groups as well. A new type of soldiery (*sekban, seymen, pandur*) came into being, willing to serve for little pay and without privileges. One result of this development was especially detrimental to public security and led eventually to the catastrophe of the *kırcali* period at the end of the eighteenth century: marauding bands of deserters in time of war or unemployed mercenaries in time of peace would ravage the countryside. The *derbendci*, inadequate in number, could not cope with the new situation. Some of them abandoned their mountain settlements altogether; others were forced to take a somewhat ambivalent attitude towards brigandage.[227] The frequent violation of their rights by provincial officials in the seventeenth century was not very conducive to making the highways safer. The functions of the *derbendci* were gradually taken over by mercenary *pandur* detachments, until in the 1830s watch-towers in mountain passes were built, manned mostly by Albanian gendarmes.[228]

Mercenary Christian *martolos* units, although no longer of military importance on the border, remained nevertheless the main security force in the interior throughout the seventeenth century and in some areas even until the Greek Revolution.[229] Initially, *martolos* troops proved to be quite effective against brigandage. In time, however, this service became demoralized, not least because the authorities found it expedient to appoint pardoned haiduk chiefs as *martolos* commanders.[230] In the long run, a certain collaboration between bandits and *martolos* was thus inevitable.

---

225. Sergije Dimitrijević, *Dubrovacki karavani u južnoj Srbiji u XVII veku* (Belgrade, 1958), p. 73.

226. Ibid., p. 75. Cf. also Antoni Podraza, 'Bauernbewegungen in den Karpaten vom 16. bis zum 18. Jahrhundert', in Heckenast, *Aus der Geschichte der ostmitteleuropäischen Bauernbewegungen*, p. 127.

227. Cf. Aleksandar Matkovski, 'Eden nepoznat bunt vo selo Gavato od juli 1639 godina', *Prilozi*, 1: 2 (Skopje 1970), pp. 57–60.

228. Herbert Wilhelmy, *Hochbulgarien*, vol. I: *Die ländlichen Siedlungen und die bäuerliche Wirtschaft* (Kiel, 1935), pp. 157–60, 173–4; Bistra A. Cvetkova, 'K voprosy o polozhenii derventdzhiiskogo naseleniia v bolgarskih zemliah v period tureckogo gospodstva', *Uchenye zapiski Instituta slavianovedeniia*, 20 (1960), pp. 216–20; Cengiz Orhonlu, *Osmanlı İmparatorluğunda derbend teşkilatı*, pp. 90–93, 111–17, 128; Stojanovski, *Dervendzhistvoto*, pp. 106–17.

229. Vasić, *Martolosi*, pp. 94–141.

230. Ibid., pp. 173–5.

The relations between the 'armatoli' and the 'klephts' in Greece are exemplary of this development. As one author put it, the 'distinction between the klephts, the robbers, and the armatoli, the licensed armed Greeks, was hardly noticed by the Greeks of the plains, although later history was to build up an image of the klephts as patriots and freedom fighters'.[231] The allegiances of klephts and armatoli were shaped primarily along the lines of family ties which were very strong in a pastoral society.[232] Apart from their own feuds, they felt obliged to interfere in the armed clashes of their relatives and friends. This kind of fighting took place each year and apparently was considered to be a normal affair; as Kolokotronis put it, 'one must help one's own people for one or two months during the summer'.[233] Obviously, such quarrelling could only be carried on at the expense of the peasantry. During the Revolution, when the klephts were altogether unchecked, the situation in the countryside became even worse. The fierce mountaineers of the Mainote Peninsula descended into the plains of the Peloponnese. 'They ruthlessly plundered the settled Greek villages and left a trail of destruction in the areas through which they passed.'[234] Makriyannis, another leader of the Revolution, deplores this situation in the following words: 'What I saw grieved me. We were turning our revolution into a school for brigands, and our country has become like the foul bedstraw of shameless men.' He was, however, unable to hold back his own men from pillaging Greek villages: 'I feared they would rob me too.'[235]

Haiduks and klephts could be easily used as instruments in the game of international power politics. Already at the beginning of the seventeenth century, they were involved in schemes for 'liberating Constantinople'.[236] For example, Karposh, a one-time haiduk who had risen to the rank of an Ottoman *martolos* chief in Macedonia, rebelled against the Porte in 1689, as the Austrian army was advancing upon Skopje. It is noteworthy that Emperor Leopold I had sent him the insignia designating him the 'Prince of Kumanovo'.[237] That such people showed an increasing readiness to collaborate with the European Powers against the Ottomans had to do not least with the sultan's decreasing capacity to offer them martial fame and rich material spoils. The loss of prestige due to repeated military defeats was in the long run bound to undermine the ability of the Porte to 'exercise effective control over all armed forces, regular or auxiliary, Moslem or Christian'.[238]

231. William St Clair, *That Greece Might Still Be Free. The Philhellenes in the War of Independence* (London, 1972), p. 8.

232. Alexis Politis, 'Brigandage – excédents économiques – élevage: Hypothèses pour une définition de l'interimbrication de ces éléments dans un circuit commun (XVIIe–XIXe s.)', in *Economies méditerranéennes équilibres et intercommunications, XIIIe–XIXe siècles*, vol. II (Athens, 1986), pp. 155–70.

233. Th. Kolokotronis, *Memoirs from the Greek War of Independence 1821–1833* (Chicago, 1969), pp. 90f.

234. St Clair, *That Greece Might Still be Free*, p. 36.

235. *Memoirs of General Makriyannis 1797–1864*, ed. and trans. H. A. Lidderdale (London, 1966), p. 57.

236. Cf. Bistra Cvetkova, 'Les Bulgares et la situation politique internationale au XVIIe siècle', *Bulgarian Historical Review*, 6: 2 (1978), pp. 35f. For a dispassionate evaluation of the political motives and factors in this period see Peter Bartl, *Der Westbalkan zwischen spanischer Monarchie und Osmanischem Reich: Zur Türkenkriegsproblematik an der Wende vom 16. zum 17. Jahrhundert* (Wiesbaden, 1974), pp. 81–199.

237. Dragan Tashkovski, *Karposhevoto vostanie* (Skopje, 1951); Ivan Katardzhiev, *Aidutskoto dvizhenie i Karposhovoto vostanie vo XVII vek* (Skopje, 1958).

238. Stephen Fischer-Galati, 'Military factors in Balkan revolutions', in Király and Rothenberg, *War and Society in East Central Europe*, p. 184.

Traditional military and semi-military groups remained a serious socio-economic and political problem in the Balkan countries even after Ottoman rule. In Serbia, Milosh Obrenović was confronted with a vigorous haiduk movement which at times threatened the very foundations of the emerging Serbian statehood and was suppressed by such draconian punishments as executions, torture, confiscation of property, internment of relatives, and holding the villages collectively responsible for acts of brigandage in their neighbourhood.[239]

The authority of the young national state of Greece was already challenged by the rebellions of 1834 and 1836, in which banditry played a prominent role. By recruiting men from traditional military groups to pursue the brigands, the Greek government resorted to a time-honoured method of allaying popular discontent. It was suspected that klephts and armatoli 'had encouraged these revolts as a way of forcing the government into dependence on them'.[240] The new ruling elite came to realize that men accustomed to the traditional military way of life had an aversion to cultivating the soil. Such persons had only the choice between some petty government post and brigandage.[241] It was obvious, furthermore, that 'the large nomadic population of shepherds often served as accomplices or protectors of the brigands . . . [and] that helpless peasants often aided the brigand only to escape his wrath'.[242] Having tried unsuccessfully to eradicate banditry by applying the principle of collective responsibility of the communities, the Greek government reached the point in 1839 of considering the reinstatement of the old system of armatoli: the communities 'would hire brigands to pursue other brigands. This method would partially eliminate one of the causes of brigandage – insufficient means of livelihood – and would benefit by the hired brigand's inside knowledge of the system.'[243]

PEASANTRIES AND AGRICULTURE AT THE END OF THE OTTOMAN ANCIEN RÉGIME: FIRST HALF OF THE NINETEENTH CENTURY

The Ottoman reforms of the nineteenth century were in a sense an attempt to reinstate the lost positions of the central bureaucracy. For that reason, the 'alliance pact' of 1807 was bound to remain a piece of paper. Its spiritual father,

239. Nikola Sotirovski, 'Za opshtestveno-ekonomskiot karakter na aidutskoto dvizhenie vo istoriiata na nashite narodi', *Godishnik na Pravniot facultet vo Skopje*, 9 (1964), pp. 271–80; Vladimir Stojančević, *Milosh Obrenović i njegovo doba* (Belgrade, 1966), pp. 116–20; Toma Zhivanović, *Zakonski izvori krivichnog prava Srbiie i istoriiski razvoi niegov i niegog krivicnog pravosudia od 1804 do 1865* (Belgrade, 1967), pp. 463–66.

240. John A. Petropulos, *Politics and Statecraft in the Kingdom of Greece 1833–1843* (Princeton, NJ, 1968), p. 252.

241. Ibid., p. 213.

242. Ibid., p. 309. For an interesting analysis of the role brigandage played in Greek irredentist policies see John S. Koliopoulos, *Brigands with a Cause. Brigandage and Irredentism in Modern Greece, 1821–1912* (Oxford, 1987).

243. Ibid., p. 310. On brigandage in Bulgaria, a country that reached autonomous statehood in 1878, see Bernard Lory, 'Problèmes du brigandage en Bulgarie 1878–1883', in *Bulgarskata durzhava prez vekovete (Purvi Mezhdunaroden kongres po bulgaristika: Dokladi)*, vol. I (Sofia, 1982), pp. 510–15.

Alemdar Mustafa Pasha, had been Grand Vezir for only a few months when the mutiny of the janissaries cost him his life. Sultan Mahmud II succeeded, in the face of the growing Russian danger and the spread of nationalistic ideas among the Christians of the empire, in gathering Muslim urban opinion round him. After the liquidation of the Janissary Corps (1826), the central government had in the emerging modern army a suitable instrument to crush the power of the *ayans*. With the exception of Egypt, whose ruler Mohammed Ali could not be subjugated, all other provinces of the empire came again under the direct control of the Sublime Porte.

Rural life in the empire could not remain unaffected by these processes. The edict of 1839, which formulated the policies of the 'reform party', also promised – albeit prematurely – the abolition of tax-farming. The adherents of reform aimed at simplification and rationalization of the tax system. All differences in status relating to geographic, class and personal background were to be abolished. Their hope was that such a reform would raise state revenue and help strengthen central authority. Along with the establishment of a Ministry of Finance wide-scale cadastral surveys, population and property censuses were envisaged.[244]

Most interesting among them were the censuses carried out in 1845/46 of 'property, land, animals and income', the results of which were registered in the *Temettü' Defterleri*. Establishing the true state of the economic capacity of the tax-paying population was intended to serve a more equitable allocation of taxes. An interesting aspect of the survey was that it was accomplished by the representatives of the local peoples; thus, village headmen and members of the elders' councils as well as imams and priests participated. Apart from registering agricultural lands, vineyards, gardens, olive orchards, cows and donkeys, sheep and goats and even poultry, income from various trades and professions was also recorded.[245]

Of greater consequence was a new Land Code promulgated in 1858. At a first glance, little seemed to have changed: the law continued to distinguish between five landholding categories: *mülk*: free property; *miri*: state land; *mevkufe*: land of the religious foundations; *metruke*: public land such as roads, markets, pastures, forests; *mevat*: no man's land, fallow land. The usufruct of the *miri* land was granted to the peasants who actually worked and possessed it for an unlimited period of time. But, as was the case in the classical system, the peasants were expected to continue to cultivate the land and not to change its character by planting trees or constructing buildings on it.

244. Fikret Adanır, 'Ondokuzuncu Yüzyıl Ortalarında Foça Kasabasında Kazanç ve Vergi (1262/1846 tarihli *Kal'e-i Foça-i Atik Temettüât Defteri* temelinde bazı gözlemler)', in Foça Belediyesi (ed.), *Geçmişten günümüze Foça* (Ankara, 1997), pp. 5–14.

245. Stanford and Ezel Kural Shaw, *History of the Ottoman Empire and Modern Turkey*, vol. II: *Reform, Revolution, and Republic: The Rise of Modern Turkey, 1808–1975* (Cambridge, 1977), pp. 95f. On the use of *temettü' defterleri* as sources for historical research, see Tevfik Güran, *Structure économique et sociale d'une région de campagne dans l'Empire ottoman vers le milieu du XIXe s. Etude comparée de neuf villages de la nahiye de Koyuntepe, Sanjak de Filibe* (Sofia, 1979), pp. 49f.; idem, 'Ondokuzuncu yüzyıl ortalarında Ödemiş kasabasının sosyo-ekonomik özellikleri', in *Ord. Prof. Ömer Lütfi Barkan'a Armağan* (Istanbul, 1985), pp. 301–19. For a successful use of temettü' registers see also Svetla Ianeva, *L'artisanat et les corporations de métier dans la partie centrale des Balkans pendant la première moitié du XIXe siècle* (PhD, European University Institute, Florence, 1996).

On the other hand, the political and economic conditions of the period were such that the state could not avoid liberalizing the economy to a certain extent. Already the Anglo-Turkish Commercial Convention of 1838 obliged the Ottoman government to introduce free trade in the empire. And with the Straits Convention of 1841 and the Treaty of Paris of 1856 the empire accepted a *de facto* trusteeship by European Powers. This growing influence of Europe left its mark on the second fundamental document of Ottoman reform, the *hatt-i hümayun* of 1856, in which the wishes of European entrepreneurs were fulfilled to let them participate in the development of transport, agriculture and industry in the Near East. This liberalization process continued and reached its apogee in 1867 with a law which permitted foreigners to acquire agricultural land in the Ottoman Empire.

These last measures served also to reconcile Muslim landowning interests with the bureaucracy. According to Article 130 of the Land Code of 1858 the lands of a village commune could not be converted into a *çiftlik* estate if the place was still inhabited. If the place was deserted, however, it was possible to register the land legally as *çiftlik*. Since most of the *çiftliks* were established on uncultivated land, the above stipulation of the Land Code was tantamount to a *post-factum* sanctioning of the conversion of state lands into private property.

***

The impact of the Land Code of 1858 is still the object of lively controversy among specialists. Did it really reflect an effort 'to reassert the state's right to land through the establishment of a regime of state ownership', an effort that ended, against all intentions, 'by enlarging the scope of private land ownership' in the empire?[246] Or were the results rather the other way around, as has also been asserted, namely that the 1858 Land Code represented 'a culmination of re-centralisation', which excluded the 'dispossession of the peasantry as an historical possibility . . . thus rendering impossible the development of capitalist agriculture with wage labour'.[247] It is just as futile to look for unanimity on the consequences of the Land Code of 1867 which stipulated that 'foreign subjects [were] allowed, with the same title as Ottoman subjects and without any other condition, to enjoy the right to possess immovable property, urban or rural, anywhere within the Empire . . . on submitting to the laws and regulations which govern Ottoman subjects themselves'.[248] One thing, however, is clear: the reforms initiated since the 1830s put an end to the Ottoman *ancien régime*.

246. Kemal H. Karpat, 'The land regime, social structure and modernization in the Ottoman Empire', in W. R. Polk and R. L. Chambers (eds), *Beginnings of Modernization in the Middle East: the Nineteenth Century* (Chicago/London, 1968), pp. 69–90, here p. 86. The author thinks that the bureaucracy wanted more state control, but that the result was increased privatization of land.

247. Çağlar Keyder, 'The cycle of sharecropping and the consolidation of small peasant ownership in Turkey', *The Journal of Peasant Studies* 10, 2/3 (1982/83), pp. 133f.

248. R. C. Tute, *The Ottoman Land Laws with a Commentary on the Ottoman Land Code of 7th Ramadan 1274* (Jerusalem, 1927), p. 140.

Map 10.1 Scandinavia

CHAPTER TEN

The Peasants of Scandinavia, 1300–1700

David Gaunt

Scandinavia encompasses Denmark, Finland, Iceland, Norway and Sweden. The distance from south to north extends beyond the Arctic circle and thus goes to the very margins of where agricultural production is possible. Many of the peasants in historical Scandinavia were compelled to combine work in the fields with herding, fishing, hunting and by-employment; and in large areas growing crops played a secondary role in the peasant economy.

No Scandinavian term translates exactly into 'peasant'; instead the generic term in use is *bonde* which originally meant a dweller on the land. The corresponding Finnish term *talonpoika*, which translates as 'son of the house', also refers to a resident. *Bonde* can be used for self-owners, tenants and modern farmers; what is common is that these individuals work the land themselves and live from its produce; they differ in whether they own or rent the land on which they dwell. The various forms of ownership probably caused few differences in daily life between neighbours, but the varying distribution of natural resources and other ecological factors had a decisive role in shaping different regional lifestyles.

The Nordic peoples were primarily coastal peoples and were equally at home on land or water. As a rule, the farther north one travelled the more important became the sea and waterways as ecological resources. Access to water brought with it ease of transport in boats or on sledges over the frozen ice. Ease of transport also meant that Scandinavian peasants were perhaps more mobile than peasants on the European continent. Access to boats and knowledge of navigation meant that many peasants could themselves take their wares to distant markets.

Up to ten thousand years ago the Fenno-Scandinavian region was covered by a three kilometre-thick ice-pack. Because of this the surface of Scandinavia was tilted and some northern areas are now rising while some southern areas are sinking. At its greatest, land is rising at a rate of a metre each century and many waterways and lakes used in Viking times have now become insignificant. Because of the ice-pack most Scandinavian soil is either sand or clay sediment with little organic content.

THE TWO EMPIRES

The political history of Scandinavia is the story of two rival empires. The western empire was built on the Danish royal house which from 1389 to 1814 also ruled Norway. The eastern empire was organized around the Swedish royal house which up to 1809 also ruled Finland. Of the two, the Danish empire was the more successful, but was ultimately overtaken in the seventeenth century when the Swedes attained a brilliant yet short-lived period as a great power. Denmark and Norway balanced on the trade lanes between the North Sea, the Baltic and Muscovy and became closely linked to foreign markets. In contrast Sweden and Finland entered later into large-scale international commerce.

The medieval Danish territories also included part of Schleswig and Holstein in Germany. Estonia was a Danish colony from 1219 to 1346. Most of what is now southernmost Sweden was under Danish rule up to the mid-1600s. The Danes also controlled Norway, Iceland and Greenland, as well as the Atlantic island-groups of the Faroes, Shetlands and Orkneys. This vast territory was a continuation of the Atlantic empire created by the Vikings. The governments of Denmark were up to the mid-1600s dominated by the aristocracy who used their power to advance their own interests and who opposed strong central interference. Denmark fought almost continual wars from 1610 to 1650, and when they finished the country was in an abysmal state, its trade was in shambles, the population was reduced, much farm land lay in waste and it never regained its former greatness.

In the east, Sweden thrived after 1520 when a revolt against the common Nordic rule put Gustavus Vasa on the throne. He began building up a centralized national state and mobilized the support of the peasantry to tame the ambitions of the aristocracy. Sweden expanded east and south in a drive to rule the Baltic coast and came into conflict with all neighbouring countries. It is assumed that the motive was economic: to command the wealthy trade going westwards to Amsterdam. By 1700 Sweden had won seven provinces from Denmark-Norway (the most important of these was Scania, a rich agricultural region) and had pushed the Finnish border beyond present-day St Petersburg. It ruled Estonia, Ingermanland and Latvia in the Baltic, along with Pomerania and Mecklenburg on the German coast.

As was the case in much of Europe, the period from 1300 to 1700 in the Scandinavian countries divided broadly into four phases. First, the agrarian crisis arose from a combination of plague, diminished population and perhaps climate change. Very extensive (more than 40 per cent) desertion of farm land took place throughout Norway and parts of Jutland; extensive (25–40 per cent) desertion took place in many parts of Denmark and part of southern Sweden. Least affected by population decline were Finland, Iceland and most of Sweden. During this time peasants were relatively well off as land was readily available. Slavery disappeared and tenant rents were lower. Second, between 1400 and 1550 a period of reconstruction occurred and landholders began pressing more work and outlay from the peasants. A few nobles built up large holdings of land. Export of cattle, fish and butter was profitable, whilst grain was cheap. Third, in the century from 1550 to 1650 governments supported the flourishing of a landed nobility with demesne farms and wide privileges. The prices of agricultural goods rose up to the 1620s, but the price of fish fell. An intricate system of privileges gave the nobles great power over their tenants and many self-owners sold their farms. Nobles ran estates with an eye to selling the produce, whilst many tenants had their dues changed into unpaid labour. Lastly, the period from 1650 to 1730 was marked by state concern with 'conserving' the peasantry from impoverishment. The Thirty Years War and its aftermath caused great destruction in Denmark and Finland and, to make matters worse, international prices for farm products fell. Demesne privileges, such as freedom from taxation, were removed in Denmark; in Sweden the state confiscated much noble land and small noble estates declined. Large numbers of Norwegian tenants became self-owners through the sale of Crown land.

ECONOMIC TRENDS

The production of Scandinavian peasants was closely linked to the structure of European markets for trade in agricultural produce. Many definitions assume that peasants were reluctant to go to market and that if they did, occasionally, have anything to sell it was because of sheer luck; if they planned to sell their produce they were no longer authentic peasants. Lack of market participation is not a very useful criterion in Scandinavia as interest in trading was widespread and peasants had many opportunities for by-employment which could balance the manifest risks of crop failure in a cold climate. Commercial opportunities often led to changes in the nature of peasant livelihood as all parts of Scandinavia kept in contact with and were in confrontation with foreign interests. Up to the late sixteenth century this was usually the Hanseatic League with its major cities Lübeck, Danzig and Tallinn (Reval). Holland emerged as a market for the western parts of Denmark and Norway during the 1400s and the English fought with the Germans over the Icelandic trade. In general, the highest international prices for Scandinavian wares were obtained in western Europe, whereas prices in nearby northern Germany were lower; lowest by far, though, were the prices of local domestic markets. Great profits were to be had in the export trade since many articles like furs and dried fish fetched high prices relative to their weight; but Scandinavians had little chance to compete against the cheap prices of Polish grain.

The north German towns were the major medieval markets for Danish butter, cattle and herring, for Norwegian cod, Finnish furs and Swedish iron. The large merchants and craftsmen in the Nordic towns were more likely to be Germans than Scandinavians and the prices paid were set by the Germans. In many towns there were two mayors: one each for the natives and the Germans. Heavy salting was the universal medieval method for preserving foodstuffs and most food was extremely salty. This was the only commodity all peasants needed but which only a few living on the Atlantic sea-coast could produce themselves. Thanks to cheap salt from nearby mines, Lübeck came to dominate trade in the region.

The medieval Danish-Norwegian realm relied on the export of foodstuffs. The Danes did have a small grain surplus but it was a trivial player in the international grain market; more important were tens of thousands of live cattle exported every year and large summer fisheries which sold thousands of shiploads of salt herring. At first the cattle were driven in droves to market where they arrived exhausted; later on they were either sent by ship and arrived while still fat or were pastured on salt-marshes on the north German coast before selling. The Norwegian fisheries specialized in dried fish, mostly cod, which was sold to Germany and Amsterdam. Much of the Danish grain was sent to Norway which had a constant demand. Thus the Danes became purveyors of expensive food in the form of meat, butter and fish. There was a possibility to import luxury wares and these turned up even in peasant households. However, demand for expensive food was more varying than for a basic necessity like grain for bread.

Norway was the nearest forested area to Holland and England, and timber for building houses and ships became its prime rural export in the 1500s, which compensated for the falling demand for fish after the Reformation. The 1666 Great Fire of London was said to have 'warmed the hearts of the Norwegians'. Peasants built small water-powered saw-mills in streams and cut up timber from their own forests. By 1680 there were an estimated 1700 saw-mills at work and a 'lumber-nobility' (*plankadel*), i.e. a local peasant aristocracy, had grown up as a few enterprising peasants came to own a multitude of saw-mills. The commercial success of fishing and forestry, and the small scale of agriculture, gave Norway a strangely modern twist as peasant life was monetarized to the extent that some wealthy peasants were actually buying foreign grain, while others starved. In 1684 a commission sent to investigate the plight of the peasantry described them as being 'forced to eat their bread in poverty and misery, so that they and the country run the risk of ruin'.

The Swedish economy was also linked by exports to urban markets. The mining and manufacturing of iron and copper was undertaken in a wide area in the middle of Sweden termed the *Bergslagen* (the 'Mountain-law' which has the same meaning as in the Danelaw of England). The greater part of the iron was produced by peasants who lived on farms and cooperated in village-based teams to work the mines and furnaces during the agricultural off-season. The iron and copper could be used for manufacturing military weapons, naval equipment and building products. Although far from insignificant before, metal production really took off in the mid-sixteenth century, after capital and know-how, which raised the scale and quality of production, were imported from Holland and Germany. For most of the 1600s Sweden was Europe's leading producer of iron and copper.

Swedish agricultural production habitually failed to meet the demand from the mining districts, but within the country those provinces which had a surplus sent it to the miners. Live cattle were also sent to the mining districts and arrived in droves from the western and southern provinces. Salted fish came from the Baltic and the Gulf of Bothnia. Grain came from wherever it could be got. Before 1600 proto-industrial wares such as textiles and carved wooden utensils became a regional speciality in Västergötland south-west of Stockholm. Peasant households would weave and carve in the off-season. From here pedlars transported and sold the wares in the mining districts as well as in nearby parts of Denmark (Halland) and Norway (Bohuslän).

REGIONAL AGRICULTURAL SYSTEMS

Agrarian production was stable throughout the period from 1300 to 1700. Traditional technology combined with weak draught animals, poor drainage of fields and too little manure for fertilization kept yields low and fields were often in fallow. Most of Scandinavia had a two-field system of agriculture; only eastern Denmark and central Sweden had the three-field system. In the two-field system, one field was in use while the other was in fallow; the fields were thus at rest every other year. In the three-field system two fields were in use while one was in fallow; the fields were thus at rest every third year. Unless the supply of manure was large, the three-field system could only succeed on naturally very fertile soil. Thus this system was often limited to the richest agricultural districts. Sometimes the three-field system has been seen as an advanced form of agriculture calculated to increase total production, but it is actually just the logical result of needing one field for spring planting of rye or barley, a second for autumn planting of rye with a third in fallow; at the same time, the two-field system was not necessarily backward. Change to a three-field rotation depended on having an increased supply of manure, otherwise the fields would quickly become barren. A one-field system existed in peripheral areas and involved planting one field which after harvest was left in fallow for several years, and next season a new field was selected from the many resting fields. Peasants needed to have extensive holdings since only a small proportion would be sown; the one-field system was typical for areas with many cattle and therefore much manure.

Barley was the main medieval crop, whilst rye attained a leading position in early modern times. On poor soils a small amount of oats was grown and in the mining regions it was fed to the horses. Barley needs a long growing season, but can only be planted in the spring. The transition to rye seems to begin in the late thirteenth century in Norway and Denmark and may be related to the shift to colder and damper weather. Rye gave a slightly smaller yield, but it could be planted in the autumn and thus had an early start when the spring began. However, the sprouts were easily damaged if standing water froze in the cold spring nights. The usual technique to combat standing water was to plough so that high-backed ridges were formed which helped the water to run off.

Archaeologists find evidence for such high-backed fields in the late Middle Ages, but not earlier.

Barley made a flat bread which was quite durable. It could also make porridge and beer, and it could be given to the animals as fodder. Although it fetched a high price, little wheat was grown anywhere in Scandinavia, because it was difficult to combine growing rye and wheat in adjacent fields. Wheat seed corn was hard to keep pure, because rye spread like a weed and its seed would mix with the wheat. As wheat was less hardy, the proportion of rye increased quickly; a Swedish writer of the early 1500s explained 'wheat turns into rye after three harvests'.

Most of the Scandinavian interior was still being cleared for settlement during this period. Peasants were thus split into those who lived in long-settled agriculturally specialized regions, and those who lived in frontier-like newly opened areas. Regional differences determined their social, political and economic well-being. The differences between old and newly settled regions within the same nation could be greater than the differences between countries.

The history of settlement is very different between eastern and western Scandinavia. For most of Atlantic Scandinavia the late Middle Ages was a period of catastrophe with slow recovery starting in the 1500s; Iceland and Norway regained independence only in the twentieth century. Eastern Scandinavia expanded throughout the period except for temporary set-backs caused by wars, disease or famine. Yet population generally grew slowly and averaged less than 1 per cent per annum at best.

Especially in Norway and on the Atlantic islands the Gulf stream influenced the climate and gave temperatures much warmer than was normal at such latitudes. Altitude limited settlement in Norway and Iceland as the coastal strips best suited to farming led rapidly into high mountains. Farming above 200 metres over sea-level was risky as temperatures fell and the growing season shrank for every metre higher up the fields were situated. The oldest settled areas, with the best soil, with easily tilled fields and with nearby fishing, were on the waterfront and at the mouths of the fjords. Later settlement moved inside the fjords and upwards onto the mountainside which made life more arduous.

Climate changes occurred many times, and until recently a popular theory held that medieval abandonment of villages was due to a shift to a drastically colder climate. While there is much evidence for a worsened climate, this explanation has been challenged since population decline and desertion of villages was not universal, but showed considerable regional disparity even in the most northerly locations. Although climate variation was not the main source of settlement fluctuation in the Middle Ages, it did have great influence. The Viking discoveries of the tenth and eleventh centuries took place during a warm period which allowed colonization even on Greenland. Change to a colder climate took place in the fourteenth century. A slight betterment came in the sixteenth century, but was followed by a worsened climate in 'the little ice age' of 1570–1650. Of the two cold periods the medieval one made the most lasting impact.

The redistribution of settlement along the Atlantic coast was not just a matter of the change to a colder climate. Iceland had stopped flourishing and, after a period of anarchy, in 1264 voluntarily subjected itself to the Norwegian king. Major volcanic eruptions in 1300 and 1362 covered large areas with ashes. According to a saga from 1350 'grain grows in few places in the south, and it is merely barley'. Thereafter arable farming became impossible until the potato was introduced. For a time, even herding animals became difficult and wool ceased to be the principal export item. The Black Death came to Iceland in 1402–4 and in 1494–95. During most of the period studied here the Icelanders lived from grazing animals and fish which they traded for grain from continental Europe. The main product was dried fish, mostly cod. The most attractive and highest taxed farms were those located on the coast near fishing grounds. Sites which were high in the hills, far from the sea and where soils were infertile, often became deserted. Lack of timber for building ships placed Icelandic trade in the hands of foreign shippers who established prices arbitrarily. Commerce was dominated first by the Hansa, then by the English and finally by the Danes. Years could go by without a single ship putting in. This put Iceland in a calamitous position. In 1695, 94 per cent of the population were tenants, whilst a minority of 7 per cent owned 45 per cent of the land.

Norway divides broadly into two regions depending on the main livelihood. 'Fishing-Norway' along the western and northern coasts thrived during the Middle Ages. 'Farming-Norway' in the south and around Oslo flourished with the rise of the timber trade in the early modern period. The two regions were isolated from each other by high mountain ranges. It is impossible to perceive of Norway as anything but a collection of local communities loosely held together by political and administrative traditions. Norway began to have political and economic problems in the late 1200s and in 1349 the Black Death struck killing over half of the people including most higher clerics and many officials. Due to the loss of population the income of the Crown and nobility plummeted and the country became defenceless. Bergen, the foremost town, was plundered several times and Norway was inevitably forced to find foreign allies. By the Reformation the nobility had all but died out and the country no longer had its own king.

Reduced population accounted for the desertion of farms. Because entire families often died in the plague, many farms were left without an heir. The plague probably struck rich and poor families equally, so one can expect farms without heirs to be evenly spread. However, settlement was vacated in a systematic way. Recently created farms on the worst sites were abandoned – this meant farms at high altitudes or deep inside the fjords. The older settlements – on the coast and near the sea-level – which had better conditions for agriculture survived because peasants from the fringes moved to take up vacated farms. In Trøndelag, north of Bergen, three-quarters of the farms started in the High Middle Ages had been deserted by 1450. Another calculation gives a fall in all of Norway from 55,000 farms before the crisis to less than 25,000 in 1520. In the course of the sixteenth century population rose steadily. The greatest repopulation occurred in areas previously deserted; many of these reclaimed farms were, of course, just as perilous as they were before the plague. The cause of this growth is not exactly known, but the virulence of plague diminished, thus indicating that the inhabitants had attained some biological immunity.

The plague also struck Denmark in the fourteenth century, although nowhere near as severely as in Norway. Farms were deserted, and there was systematic abandonment of recent and peripheral settlement. It is estimated that between a third and a quarter of the villages colonized in the Middle Ages were derelict in northern Zealand and nearly half of all land was deserted in southern parts of Jutland. The agrarian crisis actually began in the 1320s and thus pre-dated the Black Death. However, the plague definitely worsened the situation. Danish agriculture was affected in several ways. It became difficult to get farm-labourers or tenants. The main concerns for landowners were enticing peasants to become tenants and then restricting their mobility. Initially this lead to a lowering of the fees and rents of the peasants to make tenancy attractive. In the course of the 1400s tenants began to be 'tied to the soil' under the pretence of needing protection, so that they could not easily move away. Prices for cattle increased by 50 per cent from 1390 to 1465 and many nobles began to combine collecting rent with cattle-breeding. Increased grazing was also a way of getting on with fewer labourers.

Denmark divides into two parts: the long peninsula of Jutland in the west and the large islands of the east. In the Middle Ages the number of inhabitants was greater in Jutland than on the islands, but by the seventeenth century the island population had grown faster than that of Jutland. Part of this shift was caused by the growth of Copenhagen as capital in tandem with the expansion of demesne farming on the islands. Jutland was hard hit by natural disaster in the form of a spreading desert as sand dunes buried many parishes. In some areas nearly a third of the medieval churches were abandoned. From 1500 to 1650 Danish population growth was considerable without being spectacular and led to the breaking of new land on Jutland and to the emergence of a landless proletariat on the eastern islands.

Finland was a sparsely settled wilderness which Swedes and Russians fought over until a peace treaty in 1323 awarded Sweden most of the country. Permanent field agriculture was concentrated to the south-west corner and a few parish churches and monasteries were to be found there, as well as Turku (Åbo), the first town. The vast forests were not yet witness to much permanent settlement, but they certainly were inhabited with many people moving to and fro, hunting and gathering. The weather was subject to frost and drought, and in the seventeenth century one-third of all harvests failed in north Österbotten. In the severe famine between 1695 and 1697 a quarter of the population died, mostly because of illness related to poor nourishment.

Finland too divided into two regions: a small southern region featuring traditional arable farming, permanent settlement and some demesne estates; and a large region featuring swidden farming, moveable settlement and few nobles. Outside the south-west most Finnish farms came about through swidden, that is, the preparation of fields by burning the forest and sowing rye in the ashes.

Swidden could give extraordinary crop yields – sometimes ten to twenty times as much as the seed – but the soil quickly became infertile. New swidden fields had to be prepared all the time. This created a migratory form of agriculture which moved ever deeper into the forest. Ownership of land was not recognized: the customary law read 'Whosoever gets there first, owns the swidden'.

The Finns pioneered a new kind of swidden suitable for the sandy soils of coniferous forests. Up to the late Middle Ages swidden was practised solely in deciduous forests. Swidden here was easier, gave better yields and could be used through many seasons. The coniferous forests differ because both the soil and the ash were poorer, so the fields quickly became barren. The new *huuhta* method of swidden in pine and fir forests is assumed to have been the secret for opening the interior of Finland. It involved much heavy labour since the field could only be used once for rye and then once again for oats, after which the field was abandoned. Preparations began at least four years before the field could be sown. In the first year the bark was cut and the trees left standing to dry. In the second year the forest was burned. In the third year the ash was allowed to sink into the soil. In the fourth year seed was sown. The peasants had to have many swidden fields in various stages and they had to be ready to move once the woods were destroyed.

The Finns became so expert at colonizing the forest that many were shipped over to Sweden to clear the forest where they kept on going until they crossed the Norwegian border. About half of the population of the short-lived colony New Sweden along the Delaware river in America were in fact Finns. They are credited with introducing the log-cabin to the American pioneers. Colonization based on trapping and swidden led to a great population increase in Finland. However, in the sixteenth and seventeenth centuries the country was often hard-hit by disease and famine. Swidden could be successful on poor sandy soil; but when farmers were compelled to use the poor soils as permanent fields many found conditions exceedingly difficult. In 1560 a series of wars against Russia began and most involved campaigns on Finnish territory, which brought with it widespread destruction. In 1560 there were 34,000 farms; their number fell to 27,500 in the 1630s and only amounted to 32,000 in the 1690s. In the 1610s about 6,000 farms were registered as 'deserted' since the occupants either could not or refused to pay their taxes.

Finland did not usually have a grain surplus, but other peasant produce was exported. Trapping for furs, mostly marten and squirrel, was characteristic of the Middle Ages; beaver pelts were fashionable in the seventeenth century. A positive aspect of the seventeenth-century wars was the demand for tar and pitch for shipbuilding. Tar was a rural product made by slowly burning tree stumps in large ovens. In most years more than a hundred thousand barrels were exported.

Sweden too was divided into regions. The Dal river, situated about 150 kilometres north of Stockholm, was a cultural border; north of it deciduous forests were rare: there were neither nobles nor tenants and dairy products were just as important as grain. The medieval agrarian heartland of Sweden was in the centre around Stockholm and Lake Mälar. Together with the province of

Östergötland somewhat to the south, these were the areas where flat clay plains normally yielded a surplus of grain. It was also here that demesne estates were built. Along the coast and rivers of the north there was a thin settlement of peasants who combined farming, animal husbandry and fishing. Fishing here was not as plentiful as in the North Atlantic, yet there was always a market for salted herring and salmon. In the north many peasants also had distant shielings in the hills where the cattle were sent to graze during the summer.

There was sparse settlement in southern and western forests. Grain could be grown, but the main sustenance came from milk products and cattle. An export market for cattle and for butter existed in northern Germany, which was easily accessible as the natural trade routes followed the rivers which flowed south. However, the mouths of these rivers were in Danish provinces and Sweden tried to stop this export and redirect it northwards. Thus the peasants living on the border had special economic interests which often placed them in opposition to the government.

The mining districts were situated in hilly forested regions where the soil was neither plentiful nor very fertile. Mining and manufacture of iron was normally a peasant by-employment pursued after harvest and before spring ploughing. Grain growing and tending animals was done in the summer season. Peasant households needed much labour and the yield of the fields was insufficient, so there was always a demand for foodstuffs. Another by-employment was the preparation of charcoal in winter to be used in the iron-forges. Vast amounts of charcoal came from burning wood in special kilns. Because charcoal turns into dust in shaking wagons, its production was limited to the immediate proximity of the forges. Other peasants specialized in transporting foodstuffs and iron products between the harbours and the mining districts.

Population grew throughout the period, but with varying intensity. Temporary set-backs happened after pestilence and famine. Famine was usually the result of crop failure due to bad weather. Plague broke out with a certain regularity, but became gradually less virulent. The last outbreak was in 1710. There is no indication that agricultural production changed radically, so population growth was directly related to expansion of settlement and the opening of new farms.

LANDED SOCIETY

Local Viking chiefs formed an embryo from which a feudal-type nobility developed out of the warriors who formed the king's *hird*. In the thirteenth century, the military system which was built around the long-boat was transformed into a defence built on armed knights. Previously each community was responsible for maintaining, equipping and manning a long-boat. Every able-bodied male was obliged to serve in the boats. The armed knights made the long-boats redundant and the former duty of peasants to sail in the boats was commuted into a land-tax on each holding. Danes and Swedes who promised to do knight service in full armour and with a war-horse were given freedom from the land tax and this freedom was extended to their tenants. This did not mean that these peasants paid nothing; rather, the nobles would collect the revenues of the tenants expressly to finance their weapons and mounts.

The mountainous terrain of Norway placed heavily armed knights on horseback at a disadvantage. There were thus few military incentives to give the nobles the income from a great number of farms. The nobles received income from the entrance fines of the tenants, but not from their taxes. Most Norwegian nobles were thus poorer than their Danish and Swedish peers and many disappeared into the ranks of the peasantry. Iceland never really had a feudal nobility at all, although local chiefs owned much land.

Land in southern Scandinavia tended to be concentrated in the hands of a small number of very wealthy landowners. The nobility of Denmark-Norway comprised only a few hundred families and each family usually owned many estates and had tenants in many villages. The noble population here fell from 2,200 in 1550 to 1,000 in 1720. In contrast, the nobility of Sweden-Finland numbered thousands of families, but only the most ancient of them had large holdings. Swedish monarchs repaid debts by ennobling the families of bureaucrats, judges, merchant-capitalists, bishops and military; a small number of these received enormous donations. The bulk of this new nobility had to select holdings from peripheral areas poorly suited to demesne farming. The ranks of the noble population swelled to over 9,000 in 1750. The nobility was largest and poorest in Finland; because of its strategic importance as a buffer against Russia, whoever fought as a knight gained noble privileges for his land, although he might be denied admission to the House of Nobility. The Scandinavian nobility was thus very heterogeneous and ranged from the wealthy Danes in their impressive renaissance manors and landscaped parks to the lowly Finns, some of whom lived in houses indistinguishable from peasant dwellings.

Besides the nobility another major landowner was the Crown. Crown peasants were tenants, but their possession became inheritable very early. The Crown often demanded labour service to build castles and maintain roads. Crown land had its greatest extent in Sweden and in Denmark; in both Finland and Norway the Crown land was less than 10 per cent. In the Middle Ages the Church was a large landholder, but during the Reformation most of the monasteries were closed and almost all Church-held land was confiscated. Much land had been donated to the Church in the period after the Black Death, and the churches of Norway and Iceland became extensive owners of small pieces of land scattered throughout the country. In 1500 a third of the land in Denmark and Sweden belonged to religious corporations. By the 1560s the Crown owned 28 per cent of all land in Sweden, and in Denmark the proportion was even greater. In Iceland the Church, with about 45 per cent of all land, continued to be a major landowner long after the Reformation.

Denmark and Norway are the only places where townsmen established themselves as large landowners before 1700. This is related to the decline of the political power of the aristocracy. The noble privilege of being the sole owners of manorial estates was revoked after 1660 when a coup d'état brought absolutism to Denmark. The townsmen had supported the coup and defended the king. The sole economic resource available to reward the townsmen was access to manorial estates.

FORMS OF PEASANTRY

Peasants can be divided into those who owned their land and those who were tenants and worked the land of landlords. Older historians would sometimes contrast these differences in terms of 'free and unfree', 'independent and dependent', sometimes even in terms of 'free versus slave'. Nineteenth-century historians tended to idealize the self-owner peasant as forming the basis of democratic society with local citizenship rights, and they believed that in Viking times the peasants were all self-owners. Such original independence was presumed to have been destroyed by aristocratic pressure aimed at seizing the land of self-owners and turning them into bonded serfs. The historians particularly magnified the degree of servitude and repression to which the tenants were subjugated. Modern Scandinavian historians are more cautious in their judgement of the degree of restraint the tenants experienced and point out that already in 1300 only a small minority of Danish peasants were self-owners, thus there could not have been a massive loss of independence in this era.

As a rule, few peasants of southern and western Scandinavia owned land, while most of those in northern and eastern Scandinavia did own the land they worked. Regional exceptions to this rule did occur: self-owners were a large minority in Jutland; there were many tenants in northern Norway and Iceland. With few exceptions the large estates were situated in areas with bountiful soil, which were also places of early settlement and with extensive arable fields. By the late 1600s demesne estates were evenly dispersed over Denmark and accounted for 9 per cent of the land. In Sweden 6 per cent of the agricultural area was demesne land with concentrations in Scania and the eastern central regions; estates were rare north of latitude 60°. Norway had only a few estates, amounting to 1 per cent of the land. Finland's demesnes covered 7 per cent of the land and there were none north of latitude 62°.

Self-owners paid taxes directly to the Crown and in Sweden and Finland they were even known as 'tax-peasants' (*skattebönder*). They could lose the land if they failed to deliver the taxes for three years. Pioneer farms were tax-free for the first years of settlement. The peasantry owned the least amount of land in Denmark. In 1300 it is estimated that only 12 per cent of the peasants were self-owners. In the course of the following centuries the proportion of self-owners nearly disappeared and by 1750 they accounted for less that 1 per cent of the land. In the 1600s 33 per cent of the peasants in Norway were self-owners, as were 50 per cent of the Swedish and 95 per cent of the Finnish peasantry. These proportions fell rapidly and by 1700 only 31 per cent of the Swedish, 23 per cent of the Finnish and 32 per cent (1721) of the Norwegian land was worked by a self-owner.

Norwegian tenants have sometimes been referred to as 'free tenants' since the lords could seldom demand day-labour from them, there was life-time tenancy and the heirs of a tenant could claim to assume possession. Tenants could also own part of the farm even if they did not own all of it. A combination of inheritance practices, sale, mortgage and religious donations led to the partitioning of the farms between a great number of part-owners. Landed inheritance was not partible, but if the heir was unable to pay the co-inheritors their legal share, they received a proportion of the rent in proportion to their share in the inheritance. Fractions of farms were sold in order to pay taxes and small pieces were given as 'soul-gifts' to the Church in the panic after the Black Death. Probably half the land in Norway was actually in peasant ownership, but few owned all the land on their holding. This situation somewhat improved in the late 1600s when the Crown sold land to the peasants.

The reduction of self-ownership in Sweden and Finland was a result of layer upon layer of failed attempts to solve the financial crisis of the nation-state. As the state was almost continually at war from 1560 onwards, the need for money was incessant and ultimately the state's only large resource became the land-tax. Several financial solutions involved the pawning of the taxes of the free peasants to nobles, merchants and officers and these holdings could gradually be transmuted into leases or ownership. Some self-owners sold their land to nobles in order to get protection from rising extraordinary taxes and the much-dreaded military conscription.

HOUSEHOLD, FAMILY AND SELF-GOVERNMENT

Except for those in eastern Finland, the Nordic families and households were of the western European type. This meant that men and women married late and had small families: in the Lake Mälar region near Stockholm women were between twenty-five and twenty-eight years old and men between twenty-seven and thirty-one years old at first marriage in the seventeenth century. About 10 per cent of the women never married. Household size was small and nuclear households were a majority. About half of all households had servants. There was also a considerable amount of geographical mobility over long distances and many peasants lived on tenancies over fifty kilometres distant from their places of birth. Many of the unmarried women had spent time in Stockholm as maid-servants.

The timing of marriage was greatly influenced by economic considerations because newly married couples were expected to set up separate households from their parents. Therefore they needed to wait until they could inherit, unless they could otherwise get hold of land. Widows and widowers with a farm were attractive marriage partners and it was common for young men to marry widows who were much older. Establishing a new household was expensive and in some areas the bride and groom were given seed corn, animals and equipment as wedding presents from their unmarried neighbours; but these were not straight gifts – they were really a kind of credit and the couple was obliged to return each gift (with interest) when the givers themselves married. One effect of the late ages at marriage was that wives experienced fewer pregnancies than they would have if they married earlier and this, along with high infant mortality, contributed to small family size without use of contraception. In addition, late age at marriage meant that the young people, and not their parents, selected their partners. In northern Scandinavia boys visited the girls in their rooms at night and 'bundled' under the bed-covers, yet with their clothes on. In this way young people met and made independent friendships leading to marriage. This pattern of free choice of partner was limited to regions with little social stratification; in Denmark and southern Sweden where there were many landless inhabitants parents had stronger control and bundling was unknown.

Peasant households were units of production and consumption. The more work there was to do, the more workers were needed and thus the larger became the household. A division of labour was based on gender. Men, as a rule, did the work in the fields, in transport and at market. Women worked in the home and barns and with children. Women often assumed the bulk of male work if no man was around, for instance if he was away at the fishing grounds, but the opposite was not always true.

In principle, the size of the farm indicated how much work there was to be done and the Swedes had standards limiting the number of adults permitted on farms of various sizes. If the farm was small or if it was a cottage attached to an estate, it could not usually support a large household. Peasants working for demesne estates might find that they could not support a large household because they seldom had food to spare. Estates usually hindered peasants from developing by-employment and instead encouraged the settlement of specialist craftsmen. The self-owners, in contrast, were jacks-of-all-trades and avoided craftsmen. Although the normal age for leaving home was then fifteen, poor families were often forced to send their children away before puberty to work as servants. Landless agricultural labourers and fishermen too had very small households.

Particular cases arose if the household also performed labour-intensive non-agricultural work. For instance miner-peasants combined farm work in the spring and summer with the autumn and winter tasks of cutting timber, burning charcoal, working the mines, transporting ore and tending the furnaces. Often large teams were needed to accomplish such tasks. Tasks usually had to be done under stress and in a very short period of time. Running forges was limited to the spring flood, about three weeks, and during this time the work went on day and night and the peasants slept and ate in the forge. The households of peasant-miners needed a larger workforce than the extent of the fields warranted. In the seventeenth century in the Lake Mälar area the households of miner-peasants had on average 6.5 persons, whereas in parishes dominated by manors the household size was 4.0.

Inheritance in most of Scandinavia went to all of the children, both sons and daughters, although the daughters' portions were half the size of the sons'. Landed property was not partible, so one child (if there were no sons it would be a daughter) would assume possession and the other heirs would be given their part in cash, seed corn, cattle, out-lying fields, or help in clearing new fields. The dowries given at marriage were considered a pre-instalment on inheritance. A legal principle of the Middle Ages (but which ceased later) was that distant relatives had a 'birth-right' which gave them priority as buyer when a kinsman sold land.

In most of Scandinavia self-owners transferred land to children before death and widows could even transfer tenancies. Formal retirement contracts between the adult children and the older generation were legally registered at the local courts. As a rule the medieval contracts were very simple and stated the transfer of the land in return for which the inheritor was to give food, lodging and care to the parents. By the seventeenth century the contracts began to detail exact annual amounts of grain, butter, pork, firewood, clothes and so on to be given. Sometimes the terms of contract could be quite stiff and contain provisions about paying off the co-heirs. A sister might get a cow and help with the cost of a wedding. A brother might get help to clear new land. The retired peasants would normally get a cottage and eat and sleep independently.

A different kind of family existed in the swidden areas of Finland. Here land was so readily available that property rights hardly existed and inheritance of land was inconceivable. Instead the family stayed together in the male line and women were married into other households. Unlike the rest of Scandinavia which used patronymics, in Finland surnames became necessary to identify relatives who lived far away. Ages at marriage were young, which caused a rapid rate of population growth and large family size. Swidden farming was arduous work and gave incentive to keeping a large workforce. Distances to hunting grounds and to towns were very great so at any point in time many members of the household would be absent. Large and complex households could include over twenty members. It was not unusual to find that three generations were living together and that many of the sons were married and lived on the same farm. Decisions on family matters were made collectively under the leadership of the oldest male and female. Usually the household would share the same dwelling throughout the winter, but the teenagers and young adults would move to separate sleeping-sheds as soon as weather permitted.

Scandinavians had an elaborate system of self-government. Local law courts, called *ting*, with a jury of twelve men, existed since at least the Viking era; these had jurisdiction over a small territory and judged in both criminal and civil cases. The criminal cases heard were those in which the victim or the victim's family could not settle through feuding; family feuds, however, did not survive the medieval period. Civil cases primarily involved sale of land because all transfers had to be legally registered. National laws were codified on the basis of written provincial law codes in Norway (1274–76), Iceland (1281, but actually earlier) and Sweden-Finland (1350 and 1442). The national codes were consulted by the chairmen of the courts in each jurisdiction. In Sweden and

Finland the court meetings could be used for electing local representatives to the Estate of Peasants at the Riksdag. These were often wealthy peasants since they were expected to pay themselves the cost of travelling to and lodging in Stockholm. The Estates could not propose legislature, but they diligently used their right to deliver letters of grievance and thousands were registered between 1500 and 1700. Neither the Danish nor Norwegian peasants belonged to an Estate, but the peasants used the court meetings as occasions to express their grievances.

The parish was the lowest administrative unit of the Church. Parishes were quite small in central agricultural areas, but could be very large in the pioneer areas. Parish meetings and councils under the direction of the priest continued even after the Reformation when, with some feudal exemptions, parishes gained the right to appoint their priests. Parish meetings dealt with economic matters such as repairing the church building and distributing the tithe to the poor. In the 1600s some parishes had poor-houses and school-houses which the council would plan. Crimes against morality such as adultery, fornication, witchcraft, superstition and blasphemy could be taken up in the parish meeting before coming to the local court.

Village assemblies under the direction of an elected alderman kept order within the village. Some of the village by-laws were written down in the 1600s. These dealt with the timing and planning of cooperative activities such as mending roads and fences, driving cattle to pasture and use of the commons. At times the village appointed its own tax-collector who would be responsible for quartering royal officials.

TAXES, RENTS AND LABOUR SERVICE

Self-owners paid land taxes to the Crown and so did the Crown peasants. The tenants of the Church and the nobility paid a combination of rents and fees to the owners of the land. Tenants paid an entry fine when they came to a new tenancy; some historians liken this to a deposit since the landlord supplied the house, tools, animals and seed, and a fee was paid when leaving. The size of these payments was subject to negotiation and landlords could not demand too much or the prospective tenant would go elsewhere. One seventeenth-century Danish observer saw in this fine a formal recognition of what he termed the 'feudal sovereignty' of the landlord. Fines were also paid upon renewal of the tenant relationship when the lease expired. The size of tax and rent payments by peasants appears to have been small in 1300.

Tax-systems were conservative and seldom underwent radical reorganization. Instead, when new taxes were introduced they were simply added to the old ones. By the seventeenth century a peasant could be paying an amazing number of sums calculated in various ways. Some were to be paid by the farm as its proportion of the village fields: this was the medieval rule for assessment.

Some, like the tithe, were a proportion of the yield; others were based on nominal evaluation of the potential capacity of the farm – this was the principle of the 1500s. New in the 1600s were individual taxes such as the poll-tax for each adult, a tax for each cow and a luxury tax on each glass window. Some were to be paid in coin, some in produce and some in personal service (such as building roads and fortresses). Most dreaded was personal service as a soldier because the chances of returning alive were slim. Some self-owners actually sold their land to nobles as this doubled their chances of avoiding military service.

The Swedish Crown was very interested in being paid in kind – grain, butter, meat, fowl, timber and the like – to royal storehouses, which was a wise policy in a time of rising prices, and in personal service in the form of soldiers conscripted from the ranks of the village male population. The taxes of the Danes and Norwegians were simpler with most dues going to a single payment. This tax was set at a third of the amount of seed sown. Since average harvests gave three times the seed corn, this meant one-ninth of the harvest.

Up to 1500 most landlords did not bother with the daily management of the fields and lived from the revenue of the tenants and from sale of cattle. After this point in time they began to interest themselves in the details of arable farming. Landlords who simply raised the rents and fines would quickly discover that the peasants became paupers and the land became barren. The best recourse was to increase the size of the demesne farm, and substitute day-labour from the tenants for their rents. Landlords tried to assemble their holdings to a unified territory to achieve an economy of scale. Once holdings in a village were concentrated the tenants could be turned into field-labourers. Such estates represented a revolution in scale and efficiency, yet they hardly improved upon medieval agricultural methods.

Peasants living close to manorial estates were those who were most affected by the new methods of organizing demesne agriculture. The nobility were well aware of the economic advantages of the east European estates, which had vast fields worked by peasants, but to institute that kind of demesne farming landowners needed absolute control over entire villages. This was difficult to attain in Scandinavia because of the open-field pattern of the villages with large fields and meadows surrounded by common fences. There were no fences between the strips and the main work tasks such as ploughing and harvest were done at the same time. Within the field each peasant had many small strips in proportion to the size of the holding. In order to alter agricultural production in an open field a landowner must own the whole village. Usually a nobleman's property was widely dispersed over many villages, while he seldom had complete control over any particular one of them. Three or four different noblemen might even be rivals over the possession of a single village. Some nobles exchanged land with each other in order to gain local control, but this was not a universal process.

Estate-owners who owned entire villages gained the right to establish their own feudal courts and judge crimes in the jurisdiction. Only a few such courts existed in Denmark and they could not give death sentences – unlike the case in Holstein. As a consequence Danish estate-owners could not ordinarily be as aggressive as they might have liked. A manor owner could also give a reasonable amount of punishment to his peasants. The most notorious form was known as riding the wooden horse – sitting astride a sharp plank with heavy weights attached to the feet and arms.

Despite these problems, demesne estates came to cover 9 per cent of the Danish land and a few vast estates emerged. Largest in Scandinavia was Gisselfeld in Zealand which had 460 hectares of arable fields. Between 1525 and 1750, 264 villages disappeared by being enclosed within Danish estates. The peasants could be removed to other farms, the buildings torn down. The fields, barns and stables were tended by agricultural labourers, who also did the threshing. Some of these lived at the great house, others lived in cottages with land on the outskirts. A landless group of agricultural labourers grew up around the manors and they were employed during the peak season. Peasants who lived nearby were obliged to do unpaid service a specified number of days each week. In the 1500s one day per week was usual; in the 1600s two days each week were the rule in Denmark. Swedish peasants had fewer days of labour. Peasants who lived closest to the manor did many days of unpaid service and performed the bulk of the field work; those who lived within ten kilometres, but outside the manor limits, had fewer days and did the bulk of the transport with their own draught animals and wagons.

Most landlords were exercised by the question of how to find peasants to work for them. Getting rid of unsuitable peasants was subordinate to finding a stable and reliable workforce. Gradually, terms of tenancy were improved, leases became longer and arbitrary eviction was limited. When tenants were removed it was usually connected with reorganization of the fields and they were given other farms, but there are some examples in the eighteenth century of peasants being simply sent away without aid in relocation. During the agrarian crisis landowners had great difficulty in getting tenants for the deserted farms, especially if they had been abandoned for a long time. In order to attract tenants the lifetime lease was introduced and this gave the Crown peasants security to remain on the tenancy for the rest of their lives and to transfer the land to a child. This was an improvement over medieval tenancies which usually were as short as six years. Several times in the 1520s it was decreed that no lease was to be shorter than eight years and no peasant family could be removed as long as they maintained the farm, paid the rents and were obedient.

A kind of personal dependence for tenants was the eastern Danish institution called *vornedskab*, meaning protection. Male tenants were 'protected' by the landlords; in return the peasants must be loyal and remain on the lands of their lords. They could not break contract to move elsewhere and the lord could force tenants to accept inferior holdings. Some nineteenth-century historians interpreted this as a form of slave-like dependence since it tied tenants to lifetime service of their landlords. However, modern historians judge *vornedskab* less harshly since it had some advantages for the tenants (who gained security). It originated in the fifteenth century against the background of the many deserted tenancies and lasted until 1702 when it was prohibited. *Vornedskab* bound peasant families to remain in the villages where they were born. If they ran away they could be forced to return and the sons of tenants had to remain in the service of the landlord on whose land they were born. Tenants did try to run away – in 1681 a group of forty ran away from the estate of Svaneholm. Some nobles actually sold tenants to each other; a normal price was sixty marks (equal to twelve oxen). Letters of emancipation exist which show that freedom from *vornedskab* was granted as a special personal reward. Despite this restraint on movement and economic independence, the Church records bear witness to migration of peasants from Jutland, where *vornedskab* was not practised, to Zealand, where it was practised, to become tenants.

In Norway nobles did not have access to the taxes of their tenants; instead they invented in the 1500s a fee to be given every third year. The creation of demesne estates was difficult because individual farms were far away from each other. In Iceland, landowners interested themselves in grazing rather than growing crops. They obliged the tenants to take in additional cattle to feed and tend; sometimes the number of these cattle could be so great as to hinder the grazing of the peasant's own stock.

BUYING AND SELLING

Whether the actions of peasant and nobles were profitable is close to impossible to assess. The best archive sources are those of the medieval monasteries and thus belong to the period before demesne farming. A few private owners kept accounts, and while they were accurate about purchases they exempted many essential costs of production, for instance day-labour, which was unpaid. Whether the large noble estates were in the long run profitable is doubtful. Changing the scale of production from several small farms to one big farm did not necessarily increase the efficiency of grain farming; on the contrary, small farms run by highly motivated peasants usually had better results than big farms run with day-labourers. In Denmark crop yield on demesne fields averaged about 3:1, whilst the tenant fields gave more than 4:1.

The only product that was quantitatively and qualitatively improved by larger scale was butter. Cows gave little milk so peasants saved cream for many days before they had enough to churn and the result was often sour, dirty and not very tasty. Beginning in the 1630s some estates around Copenhagen began to specialize in butter and hired Dutch specialists. They had large barns, clean utensils and enough cream to make butter daily. The establishment of these dairy farms was dependent upon the growth of Copenhagen as a market and regular transportation to town.

It is risky to say much about the peasant economy in general. However, by accident a number of account books have been preserved from south-western Jutland in the sixteenth century. These were kept by wealthy peasants who were engaged in trade and who had large sums of money going through their hands. An account book from the Højer farm in 1544–46 records the trading of a son who was building up capital in order to marry. He was murdered and the book was taken as evidence in a trial.

Anders Ogels lived on his father's farm but travelled far in the countryside even to distant places like Scania and Hamburg. Mostly his trading brought him to Ribe and to fishing villages. As a middleman he bought fish in bulk and sold urban goods. Some 106 individuals dealt with him during the two years: they were close relatives, neighbours and residents of nearby villages. His merchandise was a mixture of cheap goods and luxury wares. Cloth was the largest item – he had a selection of foreign cloth termed as 'Red English', 'Brown English', 'Leiden', 'Black Leiden' and 'Red Harderwijk'. He also sold some finished goods like hats and smocks and a few luxuries like pepper (for his father) and saffron and rice (for his sister). One fisherman who sold him herring and dried fish received in exchange salt, cheap cloth, a hat, some hemp and a small cash loan. That Ogels also sold 201 horseshoes gives an idea of the rural nature of his network. There was small profit out of this and the territory was large. Over a hundred customers bought small amounts, but there was a fair amount of high priced goods.

Backe Detlefsen owned a large farm in Maas north of Husum in Schleswig. He kept an account book in 1569–76. His farm was near the great cattle-droving path from north Jutland to Holland and he bought oxen from the drove, fattened them and sold them. Usually he could get a selling price 25–50 per cent above what he originally paid. In 1569–71 he sold sixty-three oxen and bought forty-five which gave him an annual profit amounting to hundreds of marks. When the Dutch revolt broke out in 1572 cattle exports were threatened and he ceased immediately fattening cattle and began to raise horses and cows for local markets instead. He had five sons and transactions with each were entered in the book. There was a common family economy, but expensive purchases were to be accounted for when inheritance was to be divided. Aside from some silk cloth bought by a son in Amsterdam, most money was invested. Together with another peasant, Detlefsen used 955 marks in building a cargo ship with timber bought from peasants further inland. In 1574 on its first long voyage the ship sailed to Danzig to buy grain which was in greater demand than cattle.

Most Scandinavian governments from the 1500s followed a mercantilist policy and combated the free trading of peasants and tried to compel them to sell only in local towns. Many new towns were founded in Sweden in the 1600s and the peasants were forced to use them. Merchants were given the privileged position of trading with foreign markets and at times even this was limited to only a few staple towns. In most countries only nobles could trade freely with the produce of their land. However, peasants did know about markets. Peasant entrepreneurs such as the two above had a regional influence through buying, selling and giving credit. The effect of economic specialization such as cattle or fishing could thus have a spin-off affecting neighbours who did not directly participate on the market.

An account book from a parish priest in Scania in 1623–36 illustrates his function as a transmitter of wares between different specialized regions: the grain-growing plain where he lived and grain-poor forest and fishing districts. The account book was written inside the tithe register and included 1,680 entries for 353 persons living in sixty-five villages. His economy was a mixture of wares and money – one-third of the transactions were in cash.

As befits a priest, he was not an entrepreneur, but rather functioned as the community insurance agent. When in need, his neighbours could borrow wagons, lumber, fence-poles, leather, chalk, oats, beer, shoes. Each spring the priest loaned out on average seven barrels of seed corn. The peasants do not appear to have left any collateral for these loans, nor did they give interest when they repaid. Trade with the nearest town was a protracted affair. In November 1629 he delivered two barrels of oats to a merchant in a nearby harbour town, for which he was paid six marks as an advance on the next delivery. One month later he received a half barrel of salt worth six marks and after another month the priest sent two more barrels of oats. Such extended relationships were typical and created personal bonds between the producer and merchant.

The priest had standing exchange relations with peasants from forest villages thirty kilometres to the north. They would regularly deliver boards and planks, thatching straw, tallow and butter. In return he gave them grain (about a quarter of all that he sold). In nearby fishing villages the priest traded grain for large amounts of salted fish – on average seventy-seven kilograms per adult each year. Fish must have been on the table every day. Account books like this indicate that exchange within regions could be very important, even if cash was not always involved.

Relationships between town merchants and peasants were latent with conflict. Merchants had warehouses to which the peasants delivered their harvest in exchange for other goods and little cash changed hands, but the peasants risked becoming permanent debtors. The indebtedness of Norwegian fisher-peasants to the merchants of Bergen was legendary. Merchants bound the peasants by giving credit when harvests were poor. In Finland these personal ties developed into an extreme system of dependence called *majmiseri* after the word for giving lodgings. Finnish peasants usually had far to travel to a town and therefore needed to sleep over, so the merchants offered free lodging, food and drink for their customers. Eventually the merchants even began to pay the cash part of the peasant taxes. In Österbotten 80 per cent of the peasants in 1679 were bound by debts to a handful of very wealthy merchants.

PEASANT UNREST

Large peasant rebellions occurred between 1400 and 1600. The most spectacular Scandinavian revolts coincided with widespread unrest throughout Europe. Peasants were in a constant state of agitation against individual officials, priests, landlords and kings. This endemic agitation could break out in rebellion and wars, sometimes with surprising initial success for the peasants, but always finishing in defeat.

Dissatisfaction was directed at the level of taxes, especially the extraordinary taxes and contributions exacted during times of war. Even the landlords' tenants had to pay contributions in an emergency. In such circumstances the peasants demanded a return to the customary level of taxes. Rebellions in Scandinavia usually started in the periphery. In Denmark it was the northern part of Jutland, in Finland the northern province of Österbotten, in Sweden the distant provinces of Dalarna in the west and Småland in the south. As a rule the social animosity of the peasants was focused on attacking noble estates and royal castles.

Older explanations of why peripheral areas were the most volatile stress that regional economic interests were in conflict with those of central governments and that revolts came after government interference with regionally based foreign trade. The peasants of Österbotten who revolted in the 1590s dominated the export trade in tar and pitch. Northern Jutland was better placed for trade with Norway and the Netherlands than was central Denmark. The fortunes of the peasantry of Dalarna were closely linked to the conditions of the mining districts. In Småland peasants had much closer and better trade relations with northern Germany than with Stockholm.

A series of revolts, the Engelbrekt peasant war of 1434–36 in Sweden, the Gråtopp revolt of 1435 in Norway and the north Jutland uprising of 1441, toppled King Erik of Pomerania from the throne of the joint Scandinavian kingdoms. There was even a little-known local revolt in 1438 in Finland led by a 'peasant king' named David. The Swedish revolt began in the summer of 1434 in the mining districts and brought together a coalition of miner-peasants and other self-owners. The leader, Engelbrekt Engelbrektsson, was of German extraction and was perhaps related to the lower nobility. Ostensibly the peasants protested over the brutality of their Danish-born governor, but in reality the district was suffering economically as the king (who resided in Denmark) waged war with Lübeck about the southern border of Denmark. Both the export of iron and the import of grain in Sweden were dependent on the Germans and suffered as the war drew on. The king built up a centralized administration with officials loyal to him alone (i.e. by using foreign rather than local officials) and whose duty it was to squeeze the peasants for more taxes.

The peasants began by attacking and burning royal castles and in a few months they reached Stockholm. A Hanseatic visitor compared the peasant siege of Stockholm with his recent experience of the Hussite siege of Danzig. At this moment the Swedish aristocracy and armed knights allied themselves with the peasants to prohibit any more foreign appointments. By the beginning of 1435 almost all royal castles in Sweden had been conquered and raids into Danish provinces had taken place. Engelbrekt was admitted into the Council of the Realm, but he was soon assassinated. The revolt continued for some time and noble estates were burned. In the long run the aristocracy won and gained the right to official appointments; the peasants, however, lost the right to bear arms.

In 1436 the revolt spread to Telemark (a province with many self-owners) in Norway. The issues of brutal foreign-born officials and new taxes were also points of contention here. Peasants complained of 'illegal heavy taxes which brutal officials have placed on top of the correct old taxes'. The nobility joined in to gain precedence to official appointments, which was quickly granted them. The peasants, however, continued to be angry. A peasant, Hallvard Gråtopp, marched with a large group towards Oslo. They destroyed a farm belonging to the mother of a hated official before they were defeated. The leaders were executed and all inhabitants of Telemark, including persons who had not revolted, received heavy fines. 'Rich and poor, young and old as well they who sat at home, as they who ran with Gråtopp' were forced to deliver one cow.

Danish peasants revolted in 1438 in Jutland, and in 1440 in Zealand and Funen. These revolts were directed almost entirely against noble and Church landowners. Grievances concerned the high level of payments and the removal of peasants to enclose the land for grazing cattle. The rising in northern Jutland in 1441 was directed against large estates; for instance, the largest holding in the area held by the Gyldenstjerne family (made famous in Shakespeare's *Hamlet*) was destroyed. This family had been concentrating its possessions to create a large territory, and they were also trying to get control over shipping to Norway and the cattle trade. Perhaps inspired by the Hussite armies, the rebels created a wagon-circle fortress in a place called Sankt Jørgensbjerg and several battles were fought here after the estates had been burned and some landlords killed. What actually happened in the final battle in which the peasants were defeated is unknown, but the event lives on in folk-song. Afterwards, a great number of farms were confiscated.

The peasant rebellions of the 1400s were unsuccessful protests against new economic pressures. In Denmark the social position of peasants declined, payments began to rise and the first steps on the way to *vornedskab* were taken. In Norway and Sweden the peasants helped aristocrats to combat the ambitions of the Crown, but subsequently the peasants were repressed and disarmed. However, social animosity thrived; the English revolt slogan 'When Adam delved and Eve span, who was then the gentleman?' rhymed in Swedish too and made its first written appearance in Scandinavia in 1460.

A serious peasant war raged in 1542–43 with its base in the southern Swedish province of Småland. The leader Nils Dacke was a peasant who was outlawed after killing a bailiff in a conflict over a farm. In the forest between Småland and the (at that time) Danish province of Blekinge he joined other renegade peasants. Some peasants had been in arms against the government since 1537 because of prohibitions against traditional border trade. In spring 1542 the peasants began to attack royal officials and some farms held by nobles. After the first success the revolt spread northwards into the bread-basket of Östergötland. The peasants were strong enough to withstand the first noble-led military attacks and they were undefeated up to November when an armistice was arranged. By that time Dacke was in contact with foreign powers with an eye to removing the Swedish king, Gustav Vasa. Thus a simple peasant revolt turned into a real threat to the new Protestant nation-state. With the help of Danish and German mercenary troops the revolt was crushed and Dacke killed.

A simultaneous Danish revolt was that led by 'Skipper Clement' in northern Jutland. This region had rebelled in the 1440s and was one of the few areas where there was still a significant number of self-owners. The Danish nobility had just forced out the Danish King Christian II who appealed to the peasantry for support against the nobility. Clement, a ship's captain who plied the route to Norway, began in 1534 what was to be the last peasant revolt in Denmark by seizing the town and castle of Ålborg. After a few weeks the revolt had spread to all of northern Jutland. The rebels put in their own officials, nobles fled and many estates were burned. One army of local nobles was defeated, before a larger army crushed the peasants in a bloody battle. The self-owners in forty-nine judicial districts were condemned to death. This sentence was commuted to seizure of their farms but they were able to remain on the land as tenants.

The largest Finnish revolt was the War of the Clubs in the late 1590s. Until the 1550s most peasants here had been left to fend for themselves. With the rise of the nation-state they began to be brought under a central administration and an aggressive hierarchy. The revolt started in Österbotten in what seems to have been a planned attack against a local garrison. Dissatisfaction concerned having to quarter – that is, feed, clothe and lodge – the soldiers stationed there. Quartering could lead to being eaten out of house and home and there were at that time many derelict farms which were too poor to pay taxes. The peasants in Österbotten were self-owners who sold tar as a by-employment. Several separate bands with one man from each farm marched on Turku to remove the governor. It was thus a protest against the claims of the state, not of the nobility. Unfortunately the peasants were no match for the well-armed soldiers sent out to meet them. More than three thousand lost their lives and many villages were burned. After the peasants had handed over their weapons, they were slaughtered on the spot.

The causes of peasant uprisings are often attributed to reaction against increased taxes. This argument assumes that peasants are basically conservative and wish to withhold the product of their labour as much as possible. This is easier to state than to prove. Since peasants were always taxed more than they would like, additional factors must have entered when revolts actually broke out. Most landowners – except those who wanted to enclose peasant farms – did not wish to push the peasants off the land. In the revolts described here, protest was made against the repercussions of politics which disturbed commerce and led to extraordinary outlays for foreign mercenaries. Large wars erupted when noble groups were in opposition to absentee kings and united forces with the peasants.

Although by the 1600s the big revolts were over, peasants continued to be easily riled. Officials, tax-collectors and even the odd cleric came to be lynched. The nation-states began to reorganize the legal system with appeal courts and peasants had a slight chance of winning suits against their landlords. In Sweden and Finland self-owners were drawn into the Riksdag through the Estate of Peasants, and there they could express their complaints in petitions of grievance. Several times during the 1640s the Estate of the Peasants gave effective voice to its opposition to the Crown's prevailing doctrine of supporting the

336

nobility. After this period the Estate of the Peasants became an essential factor in Swedish political life.

FURTHER READING

There are no comparative works in English on the history of the peasantry of Scandinavia. Readers wishing to go further can, however, consult several English-language journals. The *Scandinavian Economic History Review* often includes articles on commerce, prices, organization of labour and accumulation of capital. The *Journal of Scandinavian History* prints articles on family, inheritance, population mobility and peasant unrest. Those who are interested in folklore and anthropological perspectives should also consult *Ethnologia Scandinavica*.

There are some works in English. Very worthwhile is W. R. Mead, *An Historical Geography of Scandinavia* (London, 1981) which covers the entire period since the Viking era. A work that delivers much more social information than the title indicates is Svend Gissel, Eino Jutikkala, Eva Österberg, Jørn Sandnes and Björn Teitsson, *Desertion and Land Colonization in the Nordic Countries ca. 1300–1600* (Stockholm, 1981). Developments in early modern Denmark are described in Thomas Munck, *The Peasantry and the Early Absolute Monarchy in Denmark 1660–1708* (Copenhagen, 1979).

Those who can read a Scandinavian language will find Eino Jutikkala, *Bonden – Adelsmannen – Kronan. Godspolitik och jordegendomsförhållanden i Norden 1550–1750* (Copenhagen, 1979) to be a very relevant comparative survey. The best all-round national description of an older agrarian society is Fridlev Skrubbeltrang, *Det danske landbosamfund 1500–1800* (Odense, 1978).

Counties of England

1	Northumberland	14	Rutland	27	Hertfordshire
2	Cumberland	15	Norfolk	28	Essex
3	Lancashire	16	Herefordshire	29	Somerset
4	Westmorland	17	Worcestershire	30	Wiltshire
5	Durham	18	Warwickshire	31	Berkshire
6	Yorkshire	19	Northamptonshire	32	Greater London
7	Cheshire	20	Huntingdonshire	33	Surrey
8	Derbyshire	21	Cambridgeshire	34	Kent
9	Nottinghamshire	22	Suffolk	35	Cornwall
10	Lincolnshire	23	Bedfordshire	36	Devon
11	Shropshire	24	Gloucestershire	37	Dorset
12	Staffordshire	25	Oxfordshire	38	Hampshire
13	Leicestershire	26	Buckinghamshire	39	Sussex

Map 11.1 England

CHAPTER ELEVEN

The English Peasantry, 1250–1650

Richard M. Smith

The historiography of the English peasantry has frequently assumed the form of a discussion of the processes whereby that peasantry was transformed and effectively 'lost' as a consequence of a precocious development of agrarian capitalism when comparisons are made with conditions prevailing in other European societies.[1] This process, for obvious reasons, has been of particular interest to Marxists, who have occupied a prominent, perhaps pre-eminent, role in the debate through their construction of overarching accounts of, and explanations for, this change.[2] Non-Marxists, while certainly not inactive in this field, have more often than not served to question or dispute particular aspects of the Marxist account rather than to offer fully substitutable interpretations. However, there has been one particularly strongly argued, although conceptually extreme, counter-argument to the Marxist position associated with Professor Alan Macfarlane, who has attempted to deny the basic premises of the former school, which argues for a transition from 'feudalism to capitalism', by refusing to accept the existence of a peasantry in the so-called feudal phase of English history. Macfarlane has argued that since the twelfth century, at least, English rural populations displayed behavioural traits that were symptomatic of a deeply embedded competitive, individualistic and 'capitalistic' value system which disqualified them from categorization as peasants.[3]

Macfarlane's thesis, while not without its supporters, has been dismissed by the central theorists of both Marxist and non-Marxist persuasion, although for rather different reasons which serve to bias the discussion of the salient attributes of English 'peasant' society when considered alongside other peasantries.[4] In many respects the teleological emphasis or priorities that dominate both the

1. A. H. Johnson, *The Disappearance of the Small Landowner*, 2nd edn (Cambridge, 1963); H. J. Habakkuk, 'La disparation du paysan anglais', *Annales ESC*, 20 (1965), pp. 649–63; W. G. Hoskins, *The Midland Peasant* (London, 1957).
2. K. Marx, *Capital*, vol. II (Everyman edn, London, 1930), pp. 800–1, 803, 829–30; M. Duggett, 'Marx on peasants', *Journal of Peasant Studies*, 2 (1975), pp. 167–8; K. Collins, 'Marx on the English agricultural revolution: theory and evidence', *History and Theory*, 6 (1967), pp. 351–81; D. Grigg, *The Dynamics of Agricultural Change* (London, 1982), ch. 14.
3. A. Macfarlane, *The Origins of English Individualism* (Oxford, 1978).
4. R. Hilton, 'Individualism and the English peasantry', *New Left Review*, 120 (March–April 1980); L. Stone, 'Goodbye to nearly all that', *New York Review of Books* (19 April 1979).

'transition theory' and the 'continuity theory' (in the manner of Macfarlane) have resulted in a relative neglect of the economic and social attributes of the English peasant *per se*. That said, agricultural and rural history have for long been thriving fields of historical enquiry and in many respects English historians are uniquely equipped to pursue these matters, particularly within the later medieval period, because of the richness of the relevant sources that derive from the workings of the English manor.[5]

This chapter, given the constraints of space, will consider a certain number of the issues raised by the study of the English peasantry from a perspective of the manor and the legal sources that its existence has generated from the thirteenth century. It will be argued that this institutional context which has determined so much of the documentation available has set the terms of the research agenda and has given to law, both customary and common and the relations between the two in so far as the issue of 'property' is concerned, a dominant role in the debate.

In Marxist analysis a distinction is frequently drawn between those relations of production that are associated with communal property and those associated with private or individual property. In the former, individuals have access to land or to resources attached to it through their membership of a group. In medieval England property tenure was not vested in groups other than through various forms of joint-possession by which 'groups' had contracted to hold land or had inherited land as a set of individuals. In some circumstances individuals might have certain common rights such as on the village waste for pasture, or within woods for pannage or fuel-collecting. Access to those rights, however, was not acquired through membership of a group or residence within a village. Those rights were acquired through prior possession of land as an individual – land, furthermore, which was usually held as a tenancy from a manorial lord in return for the payment of some form of rent, whether in kind or cash, and, depending on the status of the tenant, the rendering of labour services.[6] These 'charges' upon land that had to be made to social superiors, of course, served to define one of the most fundamental characteristics of peasantries as they have been specified by leading and highly influential commentators such as Eric Wolf or Daniel Thorner.[7] The latter authorities also draw attention to the need when discussing such peasantries to consider them with reference to the wider social formations of which they are part. As Wolf notes, 'it is only when the cultivator becomes subject to the demands and sanctions of power-holders outside his social stratum that we can appropriately speak of peasantry'.[8] It follows too from such a definition that while the majority of the working population are agriculturalists and that family-labour farms are the most representative units of production, there is no necessary absence of towns

5. P. D. A. Harvey, *Manorial Records* (London, 1984); Z. Razi and R. Smith (eds), *Medieval Society and the Manor Court* (Oxford, 1996).

6. A useful review is to be found in S. H. Rigby, *English Society in the Later Middle Ages: Status, Class and Gender* (Houndmills/London, 1995), ch. 1.

7. E. Wolf, *Peasants* (Englewood Cliffs, NJ, 1996); D. Thorner, 'Peasant economy as a category in history', in T. Shanin (ed.), *Peasants and Peasant Societies* (Harmondsworth, 1988), pp. 62–86.

8. Wolf, *Peasants*, p. 11.

and markets.[9] Indeed their presence might be regarded as essential, particularly as they constituted the sites at which exchanges took place through which agricultural products were sold to furnish the cash resources that formed part of the levy placed by landlords on peasant 'surpluses'. These essential elements in Marxist accounts have in many cases been particularly effective in establishing a coherent set of terminological definitions that lend themselves to measurement and empirical testing. However, before this discussion proceeds to consider in detail the evidence bearing upon these features of English medieval rural society and the ways in which they were sustained or altered in subsequent centuries, it is necessary to give further attention to issues surrounding notions of property, tenure and the law which served to define some of the key issues that have emerged in the debate about English peasantries and their transformation.

PROPERTY AND TENURES

One central issue concerns the place of tenant rights under the manorial system. Some peasants were technically free of lordship, although such individuals constituted a minority of the population of high and late medieval England, notwithstanding a noteworthy presence in certain regions, especially in the eastern parts of the country. Such allodial land, to use a term more familiar to historians of continental Europe, held notionally only from the king himself, was 'the fullest ownership that there can be'.[10] In the Domesday Book of 1086 land displaying this tenurial character was far from prominently visible, since so much of the land of England in that record is identified in terms of its tenure from a superior lord. *Allodarii*, where identifiable in Surrey, Sussex, Hampshire and in particular Kent, may have been equivalent to sokemen – those freemen who loomed so prominently in the eastern counties of England.[11] In the Hundred Rolls of 1279 that survive for parts of six English counties – disproportionately located in the Midlands – freemen occupied about 30 per cent of the arable, although they were decidedly heterogeneous in the characteristics they displayed, judged by the size of the holdings in their possession. They varied from substantial peasant freeholders paying token rents who were to all intents and purposes owner-occupiers, to smallholders who were very poor but personally free.[12] Both Vinogradoff and Kosminsky regarded this group as being distinguished by low rents and the absence of any obligation to

9. C. Dyer, 'Were peasants self sufficient? English villagers and the market 900–1350', in E. Mornet (ed.), *Campagnes médiévales: l'homme et son espace. Etudes offertes à Robert Fossier* (Paris, 1995), pp. 653–66.

10. L. Mussuet, 'Réflexions sur *alodium* et sa significance dans les texts normands', *Revue historique de droit français et étranger*, 4th series, 47 (1969), p. 606.

11. F. W. Maitland, *Domesday Book and Beyond: Three Essays in the Early History of England* (London, 1960 edn), pp. 191–2.

12. E. A. Kosminsky, *Studies in the Agrarian History of England in the Thirteenth Century*, trans. R. Kisch (London, 1956), pp. 198–206; P. Vinogradoff, *Villainage in England: Essays in English Medieval History* (Oxford, 1892), pp. 325–53.

perform week-work. Indeed obligations to a manorial lord were often little more than courtesy or token payments, in the form of such eccentric items as barbed arrows or gilt spurs.[13] They were often also distinguished, especially in East Anglia and Kent, by their practice of partible inheritance, settlement in scattered farmsteads or hamlets surrounded by enclosed fields. These attributes stand in contrast to those shown by customary tenants who resided in nucleated villages so strongly associated in 'champion England' with open field systems, relatively strict landlord control, regularly organized and fully virgated customary or villein properties, and impartible inheritance.[14] A sizeable proportion of the freemen of England in the thirteenth century were located on 'new land' that had been won from forest and fen in the two centuries after the Norman Conquest.[15] They were frequently to be found on the margins of settlements where there was an ever-present possibility of adding odd acres or slivers of land as colonization progressed outwards from an earlier-settled core. A distinguishing feature of those areas where pockets of freemen congregated was that they were often environments in which it was possible to graze wasteland or marsh or to engage in 'hunting and gathering' to supplement modest incomes from rather restricted quantities of land devoted to arable farming or in which it was possible to exploit mineral resources (e.g. Cornish tin-mining areas).[16] Indeed the availability of these supplementary sources of income often reveal these areas, when their assessed taxable wealth is taken into consideration, to have been relatively affluent – another factor making their inhabitants more independent of lordship or of work on demesne farms. Lords in such circumstances were either unable, or found it unneccesary, to charge freemen labour rents to service the arable cores of their directly managed demesne farms.[17]

The modal English peasant was a tenant of the king, of an ecclesiastical, monastic or lay (non-royal) landlord. In many instances the peasant would have been a tenant of a hybrid holding which, while in a strict legal sense a tenancy, also displayed certain property rights more generally associated with freehold tenure. For most peasants, whether they rented their land from the king, Church or private landlord, their holdings were normally linked in one way or another to a manor or manors. The manorial system was a composite of seigneurial and tenant rights since the manor was generally an amalgam of demesne and peasant tenures.[18] The demesne was in the lord's full possession or ownership but the lord was only the final, rather than overall, owner of the tenure. This distinction between demesne and peasant tenure opens up the ever-present possibility of two basic tenant types. Tenures associated with the demesne which were

13. Tidenham: *Victoria County History Gloucestershire*, X, p. 68.

14. R. J. Faith, 'Peasant families and inheritance customs in medieval England', *Agricultural History Review*, 14 (1966), pp. 78–86.

15. J. A. Raftis, *The Estates of Ramsey Abbey* (Toronto, 1957), pp. 71–5.

16. J. Hatcher, 'New settlement: south western England', in H. E. Hallam (ed.) *The Agrarian History of England*. vol. II: *1042–1350* (Cambridge, 1988), pp. 234–45.

17. M. McIntosh, *Autonomy and Community: The Royal Manor of Havering 1200–1500* (Cambridge, 1986), pp. 90–103.

18. For an important article that has greatly influenced the discussion in this chapter see M. L. Bush, 'Tenant right and the peasantries of Europe under the old regime', in M. L. Bush (ed.), *Social Orders and Social Classes in Europe since 1500* (London, 1992), pp. 136–57.

leased by landlords were fundamentally distinctive, since those who rented such property were likely to be leaseholders in a sense that accords with contemporary usage in so far as the property was held on a contractual basis, whereby the length of the lease was specified, so that its termination and the holding's reversion to the landlord would offer obvious rack-renting possibilities to the latter.

In contrast, the tenure holder was by no means just a tenant, since linked to the tenure were certain 'proprietary rights'. The tenure holder could transfer his tenure to his 'heir' both in the form of *inter-vivos*, as well as *post-mortem*, transfers and was potentially able to 'sell' or 'lease' such land to non-family members. However, such transfers could only be effected by one party through its surrender 'into the lord's hands' and by the other party being formally 'admitted' to it – an admission recognized by the incoming tenant who would generally do fealty and pay a fine. The tenure holder would pay his lord a set or 'certain' rent, a rent in theory fixed in perpetuity as a manorial custom (*secundum consuetudinem manerii*) which was in no sense economically determined. In certain circumstances, especially in open-field communities, tenure holders had use of areas of the manor when not under cultivation, i.e. waste, common pasture, fields after the grain and hay harvests, fallow land and the grassed-over areas dividing the arable lands, and gathering and grazing rights in the woods. These rights did not normally extend automatically to cottagers without land or to individuals leasing demesne lands. Tenure holders were required to attend sessions of the manorial court which thereby made them eligible to participate in the management of the manor alongside the lord and his officials. As potential holders of elected offices in the manor and jurors with the responsibility for fixing byelaws and trying cases, tenure holders possessed a stake, albeit with markedly differentiated opportunities within the group, in the machinery of local government and retained a hold on some of the political power rendered by it.

The presence of tenure holders in possession of a certain constellation of rights implied that the manorial system offered to them an array of benefits as well as disadvantages, the relative balance between which was by no means stable over time. Tenant rights were clearly a benefit to tenure holders in phases of population growth when inflation rates rose. Under such conditions landlords might be seriously disadvantaged by the reduced value of those resources as a consequence of the fixed character of customary rents. It was during these episodes that security of tenure and access to common rights thwarted the landlords' efforts to extend demesne cultivation or to convert blocks of tenancies into units yielding economic rents. In inflationary epochs there would be considerable opportunities for substantial peasants with 'hereditary' possession of their farms and paying low rents (relative to those determined by market forces) to accumulate sufficient resources to employ labour. Such labour might be used both to perform whatever labour services the tenant owed to a demesne farm and to work a holding that may have reached a size significantly larger than what could be farmed by the use of family labour alone.

For the peasantry the specific value of these tenure rights depended upon the lord's ability to circumvent or counteract the fixed rents by levying other charges upon the tenantry. An array of such charges which were variable and to a degree arbitrary was potentially available to be levied and was, of course, more apparent under conditions of serfdom. Such charges might be levied when a serf married, or moved off the manor, or sought to place his son in school, or sold land or entered into a holding following a parental death. The arbitrary character of these payments did offer to landlords the potential to exploit their tenants, in spite of the rights of the latter to hold a landed resource at fixed rents and the opportunity to pass it on to offspring as an 'inheritable possession' or to sell or sublet it to others on condition that the transaction passed through the conduit of the manorial court and/or was overseen by the lord or his estate officials. The lord's ability to raise these 'casualties' and the intensity with which they were levied were factors that might, under specific circumstances, undermine the tenant's economic viability and tenurial security.

Certainly the right to inherit property, the ownership of which did not reside with the holder or heir, may seem to have solved the problem of long-term economic security for the tenure holder. The longer-term security offered by such an arrangement would depend among other things on the freedom of lords to raise casualties or levies. How free landlords were to impose such charges would determine not only the extent to which they were able to compensate for income shortfalls created by the fixity of customary rents in inflationary periods, but would also potentially determine the extent to which they could effect economic blows on the tenantry sufficient to necessitate forfeiture of their holdings to the landlords who might thereafter incorporate them into the demesne or leasehold sectors of the manor from which economic rather than customary rents could be extracted. When custom restricted the lord's freedom to raise casualties or when peasants showed resolve in defending their rights either through use of the law courts or by the use of physical violence, tenant right acquired considerable value, especially in periods of inflation such as in the late thirteenth and early fourteenth centuries or in the late sixteenth and early seventeenth centuries. The capacity of landlords to increase the value of casualties to them might also depend on the extent to which the tenure holders were involved in market-based farming. To the extent that the tenure holders remained insulated from the market and that market for agricultural produce was restricted largely to output from the demesne sector, landlords had less room for manoeuvre in their efforts to increase the value to them of tenancies in the customary sector.

However, tenure holders might in theory be in a position to realize the benefits of their proprietary rights by subletting, selling or buying land. In particular, if the charges associated with such transfers fell well below the economic value of a tenure, the occupying peasant was particularly well placed to make a profit. The principal beneficiaries were those peasant households occupying holdings with an acreage larger than that needed to meet their own subsistence requirements. Indeed the incentive for the more comfortably situated holders of tenant rights to acquire land from other tenure holders less well placed than themselves would be great. In periods of rising prices and associated relative falls in wage rates, those tenants holding substantial acreages of customary land would be in a good position to benefit from hiring labour in an overstocked 'market', swollen by the inclusion of a growing number of landless persons as a consequence of accompanying demographic growth. The gains to investment of such labour on moderately large holdings were considerable. Likewise under these conditions landlords may have been very well disposed to the conversion of labour services into cash sums, and with the cash thereby raised to seek cheap labour on the 'open' market. Such labour might constitute a labour force better disposed to expend effort than the recalcitrant, foot-dragging servile labour rendered in the form of customary services. However, it might be supposed that for many holders of customary land the principal benefit to accrue as a consequence of being located in the customary sector was insulation from the need to participate in inflated land markets or to sell their labour in markets from which the returns on wage-paid work was declining. Indeed such tenant rights might under certain conditions have led to a diminution of the landlord's paternalistic control over the lives of those holding land on those terms.

In providing conditions in which it was clearly possible for those with tenant rights to hold on to surpluses, to proceed to build up capital, particularly in land, or to derive profits from money-lending or through serving a growing market for foodstuffs provided by a burgeoning landless group, it has been suggested that such tenurial arrangements reduced the possibility of large-scale class exploitation as far as landlords and peasants were concerned. Such a view is certainly plausible, although it may lose sight of other factors stimulating growing differentiation within the peasantry under these circumstances. Freeholders, especially those with modest holdings and those holding land on leases that were negotiable, or at the lord's will, were more vulnerable in these conditions since they lacked the protection offered by custom, as did serfs who had through desperation taken on land held under similar terms. They would have been poorly placed to accumulate gains accruing from differences existing between the levels of customary and economic rents. Other things being equal, a system of tenant rights might be supposed to create widening differences of well-being within the peasant sector as a whole, especially during periods of rising population and prices.

While tenant rights under specific conditions could insulate substantial sectors of the peasantry against unimpeded landlord exploitation, it would be naive to suppose that tenant rights were an effective protection against peasant privations and suffering. The peasantry was not just at risk as a potential prey of landlords within the landed aristocracy. The state or Crown as well as the Church were potentially ever-present agents of surplus removal from the peasant sector. Royal taxes and ecclesiastical tithes could function to siphon off surpluses from what would have been relatively comfortably situated holders of tenant rights. Furthermore, high rates of population growth, particularly if they gave rise to the fragmentation of holdings and occurred in periods of deteriorating climate associated with harvest shortages, could quickly bring about widespread misery to holders of tenant right and leaseholders alike.

So far this discussion has focused principally on the impact on a peasantry of the existence of substantial proportions of the population holding land under a system of tenant rights. Landlords understandably sought to narrow the difference between what custom allowed and what could be regarded as a fair return on rented land. Peasants might resist with the principal aim of upholding their rights which were largely, if not exclusively, focused upon the preservation of custom. This tension within the manorial system is not always accorded sufficient attention or recognition in the substantial body of scholarship devoted to it. As a system the manor is too frequently presented exclusively as an exploitative institution, very much geared to the landlord's interest and nothing but harmful to the peasant. Yet it was, particularly given the widespread presence of tenant rights, an institution that was from a landlord's perspective ripe for dismantling or abolition. As argued above, it was during periods of high inflation that the interests of landlords might be served by expanding the size of the demesne and by the introduction of more leasehold at the expense of tenant right. However, it was usually in periods of demographic decline, deflation and low rents (falling demand for tenancies) that opportunities available to landlords increased, enabling them to expand the area of land in demesne, by incorporation into it of tenant-right lands or the conversion of such tenancies into leaseholds. Such were the conditions of the fifteenth century. Much ink has been spilled in describing the conditions that purportedly extended leasehold at the expense of tenant right throughout the fifteenth and the sixteenth centuries. This extension, simultaneously with a growth in mean holding sizes and the relative shrinkage of the overall share of agriculturalists farming self-sufficient family-staffed holdings, is a 'classic theme' in English agricultural history. It might be supposed that by this phase landlords had effectively destroyed tenant right and had done so to an extent that was unique in its thoroughness when compared with most other areas in Europe, and particularly when the comparison is drawn with England's near neighbour France. Such developments serve as a thematic focus for the significant debate that was rekindled twenty years ago by Robert Brenner and continues to intrude into most discussions of English peasantries in the late medieval and early modern periods.[19]

The above preoccupation has to a very great extent imbued so much of the discussion with a readily recognizable theme: the essential English peasant is viewed as a member of that group within the rural populace that held land under tenant right, whether as a customary tenant of the thirteenth or fourteenth centuries or as a copyholder of the sixteenth century. The focus has been on the advantages and especially the disadvantages of serfdom to that peasant category before the late fifteenth century and how certain short-term advantages accruing to a fifteenth-century version of this tenant type (i.e. copyholder) were eroded in Tudor and Stuart England to such an extent that England became a 'peasant-free zone', possessed of a rural society made up largely of estate-owners and their large-farmer tenants who worked their properties with a body of wage-paid labourers who came to be the typical inhabitants of village communities. Interspersed within this debate is another theme which is reflected

---

19. R. Brenner, 'Agrarian class structure and economic development in pre-industrial Europe', in T. H. Aston and C. H. E. Philpin (eds), *The Brenner Debate* (Cambridge, 1985), pp. 10–63.

in the notion of the rise of the yeoman farmer as a precursor of capitalist agriculture and the role such persons fulfilled in dissolving what was essentially a peasant, non-capitalist farming system. This was supposedly achieved through benefits accruing to them from their tenure of leasehold tenancies and their rise to dominance as a recognizable stratum of 'village notables' socially and economically differentiated from what had previously been a far more homogeneous village community and culture. As part of this process they became more outward-looking in their world view and aligned themselves with the aims and aspirations of an intrusive state machinery extending its tentacles into the provinces from an increasingly powerful London-based central government of the Tudors and Stuarts.[20]

PROPERTY AND THE LAW

It might be argued that the somewhat theoretical discussion of manorial land in terms of a fundamental division between demesne and tenant right in the previous section of this chapter paints too optimistic an account of the conditions applying to the bulk of the peasantry holding their property under such terms. This apparent optimism, some could claim, was decidedly misplaced in the thirteenth and fourteenth centuries. For it was in that period, following a series of legal developments which had their origins in the twelfth century along with significant demographic growth, that peasant living standards were dragged down by several notches. An assessment of these arguments depends a great deal on how the role played by the Crown within the context of a precociously centralized English state is to be interpreted. The English Crown's complex relationship with the larger landlords by 1200 led to a curtailment of the latter's influence.[21] They had lost a great deal of their jurisdictional authority in their own seigneurial courts as royal courts had absorbed a large share of their business and in the process had imposed a set of common standards which had made them attractive to large swathes of the population. This had been achieved by granting all freemen access to royal courts – a development that required simultaneously a clearer definition of unfreedom or villeinage, since persons so deficient in status were not recipients of this privilege and were as a consequence of their villeinage left 'unprotected' against arbitrary seigneurial actions. Furthermore, since such 'villeins' possessed no access to any curial arena, other than the private courts of their landlords, it is frequently assumed that in

20. A succinct statement of this view is conveniently to be found in K. Wrightson, 'Aspects of social differentiation in rural England *c.*1580–1660', *Journal of Peasant Studies*, 5 (1977), pp. 34–47. For some sceptical thoughts see R. M. Smith, ' "Modernization" and the corporate medieval village community: some sceptical reflections', in A. R. H. Baker and D. Gregory (eds), *Explorations in Historical Geography: Interpretative Essays* (Cambridge, 1984), pp. 140–79, 234–45.

21. For authoritative discussions of these developments see S. F. C. Milsom, *The Legal Framework of English Feudalism* (Cambridge, 1976); R. C. Van Caenegem, *The Birth of the English Common Law*, 2nd edn (Cambridge, 1988); J. Hudson *Land, Law and Lordship in Anglo-Norman England* (Oxford, 1994).

their efforts to secure their rights in the matters of conflict resolution and security of tenure, the odds were indubitably stacked against them.

There is no doubt that the legal reforms introduced in the late twelfth century made the business of going to the royal courts to recover land (in particular) a much less costly and rapidly expedited affair. Peasants had much business that needed settling: labour services that had been unreasonably demanded, land lost in the anarchy of Stephen's reign, and a whole range of complaints against their neighbours. One, in particular, of the new legal remedies seemed ideally suited to their needs and they were among the first to use it. S. F. C. Milsom concluded on the basis of his analysis of the early plea rolls that modest peasant landholders were enthusiastic users of the new writ of novel disseisin, whereby a tenant could recover land from which he had been evicted without due process.[22]

How the royal courts eventually resolved which category of peasant or peasants should retain access to them is beyond the remit of this chapter, but a significant group of peasants was in principle restricted to the lord's private manorial court as the setting for dispute resolution between themselves and their seigneurs. Rosamond Faith, in a recent highly important and challenging book, presents arguments (which still have to be fully digested by this present author) for the highly plausible suggestion that what came to be a decisive criterion of unfree tenure was the owing of labour rent which was uncertain or unfixed (*incerta*) – a situation 'where one cannot know in the evening the service to be rendered in the morning', that is, one where one is bound to do whatever one is bid. Faith is convinced that the 'uncertain' work, the nature of which was unknown until the bailiff's orders were given, was week-work, the regular obligation to work on the demesne so many days at unspecified tasks.[23]

Such legal ring-fencing undoubtedly gave rise to a profound sense of loss among those peasants whose status and horizons were so stringently narrowed, having been temporarily widened by the initiatives arising with the Angevin reforms of the 1160s.[24] However, it would be too limiting a portrayal of peasant existence to view the unfree as permanently banished to a legal world that was fundamentally detached from royal justice altogether. Furthermore, some students of late medieval rural life have further developed certain of the somewhat theoretical notions presented in such skeletal form above, particularly those that relate to the contrast to be drawn between the circumstances of peasants holding land under a system of tenant rights (customary tenure) and those under leasehold (contractual) tenure.

On the latter issue John Hatcher, in a provocative but timely essay, draws attention to a number of benefits that did accrue to the 'unfree' as a consequence of their tenure of land on customary terms, thereby downplaying the

---

22. S. F. C. Milsom, Ford Lectures, Oxford 1988; G. D. G. Hall (ed.), *Treatise on the Laws and Customs of England, Commonly Called Glanvill* (Oxford, 1965).

23. R. J. Faith, *The English Peasantry and the Growth of Lordship* (London, 1997), pp. 259–65.

24. C. Dyer, 'Memories of freedom: attitudes towards serfdom in England, 1200–1350', in M. Bush (ed.), *Serfdom and Slavery. Studies in Legal Bondage* (London, 1996), pp. 277–95. The definitive study is, however, P. R. Hyams, *Kings, Lords and Peasants in Medieval England: The Common Law of Villeinage in the Twelfth and Thirteenth Centuries* (Oxford, 1980).

more unpalatable aspects of labour services and the other universally disliked charges such as tallage and merchet that were carried by those possessed of villein status. Hatcher, deploying a substantial array of evidence, notes how customary tenures protected tenants under the inflationary conditions prevailing before *c.*1320. The contrast between customary acres held in villeinage on the Cambridgeshire, Suffolk and Norfolk manors of the Bishop of Ely in 1251, renting at rates between 1d. and 4d. and those peasants holding *ad voluntatem domini* who paid rents as high as 1s. 5d. per acre is indeed striking. At Halesowen (Worcestershire), for example, a low customary fine of 13s. 4d. per virgate was charged upon inheritance, but when a villager acquired a holding without a right of inheritance he was likely to be charged at a rate much closer to the true market value. On this manor in 1294 Henry Osbern was fined £6 13s. 4d. rather than 6s. 8d. for entry into a half-virgate previously held by Thomas Robin; when William Lee in 1310 acquired a vacant quarter-virgate holding from the lord he paid a fine of £2 7s. rather than 3s. 4d. The marsh lands which the monks of Christ Church Priory, Canterbury, reclaimed and embanked in Kent were let out at competitive leasehold rents which were as high as 2s. 7d. per acre, when compared with the average *gafol* of 1d. an acre and *mala* of 3d. an acre received from their customary tenants. Hatcher's relativist treatment of villeinage and custom marked a major step forward and did open up the possibility of seeing how those holding under such tenure might have been able to benefit from their 'protected' position, which would have ensured that their 'fixed costs' barely changed while the potential income from the surplus produce of their holdings would have risen considerably for much of the thirteenth and early fourteeth centuries.[25] It is as a consequence of this process that there existed noteworthy potential for growing social differentiation within the peasant communities of late thirteenth- and early fourteenth-century England and the emergence of a readily recognizable stratum of 'proto-yeomen' farmers who unfortunately have sometimes been too readily and disparagingly equated with those *kulaks* encountered in very different times and places.

Hatcher's approach, however, tended to view custom largely from the perspective of rental arrangements, leading understandably to its treatment as a static phenomenon, in much the same way as legal historians viewed villeins, damaged by the emergence of the common law, as restricted to a customary law that was static and less innovative and potentially advantageous than the law available to freeholders in the king's court. In this way, the customary sector is presented as hermetically sealed from the influences of exogenous forces, serving as a frictional drag by which men sought to 'justify and perpetuate the present in terms of the past'.[26] Such an approach may appear too readily disposed to treat the customary tribunal of the seigneur which administered villein tenures, the terms under which they were held and their transfers between lord and tenant and tenant and tenant, as an institution lacking any means of communication with the royal courts. This view, which is fundamentally in error,

25. J. Hatcher, 'English serfdom and villeinage: towards a reassessment', *Past and Present*, 90 (1981), pp. 3–39, especially, pp. 14–21.
26. Ibid., p. 23.

fails to address a highly distinctive feature of medieval English rural society which had very significant implications for peasant circumstances as they developed over the subsequent five centuries. Furthermore, in acknowledging the existence of the royal courts and their impact on manorial courts we can more readily understand the processes giving rise to the distinctive, possibly unique, documentary evidence from English manorial courts that in so many other European contexts appear to have left no written records whatsoever.

It has been argued that the emergence of a 'common law of villeinage' troubled landlords not just because it required them to create a clearer definition of their serfs whom they and those courts deemed ineligible to use the royal courts, but it also required lords to keep a fuller record for these courts, since the precision of pleading in the *curia regis* increasingly demanded a written proof of villein status. Such necessities may have induced lords to keep a record of manorial court proceedings. Furthermore, lords wished to retain the larger part of the business in manorial courts provided by the personal plaints of free peasants who were increasingly attracted by the facilities now more readily and effectively offered by the higher courts. This growth in inter-curial competition may have been a major incentive driving lords to establish written court records which probably began to be found in a sizeable number of manors in the 1250s – a practice that expanded greatly in its geographical extent in the 1270s.[27]

The landlords' need to compete with royal courts for litigants in curial matters both intensified record-keeping and served as a stimulus for the introduction of important novel legal procedures in those courts. Landlords in seeking to encourage peasant freeholders to attend their courts were obliged to refashion them so that they came to resemble more clearly the king's court in certain, if not all, key respects. Any student of those ostensibly 'peasant courts' of the manor is obliged to consider the degree to which legal innovation in the royal courts extended downwards and thereby created a 'system' from which the unfree peasantry were not excluded. Furthermore, the social and economic consequences that followed the simultaneous shift from an oral to a written customary law were of considerable significance to the English peasantry. Such a shift had in fact occurred in the higher courts perhaps three generations previously.

Maitland over a century ago had indicated that he was aware of some of these developments, particularly the observation that there was an 'intrusion of new elements, presentments by jury and trial, elements hardly compatible with their old constitution'.[28] He was definitely correct in this observation, although it was a remark whose consequences few subsequent commentators seem to have appreciated. More recent research by an emerging body of medievalists, who have expended considerable efforts on detailed analyses of the contents of manorial court proceedings, reveals that in the earliest written records of those courts the entire body of peasants who acted as court suitors undertook the roles of 'fact-finder' and 'judgement-renderer' while the lord's steward

---

27. Z. Razi and R. Smith, 'The origins of the English manorial court rolls as a written record: a puzzle', in Razi and Smith, *Medieval Society and the Manor Court*, pp. 36–68.
28. F. W. Maitland (ed. and trans.) *Select Pleas in Manorial and Other Courts* (Selden Soc. 2, 1889), p. lxviii.

presided over them more as moderator than judge. The plaintiff brought his 'complaint witness', whose role was to support the claim, and the defendant introduced his own oath-helpers (variable in number from manor to manor) to assert the truth of the latter's denial of the charge. In such a procedure it is clear that recourse to 'fact' was limited and was in essence little more than a compurgation 'ritual'. There is evidence from the earliest court rolls that compurgation was not employed for land disputes when one or other of the disputants paid a fine to have an inquest, usually made by the whole body of suitors into the 'facts'.[29] From the 1250s it is clear that some courts had introduced inquest juries of twelve persons for land disputes and it is obvious that this was a development paralleling the emergence of the inquest jury in the royal courts which had been firmly established by 1200. The inquest jury in manorial courts rapidly extended its role into curial business concerned with personal plaints, and the undoubted authority on these matters, John Beckerman, sees the first quarter of the fourteenth century 'as the heyday of jury trial in English manor courts' – a development he regards as stimulating the use of documentary proof as evidence in the establishment of 'custom', particularly relating to those who held their land under tenant right.[30] Beckerman's pioneering work is of very great importance in drawing attention to the manner in which the emergence of written records of court proceedings served to reduce the interpretative variance surrounding the rights of parties, whether lord or tenant.[31] Another innovation which also owes its origins to reforms made in the late twelfth century by Henry II was the use of presentment juries as a way of investigating and punishing breaches of manorial custom or infringement of seigneurial rights, although the person presented in this fashion was almost invariably summarily convicted.[32] These procedures were taken up initially much more rapidly in those courts of the manor specifically dealing with offences against the King's peace (the view of frankpledge) and were somewhat sluggishly introduced into the more frequently held courts dealing with seigneurial rights and manorial custom.[33] This delay reflected, it might be suggested, some peasant resistance to the procedure since it was a development which, given the use of summary conviction and the vesting of authority in a small group, often from the most affluent and powerful members of the local peasant elite, strengthened the lord's position *vis-à-vis* the jurors' lower-status neighbours who most likely suffered some weakening of their civil protection.[34]

Notwithstanding the above-mentioned setback as a consequence of one particular form of jury practice, other developments in the legal instruments at the disposal of these courts brought numerous benefits to the peasants by

29. J. S. Beckerman, 'Procedural innovation and institutional change in medieval manorial courts', *Law and History Review*, 10 (1992), pp. 197–212.

30. Ibid., p. 214.

31. Ibid., pp. 219–26.

32. Maitland had noted the link between Henry II's reforms and the adoption of presentment procedures in the leet courts or views of frankpledge in his introduction to *Select Pleas in Manorial Courts*, p. xxxvi.

33. R. M. Smith, 'Some thoughts on "hereditary" and "proprietary" rights in land under customary law in thirteenth and early fourteenth century England', *Law and History Review*, 1 (1983), pp. 104–5.

34. Beckerman, 'Procedural innovation', pp. 232–4.

providing means of recording and defending economic transactions of indescribable variety. Of particular relevance to this present discussion is that these suitors, both free and unfree, derived very considerable and enhanced security in their tenure of customary land by inheritance and transmission through alienation and lease. We can observe a noteworthy trend through the late thirteenth and early fourteenth centuries towards a standardization of terms and forms of conveyancing procedures which were either responses to influences emanating from, or replications of, forms employed by the common law. If one considers the terminology in use in the earliest court rolls relating to property transfers alongside those employed in the early fourteenth century, the extent of the changes is clearly evident. By 1300 for the permanent transfer of customary land by peasants, that is sale with rights in perpetuity, the 'surrender and admittance' was the accepted procedure. The fully developed form of 'surrender and admittance' allowed villeins to transfer land among themselves. An unfree peasant was forbidden to surrender, sell or lease directly to another, irrespective of the recipient's status, since it was his manorial lord who was possessed of seisin at common law. However, a villein was able to surrender to his lord, who subsequently could proceed to grant seisin to another party. This usage in what, by the last decade of the thirteenth century, was a remarkably standardized form was most likely a development that helped to stifle any possible use of these records in the extension of common law remedies and the granting of free status to unfree peasants. This was achieved, notwithstanding that as part of the standardization customary lands were increasingly granted to a purchaser or incoming tenant *sibi et heredibus suis*.[35] Such grants should certainly not be interpreted to mean, as did Bracton, that an enfeoffment by a lord of his villein *sibi et heredibus suis* implied manumission because it was a recogniton that an individual had heirs.[36] It was, however, a clear acceptance of one key feature of tenant right – the expectation that property held under these terms could proceed within that family to kin according to customary inheritance rules. As Barbara Harvey states, 'the customary tenant of the period admitted with the words *sibi et heredibus suis* may be deemed to have possessed a fee simple interest in land'.[37]

The changes regarding the terminology of, and procedures for, transfers of customary land reflect reforms relating to conveyancing practices under the common law at the end of the thirteenth century. The statute *Quia Emptores* in 1290 made substitution the accepted form for grants in fee simple. Previously subinfeudation had been the usual practice.[38] One purpose of this change was the assignment of direct responsibility for rents and incidents to the new tenant and the requirement of the incoming tenant to pay an entry fine which mirrors some features of 'surrender and admittance' concerning customary land in manorial courts. It constitutes a development that had been regarded

---

35. Smith, 'Some thoughts', pp. 107–12.
36. F. W. Maitland (ed.), *Bracton's Note Book* (London, 1887), pp. 24, 170, 194b.
37. B. Harvey, *Westminster Abbey and its Estates in the Middle Ages* (Oxford, 1977), p. 279.
38. S. F. C. Milsom, *Historical Foundations of the Common Law*, 2nd edn (London, 1981), pp. 114–15.

as forming an element in a broader change in conveyancing practices involving both freehold and customary land in the middle of Edward I's reign. Some land-lords may have been alarmed by the similarity with, and the apparent simult-aneity of, these developments apparently occurring in both legal 'sectors'. For instance the consistently conservative administration of the Abbey of St Albans appears to have been particularly sensitive to the possibility that transfer of villein tenements by surrender and admittance could come dangerously close to resembling the procedure of substitution which *Quia Emptores* had made the accepted form for the transfer of free tenements. On this estate an adaption, which was an evident response to this concern, emerged as land so transferred was stated to be held *ad voluntatem domini* or *in villenagio* or *per virgam* to ensure that villein grants could not be mistaken for grants of free tenure.[39] It has been noted that the links between central and seigneurial courts followed from the fact that the seneschals who presided over the abbot's own court for his unfree tenants were also likely to represent the abbey in the king's courts. Doubtlessly, *Quia Emptores* gave this development additional momentum and presentment procedures served to embed it more deeply as a conventional and routinized practice.

A particularly noteworthy instance of the incorporation of the common law of land-conveyancing into manorial courts and into the procedures relating to customary land is provided by the entail. The statute *De Donis* of 1285 pro-tected the intention of donors from subsequent frustration. It ordained that when land was granted to a man and his wife and the heirs of their bodies, or to one person and the heirs of his or her body, the will of the donor *in forma donis* was to be observed. It is noteworthy how rapidly the transfer of custom-ary land with conditional arrangements reminiscent of *De Donis*, in theory only applicable to freehold, become observable in manorial court proceedings of the 1280s and 1290s.[40]

It has also been noted that at approximately the same time as *De Donis* it became a not uncommon practice among the more substantial freeholders to establish jointure arrangements.[41] When formally executed, jointures ensured that the land in question would be held in joint tenancy for their two lives by husband and wife, and by the survivor alone after the death of the other

---

39. L. Slota, 'Law, land transfer and lordship on the estates of St Albans Abbey in the thirteenth and fourteenth centuries', *Law and History Review*, 6 (1988), p. 123.

40. Maitland perceptively observed an example of entail in the 1291 manorial court proceedings of Weedon Bec in Northamptonshire and remarked on its proximity to the recently enacted *De Donis*: see *Select Pleas in Manorial Courts*, p. 40. In the manor court of Redgrave, Suffolk, in 1290 three land transactions involving customary land make reference to remainders for other lives in the event of the donees dying without heirs of their body: R. M. Smith, 'Women's property rights under customary law: some develop-ments in the thirteenth and fourteenth centuries', *Transactions of the Royal Historical Society*, 5th series, 26 (1986), p. 188. In an analysis of the St Albans manor courts of Park and Codicote in Hertfordshire, 31 of 33 entails in the former and 45 of 48 in the latter manor occurred after 1285, Slota, 'Law, land transfer and lordship', pp. 125–6.

41. It has been observed that among gentry and lawyer families that the formal execution of jointures, strictly defined as land held in joint tenancy for their lives by husband and wife and by the survivor alone after the death of one partner, were not much older than Edward I's reign, see K. B. McFarlane, *The Nobility of Later Medieval England* (Oxford, 1973), p. 65.

partner. Such arrangements involving customary land and married customary tenants can be found in manorial court rolls from the 1290s.[42]

Another development bearing more directly on the monitoring of female rights in customary land than jointure also has its origins in the king's court. The common law established a formal procedure to record land transfers made by husbands in the course of a marriage. A formal procedure involving the examination of the wife in the court and the levying of a fine in the event of her land being conveyanced to a third party ensured that her subsequent claims over land in her own right were barred.[43] It is noteworthy that in the earliest court roll series from the 1240s through to the 1270s land transfers are rarely recorded as being undertaken by conjugal pairs and no written record was preserved of the wife's attitude to such transactions in land to which her dower attached.[44] In the last two decades of the thirteenth century manorial courts began to adopt a practice of formal examination of the wife to establish her agreement to such sales in which she and her husband had joint rights.

All these developments – surrender and admittance, entails, jointures, and the formal examination of married women when they disposed of property with their spouse – reveal how intimately related were manorial and royal courts by the early fourteenth century. They suggest the obvious possibility of a move towards the standardization of customary procedures concerning the tenure and transfer of land. While the variability of patterns from place to place should not be understressed or ignored, they nevertheless reveal some detectable common denominators across English manors regarding the options of unfree peasants which would surely have been less apparent if manorial custom had not come under the influence of the king's court and a written record of its proceedings not been kept.[45]

While the clarification of tenancy terms from the lord's point of view served to provide greater protection of his own 'rights' in and claims for services and fines from his tenants of customary land, certain gains also accrued to his tenants. First, the unfree peasant came to possess a fuller written statement of the terms of his tenancy which ensured an improvement of his security in relation to his lord, his kin and his neighbours, all of whom subsequently had fewer opportunities to act arbitrarily. Second, following the reduced ambiguity surrounding the status of land held subsequent to a transaction, men may have been more readily disposed to enter into such arrangements and hence the market for land may have been greatly stimulated. Indeed manor courts in the eastern and south-eastern counties of England do show a significant growth

42. Smith, 'Women's property rights', pp. 184–7, and for further developments in the late fourteenth and early fifteenth centuries, see R. M. Smith, 'Coping with uncertainty: Women's tenure of customary land in England c.1370–1430', in J. Kermode (ed.), *Enterprise and Individuals in Fifteenth-Century England* (Stroud, 1991), pp. 43–67.

43. F. Pollock and F. W. Maitland, *The History of English Law Before the Time of Edward I*, vol. II, (Cambridge, 1895), p. 413 and J. S. Loengard, ' "Of the gift of her husband": English dower and its consequences in the year 1200', in J. Kirshner and S. F. Wemple (eds), *Women of the Medieval World* (Oxford, 1985), pp. 143–67.

44. Smith, 'Women's property rights', pp. 179–80. For similar features detectable in the earliest rolls of the *curia regis*, see the comments of G. D. Hall in his review of *Curia Regis Rolls of the Reign of Henry III, 9–10 Henry III* (London, 1957) in *English Historical Review*, 74 (1959), p. 108.

45. R. H. Britnell, *The Commercialisation of English Society 1000–1500* (Cambridge, 1993), pp. 140–4.

in the turnover of parcels of customary land in the late thirteenth and early fourteenth centuries, although it is a trend upon which were superimposed at quite frequent intervals a series of short-term surges of 'distress-related' land sales in years of deficient harvests.[46] Of course, in considering the possible effects of such legal innovations on the propensities of unfree peasants to enter such arrangements and of lords to sanction them, it becomes extremely difficult to distinguish cause from effect. This conundrum is especially pronounced since those legal innovations were most readily evident in the manors of the eastern and south-eastern counties where it is also clear there existed a more active land market in customary holdings, or parts of them, than was present in the midlands and the south-west of England.

One should not draw the conclusion that the growing incidence of surrender and admittance procedures in the transfer of villein land along with tenure by the purchaser and his heirs (*sibi et heredibus suis*) coincided with any substantive change in status at common law of either the villein or his land. The surrender and admittance procedure must be viewed exclusively in terms of economic and legal implications for villein tenure. Of course, the existence of such a procedure does not preclude the possibility that the lord might prevent the splintering of the villein holding by declining permission to alienate anything but a 'full land' or complete tenement. In fact, there might be considerably less danger of villein land converting to freehold if these constraints were imposed. Furthermore, as John Hatcher has stressed, the point of admission was a potentially profitable moment for the lord. This has major implications for a peasant 'market' in unfree land. As Hatcher has argued, one prime requisite for an active market in unfree land among the customary tenantry, particularly in the century before the Black Death, was that the land conveyed had a value over and above the seigneurial burden which went with it.[47] In assessing that 'value', all the elements which constitute the seigneurial burden must be taken into account. In one major study of the customary tenants of Westminster Abbey, who were distributed in manors located across large tracts of the eastern, southern and midland counties of England, Barbara Harvey concludes that in aggregate, these charges constituted 'a very effective antidote to the fragmentation of customary holdings'.[48] The monks of Westminster opposed fragmentation because they conceived of the holding in its entirety as a necessary portion for a household, and they were unwilling to bother to collect rents and administer fractions of holdings. She suggests that the conditions of tenure on their estate ensured that the vendors in transactions would derive little profit from the deal: if a higher entry fine or

---

46. B. M. S. Campbell, 'Inheritance and the land market in a fourteenth-century peasant community', in R. M. Smith (ed.), *Land, Kinship and Life-Cycle* (Cambridge, 1984), pp. 87–134; R. M. Smith, 'Families and their land in an area of partible inheritance: Redgrave, Suffolk 1260–1320', in *Land, Kinship and Life Cycle*, pp. 135–95; R. M. Smith, 'Transactional analysis and the measurement of institutional determinants of fertility: a comparison of communities in present-day Bangladesh and pre-industrial England', in J. C. Caldwell, A. G. Hill and V. J. Hull (eds), *Micro-Approaches to Demographic Research* (London, 1988), pp. 215–41; C. Clarke, 'Peasant society and land transactions in Chesterton, Cambridgeshire, 1277–1323' (unpublished D. Phil thesis, University of Oxford, 1985), ch. 4; P. R. Schofield, 'Dearth, debt and the local land market in a late thirteenth-century village', *Agricultural History Review*, 45 (1997), pp. 1–17.

47. Hatcher, 'English serfdom and villeinage', p. 21.

48. Harvey, *Westminister Abbey*, p. 302.

licence fee was not demanded from a purchaser than from the tenant who took customary land by inheritance, and there is nothing to suggest that he paid less, these changes make it less likely that the yield from the land would be adequate to render the whole procedure sufficiently rewarding economically for the potential buyer or seller.[49] Therefore, the unwillingness of the monks to permit fragmentation, the large size of units, low capital resources of potential purchasers and the high cost of land in relation to the yield combined to thwart an active market in customary tenancies. Harvey concludes her arguments by stating that 'as a rule the destination of substantial holdings on the manors of Westminster Abbey was decided outside the nexus of market transactions . . . only small amounts (mainly of assarted and free land) were transacted in the ways that were not detrimental to the virgated structure of holdings that "family and feudal sentiment" both cherished'.[50] Of course, acceptance of the logic of this argument would require some evidence on the value of customary land as a productive agricultural asset. It would also require information on the price paid by the purchaser to the vendor in relation to the customary payments made by both the purchaser and the vendor to the lord. There is, in fact, a reason to suppose that the circumstances applying to the customary land on the Westminster estates were not the only or indeed the most frequently encountered because, to use Harvey's phrase, a different combination of both 'family and feudal sentiment' could produce different patterns of behaviour under customary law. Establishing the 'value' of land to buyers and sellers in customary transfers is no straightforward matter since the form of the surrender and admittance entry in a court roll conceals entirely the actual details of the transaction involved. Sales, gifts, exchanges and leases can frustratingly all look alike. Ordinarily, it is only from litigation in the courts that we can glimpse the factual situation behind these clinically austere sources.

It is necessary to take account of the financial benefits, which could assume varying forms, derived by landlord as well as unfree peasants in such 'sales'. It is clear that within lay and ecclesiastical estates in East Anglia and the east Midlands highly active land 'markets' existed. In the case of two estates that have received quite detailed investigations, those of the Benedictine Abbeys of Crowland and Bury St Edmunds, rents and services were levied on customary tenancies that were comparable with those paid by the villeins of Westminster Abbey.

In the Abbot of Bury St Edmunds' case it can be seen that the annual income from licence fees paid to 'register' instances of surrender and admittance relating to customary land constituted on some manors in 1260 approximately 30 per cent of the value of fixed (assize) rents from customary tenancies, but from 1290 to 1320 generated money sums worth almost 70 per cent of those derived from fixed rents. Inflation and demand for land over the period were most likely inclining this estate administration not to stifle the land market that was helping to minimize the potential loss of income that the intransigencies of

49. Ibid., pp. 302–3.
50. Ibid., p. 317.

customary tenant right were capable of imposing on the situation. On this same estate an entry fine of 6d. per quarter-acre was common in this period, with a tendency by the second decade of the fourteenth century for it to double to 1s. The assize rental cost of customary land was on average about 5d. per acre. If the attached services are converted to a monetary value they appear to vary between 4d. per anum for holdings with minimal service obligations to 1s. 4d. per acre for holdings with very heavy week-work. Fixed rents would seem to have varied from 9d. to 2s. 6d. per acre *in toto*, but such land 'sold' for values that were often twelve to twenty times the value of the annual customary charge per acre. Under such conditions it is perhaps understandable that this particular landlord appears increasingly to have sought to augment his income by expanding the non-customary component in his total manorial revenue.[51]

On the east Norfolk lay manor of Coltishall an extremely active market in small-sized units of land was associated with a tenant population holding very small units – a modal holding of about two acres. Such a rural population, however intensively they may have worked their land, would have needed to supplement household incomes by off-farm work. It is perhaps no coincidence that this manor is lodged within an area of England that has now been revealed to have some of the most productive manorial demesnes in the whole country, securing very high yields per acre, but achieved by exceptionally heavy labour imputs. Obviously the 'surplus' labour deployed on these demesnes did not derive primarily from customary services. Instead it was made available by a burgeoning tenant population that simultaneously fostered, and was also the product of, an active land market with exceptionally important implications for the development of a highly distinctive regional economy.[52] It seems that a sizeable proportion of the labour services on the estates of the Abbot of Bury St Edmunds were not taken in kind but 'sold back' to the tenants for their cash value. Under these conditions it would seem that landlords might not have been so preoccupied with maintaining holdings in unfragmented conditions and hence more readily able to meet service obligations.[53] Here too, contrary to some of the views about the reasons for limited wealth accumulation in peasant society, there were no prohibitions by the landlord on the acquisition by individuals of more than one holding.[54]

Of course these East Anglian manors shared in common the practice of partible inheritance on customary land which may have helped to create property units of a size highly conducive to an active land market. It has, however, proved difficult to identify the causal relationships between the presence of partibility and an active peasant land market. One effect of the market in land may have been to mitigate the erosional influence of partible inheritance on the fragmentation of holdings, since partibility in practice only applied to the land

51. Smith, 'Some thoughts', pp. 115–18.

52. B. M. S. Campbell, 'Agricultural productivity in medieval England: Some evidence from Norfolk', *Journal of Economic History*, 43 (1983), pp. 379–40.

53. Smith, 'Some thoughts', p. 119.

54. Smith, 'Families and their land', pp. 360–72 and idem, 'A periodic market and its impact upon a manorial community: Botesdale and the manor of Redgrave, 1280–1300', in Razi and Smith, *Medieval Society and the Manor Court*, pp. 450–82.

of which an individual died seised and, in theory, would only lead to subdivision if there was more than one heir. It has been shown that under the demographic conditions applying in much of England before the Black Death, 'surplus' sons could potentially have supplemented their inheritances by purchasing 'surplus' land left by men dying without an heir or by marrying into families where there was no heir but an heiress.[55] None the less, such an argument does assume that markets for land and marriage markets involving heiresses worked to stabilize the social *status quo*. Destabilization might have been a more likely outcome as landed heiresses married heirs or non-heirs with landed resouces. A different assessment of the impact of partible inheritance would arise if stress were placed on its role in dividing holdings to levels below which they were no longer capable of sustaining a family farm. Individuals so situated were eventually forced, perhaps as a consequence of bad harvests or heavy taxes, to release their lands onto the market. Such conditions were relatively commonplace in the late thirteenth and early fourteenth century and have received their most careful consideration by scholars working on East Anglia where 'distress sales' in bad harvest years in the 1290s and early 1300s were capable of reaching dramatically high levels within the customary tenantry – a pattern intensified perhaps by the high taxation rates imposed at that time.[56] For the most part these sales took land outside the kin group and the end result was an intensification of social differentiation with financial advantages accruing to both the relatively small group of purchasers and to the local landlords whose income from entry fines or licence fees rose to particularly high levels in such years. In fact, it has proved possible to document instances of changes in inheritance customs which may have favoured such developments. For instance, we know of a shift from impartible to partible inheritance in the thirteenth century when a jury of trial in a land dispute in the Norfolk manor of Gressenhall reported that the custom had been altered because the lord's seneschal *vellet habere plures tenentes*.[57]

On the Cambridgeshire manors of the Abbots of Crowland a further example indicating the importance of landlord attitudes to practices regarding the devolution of property within the peasantry may be considered. Evidence concerning widows of peasant property-holders in these manors reveals that, although it was the 'custom' that a widow forfeited her holding if she remarried, in the early fourteenth century over 51 per cent of recorded marriages in that manor involved the remarriage of widows with their land. The lord without doubt benefited from the additional revenue brought by the high entry fines paid by grooms in these marriages. He was willing to generate additional income through enhanced fines paid for the marital link itself and the access to the widow's land it made possible, rather than deliberately inducing high fertility by encouraging first marriages, offspring from which might sustain the ranks of a *corvée*

---

55. Smith, 'Families and their land', pp. 365–69 and idem, 'Some issues concerning families and their property in rural England 1250–1800', in *Land, Kinship and Life-Cycle*, pp. 38–62.

56. Schofield, 'Dearth, debt and the local land market', pp. 15–17.

57. J. Williamson, 'Norfolk: thirteenth century', in P. D. A. Harvey (ed.), *The Peasant Land Market in Medieval England* (Oxford, 1984), pp. 57–8.

labour force for his demesne. Yet such revenue-raising possibilities might not have been possible if women, once widowed, had been unable to retain property in their own right as their husband's 'heir', and cannot therefore be seen solely as the product of untrammelled landlord power. Worthy of our attention is the fact that marital access to these widows was confined, as a consequence of the high entry or marriage fines levied on persons marrying such females, to the sons of the wealthier members of the local customary tenantry – usually the sons of full-virgaters. Such constraints certainly helped to prevent the movement of land down the social scale in a resource-scarce situation, in the period between c.1290 and c.1330. The lord's freedom to act in these circumstances was strictly limited by the economic climate, for with declining property values in the second half of the fourteenth century, widow remarriage diminished and, in outward appearances at least, the old 'custom' of an apparent prohibition on the marriage of widows with land reasserted itself.[58]

The case studies from East Anglia discussed above suggest the existence of considerable flexibility in practices relating to 'customary' land and indicate some needed caution in assuming that those holding under tenant right were encapsulated in a world without change, notwithstanding the very considerable legal protections that, it has been suggested, derived from holding land under such terms.

The above instances suggest that there was no necessary reason why landlords should insist on a continuity of holding sizes or structures, nor of family associations with them. The implications of this observation run deeper still, since there is no reason why in an ostensibly peasant society there should be any assumption about continuity of peasant familes with the land that they farmed. There were very considerable regional divisions in England and large tracts of the Midlands and central-southern England did not display characteristics akin to those that have been described for manors and peasantries from the eastern counties. In the former areas a land market involving transfers between unrelated individuals was very muted in its development in the thirteenth and fourteenth centuries. In a sizeable number of case studies involving manors or whole estates located away from the eastern and southern regions it is commonly reported that restrictions were imposed on tenants which prohibited the fragmentation of standard-sized landholdings leading to a noteworthy predictability in the presence of full-, half- and quarter-virgates.[59] In contrast, the eastern areas of England almost invariably reveal holdings described in acres and rods with no specific size exhibiting numerical dominance. Many such studies have noted hostility on the part of Midlands landlords to the fragmentation of such holdings, although there may have been a 'market' in small parcels of land that fell outside the virgated structures which it has been argued actually

58. For a full discussion of this case see J. Ravensdale, 'Population change and the transfer of customary land on a Cambridgeshire manor in the fourteenth century', in Smith, *Land, Kinship and Life-Cycle*, pp. 197–225.

59. For example, E. King, *Peterborough Abbey 1086–1310: A Study in the Land Market* (Cambridge, 1973), pp. 107–25; G. C. Homans, *English Villagers of the Thirteenth Century* (Cambridge, MA, 1941), ch. 16; P. D. A. Harvey, *A Medieval Oxfordshire Village: Cuxham 1240–1400* (Oxford, 1965); R. J. Faith, 'Berkshire: fourteenth and fifteenth centuries', in Harvey, *The Peasant Land Market in Medieval England*, pp. 107–58; Harvey, *Westminster Abbey*.

facilitated the preservation of the regularized pattern. Here we have a highly plausible, if somewhat functionalist, argument that the market, to the extent that it existed, preserved a peasant social structure, rather than transformed it through furthering social differentiation, as may have happened in East Anglia.[60] It may not have been a coincidence that, in addition to their reluctance to sanction the splitting of holdings, landlords of Midland manors effectively imposed impartibility, since it can be shown that freeholders in this area practised partibility and part of the land market in small pieces was focused upon acquisition of land for sons other than the designated heir.[61] In fact, Zvi Razi would see these as characteristics that served to create a functionally extended peasant family in these regions, whereas nuclearity may have been more readily generated in the eastern counties with a lower place for kinship and a larger role for contractual or market-based relations in everyday life.[62] It might, furthermore, be suspected that far greater use was made of labour services supplied from labour forces resident within the households of those occupying the standard holdings in the Midland areas, and correspondingly less use made of wage-paid labour than on the demesne farms in the eastern regions.

DEVELOPMENTS AFTER THE BLACK DEATH

How does the picture of English peasant land tenure, specifically focused upon customary tenants in manorial courts that none the less came under the influence of the king's court which operated as an innovative force regarding land law, change during the cycle of demographic decline and subsequent recovery in the three centuries after the Black Death? Do the regional contrasts between the eastern counties with a more active market in customary land and the Midlands and central southern England with greater regularity in holding sizes and less evident landlord enthusiasm for a market in holdings or parts of holdings continue to be detectable? Do the Crown or the common law have any further role to play in determining the character of tenant rights in the customary or non-freeholder sector?

One development was clear and is given great emphasis in the historiography of the English peasant. The capacity of landlords to exercise coercive power over their peasantry was severely diminished in the depopulated and depopulating England of the century and a half after 1349. There was eventually an end to villeinage, labour services were no longer extractable and a combination of escalating labour costs and falling prices made it no longer possible for the demesnes to provide their owners with adequate incomes under a form

---

60. King, *Peterborough Abbey*, p. 124.

61. Faith, 'Peasant families and inheritance customs', p. 85; C. Dyer, *Lord and Peasants in a Changing Society: The Estates of the Bishopric of Worcester 680–1540* (Cambridge, 1980), pp. 106–7; Faith, *The English Peasantry and the Growth of Lordship*, pp. 135–7; Harvey, *The Peasant Land Market in Medieval England*, pp. 189–206.

62. Z. Razi, 'The myth of the immutable English family', *Past and Present*, 140 (1993), pp. 3–44.

of direct management. Hence they were let to farmers and/or leased in parcels to a peasantry that was now experiencing a veritable glut in the supply of land. One consequence of this 'buyers' market', as far as it concerned peasant land-holdings, was the proliferation of a varied array of tenancy types. The late fourteenth and early fifteenth centuries saw the abandonment of villein tenure and its replacement by tenancies at will or for short terms of years, particularly when demesnes were broken up to be let to manorial tenants.[63] Landlords may have opted for these arrangements in expectation that pre-plague conditions would eventually re-establish themselves. Tenants may have been willing to take on tenancies for restricted periods since they were frequently perceived to be fundamentally unlike hereditary customary properties which from their perspective still had disagreeable associations with serfdom. Furthermore, such impermanent arrangements were fully compatible with the desires of a peas-antry that revealed higher levels of mobility as it 'shopped around' for the most favourable tenancy terms available. In addition, under the new demographic conditions inheritance was increasingly uncertain within family lines. Fathers were frequently not succeeded by sons since they had either not survived to do so, or had moved on to take up land often held on non-hereditary terms and for favourable rents, and with increasing likelihood of not carrying the stigma of villeinage, nothwithstanding its greatly diminished material disadvantages as labour services and other arbitrary exactions withered away. Indeed there has long been a stress on this period as a moment when a bond between family and land was broken – the removal of a major prop that constituted an essential attribute of an authentic peasantry. Furthermore, others have stressed that this was a phase when what had once been a functionally extended peasant family was eventually lost from those areas of 'champion' England where open-field farming and strong manorial controls co-existed.

By the sixteenth century in addition to freehold, three major tenures had emerged under which the bulk of the English peasantry held its land – copyhold of inheritance, copyhold for lives and beneficial leases.

Copyhold was the most widely discussed of these tenurial categories since it is often described as if its tenure was equivalent to a free person holding land in villeinage in the thirteenth or fourteenth centuries. It is also assumed that the copyholder held his land at the will of the lord according to the custom of the manor. Like customary tenures of the earlier period, land transfers under copyhold were achieved through 'surrender and admittance' in the manorial court. 'Copyhold' as a term for this type of tenure reflects the actual practice developed first in the fourteenth century whereby a person holding a tenancy under terms of surrender and admittance was given a copy of the relevant manorial court roll entry recording the admission as 'proof of tenure'.

There were two principal categories of copyhold – copyholds of inheritance and copyholds for lives. The former category of copyhold was widespread over East Anglia, south-east England and the east Midlands, and the latter was much more common over regions further to the west and north. The major difference

---

63. R. H. Hilton, *The Decline of Serfdom in Medieval England*, 2nd edn (London/Basingstoke, 1993).

between the two copyhold types concerned a right to renewal when the terms expired. With copyholds of inheritance, the tenant paid a small annual rent and a more substantial fine when the property was sold or when it passed to an heir. Sometimes the fine was fixed by custom and sometimes it was arbitrary. In theory, just as under villein tenure, a landlord could make the transmission problematic for the incoming tenant by setting an entry fine that was cripplingly high and in practice unpayable.

Copyholds for lives were not heritable over the longer term. They were usually grants for three lives – often the peasant husband, his wife and a son. Usually when the son initiated his family he surrendered his copyhold and was readmitted with a new copy specifying himself, his wife and son as the three tenants. He paid a fine which was, in theory, arbitrarily determined for the extension of the agreement. Unlike copyhold of inheritance, such an agreement need not have been automatically renewed.[64]

A long-standing and far from fully resolved debate has preoccupied English historians concerning the implications of the growth of copyhold.[65] It has often been stressed that it was essentially an *ad hoc* arrangement established without any clearly structured and repetitive forms or rules, since it was negotiated on a manor-by-manor basis, and had no guarantee from the royal courts to be a long-term and secure form of tenure. It is sometimes supposed that in the land-abundant conditions of the fifteenth century there had been no pressures to test whether it offered much protection against arbitrary landlord action. Robert Brenner has given the growth of this tenure pride of place in his arguments about the destruction of a peasantry that had failed to gain a secure legal title when serfdom dissolved. This failure ensured that thereafter rural England had embarked on an irreversible journey towards fully fledged agrarian capitalism. This inability to achieve a secure form of tenure in the aftermath of villeinage's collapse implied that peasants would not eventually have the means to withstand the efforts of landlords who wished to engross or enclose their holdings as they proceeded to create the large farms, which would be essential for fully fledged capitalist enterprises. In achieving their 'victory' over the peasantry, landlords, according to Brenner, had been aided by the Crown which had declined, whether passively or actively, to establish freehold for those holding under customary tenures or copyhold of both types. Another process aiding the displacement of a peasantry from occupancy of their land, whether held under customary or copyhold tenure, arose from the influence of demography. Given the substantial shortage of tenants in the late fourteenth and fifteenth centuries, lords were able to take holdings which escheated to them and to incorporate them into their demesnes, subsequently letting them on contractual terms which would enable the tenants' removal at a later date by use of excessive fines.[66]

64. For an excellent succinct account of tenurial changes see Harvey, *The Peasant Land Market*, pp. 328–38.

65. The *locus classicus* is R. H. Tawney, *The Agrarian Problem in the Sixteenth Century* (London, 1912).

66. Many of the above issues are developed at length in the various contributions in Aston and Philpin, *The Brenner Debate*.

The 'Brenner thesis' has excited a great deal of interest and much supportive as well as critical comment. Much of this discussion has been pursued at a rather general level – a feature not helped by the fact that detailed research on processes relating to land-holding and the devolution of properties within the peasantry in the period from 1350 to 1700 has been more limited in quantity than that concerned with the earlier period. Inevitably, when detailed work has been undertaken the results highlight significant qualifications to Robert Brenner's broad-brush treatment of the subject.

Brenner gave relatively limited attention to issues concerning regional variations in England and his account both of villeinage and its adverse consequences, as well as developments during the phase of copyhold tenure, failed to confront conditions in the eastern counties where it might be claimed fully fledged capitalist agriculture established itself earliest and most extensively. Case studies of peasant land tenures in East Anglia raise many interesting points. It has already been argued above that this region was particularly marked by active land markets in the century before the Black Death, and that manors held by landlords of varying levels of wealth and political power introduced into their curial practices concerning customary land many innovations that had emerged initially in the royal courts. Such openness to influences from higher echelons within the curial system implied that their tenantry was endowed with securer terms of tenure than if their manorial courts had been more introspective affairs. This process went still further in the later fourteenth and fifteenth centuries.

Mention has already been made of jointure arrangements and entail as fourteenth-century developments which certainly became far more pervasive within the peasantries of eastern England after the Black Death, although their origins pre-date that shock, and cannot be attributed fundamentally to subsequent loosening of landlord authority, although their greater and speedier spread in this area may have done so, since the deployment of these instruments gave tenants greater choice in the way they devolved their land-holdings. Another development that in some places can be documented from the earliest decade of the fourteenth century was the so-called 'death-bed transfer', occurring when a peasant 'languishing near death' (*languens in extremis*) or 'on his death bed' (*in mortali lecto*) gave specific instructions to a 'third party', who was sometimes a manorial officer (usually the reeve or bailiff), or other persons who were likely to be witnessed by other tenants, concerning the disposal of his or her landed assets following his or her death. At the subsequent court, the 'third party' was to ensure that the tenement was granted to the recipient by the process of 'surrender and admittance'. In effect, seigneurial interest in this procedure continued to be strong as the surrender and admittance ensured that the court roll entry concerning the transaction made it clear that the land was held, usually at the lord's will, and that seigneurial levies (i.e. entry fines) were taken. As a recent study, drawing heavily on evidence from fourteenth- and fifteenth-century Essex and Norfolk and concerned largely with the legal theory of this device, has noted, the most distinctive feature of such transfers is that they occurred outside the court and seem to have been an acceptance of a villein's right to make an oral will relating to his or her customary or copyhold property. Indeed, unlike other *pre-mortem* arrangements for the transfer of property, and in obvious contradistinction to the *post-mortem* inheritance custom, they allowed an individual to delay the decision on the devolution of property to almost the last possible moment before death.[67] It should be noted that customary tenants, certainly from the 1290s in many parts of eastern and south-eastern England, had employed the entail which allowed individuals to grant land to another or others and the heirs of the grantees' bodies. While this could be used by an individual to fulfil very specific wishes with regard to the devolution of the property after his or her death, and although the remainder might go to the donee after the donor's death, thereby not depriving him of the employment of the land in his own lifetime, it did not facilitate a 'change of heart'.[68]

In jointure, entail and the deathbed transfer we can observe peasants holding customary tenancies by the close of the fourteenth century and increasingly able to deploy devices which students of the later medieval English nobility and gentry have come to regard as fundamental in any discussion of family strategies concerning the provisions made by men for their wives and children and maintenance over the longer-term integrity of their estate.[69] Under conditions of rapidly improving ratios of land to people, that were driven both by the demographic decline and the leasing of demesne lands, there was an ever-rising proportion of land that did not move between related parties in *inter-vivos* transfers secured by 'surrender and admittance'. In a sample of manors from Norfolk, Suffolk, Essex and Buckinghamshire in which it has proved possible to trace transfers relating to 2,869 acres of customary land in the first decade of the fifteenth century, it seems that less than a third of that land passed by means of *post-mortem* inheritances within the family. The remainder of the land (59 per cent) moved between living persons, the overwhelming majority of whom were unrelated. Approximately 15 per cent of the land that was transferred was, however, granted principally to kin by individuals close to death utilizing the out-of-court device of the death-bed transfer. Statistical aggregations of this kind, however, fail to reveal the complex arrangements that individuals were able to construct for themselves or their families. For instance, at slightly later dates in the fifteenth century in the Abbot of St Albans' manor of Winslow (Bucks.) the intricacy of the arrangement becomes amply apparent when the death-bed transfers can be observed alongside the evidence bearing upon testamentary devolution of chattels and the 'intestate' inheritance of property according to manorial custom that had not been previously redistributed. In the records of the Winslow manor court we can observe how the full-virgater John Jankyn in 1430 gave half an acre of meadow to his widow Alice, and granted a further half an acre to his son William, to whom seven years earlier he had given a virgate and a messuage by 'surrender and admittance'; the

67. L. Bonfield and L. R. Poos, 'The development of the death-bed transfer in medieval English manor courts', *Cambridge Law Journal*, 47 (1988), pp. 403–27.

68. Smith, 'Coping with uncertainty', p. 45.

69. C. Given-Wilson, *The English Nobility in the Late Middle Ages* (London, 1987), pp. 143–4.

remainder of his estate, which included a virgate of land, a toft and a further half acre, of which John Jankyn died seised, passed according to manorial custom to his son John, who paid the death duty of a horse valued at a mark. In the proceedings of the same court John Jankyn's will had been enrolled. This specified that six bushels of grain were to go to his daughter-in-law, a further two bushels to his granddaughter Matilda. His sons William and John were made their father's executors. From the same manor we can see how provision for the present might be made in conjunction with arrangements to secure satisfactory outcomes in the after-life. Ralph Wengrave of Winslow in 1433 on his death-bed gave his wife Emma a croft of half an acre and granted her the substantial rump of his property containing a messuage with its adjacent land of two acres, a toft, half a virgate, a cottage and two acres, another messuage and two acres, and twenty acres along with one and a half acres of meadow until her son John came of age. He also specified that if John were to die then the property was to go to Joan, his eldest daughter, who, if she died, was to be succeeded by Joan, his youngest daughter, who in turn was to be succeeded by Emma, the widow, if by then she was still alive. If Emma should outlive the specified heirs then she or her executors were instructed to see that the property at her death was sold for the benefit of the souls of Ralph and his family. We can note the particular attention given in these examples to provisioning the widow and the care taken to allocate resources to other offspring, sons and daughters. Essentially similar principles of confining kin recognition to spouse and immediate offspring distinguish the actions of the much more humble tenant of the Abbot of Bury St Edmunds, Robert Littlebury of Redgrave, Suffolk, whose cottage and its adjacent curtilage he granted in 1404 to Matilda, his widow, and after her death to John, their son, However, if John were to die before Matilda, she was to arrange to have the property sold at her death for the benefit of their souls. Other means of securing the position of the widow were provided by jointure arrangements and an increasing proportion of *inter-vivos* transactions in which purchasers were found to be husband and wife pairs – a means of ensuring that a wife would have land in widowhood, if pre-deceased. A widow holding land under such arrangements would frequently have avoided the payment of entry fines or heriots on her husband's death.[70]

Other work on East Anglian communities concerned with land held by copyhold of inheritance in the second half of the fifteenth and first half of the sixteenth centuries reveals even greater flexibility in the means by which land was transferred. Over this period it is possible to observe a still greater shrinkage in the proportion of land transferred through *post-mortem* means and a larger share through death-bed instructions. Furthermore, a widening array of means of transferring customary land is detectable, such as joint tenures between groups of unrelated men, mortgage arrangements, and increasing use of wills to grant customary properties. At the same time the proportion of land transferred within the family continued to shrink to particularly low levels. It

---

70. Smith, 'Coping with uncertainty', pp. 50–4. See, too, E. Clark, 'Charitable bequests, death-bed land sales and the manor court in later medieval England', in Razi and Smith, *Medieval Society and the Manor Court*, pp. 143–62.

is clear that these developments reflect an ever-widening set of choices available to a population less subject to manorial control. However, it would be incorrect to state that these devices owe their origins to changes in this era of enhanced freedom, since they had penetrated into customary courts from higher curial echelons when villeinage was 'alive and well' in the early fourteenth century. Their subsequent diffusion was no doubt aided by the loosening of controls and the disappearance of serfdom over the course of the fifteenth century.

More recent work on Norfolk has revealed that copyholders were able to combine a mixture of devices available through the manor court and through wills to expedite complex devolutionary strategies which enabled them to provision kin with land, or to exclude kin from it, to sell land to non-kin, to endow kin with cash rather than land, or to allocate land to a designated heir who thereafter would be obliged to sell the property concerned to endow other siblings with cash. Under no circumstances is there any suggestion that copyhold of inheritance did not allow these individuals to treat their land as if it were a fee simple resource. Furthermore, from information relating to the sums of money that passed between 'purchaser' and 'seller' it is evident that copyhold land possessed a value that greatly exceeded the rents and entry fines that landlords levied upon it. The value of that land increased sharply after 1550 when it has also been observed that the proportion of land moving within the family began to increase notably from its late medieval low point. In the Norfolk manor of Hevingham more land moved within the family between 1544 and 1558 than at any time since the late thirteenth century. Similar increases in the level of intra-familial transfers have been observed in parts of midland England over a comparable period in the sixteenth century.[71]

Dr Jane Whittle, who has advanced our understanding of these developments most profoundly through her comparative analysis of East Anglia and the Midlands, notes a number of contrasts to be drawn between these regions from the early fourteenth century to the early sixteenth century. In East Anglia, in particular, she perceives that with the widening array of choices at the disposal of copyholders in the fifteenth century – a development that had grown steadily over the previous two centuries – they were able to side-step the operation of manorial custom by granting the bulk of their property as they wished, and an increasing share of this was undertaken outside the confines of the manorial court through death-bed procedures. However, a more fundamental point made by Whittle is that essential characteristics of the land market in customary or copyhold property were changing. She acknowledges the existence in East Anglia

71. Reported in a seminar paper entitled 'Individualism and the family-land bond: a reassessment of land transfer patterns among the English peasantry *c.*1270–1580 (forthcoming *Past and Present*) delivered by Dr Jane Whittle, University of Exeter, at the Cambridge Group for the History of Population and Social Structure, 25 November 1996. For other instances where a rise in intra-familial land transfers has been identified in the sixteenth century see, Macfarlane, *Origins of English Individualism*, pp. 28–9, C. Dyer, 'Changes in the size of peasant holdings in some west midland villages', in Smith, *Land, Kinship and Life-Cycle*, pp. 284–5; G. Sreenivasan, 'The land-family bond at Earls Colne (Essex) 1550–1650', *Past and Present*, 131 (1991), p. 10. For more general remarks on the failure of historians to exercise caution in their comments about emotional attitudes to land displayed by kin groups in the light of the contrasts between the fifteenth and the sixteenth century see Smith, 'Families and their properties', p. 59.

of a very active land market, based on *inter-vivos* transfers from the late thirteenth century, but notes that a relatively large share of land was then transferred according to manorial custom by *post-mortem* means. This was a major difference over the sixteenth century when individuals could devise strategies and implement them before death. In addition there was a significant increase in the mean size of transactions which in the sixteenth century were seven to ten times larger than they had been in the late thirteenth century, when they were rarely more than an acre in area. Another difference that distinguished the later period was the increasing presence of wealthy individuals, including townsmen, clerics and gentlemen, in the market for copyhold property – indicative of a shift of attitude. No longer was customary land encumbered with financial charges associated with villeinage and, perhaps of greater significance still, this land no longer carried with it the stigma of serfdom. The rising size of land transactions reflected the greater wealth of those who now participated in the market, as well as the impact of engrossment of holdings that had occurred cumulatively over the fifteenth century.

A particularly important element in Whittle's argument is that the family-land bond was never particularly strong. It certainly fell away from what had earlier been relatively low levels after the Black Death and rose sharply after 1550 in a market that was becoming decidedly less 'peasant-like'. Indeed she is surely correct to argue that a strong bond between family and land cannot be used as the distinguishing characteristic *par excellence* of a peasant society, since peasants in this part of England had shown themselves quite capable of devising strategies that both made elaborate provisions for family members in, as well excluding them altogether from, land which was in their possession to grant. What is of more fundamental significance is the nature of lordship and the institutional constraints limiting the peasant's freedom of action. Strong land–family bonds are more likely a reflection of limited freedoms and landlord intransigence.

In the comparison she draws between the Midlands and East Anglia this point is effectively developed. Not only before the Black Death did landlords in the former region place obstacles in the path of a peasantry that was obliged to retain a highly regularized landholding structure from which labour services were drawn, but in the fifteenth century, too, the two regions were distinguished by possessing rather different forms of copyhold. Copyhold of inheritance, so prevalent in East Anglia, permitted tenants to grant or sell their land to 'assignees' who were frequently unrelated or to 'heirs' if they so desired, and the tenure derived was indefinite with no time limit placed upon it. As Whittle perceptively notes, 'copyhold of inheritance was valuable because it could be bought and sold, rather than because it could be inherited'. The predominance of copyhold for lives and leases for specified terms of years in so many areas away from the east of England did mean that in the fifteenth century most customary land and demesne leases were relatively insecure and were tenures that could not be held indefinitely. Under such conditions lords were in a far stronger position to choose or bar new tenants, and it would be far more likely for that reason alone that a customary inheritance provided an individual with his best chance of entering a property with landlord approval. A corollary of this was that customary properties had far less value as a tradeable asset in these areas – a feature which was both a cause and a consequence of the poorly developed land market.[72]

The regional differences we have discussed above under which customary tenures were held would appear to have sustained remarkably durable contrasts in the character of peasant land tenures and associated land exchange systems from the thirteenth into the early sixteenth century. It might be supposed that, given this apparent geographical intransigence, it would be in the areas marked by a predominance of copyhold for lives and beneficial leases that conditions most conducive to landlord actions of the type posited by Brenner would be readily detectable, and where the destruction of the peasantry would have proceeded most rapidly. However, it has been said in relation to England's early modern agrarian development that 'one reason why Brenner inflates the role of the large capitalist farmer at the expense of the part played by the peasant is that he correspondingly under-estimates the latter's legal position'.[73] This view might serve as a *leitmotiv* for this chapter as a whole, since throughout the above discussion it has been argued that the presence of the royal court has served not so much as a curial arena concerned solely with the rights of freeholders but did, over the later medieval centuries, operate as an influence that frequently determined the ways in which legal instruments at the disposal of manorial courts developed and broadened the range of options available to an English peasantry holding under customary tenures. It is important to stress that this influence may well have been more readily evident in the eastern regions, which later in the fifteenth and sixteenth centuries also came to be distinguished by the presence of the most secure form of copyhold – copyhold of inheritance. The regional geography of copyhold categories remains a perplexing and unresolved problem, but the explanation for those spatial patterns may well eventually be found to derive from the developments in manorial courts in the thirteenth and fourteenth century which have been given such extended consideration in the first part of this chapter.

It most definitely seems, contrary to older opinions, that interventions by royal courts expanded the proprietary interest of the copyholder still further in the sixteenth century. Notwithstanding a rather different reality when observed in the membranes of manorial court rolls, particularly as it concerned land transferred *sibi et heredibus suis*, land held in villein tenures in the thirteenth and fourteenth centuries had been considered by the common law courts to be tenancies at will and their tenants had no access to those courts if lords took it upon themselves to evict them. By 1600 copyholders could recover possession of their land if a lord did take such action, provoking Robert Allen to comment that this change 'converted villeins into peasant proprietors'.[74] Parliament in the sixteenth century, as Richard Hoyle observes, could have abolished copyhold

---

72. Ibid.
73. P. Croot and D. Parker, 'Agrarian class structure and the development of capitalism: France and England compared', in Aston and Philpin, *The Brenner Debate*, p. 82.
74. R. C. Allen, *Enclosure and the Yeoman: The Agricultural Development of the South Midlands 1450–1850* (Oxford, 1992), p. 68.

and established leasehold in its stead, swept away customs whereby fines were fixed, and declared them to be arbitrary. However, it did not do so. Hoyle also points to other contexts, particularly those to do with enclosure and depopulation in the early sixteenth century, when Parliament did intervene, although to the advantage of tenants and against the economic interests of the landlord. The courts were generally willing to accept the equitable claims of tenants against lords, and where they were rejected judges requested landlords to act leniently with respect to tenants. Furthermore, peasant tenants might have been more severely disadvantaged in the matter of precedent since, in theory, customary tenancies could have been downgraded to tenancies at will if it were possible to show that at some earlier time they had been leasehold land or demesne. Likewise, customs claiming fixed fines could be overturned if at some previous phase fines could be revealed to have been variable. Certainly Parliament made no effort to introduce a statute of limitations thereby allowing landlords, in principle, to produce evidence from the relatively distant past, even where current practices may have existed for many generations. It might therefore be supposed that a lord who could prove that the customary tenants had previously held by lease could destroy their claims to hold by copyhold of inheritance, or those who had earlier utilized variable fining practices could abolish any rights to fixed fining.[75] Indeed Charles Gray has argued that in the sixteenth century the courts accepted that any proof of changes of tenurial status after 1189 could destroy copyhold.[76] But what is particularly noteworthy, as Hoyle remarks, is that 'there is little evidence that [landlords] turned archivists to defeat their tenants' titles'.

It must be acknowledged that the issue of excess fining as a means by which lords were able to expel tenants has generated no evident unanimity of opinion among historians, although there is a noticeable reluctance to endorse some of the more extreme claims of Tawney on this subject.[77] Brenner, while aware of the view that equity courts could intervene on behalf of tenants to limit excessive fines, noted that no instances of Chancery doing so before 1586 could be discovered.[78] Hoyle notes, however, that this view remains tenable only because the debate has been conducted with reference to the published reports, of which there are none for the mid-sixteenth century, rather than the records of the courts. He observes, too, that the Chancellors had certainly ruled on fines by c.1550, although it is still unclear, given the current state of research, how frequently this happened and how Chancery responded.[79]

Hoyle, like Croot and Parker, is adamant that Brenner has presented far too depressing a picture of the customary tenant's or copyholder's position *vis-à-vis* the Crown or the state, since the state is more accurately 'seen as possessing

75. R. W. Hoyle, 'Tenure and the land market in early modern England: or a late contribution to the Brenner debate', *Economic History Review*, 2nd series, 43 (1990), pp. 4–12.

76. C. M. Gray, *Copyhold Equity and the Common Law* (Cambridge, MA, 1963), p. 201. See, too, P. W. F. Large, 'Economic and social change in north Worcestershire during the seventeenth century' (unpublished D.Phil thesis, University of Oxford, 1980), pp. 19–23.

77. E. Kerridge, *Agrarian Problems in the Sixteenth Century and After* (London, 1969), pp. 38–9

78. Aston and Philpin, *Brenner Debate*, pp. 47–8, 296.

79. Hoyle, 'Tenure and the land market', p. 5.

a concern for the well-being of tenants which led it to intervene in the affairs of landlords and tenants both over enclosure and over fines'.[80] This is a view voiced even more forcefully by Professor Robert Allen when he stresses the growing security of tenure of copyholders, who by the end of the sixteenth century pursued cases of eviction by resort to the writ of ejectment, previously an instrument only available to freeholders. Likewise, he sees the decision to cap entry fines for heritable copyholds as very advantageous to the peasantry. He stresses similar protection that was emerging to establish security of tenure for those holding land by beneficial leases which he regards as a development mirroring the improved status of copyholders.[81] For Allen the early seventeenth century marks 'the high point of peasant proprietorship' as a consequence of legal developments in the preceding century, when the acreage of land farmed by those who might be justifiably described as 'owner-occupiers' took a giant stride forward to reach unprecedented levels.[82]

The emphasis in the writings of scholars whose work we have cited as representing a set of counter-arguments to the views of Robert Brenner has been on institutional changes that served to protect a peasantry, or more specifically, facilitated the emergence of what many have regarded as the most distinctive feature of sixteenth- and seventeenth-century English rural society – the English yeoman. This is not, however, to deny that this emergence was the product of growing social differentiation within the ranks of the peasantry and an associated reduction in the overall number of copyholders as engrossment took place. The emphasis, none the less, is on the fact that this was a process engineered by the copyholders themselves in a legal context relating to land tenure that was highly favourable to such processes.[83] When such propitious circumstances are set alongside prevailing economic conditions associated with rising agricultural product prices and land values, driven by rapid demographic growth, taking population levels once more closer to their medieval maxima, it is apparent that only those villagers with adequate resources were able to expand the size of their holdings. It is clear, too, that at the moment of the new seventeenth-century demographic peak, unlike the early fourteenth century, land tenurial terms for the English peasantry were far more favourable to wealth accumulation by certain sections of that group, helped also by particularly low levels of taxation.[84] Allen treats these conditions as a vital prerequisite for what he terms the 'yeoman's agricultural revolution', during which he believes total grain output and yields rose along with national income.[85] It is particularly noteworthy that these conditions endowed the early modern English demographic regime with characteristics that distinguished it from that of the late thirteenth and early fourteenth centuries and that to be found (with the exception of conditions experienced by the Dutch) over a great deal of Europe in the late

80. Ibid., p. 6.
81. Allen, *Enclosure and the Yeoman*, pp. 68–70.
82. Ibid., p. 72.
83. Croot and Parker, 'Agrarian class structure and the development of capitalism', p. 85. See, too, M. Spufford, *Contrasting Communities* (Cambridge, 1974), pp. 76–85.
84. Croot and Parker, 'Agrarian class structure and the development of capitalism', p. 89.
85. Allen, *Enclosure and the Yeoman*, p. 21.

sixteenth and early seventeenth centuries. England was remarkable for an absence of harvest-induced mortality surges and the only regions that did display some susceptibility to those difficulties were confined to certain peripheral pastoral-farming areas where many of the developments regarding land tenure on which this discussion has focused were less relevant or evident.[86]

Whether this favourable relationship between population and resources, particularly when comparisons are drawn with continental Europe (once again excepting the case of the Dutch), stems at base from the legal responses of government over the long sixteenth century, when the royal courts came more emphatically to protect the tenures of copyholders and leaseholders, remains difficult, perhaps impossible, to establish. It provides a matter of recurrent debate among English early modern historians, but it reveals why discussions of the English peasantry have been dominated by, indeed have almost become in their entirety, a sub-branch of legal history. Such concerns have absorbed the bulk of this present discussion which, it should be stressed, sees no case for not regarding England unambiguously as a peasant society in which 'owner-occupancy' reached its apogee early in the seventeenth century.[87]

86. J. Walter and R. Schofield, 'Famine, disease and crisis mortality in early modern society', in J. Walter and R. Schofield (eds), *Famine, Disease and Social Order in Early Modern Society* (Cambridge, 1989), pp. 68–73.

87. In adopting such a position this argument reaches back to a pre-First World War terminological usage associated with those scholars who considered the peasantry to be small freeholders, copyholders and farmers, with the yeomen in the vanguard. See G. Slater, *The English Peasantry and the Enclosure of the Common Fields* (London, 1907) and W. Hasbach, *The History of the English Agricultural Labourer* (1908). Such views are considered in a broader discussion by J. V. Beckett, 'The peasant in England: a case of terminological confusion', *Agricultural History Review*, 32 (1994), pp. 113–23.

CHAPTER TWELVE

The Historical Geography of
European Peasantries, 1400–1800

John Langton

The prospect of reading, thinking over and writing about essays in English incorporating recent research in many languages on peasants spread from Finisterre to the Urals, and from the North Cape to Sicily, was mouth-watering. Doing the reading and trying some reflection has brought dry-mouthed apprehension: at the end of a feast of scholarship and argument served with great panache comes, it seems, a poisoned chalice. To write a closing chapter is not problematical simply because the book contains so much adept reasoning and so many intriguing case studies that generalization (let alone synthesis) would require more wisdom than I possess. It is worse than that, for a number of reasons.

THE EXPLOSION OF VARIETY

As requested, each author has deliberately demonstrated for their allotted territory that peasantry varied widely across space and changed through time. Inexorably, each chapter adds another segment to an already kaleidoscopic picture. It is easy to appreciate the impatience, even irritation, made more or less explicit by different authors, at the alacrity with which writers who are less fully involved in historical scholarship generalize about peasants and peasantry. In effect, each chapter warns of the futility of attempting what I was asked to do.

As the Introduction sagely anticipated, even the validity of the term 'peasant' is disputed. And it is undoubtedly true that the non-English words which are translatable into 'peasant' for comparative convenience might well have represented different modes of existence and carried different evaluative connotations from one part of Europe to another.[1] The etymologies of *bauer*, *bonde* and *husbandman*, for example, seem to imply service, land cultivation and household headship, the fundaments of a socio-economic system, whereas *paysan* and *paesano*

---

1. As well as from time to time, which is also true of the word 'peasant' itself as used in English. Raymond Williams, *Keywords: A Vocabulary of Culture and Society*, 2nd edn (London, 1976), pp. 231–2, and J. V. Becket, 'The peasant in England: a case of terminological confusion', *Agricultural History Review*, 32 (1984), pp. 113–23.

stem from the same Latin root as 'pagan' and convey, besides rural living, a sense of being outside from, rather than basic to, something greater. Not just general model-building, but even expression in a common language acts to distort empirical circumstances, however faithfully and minutely we might try to depict them. Comparative study requires a single word for the commonfolk[2] who comprised the vast majority of people in western Europe at this time, and 'peasant' is probably the best. None the less, it would be negligent not to acknowledge that the extensive use of alternatives such as 'villagers', 'countryfolk' and 'subalterns' by some authors is more than a stylistic device.

Again as the Introduction predicted (perhaps even urged), the abstract conception of 'peasantry', decribing a singular mode of economic operation, social organization and cultural expression, is more deliberately called into question in more chapters. One of the most striking aspects of the book to someone who has dabbled in generalizing about peasantry[3] is the number and ingenuity of the ways in which its essential, even defining, aspects are shown not to have pertained among the peasants of Europe at this time. They might live in towns, not the countryside; not be subsistence farmers, but reliant on crafts and/or trade; not dwell in autarkic self-provisioning households, but in specialized units within systems of exchange; not rooted to the soil on which they were born, but highly migratory; not communally harmonious, but competitively individualistic; not snugly bound into families with imperatives to support all their members and perpetuate themselves across generations, but jealously tenacious of personal shares; not cloddishly conservative, but cleverly innovative; not placidly following routines enshrined in irrevocable custom, but violently wilful; not politically powerless, but capable of exploiting their lords, and even bringing down governments. What received wisdom leads us to expect in each of these oppositional pairs can also be found in the book, and any *a priori* generalization could be validated by 'cherry-picking' from it; but that would fly in the face of the authors' own intentions and abuse the privilege of having the last word.

So far, this litany of difficulties has been based in the sheer variety of historical experience which the book reveals. Historiographical diversity presents another set of barbs to puncture synthetic ambition. Chapter headings and subheadings show different foci of interest and rhetorical structures. It would have been perverse to expect chapters to be written in easily intercommensurable ways. No one can write a fully impartial, utterly comprehensive and evenly balanced account of anything, and historians are disputatious by profession. That is the hallmark of their worth. Each author scrupulously explains why the substantive

2. The term used by Börje Hanssen, 'Commonfolk and gentlefolk', *Ethnographia Scandinavica*, 1976, pp. 67–100. As an alternative which in English has no happy singular and carries unpleasant resonances from '*das Volk*', it brings its own problems, as do all other conceivable terms.

3. As in the Introductions to Colin G. Clarke and John Langton (eds), *Peasantry and Progress: Rural Culture in the Modern World* (School of Geography, University of Oxford, Research Paper, 45) (Oxford, 1990), pp. 5–12, and Göran Hoppe and John Langton, *Peasantry to Capitalism: Western Östergötland in the Nineteenth Century* (Cambridge, 1996), pp. 1–39; Langton, 'Habitat, economy and society revisited; peasant ecotypes and economic development in Sweden', *Cambria*, 13 (1986), pp. 5–24, and idem, 'The origins of the capitalist world economy', in Ian Douglas, Richard Huggett and Mike Robinson (eds), *Companion Encyclopedia of Geography: the Environment and Humankind* (London, 1996), pp. 206–27.

contents of their chapter lean in a particular direction and how other authorities in their field have dwelled more heavily on other aspects of the subject, or interpreted the same one differently. But to articulate the diversity of preoccupations and judgements does not reduce their potency to frustrate an endgame.

Some of this historiographical diversity comes from the concentration of particular kinds of written sources in particular places: Russian censuses, Austrian inventories, Scandinavian peasant business records, English manor court rolls, German law codes, east European estate accounts, or Spanish literary dramas, for example. Invariably, they are difficult to use and easy to misinterpret. The vastly increased expertise and research effort recently concentrated on many of these sources is fundamentally altering the messages they convey, and these projects give distinctive casts to research in different parts of Europe. More prosaically, variability in source materials alone can account for methodological differences between chapters, such as the extent to which detailed case studies, quotations from contemporary observations or quantification are used. It also affects choices about which aspects of peasantry are stressed and which are given shorter shrift, and the rigour with which generalizations about those attributes can be put to the test: definitive conclusions about peasant serfdom, household structure, inheritance strategies or market behaviour can only be drawn if manorial estate accounts, census data, wills and inventories, or peasant account books exist. Each chapter must, therefore, appear somewhat lop-sided relative to the others, and lean in different directions and at different angles towards *a priori* theoretical speculations.

Variable source materials are not the only reason for this. It is quite evident that the preoccupations of the scholars whose work is brought together by each author have varied from one part of Europe to another. Histories vary not only because of what they are written from, but also because of why they are written. Always they are fitted, more or less overtly, as support or critique, into bodies of contextual literature – into coherent 'peoples' stories'. Although there were not, and could not have been, 'national peasantries' in the past, national histories tell coherent stories about them. It would be silly for me to try to describe how, let alone explain why, these stories have varied across Europe; but it would be inattentive not to recognize that the preoccupations and evaluative frames of reference of different chapters do, to some extent, reflect such differences. Some of the authors explicitly say so, as they set out to question stereotyped beliefs about the 'developed' north and 'backward' south in Italy; about 'peasants as victims' east of the Elbe; about the cultural benignity and economic potency of free peasant 'salts of the earth' in Austria; or about the ineffectuality of peasantry in England and Italy. The chapters on Spain and France are aimed at explaining how it can be believed that peasantry combined the ostensibly incompatible historical roles of obstructive boor and moral guide.

Stereotypes are less evident when they are not painted as targets, but they are none the less always there, and how peasantry has been fitted into the stories of European peoples clearly differs radically. A vitally constitutive figure of celebrity in the histories of Western Germany and Scandinavia, of paradox in Spain and France, and of lament in Poland, Russia and (at least, southern)

Italy, it seems incidental, even accidental, to the distinguishing features of England and Austria. The sometimes uncomfortable dissonances where authorial jurisdictions overlap, as in German Austria and Poland, are valuable reminders that histories are composed by historians whose ideas are influenced by other historians, not given pristine by source materials.

With less confidence, another differentiating historiographical influence might be discerned. Perhaps an Anglo-American provenance is betrayed in chapters where it is an article of faith that greater involvement in untrammelled commodity exchange could bring nothing but good, was the only possible source of progress, and can be used to calibrate the historical significance of peasantry, its material welfare and moral value.[4] Even less confidently: perhaps differences in the authors' own personalities show through variations in the extent to which they engage directly with, and their attitudes towards, theoretical arguments about peasantry and generalizations about the early modern period of history? Whatever the reasons, the net effect is to side-step or destroy all the templates which might have been used to organize a concluding statement. The notion that peasantry was 'transitional' – between feudalism and capitalism, or towards modernity or, Whiggishly, towards some specific subsequent national characteristic – is sedulously demolished in a number of chapters. The organizing principle of 'free west' and 'servile east' is debunked. So is the 'world-system' model. 'Biological' explanations of peasant character and behaviour – in response to the aetiology of disease-bearing organisms, the imperatives of human reproduction, the natural ecology of the resource bases they used, or combinations of all three – are shown, in one chapter or another, to be untenable.

Thus, 'all that was solid melts into air'.[5] It is not simply that the peasantry in different parts of Europe had a different story, nor even that within any one part of Europe there are different stories for different groups of peasants, but that for each particular peasantry a number of different, equally valid, stories can be written. Perhaps it was in anticipation of this that the editor asked someone from outside the disputatious historical canon to have the last word.[6]

THE CONTAINMENT OF VARIETY

The kaleidoscope's pieces are heaped high, wide and jumbled on the workbench. What is needed is a frame to contain them and, within it, a structure to articulate the pieces so that they can be moved around in search of patterns.

4. If this is indeed so, it is rather paradoxical because empirical work on rural societies in eighteenth- and nineteenth-century England and North America themselves increasingly stresses the importance of persistent 'pre-capitalist' non-market orientated aspects of farming there. E. P. Thompson, *Customs in Common* (London, 1991); Allan Kulikoff, *The Agrarian Origins of American Capitalism* (Charlottesville, VA, 1992). Winifred B. Rothenberg, *From Market Places to Market Economy: The Transformation of Rural Massachusetts, 1750–1850* (Chicago, 1992) is an example of the older view.

5. Marshall Berman, *All That Was Solid Melts Into Air* (New York, 1982).

6. The post-modern *zeitgeist* haunts geography, too, and other geographers would have set about this task in different ways.

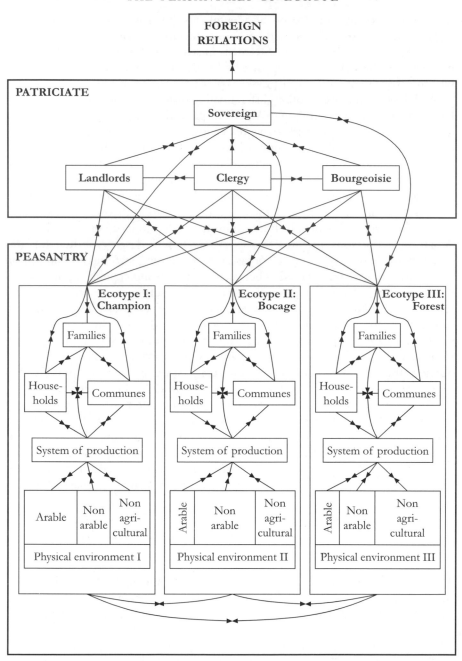

Figure 1 The components of peasantry

Figure 1 is a diagram of the subjects given most prominence in the book.[7] Although different chapters focus on different parts of what it depicts, they agree unanimously with the basic theoretical proposition about peasantry set out in the Introduction and represented by the highest-order difference on the diagram. In abstract anthropological terms, 'peasant society is part society':[8] peasantry is the productive part of a whole agrarian society which necessarily includes other groups which have the power to take some of what it produces. In concrete historical terms, all the authors show that what peasantry comprised depended on how, exactly, it was exploited by landlords, churches, urban communities and sovereigns. The diagram recognizes that each component of the patriciate[9] was linked in its own way to the peasantry. It also recognizes, in its topmost element, that each part of the patriciate gained some of its character from external relationships, such as international warfare or trade. Because of their links to the patriciate, peasant histories could not be 'immobile', comprising an endlessly recurring sequence of centuries-long cycles of natural increase until over-population brought collapse to recreate the initiating conditions.[10] However autarkic their aspirations (which is itself, as we have seen, questionable), their links with the patriciate dragged them into the theatres of European history.

All authors also stress what is represented by the bottom half of the diagram. Peasantry varied according to the resources offered by the natural environment, expressed in different kinds of farming systems, which entailed differences in family composition, household structure, and the form and function of communal institutions.[11] The sets of resources represented are heavily restricted by available space: even in these gross terms, alpine and coastal environments would yield different economic systems, and through that, different kinds of family, household and communal structures. However, the diagram does show – contrary to many models of peasant demography and culture, but as many of our authors stress – that families and household labour groups were not the same things, and also what Rebel particularly emphasizes: that 'peasant ecotypes', as properly defined,[12] are the result of interaction between environmental *and* patrician influences. Just as peasantry must differ between different environments over which exactly the same powers held sway, so must it between identical physical environments under different structures of domination.

To accord with the book's arguments, the diagram must be complicated further. Nearly all of the lines representing relationships between elements of the system carry double-headed arrows, implying reciprocal influence: the power

7. It is a much modified version of that presented in Langton, 'Habitat, economy and society'. I am very grateful to Ailsa Allen, of the Oxford University School of Geography Cartography Unit, who drew the figure which appears here.

8. Robert Redfield, *Peasant Society and Culture*, 2nd edn (Chicago, 1960), pp. 23–39.

9. It is difficult to think of a better collective term for the groups who exercised power over the peasantry. Clearly, 'state' is not a suitable alternative, because it precludes the overlapping independent jurisdictions between different components which still existed over much of Europe in early modern times.

10. As asserted, for example, in Emmanuel Le Roy Ladurie, 'Peasants', in Peter Burke (ed.), *The New Cambridge Modern History*, vol. XIII (Cambridge, 1979), pp. 115–64.

11. Benjamin S. Orlove, 'Ecological anthropology', *Annual Review of Anthropology*, 9 (1980), pp. 235–73.

12. Orvar Löfgren, 'Peasant ecotypes: problems in the study of ecological adaptation', *Ethnologia Scandinavica*, 1976, pp. 100–15.

of a landowning nobility, for example, would both cause and result from the facility with which it could extract tribute from peasantry under its sway. One of the things on which the book is most insistent is the two-way relationships between the upper and lower parts of the diagram: peasants were by no means powerless. From perpetual resistance to patrician control through foot-dragging, dissimulation and feigned stupidity – the 'weapons of the weak'[13] – to intermittent outbursts of rebellion and revolt, they were active historical agents throughout Europe. It may well be that influence flowed predominantly in one direction through some relationships for most of the time: for example, from systems of farming to kinship systems, household composition and communal structure. Even so, Melton shows that the Russian commune gained much of its form and power from the system of revenue-raising imposed by tsars in the eighteenth century, and then affected farming systems through the redistribution of holdings, and Rebel shows how Austrian inheritance laws affected the form of family households, which, again, had important implications for the system of peasant farming.

The diagram is not only deficient because it does not show the different strength of influences flowing in opposite directions between the components, and their possible switches through time, but in at least one other respect as well. It depicts peasantries as 'little communities', whose external economic contacts were always mediated through the patriciate. The lines at the bottom of the diagram imply that commodity exchange only occurred directly between peasants within particular political systems. However, even in theory they engage in long-distance direct exchange,[14] as the book shows that they did in practice.

So, over-complicated though it might seem at first glance, Figure 1 is a severe simplification of the components and relationships dealt with in the book. It is just because these were so complicated that European peasantry was very varied and changed in different ways from place to place and time to time. Moreover, it is just because each aspect of peasantry depicted on the diagram was, in one way or another and more or less directly, linked with all the others in ways which are too complex to be fully decyphered that there can be so much argument and uncertainty about the nature and causes of this variety. These systems were like those of meteorology, where vast differences in weather can stem from one butterfly flapping its wings, or those of warfare, in which kingdoms can be lost for want of a nail.

A HISTORICAL GEOGRAPHICAL STRUCTURE

How can the historical geography of such a complex phenomenon be described? What is the irreducible minimum it must comprise? History as subject has two

---

13. James C. Scott, *Weapons of the Weak: Everyday Forms of Peasant Resistance* (New Haven, CT, 1985).
14. Manning Nash, 'Market and Indian peasant economies', in Teodore Shanin (ed.), *Peasants and Peasant Societies*, 1st edn (Harmondsworth, 1971), pp. 161–77.

components. It is about how different aspects of life affect each other at a particular time (about 'periods') and about how things change in patterned ways as time passes (about 'trends'). Geography has a congruent duality. It is concerned with how different aspects of life affect each other at particular locations (about 'places') and about how things vary across the earth (about 'spatial patterns'). This multidimensionality makes historical geography a 'still greater mystery' than either parent discipline,[15] but it is clear, at least, that a historical geography must say something about the unity of the period and the place, as well as about changes and spatial variations in the subject of concern.

What gave the early modern period in Europe the unity and singularity which make it reasonable to look for coherent and intelligible trends and patterns in its peasantry? What were the main general trends and patterns, and why did they evince so much variety? What follows pulls out three parameters which underlay the variability revealed in the book. Each one alone, with the other two absent, might have produced simple trends and patterns among the components of peasantry; but they must produce apparently bewildering complexity when combined together. The kaleidoscope is complete: overlaying just three primary colours, each varying in shade across identically shaped pieces of transparent film, is enough to produce all possible colours, arranged in the most complex of patterns, even without random spattering from the black of chance and the white of individual human agency.

The Photosynthetic Constraint[16]

It is appropriate to deal first with a universal attribute of the productive elements and relationships depicted on the bottom part of the diagram. Even if biological theories of history are eschewed, it must be acknowledged that *the* major continuity of human history is that 'humankind cannot escape from the biological need to sustain itself'[17] – as all peasants did every time they they recited the Lord's Prayer.

The early modern period came before the industrial revolution. This is not to say that industry did not exist, but simply that the stocks of mineral energy contained in the Earth had not yet been brought into wide use. Human beings were still 'ecosystem people',[18] dependent for their metabolism, reproduction, movement and recreation on tapping the flow of solar energy as it coursed

15. Chris Philo, 'History, geography and "the still greater mystery" of historical geography', in Derek Gregory, Ron Martin and Graham Smith (eds), *Human Geography: Society, Space and Social Science* (London, 1984), pp. 252–81.

16. This phrase is taken from E. A. Wrigley, 'The classical economists, the stationary state, and the industrial revolution', in Graeme D. Snooks (ed.), *Was the Industrial Revolution Necessary?* (London, 1994), pp. 27–42, quote at p. 33.

17. T. L. Steinberg, 'An ecological perspective on the origins of industrialization', *Environmental Review*, 10 (1986), pp. 261–76, quote at p. 267.

18. G. A. Klee, 'Introduction', in idem (ed.), *World Systems of Traditional Resource Management* (London, 1980), pp. 1–2.

through nature. Food, clothing, shelter and fuel, the four necessities of life, were derived by harnessing the power of wind and flowing water and, mainly, by growing plants and raising animals: that is, through sedentary agriculture, rather than mobile hunting and gathering.[19] Everywhere except at its extreme northern and southern margins and at high altitude, Europe has a temperate seasonal climate, suitable for grain crops. Wheat, barley and rye will grow from central Spain to southern Finland, and towards northern and highland margins with insufficient sunlight for them to ripen, oats and pulses thrive. Although grain harvests were nowhere absolutely secure because fluctuations in climate from year to year are endemic in temperate latitudes, the immoderate swings of climate which can bring total devastation to huge areas in the Tropics and on eastern continental margins are impossible.[20]

Before the industrial revolution, unlike since, it was not possible to use more energy in agriculture than agriculture produced: rather than using stocks of mineral energy to increase the photosynthetic flow from the land, all energy for every purpose must come from that flow.[21] Compared with mineral fuels, agricultural sources of energy are very meagre.[22] In Europe before the industrial revolution, the average amount of energy available per head per year was about 26,000 kilocalories (barely twice as much as in about 5,000 BC, just after agriculture first developed); by 1900 it was 77,000 (in 1960 it was 230,000).[23] Average population densities of little more than five per square kilometre were possible.[24] Not only was little energy available anywhere, but most of it was locked up everywhere in sustaining the flow, because agriculture has a very high ratio of energy consumed to energy produced.[25] It is unlikely that so much as one-third was free for consumption outside production.[26] We have seen that harvest:seed ratios of only 2:1 were common, and although they ranged up to 6:1, such high yields were rare, needing not only land of exceptional fertility but also the application of huge amounts of highly coordinated human labour

---

19. Just as some coal was already used, so some hunting and gathering still occurred. It was a less effortful way of deriving a more varied sustenance than farming but, as we have seen, in our period it was only a feasible basis of subsistence on the margins of Europe, where population was sparse enough to permit it. Wild produce from forests and wastes yielded about 10 per cent of the subsistence of medieval peasants, even in densely settled areas. M. N. Cohen, *The Food Crisis in Prehistory: Overpopulation and the Origins of Agriculture* (New Haven, CT, 1977) and Robert Fossier, *Peasant Life in the Medieval West* (Oxford, 1988), p. 117.

20. Eric L. Jones, *The European Miracle: Environments, Economies and Geopolitics in the History of Europe and Asia* (Cambridge, 1981).

21. Wrigley, 'The classical economists', p. 31.

22. Brinley Thomas, 'Escaping from constraints: the industrial revolution in a Malthusian context', *Journal of Interdisciplinary History*, 15 (1985), pp. 169–94. It takes one acre of woodland to supply, as crop, as much heat energy as one ton of coal; England would have had to be half-covered in forest to supply an equivalent amount of energy to that already provided by coal in 1800. Wrigley, 'The classical economists', p. 34.

23. E. Cook, 'The flow of energy in an industrial society', *Scientific American*, 225 (1971), pp. 135–45; Leslie A. White, 'Energy and the evolution of culture', *American Anthropologist*, new series, 45 (1943), pp. 335–56.

24. E. S. Deevey, 'The human population', *Scientific American*, 203 (1960), pp. 195–205.

25. E. A. Wrigley, 'Energy availability and agricultural productivity', in Bruce M. S. Campbell and Mark Overton (eds), *Land, Labour and Livestock: Historical Studies in European Agricultural Productivity* (Manchester, 1991), pp. 323–39.

26. Cook, 'Flow of energy' and Patricia Crone, *Pre-industrial Societies* (Oxford, 1989). In modern rural India, 82 per cent of total energy use is directly related to food production, 50 per cent in the economy as a whole. I. G. Simmons, *Changing the Face of the Earth: Culture, Environment, History* (Oxford, 1984).

and animal power (which also had to be fed).[27] Even in the nineteenth century, yields per unit of farm labour in continental Europe varied only between 0.25 bushels per acre in Austria and Hungary to 0.48 in France – half those in England and the USA, where much more animal and mineral power were used.[28] It is only an exaggeration, not a wrong categorization, to describe the economy of pre-industrial Europe as subsistent: although some people did not grow their own food and those who did produced other things as well, most of the energy in the system was locked up in the lives and work of the people and animals producing it.

The only ways of increasing soil fertility were also organic. So were the raw materials of the industries which might in principle have yielded large economies in energy use through the specialization and subdivision of labour. Like everything else, wool, flax, leather, timber, charcoal and ores were produced by jack-of-all-trades peasants who had to plough, sow, reap, mow, herd, spin, weave, sew, cook, whittle, hew, and do countless other things as well.[29] Industry was, therefore, limited in extent and capacity because its inputs were produced from the land by human labour which, as Adam Smith as well as the Physiocrats pointed out, was necessarily unspecialized.[30]

The impossibility of getting much more from nature than was needed to feed the producers had some inescapable consequences. It meant that they must be in a large majority, and live meanly and carefully, aiming to maximize the minimum output their efforts might yield,[31] preoccupied with the harvest and the aspects of their lives linked to producing it, determined to maintain the systems of organization which precariously ensured it, reticent to give up any share of their work or what it produced.[32] In extreme youth and age, everyone has to be fed through the effort of others. The 'West European family'[33] of parents and their children in unitary households, which is shown here to have existed over almost the entire continent, was at least in part a response to that. Its complex relationships between land resources, nuptiality rate, age at marriage,

---

27. Wrigley attributes the doubling of output per man in English agriculture between the early sixteenth century and 1800, and its being between 50 and 100 per cent higher in England than in France in 1800, to heavier use of horses and oxen. Wrigley, 'Energy availability', p. 327. Such differences in yields had a dramatic impact on marketable surpluses: 'when the yield doubles, the persons fed nearly triples, and the nonagricultural population that could then be supported increases sevenfold'. Jan de Vries, *The Economy of Europe in an Age of Crisis, 1600–1750* (Cambridge, 1976), pp. 35–6.

28. Yield figures are from Gregory Clark, 'Labour productivity in English agriculture', in Cambell and Overton, *Land, Labour and Livestock*, p. 213.

29. Boguslaw Galeski, 'Farming as an occupation', in Teodore Shanin (ed.), *Peasants and Peasant Societies*, 2nd edn (Oxford, 1987), pp. 135–50.

30. Wrigley, 'Energy availability', p. 324. One of the reasons for low labour productivity in farming on the continent might well have been that peasants there were simultaneously involved in producing many more other things as well compared with English farm labourers.

31. 'Typically, the peasant cultivator seeks to avoid the failure that will ruin him rather than attempting a big, but risky, killing . . . his behavior is risk-averse.' James C. Scott, *The Moral Economy of the Peasant: Rebellion and Subsistence in Southeast Asia* (New Haven, CT, 1976), p. 4.

32. F. G. Bailey, 'The peasant view of the bad life', in Shanin, *Peasants and Peasant Societies*, 2nd edn, pp. 284–98; James C. Scott, 'Peasant moral economy as a subsistence ethic', in Shanin, *Peasants and Peasant Societies*, 1st edn, pp. 304–9.

33. John Hajnal, 'European marriage patterns in perspective', in D. V. Glass and D. E. C. Eversley (eds), *Population in History: Essays in Historical Demography* (London, 1965), pp. 101–43.

marital fertility, inheritance strategy, and arrangements between retired parents and inheriting kin ensured rapid population growth in the fifteenth and sixteenth centuries as land abandoned in the fourteenth was recolonized. It also ensured rapid population growth in newly colonized regions during later centuries, when the demographic slowdown which this family system serves to create as free land dries up was occurring in the old heartlands of settlement.

Similarly, the paramountcy of getting enough to eat made individual families willing to cooperate in networks of extended kin or in communes, where sharing property, effort and output had the side effect of reducing differences between families.[34] Exchange with people outside the confines of consanguinity and neighbourhood was also necessary to get things which could not be produced locally: salt and iron at a minimum but, as we have seen, even grain itself in the Scandinavian peninsula, Finland and Russia, on or beyond the environ-mental margins of grain production where metals, wild foodstuffs and other forest products such as tar could be produced in relative abundance. These non-neighbourhood exchanges were facilitated by markets and fairs, or the seasonal itinerancy of some members of the peasant family.[35]

Not only could families of sedentary cultivator-herders reliably produce their own subsistence, but also enough surplus to support warrior and religious groups who promised the predictability, order, and security of property rights essential to sedentary people who depend on one short harvest for a whole year's food.[36] On the other hand, they needed to work unmolested and undistracted in one small area over the whole year in order to do it. There was a peculiarly intense symbiosis between lordship and peasantry in temperate Europe. However, the inevitable meagreness of any surplus above the subsistence needs of producers meant obsessive effort, ingenuity, desperation and violence in patriciates' quest for ever-greater shares as their needs increased.

The early modern period of European history is conventionally marked off from prior pre-industrial times by the emergence and eventual domination and interaction of distinctive means of achieving patrician command over energy surplus to the needs of its agricultural producers. Economically, it was the period of 'urban renaissance', when merchants devised ways of tapping, trans-forming and circulating more of the surplus through markets. Even so, inde-pendent cities, and associations of them such as the Hanseatic League, generally lost power relative to another institution whose appearance and development characterizes early modern Europe. Politically, the period was distinguished by the rise of absolutist nation-states with the ability to command tribute and manpower through non-market mechanisms from territory under their control, in return for the promise of order, justice and protection. Although they varied greatly amongst themselves, these states differed fundamentally from political

34. Randall McGuire and Robert McC. Netting, 'Levelling peasants? The maintenance of equality in a Swiss Alpine community', *American Anthropologist*, 9 (1982), pp. 269–90.

35. Jan Lucassen, *Migrant Labour in Europe 1600–1900* (London, 1987).

36. R. T. Anderson, *Traditional Europe: A Study in Anthropology and History* (Belmont, CA, 1971); C. M. Arensberg, 'The Old-World peoples: the place of European culture in world ethnography', *Anthropological Quarterly*, 36 (1963), pp. 75–99.

systems of earlier times and other parts of the world,[37] and were similar in basic structure, each being composed of a sovereign power and the three Estates of nobility, Church and bourgeoisie, coordinated through parliaments.[38]

These economic and political trends were linked by growth in the use of money: in commodity exchange (instead of barter), in tribute payment (instead of command-in-kind and *corvées*), and in the military and administrative activities of sovereigns and other Estates (instead of feudal fealties and other hereditary and oath-bound services). Whether or not peasants were involved in selling goods was as much due to the form in which the patriciate preferred to receive its dues as it was to the peasantry's own inclinations – which is why it is inappropriate to read off their susceptibility to capitalist market exchange from the form in which obligatory transactions with the patriciate were fulfilled.[39] It is ironic (not to say tragic) that the institutions of family, commune and market, developed to ensure more secure peasant subsistence, provided the instruments through which patricians were able to abstract more and more peasant surplus product in the form of money through taxes, rents, bequests, tithes and profits.

In sum, we might well demur at calling this period 'transitional', not only because this implies that its characteristics depended on what came before and after, rather than being intrinsic to itself, but also because (except, perhaps, in Britain) early modern Europe was, in fact, a *culmination* of pre-industrial organically derived human economy. That is what gave it an underlying unity and continuity with the past. A basic similarity in the methods devised by non-producers to take and deploy ever-greater shares of that economy for their own purposes in the form of money is what distinguished this period from medieval times, and Europe from the rest of the early modern world.

That is our first primary colour: the dependence of the whole system on annual grain harvests which could produce little energy surplus to that needed in production. Its shade varied a great deal across the continent. How much energy could be produced, what share could be taken by the patriciate, and the facility with which it could be transformed into money, differed from place to place according to the natural environment in which the peasantry worked. Because of latitude, shape, internal topographical contrasts and position relative to ocean currents, natural environmental variations are greater in Europe than over any other equal portion of the Earth's surface: its massive environmental variety also makes Europe a singular part of the world.

An important broad contrast existed between Europe north and south of the Massif Central, Alps and northern Balkans. Southward, greater dryness

37. Jones, *European Miracle.*

38. A. R. Myers, *Parliaments and Estates in Europe to 1789* (London, 1975). As the authors of earlier chapters show, variations in the relative power of the sovereign and constituent Estates had enormous significance for the fate of the peasantries they ruled, as did the fact that Sweden had a fourth Peasant Estate.

39. For example, in some parts of Ireland in the nineteenth century, linen was produced from flax crops deliberately to provide money income with which to pay rent, while in other districts 'all the spring rents were made . . . of the pigs. The autumn rents would either be made of butter, or a little corn if they had it.' Michael Beames, *Peasants and Power: The Whiteboy Movements and their Control in Pre-Famine Ireland* (Brighton, 1983), p. 4.

and heat give light soils which are easily worked but relatively poor in natural nutrients except in well-watered and silted river valleys, which are extremely fertile. To the north rain is more plentiful, sunshine is less reliable, and riverine land tends to be waterlogged; but more luxuriant natural vegetation and the effects of glaciation in areas marginal to the ice masses themselves (which eroded the surface to bare rock) produced rich heavy soils. Ploughing must be deep to return rain-leached nutrients to the surface and needed much more energy: teams of eight oxen with two men per plough, compared with a single mule and one man in Mediterranean Europe, and many more ploughs per acre. The rapid natural revival of herbage in the wetter north meant that fields left fallow could be grazed and manured by oxen and other cattle; but the cessation of plant growth in winter made it difficult to keep them all year without depleting human food, and careful regulation of herbage and fodder supplies were therefore crucial aspects of farming north of the Alps. In many northern areas, so was effective field drainage, whereas bringing water to crops might be equally important in the south.

Most cultivated land was carved out of natural forest, which survived to differing extents – generally more thickly towards the north and east – to supply timber, fuel, grazing, game, berries, nuts and fungi, and permit further colonization for agriculture. Tree species varied in type and the uses to which they could be put in reflection of the natural environment, but nearly everywhere woodland and planted trees or bushes of some kinds could grow: from citrus fruit, vines, olives and chestnuts in the south to apples, hops, raspberries and hazelnuts in the north. Bare moor and mountainsides above the tree-line were moist enough to provide summer pasture for cows, sheep and goats, whilst low-lying swampland was dry enough in summer for cattle. Fish were seasonally available near coasts and the banks of lakes and rivers. Everywhere, something besides grain could be gathered at one time of year or another as a partial insurance against crop failure and to provide other foodstuffs and the raw materials needed for shelter, clothing, tools and equipment.

The extreme convolution of Europe's topography produced intricate variations within the broad north–south gradation of climate and biogeography. Grain crops were more dependable on northern plains; upland and woodland areas interspersed within the plains were better suited to pasturing animals, and grain was less important in total output; in Alpine regions and mountainous parts of the Mediterranean basin, each small area had its own 'vertical north' and an enormous variety of natural resources; whilst along coasts and in northern forests wild food might be abundant but grain crops very thin and unreliable. In upland areas, water power could be harnessed as a supplement or substitute for human and animal power, and on coasts and in mountain passes, peasants had access to resources through piracy or brigandage of patricians' trade, or by themselves engaging in organizing the exchange which, to some extent, was encouraged by environmental diversity.[40]

40. As in Central America, where physical geography was similarly very varied. Nash, 'Peasant market'. See also Marc Bloch, 'Natural economy or money economy: a pseudo-dilemma', in Marc Bloch, *Land and Work in Medieval Europe: Selected Papers by Marc Bloch* (Berkeley, CA, 1967), pp. 220–43.

To best guarantee subsistence, people must do different kinds of work and organize their effort in different ways in different environments. As we have seen, the little systems depicted in the bottom half of Figure 1 could have very different social attributes in consequence: households with upwards of twenty kinsfolk in forest Finland, but with only between five and ten people, some of them non-kin, on grain-rich plains;[41] strong communes on the plains, where the grain harvest was relatively most important and most tied in with animal husbandry for power and manure, but much weaker (even non-existent) ones where it was less so. In consequence, the means and effectiveness of the patriciate's interaction with peasants differed widely: communal open-field grain farmers were more easily tapped for their surplus through labour services or rents, for example, than upland, Alpine or coastal peasants, whose economies were more diversely sourced, and who had to move about to effect them. On the other hand, the strong communes of grain-farming regions provided a fertile matrix for the growth of determined peasant resistance to increased landlord exactions.

Notwithstanding this environmental diversity and its differentiating consequences, one constant applied everywhere. Every chapter in the book emphasizes that the seasonality of plant and animal growth had a very important universal implication. The kind and amount of work needed to produce crops varied widely over the year:[42] much more labour and animal power was necessary for winter and spring ploughing, especially in the north, and to get the harvest home quickly and in time, again especially in the north where weather was less propitious. Many units of labour and animal power needed only for short spurts of work in grain farming had to be fed and kept all year. Different ways of harmonizing this seasonal dissonance accounted for much of the variation in peasantry from one part of Europe to another. Some, but not all, were only appropriate in particular kinds of environment. Communal ploughing, reaping and pasturing practices;[43] work and residence in towns, forests, mountains or fishing grounds during lulls in the farming year; working up saleable by-products at home when fieldwork was slack: any of these strategies might provide a solution.

The more self-sufficiency was aimed at, the less acute was the problem posed by seasonality, because the more it was necessary to produce other things besides grain, through animal husbandry; fruit tending, gathering and preservation; fibre spinning, cloth making and sewing; building and fencing; and making and mending utensils, tools and equipment for farm, domestic and craft use. Again, the extent to which these things could be done depended on the particularities

---

41. The relationships between ecotypes and family structures is dealt with in Richard L. Rudolph (ed.), *The European Peasant Family and Society: Historical Studies* (Liverpool, 1995), esp. pp. 26–63.

42. The significance of seasonality in peasant life was reflected in the importance of calendar customs marking passage from one season to another in peasant ceremonial behaviour. It has also been pointed out that the timing of peasant protest movements was strongly seasonal because of the inescapable influence of the farming calendar on every aspect of peasant behaviour. Robert Bircher, 'Peasant resistance and the defence of servitude rights in Russia's south west, 1890–1914' (D Phil Oxford, 1996), pp. 225–6.

43. Carl Johan Dahlman, *The Open Fields and Beyond: A Property Rights Analysis of an Economic Institution* (Cambridge, 1980).

of the environment occupied, but where they were possible some were naturally complementary in seasonality to farming, and others could easily be made so. All of them had opportunity costs approaching zero in large farm households, and subsistence, cash or industrial crops of very high labour intensiveness would be raised by peasant 'self-exploitation' through inordinately long hours of work if they expedited the seasonal mix of farming and other activities. Conversely, the more a farm concentrated on the production of one specialist crop for sale, satisfying its consumption needs through exchange, the more acute the problem of seasonality became.[44] Rather than large self-sufficient households full of two or three generations of more or less closely related kin and others who could usefully be doing something else, maybe even somewhere else, when not harvesting, the optimum for specialist producers was a small permanent household of husband, wife and one or two children, massively afforced during the harvest.

But where could the extra harvest labour come from, and how could the risk and cost of depending on outsiders be minimized? Again, as we have seen, different solutions were devised in different parts of Europe at different times. In Spain and Italy, towns could be relied on to provide it. In England, independent rural households of landless labourers were the main source, and the book shows that such families were much more common everywhere else, too, than in a 'model peasantry', and just as abject and impoverished as those in England.[45] But it also demonstrates that where governments depended for taxes and conscripts on peasant households, non-landed rural families were made illegal. Servantship survived much more strongly there, and specialist grain production was a less easy option for peasant households.

The Tyranny of Distance

The inordinate amount of energy needed to move people, food, fuel and goods affected systems of peasant production directly. Perhaps more so, it shaped the components and interactions depicted in the top half of Figure 1, relating to the patriciate, which then fed back to influence peasant production indirectly.

According to the nineteenth-century north German estate-owner and economist J. H. von Thünen, the food eaten by two drivers and four horses in conveying a waggonload of grain and then returning to their origin exhausted the entire capacity of the load in fifty to a hundred kilometres, depending on terrain.[46] For fuel, the distance over which the value of the load was exceeded by the cost of transporting it (in other words, at which its price doubled) was

44. Galeski, 'Farming as an occupation' deals with the wide range of social and cultural changes that occurred when farmers became 'professionalized', aiming at the maximum output of a specialist crop for sale.

45. At a time when the market is in such ideological ascendancy, it is worth recalling the outrage of European commentators at the plight of English farmworkers who embodied the operation of a labour market in the eighteenth and nineteenth centuries. W. Hasbach, *A History of the English Agricultural Labourer* (London, 1920).

46. Quoted in E. W. Fox, 'The argument: some reinforcements and projections', in Eugene D. Genovese and Leonard Hochberg (eds), *Geographic Perspectives in History* (Oxford, 1989), pp. 331–42, esp. p. 333.

one-tenth as far.[47] According to other calculations, these distances were rather greater,[48] but it is incontrovertible that bulky commodities could not be hauled long distances overland before railways applied mineral energy to the task.[49] In early modern times, agricultural surpluses were of very little value except near to navigable water, and large towns could only exist on waterways because of the otherwise inordinate difficulty and cost of getting energy, in the forms of food and fuel, to them.[50]

This imposed a powerful constraint upon the extent to which peasants could depend upon market exchange. In these circumstances, specialized cash crops could not provide a secure livelihood: 'one cannot live on butter, cheese and cabbage alone: and one cannot live on hemp, madder, flax and coleseed at all',[51] and grain could not be hauled over long distances in exchange for them. Rural energy surpluses, wind and water power could be used to work on farm produce or minerals to create things of much greater value per unit of weight, such as cloth,[52] wine, oil and metalware, which could be traded over long distances in exchange for other precious goods. However, for the same reason, the geographical tyrant's sway could not be escaped in this way, either. Fox points out that there are two types of trade:

The pound of pepper brought from the Indies to some Rhineland prince might have made a handsome profit for the merchant, but it added nothing to the 'net product' of the Rhineland. Rather, its transport consumed energy all along the route. In more general historical terms, this means that the growing luxury trade of the Mediterranean did not actually enrich Europe or enlarge the economic units of which Europe was composed; rather, it was attracted by Europe's growing agricultural surpluses, which it tapped without adding to the real wealth of the agricultural community.[53]

Coupled together, the high ratio of energy consumed to energy produced in agriculture, the tendency towards self-sufficiency induced by seasonality in the natural environment, and the need for energy in transportation, ensured that traded goods could not nearly have amounted to 30 per cent of total output if the producers had to grow their own food and haulage needed man or animal power.

47. Paul Bairoch, *Cities and Economic Development: From the Dawn of History to the Present* (London, 1988), p. 14. In the eighteenth century, even without allowing for transport costs, it would have taken 10,000 square kilometres of forest to supply the annual fuel needs of a European city of 100,000 people.

48. Bairoch, *Cities*, pp. 11–12.

49. It can be argued that this state of affairs did not end until the innovation of motor trucks in the twentieth century. Richard Rosecrance, 'The commercial society and international relations', in Genovese and Hochberg, *Geographic Perspectives*, pp. 315–30.

50. London – by no means the largest European city of the time – depended on water transportation for firewood by 1400, and for grain by 1500. James A. Galloway, Derek Keene and Margaret Murphy, 'Fuelling the city: production and distribution of firewood and fuel in London's region, 1290–1400', *Economic History Review*, 49 (1996), pp. 447–72, and James A. Galloway and Margaret Murphy, 'Feeding the city: London and its agrarian hinterland', *London Journal*, 16 (1991), pp. 3–14.

51. Jan de Vries, *The Dutch Rural Economy in the Golden Age, 1500–1700* (New Haven/London, 1974), p. 164.

52. Which was about 80 times more valuable than wheat and 2,000 times more valuable than firewood. Bairoch, *Cities*, p. 14.

53. Fox, 'The argument', p. 333. He categorizes the difference as being between long distance 'commerce' and short-distance 'trade', p. 332.

Away from navigable water in what Fox called 'agricultural kingdoms',[54] peasants could not neglect their own food harvest or fuel gathering, however tempting the returns on worked-up goods. They could not *depend* on exchange, and did not, therefore, '*compete* in terms of their productive powers'.[55] Commodity exchange could have little more significance for peasants than self-provisioning from gardens and allotments does for proletarians. For dependable subsistence, they must shun the market as completely as possible: when they had some crop to sell after an unusually good harvest, prices were at rock-bottom, whereas when they needed to buy after an unusually bad one, prices were sky-high. Even peasants who concentrated their efforts on food production must, therefore, because of the vagaries of weather as well as to satisfy the requirements of landlords, resort to the market at times, but they could never equalize the value of the food surplus and food deficit years through market exchange. So, 'we are sure to go astray, if we try to conceive of peasant economies as exclusively "subsistence" oriented and to suspect capitalism wherever the peasants show evidence of being "market" orientated';[56] 'while the idea of exchange must be very nearly as old as man . . . we must not make the mistake of assuming that all the world has the bargaining propensities of a twentieth-century American schoolboy . . . For the market system is not just a means of exchanging goods; *it is a mechanism for sustaining and maintaining an entire society*.'[57] Under the constraints imposed by dependence on photosynthesis and the tyranny of distance, it simply could not do so, and the marketplaces in which goods were exchanged did not operate like the price-fixing markets of Classical economic theory, where atomized individuals independently pursue their self-interests, but more to bolster local community solidarities, until the nineteenth century.[58] This absence of a market *system* was another reason why peasants widened the portfolio of resources they used as far as possible, and explains something else shown in many chapters: why, as a peasant economy becomes marketized, middle-sized erstwhile subsistence farms disappear, to be replaced by many fewer ones, big enough always to have something to sell, and therefore gain from dearth.[59]

However, this can only occur if foodstuffs can be moved cheaply and reliably, which was impossible before the nineteenth century except in what Fox called 'commercial kingdoms', where the coast or rivers allowed energy from the wind and the buoyancy and flow of water to be used in transportation. There, as in sixteenth-century Tuscany, the proportions tied up in production

54. Fox, 'The argument', p. 332.

55. Robert Brenner, 'The origins of capitalist development: a critique of neo-Smithian Marxism', *New Left Review*, 104 (1977), pp. 25–92, quote at p. 37, emphasis added.

56. D. Thorner, 'Peasant economy as a category in History', in Shanin, *Peasants and Peasant Societies*, 2nd edn, pp. 62–8, quote at p. 65.

57. Robert Heilbroner, *The Worldly Philosophers: The Lives, Times and Ideas of the Great Economic Thinkers*, 6th edn (London, 1991), p. 27, emphasis in original.

58. 'For too long the market has been seen as the *deus ex machina* of modernism, because an essentially instrumental model has been imported from the discipline of economics by historians'; Craig Muldrew, 'Interpreting the market: the ethics of credit and community relations in early modern England', *Social History*, 18 (1993), pp. 163–83, quote at p. 183.

59. Hoppe and Langton, *Peasantry to Capitalism*, pp. 2–3.

and free for exchange could be reversed.[60] It was simply not possible for this to happen in most parts of Europe. Where the iron industry gave rise to large populations in poor agricultural regions of Sweden, the owners of furnaces and forges often ensured their grain supply by purchasing agricultural estates on the plains, or providing it directly in other ways, and supplied most of their workers' food through truck shops, simply because the market could not be relied on.[61] However responsive peasants themselves were to the benefits of deriving comparative advantages through exchange,[62] the overland haulage of foodstuffs consumed too much of the little energy left after fuelling the work of producing them.

When peasants have to supply their own subsistence, then neither food nor the land and labour needed to produce it can become commoditized: the basic elements of capitalist market economy could not develop.[63] Neither could the use of money as simultaneously a medium of exchanging, measuring and accumulating wealth, which is another requirement of a fully fledged market economy. Because so little of peasant output could be exchanged, there was little coin in the countryside, and any there was existed in denominations far too large to be of use in the daily small exchanges within peasant communities.[64] Anyway, these transactions were individually too infrequent for relative values to be fixed,[65] and the termination of a transaction by paying cash was 'alienating', destroying the social obligation exchange otherwise entailed.[66] These are the reasons why surviving records in Denmark and southern Sweden show that most peasant exchange was in the form of barter on indefinitely long-term uncosted credit. Just as land and labour were hoarded to guarantee subsistence, so money was hoarded to provide dowries or inheritance portions, or as insurance against dearth, or to buy more land for the same purpose, or it was spent 'irrationally', the better to guarantee subsistence by accumulating social obligations.[67] Indeed, the sale of commodities and seasonal labour could be used as part of the general peasant strategy of subsistence risk minimization, preventing the penetration of market exchange into the more fundamental aspects of life concerned with the production of subsistence foodstuffs and the

---

60. Even so, Epstein's (above, p. 102) calculations that only 40 per cent of the population of the Florentine Republic in the early fifteenth century were self-sufficient in food, and consumed only 15 per cent of total agricultural output, do lead one to wonder what the producers did when not harvesting, what they ate, and how they cooked and kept warm.

61. Hoppe and Langton, *Peasantry to Capitalism*, p. 210.

62. As described, for example, by Melton in nineteenth-century Russia (above, pp. 255–7).

63. Karl Polanyi, *The Great Transformation* (Boston, MA, 1957).

64. Peter Spufford, *Money and its Uses in Medieval Europe* (Cambridge, 1988). There were only about £3 of coins per person in circulation in late seventeenth-century England. Muldrew, 'Interpreting the market', p. 171.

65. Hanssen, 'Commonfolk and gentlefolk'.

66. Mick Reed, ' "Gnawing it out": a new look at social relations in nineteenth-century rural England', *Rural History*, 1 (1990), pp. 83–94; David Harvey, 'Money, time, space and the city', in idem, *Consciousness and the Urban Experience: Studies in the History of Capitalist Urbanization* (Oxford, 1985), pp. 1–35. Reddy argues that monetized market exchange always disadvantages people with little to trade, who therefore prefer alternative modes of exchange for reasons which are soundly economic. William M. Reddy, *Money and Liberty in Modern Europe* (Cambridge, 1987).

67. Hoppe and Langton, *Peasantry to Capitalism*, pp. 8 and 17–18.

retention of the land and family labour needed to do it.[68] Production of non-subsistence goods for the market, as in the process of proto-industrialization, might thus help to preserve peasantry as a way of life, rather than destroying it if, as was usual because of the tyranny of distance, markets could not be relied upon for the supply of food.[69]

Even if peasants had converted everything surplus to their subsistence needs into easily tradable forms, rather than accumulating large ceremonial funds of alcohol, other highly wrought and precious foodstuffs, clothing and so on,[70] and converted it into money which was not hoarded or locked into inflated prices of farmland, there would still be very little for others to struggle over, and most of what there was would still be close to the land. Hence the vigour of the strategies of merchants, landlords, churches and sovereigns to increase their relative shares of peasant output itself and to encourage the colonization of new land, and the extreme and expensive violence that sovereigns were willing to wage for more territory to increase the number of peasants under their sway at the expense of other sovereigns. The macro-economic and political distinguishing features of early modern Europe – the growth of cities, with their merchants, craftsmen and rich ecclesiastics dependent on money income, and of absolutist states, with their splendid sovereigns in opulent courts, complex administrations and large well-equipped armies – were expressions of the increasing success of the instruments through which small peasant surpluses of low intrisic unit value were tapped at source by the patriciate.

These instruments varied greatly between agricultural and commercial kingdoms. In the former, power was exercised 'areally' because it was 'relatively easy for individuals or groups to travel overland along an unobstructed path if supplies were available on the way, [but] it would be . . . difficult to move staple foods or fuel . . . [E]conomic co-operation would be restricted while governmental or military activity would not'. So, 'human effort was dispersed over as wide an area as possible, in order to bring the maximum amount of territory under cultivation and taxation'.[71] In contrast, places on or near to waterways formed linear networks with nodal points at which people, activity and wealth were concentrated in cities because 'heavy goods could be transported easily . . . but less flexible travel would tend to hamper military or administrative effort' and political control and taxation were less easy to effect. Comparatively, 'the areal form would have gross advantages in a military confrontation, and the linear would enjoy even greater superiority in an economic or monetary one'.[72]

68. Ann C. Mayering, 'Did capitalism lead to the decline of the peasantry? The case of the French Cambraille', *Journal of Economic History*, 43 (1983), pp. 121–8.

69. Derek Gregory, '"A new and different face in many places": three geographies of industrialization', in R. A. Dodgshon and R. A. Butlin (eds), *Historical Geography of England and Wales*, 2nd edn (London, 1990), pp. 351–99.

70. Peasants produced for three different 'funds': not only for subsistence, but also for tribute in the form of rents, taxes, tithes and so on, and for the ceremonies through which social relations were articulated. E. R. Wolf, *Peasants* (Englewood Cliffs, NJ, 1966), pp. 4–10.

71. Fox, 'The argument', pp. 331 and 334.

72. Ibid., pp. 331–2 and 334. The developments in military technology which gave a decisive advantage to large infantry formations during this period are discussed in Paul Colinvaux, *The Fates of Nations: A Biological Theory of History* (Harmondsworth, 1980).

The balance of power amongst the three Estates, and between them and the sovereign, differed accordingly. Landlords held the fiscal levers of the first and second, merchants and bankers those of the third. Landlords were more easily usurped or bypassed than merchants in the search for revenue by absolutist sovereigns because they could tax sedentary peasants directly, whereas the sources of trade were distant, nebulous and often foreign. So, the absolutist state suppressed mercantile institutions and trade so that wealth could be fixed on the land, in peasant hands from which it could be taken with facility; the peasantry was heavily exploited, but because it was politically necessary, its existence was secure. In commercial kingdoms, peasantry was not available for taxation or conscription. The direction of causal influence between the freedom of peasantry from taxation, weak state finances, the balance of power between Estates, and the growth of trade in 'commercial Europe' ran in all directions,[73] but whatever the ultimate motive force, state finances based in exactions from the fruits of trade meant that peasantry was not protected by the sovereign power.

Europe was not split neatly into 'inner agricultural' and 'outer commercial' parts. Both types of socio-economic system coexisted everywhere – hence the dissatisfaction of some of our authors with the world-system model of economic development. None the less, each of its polities gained a characteristic cast as one or the other came to dominate its institutional structure during early modern times.[74] We have seen that water transport was of great economic and strategic importance in the parts of eastern and central Europe where rivers could carry cargo from the interior to the Baltic and Black Seas. But access to and and egress from both seas was under foreign control, and the ratio of miles of coast and navigable river to land area was infinitesimal compared with western Europe,[75] accessible to minuscule proportions of territory. In consequence, Melton points out, Russia was a 'peasant state', 'whose existence depends on its peasant population to supply the revenue, labour, rents and conscripts that support the ruler and his civil/military elite'.[76] All of eastern and central Europe was in the agricultural kingdom, with republics of commerce on Europe's southern and north-western littorals and, as Robisheaux and Rebel show, along the Rhine and its tributaries and across the Alpine passes of Austria. Britain and Holland were the archetypes of the latter, where the taxation of trade and consumption rather than production was associated with the development of commercial farming, and the end of peasantry. In Switzerland, the wide resource base of Alpine peasantries and their ability to resist control by landowners and sovereigns combined with the control of long-distance trade through mountain passes to give a unique political outcome.

73. Bruce G. Carruthers, *City of Capital: Politics and Markets in the English Financial Revolution* (Princeton, NJ, 1996).

74. Fox developed his model to explain early-modern French political characteristics, in which areal influences were predominant. E. W. Fox, *History in Geographic Perspective: The Other France* (New York, 1971).

75. As well as its extensive coastline, relatively tiny Britain had 7,200 miles of navigable inland waterway in 1850, France 4,170 miles in 1847, and Germany 6,600 miles in 1914, whereas the whole of Russia had relatively little coastline and contained only 500 miles of inland waterway in 1914. Simon P. Ville, *Transport and the Development of the European Economy, 1750–1918* (London, 1990), p. 31. Maybe it is not surprising that so little grain was exported from Belorussia in the seventeenth century, cf. Melton, above, p. 241.

76. Ibid., p. 263.

The wars of the seventeenth and eighteenth centuries caused the states engaged in them to accentuate their agricultural characteristics in pursuit of greater and more securely sourced revenue and soldiers.[77] The systems of peasant exploitation in place by the end of our period were not inert survivals from medieval times, but developing responses to the interaction of early modern human ecology and political economy. Inevitably, in 'agricultural Europe' peasantry was more heavily exploited and more assiduously preserved, from Sweden through continental Europe to Italy, but trade was either discouraged or more rigorously channelled so that it, too, could be mulcted. We have seen that variations in the relative power of landlords, Church, townsmen and sovereigns caused wide differences in the effects of this on the peasantry. In France, Russia, Brandenburg-Prussia and Sweden, relatively powerful sovereigns guarded the peasantry from the competing exactions of the nobility, Church and towns. Even so, in each of them except France, as more extremely in Poland and Hungary, where landowners had much more power relative to the Crown, manorial estate production based on peasant labour services was developed by the nobility. As we would expect from the energetics of grain transportation, much of this was to satisfy the consumption of the manor owners and their retainers, not for exchange. However, these estates reached their apotheosis in limited areas near water transport routes, where extremely heavy feudal services of labour and animal teams, fed from serfs' work on leasehold land, produced grain harvests for sale through the hands of foreign merchants in the Baltic ports of western Europe.

Even there, though, things were not quite what we might have expected. The chapters on eastern Europe contain many surprises. Serfdom was common only on noble land: royal and Church estates tended to be farmed by unservile peasants, who might provide money rents. Large-scale manorial production through servile labour was easily installed only on newly settled land, of which there was a great deal east of the Elbe (much less on the plains of Sweden) where suitable village structures could be created from the start by landowners given unusually generous privileges in return for holding and defending the land for the sovereign. In such areas, peasants were willing to give up freedom and a large part of their labour in exchange for food in hard years, access to the lords' resources of pasture and timber (through what came to be known as 'servitudes'),[78] and protection when political contol disintegrated, as it was prone to do there, just as they were willing to submit to the discipline of communes to provide security in a particularly uncertain world. The frontier was also a double-edged sword: peasants could flee to other estates, or further, to borderlands where revolt was endemic. Hence the imposition, but also the incomplete effectiveness, of restriction of their freedom to move by enserfment.

77. The cost of financing wars, on top of the massive economic destruction and disruption they caused, was enormous in absolute and relative terms. For example, British canal construction 1750–1820, by far the biggest economic investment of the time, cost only about 2 per cent of what Britain spent on the French wars 1793–1815. Peter Mathias, 'Financing the industrial revolution', in Peter Mathias and John A. Davis (eds), *The First Industrial Revolutions* (Oxford, 1989).

78. Bircher, 'Peasant Resistance'.

Even where this was effective, Lithuanian serfs sold flax, hemp and thread though peasant merchants in Riga, central Russian serfs made and sold a vast array of craft wares southwards, and everywhere serfs bought and sold land, and hired wage labour to work their own holdings as they were forced to spend more and more of their own days on their lords' demesnes. It was not only in western Europe that a differentiated peasantry and the trading of land, labour and commodities emerged. The big difference was that in the east it was merely supplementary to an economic system where most land and labour – on the lords' demesnes – were locked into non-market mechanisms which channelled most of the fruits of commodity exchange into landlords' pockets.

In other parts of 'inner Europe', generally to the west, and predominantly so in France and western Germany, the grip of landlords on peasant surpluses was weakened in and after the fourteenth century by inflation, which reduced money rents to tokens of ultimate lordship. Peasants became free there, and were more capable of generating the long cycles of demographic growth to the point of overpopulation and collapse which are supposed to be characteristic of peasantry everywhere. These were the regions of 'classical' European peasantry, but even there increased abstraction of surpluses occurred through a variety of alternatives to land rent, such as taxes, conscription, tithes, lords' hunting rights, reversionary rights on the failure of heirs, monopoly milling and distilling rights and tolls, and market dues payable to townsmen. Everywhere, however, the need for peasants to concentrate on producing their own subsistence, which was inescapable in economies based on human and animal power derived from incoming solar energy for production and transportation, not only restricted the tradable surplus, but also prevented the appearance of market exchange in land and labour, and discouraged the use of money for purposes other than the payment of patrician impositions, hoarding for insurance, or the acquisition of trifles.

In parts of 'commercial Europe', there were tendencies towards the same ends, from Spain through Italy to Austria. Where the bourgeois Estate was relatively weak, as in Spain, its privileges were reduced further. Where it was overweeningly strong, as in northern Italy, it transmuted itself into a version of landlordism, reduced dependence on trade whilst taxing it further through border tolls, and as Epstein shows, impoverished the southern Italian regions with which it had traded in the process. In between these extremes, where towns were powerful they generally seem to have acted as a brake on peasant production for exchange by legally monopolizing the right to manufacture and trade goods, although in England, where pre-industrial towns were generally very small and massively primate London had other fish to fry, this did not happen.[79] In parts of 'commercial Europe', too, where markets for surpluses were readily available, the power of landlords over the peasantry usually increased hardly

---

79. It is none the less worth remembering that some London guilds were still trying to exercise their legal right to control production throughout England, or monopolize the sale of what was produced, in the late seventeenth and early eighteenth centuries. John Hatcher and Thedore C. Barker, *A History of British Pewter* (London, 1974), and D. W. Jones, 'The "hallage" receipts of the London cloth markets, 1562–*c*.1720', *Economic History Review*, 2nd series, 25 (1972), pp. 567–87.

less than in eastern Europe. Danish manors were little different from those of Poland, and on Spanish and Italian latifundia and Irish and English gentry estates, production for the market brought large specialized farms worked by sharecroppers, tenant labour services, or wage-labourers in abject poverty, even though prosperous intermediaries, like English yeoman farmers, might also be precipitated in the drive to increase landlord's money income. It was only where legal restrictions on rural landlessness, peasant inheritance practices, and rural manufactures and trade did not exist that peasant subsistence farming ceased to be the basis of economy, even in 'commercial Europe'.

As 'agricultural Europe' pushed southwards and eastwards in search of more resources, and some parts of 'commercial Europe' retrenched as Mediterranean colonies were lost to the Ottoman advance, other parts of outer Europe searched across the Atlantic. Vast 'ghost acres'[80] were captured by Portugal, Spain, Holland, England and, to a lesser extent, France. Their acquisition was much cheaper in money and manpower than war and conquest in Europe, and conflict between the conquerors themselves caused no destruction at home. But the outflow of emigrants could shift radically from being a relief of subsistence pressure to become a drain on vital manpower, as in Spain and especially Portugal, and the import of colonial bullion was not an unmixed economic blessing. Even for England, where landlords colluded with urban and government interests to produce the 'gentlemanly capitalism' which stimulated regional specialization in production and exchange not only along its own rivers and seaways, but across a large part of the globe,[81] the dismal conclusions of Quesnay, Malthus and Adam Smith about the sharp limit on economic wealth in an economy dependent on organic energy still held.[82] To be sure, the introduction of potatoes and maize greatly increased energy output in many parts of Europe, and access to waterways allowed significant gains to be made from the exploitation of comparative advantages through trade; but it was only access to mineral energy through the industrial revolution which could breach the low energy ceiling, and it was only after the innovation of steamships that colonies could provide basic foodstuffs and other forms of energy in large amounts.[83]

There were enormous differences within, as well as between, the 'two Europes' produced by the tyranny that distance held over organically based economics through the need to consume energy in order to move it. This second primary colour was as intricately shaded across Europe as the first, but in a different pattern. Overlain, they richly compounded the variety of Europe's peasant ecotypes. This variegation was heightened further by the admixture of a third primary colour, which was shaded across Europe in yet another pattern.

80. Jones, *European Miracle*.

81. Andrew Porter, review article 'Birmingham, Westminster and the City of London: visions of Empire compared', *Journal of Historical Geography*, 21 (1995), pp. 83–7.

82. Brinley Thomas deals with the 'population explosion and energy crisis' in Britain in the second half of the eighteenth century in 'The end of the charcoal iron age', in his *The Industrial Revolution and the Atlantic Economy* (London, 1993), pp. 60–80.

83. Brinley Thomas, 'Britain's food supply, 1760–1846: the Irish contribution', in idem, *The Industrial Revolution*, pp. 81–99.

Christendom

Christianity gave powerful singularity to Europe, which comprised virtually the whole of Christendom. All of what was effectively European at any particular time in our period, rather than Ottoman, Tatar or Moorish, was Christian. Areas were Europeanized as they were converted to Christianity, and Christendom expanded its geographical range through European conquests in other continents. European culture was Christian culture; its ideologies were shot through with Christian moral philosophies which set limits, however broad, on the beliefs, conceptions and behaviour of patricians and peasants alike. Kings and emperors were anointed with Christian authority and responsibilities, and right through to the other end of the spectrum marriage was sanctified as an indissoluble union, and the patriarchal nuclear family was sanctioned by the Church as the primal unit of peasant social organization.[84] The idea that the top and bottom of the social pyramid were joined through an immutable hierarchy, with reciprocating rights and responsibilities between each structural level, and without sanction for arbitrary despotism such as that of the Muslim Ottomans, gained authority from St Augustine's vision of the City of God.

Although its mission and administration required literacy, the Catholic Church relied on and encouraged oral communication in relation to its flock,[85] stressed communalism in its practices of worship and organization, and portrayed the forests which provided a chance of freedom as havens of demons and outcasts. Its calendar of holy days celebrated in parish churches meshed with and sanctioned the seasonal rhythms and localism of peasant life, and its doctrines of cyclical time and human fall from past perfection, which militated against any conception of earthly improvement, chimed well with peasants' own experience of the world, which produced backward-referencing cultures of survival, rather than future-oriented cultures of progress.[86] The Church taught the paramountcy of spiritual over material concerns, the charitable duty to give away surplus wealth, and devotion to the welfare of others in daily life: 'the idea of the propriety (not to say the necessity) of a system organized on the basis of *personal gain* had not yet taken root . . . [and so] a separate, self-contained economic world had not yet lifted itself from its social context.'[87] It could not do so whilst ideas of 'fair exchange', 'just prices', the right to charity, and the entitlement of all to support from community resources still permeated European culture as deeply as they did during our period.[88] This 'galaxy of strong and interconnected concepts', albeit honoured as much in its breach as in its observance, and the joint hegemony of land and Church it supported, 'proved remarkably durable, outlasting both Renaissance and Reformation, at least in Catholic Europe',

---

84. Jack Goody, *The Development of the Family and Marriage in Europe* (Cambridge, 1983).

85. For the cultural importance of exclusively oral communication in peasantry, see Kazimierz Dobrowolski, 'Peasant traditional culture', in Shanin, *Peasants and Peasant Societies*, 2nd edn, pp. 261–77.

86. John Berger, 'Historical afterword', in idem, *Pig Earth* (London, 1979), pp. 195–213.

87. Heilbroner, *The Worldly Philosophers*, p. 24, emphasis in original.

88. Gregory Claeys, *Machinery, Money and the Millennium: The New Moral Economy of Owenite Socialism, 1815–1860* (Oxford, 1987).

where it survived until well into the nineteenth century.[89] Elsewhere, 'the essential turning point . . . from an earlier self-image as *Respublica Christiania* to a concept of Europe as the unique realm where justice, order and secular humanism could flourish' came as late as the mid-eighteenth century; only then could 'the cellular, diversified and non-hierarchical space of medieval Europe [become] the hierarchically differentiated space of secular humanism'.[90]

The Church was able to fulfil its ideological role through ministration to everyone in society because it comprised one of the political Estates, allocated that particular function and the rights over resources necessary to do it, in all parts of Europe. In the Papacy and its universal Latinate ministry and administration, the Church gave an expression of European homogeneity which was far more potent than that of the parallel temporal institution of the Holy Roman Empire. Like our other two primary colours, it became much more variegated as the period passed. Indeed, this fissipatory process, too, can be used to mark off early modern from medieval Europe, as Catholicism shattered into Protestant sects in northern parts of the west, was halted eastwards by the espousal of Orthodoxy by the Russian tsars, and was pushed north-westwards out of the Balkans by the Ottoman Empire.

Because its was an eternal corporation which could never fail to have an heir, but benefited from the failure of heirs among the devout, the Church accumulated large landed estates,[91] run by devoted and literate agents, often with the uncosted labour of monks. In many parts of Europe, these estates were exemplars of current best-practice methods of cultivation. As units in a Europe-wide hierarchical organization, funnelling wealth upwards through stages to Rome, Church estates were necessarily engaged in converting output to goods, services or money which could be sent over long distances. The Church also 'contributed to long-distance trade indirectly, through its improvement of routes for easing the passage of pilgrimage and the flow of church business and tithes'.[92] However, in so far as tithes were the means through which the secular clergy were supported, the Church's influence on peasant farming might turn out to be conservative, not only because of the resentment caused by having to produce for someone else's use, but also because the expression of tithes as proportions of products of particular kinds obstructed changes in peasant farming systems.

The Reformation shattered this unified structure. The Bible provided ample validation for opposition to unjustly exercised authority,[93] and John Ball's stirring biblical justification for revolt spread through Europe in one direction, as Hussite

89. Huw Ridgeway, 'Medieval mentalités', *Journal of Historical Sociology*, 4 (1991), pp. 175–81, quotes at pp. 177 and 178.
90. Michael Heffernan (after Anne Buttimer), 'Geography and enlightenment', *Journal of Historical Geography*, 22 (1996), p. 476.
91. Ranging from 10 per cent of the area of France and 15 per cent of Italy as a whole, through 25 per cent of Picardy and Laonnais to 56 per cent of Bavaria. Norman J. G. Pounds, *An Historical Geography of Europe 1500–1840* (Cambridge, 1979), p. 161.
92. James E. Vance, Jr, 'Transport and the geographical expression of capitalism', in Genovese and Hochberg, *Geographic Perspectives*, pp. 119–43, quote at p. 123.
93. Christopher Hill, *The English Bible and the Seventeenth-Century Revolution* (London, 1993).

and Lutheran doctrines coursed in others. These revolts, and the Thirty Years War which represented the battle between Catholicism and Protestantism at the level of state power, were immensely destructive economically, injecting a further dose of insecurity into systems of peasant livelihood where the wars were actually fought, and causing large increases in taxation and rents everywhere (except in England which, because the Crown could not raise the revenue for it, did not join in the continental conflict, although it had its own domestic Civil War). However, where Protestantism was sanctioned by sovereign powers, as in much of northern Europe, there were large influxes of population after the wars, which could be encouraged to settle empty land or introduce useful crafts,[94] and large religious estates came into Crown hands. These could be used to remunerate state officials in kind, as in Sweden; if they were sold, as in England (where more than one-quarter of farmland was in Crown hands in 1540, largely as a consequence of religious confiscations), they provided a huge windfall of revenue, and a powerful stimulus to the notion that lands could be considered as an investment among the gentry who borrowed heavily to buy them.[95] In Orthodox Russia, too, the Crown gained enormous areas of land from the Church, which it could use as an additional source of income to taxation. Protestant and Orthodox state churches gave firm ideological buttresses to sovereign power, whilst at the same time Protestant Hobbesian doctrines about how power must be exercised for the common good to be acceptable curbed it. Unified national churches also strengthened state organization, as their structures were used as agencies of secular as well as religious administration, and provided a rallying point for revolt against foreign domination, as against Catholic Polish and Lithuanian landlords by the Orthodox peasantry of Ukraine. In Britain and Scandinavia, the representative vestry meetings though which Protestant church administration was done provided an alternative to landlords' manor courts for the institutional organization of peasant life. It was there that the poor relief policies necessary for landless labourers to survive all year were implemented.

Protestantism sapped at four of the foundations of Catholic peasant non-material culture. Community rather than individuality, resignation rather than confidence in the power of action, unquestioning reliance on customary models from the past, and the oral transmission of culture were all prey to Protestant ideology. These same traits fissipated the unity of churches, their teachings and authority, and injected a strong anti-authoritarian tendency into societies generally. Bible-reading produced ' "the Village Hampden". – The whole cast of his character was formed by the Bible . . . Acts of parliament which appeared to him to clash with the laws laid down in it, as the word of God, he treated with contempt – he maintained that the Fowls of the air and the fish of the sea were free to all men.'[96] Sectarian organization came from below and gave its leaders

94. For the importance of this in the diffusion of technology, see W. C. Scoville, 'Minority migrations and the diffusion of technology', *Journal of Economic History*, 11 (1951), pp. 347–60, and idem, *The Persecution of Huguenots and French Economic Development 1680–1720* (Berkeley, CA, 1960).

95. G. E. Mingay, *The Gentry: The Rise and Fall of a Ruling Class* (London, 1976), pp. 44–50.

96. Thomas Bewick, *A Memoir* (1862; repr. Oxford, 1979), p. 25.

an authority which was of, rather than above, their local community. The Church became an agent which could mobilize demands for change from common people, rather than one which explained through its teachings and demonstrated in its practices why change was neither possible nor desirable. Perhaps this was at least part of the reason why in countries which seceded from the authority of Rome, Established Protestant sects (or Orthodoxy) were used, to a greater or lesser extent, as a channel through which national political, social and economic doctrines could be communicated to the populace at large.

It was an old orthodoxy of European history that Protestantism, especially in its Calvinist version (as in Switzerland, France, Holland and Britain[97]), was linked to the rise of capitalism.[98] In fact, it is impossible to generalize about this without neglecting important exceptions, and any attribution of causality risks circular argument: how far were the religious tenets and world-view of Protestantism responsible for the cultural characteristics of its adherents, and how far did the pre-existing cultural characteristics of certain social groups or regions predispose them to embrace it?[99] However, the promulgation of literacy by Protestant sects generally, and the related stress on each individual's access to truth through unmediated effort because God's grace is innate equally in every person,[100] do seem to be intelligibly linked to the ideology of a fragmented society of atomized individuals acting for their own ends, which the capitalist market economy requires in order to function.[101] Certainly, it was thought (at least by some) at the time that in Protestantism 'the Rules of Religion and the Rules of social Industry do perfectly harmonize',[102] and Zürich (home town of Zwingli, the supposed co-founder of 'the Protestant work ethic') did produce 'an early industrial entrepreneurial type . . . who combined competence in business with his firm, almost puritanical, religious faith to achieve a more elevated aim in life . . . The hand of God directed the course of manufacture and rich business profits were recognised and valued as the blessings of God.'[103] The Welsh Calvinistic Methodist migrants who set up the iron industry in southern Ohio were strikingly similar.[104]

97. Because of its belief in predestination, Calvinism normally promoted both social inequality and quiescence in the face of civil authority. The Arminian version of Calvinism which came to dominance in the Low Countries and England excluded belief in predestination. Emmanuel Todd, *The Making of Modern France: Politics, Ideology and Culture* (Oxford, 1991), pp. 51–3.

98. Max Weber, *The Protestant Ethic and the Spirit of Capitalism* (1904–5; Eng. trans., London, 1930); R. H. Tawney, *Religion and the Rise of Capitalism* (London, 1926).

99. Todd, *The Making of Modern France*, pp. 40–54. English contemporaries remarked on the close relationships between pastoral farming regimes with domestic industry and Puritanism, and it seems generally to have been acknowledged at the time that 'mountains breed piety'. John Aubrey, *The Natural History of Wiltshire* (1685; repr. Newton Abbot, 1969), p. 11; Joan Thirsk, 'Seventeenth-century agriculture and social change', in idem, *The Rural Economy of England* (London, 1984), pp. 183–26; David Underdown, *Revel, Riot and Rebellion: Popular Politics and Culture in England 1603–1660* (Oxford, 1985), and Christer Ahlberger, 'Home industry and rural millenarianism in early nineteenth-century Western Sweden', in Mats Lundahl and Thommy Svensson (eds), *Agrarian Society in History: Essays in Honour of Magnus Mörner* (London, 1990), pp. 184–200.

100. Walter Ullmann, *The Individual and Society in the Middle Ages* (London, 1967), pp. 135–9.

101. Reddy, *Money and Liberty*, p. 74.

102. Josiah Tucker, 'Instructions for Travellers' [1758], repr. in R. L. Schuyler (ed.), *Josiah Tucker: a Selection from his Economic and Political Writings* (New York, 1931), p. 206.

103. Rudolf Braun, *Industrialization and Everyday Life* (Cambridge, 1990), pp. 9 and 132.

104. Anne K. Knowles, *Calvinists Incorporated: Welsh Immigrants on Ohio's Industrial Frontier* (Chicago, 1996).

In so far as it is true that different systems of religious beliefs had different social and economic consequences, another very strong shading of difference emerged across the peasant ecotypes of early modern Europe.

CONCLUSION

This chapter might well have been organized differently. Each component of Figure 1 could have been dealt with in turn, to show how it varied across Europe and changed through time. Perhaps that would have been a better way of conveying the increasingly rampant variety revealed in the substantive chapters of the book, more ostensibly in sympathy with the burden of its argument, and more suited to giving the geography of patriciates the due it deserves for its role in differentiating peasantry across the continent. However, co-extensive variation of the three simple and basic parameters discussed above could produce enormous variety, just as overlaying three primary colours exhausts every chromatic possibility. Yellow, blue and red themselves disappear when mixed in varying proportions, and so did each of the characteristics dealt with here, so that the intricacy of the differences displayed in earlier chapters is not inconsistent with the geographical and historical constancy of the effects of the photosynthetic constraint, the tyranny of distance, and Christianity.

Even so, it might still seem perverse, given the arguments in the rest of the book, to have chosen factors which operated so severely to constrain the possibilities of peasantry: to prevent, rather than enable, the emergence of features which are most characteristic of our own lives in the present. All the authors show that much changed during the period, corroborating Löfgren's observation that peasantry is a process, not a structure.[105] This was inevitable because peasantries interacted with both the physical environment and patriciates, changing and being changed by each other in the intricate ways represented in Figure 1. Consequent advances in the techniques of harnessing human, animal, wind and water power to production and exchange significantly increased the energy available per head over the period, population increased massively, and the peoples of Europe erupted westwards and southwards across the oceans and eastwards across the steppes. None the less, early modern peasantry represented the end of 'the old order' of European agricultural civilization,[106] and disappeared with the emergence of the new industrial one, which had only just begun, at the north-western end of 'commercial Europe', by 1800.

We end where we began: in the coils of historiography. The past can be used to mirror ourselves. From the vantage of our own energy-rich, globalized, secular world, maybe we cannot help looking for – and finding – harbingers of its coming. However, if we choose to emphasize how different peasantries were

105. Orvar Löfgren, 'Historical perspectives on Scandinavian peasantries', *Annual Review of Anthropology*, 9 (1980), pp. 187–215.
106. Jerome Blum, *The End of the Old Order in Rural Europe* (Princeton, NJ, 1978).

from each other in the past, then, surely, we must also emphasize the ways in which that past differed from our own world: perhaps 'the value of historical study lies in the opportunity it gives us for self-estrangement, the chance to recognize ourselves in what we are not'?[107] The stark primal distinction between then and now is a human ecological one: the utter dependence upon organic resources for energy for human use is what created peasantry. The increased abundance of other sources of energy brought into being new systems of socio-economic organization, and the departure of peasantry from history.[108] While organic dependence continued, so must peasantry; necessarily varied from place to place and changing through time, but constant in the implacability with which the need for most people to produce their daily bread for themselves affected all other aspects of their own, and everyone else's, lives.

---

107. John Barrell, *Painting and the Politics of Culture* (Oxford, 1992), p. 5.

108. 'Peasants are the victims of modernity . . . The period 1950–75 witnessed an epochal shift in which the peasantry became for the first time a global minority.' Michael Watts, 'Peasantry', in R. J. Johnston, Derek Gregory and David M. Smith (eds), *The Dictionary of Human Geography*, 4th edn (London, 1994), pp. 436–7.

Index of Names and Places

(Including battles, conventions, leagues, peace treaties, revolutions and wars; for land codes, laws and statutes, see Select Subject Index.)

Abel, Wilhelm 114, 120, 122, 152, 202, 203, 237
Åbo, *see* Turku
Abruzzi 75, 95
Adanır, Fikret 3, 18
Adrianople 291
Aegean Sea, region 50, 273, 289, 290, 293
Agnadello, battle of 78, 83
Ahmed I, sultan 304
Aistersheim estate (Upper Austria) 219
Akka, plain 289
Akkerman 299
al-Andalus 50, 51
Albania, Albanians 272, 275, 276, 277, 283
Ålborg, castle, town 336
Alemdar Mustafa Pasha, ruler of Rusçuk 301, 309
Alentejo (Portugal) 56, 64
Alexander II, tsar 266
Algarve 51, 64
Allen, R. C. 368, 370
Alps (region) 383, 384
    Austrian alps 193, 209, 212, 391
    Bavarian alps 112, 114
    Dinaric alps 272
    French alps 23
    Italian alps 84, 105

    Swiss alps 112, 391
    Transylvanian alps 273
      Stari Planina 273
Alpujarras mountains 50, 64
Alsace 112, 118
Amiens 33
Amsterdam 316, 332
Anatolia 272, 273, 274, 279, 282, 283, 284, 287, 288, 289, 292, 293, 295, 299, 303
Andalusia 51, 54, 56, 62, 64, 65, 66
Anglo-Turkish Commercial Convention (1838) 310
Anjou 22
Antioch 288
Apennines 76, 80, 84
Apulia 80, 92, 93, 95, 96, 97, 100, 105
Aragon, crown of, territory 50, 52, 53, 54, 56, 61, 62, 63, 64, 275
Archangel 237
Artola, Miguel 64
Asia Minor, *see* Anatolia
Assumption (Cañas), monastery 60
Astrakhan 256
Asturias 59, 65
Athos, monasteries 290
Attica 275, 292
Augsburg 116, 202, 211–12
Austria, Federal Republic of 138, 191

Austrian duchies, regions
    Inner Austria 201, 205, 206, 209, 217
    Lower Austria 202, 213, 215, 220,
        221
    Upper Austria 205, 206, 212, 213,
        214
    see also Burgenland; Carinthia;
        Carniola; Styria
Austrian Succession, War of 222
Austro-Hungarian empire, see Habsburg
    lands
Auvergne 28, 35
Ávila 54, 67

Baki estate 260–1, 264, 266
Balearic Islands 55
Balkans, peninsula, region 193, 270, 272,
        273, 274, 275, 277, 279, 280,
        282, 283, 284, 286, 287, 288,
        289, 296, 299, 301, 302, 305,
        306, 383, 396
Ball, John 396
Baltic Sea, region 164, 217, 241, 314,
        317, 391, 392
Bamberg 134
Barcelona 54
Bariatinskii, prince 255
Barkan, Ömer Lûtfi 270
Basque country 56, 57, 59
Bavaria 111, 118, 119, 123, 126, 134,
        135, 139, 140, 204, 211, 217–18,
        220, 236
Beckerman, John 351
Behar, Ruth 59
Belgium, see Low Countries, southern
        Low Countries
Belgorod Line 248–9
Belgrade 272
    Pashalik of Belgrade 302
Belorussia 228, 229, 240–4, 246, 252–3,
        254, 391
Bender 299
Bergamo 78
Bergen 319, 323
Bergslagen (Sweden) 316
Bertaut, François 54

Beypazarı (near Ankara) 288
Bezhetskaia district, 233
Bierbrauer, Peter 138
von Bismarck, Otto 192
Black Forest 112, 114, 118, 123, 139, 141
Black Sea, region 293, 391
Blekinge, province 335
Blickle, Peter 138, 204
Blum, Jerome 233, 238
Bohemia 111, 112, 120, 193, 202, 204,
        205, 208, 211, 212, 215, 217,
        220, 221, 222, 224, 237
Bohuslän (Norway) 317
Bona Sforza 242
Bosnia 272, 287, 301
Bothnia, Gulf of 317
Boyabat (near Sinop) 288
Brabant 18
    see also Low Countries
de Bracton, Henry 352
Brandenburg 112, 148, 163, 166, 168,
        169, 174, 175, 230, 236, 259
    Altmark 165, 177
    Mittelmark 169, 177
    Neumark (New Mark) 177
    Uckermark 174, 175, 177
Brandenburg-Prussia, see Prussia
Braudel, Fernand 58–9, 269–70, 273
Brazil 56
Breisgau 116
Brenner, Robert 14–17, 210, 346,
        362–3, 368, 369, 370
Brescia 78, 89
Brest (Poland) 242
    Union of Brest (1596) 245
Britain, British Isles 14, 18, 391, 397,
        398
Britnell, Richard H. 15
Brittany 22, 28, 32, 33, 35, 40
Bruck an der Mur 212
Bruckmüller, Ernst 191
Brueghel, Pieter, the Elder 67
Brumont, Francis 67
Brunswick 120
Buckinghamshire 364
Bug, river 241, 253

Bukovina 192
Bulgaria 277, 297, 299, 302
  second tsardom (1187–1393) 275
Bureba 55, 67
Burgenland 202
Burgos 51, 54
Burgundy 22, 34, 35
Bursa 291
Bury St Edmunds, abbey 356, 357
  Redgrave manor (Suffolk) 353
  Littlebury family 365
Bushkovitch, Paul 235
Byzantium 274

Calabria 80, 81, 84, 90, 92
Calahorra 54
Calderón de la Barca, Pedro 49
  El alcalde de Zalamea 49
Cambridgeshire 349, 358
Campania 93
  see also Naples
Campbell, Bruce M. S. 15
Cantabria 59, 60
Canterbury, priory of Christ Church 349
Capitanata 93
  see also Apulia
Caribbean 14
Carinthia 201, 202
Carniola 202, 213
Carsten, F. L. 147
Castile 49, 50, 52, 53, 56, 59, 61, 64,
    65–6, 67, 68, 70
  Mesetas 51
  New Castile 51, 54, 62, 65, 68
  Old Castile 51, 62
  Sierras 51, 71
Catalonia 50, 56, 57, 58, 59, 60, 61, 69,
    71, 72
  Old Catalonia 52, 57, 60
Câteau-Cambrésis, peace of 86
Catherine II, tsarina ('the Great') 254
Caucasus 254
Çemişgezek 285
de Cervantes, Miguel 49, 71
  Don Quixote 49, 71
Chalkidiki 290

Champagne 201
Charlemagne 5
Chayanov, Alexander 8–9
Chios 290, 297
Christian II, king of Denmark 336
Christian, William, Jr 69
Cicilian plain (Çukurova) 283, 288
Cole, John 199–200
  see also Val di Non
Collantes de Terán, Antonio 54
Cologne 120
Coltishall manor 357
Constantinople, see Istanbul
Conze, Werner 243
Copenhagen 320, 331
Córdoba 65
Corinth 284
cossacks 245, 249, 250, 253, 265
Covaleda 63
Cremona 78, 89
Crete 297
Crimean War 266
Croatia 287
Croot, Patricia 369
Crowland, abbey 354, 358
Cuenca 54, 57
Çukurova, see Cicilian plain
Cumans 275

Dacke, Nils 335
Dal, river 321
Dalarna, province 334
Dalton, George 8
Damascus, 300
Danube, basin, region, river 112, 193,
    201, 272, 288, 293, 298
Danzig 156, 157, 164, 178, 315, 332, 334
Dardanelles 276
David, 'peasant king' in Finland 334
Delaware, river 321
Delibes, Miguel 49
  Los santos inocentes 49
Demirhisar 287
Denmark, Danes 313–17, 319, 320, 322,
    323–4, 326, 328–30, 331–2, 334,
    335–6, 389, 394

Detlefsen, Backe 332
Diesdorf, nunnery 165–6
Divriği 282
Dniepr (Dnepr), river 244, 245, 249,
    252–3
Dniester (Dnestr), river 244, 299
Dodgshon, Robert A. 7
Don, river 265
Dósza, György 214
Drama 287, 289
Dubrovnik, see Ragusa
Duero, river, valley, 51
Duruelo 63
Dušan, Stefan 276
Dutch Republic, see Low Countries,
    northern Low Countries
Dvina (western), river 241
Dyer, Christopher 16

East Anglia 342, 356, 357–8, 359, 360,
    361, 363, 365, 366–7
Edward I, king of England 353
Eifel 112
Elbe, river 111, 112, 114
Ellis, Frank 1, 8, 10
Ely, bishopric, manors of 349
Emilia 91
Engelbrektsson, Engelbrekt 334
Engels, Friedrich 153
England 6, 13, 14–17, 33, 36, 84, 94,
    108, 123, 316, 319, 339–71,
    374, 375, 381, 386, 393, 394,
    397
  East Anglia, see s. v.
  eastern England 363
  Midlands, see s. v.
  south-east England 361
  English Civil War 397
Epiros 273
Epstein, Stephan R. 9, 11, 393
Erik of Pomerania, king of Denmark-
    Sweden 334
Erzgebirge 111
Essex 363, 364
Estonia 314
Euboea 276, 284

Examinis, Catalan writer 71
Extremadura 63, 70

Faith, Rosamond 348
Faroe Islands 314
Fener 289
Ferdinand, king of Aragon 49
Ferrer i Alos, Llorenç 58
Fertile Crescent 272
Finland, Finns 228, 313–15, 320–1,
    323–4, 327, 333, 334, 336, 380,
    382, 385
Flanders 18, 22, 32
  see also Low Countries
Florence, city, territory 11, 75, 77, 79,
    82, 83, 84, 89, 103, 389
  Catasto (1424–27) 78, 102
Foster, George M. 197
Fox, E. W. 388
Fra Bernadina, 'missionary in Serbia'
    306
France 15, 21–47, 84, 93, 111, 112, 119,
    123, 258, 346, 374, 391, 392,
    393, 394, 398
Franco, Francisco, generalissimo 49
Franconia 112, 114, 118, 119, 120, 121,
    123, 124, 126, 134, 137, 139
Frankenburg 214
Frankenwald 112
Franz, Günther 204
Frederick II, king of Prussia
    ('the Great') 149
Frederick William I, king of Prussia 149
Freedman, Paul H. 61, 71
Freiburg im Breisgau 116
French Revolution 23, 46–7
French Wars of Religion 25
Friesland 114, 119, 122, 126
Frisia, see Friesland
Friuli 84, 100
Fuenteovejuna 49
Funen 335
Fyodor, tsar 250

Gabelbach 119
Gagarin estate 258

Galiani, Ferdinando 102
Galicia (Poland) 244, 251
Galicia (Spain) 51, 59, 66, 68, 70
Galilee 289
Gallejones de Zamanzas 60, 68, 72
García de Cortázar, José A. 55
Gaunt, David 4
Gdańsk, see Danzig
Genoa 77, 201
German Democratic Republic 153–4
Germany 27, 36, 84, 111–42, 202, 204,
    233, 258, 315–16, 322, 334, 374,
    391, 393
  east-Elbian Germany 111, 112, 121,
    126, 133, 138, 145–54, 162–70,
    172, 173–82, 188–9, 230–2, 237,
    239, 248, 374, 392
Gerona 61
Gnieszno, archbishopric 171
Golovkin, count 250
Gorky, Maxim 266
Granada 50, 64
Gråtopp, Hallvard 334, 335
Gray, C. M. 369
Greece 93, 273, 298, 307, 308
  Greek Revolution (War of
    Independence) 306
Greenland 314, 318
Grodno 242
Grüll, Georg 219
Gubec, Matija 214
Guerre, Martin 24
Gustavus I Vasa, king of Sweden 314, 335
Guyenne 23
Gyldenstjerne family 335
Gyula, sancak 283

Habsburg, house of 191, 200, 202, 295,
    305
  Charles V 71
  Ferdinand I 213, 287
  Francis I 225
  Joseph II 222, 223–4, 225
  Leopold I 212, 213, 307
  Leopold II 225
  Maria Theresia 219–20, 222, 225

  Maximilian I 212
  Philip II, king of Spain 58, 69, 70
  Rudolph II 213
Habsburg lands 191–225, 249–50, 287,
    302, 303, 374, 375, 378, 381, 393
  see also Austrian duchies, regions;
    Bohemia; Hungary
Hagen, William W. 14
Halesowen 349
  Lee, William 349
  Osbern, Henry 349
  Robin, Thomas 349
Halland (Denmark) 317
Hallein 202
Hallstatt 202, 212
Hamburg 217, 221, 332
Hampshire 341
Hanover 136
Hanseatic League 315, 319, 382
Harput 283
Hatcher, John 348–9, 355
Harvey, Barbara 352, 355–6
Hauenstein 139
von Haxthausen, August 263
Henning, Friedrich-Wilhelm 136
Henry II, king of England 351
Hercegovina 272
Hesel 119–20
Hesse 112, 118, 119, 123, 126, 134, 135
Hilton, Rodney H. 16
Hobsbawm, Eric 254
Hoch, Steven 258
Hoffmann, Alfred 214
Hohenlohe 117, 122, 123, 129, 134
Hohenzollern dynasty 149
  see also Prussia
Holstein, see Schleswig-Holstein
Hörnigk, J. W. 220
Holland, province 18
  see also Low Countries
Hoyle, R. W. 368–9
Hundred Years War 24
Hungary 192, 194, 201, 204, 205, 209,
    211, 214, 215, 217, 220, 222,
    250, 253, 283, 284, 304, 305,
    381, 392

Hunsrück 112
Hussites 205, 207, 334, 335, 396–7
Husum 332

Iberia 18, 49–73, 84, 93
Iceland 313–15, 318–19, 323–4, 327, 331
Île-de-France, see Paris, Paris basin
Imbros 290
Imhof, Arthur E. 119
Indies, East 387
Indies, West, see Caribbean
Ingermanland 314
Ingrao, Charles 191–2
Ireland 14, 18, 383, 394
Isabella, queen of Castile 49
Ischl 212
Istanbul 290, 291, 292, 307
István Bocksai, prince of Transylvania 305
Italy 10–11, 50, 75–108, 118, 119, 193, 194, 201, 202, 217, 220, 287, 291–2, 374, 386, 392, 393
Ivan III, tsar 232
Ivan IV, tsar ('the Terrible') 232, 234, 235, 238

Jaén 65, 68
Jagiełło dynasty 208
Joseph-Volokolamsk monastery 240
Judenburg 201
Justi, J. H. G. 219
Jutland 314, 320, 324, 331–2, 334, 335, 336
    Højer farm 331–2

Kafka, Franz 222
    Das Schloß (The Castle) 222
Kaluga 235
Kamchatka (eastern Siberia) 228
Kara Ferye, see Verria
Karlovci 305
Karposh, haiduk, 'prince of Kumanovo' 307
Kautsky, Karl 101
Kemah, sancak 283, 285

Kent 341, 342, 349
Kiev 229–30, 244
Kili 299
Klaipeda 241
von Kleist family 178–9
Kmel'nitskii, Bogdan 245, 252, 253
Knapp, Georg Friedrich 147–52
Knighton, Henry 17
Koblenz 120
Kolokotronis, Th. 307
Komotini 289
Konya 273
Kosminsky, E. A. 341
Kostroma, province 260
Krakow 240
Kratovo 287
Kremsmünster, abbey 202
Kula, Witold 160
Kustendil 287, 302
Kursk, province 255

Laimbauer, Martin 214
Lake Mälar 321, 325, 326
Langton, John 8, 13, 18
Languedoc 23
L'Aquila 81
Laslett, Peter 69, 93–4
Latin America 14, 56
Latvia 314
Lazio 75, 76, 94, 99
Leipzig 217, 221
Lenin, Vladimir Il'ich 159
León 59, 60
Le Roy Ladurie, Emmanuel 202
Lieven, prince 266
Liguria 80
Limnos 290
Linz 202, 212, 214, 219
Lisbon 54, 56
Lithuania 171, 227, 228, 229, 240, 241, 242, 243, 244, 245, 253, 393, 397
Livonia 236, 237, 241
    Livonian War (1558–82) 234
Lodi 107
Löfgren, Orvar 399

Logroño 54
Loire, river 22
Lombardy 10, 76, 78, 84, 90, 91–2, 93,
      95, 103, 104, 105
London 219, 393
    Great Fire (1666) 316
Lorca 57, 64
Lorraine 112
Louis XIV, king of France 40, 42
Low Countries 18, 112, 115, 118, 176
    northern Low Countries
        (Netherlands) 11–13, 16, 18,
        315, 316, 332, 334, 391, 394,
        398
    southern Low Countries (Belgium)
        18
Lower Saxony 118, 126
Lübeck 315, 316, 334
Lublin, Union of (1569) 245
Lucca 82, 94
Lusatia 148, 177
Lütge, Friedrich 133
Luther, Martin 138, 397

Maas (Husum) 332
Macartney, C. A. 225
Macedonia 273, 277, 282, 284, 289, 291,
      300, 307
Macfarlane, Alan 16–17, 339–40
Machiavelli, Niccolò 83
Maçuka 289, 290
Magdeburg 177
Mahmud II, sultan 301, 309
Main, river, valley 112, 115
Maine 22, 32
Mainote Peninsula 307
Mainz 134
    Public Peace of Mainz (1152) 6
Maitland, F. W. 17, 350
Makriyannis, general 307
Malthus, Thomas 394
Manisa 289
Mantua 82
Marches, the (Italy) 75, 80, 91
Maremma 93, 99
Maritsa valley 288

Marmara, Sea of 293
Marseilles 201
Marx, Karl 21
Massif Central 383
Matute (Rioja) 60
Matzouka, see Maçuka
Mazovia 163, 164, 170
Mecklenburg 112, 148, 149, 157, 168,
      174, 175, 177, 314
de Medici, dukes of Florence 79
    duke Cosimo 83
    see also Florence
Mehmed II, sultan 280, 284
Melton, Edgar 17, 378, 391
Memel, see Klaipeda
Memmingen 116
Menlik 289
Menshikov, prince 250
Messina 81
Metz, siege of 71
Midlands (English) 341, 359–60, 361,
      367
Milan, city, territory 75, 78, 79, 91
Military Orders:
    in Prussia 156, 164
    in Spain 51, 64
        Order of Calatrava 49
Milsom, S. F. C. 348
Mistra, despotate 275
Mitterauer, Michael 198
Mohammed Ali, ruler of Egypt 309
Moldavia 244, 305
Montenegro 272
Morava, river, valley 273, 298
Moravia 220
moriscos 50, 52, 61, 64
Moscow, city, province 227, 229, 230,
      232, 233, 240, 255, 257
    see also Muscovy
Mosel (Moselle), river, valley 118
de Moxó, Salvador 70
Mudejars 51
Murad I, sultan 280
Murcia 51, 58, 64
Muscovy 229, 230, 232, 234, 235, 237,
      242, 248, 249, 250, 314

Naples, city, kingdom 61, 75, 76, 80, 82, 89, 95, 99, 100, 103, 104
Napoleon Bonaparte 149
Navarre 50, 60, 63
Neckar, river, valley 115
Neckarhausen 116, 130, 132
Netherlands, see Low Countries, northern Low Countries
New Sweden 321
Nieman, river 241
Niklashausen 137
Nizhnii Novgorod, region 257
Nocera 85
Norfolk 349, 357, 358, 363, 364, 366
    Gressenhall manor 358
    Hevingham manor 366
Normandy 22, 24, 29, 32, 33, 38, 40
North Sea, region 314
Northern Wars (1655–60; 1700–21) 246, 251, 252
Norway, Norwegians 313–19, 320, 321, 323–5, 327–8, 329, 333, 334–5, 336
Novgorod 227, 228, 230, 232, 234, 236
Nuremberg 202

Obrenović, Milosh 308
Ochsenhausen 137
Odenwald 112
Oder, river 177
Ogels, Anders 332
Ohio 398
Oporto, see Porto
Orkney Islands 314
Oslo 319, 335
Osnabrück 127
Österbotten, province 320, 333–4, 336
Östergötland 335
Ottoman lands, Ottomans 18, 269–310, 394, 395, 396
    Ottoman dynasty 274, 276–7
    Ottoman War against Russia and Austria (1787–92) 301

Palatinate, see Rhineland-Palatinate
Palestine 284, 285, 289, 304

Panayot Benakis, prince of Kalamata 303
Pannonia 209, 273
    see also Austrian duchies, regions; Hungary
Papal States 75, 82, 86
Paré, Ambrose 71
Paris 22, 24, 25
    Paris basin 23, 26–7, 30, 31, 36, 39, 41, 43
    Treaty of Paris (1856) 310
Parker, David 369
Patras 298
Paul I, tsar 263
Pavlovo 257
Pechenegs 275
Peloponnese 277, 283, 284, 303
Persia 294
Perugia 84, 85, 103
Peter I, tsar ('the Great') 246, 247, 250, 251
Petrovskoe 258–9, 260, 261
Philippopolis 289
Physiocrats 381
Picardy 32
Piedmont 84, 95, 104, 105
    see also Savoy
Pindos 273
Pinsk 242
Pisa 201
Po, river, valley 76, 89, 91, 104
Podolia 230, 244, 253
Poland 145–7, 154–60, 162–4, 170–3, 175–6, 178, 182–9, 227, 228, 232, 237, 239, 240, 241, 242, 243, 244, 245, 247, 248, 315, 374, 375, 392, 394, 397
Polanyi, Karl 8
von Polheim, Wolfgang 213
Pomerania 112, 148, 157, 168, 314
    Prussian Pomerania 177
    Swedish Pomerania 177
Popkin, Samuel L. 197
Porto 66
Portugal 18, 50, 51, 52, 53, 54, 55, 56, 62, 66, 68, 394

Postan, M. M. 17
Poznań 170
Principato 81
Provence 23
Prussia (Brandenburg-Prussia, electorate; afterwards kingdom) 149, 152, 173, 176–8, 189, 228, 247, 392
    Duchy of Prussia (East Prussia) 148, 177, 230
    Royal Prussia 164
Pskov 227, 231, 232
Pugachev, Emelian 265
Pyrenees 23, 50

Quesnay, François 394

Raab, Franz Anton 224
Raczyński estates, family 182–8
    at Grylewo 188
    at Prosna 188
    at Stobnica 188
    at Sycyno 187–8
    at Szamocin 188
    at Wyszyna 188
    peasants 186–7
Radiłoło 291
Radomir 287
Radziwiłł family 240
Ragusa 292, 306
Ravensburg 116
Razi, Zvi 360
Razin, Stenka 265
Rebel, Hermann 377, 378, 391
Reher, David 54, 57
Revolution of 1848 (Germany) 150
Rhine, river 112, 115
Rhineland 115, 117, 118, 123, 126, 139, 204, 387, 391
Rhineland-Palatinate 118, 119, 126
Rhodopes 273
Ribe 332
Riga 241, 393
Rioja 66
Romania 227
Robisheaux, Thomas 391
Rome 86, 103, 273, 396

Rosenberg, Hans 146, 147
Ruiz, Juan 71
Ruiz, Teófilo M. 18
Rum Vilayeti 280
Rumelia, see Balkans
Russia 17, 157, 227–66, 321, 323, 374, 378, 382, 391, 392, 393, 397
Russo-Ottoman War 301
Rutkowski, Jan 154, 156–60

Saint Albans, abbey 353, 364
    Codicote manor (Herts) 353
    Park manor (Herts) 353
    Winslow manor (Bucks) 364
        Jankyn family 364–5
        Wengrave family 365
Saint Augustine, bishop of Hippo 395
Saint Petersburg 228, 314
Saint-Quentin 33
Saint Roch (Roque) 69
Saint Sebastian, 69
Salonika 273, 287, 292
Salzburg, city, territory 204, 206
Salzkammergut 202, 212
Samogitia 241
Samokov 297
Sandžak 272
Sankt Jørgensbjerg 335
Santa María del Monte 59, 60
Santa María la Real de Aguilar de Campóo, monastery 56, 68
de Santillana, Marquis 71
    Serranillas 71
Sapieha family 240
Sardinia 95
Savoy 82, 201
Saxony 111, 112, 116, 117, 120, 121, 122
Scandinavia 4, 313–37, 374, 382, 397
Scania 314, 324, 332–3
Schleswig, see Schleswig-Holstein
Schleswig-Holstein 148, 157, 168, 177, 228, 314, 330, 332
Schwalm 130
Scotland 14, 18
Scott, James C. 197

Segovia 54, 56
Seine, river 22
Semevskii, V. V. 227
Serbia, Serbs 276, 302, 303, 306, 308
Seres 273, 289
Seville 54, 65
  San Gil 54
  San Julián 54
  Santa Lucía 54
  Triana 54
Schapiro, A. L. 238
Sheremetev, count 250
Shetland Islands 314
Siberia 245
Sicily 75, 80, 82, 84, 90, 92, 93, 95, 97,
  99, 157, 201, 273
Siderokapsa 287
Sigismund I, king of Poland 242
Sigismund II Augustus, king of Poland
  242
Silesia 148, 163, 177, 202, 205, 220
'Skipper Clement' 336
Skopje 273, 306, 307
Slovakia 202, 227
Slovenia 214, 272
Småland, province 334, 335
Smith, Adam 220, 381, 394
Smith, R. E. F. 17
Smith, Richard M. 17, 94
Smithfield 17
Sofia 287, 297
Sophia, regent of Russia 246, 250
Soria 63, 70
South-East Asia 10
Soviet Union (USSR) 9
Spain 24, 119, 374, 380, 386, 393, 394
  under the Bourbons 50
  under the Catholic monarchs 49
  under the Habsburgs 25
  see also al-Andalus; Habsburg, house
    of; Iberia
Spaso-Prilutsk monastery 247
Spittler, Gerd 263
Srem, sancak 284
Stavenow, lordship 178–82, 183, 188
Stephen, king of England 348

Steward, Julian 199
Stockholm 317, 321, 325, 328, 334
Straits Convention (1841) 310
Styria 201, 202, 213
Suffolk 349, 364
Šumadija 272
Surrey 341
Sussex 341
Swabia 112, 114, 116, 117, 121, 122,
  139
Sweden, Swedes 246, 313–18, 320–6,
  327–8, 330, 332–3, 334, 335,
  336, 383, 389, 392
Switzerland 36, 112, 136, 138, 204, 391,
  398
Syria 272, 283, 287, 288

Tallinn 315
Tambov, province 258
Tatars 244, 248, 249, 275, 395
Tawney, R. H. 369
Telemark, province 334, 335
Terra di Bari 81
Terra d'Otranto 81
Teutonic Knights, see Military Orders, in
  Prussia
Thasos 290
Thessaly 273, 275, 277, 289
Thirty Years War 40, 118, 119, 120,
  125–6, 134, 135, 140, 149, 169,
  236, 315, 397
Thorner, Daniel 340
Thrace 273, 277, 288
von Thünen, J. H. 386
Thuringia 112, 117, 121, 122, 134
Tierra de Campos 66
Tikhonov, Iu. 248
Tilly, Charles 46
Timur i Leng (Tamerlane) 277
Tirol 112, 192, 199–200, 202, 204, 205,
  213, 221
de Tocqueville, Alexis 46
Topolski, Jerzy 170
Toulouse 28, 38
Trabzon 290
Transylvania 250

Trent (Trento) 84, 90
Trøndelag 319
Tsarevo-Konstantinov monastery 232, 239–40
Turcomans 274, 277, 286, 289
Turkey, Republic of 269, 273
Turku 320, 336
Tuscany 10, 75, 76, 78, 80, 84, 91, 94, 102, 106, 388
Tver 233
Tyrrhenian coast 95

Udine 100
Ukraine 156, 171, 228, 229, 230, 244–7, 249, 250, 252–3, 254, 397
Ulm 116
Umbria 75, 91
Upper Palatinate (Franconia) 116
Upper Rhine 112, 115, 117, 121, 122, 124, 137, 139
Ural mountains 227, 228, 265
Urbino 82

Val di Non 199–200
    Sankt Felix 199–200
    Trett 199–200
Valencia 50, 51
Valladolid 68
Valle d'Aosta 84
Vardar, river, valley 273, 298
Varna 287
Vassberg, David E. 64
Västergötland 317
de Vega, Lope Felix 49
    Fuenteovejuna 49
Venice, city, territory 75, 76, 77, 78, 79, 82, 83, 85, 86, 89, 90, 91, 99, 100, 103, 104, 105, 107, 108, 201, 275, 302
Ventosa 60
Verona 78
Verria 289, 300
Vetluga, region 260, 261
Viatka 228
Viazzo, Pier Paolo 198
Vidin 281, 302

Vienna 201, 214
Vikings, Viking era 313, 318, 322, 324, 327
Vinogradoff, Paul 17, 341
Vistula, river 156
Vlachs 275, 276, 277, 286, 287, 288, 305
    'Valachia' 275, 306
    Black Valachia 275
    Magna Valachia (Valachia Maior) 275
    Old Valachia 275
    Rhodope Valachia 275
    Upper Valachia 275
    Valachia Minor (Aetolia, Acarnania) 275
    Valachia Minor (Oltenia) 275
    Valachia north of the Balkan range 275
    White Valachia 275
    see also Wallachia
Vladimir, province 255
    Vladimir-Kostroma textile region 257
Vogelsberg 112
Vojvodina 305
Volga, region, river 227, 228, 255, 256, 257, 265
Volhynia 229–30, 244, 253
Vologda 235, 247–8
Vorarlberg 205
Vrsac 305
de Vries, Jan 11–13, 16

Wales, 14, 18
    Welsh in Ohio 398
Wall, Richard 198
Wallachia 275, 305
Wallerstein, Immanuel 271
Weber, Max 6, 147
Weis, Eberhard 111
Weser, river 112, 114
Westminster abbey, estates of 355–6
Westphalia 111, 112, 116, 118, 126
Wetterau 112
White Mountain, battle of (1620) 205
Whittle, Jane 366–7
Wolf, Eric R. 2–4, 6, 197–200, 340
    see also Val di Non

Wolfenbüttel 120
Wright, William E. 224
Württemberg 117, 118, 119, 120, 124,
    126, 127, 130, 134, 135, 137
Würzburg 134
Wyczański, Andrzej 171

Yürüks 287, 289, 305
    see also Turcomans

Zealand (Danish province) 320, 330–1,
    335
    Gisselfeld estate 330
    Svaneholm estate 331
Zeeland (Dutch province) 18
    see also Low Countries
Zihna 287
Zürich 398
Zwingli, Huldrych 138, 398

Select Subject Index

Agricultural systems 56, 66, 88, 93, 114,
    228, 274, 288–9, 292, 381
  capitalist agriculture 12, 14, 16, 88,
    142, 160, 347, 362–3
  ecotypes 4, 198–200, 377
  productivity 26, 91, 106–8, 115, 124,
    228–9, 230, 231, 259, 260, 331,
    380–1

Banditry 70, 85–7, 104, 271, 295–6,
    304–8
Black Death (1348–51) 14, 15, 52, 88, 89,
    90, 163, 202, 230, 319–20, 325
  subsequent outbreaks of plague 24,
    67, 118, 124, 319, 322
Bondage, see serfdom
Brigandage, see banditry

Çiftliks, see latifundia
Communes (parish, peasant, valley,
    village) 6, 7, 36–7, 53, 60, 62,
    114, 128–9, 136–7, 156, 204,
    206, 207, 213, 231–2, 252,
    262–5, 328, 378
Cottagers, cottars, see labourers

Demesne agriculture, see latifundia
Demography 14, 89, 104, 117–19,
    121–2, 125, 181, 216, 234, 246,
    249, 252, 254, 259, 292, 318,
    320, 322
  Malthusian theories 11, 26, 120, 124,
    202

population statistics
  in France 22, 24–5
  in Germany 117
  in Iberia 53–6
  in Italy 81
  in the Ottoman lands 292
  in Poland 184
  in Russia 235

Family structures 36, 43–5, 56–7, 93–5,
    97, 129–30, 180–1, 183, 185, 200,
    219, 221, 230, 243, 259–60, 271,
    302, 325–6, 327, 381–2, 385
Farm sizes, types 51, 62, 91–2, 95,
    178–80, 183, 185, 230, 242–3,
    249, 282, 283, 326
Field systems 65, 115, 149, 156, 175
  one-field system 317
  three-field system 65, 228, 258, 317
  two-field system 65, 317

Gutsherrschaft, see lordship: Germany
Gutswirtschaft, see latifundia

Haiduks 250, 253–4, 304–6, 308
  see also banditry

Industrial crops, see rural industries
Inheritance customs
  impartible 123, 198, 325, 342, 360
  inter vivos 216, 327, 343, 364, 365, 367
  partible 27–8, 57–8, 123–4, 127, 198,
    357–8, 360

Labour services, *see* labourers; latifundia; serfdom

Labourers (day-, landless, migrant, seasonal, wage-) 29–30, 53, 54, 64, 72, 81, 87, 98, 99, 100, 122, 128, 150, 152, 156, 158, 160, 161, 168, 169, 174–5, 177, 194, 209, 217, 230, 236, 252, 261, 329, 330, 343, 346, 360, 386, 394

Latifundia 14, 49, 51, 64–5, 88, 95, 146–89, 232–3, 239–41, 242, 247–8, 250, 256–8, 322, 324, 329–30, 393–4
  Çiftliks 298–301, 303
  Gutswirtschaft 151–2, 157, 159–60, 166–72, 174, 189, 215
  robot estates in the Habsburg lands 211, 214
  Wirtschaftsherrschaft 214–15

Land codes, laws and statutes:
  England
    De Donis 353
    Domesday Book 341
    Quia Emptores 352–3
    Statute of Labourers (1351) 15
  Germany: *ius Theutonicus* 156, 162, 163, 164
  Ottoman lands
    ius valachicum 275, 277
    Land Code (1858) 309, 310
    Land Code (1867) 310
    Serbian Land Code of Stefan Dušan 276
  Russia
    Law Code (1497) 238
    Law Code (1649) 238
  Spain: *Siete partidas* 57

Literacy 38–9, 46

Lordship
  in France 34–5
  in Germany 133, 145–6
    Grundherrschaft 133, 150–1
    Gutsherrschaft 150–1, 157
  in Iberia 52, 59
  in Italy 79–82

Manorialism, east-Elbian commercialized, *see* latifundia, *Gutswirtschaft*

Markets 16, 27
  credit markets 98–101
  land market 123, 356–60, 368
  peasant involvement in 2, 7–9, 28, 31, 95–6, 101, 115, 123, 127–8, 131, 178, 206, 220, 259, 261, 291, 315, 332–3, 341, 387, 389–90

Marriage, *see* demography; family structures

Mesta, the, *see* transhumance

Mining 122, 193, 202, 342
  peasant-miners 122, 326
  salt-mining 202, 212

Nomadism 274, 288, 289

Peasant rebellions 40–1, 84–5, 104, 137, 138–9, 140, 206, 213, 214, 218, 234, 245, 249, 265–6, 295, 301, 303–5, 333–6
  England: Peasants' Revolt (1381) 17
  France
    Jacquerie (1358) 21
    revolts in Brittany (late 17th c.) 40
    revolts in Normandy (mid-17th c.) 40
    revolts in South-West France (16th–18th c.) 40
  Germany
    in Bavaria: Bavarian Peasant Rising (1705) 139
      Haag revolt (1596) 139
      Upper Bavarian Revolt (1633–4) 139, 140
    in the Black Forest: Saltpetre Wars (1725–27; 1738; 1743–5) 139, 141
    Peasants' War (1525) 17, 41, 116, 134, 137–8, 140, 141, 153, 213
    in Swabia: Ochsenhausen revolts (1496; 1502) 137
    on the Upper Rhine: Bundschuh conspiracies (1502; 1513; 1517) 137

in Württemberg: Poor Conrad
Rebellion (1514) 137
Habsburg lands
in Bohemia: revolts (late 17th c.)
218
in Carniola: revolt (1515) 213
in Hungary: Dósza Rebellion
(1514) 214
in Slovenia: Gubec Revolt (1573)
214
Upper Austrian Peasants' War
(1626) 213
Italy 84, 104
in Calabria (1459) 84
in Florence (1425–27) 84
in Friuli (1511) 84
in Naples (1647–8) 84–5
in Perugia (1525) 84–5
in the Veneto (1509) 85
Ottoman lands
in Anatolia: Celâlî Revolts (1603;
1610) 295
in the Balkans: Kircali Revolts
(1787–92) 301
Russia 234, 265
Cossack Rebellions (1590–1; 1595;
1635–8) 245
Pugachev Rebellion (1773–5) 245
Razin Rebellion (1667–71) 265
in the Ukraine: Kmel'nitsku
Rebellion (1648–52) 245, 249,
252–3
Scandinavia 333–6
in Denmark
Jutland Revolt (1438) 335
North Jutland Uprising (1441)
334
'Skipper Clement' Revolt (1534)
336
Zealand and Funen Revolt
(1440) 335
in Finland
'peasant king' David's Revolt
(1438) 334
War of the Clubs in Österbotten
(1590s) 334, 336

in Norway: Grâtopp Revolt in
Telemark (1435) 334–5
in Sweden
Engelbrekt Peasant War
(1434–6) 334
in Småland: Dacke Revolt
(1542–3) 335
Peasantries
peasant ecotypes, see agricultural
systems, ecotypes
'peasant mode of production' 11–12
terminology 5, 21, 194–5, 313, 372–3
Population, see demography
Proto-industrialization, see rural
industries
Putting-out system 12, 116, 211, 217
see also rural industries

Religion 37–8, 68–9, 119–20, 130, 132,
135, 138, 139, 218
rural clergy 37–8, 131
Rural crafts and industries 32–4, 46,
67, 103–6, 124–5, 126–7, 129,
132, 216, 218, 241–2, 255,
256–7, 261, 290, 298, 383,
389–90
industrial crops 23, 63, 91–2, 105,
115, 116, 243, 289, 292, 297
textiles 32–4, 54, 123, 217, 220, 231,
292
silk 8, 23, 51, 75, 92, 297

Serfdom 14, 16, 52, 61, 88, 111, 121,
133, 287, 392–3
in east-Elbian Germany and Poland
('second serfdom') 151, 153,
169, 175, 178
in England 344, 345–6, 347–50,
352–3, 355, 362, 363, 366–7
in the Habsburg lands 192, 196, 206,
208–9, 223–4
in Old Catalonia 60–2
remença 61
in Russia 227, 232–3, 237–40, 242,
244, 246, 251, 253, 254, 255,
257, 261, 263, 266

in Scandinavia 324
  Vornedskab in Denmark 330–1
in South-West Germany ('local
  serfdom') 121, 134, 151
Sharecropping 10–11, 31–2, 84, 88, 91,
  92, 98, 100, 106, 108, 252, 271,
  302
Silk-manufacturing, *see* rural industries,
  textiles
Slash-and-burn husbandry, *see* swidden
Sorcery, *see* witchcraft
Specialization of production 11–13, 93,
  101, 103, 387
  see also 'peasant mode of production'
Swidden 3, 260, 320–1, 327
Székely 250
  see also banditry

Taxation (state, territorial) 40–1, 77–9,
  126, 134, 135, 140, 149, 152,
  177, 180, 235–6, 251, 278–9,
  281–5, 290, 296–7, 324–5, 328,
  329

Tenure
  copyhold 346, 361–2, 363, 367–70,
    371
  customary 13
  fixed-term 60, 67, 88, 361
  freehold 341, 361, 371
  hereditary 13, 67, 121, 129, 137, 156,
    158, 165, 169, 173, 175, 177
  leasehold 13, 87, 165, 169, 175, 207,
    346, 347
  villein 362
Transhumance 62–3, 66, 76, 90, 92, 93,
  275, 277
  the Mesta 62–3

Village types 112–14
Villeinage, *see* serfdom, in England
Viticulture 8, 22, 51, 66, 92, 115, 122,
  123, 128, 290, 291, 292

Witchcraft 38, 131, 141

Yeomen 13, 21, 347, 349, 370, 371, 394